From SAND CREEK *to* SUMMIT SPRINGS

— COLORADO'S INDIAN WARS —

Linda Wommack

Caxton Press

© 2022 by Linda Wommack

All rights reserved. No part of this book may be reproduced in any manner without the express written consent of the publisher, except in the case of brief excerpts in critical reviews and articles. All inquiries should be addressed to:
Caxton Press, 312 Main Street, Caldwell, ID 83605.

First Edition
ISBN # 978-087004-643-8
Library of Congress Control Number: 2022933886

CIP Information available at Loc.gov

Cover and book design by Jocelyn Robertson

Printed in the United States of America
CAXTON PRESS
Caldwell, Idaho

Dedicated to the late John L. Sipes Jr.
Southern Cheyenne Tribal Historian
My friend and mentor
Rest In Peace Noble One

And to the late Pat Mendoza
Who pointed the way

And to Mo-chi
Whose life after Sand Creek was the true Song of Sorrow

TABLE OF CONTENTS

Foreword   *1*
Acknowledgments   *9*
Introduction   *11*
Epilogue   *503*
Bibliography   *507*
Index   *515*

Prelude to War   15

The Sand Creek Massacre   73

Revenge, Raids and the River   145

For Peace or War   197

The Battle of Beecher Island   235

Battle of Summit Springs   299

Defiance, Death and Despair   353

The Battle of Milk Creek
and the Meeker Massacre   389

— FOREWORD —

The Sand Creek Massacre of November 29, 1864, was not the largest or even the most brutal assault on American Indians by whites in American history, but it did come to symbolize the failure of American Indian policy and the worst instincts of "settler colonialism." First, it was clearly an act of betrayal directed against people who were assured that they were in a "place of safety." Second, it was an indiscriminate slaughter of men, women, and children in which no quarter was given, followed by extensive mutilation of the dead. Third, it produced something that its perpetrators thought was impossible for the Plains Indians—a winter war that extended into the summer of 1865 and cost $30,000,000. Fourth, in the midst of the Civil War, it produced two congressional investigations and a military commission resulting in three separate condemnations of Sand Creek as a "cowardly and cold-blooded slaughter."

Sand Creek launched the most extended debate over Indian policy since Indian Removal. It undermined Native trust in American promises, invigorated the Indian reform movement as Exhibit A of policy failure. It caused the removal of the commissioner of Indian Affairs and the governor of Colorado. At the Treaty of the Little Arkansas in October 1865, the government acknowledged its responsibility for the Sand Creek Massacre and agreed to pay reparations to the survivors and families of the victims of Sand Creek. Still, the tribes remained in limbo—and conflict—through the rest of the 1860s. The promised new reservation was delayed, which had the effect of prolonging the conflict—adding new chapters of violence and distrust in Hancock's War, another impotent treaty at Medicine Lodge, Beecher's Island, Washita, and Summit Springs, while spreading the war into the lands above the North Platte.

In fact, it can be argued that the Sand Creek affair set in motion or exacerbated the conflict with the plains tribes from Texas to the Canadian line, disrupted tribal organizations, and deepened the anti-Indian sentiment in the West. The shadow of the Sand Creek Massacre hung over federal Indian policy, military operations in the West, and the Indian reform movement for the rest of the nineteenth century. The story is a reminder of the potential for evil in every person and that the tethers which hold right and wrong in check are fragile. It is a story which reveals conscience as well—courage, strength, sacrifice, even nobility.

Civilization is self-defined, and for most of human history, unquestioned by those who claim it and define it. Its definition invariably assumes a superiority of the "civilized" over other groups and "higher" claims to knowledge and resources in contrast to civilization's "native twin," savagery. Civilizations look down on those "others" who are different. As the German historian Jurgen Osterhammel notes, settled people look down on nomads, urban societies look down on rural societies, literate societies look down on illiterate societies, rich societies look down on poor societies, complex religions look down on "pagans" and animists, and societies with greater reliance on science and technology look down on more "primitive" and less sophisticated ways of life. In other words, there is an inherent arrogance of the "civilized" toward the "savage," even among those whose civilized instincts are benevolent and well-intentioned.

Osterhammel writes: "The less civilized are a necessary audience for this grand theater for the civilized need the recognition of others, preferably in the form of admiration, reverence, and peaceful gratitude. They can live with envy and resentment if they have to; any civilization must arm itself against the hatred and aggressiveness of barbarians. The sense of worth felt by civilized people arises from an interplay between self-observation and attention to the various ways that others react to them, with an awareness that their own attainments are constantly at risk." Civilizations over time have usually felt an obligation to spread their values and way of life. By presuming the superiority of one's way of life, one defines progress by the transmission of one's norms, institutions, and values to others. The Europeanization of civilization carried with it a triad of Judeao-Christian assumptions—identity as a "chosen people," a responsibility to subdue the earth, and the concept of a "promised land."

The penetration of the "New World" in the fifteenth and sixteenth centuries was justified by a "right of discovery" and the conquest of the savage inhabitants of the new empires Europeans sought to build. Rooted in religious, political, and economic assumptions deemed to be superior, the civilizers justified themselves as saviors who would make the world a better place by the spread of their way of life to the barbarians they encountered. Unfortunately, the indigenous populations of the Americas did not share the Europeans' perceptions of themselves. They had their own views of the natural order of things. With few things in common and different ways of seeing the world, conflict was inevitable and persistent between European interlopers and the indigenous peoples of the Western Hemisphere.

By the time the United States of America was created, a pattern had developed which would dominate the course of Indian-white relations. On the one hand, there was a well-intentioned effort under both the Articles of Confederation and the Constitution of 1787 to pursue peaceful relations with the indigenous tribes. George Washington, Thomas Jefferson and especially Henry Knox, the Secretary of War, under both the Articles and the Constitution, desired to deal fairly with the tribes. Knox pronounced the right of conquest to be a failure and proclaimed that land should not be taken from them except by their consent. Anything less, he said, would "fix a stain on the national reputation of America." Washington and Jefferson agreed, and Washington saw the settlers usurping Indian lands as "a parcel of banditti." The West, he said, had become "a grand reservoir of the scum of the Atlantic States." But there were two flaws in the system. Even the best-intentioned policy makers assumed that the Indians would eventually give way to American expansion. More importantly, the government lacked both the power and the will to stop the settler invasion. By 1800, settlers outnumbered Indians in the Ohio Country eight to one.

Anti-Indianism took on an increasingly darker hue in a vast literature that defined Native character, behavior, and warfare in the most savage ways. As historian Peter Silver has written: "Anti-Indianism was the result not of a realistic calculation of the national interest but of a vacuum of policies and power at the federal level. Amid popular demands that vacuum came to be filled by dreams of Indian treachery and American suffering—dreams that always returned to the prosects of new lands...." The diversity of Native cultures disappeared into a negative stereotype of all Indians as "murderous savages."

In the lengthy history of Settler-Indian wars in what became the United States, it took nearly three hundred years to push the Native tribes from the Atlantic coast beyond the Mississippi River. That bloody saga was more balanced than many histories suggest.

Native resistance, especially in the Trans-Appalachian West, was surprisingly effective. Eventually, the sheer size of settler migration determined the outcome. Despite official policies that sought to protect American Indian rights, white settlement continued unabated. Indian Removal seemed to secure and stabilize Indian affairs, but it proved to be a false dawn. The Great Plains were still identified as "the Great American Desert," and the far West would be decades in developing—or so policy makers believed. But the Texas Revolution soon followed, and in 1846, the Mexican-American War began. Two years later, the Treaty of Guadalupe Hidalgo ceded more land to the United States, followed quickly by the discovery of gold in California. Three hundred thousand settlers soon flooded California and the great routes, the Overland Trail and the Santa Fe Trail.

Most were merely passing over the Great Plains, but they had a dramatic impact on the natural environment. Accounts of the river routes west in the 1830s talked about the timber along the creeks and rivers, reported ponds and seeps, providing bountiful water, recorded an abundance of horses and wild game, and even spoke admiringly of the plains Indian lifeway. Twenty years later, settlers rushing to Colorado to find gold found a very different environment. Ponds and seeps were drying up, grass was drying up, animal life was reduced, and timber was so scarce that settlers dismantled burial scaffolds for wood to build fires. The "trails" were becoming swaths of barren land. The Colorado Gold Rush swept over unceded Indian lands, ignoring existing laws, and American politics focused on "free soil" in Kansas and Nebraska. The very notion of protected Indian lands was naïve in the extreme.

Then came the Civil War—and more changes. Through the 1850s, the regular army patrolled the overland trails as a kind of police force. They were led by West Point officers and saw their role as peacekeepers. With the outbreak of the Civil War, the regular army was ordered east to form the core of the armies preparing to fight. They were replaced by volunteer regiments commanded by prominent citizens. Now, the army was composed of the settlers themselves and shared their opinions of the Indians. What is perhaps most remarkable is the number of officers and enlisted men who despised the conduct of officers like Chivington and events like Sand Creek. With the end of the Civil War, settler migration renewed, accelerated by the demand for railroads and the rapid industrialization that paralleled Southern Reconstruction.

The unsettled conditions left on the plains by Sand Creek

and its aftermath hastened the return of the regular army to the frontier. The Civil War had not prepared the military entirely for its new mission, and it struggled somewhat, restrained by cautions about noncombatant casualties and limited by policies that sought to prevent Sand Creek-like events. For men like William Tecumseh Sherman and Philip H. Sheridan, the mission no longer involved temporizing the relationship between Native tribes and the government. Rather, the generals became the agents of industrialization and subjugation of the tribes to clear the way for civilization. Clearing the land and forcing the tribes onto smaller and smaller reserves were the goals, and soldiers chafed under civilian insistence that these things be achieved with proper respect for the rules of war. The ultimate advantage was not strictly military. Sherman himself attributed the conquest of Native resistance to the sheer volume of migration, industrialization, and the railroad.

Linda Wommack adds an important personal dimension to her narrative account of the massacre and its aftermath. It is essentially an account of Colorado's "Indian problem." It is in many ways a reflection of the centuries-long conflict between white preoccupation with land and Native defense of their lifeway on the land. But this account is not so much a matter of policy or philosophy or cultural differences. Wommack's account is personal. It is about individuals, white and red, and their ways of seeing. Hers is a story of the "war in the dooryard" that characterized much of the history of the Indian wars. Wommack reminds us that the Cheyennes and Arapahos were warrior tribes responding to an invasion they could not have imagined a decade before and determined to hold on to their life way. Many fought desperately, and others sought peace consistently. Also found here are settlers who saw themselves as victims rather than interlopers, who saw themselves as having a right to claim what they perceived as "empty land" and make new lives for themselves on the frontier. They justified their actions, including the atrocities at Sand Creek, as fair reprisal for Native resistance to their invasion.

Stripped loose from grand design (of which she is aware), Wommack's story is about ordinary people, whose opinions and actions were driven by experience and inheritance. They explained what they felt based on fear, anger, revenge, community, conscience, and belief. It is dangerous to oversimplify and make this simply a question of whites and Indians, of "good guys" and "bad guys." These characters were not of one mind. At Sand Creek, at least two companies of the First Colorado Cavalry took little part in the massacre, and afterward more officers and enlisted men condemned what had happened. Less well-known is the number of "Thirdsters," members of the one-hundred-day regiment, the Third Colorado Cavalry, who were repulsed by what happened. One soldier who enlisted hoping to find a child who had been captured in the summer war of 1864, stopped fighting after the initial assault on the village, as he watched the slaughter of noncombatants, saying that he did not enlist to kill unresisting women and children. Others refused to participate in the killing of noncombatants after the fight was over and the mutilation of the dead commenced. Three of the officers of the First Colorado Cavalry who had the most to do with exposing Sand Creek as a massacre were members of the clique of officers considered to be closest to Colonel John M. Chivington, who was the architect of the slaughter. One soldier went so far as to say that he was surprised that Chivington was not killed by angry soldiers.

Wommack details the character and conduct of individuals from chiefs and officers to settlers and captives to policy makers and politicians. Here is the story of Mochi, a Cheyenne woman who lost her family at Sand Creek and became a Cheyenne warrior to avenge their deaths. Here is Black Kettle, the Cheyenne peacemaker, who worked for accommodation only to be killed at the Washita, one day short of four years after the Sand Creek affairs. Here are portraits of Roman Nose and Tall Bull, Cheyenne chiefs who died at Beecher's Island and Summit Springs. Here are accounts of woman like Nancy Morton, Laura Roper, Lucinda Eubanks and others with stories that range from understandably bitter to surprisingly forgiving. Told with balance and in their own words from firsthand accounts, the war for the central plains becomes very human.

When, at last, the author brings to an end the story of the Cheyenne and Arapaho resistance, Wommack adds a fitting epilogue with the story of the fate of the Utes, who, a decade after Summit Springs, were finally expelled from Colorado like the Cheyennes and Arapahos before. The Utes had sought to accommodate the whites, and one of their chiefs, Ouray, consistently worked for peace, but despite the different path the Utes chose, their story followed an all too familiar path. White Coloradans wanted their land and decided that "The Utes Must Go." An agent named Nathan Meeker was chosen to help transform the Utes. Soon a debate was in full swing to decide their fate. One of Colorado's senators, Nathaniel Hill, defended the Utes, especially Ouray, but the state's other senator, Henry Teller, dismissed Ouray as a "renegade chief." When Hill defended him, Teller offered a revealing response: "Gentlemen may talk as they choose of his ability and his devotion to the whites; he is an Indian, with an Indian heart and with Indian blood; and he is looking for what he thinks is in the interest of his tribe. He knows his people do not want to be civilized; he is looking to keep his government stipend."

The situation deteriorated until troops were dispatched to impose order. The Utes and Agent Meeker urged them to proceed with caution, but on September 29, there was a fight between Utes and the soldiers and an attack on the Indian agency. Agent Meeker and ten others were killed, Meeker's wife, Arvilla, and daughter, Josephine, were captured along with the family of another employee of the agency. "Meeker's Massacre" and the Milk River Fight became known as the Ute War. The captives were eventually released, and the Meeker women gave interesting and deeply personal accounts of their captivity. Eventually in 1880, the Utes were expelled from Colorado and resettled in Utah. What is surprising is how little things had changed. Henry Teller, who had defended the Sand Creek Massacre, still clung to the anti-Indian stereotype as his measure of all Indians. He did not speak of Utes or Cheyennes or Arapahos but mythical savages that helped him to justify his prejudices and his greed.

Linda Wommack provides insight into human nature, its conscience and its folly, adding a vital dimension to an important story.

~ *Gary L. Roberts*
Emeritus Professor of History
Abraham Baldwin Agricultural College
Tifton, Georgia

— ACKNOWLEDGEMENTS —

There are many people who have helped with this project over a span of fifteen to twenty years. First on that list is Mr. William Dawson who owned the land where the National Park Service has designated as the Sand Creek Massacre site. What originally started as a "site seeing" trip soon turned into many trips to gain information and insight through Bill's keen perspective. Soon a friendship developed and as I learned more the beginnings of this manuscript were formed in my mind.

Bill Dawson introduced me to Laird and Colleen Cometsevah, descendants of Sand Creek victims. Through them I learned much of the Cheyenne culture. During one trip to a reservation area of Clinton, Oklahoma, I met a man who would add to that understanding in immeasurable ways. His name was John Sipes, Jr. He was the Cheyenne Tribal Historian for many decades. He also was the descendant of a Cheyenne Dog Soldier, Medicine Water, and his wife, Mo-chi, pronounced mo-ki. Over the next several years we visited often. He taught me the ways of the Cheyenne way of life and shared his family oral history with me. We became very close and soon he was sending me boxes of his research on a regular basis. Today I have most of his research, documents and photographs; products of his life-long work. It is my hope that in bringing forth his family story I have satisfactorily fulfilled a promise of long ago.

Another man who showed me the way was Pat Mendoza. He walked in two worlds and struggled to understand both. Along his journey, he taught me many aspects of the Cheyenne way.

Others helped with my research. First among them is Dr. Jefferson Broome. Over the years he has shared his research with me, explained his findings and helped me to understand military strategy and policy. His explorations of many of these battle sites is extraordinary and his knowledge is quite impressive. Walking the sites of Summit Springs, Beecher Island and the Hungate homestead where those murders took place gives one a true sense of time and place.

I am indebted to Jeff Broome for reading and correcting my manuscript, offering suggestions and adding additional information. John Monnett, author of "Battle of Beecher Island," also read my work and contributed his thoughts and ideas.

I am also grateful for the keen insight of Gary Roberts. His expertise in the Sand Creek matter is immeasurable and welcomed. His kindness in writing the forward is much appreciated.

The kind folks at the National Park Service were instrumental in providing insight to their interpretations of the Sand Creek Massacre and the Washita battle site. They also provided some of the photographs used in this work. Jefferson Broome also provided many photographs as did the Fort Wallace Museum. Coi E. Drummond-Gehrig, photo editor at the Denver Public Library Western History Department, once again used her expertise to find excellent photographs. And finally, Deb Goodrich with the Fort Wallace Museum went above and beyond the call for me with documents, information and photographs.

Finally, my copy editor, Connie Clayton, never let me down and expertly made this manuscript much better. And to Scott Gipson of Caxton Press, my publisher for over twenty years: Thank you for continuing to believe in me.

As John Sipes once told me, "The spirits are with you and this is something that was meant to be."

May you enjoy the effort.

~ Linda Wommack

— INTRODUCTION —

The Indian wars in Colorado were a tumultuous time in the state's history. Each side fought for that which they strongly believed. American government and military policy versus the Indian struggle to keep their way of life, caused it to become a culture war that neither side could win.

These struggles are revealed through government documents, Indian oral history, and eye witness accounts.

As with any conflict there are casualties of war. Several female captives of the Indians were later killed, but many were rescued and went on to tell their stories. Their words tell a terrifying tale of the Indian wars.

Conversely, one captive, Josephine Meeker, when rescued went on to write articles describing the plight of the Native American. She gave lectures and became an early supporter for Native American rights.

Another woman who fought for the Indian way of life, did not have a positive outcome. Mo-chi's parents were killed at the Sand Creek battlefield. Mo-chi took her father's firearm and declared war on the white man. She became the first female Cheyenne warrior. Twenty years later, almost to the day, Mo-chi surrendered to save her people from starvation, only to be sent to a land far away from her Colorado homeland—she was sent to a dank, dark prison in Florida.

From SAND CREEK to SUMMIT SPRINGS

— COLORADO'S INDIAN WARS —

Linda Wommack

The Overland Trail travelers and Plains Indians moved along the Overland Trail and South Platte River Road in harmony – at least for a time. *Denver Public Library (DPL)*

— PRELUDE TO WAR —

Colorado Territory was created and granted by the U. S. Congress on August 1, 1861. William Gilpin, selected by President Abraham Lincoln, became the territorial governor. One of Gilpin's first acts was to formally organize the First Regiment of Colorado Volunteers. The purpose was to aid in the Civil War effort, as well as protect Colorado citizens against increased danger from roaming bandits and marauding Indians. Gilpin requested federal funds, but his pleas fell on deaf ears. In a time when the country was at civil war, there was no federal money to spare.

This period in Colorado history was one of marking time between two diverse cultures that would eventually explode into warfare.

The summer of 1861 had been a hot one with rumors swirling of a Confederate attack. Posters were hung at Denver street corners with offers to buy percussion caps and ammunition for use against the Confederate forces.

One of the largest recruiting centers in the territory was at the mining settlement of Central City. Captain Samuel Tappan, with his persuasive persona, effected the enlistment of over one hundred men in a twenty-four hour period. One of those men, Silas Soule, not only chose to enlist with the First Colorado Volunteers he actually fully supported the effort by recruiting fellow miners to the cause. For his efforts, he was awarded a commission as first lieutenant of Company K, under the command of Colonel John P. Slough.[1]

Another man eager to enlist with the First Colorado Volunteers, was the former sheriff of Denver, Edward Wynkoop. Enlisting on July 31, 1861, he received a commission as second lieutenant. He would later say in a letter to his son Frank, "I went into the service to help my country in her time of trouble, not to play soldier."[2] Those words would play out not only in his military future, but for his military comrade, Silas Soule, as well.

The citizens of Colorado Territory rallied around the First

Colorado Volunteers. On August 10, 1861, several women of the mining town of Eureka, near Central City, hosted a benefit for the recruits. Lieutenant Colonel Samuel Tappan marched his troops in a parade down the dirt street. Also in attendance were Silas Soule and Edward Wynkoop. After speeches by Tappan and Wynkoop, the women presented bibles to the troops. On this day, Soule and Wynkoop formed a bond that would last through the events to come and change both of their lives forever. The *Rocky Mountain News* heralded the celebration in the issue dated the same day, calling for "a few months of active extermination against the red devils." The new regiment was mustered in on August 29, 1861, and training commenced at Camp Weld.

Soule's duties throughout his first year of service were primarily in recruiting. He traveled often between Central City and the newly constructed Camp Weld, on the southwest outskirts of Denver. By the end of that summer, John P. Slough had been promoted to colonel, commanding the First Regiment of Colorado Volunteers. Samuel Tappan had been promoted to lieutenant colonel and requested Wynkoop be given a promotion to captain of A Company after Glorieta Pass.[3] Soule now reported directly to Captain Wynkoop. For the remainder of 1861 Lieutenant Soule worked at garrison duty at Camp Weld, still under construction.

Meanwhile, John Milton Chivington, a Methodist preacher from Ohio who arrived in Denver the previous year, had been asked by Governor Gilpin to serve as regimental chaplain. However, the large, overbearing, gun-toting man of the cloth wanted a fighting commission. Gilpin agreed to the request, granting him the rank of major.

Just six months into his governorship, Gilpin began issuing drafts for needed military supplies such as clothing, weapons, housing and payroll. Gilpin had sent several requests to Secretary of War Simon Cameron, detailing the situation and asking for help from Washington. Cameron, overwhelmed with the raging war in the East, was unable to grant Gilpin's requests. He did, however, return Gilpin's letters with general advice and direction.

Although he had not been given federal aid, Gilpin assumed he had proper authorization from correspondence with President Lincoln and Secretary Simon Cameron. Therefore, Gilpin went forth with his plan. However, this was not the case. Over three hundred thousand dollars in promissory drafts had been issued by the governor to various merchants. These honest businessmen soon complained when they were refused payment by the federal government's Secretary of the Treasury.

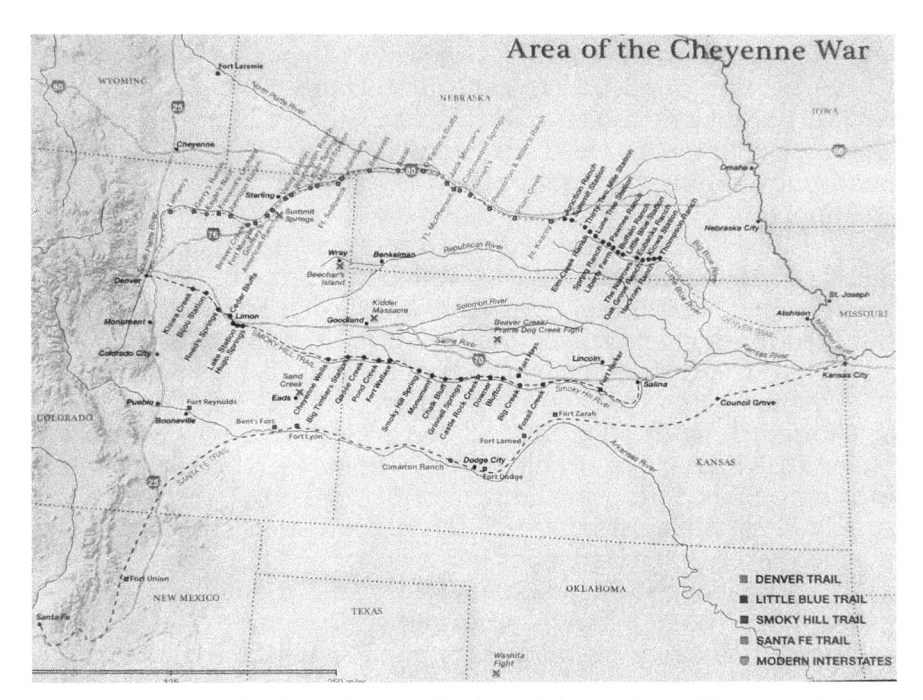

The area, primarily along the South Platte River, of the Cheyenne Indian wars in eastern Colorado. *Jeff Broome*

In early December, Gilpin was summoned to Washington, D. C. Owner and editor of the *Rocky Mountain News,* William Newton Byers, wrote scathing editorials impugning the governor's integrity and honesty. He gleefully printed all letters to the editor with similar sentiment against Gilpin. Gilpin had become an embarrassment to the Lincoln administration.

Finally, in February 1862, the First Regiment of Colorado Volunteers were about to see battle. Rumors of Confederates invading the Rocky Mountain region for the gold had been swirling ever since the war broke out the previous year. The Army of the Confederacy had plans to invade the area in an effort to drive out the Union forces. Confederate Brigadier General Henry H. Sibley, with little knowledge of the opposing military forces in the region, boldly moved forward with his plans. His troops, over a thousand, were known as Sibley's Brigade and were stationed in Texas.

The First Regiment of Colorado Volunteers drilled daily until they were fit and ready for combat. The order finally came to march south and the untested military unit proved their strength and their worth to the country. Ironically, Gilpin's previous actions would be vindicated and ridicule by the press would be proven wrong. But it came too late. By the time Gilpin's First Regiment of Colorado Volunteers were victorious in battle, President Lincoln had removed him from office. He was replaced by Dr. John Evans of Illinois.

Meanwhile, the troops were heading south. In one particular march, they traveled ninety-two miles in thirty-six hours. When they reached Fort Union, northern New Mexico Territory, over four hundred miles from Denver, they did it in thirteen days.

In the battle against Sibley's Brigade, dubbed as the "Gettysburg of the West," they defeated the Confederate forces at Glorieta Pass in New Mexico Territory over a two-day battle. Major Chivington led a bold circular maneuver taking his men, including Silas Soule, to the rear of Sibley's line, destroying his supply lines. Sibley's men were forced to retreat. Chivington and his men returned to Denver as heroes.

Surprisingly, Silas Soule also became the talk of the local media, "He [Soule] handled himself well in battle." His sense of humor and keen wit made him popular with all who came in contact with him, and his natural ease with the media made him a darling among the reporters. Ovando J. Hollister later reported:

> *"Robbins, Soule and Hardin were here, every one of them as cool and collected as if on parade."* [4]

Soule described his fighting experience at Glorieta Pass in triumphant prose to his friend Walt Whitman:

> *"As soon as we heard of the battle we made a forced march to the rescue. We marched a Reg [sic] of some 350 miles in 14 days. We marched 120 miles in three days and 80 miles in 24 hours. I think we made the biggest march on record. We understood that Sibley was making an attact [sic] on Fort Union. The word came to us about sundown after the men had marched 40 miles and had not had their supper and they threw their hats in the air and swore they would march 40 miles farther before they slept and they did. They started off singing the Star spangled banner, [sic] Red white and blue and yankee doodle [sic] so you can imagine what kind of material this Reg is composed of."* [5]

So great was Chivington's popularity that by May 1862, both Colonel Slough and Colonel Tappan had tendered a petition to Brigadier General Edward R. S. Canby, setting up a perfect promotion for Chivington, which eventually would make him commander of the entire Military District of Colorado. It was also at this time that the First Regiment of Colorado Volunteers officially became the First Colorado Cavalry.[6]

Under Chivington's command, several officers received field promotions, including Silas Soule and Edward Wynkoop. Canby promoted Wynkoop to major of the regiment, who in turn promoted Soule to captain of Company D.

Continuing his service with the First Colorado Cavalry, Soule would serve under Wynkoop throughout 1863 at Camp Weld.

In a letter to federal authorities dated November 10, 1863, Governor Evans requested federal military enforcements for Colorado Territory, and included a statement given to him by Robert North, an Indian trader in the area:

"The Comanches, Apaches, Kiowas, the northern band of Arapahoes, and all of the Cheyennes, with the Sioux, have pledged one another to go to war with the whites as soon as they can procure ammunition in the spring. I heard them discuss the matter often and the few of them who opposed it were forced to be quiet and were really in danger of the loss of their lives. The principal chiefs pledge to each other that they would shake hands and be friendly with the whites until they procured ammunition and guns, so as to be ready when they strike. Plundering to get means has already commenced, and the plan is to commence the war at several points in the sparse settlements early in the spring." [7]

Due to the military priority of the Civil War raging in the East, Governor Evans' request was denied.

On March 26, 1864, Brigadier General Robert B. Mitchell, of the Military District of Nebraska Territory, requested and received authorization for all available troops of the First Colorado Cavalry to be sent to the southern border of his district. Union Army General Samuel R. Curtis, who was also in command of all military operations in the West, sent the authorization to Governor Evans. The depleted military force in Colorado Territory meant an obvious reduction in military protection. As Indian uprisings on the plains increased, Wynkoop and Soule, with a few small troops, were often dispatched from Camp Weld to quell the disturbances.

On April 4, 1864, a few cattle herders in the employ of the freighting firm of Irwin, Jackson, & Company rushed to Denver

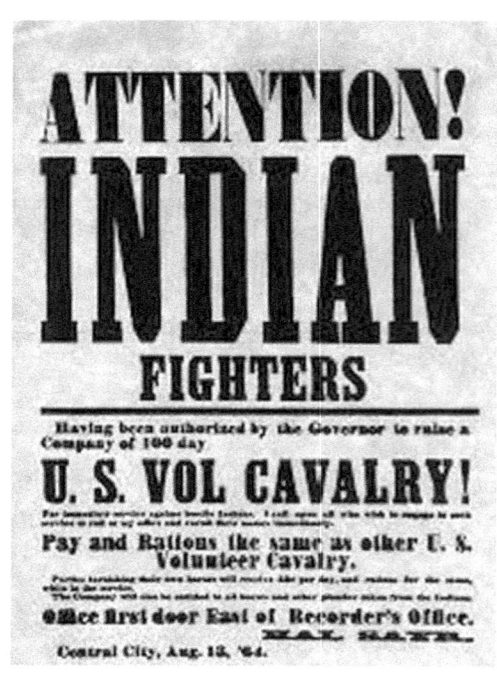

The government allowed for Colorado Territory to recruit volunteers for Colonel Chivington's army. *DPL*

City to report the theft of nearly one hundred and seventy-five head of cattle (the number differs in several accounts) from their pasture at Bijou Creek. They were sure, they said, it was Indians, specifically implicating that it was the Cheyenne. Colonel Chivington ordered Lieutenant George S. Eayre, commander of the Independent Battery of Colorado Volunteer Artillery, to recover the stolen livestock. Traveling slowly through a spring snowstorm, Eayre eventually crossed the divide between the valleys of the South Platte and the Arkansas, camping at Sand Creek. From there, the troops traveled along the creek northeast where they came upon the Cheyenne villages of Coon and Crow Chief, camped on the Republican River. The Indians, who observed the military approach, abandoned their camp. Eayre and his men recovered a few head of the stolen cattle. The troops returned to Denver City for more supplies and returned to the area a few weeks later. Eayre and his fifty-four troops were indeed well supplied; with two twelve-pound howitzers. On May 19, 1864, Eayre sent a report to Chivington which read as follows:

> "Sir,
> I have the honor to inform you that on the 16th instant, when within three miles of Smoky Hill, I was attacked by the Cheyenne Indians about one hundred strong, and after a persistent fight of 7 1/2 hours succeeded in driving them from the field. They lost three chiefs and 25 warriors killed; the wounded I am unable to estimate. My own loss is 4 men killed and three wounded. My animals are exhausted. I will remain at this post until further orders." [8]

Meanwhile, as Eayre and his troops were fighting the Cheyenne in the southeast portion of Colorado Territory, Chivington had ordered Captain George L. Sanborn, of the First Colorado Cavalry, to pursue a group of Cheyenne Dog Soldiers. Sanborn dispatched Lieutenant Clark Dunn and forty men from Camp Sanborn to Fremont's Orchard, along the South Platte River in the northwest portion of the Colorado Territory.[9] Again, the soldiers were sent to recover livestock, presumably stolen by hostile Indians.

On the evening of April 11, 1863, W. D. Ripley, a local rancher on Bijou Creek, had come into Camp Sanborn, a temporary military post on the South Platte River, to report the theft of livestock from his ranch. The following morning, Dunn and his soldiers, accompanied by Ripley, left the military camp, following the South Platte River upstream. That afternoon, approximately forty-five miles northwest of Camp Sanborn, the group observed a band of Indians watering their horses on the north side of the river, along the Crow Creek tributary. The soldiers crossed the river to meet with the Indians. In response, a few of the Cheyenne warriors rode forward to greet the soldiers. Lieutenant Dunn explained that under military order, he must disarm the men of their weapons. As the soldiers attempted to collect their weapons, the Indians resisted and backed their ponies away.

Eye-witness testimony and Indian accounts differ sharply as to what happened next. According to Lieutenant Dunn's testimony, he claimed that when he attempted to disarm the Indians, they opened fire on the soldiers. The soldiers returned the fire, Dunn said, killing "eight or ten warriors." Dunn and his troops then pursued the fleeing warriors some fifteen miles. Dunn further testified that his losses were two dead and two wounded. However, contradicting this testimony was a subsequent report of the incident written by Captain Sanborn, which stated that:

> *"Lieutenant Dunn has just arrived and reports that none of the men were killed; several of the Indians were seen to fall from their horses, but being freshly mounted, succeeded in getting them away."* [10]

Little Chief, who was involved in the battle, claimed that it was the soldiers who fired first without provocation, and then the warriors retreated from the scene, as they recognized they were out-numbered and outgunned. He also said that no Cheyenne died and only three Indians were wounded, Bear Man, Mad Wolf and Wolf Coming Out.[11]

In any case, Little Chief, along with White Antelope and many members of the Cheyenne tribe, believed that this incident was the beginning of the Plains Indian War. Others felt the same way, such as Crow Chief and his people. They arrived in Little Chief's camp a few days later, having been driven from their camp on the Republican River by Eayre and his troops. Lieutenant Augustus W. Burton, under Eayre's command, later stated that Eayre's orders were to "kill Cheyennes whenever and wherever found."[12]

In May 1863, Governor Evans learned of an Indian council including Arapaho, Cheyenne and Sioux chiefs, being held one hundred miles north of Denver City. Evans sent his trusted friend, frontiersman Elbridge Gerry, to deliver a message to the council requesting the Indians come to Denver for a meeting. Gerry obliged the governor, gathering a few of the roving bands of Arapaho and Sioux that he could find hunting along the river. However, most tribes, including the Arapaho and Cheyenne, refused to meet with the governor. Promises made by the treaty of Fort Wise two years earlier had not been kept, including an annual payment of fifteen thousand dollars to each tribe. Several chiefs, including White Antelope and Black Kettle, claimed they had never agreed to the treaty. The chiefs in the Indian council sent a return message telling the governor that their horses, still weak from the harsh winter, could not travel that far.

After delivering the Indians' refusal to the governor, Gerry, not wanting to harm his own relations with the Indian tribes, left Denver with a wagonload of goods in an effort to smooth things over.

Being rebuffed by the Indians, Governor Evans tried to spin the situation in the press. He gave the following quote to the *Rocky Mountain News*:

> *"Elbridge Gerry was acquainted with all the leading men of both the Arapaho, [sic] Cheyenne and Sioux tribes of Indians, and consequently being a very intelligent man, was a very valuable assistant to me in negotiations with the Indians."*

Less then thirty days later, not even the First Colorado Cavalry could prevent the murder of a family on Running/Box Elder Creek, some thirty miles southeast of Denver City, nor the hysteria that gripped the citizens of the territory.[13]

Nathan Ward Hungate, his wife Ellen Eliza, and their three-year old daughter, Laura, and infant daughter, Florence, had arrived in Colorado Territory with high hopes of eventually homesteading land on Box Elder Creek, also known as Running Creek. In the meantime, Hungate found work as ranch foreman for Issac Van Wormer, and moved his young family into a small cabin on the ranch. By all accounts, the Hungate family were well-respected, hard working people. They had lived and worked in the area a mere two months when the unthinkable happened.

On June 11, 1864, Nathan Ward Hungate's entire family were found murdered at their burned homestead. The throats of Ellen and her two young daughters had been slashed, their heads being nearly severed from their bodies. Ellen had been stabbed several times, scalped, and their was evidence she had been raped. The body of Nathan Hungate was later found in the west side of the creek bed, approximately one mile north of the homestead. His body had been riddled with bullets and the scalp torn off. Their home had been burned to the ground and their livestock stolen. As there had been Indian raids in the area over the past few days, those who found the mutilated bodies immediately understood that it was an act of marauding Indians.

The *Denver Commonwealth* newspaper reported the murders in grisly detail in the June 15, 1864 edition:

"Indian Depredations - Murder of an Entire Family

On Saturday night two Indians stampeded 49 mules belonging to Daniels & Brown, about thirteen miles from this city, on the 'cut-off,' while the teamsters, four in number, were preparing supper. Two of the men pursued the Indians some thirteen miles, until they came in sight of about 120 head of ponies, horses and mules, when they judiciously returned to the wagons, as the Indian camp was evidently near. On Saturday afternoon, the buildings of the ranche of Mr. Van Wormer, of this city, on Living Creek, [sic] thirty miles southeast of Denver, were burned down by Indians, as were the buildings of the next ranche. Mr. Hungate and family, who occupied Mr. Van Wormer's ranche, were barbarously murdered by the Indians. The bodies of Mrs. H and two children were found near the house. They had been scalped,and their throats cut. A later report brings news of the discovery of Mr. Hungate's body, about a mile from the same place. Moccasins, arrows, and other Indian signs were found in the vicinity. The bodies of these will be brought to the city this afternoon, and will, at the ringing of the Seminary bell, be placed where our citizens can all see them." [14]

The newspaper editor added the following to the original account of the murders:

> "Since writing the above we have had a conversation with Mr. Follett, who has just arrived from Running Creek. Mr. F. is one of the party that went after the bodies. He says that the woman was found about four hundred yards from the house, with the children both in her arms - one a babe three or four months, and one, a little girl about two years old. The bowels of the younger one were ripped open, and its entrails scattered by the sides of the mother and children. The body of the man was found about two miles from the house, but his whip was found at the ruins, and some other marks seemed to indicate that he had first been attacked there, and finding himself overpowered, had made an effort to escape."

Then, as now, a rush to be first with sensational stories often resulted in errors, not to mention the obvious flair for embellishment. However, this was the first account that suggested Hungate had fled from his home, a fact that would later be proven true.

Evans had been informed of the recent Indian depredations in the area of Box Elder Creek, the other name for Running Creek. John S. Brown and Thomas J. Darrah had rushed to Denver City to inform the governor of the Indian thefts, corroborating the *Denver Commonwealth* report of the theft of mules and horses. However, the news of the Hungate murders had not yet reached Denver City.

The governor immediately made preparations to increase military presence in the area. In a letter dated June 11, 1864, Evans ordered Captain Joseph C. Davidson, who was camped on Cherry Creek just west of where the raids were occurring, to pursue and punish the raiding Indians. [15] Darrah immediately volunteered to deliver the order.

Evans then wrote to Colonel John M. Chivington, informing him of the Indian atrocities. The letter was evidently not sent until the following day, as there was a postscript regarding the recent information he had received about the Hungate murders.

Darrah had arrived at Captain Davidson's camp the following morning, June 12. Delivering the governor's order, Davidson led a group of soldiers at first light, accompanied by Darrah, north to area where the raids had recently occurred. Following Box Elder/Running Creek, the group encountered John S. Brown and D. C. Corbin, who were searching for their stolen stock. The men joined the military search party and continued north.

Meanwhile, two neighbors who had observed rising smoke from the direction of the Hungate cabin, rode over to the area to investigate. Through his extensive research into heretofore untapped resources, Dr. Jeff Broome has recently learned that the names of the two neighbors were Johnson and Ferguson. When they arrived, they discovered the cabin had been burned to the ground. Searching the immediate area, they quickly found the bodies of Hungate's wife and two daughters. After a further search of the area, they were unable to find Nathan Hungate. In what must have been a solemn, sad and gruesome task, the men managed to take the three bodies to the nearby mill owned by Philip Gomer.

It was some time later in the day that Captain Davidson's soldiers and accompanying civilians found the burned remains of the Hungate cabin and then discovered the body of Nathan Ward Hungate. John Brown later gave the following testimony:

"There was a camp of U. S. soldiers camped on what was known as Cherry Creek...Darrah had before informing us of our loss, [stolen stock] carried an order from Capt. Maynard to have those troops to go over to Running Creek, to march from Cherry Creek to Coal Creek and back in 48 hours. We went to Box Alder [sic] and traveled about 14 miles up Running Creek, where we found the soldiers in camp eating dinner, and was also joined by Thomas J. Darrah. After dinner the soldiers saddled up and traveled up the creek, we in company with them. A few miles up the creek we found Hungate's cabin pillaged and a note pinned on the cabin, signed by a party from Gomer's Mill, containing the information that Mrs. Hungate and two children were killed; a short distance from the cabin we left the soldiers as they had to return. We then started from the station at Box Alder [sic] and while on the way, we found Hungate killed and scalped. We made a report of it in town and the bodies of the Hungates were brought into where is now Denver City, and buried."[16]

In an affidavit later provided by Thomas Darrah, Brown's account was affirmed:

"When we camped for dinner we were joined by J. S. Brown. In company with the soldiers we followed the trail of the Indians until we came to a cabin which had been pillaged on which we found a note signed by a party from Gomer's Mill, stating that Mrs. Hungate and her two children had been killed and were at the mill. We skirted around in the timber looking for Mr. Hungate but did not find him. At a short distance from the Hungate cabin we left the soldiers as they had orders to return.

We then started for the station at Box Elder and on the way found Mr. Hungate killed and scalped. We reported it to the stage station and at Denver and the bodies were brought in to where the City of Denver now is and buried."

After the men took Hungate's body to the Gomer mill, J. S. Brown and Thomas J. Darrah left for Denver City to report the murders to the governor. They arrived late in the night, at approximately 10 p.m. Following their report, Governor Evans penned the following to his original missive to Chivington:

"P.S. - Since writing the above there has arrived a messenger from Mr. Van Wormer's ranch, 10 miles south of the cut-off road, on Box Elder. He says that yesterday afternoon the Indians drove off his stock, burned Mr. Van W.'s house, and murdered a man who was in Mr. Van W.'s employ, his wife, and two children, and burned his house also." [17]

The bodies of twenty-nine-year-old Nathan Ward Hungate, his twenty-five-year-old wife, Ellen Eliza Decker Hungate, and daughters three-year-old Laura and five-month-old Florence, were placed in hastily made pine boxes at Philip Gomer's mill, for transportation by wagon to Denver City, where they were publicly displayed at the city's post office building. The bodies were later placed in pine coffins and buried in Denver City's Mount Prospect Cemetery.[18]

Fear gripped the citizens of Colorado Territory. Susan Riley Ashley lived through this trying time. She later wrote of her experience:

"Two days after the Hungate massacre, just as the home guard were disbanding from drilling on East Fourteenth Street, a man on a foaming steed galloped through our streets crying, 'Indians are coming. Indians are advancing on the town to burn and massacre. Hurry your wives and children to places of safety! Following close after this rider came men, women and children, in wagons, or carts, on horseback and on foot, all pale with fear. The news swept over the town like the wind. Women and children of East Denver were hurried to the mint; those of West Denver to the upper story of the Commissary building on Ferry Street. In those two buildings women and children congregated in every stage of dress and undress. Some came arrayed in their best, having planned for an evening with friends...The men patrolled the two points of refuge. My sister and I were in the Commissary building. Its iron shutters to windows and doors

were bolted, and at the foot of the outside stairs by which we had climbed to the upper story, two men were stationed with axes to cut the stairs away on the first sight of the red devils. To intensify the excitement three women who had looked upon the Hungate remains described that horror.

No Indians appeared, and when after midnight scouts returned from a fruitless search outside the city limits, many families returned to their homes, Others remained until the sun was high in the heavens. Few houses in the city had been locked that night and many were left with doors and windows open and lamps burned within. But so general was the belief in a fast approaching death, or a still worse fate, that no thieving was done." [19]

This account exemplifies the hysteria of the Indian threat in Colorado Territory. The citizens demanded Governor Evans to take action against the increasing Indian threat. The influential press, led by Byers and his *Rocky Mountain News*, called for the "immediate extinction of the Indians." With a stroke of predictive journalism, Byers clearly stated the views of many citizens of Colorado Territory.

Territorial politics reached an explosive level by this time. The powers at large, primarily in Denver, lobbied Washington for a second time for admission to the Union. The stakes were high and the obstacles were numerous, particularly regarding the Indians. Foremost on the minds of political hopefuls, particularly Governor John Evans and Colonel John M. Chivington, were the recent Indian uprisings. Now, with the support of the influential newspaper editor, the course was clear: eradicate the "Indian problem."

Evans had sent several requests to military enforcements, but was denied, again due to the raging Civil War in the East. The governor then sent a peace proposal to the Indian tribes of the Colorado Territory. Evans requested that all "friendly" Indians go to the various territorial forts. His proclamation, issued on June 27, 1864, read:

"Agents, interpreters, and traders will inform the friendly Indians of the plains that some members of their tribes have gone to war with the white people. They steal stock and run it off, hoping to escape detection and punishment. In some instances, they have attacked and killed soldiers and murdered peaceable citizens. For this the Great Father is angry, and will certainly hunt them out and punish them, but he does not want to injure those who remain friendly to the whites. For this purpose I direct that all friendly Indians keep away from those who are at war, and go

to places of safety. Friendly Arapahoes and Cheyennes belonging on the Arkansas River will go to Major Colley, U. S. Indian Agent at Fort Lyon, who will give them provisions and show them a place of safety. Friendly Kiowas and Comanche will go to Fort Larned. Friendly Sioux will go to their agent at Fort Laramie. Friendly Arapahoes and Cheyennes of the Upper Platte will go to Camp Collins on the Cache la Poudre.

The object of this is to prevent friendly Indians from being killed through mistake. The war on hostile Indians will be continued until they are all effectively subdued." [20]

Evans specifically instructed Indian Agent Samuel G. Colley, of Fort Lyon, to provide food and clothing to all Indians who came into his fort.[21] He further stated:

"The war is opened in earnest, and upon your efforts to keep quiet the friendly Indians as a nucleus for peace will depend its duration to some extent at least." [22]

The governor's proclamation was distributed to the Indian camps that could be located. Many of these Indian tribes complied, others did not, as their intentions were anything but peaceful. Elbridge Gerry, who had previously attempted to assist the governor with regard to the Indians, was hired by Evans to facilitate meetings with the various Indian tribes.

Gerry, described as quiet and reserved, a man of few words, for the most part, kept to himself on his farmland on the eastern plains of Colorado Territory. Possibly because Gerry was so reserved, his background is somewhat clouded in mystery. Born in Massachusetts on July 18, 1818, he spent some time during his youth at sea, and sported a tattoo of a ship on his arm. Gerry ventured west at a very early age, working as a trapper with the Sublette brothers on the Snake River, and at Jackson Hole and Yellowstone from 1839 to 1841. He later operated a trading post on the North Platte River near Fort Laramie in 1844, where he married the first of several Indian wives. As the demand for beaver pelts declined, Gerry left present-day Wyoming for Colorado Territory.

By 1853, Gerry, the first white settler in northern Colorado, had established a horse ranch at the mouth of Crow Creek, which flowed into the South Platte River. Gerry built a friendly trading business with the travelers, scouts, and the local Cheyenne

Indians, who called him "White Eyes," obtaining pelts in exchange for blankets, beads, and the like. His account books, on file at the Colorado History Center, show very detailed accounting records in an impressive descriptive handwriting.

By 1858, Gerry had built a very successful trading business along the South Platte Trail, the main road into Denver City from Julesburg. Two of the traders in partnership with Gerry were John Smith, and William W. McGaa, also known as Jack Jones. The two men traded Indian goods from Gerry's trading post near the confluence of Cherry Creek and the South Platte River. This area had became the center for mining supplies in the rush for gold riches during the summer of 1858. By the fall of that year, both McGaa and Smith had elected to stay in the river bottom land and establish the St. Charles Town Company, which became the Denver Town Company. Through his relationship with McGaa and Smith, Elbridge Gerry was introduced to the second territorial governor, John Evans. The two became close friends and allies.

It was believed by most of his contemporaries of the day that Gerry, who had the same name as the Massachusetts politician and signer of the Declaration of Independence, were related. Gerry, the statesman, later served as the vice president of the United States, under James Madison. The *Rocky Mountain News* reported that Gerry was the grandson of the famous signer, and Governor John Evans, a personal friend, stated several times that it was true. As for Gerry, he evidently didn't say much about it, as members of his own family were never really sure of the connection. Regardless of the connection, or lack thereof, the Elbridge Gerry of Colorado had, by his own accomplishments, gained the trust of Governor Evans.

In July 1864, Gerry, on behalf of the governor, held an informal council with the Arapaho and Cheyenne. In attendance were Cheyenne chiefs Bull Bear; Tall Bull; Long Chin, an uncle of George Bent; as well as Arapaho chief White Antelope. Gerry conveyed the governor's wish for peace and reiterated the invitation Evans made in his earlier proclamation, that all "friendly" Indians go to the various territorial forts. The chiefs flatly refused. Gerry later testified:

> "They said that the white man's hands were dripping with their blood, and now he [Evans] calls for a treaty." [23]

Then, just eight weeks, nearly to the day, after the murders of the Hungate family, news arrived in Denver City of a particularly violent Indian raid along the Little Blue River, a tributary of the Platte River in south central Nebraska Territory. Reaction reached points of near mass hysteria throughout both territories.

The many members of the extended family of Joseph Eubanks, Missouri natives, homesteaded along the Little Blue River and Plum Creek, tributaries to the Platte River, by the spring of 1864. The homestead was located approximately a mile and a half north of the small community of Oak. This area was the main thoroughfare for the Oregon Trail west through Nebraska Territory, as well as a southern trail through the Blue River valley, for freight and passenger stages traveling to Denver City.

Just two months after the Eubanks family arrived, a vicious attack by the Cheyenne, Arapaho and Sioux resulted in the brutal deaths of most of the Eubanks family. Other members of the family were taken hostage, treated horribly, violated, sold as slaves, or killed. It was a brutal atrocity.

It was a quiet, peaceful Sunday afternoon on August 7, 1864, when the Indians descended the nearby bluff and began their brutal attack. John Palmer, the brother-in-law of Joseph Eubanks Jr., later recalled what happened:

"In the month of May 1864 the Eubanks family composed of Joseph Eubanks, his wife, their two married sons Joseph and William with their wives also three younger sons and two younger daughters.my sister Harriet and myself settled in the state of Nebraska. The massacre of the Eubanks took place late in the afternoon between 4 and 5 o'clock...this was a Sunday evening. The Eubanks were all at their house excepting one of the younger sons who was with me - we were pulling up some hay. Young Eubanks was raking hay while I was going to a spring about a half mile distant for water. I was absent about half an hour - upon my return I found young Eubanks dead and scalped. He had been shot with arrows.

Joseph Eubanks, Jr., and his wife who was my sister - the young Eubanks just mentioned and myself lived together. About an hour before the massacre I saw Joseph Eubanks, Jr., and his wife at our house. After the younger Eubanks and myself had gone into the field Joseph Jr. left the house...He was found dead and scalped 3 days after about 1 mile from his house. Where I found the younger Eubanks dead in the hay field upon my return with the water from the spring I at once ran to the house to see if my sister was safe.

When I got to the house I saw the Indians ride to the top of a hill about 300 yards north from the house; a train of freighters was corralled about 600 yards east from the house.

I found my sister unharmed and we ran with all possible haste to the freighters. The Indians then left and I did not see any more of them. My sister and I remained with the freighters that night and the next day I went to where the Eubanks lived about 4 miles northwest of where I lived.

When I reached their house I found five dead bodies, those [of the] two younger sons aged about 14 and 16 years and a daughter aged 17 of Joseph Eubanks, Sr., William; two children of William and a boy about 7 years old, a grandchild of Joseph, Sr., were captured. All had been shot with arrows except William - he was shot in the head with a bullet. All except Joseph E., Sr., were scalped and entirely stripped of their clothes.

I with some of the freighters before mentioned buried all of them." [24]

An unnamed eye-witness account of the horrific scene not long after the slaughter comes from the archives of the University of Nebraska Library Special Collections:

"I met a party of freighters and stage coach passengers on horseback and [a] few ranchmen fleeing from the Little Blue Valley. They told me a terrible story that the Indians were just in their rear and how they massacred the people west of them, none knew how many. All knew that the Cheyennes had made a raid into the Little Blue Valley striking down all before them. Next day I passed Eubanks' Ranch; found three little children from three to seven years old who had been taken by the heels and swung around against the log cabin, beating their heads to a perfect jelly. Found the hired girl some 15 rods from the ranch staked out on the prairie tied by her hands and feet, naked, body full of arrows and horribly mangled. Not far from this was the body of Eubanks, whiskers cut off, body most fearfully mutilated. The building had been fired - ruins still smoking."

Among the dead that Palmer and the freighters buried that awful day were the aforementioned Joseph Eubanks Sr., and six of his seven sons. Joseph, Jr., who had three arrows in his back and an arrow in his arm, had also been scalped. His younger brothers, William, James, Henry, Fred, and Andrew, were all killed in similar fashion. Two of Eubanks' daughters, Sarah and Meldora (Dora,) were also murdered.

Daniel Freeman, one of the freighters who helped with the burials, later described what he saw:

"The men were scalped, their limbs unjointed, privates cut off; the women were scalped their bodies mutilated and the private parts scalped." [25]

Another witness recalled that:

"One of the females, beside having suffered the latter inhumane barbarity, was pinned to the earth by a stake thrust through her person in a most revolting manner." [26]

There were very few family members that survived the incomprehensible tragedy, and others were missing. It was surmised they faced a most horrible ordeal, possibly worse than death: they had been taken captive.

While graves were being dug for the dead Eubanks, the Indians were continuing their reign of terror in the area. The Sioux, accompanied by a few Cheyenne Dog Soldiers, including Charlie Bent and Minimic, attacked a wagon train. The ill-fated Fletcher/Morton group of westward travelers had left the Plum Creek Station the previous day. This was the only station on the Oregon Trail between Julesburg, Colorado Territory, and Fort Kearny in Nebraska Territory. The wagon train, twelve in all, included two wagons belonging to William Fletcher and his cousin John Fletcher, as well as three wagons belonging to Thomas Frank and Nancy Jane Morton. William Marble had three wagons in this group. He and his two sons, twelve-year-old Joel and nine-year-old Daniel, were accompanied by Marble's partner, James Smith and his wife. Others in the Fletcher/Morton group included Michael Kelly, and a man known only as Mr. St. Clair.

This was a new beginning for nineteen-year-old Nancy Morton, who was grieving over the recent deaths of her two children. Three-year-old Charlotte Ann and her infant baby brother, (born near Pikes Peak) both had recently died of measles. Nancy Jane Fletcher Morton, again pregnant, seemed to have enjoyed the westward journey thus far, as she later wrote:

"But this river, [the Platte] when in season of high water, assumes a beautiful appearance. Its broad bosom is dotted with islands of the

richest verdure, and adorned with gorgeous hued flowers and delicate vining vegetation." [27]

As the sun began to set on the evening of August 7, 1864, the group camped on the banks of Plum Creek, another tributary of the Platte River.

Continuing their westward journey the following morning, the Fletcher/Morton party had traveled just two miles when they were suddenly overtaken by a party of warring Indians. They didn't stand a chance. The bodies of eleven men were found scalped. It was believed that the entire party of freighters had been viciously murdered.[28]

George Bent, the older half-brother of Charlie (George's mother was Owl Woman), later said that a large camp of hostile Indians had gathered in unison against the whites. Camped near the Solomon River, members of the Arapaho, Southern Cheyenne and Sioux united under Spotted Tail and Pawnee Killer. This became known in history as the Sioux War of 1864. In ten days, August 7 through August 16, 1864, over one hundred white people were killed and several more injured. Property was destroyed, livestock stolen and telegraph lines were cut.

Due to the Indian raids, the Overland Stage Company had suspended all travel. One of the last stages to arrive at the station in Julesburg carried Mrs. Catherine Weaver Collins, the wife of William O. Collins, the military commander at Fort Laramie. She related the experience in her diary:

"We arrived here at Julesburg this morning. The [military] escort of men who accompanied us to our encampment started back to Fort Laramie... and behold! When we got here General Mitchell learned by telegraph that Indians had attacked and burned a wagon train yesterday at the Bluffs Canyon near Plum Creek Station, killing eleven emigrants, plundering and burning their wagons and taking as captive two or three women and children. It seems as if there is to be a general Indian war which will lead to the extermination of this race along this great thoroughfare. In the event of an Indian attack we were to lie down flat on the ground as soon as the wagons were corralled, so the [rifle] balls would pass over us." [29]

Elbridge Gerry was quite concerned at the increase of the Indian raids along the South Platte Trail. Chivington had previously ordered troops of his Colorado Volunteers south to patrol the Arkansas and Republican Rivers, largely leaving the northern plains and the South Platte Trail unprotected. The Cheyenne Dog Soldiers, a warring branch of the tribe, saw their opportunity and had been raiding all along the South Platte River in June and July. Many settlers lost stock in cattle and horses. On August 1, both the Junction Station and the Valley Station along the trail were also ransacked and livestock was taken. On August 7, the very day of the Plum Creek murders, more homes were burned, south of the Platte. This time, entire families were killed. Word reached Governor Evans on August 10.

Frustrated by the lack of help from the federal government, on August 11, 1864, immediately after learning of the murderous August raids in Nebraska, Evans took matters into his own hands, issuing a second public proclamation to the settlers of the territory. He called for them to organize groups for self-protection against the Indians. Colonel Chivington followed suit, directing his military officers to fire on all Indians, and ordering them to "not burden your command with prisoner Indians." The same day that Evans made his public proclamation, the *Rocky Mountain News,* back in publication following the spring flood, published this second proclamation from the governor. It read in part:

"All citizens of Colorado, either individually or in such parties as they may organize, to go in pursuit of all hostile Indians on the plains, scrupulously avoiding those who have responded to my call to rendezvous at the points indicated; also to kill and destroy as enemies of the country wherever they may be found, all such hostile Indians."

The governor's plea was too late for many on the South Platte Trail. On the night of August 19, 1864, Elbridge Gerry and his Cheyenne wife were visited by her two brothers, Long Chin and Man-Shot-By-A-Ree. Perhaps out of respect for Gerry and his great care of their sister, they warned Gerry of an impending attack along the South Platte Trail. They told Gerry that nearly a thousand warriors of the Sioux, Cheyenne and Arapaho tribes were assembled in the hills above Beaver Creek. In two days' time, they warned, the Indians would attack every station and homestead along the river road, cut the telegraph lines, and go on to destroy Denver.

Immediately, in the dead of night, Gerry saddled his horse and bravely rode the sixty-five miles to Denver, non-stop and in the cover of night, warning ranches and stations along the way, and changing horses three times. He arrived in Denver twenty-four hours later, in the middle of the night, exhausted, but determined to alert the governor. Governor Evans assembled every man who owned a gun, telegraphed the settlements that could be reached, and sent out what troops he had to the Overland Stage stop of Latham, across the river from the Gerry ranch. All along the trail homesteaders fortified their homes, corralled their livestock, or gathered at local forts.

The Indian informants were correct, for two days later the Indian warriors appeared on the bluffs above the river. Seeing the soldiers, they must have realized they had lost the element of surprise. The Indians called off their attack, when they discovered that Denver, Latham, and the settlements were prepared for the attack. Robert North had also been warning of the Indian raids for some time. In a report dated November 10, 1863, North wrote:

"Having recovered an Arapaho prisoner (a squaw) from the Utes, I obtained the confidence of the Indians completely. I have lived with them from a boy, and my wife is an Arapaho. In honor of my exploit in recovering the prisoner the Indians gave me a 'big medicine dance,' about fifty-five miles below Fort Lyon, on the Arkansas River, at which the leading chiefs and warriors of several of the tribes of the plains met. The Comanche, Apache, Kioways, [sic] the northern band of Arapahoes, and all of the Cheyennes, with the Sioux, have pledged one another to go to war with the whites as soon as they can procure ammunition in the spring. I heard them discuss the matter often, and the few of them who opposed it were forced to be quiet, and were really in danger of their lives. I saw the principle chiefs pledge to each other that they would be friendly and shake hands with the whites until they procured ammunition and guns, so as to be ready when they strike. Plundering to get means has already commenced; and the plan is to commence the war at several points in the sparse settlements early in the spring. They wanted me to join them in the war, saying that they would take a great many white women and children prisoners, and get a heap of property, blankets, &c. But while I am connected with them by marriage, and live with them, I am a white man, and wish to avoid bloodshed. There are a great many Mexicans with the Comanche and Apache Indians, all of whom urge on the war, promising to help the Indians themselves, and that a great many more Mexicans would come up from New Mexico for the purpose in the spring."

Elbridge Gerry, known as the Paul Revere of the Plains, had averted a certain disaster. The consequences were detrimental to

Gerry and his ranch. The Indians raided three times, burning the barn and stealing nearly one hundred of his prized horses. It took years, but eventually the State of Colorado did compensate Gerry for his loss, with nearly eight thousand dollars.[30]

A week later, Evans again reached out to Washington. In a letter to Secretary of War Edwin M. Stanton, dated August 18, 1864, Evans wrote:

> *"Extensive Indian depredations, with murders of families, have occurred... Our lines of communication are cut, and our crops, are all in exposed localities, and cannot be gathered by our scattered population. Large bodies of Indians are undoubtedly near Denver, and we are in danger of destruction from attack. I earnestly request that the Second Colorado Volunteer Cavalry Regiment be immediately sent to our relief. It is impossible to exaggerate our danger. We are doing all we can for our defense."* [31]

Once again, Evans' request was denied. However, the governor did receive authorization from the federal government on August 29, 1864, to recruit a volunteer regiment of soldiers for "a period of 100 days." Thus, the new Third Colorado Volunteer Cavalry Regiment came under the command of Colonel Chivington.

In the spring of 1864, Major Edward Wynkoop had been assigned commander of Fort Lyon, along the Arkansas River, in southeastern Colorado Territory. Captain Silas Soule served as acting assistant adjutant general for the First Colorado Cavalry, under Wynkoop's command. At the fort, both men learned that a band of peaceful Southern Cheyenne, under Chief Black Kettle, were camped near the fort. In an effort to clarify his duty, regarding Governor's Evans missive for peaceful Indians to seek refuge at a nearby fort, Wynkoop wrote to Chivington:

> *"I would like to receive from headquarters full and thorough instructions in regard to the course I shall adopt in reference to the Indians."* [32]

Chivington replied with commands to reinforce the military detachment, to be ready for an enemy advance from the Confederates. This was a ruse on the part of Chivington. The winds of war were blowing ever stronger.

As the Indian War was raging in Kansas and Nebraska Territory, Wynkoop became concerned over several Indian skirmishes near Fort Lyon. The first occurred on August 11, 1864, when Ordnance Sergeant Kenyon left the fort one morning in search of stray horses. Near the Sand Creek juncture, he noticed a group of Indian warriors riding toward him. Kenyon managed to make it safely back to the fort. Wynkoop sent Lieutenant Joseph A. Cramer and thirty men to search for the warriors. Approximately five miles east of the fort, Cramer and his men spotted the Indians and gave chase. The chase went on for some ten to fifteen miles before the soldiers caught up with the fleeing Indians. At that point, the warriors turned and attempted to charge the soldiers. They suddenly turned and fled again when they saw a second group of soldiers approaching Cramer's troops. The soldiers again gave pursuit. During a running fight, the men wounded four warriors and captured one pony.

On August 17, Captain Gray, of Camp Fillmore, near Booneville, received a report from a stagemaster, of an Indian raid not far from his camp. Taking thirty-eight soldiers with him, he left the camp on a reconnaissance mission. Approximately eight miles east, along the Arkansas River, the men discovered the bodies of three men. Nearby was a military ambulance and an abandoned government wagon containing the usual items, as well as female clothing and household goods. Mrs. Julia S. Lambert, the wife of the Fort Lyon's station master, later recounted the incident:

"A man named Snyder, who worked in the blacksmith shop had sent east for his wife to come to Denver where he was to meet her and bring her to the fort. The quartermaster let him take a small ambulance, four mules and a driver for the trip.

He met her and came down to Pueblo, following that branch of the stage route. When they stopped at Booneville, twenty-five miles east of Pueblo, Aunt Eliza, the old colored woman who had lived in Colonel Boone's family for many years, said, 'You all got a mighty fine head of hair for the Injuns to git, honey.' This frightened and made her nervous and she replied, 'Oh, don't say that, for I have heard such terrible stories of how they abuse the prisoners.'" [33]

According to Mrs. Lambert, the Snyder wagon group traveled to Bent's Old Fort, where they stayed for a time before going on to Fort Lyon. They never made it. Mrs. Lambert later recounted:

> "A westbound stage from Fort Lyon came upon the abandoned military ambulance. The two men had been shot and scalped and the woman was gone. It was known there had been a woman in the party as articles belonging to her were found strewn around. One of the wheel mules had been shot in order to stop the ambulance." [34]

Mrs. Lambert's account is fairly accurate, however, there were three male bodies found at the scene, not two. The men were identified as Mr. Snyder and his two teamsters. It was later learned that the murders and the apparent kidnapping of Mrs. Snyder were committed by a band of Arapaho warriors led by Little Raven's son, who was also known as Little Raven. It would not be known what became of Mrs. Snyder until nearly two months later.

On the same day as the murders of the Snyder group, Little Raven's band also raided a nearby agency, stole twenty-eight head of stock and murdered three other white people. The following day they crossed to the south side of the Arkansas River, where they raided Charles Autobees' ranch and stole several horses. Autobees, the half-brother of trapper, trader and military scout, Thomas Tate Tobin, was a well-respected pioneer of the area in his own right, and known friend to the Indians. The act of such a raid and the murders by hostile Indians was shocking to Autobees. And it continued.

The week following the attacks and raids on the Arkansas River, on August 21, another raid occurred resulting in murder. Two men, later identified only as Crawford and Hancock, were found approximately eighteen miles west of Fort Lyon. Both men had been scalped. That same day, further north, a group of Cheyenne warriors raided Elbridge Gerry's ranch, stealing over a hundred head of cattle.

Concerned over the obvious increase of Indian hostility, Wynkoop wrote a detailed report of the recent incidents to Colonel Chivington. He ended his report with the following statement:

> "My intention is to kill all Indians I may come across until I receive orders to the contrary from headquarters." [35]

On September 4, 1864, a group of soldiers were riding a few miles northwest of Fort Lyon when they encountered two Cheyenne men and one woman heading in the direction of the fort. One of the men signaled signs of peace and waved a sheet of paper in the air. The three Cheyenne were taken to the fort as prisoners. John Smith, the local Cheyenne interpreter, arrived at the fort to interpret for Wynkoop as he interrogated the prisoners. The Cheyenne, identified as Minimic (Mah-nim-ic), One-Eye and his wife, explained they had come in peace. One-Eye offered a letter of peace from some of the Cheyenne chiefs to Major Wynkoop, which was written by George Bent and addressed to Major Colley. The letter, from Black Kettle, read:

"*Cheyenne Village, August 29, 1864*

Maj' Colley, sir:
We received a letter from Bent, wishing us to make peace. We held a council in regard to it; all came to the conclusion to make peace with you, providing you make peace with the Kiowas, Comanches, Arapahoes, Apaches, and Sioux. We are going to send a messenger to the Kiowas and to the other nations about our going to make peace with you. We heard that you have some prisoners at Denver; we have seven prisoners of yours which we are willing to give up, providing you give up yours. There are three war parties out yet, and two of Arapahoes; they have been out some time and expected in soon. When we held this council there were a few Arapahoes and Sioux present. We want true news from you in return. Black Kettle and other Chiefs." [36]

The "prisoners" Black Kettle referred to were the missing Eubanks family members as well as a female and child captives from the Plum Creek raids. The adult female captives were kept in various areas of the camp but were never allowed to be together, until George Bent intervened. When Bent learned of the female and child hostages, he befriended a few of these captives in the camp on the Republican River.

One of the first he visited shortly after her capture was Nancy Jane Morton. She and her husband, Frank, were among those traveling west with the Fletcher/Morton wagon train. Nancy Morton had been severely injured during the Indian attack at Plum Creek, and was confined to a Sioux lodge. When Bent first saw her, he was shocked at the extent of her injuries. Her eyes were swollen shut and she had two gaping wounds which looked to Bent as though they were infected; one in her left side, near her armpit, the other to her thigh, both the results of arrow shots. Bent insisted that a Cheyenne medicine man immediately treat her. Mrs. Morton was given a strong broth to drink and a mixture of herbs and roots were massaged into her wounds, and raw liver was placed over her eyes. Bent returned the following day and Nancy Morton began to tell him the events of her capture. She said that she was driving the wagon team when she observed a large group of Indian warriors on a bluff on the south side of the Platte River Road. She shouted to her husband who was sleeping in the wagon as he had been up all night with guard duty. As he joined his wife on the spring wagon seat, James Smith, whose wagons were in the lead, rode back to the other wagons, warning of an Indian attack. And then the Indians attacked. They cut off the lead wagon and several warriors killed Smith and St. Clair.

Nancy watched in horror as Mrs. Smith jumped from her wagon and ran to hide in a thicket near the river. Possibly taking a cue from Mrs. Smith, Nancy leaped from her wagon perch. She said that as she landed on the ground, she hit the wheel of the moving wagon and broke several ribs. Nevertheless, she gathered herself with all the might she could muster and ran toward the river. Seeing her brother William and cousin John, she ran toward them. Just as John shouted out to her, "We're all going to be killed," an arrow was shot into his chest. He fell to the ground, landing at Nancy's feet. Blood oozed over her shoes and within seconds he was dead. She quickly ran to her brother who was hiding in a cluster of tall grass. After some time, Nancy had no idea how long, her brother suggested they return to the wagons. As William Fletcher rose to make a run for the wagons, he was shot full of arrows before her very eyes. He, too, fell near Nancy, and reportedly said, "Tell my wife Susan I am killed. Good-bye, my dear sister." [37] And then Nancy, who had exposed herself to come to her brother's aid, was shot with two arrows. Warriors surrounded her and one of them grabbed her and pulled her onto his horse. As the warring party rode away, Nancy noticed another warrior had nine-year-old Danny Marble on his horse. The Cheyenne warriors, as they were later identified, took their captives to the camp on the Republican River. During the first days of their captivity, both Nancy and young Daniel were treated in a cruel manner, including daily beatings. As Danny cried, Nancy tried to comfort him, despite her physical pain. The beatings and subsequent injuries caused Nancy to miscarry a few days after her capture. This harrowing time at camp caused Nancy and young Daniel Marble to became quite close; after all, all they had was each other.

Another female captive Bent visited was Mrs. Lucinda Eubanks. She and her two children, three-year-old Isabelle and her baby, William, Jr., were among those taken captive following the massacre near the Little Blue River. Lucinda, understandably disconsolate, eventually warmed up to Bent. Lucinda said that she was taken by a Cheyenne chief who threatened her, beat her and forced himself on her several times. Later, he traded her to a Sioux warrior named Two Face, who also beat her. Two Face then traded her to Black Foot. While Black Foot didn't beat her, his several wives did. Then, in the autumn, the Cheyenne traded for her. Bent also learned that her husband, William, had been killed before her eyes. Her daughter had been taken from her and she feared for the child's life. Concerned that she may lose her son as well, she continued to breast-feed him, afraid that if he were weaned, he, too, would be taken from her.

Bent then learned that another captive, sixteen-year old Laura Roper, who had been separated from Lucinda, had little Isabelle with her. He later recalled after his first meeting with Laura Roper, that she seemed "happy." She played games with the Indian children and laughed often. Female captives were repeatedly raped and passed from warrior to warrior.

For whatever reason, Bent said that Laura Roper was treated very differently. He also said that the Indian women delighted in combing her blond hair.[38] During his visits with her, Laura told him of the event when she was captured. She related that at approximately 4 p.m. on that fateful Sunday afternoon, William and Lucinda Eubanks, along with their two children, Isabelle and William, Jr., were escorting her back to her home, about a mile away from the Eubank's home. As the group heard the yells of warriors and the thunder of a hundred horses approaching, they ran for cover in a buffalo wallow. She said they watched as the Indians descended on the Eubanks homestead and began killing her family members near a sandbar at the river. Then the Indians swarmed the house and killed everyone in sight. As the Indians left the area, she said, they passed near where she and the others were hiding. Little Isabelle screamed. The Indians discovered the them. They watched as the Indians killed Lucinda's husband. Then she and three-year-old Isabelle Eubanks, whom she was holding, as well as Lucinda and her baby, William Jr. (a Eubanks grandson), were abducted. She said that the Indians traveled southeast. At one point, she said, they separated herself from little Isabelle. When an Indian grabbed Isabelle her by the hair and drew out his knife, Laura Roper said she grabbed the knife and that the other Indians laughed. From then on she was called "brave squaw."

Through the efforts of Bent, Lucinda, her daughter Isabelle, Laura Roper, and Lucinda's seven-year-old nephew, Ambrose

Nancy Morton on her wedding day. She was captured at Plum Creek, Nebraska Territory August 8, 1864. Her husband Thomas was killed. Nancy soon miscarried during her captivity. *Jeff Broome*

Asher, were all reunited after the Cheyenne camp moved to the Smoky Hill River and joined with the other warring tribes in the area. The women were delighted to see each other and spend time with the children. They were also saddened, yet consoling, when young Ambrose finally opened up to people he felt comfortable with and recounted with remarkable detail, how the Indians shot his grandfather, Joseph Eubanks, then pulled him to the ground, stripped him and scalped him. [39] Nancy Morton recalled years later, "We all began to cry for we all knew each others sorrow." [40] The reunion did not last long and was never repeated.

    Bent continued to visit the captives when he was able. A few days after the reunion, he visited Nancy Morton, who was now beginning to walk again. Bent brought her to the lodge of his stepmother, Island. Nancy seemed to have not particularly enjoyed her visit away from her own captive surroundings, as she later wrote:

> "Their tepee was decorated with many gorgeous decorations which looked to me very grotesque. The old squaw took me on her lap and kissed me and told me she was so sorry the Indians had killed my husband and friends, then she would caress me and tell me not to worry for she thought I would get home one day. She combed my hair and tried to comfort me all she could in her grotesque way."

    On that September day in 1864, when peaceful representatives of the Cheyenne, One-Eye, his wife and Minimic, met with Major Edward Wynkoop at Fort Lyon, Wynkoop was skeptical of their intentions, despite previous peaceful overtures displayed, particularly by One-Eye.

One of many examples was the previous July when Colonel Chivington was at Fort Lyon and met briefly with One-Eye. After the meeting, Chivington wrote a certificate of "good character" for him and instructed him to exhibit a white flag should he meet up with soldiers.[41] (This instruction by Chivington would become a crucial point in the aftermath of the Sand Creek massacre.) One-Eye, whose daughter, Amache, was married to the very prosperous rancher, John Prowers, had longed believed in peace with the white men.

Nevertheless, Wynkoop had reservations. However, after reading the letter of the peace proposal, he became intrigued. Through his interpreter, John Smith, he asked several questions, directed at One-Eye. His first question to the Cheyenne representative was asking why (according to Chivington's new orders) would he risk death to travel to the fort. One-Eye replied:

"I thought I would be killed, but I knew that the paper would be found upon my dead body, that you would see it, and it might give peace to my people once more." [42]

Wynkoop pressed on with more questions. His final question went to the sincerity of the peace proposal and the release of the female and child "prisoners." Smith interpreted One-Eye's reply as, "At the risk of his life he would guarantee their sincerity."[43] Wynkoop was persuaded by the honesty of One-Eye. He felt an obligation to attempt to rescue the white females and children held captive. By attending the Indians' council for peace, he also saw an opportunity to end the violence between the two cultures. Wynkoop reflected years later on this event and how it changed his attitude toward the Indians:

"I was bewildered with an exhibition of such patriotism on the part of two savages, and felt myself in the presence of superior beings; and these were the representatives of a race that I had heretofore looked upon without exception as being cruel treacherous, and blood-thirsty." [44]

One-Eye had informed Wynkoop that a large Indian village lay along the Smoky Hill River, approximately 140 miles northeast of Fort Lyon, in Kansas Territory. He also told Wynkoop that time was of the essence, as the village would soon break up and move to other locations for the winter.

Major Wynkoop, along with a group of 127 volunteer soldiers, including Captain Silas Soule, Lieutenants Joseph A. Cramer and Charles Phillips, and interpreter John Smith, left Fort Lyon on September 5, 1864. The military expedition included two twelve-pound howitzers, as well as the four "prisoners." Wynkoop agreed to the "prisoner" exchange for those held by the Indians. Wynkoop's "prisoners" were One-Eye, his wife, Minimic and another Indian known as The Fool.

After four days of travel, Wynkoop and his troops located the Indian camp on a fork of the Smoky Hill River, in an area known as the "Bunch of Timbers." At this point, Wynkoop sent Minimic to the camp to let them know that he had arrived per the letter of a peace proposal signed by Cheyenne chiefs.

In the meantime, Wynkoop ordered his men to set up camp, moving the wagons into a corral formation for defense purposes. As the men readied their horses to move toward the camp, several hundred Indians moved their ponies in position as well. It was a tense stand-off for quite some time, as the warriors were unaware of Wynkoop's intentions and the soldiers knew they were outnumbered by at least five to one.

The following morning, September 10, Black Kettle and several other chiefs arrived to meet with Wynkoop. Warriors escorted Wynkoop, Cramer, Phillips, Soule and Smith to a large grove of trees along the south bank of the Smoky Hill River. It was here that they were met by Cheyenne chiefs Black Kettle, Big Wolf, Dog Man, Bull Bear, and White Antelope. Arapaho chiefs present included Big Mouth, Left Hand, Little Raven and Neva. George Bent acted as interpreter for the Indian chiefs.

What became known in history as the Smoky Hill Council officially began with the Indian tradition of passing around the peace pipe, in which all in attendance participated. Wynkoop began by stating that he had come in effort of peace after receiving Black Kettle's letter delivered by One-Eye. He also said that he would deliver his four prisoners in return for the seven white prisoners held by the Indians. He further told the chiefs that it was his firm belief that this action would demonstrate the Indians' sincerity at forging a lasting peace between the two cultures. Wynkoop informed the council that while he did not have the authority to negotiate a peace agreement, he offered to escort the chiefs to Denver to meet with Governor John Evans, who was also the Superintendent of Indian Affairs, who did have such authority. Wynkoop concluded by advising the chiefs to bring their people to Fort Lyon in compliance with Evans' earlier peace proposal to the Indian tribes, requesting that all "friendly" Indians go to the various territorial forts.

Wynkoop, feeling fairly confident with the negotiations thus far, was interrupted by Lieutenant George Hardin. In a private exchange, Hardin informed Wynkoop that their camp had been besieged by heavily armed mounted warriors. They had raided the provision wagons and blocked the soldiers' access to the howitzers. Wynkoop stormed back to the peace proceedings expressing his anger over the blatant invasion of his camp by the warriors during an obvious demonstration of peace. Outraged by the action, Black Kettle immediately left the group and rode to the military camp. Confronting the warriors, he ordered them to mount their horses and leave the area. As the warriors left, they set the prairie on fire. In the smoke and haze, the soldiers packed up what they could and abandoned their position. News of the soldiers' retreat would quickly make its way back to the Indian camp which would lead to an unfortunate end for one of the white captives.

Tension was high on both sides as the peace council continued. Perhaps bolstered by the warriors' attack, Bull Bear, still angry over the murder of his brother, Lean Bear, four months earlier, rose from his seat and confronted Wynkoop, demanding he stand. He accused Wynkoop and his soldiers of lying and stealing from them when they came to him to trade in peace. He then suggested to his fellow chiefs that they were "fools" to believe that Wynkoop was sincere. Little Raven agreed with Bull Bear, urging the chiefs to continue the war. Left Hand voiced his anger, stating that he had always acted peacefully, but was ignored in his efforts.

As the hostility mounted, One-Eye rose. He said he would feel ashamed if Wynkoop was harmed. Taken aback by such hostility and accusations, Wynkoop glanced over at Black Kettle for direction. Their eyes met and Black Kettle smiled and nodded. Wynkoop later recounted the moment:

> *"He saw my bewilderment, I might say my trepidation, and his eye caught mine, he gave me a look of encouragement."* [45]

Black Kettle had allowed the chiefs to speak. Now he spoke.

He rose from his seat and approached Wynkoop. He offered his hand to Wynkoop and the major rose from his seat. Black Kettle then embraced Wynkoop twice before leading him to the center of the council. John Smith translated what Black Kettle said to his fellow chiefs:

"This white man is not here to laugh at us, nor does he regard us as children, but on the contrary unlike the balance of his race, he comes with confidence in the pledges given by the Red man. He has been told that he should come and go unarmed. He has not come with a forked tongue or with two hearts, but his words are straight and his heart single. Had he told us that he would give us peace, on the condition of our delivering to him the white prisoners, he would have told us a lie. For I know that he cannot give us peace, there is a greater chief in the far off camp of the White Soldiers." [46]

With that, Black Kettle ended the council proceedings. He shook the hands of both Silas Soule and Wynkoop, and assured Wynkoop, that he was "still, as he always had been, a friend to the whites."[47] The various Indian chiefs left for a private council and Wynkoop told Black Kettle he would return to his camp and await their decision. Black Kettle told him he and his men would not be attacked. Nevertheless, Wynkoop, Soule and other officers spent a long night on watch duty.

At near noon the following day, a group of Arapaho Indians, led by Neva, rode into the military camp with sixteen-year-old Laura Roper. Delivering her to the soldiers, they then rode away. Grateful for the return of one of the hostages, a bewildered Wynkoop spent a second night at the camp. The following day, Wynkoop noticed a group of riders approaching. Recognizing Black Kettle, he rode out to meet him.

After their greeting, Wynkoop was overjoyed when he saw an Indian woman with three white children. He later wrote:

"The feelings I then experienced I would be powerless to fully describe. Such happiness I never experienced before, never since, and do not expect to in this world." [48]

The three children were Daniel Marble, Ambrose Asher and little Isabelle Eubanks. Wynkoop took custody of the children, placing the little girl on his saddle with him. Black Kettle misinformed Wynkoop that there were two women and one child that were at Sioux camps further north, and that he had sent traders to the camps to purchase them from the Sioux. However, Black Kettle further informed Wynkoop that he had learned that the Sioux refused to free their captives and had staked them to the ground and covered them with buffalo robes in an effort to hide them. Black Kettle assured Wynkoop he would do everything he could to deliver the promised captives.

Black Kettle also informed Wynkoop of a tragic event that happened during the Smoky Hill Council. Mrs. Snyder, captured during the Arapaho raid on the Arkansas River, had hung herself the previous night in Chief Left Hand's camp. Later, Laura Roper said that the captives were told the soldiers had left the council, when they moved further away following the raid and burning of their camp by the marauding warriors. Julia Lambert, wife of the Fort Lyon's station master, later wrote of the tragic incident and quoted Laura Roper's account:

> *"I knew there were other white women in the camp. One escaped only to be recaptured and brought back after a chase of some miles. During the night she took off her calico dress, tore the skirt into strips and twisted them into a rope with which she hung herself from the lodge pole. How she accomplished this no one knew as the poles were high in the center."*[49]

It is quite possible that if Mrs. Snyder was told that the soldiers had left the council, as Laura Roper indicated, she may have thought her only hope of rescue was gone. With such perceived abandonment, she committed suicide.

The remaining captives promised by Black Kettle in his letter of peace, and reiterated to Wynkoop as he delivered the others, were Lucinda Eubanks and her young son, William Jr., and Nancy Jane Morton.

With a nod to Black Kettle in gratitude, Wynkoop took the children back to his camp.

Black Kettle and the other chiefs, including Neva, White Antelope, One-Eye, White Wolf, Bosse, Bull Bear, and Heap of Buffalo, agreed to travel with Wynkoop and his troops back to Fort Lyon. From there, they would prepare for the trip to Denver for Wynkoop's promised meeting with Governor Evans.

Back at Fort Lyon, Wynkoop, bolstered by the peaceful compromise, following the Smoky Hill Council, sent a series of reports to his commanders, including a letter to Governor Evans, dated September 18, 1864. The reports and letter to the governor detailed his latest mission, resulting in the Smoky Hill Council, and the subsequent release of four white prisoners. Explicit in Wynkoop's writings to the officials was the expressed willingness of the Cheyenne and Arapaho chiefs to meet with Evans, as Superintendent of Indian Affairs, to form a peace treaty. Additionally, in his letter to Evans, Wynkoop informed the governor that he was leaving Fort Lyon for Denver City, "immediately," with the rescued hostages as well as the peaceful Indian chiefs, who were willing to meet with the governor in an effort to conduct a peaceful negotiation to the recent conflicts.[50] This was a mission Wynkoop believed would lead to peace for all parties. The details of the Smoky Hill Council and Wynkoop's resolve to find a way toward peace are apparent in his report *to General Samuel R. Curtis:*

"*Fort Lyon, Colo, Ter., September 18, 1864.*
General Samuel R. Curtis
Lieut. S. F. Tapppan,

Sir: I have the honor to report for information of the major-general commanding that on the 3rd instant three Cheyenne Indians were met a few miles outside of this post by some of my men en route for Denver, and were brought in. They came, as they stated, bearing with them a proposition for peace from Black Kettle and other chiefs of the Cheyenne and Arapaho Nations. Their propositions were to the effect that they, the Cheyennes and Arapahoes, had in their possession seven white prisoners whom they offered to deliver up in case that we should come to terms of peace with them. They told me that the Cheyennes, Arapahoes, and Sioux were congregated for mutual protection, at what is called 'Bunch of Timber,' [sic] on headwaters of the Smoky Hill, at a distance of 140 miles northeast of this post numbering altogether about 3,000 warriors, and desirous to make peace with the whites. Feeling anxious at all odds to effect the release of these white prisoners, and my command having just been re-enforced by a detachment of New Mexico infantry sent by General Carleton, commanding Department of New Mexico, to my assistance, I found that I would be enabled to leave sufficient force to garrison this post by taking 130 men, including one section of the battery with me, and concluded to march to this Indian rendezvous for the purpose of procuring these white prisoners above mentioned, and to be governed by circumstances as to the manner in which I should proceed to accomplish the same object. Taking with me under a strict guard the Indians I had in my possession, I reached my destination and was confronted by from 600 to 800 Indian warriors drawn up in line of battle and prepared to fight. Putting on as bold a front as possible under the circumstances, I formed my little command in as good order as possible for the purpose of acting on the offensive, or defensive, as might be necessary, and advanced toward them, at the same time sending forward one of the Indians I had with me as an emissary to state that I had come for the purpose of holding a consultation with the chiefs of the Cheyenne and Arapaho Nations; to come to an understanding which might result in mutual benefit, and that

I had not come desiring strife, but was prepared for it, if necessary, and advised them to listen to what I had to say previous to making any more warlike demonstrations.

They consented to meet me in council, and I then proposed to them that if they desired peace to give me palpable evidence of their sincerity by delivering into my possession their white prisoners. I told them I was not authorized to conclude terms of peace with them, but if they acceded to my proposition I would take what chiefs they might choose to select to the Governor of Colorado Territory and state the circumstances to him, and that I believed it would result in what it was their desire to accomplish, peace with their white brethren. I had reference particularly to the Cheyenne and Arapaho tribes. The council was divided, undecided, and could not come to an understanding among themselves. Finding this to be the case, I told them I would march to a certain locality, distant twelve miles, and await a given time for their action in the matter. I took a strong position in the locality named and remained three days. In the interim they brought and turned over into my possession four white prisoners, all that was possible at the time being for them to turn over, the balance of the seven being, as they stated, with another band far to the northward. The released captives that I have with me now at this post consist of one female named Laura Roper, aged sixteen, and three children (two boys and one girl), named Isabella [sic] Eubanks, Ambrose Asher, and Daniel Marble; the three first mentioned all being taken on the Blue River, in the neighborhood of what is known as the Liberty Farm, and the latter captured somewhere on the South Platte with a train of which all the men were murdered. I have the principal chiefs of the two tribes with me, and propose starting immediately to Denver City, Colo. Ter., to put into effect the proposition made aforementioned by me to them. They agreed to give up the balance of the prisoners as soon as it is possible to procure them, which can be better done from Denver City than it can from this point.
Hoping my action may meet the approval of the major-general commanding. I respectfully submit the above report.

I have the honor to remain, very respectfully, your obedient servant,
E. W. Wynkoop
Major First Cavalry of Colorado, Commanding Post." [51]

Major Wynkoop firmly believed that Evans, in his capacity as Superintendent of Indian Affairs, who in the past had negotiated with the Indian tribes, would welcome the opportunity to settle a peace agreement with the peaceful leaders of the Southern Cheyenne and Arapaho tribes. He couldn't have been more wrong.

Wynkoop, along with a small entourage, left Fort Lyon on the morning of September 20, 1864. Included in the group were the major's wife, Louise Wynkoop, the four released children, seven Indian chiefs, and John Smith. Captain Silas Soule accompanied his commanding officer, as did Lieutenant Joseph Cramer. Forty soldiers escorted the group.

Concerned that he had not received an answer from Evans, either by telegraph or military missive, Wynkoop and his wife, escorted by Captain Soule, left the group at Booneville, traveling ahead to meet with the governor prior to the arrival of the peaceful Indian entourage.

Meanwhile, Chivington was pushing for further Indian punishment. On September 20, he wrote a letter to General Samuel R. Curtis, commander of all military operations in the West, requesting Curtis to authorize a campaign against the Cheyenne and Arapahoes in Colorado Territory.

Then, upon hearing Wynkoop was on his way to Denver with a group of peaceful Indians, on September 26, Chivington wired the following message to General Curtis, at Fort Leavenworth:

"I have been informed by E. W. Wynkoop, commanding Fort Lyon, that he is on his way here with Cheyenne and Arapaho chiefs and four white prisoners they gave up. Winter approaches. Third Regiment is full and they [the Indians] know they will be chastised for their outrages and now want peace. I hope that the major-general will direct that they make full restitution and then go on their reserve and stay there." [52]

Arriving in Denver City, Wynkoop attempted to meet with the governor but was informed that Evans was ill. The following day, Evans did meet with Wynkoop at a hotel. In the meeting, Wynkoop recounted the details of the Smoky Hill Council, the release of the four captives and the fact that Cheyenne and Arapaho Indian chiefs were on their way to meet with Evans in an effort at true peace.

Evans, somewhat impatiently, listened to Wynkoop and then replied, with regard to the peaceful Indians, that he, wanted "nothing to do with them."[53] Evans further stated, "They [the Indians] declared war against the United States." Stunned, Wynkoop again reminded Evans of his promise to the Indians. Unconcerned, Evans informed Wynkoop that he was leaving the following day on Ute Indian agency business. Wynkoop would later testify that as he pushed the issue with Evans, the governor revealed his true concern. After nearly two years of requests to the federal government, just a month earlier, he had finally received the authority to form the Third Colorado Volunteer Cavalry Regiment. In his written testimony, Wynkoop stated:

> *"Several times in our conversation in regard to the object of the Indians who were coming to see him, he made the remark, 'What shall I do with the third regiment, if I make peace?'"* [54]

With Evans' refusal to meet with the Indians, Wynkoop was at a loss as to what to do next. Then he read the lead story in the *Rocky Mountain News*. The September 27, 1864, issue reported Wynkoop's arrival with the rescued children. The article also took issue with the Indian group Wynkoop was bringing in to meet with the governor. The article stated that the Indians had "little if any influence over the 'Dog Soldiers', and it is not likely that a treaty with them would bring about peace."

Wynkoop was outraged. He went to the office of the *Rocky Mountain News* and met with owner and editor, William Newton Byers. In the next issue of the paper, September 28, 1864, Byers wrote an editorial stating:

> *"Major Wynkoop has considerably changed our opinion with respect to the pending [Indian] council. They have unquestionably had great provocation for hostilities, and we were not the first to violate friendly relations. As he [Wynkoop] is very familiar with all the circumstances, and has given the matter his especial thought we are willing to defer to his judgment."*

Later that day, the citizens of Denver lined the streets to watch the arrival of the Indians. It was quite a sight. Rows of army wagons, escorted by soldiers, brought the Indians into the city. Wynkoop's father-in-law, George Wakely, even took a photograph of the historic moment. Perhaps due to the editorial in the Rocky Mountain News, and the public interest, Evans was forced to attend the meeting at Camp Weld later that day. Neither Evans nor Chivington were pleased by this in impromptu meeting.

Nevertheless, Evans insisted on presiding over the meeting. He further insisted that United States Ute Indian Agent of the Grand River and Uinta Utes, Simeon Whiteley, take down a complete record of the proceedings. Evans told Whiteley that:

"Upon the results of this council very likely depended a continuance of the Indian war on the plains, and it was important that the minutes should be full and complete." [55]

Evans presented a cold reception. John Smith interpreted and Whiteley often stopped the proceedings to get every word. Governor Evans opened the meeting with a few remarks to the group which included Colonel Chivington, Commander of the District of Colorado; Major George L. Shoup, Commander of the Third Colorado Volunteer Cavalry; Major Wynkoop; Captain Silas Soule, and Lieutenant Joseph A. Cramer. The peaceful Indians in attendance were the leading Cheyenne chiefs, Black Kettle; White Antelope, of the central Cheyenne band; Bull Bear, leader of Cheyenne Dog Soldiers; Arapaho chiefs Bosse, Heap of Buffalo, Na-ta-nee, and Neva.

Governor Evans asked the Indians if they had anything to say. Black Kettle rose to his feet and then said - On sight of your circular of June 27th, 1864, I took hold of the matter, and have now come to talk to you about it. I told Mr. Bent, who brought it, that I accepted it, but it would take some time to get all my people together-many of my young men being absent-and I have done everything in my power, since then, to keep peace with the whites. As soon as I could get my people together, we held a council, and got a half-breed who was with them, to write a letter to inform Major Wynkoop, or other military officers nearest to them, of their intention to comply with the terms of the circular. Major Wynkoop was kind enough to receive the letter, and visited them in camp, to whom they delivered four white prisoners-one other having killed herself; that there are two women and one child yet in their camp, whom they will deliver up as soon as they can get them in. I followed Major Wynkoop to Fort Lyon, and Major Wynkoop proposed that we come up to see you. We have come with our eyes shut, following his handful of men like coming through the fire. All we ask is that we have peace with the whites. We want to hold you by the hand. You are our father. We have been traveling thro' a cloud. The sky has been dark ever since the war began. These braves who are with me are all willing to do what I say. We want to take good tidings home to our people, that they may sleep in peace. I want you to give all the chiefs of these soldiers to understand that we are for peace, and that we have made peace, that we may not be mistaken by them for enemies. I have not come here with a little wolf bark, but have come to talk plain with you. We must live near the buffalo or starve. When we came here we came free, without any apprehension to see you, and when I go home and tell my people that I have taken your hand, and the hand of all the chiefs here in Denver, they will feel well, and so will all the different tribes of Indians on the Plains, after we have eaten and drank with them.

Governor Evans - I am sorry you did not respond to my appeal at once. You have gone into an alliance with the Sioux, who were at war with us. You have done a great deal of damage-stolen stock, and now have possession of it. However much a few individuals may have tried to keep the peace, as a nation you have gone to war. While we have been spending thousands of dollars in opening farms for you, and making preparations to feed, protect, and make you comfortable, you have joined our enemies and gone to war. Hearing, last fall, that they were dissatisfied, the Great Father at Washington sent me out on the plains to talk with you and make it all right. I sent messengers out to tell you that I had presents, and would make you a feast, but you sent word to me that you did not want to have anything to do with me, and to the Great Father at Washington that you could get along without him. Bull Bear wanted to come in to see me at the head of the Republican, but his people held a council and would not let him come.

Black Kettle - That is true.

Gov. Evans - I was under the necessity, after all my trouble, and all the expense I was at, of returning home without seeing them. Instead of this, your people went away and smoked the war pipe with our enemies.

Black Kettle - I don't know who could have told you this.

Gov. Evans - No matter who said this but your conduct has proved to my satisfaction that was the case. So far as making a treaty now is concerned, we are in no condition to do it. Your young men are on the war path. My soldiers are preparing for the fight. You, so far, have had the advantage; but that time is near at hand when the plains will swarm with United States soldiers. I understand that these men who have come to see me now, have been opposed to the war all the time, but that their people have controlled them and they could not help themselves. Is this so?

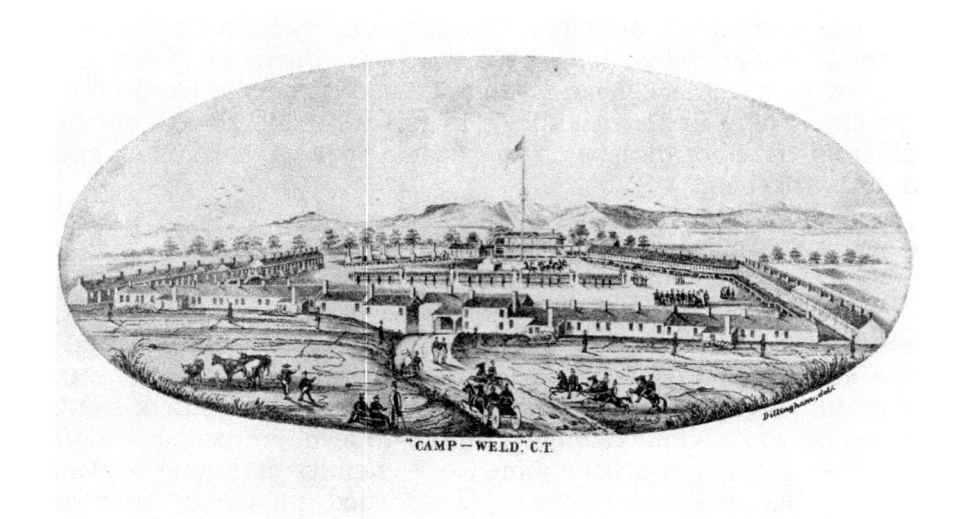

Governor Evans reluctantly met with the Arapaho and Cheyenne leaders. *DPL*

All the Indians - It has been so.

Gov. Evans - The fact that they have not been able to prevent their people from going to war in the past spring, when there was plenty of grass and game, makes me believe that they will not be able to make a peace which will last longer than until winter is past.

White Antelope - I will answer that after a time.

Gov. Evans - The time when you can make war best, is in the summer time; when I can make war best, is in the winter. You, so far have had the advantage; my time is just coming. I have learned that you understand that as the whites are at war among themselves, you think you can now drive the whites from the country. But this reliance is false. The Great Father at Washington has men enough to drive all the Indians off the plains, and whip the rebels at the same time. Now the war with the whites is nearly through, and the Great Father will not know what to do with all his soldiers, except to send them after the Indians on the plains. My proposition to the friendly Indians has gone out; I shall be glad to have them all come in, under it. I have no new propositions to make. Another reason that I am not in a condition to make a treaty, is that war is begun, and the power to make a treaty of peace has passed from me to the Great War Chief. My advice to you, is, to turn on the side of the government, and show, by your acts, that friendly disposition you profess to me. It is utterly out of the question for you to be at peace with us, while living with our enemies, and being on friendly terms with them.

Inquiry made by one Indian - What was meant by being on the side of the government?

Explanation being made, all gave assent, saying "All right."

Gov. Evans - The only way you can show this friendship is by making some arrangement with the soldiers to help them.

Black Kettle - We will return with Major Wynkoop to Fort Lyon; we will then proceed to our village, and take back word to our young men, every word you say. I cannot answer for all of them, but think there will be but little difficulty in getting them to assent to helping the soldiers.

Major Wynkoop - Did not the Dog Soldiers agree, when I had my council with you, to do whatever you said, after you had been here?

Black Kettle - Yes.

Gov. Evans - You understand, that if you are at peace with us it is necessary to keep away from our enemies. But I hand you over to the military, one of the chiefs of which is here today, and can speak for himself, to them, if he chooses.

White Antelope - I understand every word you have said, and will hold on to it. I will give you an answer directly. The Cheyennes, all of them, have their eyes open this way, and they will hear what you say. He is proud to have seen the chief of all the whites in this country. He will tell his people. Ever since he went to Washington and received this medal, I have called all white men as my brothers. But other Indians have since been to Washington, and got medals, and now the soldiers do not shake hands, but seek to kill me. What do you mean by us fighting your enemies? Who are they?

Gov. Evans - All Indians who are fighting us.

White Antelope - How can we be protected from the soldiers on the plains?

Gov. Evans - You must make that arrangement with the Military Chief.

White Antelope - I fear that these new soldiers who have gone out, may kill some of my people while I am here.

Gov. Evans - There is a great danger of it.

White Antelope - When we sent our letter to Major Wynkoop, it was like going through a strong fire, or blast, for Major Wynkoop's men to come to our camp; it was the same for us to come to see you. We have our doubts that the Indians south of the Arkansas, or those north of the Platte, will do as you say. A large number of Sioux have crossed the Platte in the vicinity of the Junction, into their country. When Major Wynkoop came we proposed to make peace. He said he had no power to make a peace except to bring them here and return them safe.

Gov. Evans - Again, whatever peace they make, must be with the soldiers and not with me. Are the Apaches at war with the whites?

White Antelope - Yes, and the Comanches and Kiowas as well; also a tribe of Indians from Texas, whose names we do not know. There are thirteen different bands of Sioux who have crossed the Platte and are in alliance with the others named.

Gov. Evans - How many warriors with the Apaches, Kiowas and Comanches?

White Antelope - A good many. Don't know.

Gov. Evans - How many of the Sioux?

White Antelope - Don't know, but many more than of the southern tribes.

Gov. Evans - Who committed the depredations on the trains near the Junction, about the 1st of August?

Arapaho and Cheyenne leaders at the Camp Weld meeting with Governor Evans and Colonel Chivington. Note: Black Kettle and White Antelope are opposite of the identification. *DPL*

White Antelope - Do not know did not know any were committed. Have taken you by the hand and will tell the truth, keeping back nothing.

Gov. Evans - Who committed the murder of the Hungate family, on Running Creek?

Neva - The Arapahoes; a party of the northern band who were passing north. It was Medicine Man, or Roman Nose, and three others. I am satisfied from the time he left a certain camp for the north, that it was this party of four persons.

Agent Whiteley - That cannot be true.

Gov. Evans - Where is Roman Nose?

Neva - You ought to know better than me. You have been nearer to him.

Gov. Evans - Who killed the man and boy at the head of Cherry Creek?

Neva - (After consultation) - Kiowas and Comanches.

Gov. Evans - Who stole soldiers horses and mules from Jimmy's Camp, twenty-seven days ago?

Neva - Fourteen Cheyennes and Arapahoes, together.

Gov. Evans - What were their names?

Neva - Powder Face and Whirlwind, who are now in our camp, were the leaders.

Col. Shoup - I counted twenty Indians on that occasion.

Gov. Evans - Who stole Charley Autobee's horses?

Neva - Raven's son.

Gov. Evans - Who took the stock from Fremont's Orchard, and had the first fight with the soldiers this spring, north of there?

White Antelope - Before answering this question I would like for you to know that this was the beginning of war and I should like to know what it was for, as a soldier fired first.

Gov. Evans - The Indians had stolen about forty horses, the soldiers went to recover them, and the Indians fired a volley into their ranks.

White Antelope - This is all a mistake. They were coming down the Bijou, and found one horse and one mule. They returned one horse before they got to Geary's then went to Geary's, expecting to turn the other one over to some one. They then heard that the soldiers and Indians were fighting somewhere down the Platte; then they took fright, and all fled.

Gov. Evans - Who were the Indians who had the fright?

White Antelope - They were headed by the Fool Badger's son, a young man, one of the greatest of the Cheyenne warriors, who was wounded, and though still alive, he will never recover.

Neva - I want to say something. It makes me feel bad to be talking about these things and opening old sores.

Gov. Evans - Let him speak.

Neva - Mr. Smith has known me ever since I was a child. Has he ever known me commit depredations on the whites? I went to Washington last year - received good council. I hold on to it. I determined to always keep peace with the whites. Now, when I shake hands with them they seem to pull away. I came here to seek peace and nothing else.

Gov. Evans - We feel that they have, by their stealing and murdering, done us great damage. They come here and say they will tell me all, and that is what I am trying to get.

Neva - The Comanches, Kiowas and Sioux have done much more injury than we have. We will tell what we know, but cannot speak for others.

Gov. Evans - I suppose you acknowledge the depredations on the Little Blue, as you have the prisoners then taken in your possession.

White Antelope - We (the Cheyennes) took two prisoners, west of Fort Kearney, and destroyed the trains.

Gov. Evans - Who committed depredations at Cottonwood?

White Antelope - The Sioux. What band, we do not know.

Gov. Evans - What are the Sioux going to do next?

Bull Bear - Their plan is to clean out all this country. They are angry and will do all the damage to the whites they can. I am with you and the troops, to fight all those who have no care to listen to what you say. Who are they? Show them to me, I am not yet old - I am young. I have never hurt a white man. I am pushing for something good. I am always going to be friends with the whites - they can do me good.

Gov. Evans - Where are the Sioux?

Bull Bear - Down on the Republican, where it opens out.

Gov. Evans - Do you know that they intend to attack the trains this week?

Bull Bear - Yes. About one half of all the Missouri River Sioux and Yanktons, who were driven from Minnesota, are those who have crossed the Platte. I am young and can fight. I have given my word to fight with the whites. My brother (Lean Bear) died in trying to keep peace with the whites. I am willing to die in the same way, and expect to do so.

Neva - I know the value of the presents which we receive from Washington. We cannot live without them. That is why I try so hard to keep peace with the whites.

Gov. Evans - I cannot say anything about those things, now.

Neva - I can speak for all the Arapahoes under Left Hand. Raven has sent no one here to speak for him. Raven has fought the whites.

Gov. Evans - Are there any white men among your people?

Neva - There are none except Keith, who is now in the store at Fort Larned.

Col. Chivington - I am not a big war chief, but all the soldiers in this country are at my command. My rule of fighting white men or Indians is to fight them until they lay down their arms and submit to military authority. They are nearer Major Wynkoop than any one else, and they can go to him when they get ready to do that.

The Council then adjourned.

> *I Certify that this report is correct and complete; that I took down the talk of the Indians in the exact words of the Interpreter, and of the other parties as given to him, without change of phraseology, or correction of any kind whatever. - [signed] Simeon Whiteley* [56]

It should be noted that during Evans' interrogation regarding the Hungate murders, Arapaho Chief Neva's response was that the murders were the acts of a small party of Arapaho, led by Roman Nose. However, this contradicted earlier information Evans had received on June 15th, four days after the Hungate massacre. Robert North, the Indian trader who was also married to an Arapaho woman, had informed the governor that small bands of Cheyenne and Arapaho Indians had been raiding the area in search of guns and ammunition, and that it was John Notnee, an Arapaho Indian, who was responsible for the deaths of the Hungate family. Evans, requesting federal military assistance, included this information in his letter to Secretary of War Stanton:

> *"Robert North, the same who made statement last autumn, now on file, reports that John Notnee, an Arapaho Indian, who was here with him and Major Colley last fall, spent the winter on Box Elder. He was mad because he had to give up the stock that he stole from Mr. Van Wormer last fall. He thinks he was with the party who murdered the family on Mr. Van Wormer's ranch and stole the stock in the neighborhood last Saturday, but thinks that the most of the party were Cheyennes and Kiowas."* [57]

Black Kettle, particularly pleased with the results of the meeting, hugged Major Wynkoop as well as Governor Evans. He was very much in favor of returning to Fort Lyon with Wynkoop and his men, as Chivington's words were very clear. Black Kettle would move his people near Fort Lyon, and "lay down their arms and submit to military authority." Caught up in the moment, the Indians agreed to have a photograph taken. It would be the only known photograph of Black Kettle. Later, a photograph of the four released captives was also taken.

Despite editor Byers' previous claim to "defer to his [Wynkoop's] judgment," the daily edition of the *Rocky Mountain News*, dated September 28, 1864, obviously agreed with the governor's position and Colonel Chivington's dismissive remarks:

"The most revolting, shocking cases of assassination, arson, murder and manslaughter that have crimsoned the pages of time have been done by the Indians, in former days and recently-nevertheless we are opposed to anything which looks like a treaty of peace with the Indians...The season is near at hand when they can be chastised and it should be done with no gentle hand."

As Wynkoop prepared for the return trip to Fort Lyon, along with the peace-seeking Cheyenne and Arapaho representatives, Chivington received a reply to his wired message from General Curtis. Dated September 28, 1864, the very day of the Camp Weld meeting, Chivington must have been very pleased with his superior's response:

"I shall require the bad Indians delivered up; restoration of equal numbers of stock, also hostages to secure. I want no peace till the Indians suffer more. Left Hand is said to be a good chief of the Arapahoes, [sic] But Big Mouth is a rascal. I fear [the] agent of the Interior Department will be ready to make presents too soon. It is better to chastise before giving anything but a little tobacco to talk over. No peace must be made without my direction." [58]

This chilling military order would soon be put in motion by Colonel Chivington, resulting in death and destruction, leaving behind the bloodiest pages in the annals of Colorado history.

Governor Evans was doing his share of damage control after the Camp Weld meeting. After finally receiving authority from the federal government to raise the Third Colorado Volunteer Cavalry Regiment, Evans was not about to let the opportunity be lost. The day following his reluctant meeting with the Indians, Evans wrote the following to Indian Agent Colley:

> *"The chiefs brought in by Major Wynkoop have been heard. I have declined to make any treaty with them."* [59]

Nevertheless, believing the words spoken at Camp Weld by the "Great Father," the Indians were escorted back to Fort Lyon by Wynkoop, Soule and the forty soldiers. At Fort Lyon, Wynkoop held an Indian council of his own, telling Black Kettle, White Antelope and the other peaceful Indian chiefs that they were free to bring their people to camp near the fort. Confident in Wynkoop's words and actions, this is exactly what the Cheyenne and Arapaho chiefs did.

Wynkoop then had a separate conversation with Black Kettle, asking him to bring the three remaining captives to the fort. Black Kettle informed Wynkoop that he was working on the matter and that it would take time, as the captives were with Bull Bear's Dog Soldiers, some distance from the fort. However, given the fact that Bull Bear was in attendance at Camp Weld and agreed to the terms offered by Evans and Chivington, and the fact that he returned to Fort Lyon with Wynkoop's group, it is a curious point of circumstance as to why Black Kettle and Bull Bear could not communicate. As for the four captives that were returned during the Camp Weld meeting, their lives were forever changed by their horrendous experience. The children were immediately taken to the Camp Weld military hospital on Ferry Street, where they were examined by military doctors. While Laura seemed to be in good health, the three younger children were all suffering from various degrees of malnutrition.

Denver City's Relief Association came to the aid of the children with donations of clothing from the community. While working with the military to find their relatives, the association also attempted to find temporary homes for the children until family members could be located. Fundraising was also done to provide funds for Laura Roper's wagon train trip to distant relatives in the East.

Perhaps little Isabelle "Belle" Eubanks suffered the most, although it was short-lived. She was never reunited with her family. In fact, she never left Denver, dying March 18, 1865. Mollie Dorsey Sanford, a young newlywed who came to Denver from Nebraska in 1860, kept a journal early in her marriage. In September 1864, she wrote that the four released captives were kept in her house for a time.

Indians, interpreters and scouts pose for a photo at Camp Weld. Kneeling are Edward Wynkoop and Silas Soule. Black Kettle is seated behind Wynkoop. The other seated Indians are Neva, Bull Bear, White Antelope and Left Hand. *DPL*

> *"Miss Roper was subjected to all the indignities usually given white captives, and the children were brutally treated by the squaws. The mother [Lucinda Eubanks] of little Bell was taken away by some distant band, and the poor little things left. She saw her father butchered, and only three years old, can and does recount the whole tragedy. I took her, thinking I might adopt her, but I could not stand it. She would wake from a sound sleep, and sit up in bed with staring eyes, and go in detail over the whole thing. She was scarred all over with the prints of arrow points that the squaws tortured her with. Dr. Brondsall has adopted her, where she will have medical care and good care otherwise."*

Little Mary Isabelle Eubanks died on March 18, 1865. The *Rocky Mountain News* reported Belle's death in the March 21, 1865 issue. Although full of errors, it did confirm arrow wounds as a cause of her death:

> *"DIED: In this city, on the 18th inst., of inflammation of the brain, MARY [Isabelle] EUBANKS, aged 4 years. This was the girl captured from [by] the Indians, on the Arkansas [Little Blue], last fall. Her death*

was caused indirectly from three arrow wounds in different parts of her body."

Meanwhile, Laura visited with the other children as often as she could. A few days after his release, nine-year-old Daniel Marble became gravely ill. Doctor A. A. Smith, Assistant Surgeon for the First Colorado Cavalry, examined young Danny. The doctor's diagnosis was typhoid fever. Doctor W. F. McClelland offered his services to treat the young boy free of charge. For unknown reasons, his offer was declined by the military. Laura's last visit with Danny was in early November, just before she returned east.

Tragically, on November 9, 1864, Daniel Marble died. He was buried in the City Cemetery on November 14, 1864. The military had not informed his mother, Ann, living in Council Bluffs, Iowa, of her son's rescue, or his death. Ann Marble learned the devastating news from a letter penned by Doctor W. F. McClelland.[60] Laura Roper learned of young Danny's death while enroute to reunite with her family. Laura wrote a letter to Ann Marble. Dated November 28, 1864, she expressed her sorrow and sympathies and promised to send a copy of the Denver photograph of the rescued children.

Laura Roper lived a long life and wrote extensively over the years of her thirty-seven days in captivity. The following account, printed in the *Nebraska Nelson Gazette* in 1929, when Laura was eighty-years-old, gives a detailed account of the young teenager's horrific ordeal:

"About one p.m. on the seventh day of August, 1864, I left my home on the Little Blue River to spend the afternoon with a neighbor by the name of Eubanks. About three weeks before, Indians had stolen some horses from my father and had committed other depredations around the country which of course had caused the people to have some fear of them. This being the case, my father told me as I left to be sure and not come home alone as the Indians might be lurking around.

I spent the afternoon at Eubanks until about 4 p.m. at which time Mr. Eubanks, his wife and two children [Lucinda, William Jr., and Isabelle, respectively,] and myself started for my home which was about one and one half miles away. We had gone about one half mile when we came to a place in the road which was called the "Narrows" because the road was so narrow in that place. Mr. Eubanks was barefooted and got a sliver in his foot and said he would stop and get it out and for us to walk on; he would overtake us. We had gone about 50 yards around the bluff when we stopped to wait for him. Just then we heard terrible yells. I said I thought it was Indians so we turned and ran back until we came in sight of Mr. Eubanks who was running toward the house. Just as we got to the edge of the sandbar the Indians shot and killed him. His two brothers that were in the house started to run up a draw and they were both killed. His sister started to run toward us; they had tried to take her prisoner and she fought them so they stabbed her in the head and killed her.

By this time we had gotten into the timber; the Indians had killed everyone at the Eubanks' house and we started for my father's house. As they passed they saw us, whirled their horses and came right to us. I had taken off my slippers and was carrying them in my hand. The first thing they did was to snatch my hat off and my slippers out of my hand. I had a signet ring on my finger and they took it off next. Then they took us by the hand and told us to come; they picked us up and put us on the horses and took us back to Mr. Eubanks' house. On the way back we saw Mr. Eubanks' sister lying beside the path. We could see where they had stabbed her; she was not quite dead but threw her arms over her head as we passed. In a few minutes another Indian came riding up with this girl's scalp on a spear dripping with blood; he was yelling like a madman.

We traveled all night; all the next day and night. About three o'clock the following afternoon we camped and ate a wild turkey they had killed on the way. I was put on a horse by myself instead of riding behind an Indian on one horse. The next day we came to a band of about 50 Indians. Then they all painted their faces, put feathers in their hair and put on their war paint regalia. Then we rode on for one and a half hours when we came in sight of their main camp of about ten thousand Indians. I was treated very nicely; one of the old squaws took me under her care. The camp moved westward traveling steadily until within a few day's ride of Fort Lyons, [sic] Colorado.

Here we camped and a few warriors went on to attempt to bargain with the soldiers that came part way to meet us. Both sides mistrusted the other; finally I was given to the soldiers in exchange for some other prisoners. I was taken into Denver where a strong wagon train was soon made up and we started back for my old home at Nebraska City. I arrived safely there and from there we went to Pennsylvania, my people's former home." [61]

Ambrose Asher, the six-year-old grandson of Joseph Eubanks Sr., who witnessed the murders of his grandfather and other family members, was a quiet boy, shy and reserved around the soldiers. However, Private William F. Smith took a shine to the lad. He asked his fellow soldiers for donations to purchase clothing and toys for the boy. Then word came from the Relief Association that Ambrose's mother was on her way to Denver. The soldiers were pleased with the news and took extra care of the boy until he could be reunited with his mother. She had funds to reach Atchison, Kansas, and the association agreed to pay for his passage to that destination. Ambrose Asher received his education, became a teamster and married Belle Harrison on February 24, 1881. The couple had five children. At some point, between 1894 and 1900, according to author, Ronald Becher, Ambrose Asher "simply disappeared." There was no record of death or indications from the family of abandonment.

The city's Relief Association had a difficult time placing little Isabelle Eubanks with volunteer families. Often ill and unable to eat, at times she seemed to do nothing but cry. Mrs. Mollie Sanford wrote in her diary, the section quoted on page sixty-four.

That diary quote, printed in the Sunday *World Herald*, June 1, 1964, is not dated. However, it must have been entered in her diary after Lucinda Eubanks death, which occurred several years after Isabelle's release by Black Kettle. It is quite possible that the remaining members of the Eubank's knew nothing of Isabelle's whereabouts or condition. In March 1865, Isabelle Eubanks died and was unceremoniously buried in the City Cemetery. It was three months later, nearly to the day, that her mother and baby brother would finally be released from their captivity.

On October 8, 1864, Major Wynkoop wrote a detailed report of the events to General Curtis. He concluded with the following observation:

> "I think that if some terms are made with these Indians, I can arrange matters so, by bringing their villages under my direct control, that I can answer for their fidelity. We are at war with the Sioux, and the Kiowas, and Comanches; these Indians, the Arapahoes [sic] and Cheyennes, [sic] tell me they are willing to lend me their assistance in fighting the Kiowas and Comanches. I know that in a general Indian war it will take more soldiers than we can possibly spare to keep open the two lines of communication, protect the settlements, and make an effective war upon them." [63]

As nearly one hundred lodges of Arapaho and Cheyenne were camping near Fort Lyon, time was of the essence. Therefore, Wynkoop sent Lieutenant Denison to Fort Leavenworth to personally deliver the report to Curtis.

In the crisp autumn of 1864, roving bands of young Cheyenne Dog Soldiers and Arapaho warriors increased their raids in eastern Colorado and western Kansas, causing further alarm among the white settlers.

Governor Evans and Colonel Chivington had to react.

The winds of war were blowing strong on the Colorado prairie.

— Chapter Notes —

1. First Regiment of Colorado Volunteer Records and Company Muster Roll, CHC.
2. Wynkoop Collection, Chavez History Library.
3. Company Muster Roll of July 29 through August 31, 1861. Transcripts of the Colorado Volunteers records, State of Colorado, Division of the Archives and Public Records.
4. Hollister, *Boldly They Rode*, pg. 70.
5. Letter dated March 1862, Charles E. Feinberg Whitman Collection, Library of Congress.
6. Colorado State Archives. This change occurred in November of 1862 and is an important distinction. Many authors have interchanged the two regiments in accounts of both Glorieta Pass and the Sand Creek Massacre. The change was specifically made to convert from infantry to cavalry by the War Department to be "more effective for Indian-fighting purposes," Glorieta Pass being military prior to the conversion.
7. The War of the Rebellion Official records, Part 1, pg. 880-882. Hereafter listed as Official Military Record.
8. Official Military Record.
9. Fremont's Orchard, approximately eighty miles northeast of Denver, was named by John C. Fremont, as the trees reminded him of apple orchards back east. It was the site of one of his many camps during his westward expeditions.
10. Official Military Record, Part 1, pg. 884-885.
11. Official Military Record, Part 1, pg. 881.
12. George Bent letters to George E. Hyde. Colorado History Center.
13. Official Military Record, Eayre to Chivington, May 1, 1864.
14. Dr. Jeff Broome has been involved with the archeological evidence of the Hungate homestead for over a decade. The precise location, on the Arapaho/Douglas County line, is identified as the N. E. quarter of Section 3, T6S, R64W, 6th p.m.
15. The devastating Cherry Creek flood of May 19, 1864, washed out the foundation of the *Rocky Mountain News* building and carried the presses downstream, never to be seen again. As editor and owner, William N. Byers rebuilt his newspaper enterprise, the *Denver Commonwealth* published articles and editorials on Byers' behalf. Thus, the atrocious murders were first reported in the *Denver Commonwealth*.

16.   Extensive research conducted by Jeff Broome reveals that Captain Davidson's military camp was most likely near present-day Franktown.
17.   Two points of reference must be made regarding this account. First is the references to both Box Elder Creek and Running Creek. This has confused historians for years. The creek is one and the same and known by both names. Second is that Brown says they followed the creek "upstream." The creek actually runs north.
18.   Official Military Record, Part IV, pgs. 319-320.
19.   Wommack, *From the Grave*. This was a section of Denver's first cemetery, now Cheesman Park. In 1892 the bodies were removed to their final resting place at Fairmount Cemetery. A small obelisk lists the family surnames as well as all four names of the murdered family. There is an additional marker inscribed with the words, "Killed by Indians 1864." This marker, originally placed at the Mount Calvary burial site in 1864, was moved to Fairmount along with the remains of the Hungate family.
20.   Ashley, "Reminiscences of Colorado in the Early 'Sixties" *The Colorado Magazine*, Volume X111, 1936, pg. 219-30.
21.   Official Military Record, Part 1, pg. 964.
22.   Samuel G. Colley was appointed Indian agent of the Upper Arkansas on August 26, 1861, replacing Colonel Albert Gallitan Boone, the grandson of famed frontiersman, Daniel Boone.
23.   Official Military Record, Part 1, pgs. 963-964.
24.   Report of the Commissioner of Indian Affairs, pg. 130.
25.   Ellenbecker, *Tragedy at the Little Blue*, pg.16.
26.   ibid.
27.   ibid.
28.   Unpublished manuscript, Nancy Jane Fletcher Morton Stevens, Iowa State Historical Society.
29.   It was later learned that Marble's older son, Joel, had taken ill before the group reached Plum Creek and had been sent back to his mother, Ann, in Council Bluffs, Iowa. Becher, *Massacre Along the Medicine Road*, pg. 252.
30.   Hyde, *Life of George Bent*, pg. 140. Grinnell, *The Fighting Cheyennes*, pg. 156. Halass, *Halfbreed*, pg.127.
31.   Archives of the Lincoln, Nebraska, Public Library.
32.   When Elbridge Gerry died in April of 1875, he was buried on a small knoll on his land, later part of the old Kuner canning plant. His marker is still there, and reads simply: "First Permanent White Settler in Weld County." Wommack, *From the Grave*.
33.   United States Senate. Report of the Secretary of War, 1867.
34.   U.S. Congressional Testimony, Edward Wynkoop, March 20, 1865.

35. The Trail, "Plain Tales of the Plains," Volume VIII, 1916. Boonsville was named for Albert Gallatin Boone, a grandson of the famous frontiersman, Daniel Boone. A. G. Boone was also a former Indian agent for the Colorado Territory.
36. The Trail, "Plain Tales of the Plains," Volume VIII, 1916.
37. Official Military Record.
38. United States Congress, Senate. Report of the Secretary of War, Sand Creek Massacre. Executive document 26, 39th Congress, 1867, Washington, D. C. Hereafter noted as the "Sand Creek Massacre."
39. Becher, *Massacre along the Medicine Road*, pg. 315.
40. Czaplewski, *Captive of the Cheyenne*, pgs. 29 and 30.
41. Ellenbecker, *Tragedy at the Little Blue*, pgs.22 and 23.
42. Becher, *Massacre along the Medicine Road*, pg. 314.
43. Czaplewski, *Captive of the Cheyenne*, pg. 20.
44. U.S. Congress, Report on the Conduct of War, Washington D.C., 1865.
45. Wynkoop, "Unfinished Colorado History, 1886"
46. ibid.
47. ibid.
48. Hoig, *The Sand Creek Massacre*, pg. 101.
49. Kraft, *Ned Wynkoop and the Lonely Road From Sand Creek*, pg. 110.
50. Wynkoop, "Unfinished Colorado History, 1886."
51. Wynkoop, "Unfinished Colorado History, 1886," pg. 95.
52. Official Military Record, sworn testimony by John Smith, dated January 15, 1865.
53. Wynkoop, "Unfinished Colorado History, 1886," pg. 102.
54. The Trail, "Plain Tales of the Plains," Volume VIII, 1916.
55. Hoig, *The Sand Creek Massacre*.
56. Official Military Record, Part III, pgs. 242-243.
57. Official Military Record, Volume XLI, pg. 399.
58. Kraft, *Ned Wynkoop and the Lonely Road from Sand Creek*, pg. 118.
59. Hoig, *The Sand Creek Massacre*.
60. ibid.
61. Hoig, *The Sand Creek Massacre*, pgs. 213-15. The *Rocky Mountain News* issue of September 29, 1864, also carried the transcript on its front page.
62. United States Senate. Report of the Secretary of War, 1867.
63. Wynkoop, "Unfinished Colorado History, 1886" and "Sand Creek Massacre." Testimony of Joseph Cramer, March 2, 1865. pg. 56.

— THE SAND CREEK MASSACRE —

Territorial Governor John Evans found himself in the midst of a political pressure cooker following his forced meeting with the Indian chiefs at Camp Weld on September 28, 1864.

During the summer, communication with the East had been cut and stage lines were stopped, due to the Indian uprisings. Supplies were practically nonexistent and prices soared. The citizens were in a state of panic and demanded Governor Evans take action. The safety of the citizens, as well as secured land prospects that would lead to eventual statehood, were at risk.

"Help Demanded From Government." "Appeal To The People." "Cavalry or Infantry."

These were just a few of the many headlines screaming for action in Colorado's newspapers. The influential press, led by William Newton Byers of the *Rocky Mountain News*, called for the "immediate extinction of the Indians." Byers further editorialized:

"The most revolting, shocking cases of assassination, arson, murder and manslaughter that have crimsoned the pages of time have been done by the Indians, in former days and recently-nevertheless we are opposed to anything which looks like a treaty of peace with the Indians...The season is near at hand when they can be chastised and it should be done with no gentle hand..." [1]

With a stroke of predictive journalism, Editor William N. Byers clearly stated the views of many citizens of Colorado Territory. Evans clearly needed a military victory against the Indians, for the safety of the Colorado citizens, as well as his own political future.

Earlier in the year, the "Union Administration Association" had been formed to create a lobbying body for Colorado statehood. Members of the group selected D. T. Towne for governor, current

Territorial Governor John Evans and Henry Teller for state senators, and John M. Chivington for state congressman. Opposition to the movement soon took a nasty turn in newspapers across the region. The *Daily Mining Journal* editorialized:

> "...the fact that our late troubles are due chiefly to the perfidy & ambition of Gov. Evans & Col. Chivington our 'Military Dictator.'"[2]

In less than a month's time, following authorization by Secretary of War Edwin M. Stanton, Governor Evans and Colonel Chivington were successful in raising the Third Regiment of Colorado Volunteers, whose service, under federal government orders, was not to exceed one hundred days. The recruits were mustered in at Camp Weld, where, under Chivington's command, they were trained for Indian battle. In a letter to Major Edward W. Wynkoop, dated May 31, 1864, Chivington wrote:

> "The Cheyenne will have to be soundly whipped before they will be quiet. If any of them are caught in your vicinity kill them, as that is the only way."[3]

Governor Evans had declared martial law and issued a general proclamation to the citizens of Colorado Territory:

> "Go in pursuit of all hostile Indians on the plains...kill and destroy, as enemies of the country, wherever the Indians may be found."[4]

Major Edward Wynkoop, as commander of Fort Lyon, had worked toward a peaceful solution when he brought the chiefs of the Cheyenne and Arapaho tribes to Denver, to meet with the governor. It could have been a brilliant success or a horrible failure. Wynkoop never imagined it would be the latter. Just two weeks after Wynkoop returned to Fort Lyon and the peaceful Cheyenne and Arapaho tribes had set up camp nearby, local citizens in the Arkansas River Valley presented Wynkoop with a signed "Memorial." Praising the Major for his peaceful efforts, the document read:

> "We the undersigned citizens of the Arkansas valley desire to further express our appreciation of your bravery, as well as your sense of right, and earnestly express the hope that the merrit [sic] which is justly your due may not go unrewarded, in official preferment, as well as the gratitude of private citizens."[5]

During this time, it seemed as if Wynkoop's efforts had indeed made a difference, as there were very few reports of Indian troubles. Even Editor Byers, a staunch supporter of both Evans and Chivington, reported the following in the October 20, 1864, issue of the *Rocky Mountain News*:

"Previously to the time that the armistice was granted to the Cheyennes [sic] and Arapahoes [sic] by Major Wynkoop, it was impossible for any person to pass over the road on the Arkansas, unless in very large parties or attended by large escorts of troops, but since that time the [Indians] *have not committed a single overt act on the said road."*

Nevertheless, things were about to change at Fort Lyon. On November 5, 1864, Major Scott J. Anthony arrived at Fort Lyon from Fort Leavenworth, carrying written orders signed by General Samuel R. Curtis, commander of military operations in the West. The general's order was simple and direct. By Special Order Number 13, Major Wynkoop had been relieved of command of Fort Lyon and replaced by Major Scott Anthony. Wynkoop was further ordered to report to District Headquarters at Fort Riley, Kansas. There is a sense of irony in this change of command. Two years earlier, the self-centered, pompous Major Anthony, then commander of Fort Lyon, had been replaced by Colonel Chivington, with Major Wynkoop. Years later, Wynkoop's son Edward, wrote that:

"Strong, hidden forces - forces that lie in safe covert to avoid danger when the soldier is at the front, but often reach forth their slimy fingers to befoul his good record - demanded that Wynkoop be punished for leaving his post of duty with his hostages." [6]

Edward Estill Wynkoop's assertion seems to have merit. Major B. S. Henning of Fort Riley wrote to Anthony:

"I am very desirous to have an officer of judgment at Fort Lyon, and especially one that will not commit any such foolish acts as are reported to have occurred there."[7]

Wynkoop would later testify that when he told Governor Evans of the rescued hostages and proposed Indian peace talks, Evans was enraged. Wynkoop testified that Evans said:

> "It would be supposed at Washington that he [Evans] had misrepresented matters in regard to the Indian difficulties in Colorado, and he had put the government to a useless expense in raising the regiment; that they had been raised to kill Indians and they must kill Indians." [8]

Major Anthony had further orders to investigate "any officer leaving the post without orders and officers [who] have issued goods, stores or supplies to hostile Indians in direct violation of orders from the General Commanding the Department." [9]

On November 6, 1864, Major Anthony sent his first report from Fort Lyon:

> "Nine Cheyenne Indians to-day [sic] sent in, wishing to see me. They state that 600 of that tribe are now 35 miles north of here, coming towards the post, and 2,000 about 75 miles away, waiting for better weather to enable them to come in. I shall not permit them to come in, even as prisoners, for the reason that if I do, I shall have to subsist them upon a prisoner's rations. I shall, however, demand their arms, all stolen stock, and the perpetrators of all depredations. I am of the opinion that they will return to the Smoky Hill. They pretend that they want peace, and I think they do now, as they cannot fight during the winter, except where a small band of them can find an unprotected train or frontier settlement. I do not think it is policy to make peace with them now, until all perpetrators of depredations are surrendered up to be dealt with as we may propose." [10]

Wynkoop had remained at Fort Lyon in an effort to insure a smooth transition. Almost immediately, he sensed there would be a stark change. Disturbed by Anthony's communique, Wynkoop explained in no uncertain terms the purpose of the Camp Weld peace talks which had resulted in the willingness of the peaceful Indians to come in to Fort Lyon. Possibly with some reluctance, Anthony initially agreed with Wynkoop's assessment. Wynkoop then arranged a meeting with the chiefs and introduced them to Anthony. He explained to them that Anthony was the new commander of Fort Lyon and assured them that their peaceful compliance following the Camp Weld talks would be upheld. Both the Arapaho and Cheyenne tribes that had followed Wynkoop to Fort Lyon believed and trusted him. They did not trust this new commander. Major Anthony's "dark disposition" and physical appearance alarmed the Indians. They referred to him as the

"Red-eyed chief." Anthony's "red-eye" condition was the result of scurvy, which he had contacted, ironically, during his first stint as commander of Fort Lyon in 1863.

Anthony assured the Indians that he believed in Wynkoop's policy. Therefore, he immediately issued rations. He further suggested that Black Kettle and Left Hand move their people to Sand Creek, approximately forty miles northeast of Fort Lyon. Anthony assured them that they would be safe there and under the military's protection.[11]

However, Anthony also instructed them to return any and all stolen livestock in their possession. The Indians, for the most part, complied with the order. Private William H. Valentine, a soldier with the First Cavalry, later reported that the Arapaho Indians, under Left Hand and Little Raven, camped across the Arkansas River from Fort Lyon. They surrendered eight mules which had been taken from the Snyder teamsters following that murderous attack in August. Valentine also provided a humorous note regarding the mules. He said they were so loud and annoying that the soldiers complained. Eventually, the mules were moved away from the fort.[12] A few days later, Left Hand and Black Kettle moved their lodges to Sand Creek. Wynkoop had a final moment with his friend and wished him well.

"The Cheyenne call Sand Creek, "Bo-no". In Cheyenne, this means dry creek, no water. The Old ones say there was no water in there."[13]

As Black Kettle rode in solitude across the wind-blown prairie of eastern Colorado, he was deeply concerned for the welfare of his people. In the crisp autumn air of 1864, Black Kettle reflected on the bloody summer which had witnessed terror and murder across the plains. Black Kettle would not have known of the editor's words in the Denver paper, but he knew the feelings of his white counterparts. Following months of raids and murders by roving bands of young Cheyenne and Arapaho warriors, the peace chief wondered if Major's Anthony's words of peace and protection were true. Because the Native Americans relied on oral tradition, there is no definitive record of Black Kettle's birth or his parentage. Researchers and historians, and even friends of his, had placed his birth anywhere from 1803 to 1812. George Bent, who married to Black Kettle's niece, Magpie, likely gave the most credible account in his memoirs. He said that Black Kettle was sixty-seven years old when he was killed by George Armstrong Custer's troops in the Indian massacre at the Washita River in 1868.[14] If this is accurate, that would place Black Kettle's birth in the year 1801. Bent also wrote that Black Kettle was the son of Swift Hawk Lying Down. While he didn't mention the name of his mother, Bent wrote that Black Kettle had two brothers, Gentle Horse and Wolf, as well as a sister, Wind Woman.[15] Black Kettle was born into the Cheyenne Tsistsistas tribe in the area of the Minnesota River valley. According to Cheyenne oral history, Tsistsistas means "The People." The Sioux, a neighboring tribe, called them the Shai ena, meaning "red talkers." Over time the Sioux word Shai ena evolved to the common name known today: Cheyenne.

According to Black Kettle's biographer, Thom Hatch, Black Kettle was approximately fourteen when he joined the Bowstrings, a soldier band of the tribe. Black Kettle participated in the ceremonial Sun Dance, a ritual of Cheyenne warriors, in an effort to gain a vision and spiritual guidance as they moved from their adolescence years into manhood and, eventually, leaders of their people. It was also at this time that Black Kettle became a member of the Crooked Lances.[16]

Shortly thereafter, Black Kettle married Little Sage Woman. By this time, Black Kettle had participated in and led several successful raids against enemy tribes. In the summer of 1838, Black Kettle led a group of warriors in pursuit of Apache, Comanche and Kiowa, who had stolen a herd of ponies from the Cheyenne. Locating the camp of the three tribes on Wolf Creek, Black Kettle and his warriors overtook the camp and recovered their stolen ponies. It was a big coup for Black Kettle. Black Kettle witnessed the peace process for the first time in the summer of 1840. The Kiowa and Comanche had expressed interest in a peace treaty with the Arapaho and Cheyenne. An initial agreement was reached and the Cheyenne tribe moved their camp near Bent's Fort on the Arkansas River. At the fort they traded for special gifts to present to the chiefs of the Comanche and Kiowa as tokens of friendship.[17] After a brief rendezvous with the Arapaho at the fort, the two tribes traveled together to the mouth of Two Butte Creek, where they awaited the arrival of the former enemies.

A few days later, Little Mountain of the Kiowa tribe led his people to the site of the peace council. After greeting his guests, Eagle Feather lit the ceremonial peace pipe and then passed it around the circle of tribal leaders. With peace declared between the tribes, the time had come to exchange presents. Leaders of the Comanche and Kiowa presented the Arapaho and Cheyenne leaders with a beautiful Indian blanket. Inside were the scalps of forty-two Cheyenne Bowstring warriors who had been killed in battle. High Back Wolf showed great leadership by refusing the "gift." He responded by saying: "Friend, these things if shown and talked about will only make bad feelings. The peace is made now; take the heads away with you and use them as you think best; do not let us see them or hear of them."[18]

Black Kettle was incredibly moved by this gesture. From High Back Wolf, he had gained much wisdom in the art of diplomacy. He would take this experience with him and work for a lasting peace for his people.

Tragedy soon struck Black Kettle's people as well as several other tribes in the American West. With the California gold rush of 1849 bringing thousands of immigrants west, so came disease. An outbreak of cholera shortly spread to the Indian camps along the westward trails such as the Overland Trail, the Santa Fe Trail and the Smoky Hill Trail. George Bent described the deadly effect it had on his people: "cramps" the Indians called it, and they died of it by the hundreds. On the Platte whole camps could be seen deserted with the tipi full of dead bodies, men, women and children. The Sioux and Cheyenne, who were nearest to the road, were the hardest hit. Our tribe suffered very heavy loss; half the tribe died, some old people say. The people were soon in a panic. The big camps soon broke up into little bands and family groups, and each party fled from the rest."[19]

Fortunately, Black Kettle and Little Sage Woman did not contract the deadly disease. As the cold winter weather seemed to kill the disease, Black Kettle moved his people to the Arkansas River where they set up their winter camp near Bent's Fort. Black Kettle welcomed the other Cheyenne bands who had survived the white man's disease. All were full of sorrow and loss. Black Kettle worked to bring the people together and reassemble a strong tribe of the Cheyenne Nation.

In September 1851, over ten thousand Indians, members of the Arapaho and Cheyenne tribes, gathered at Horse Creek, some thirty-five miles east of Fort Laramie. The purpose was to negotiate a peace agreement with the United States government. It had come about due to the desire and hard work of famed mountain man, Thomas Fitzpatrick. Known as "Broken Hand" to the Indians, Fitzpatrick had been appointed Indian Agent in 1846 for the Upper Arkansas and Platte River valleys. With the help of such peace advocates as Father Pierre Jean De Smet and frontiersman Jim

Bridger, a peace treaty was agreed to by all parties on September 17, 1851. Known as the "Treaty of Fort Laramie," or the "Treaty of Horse Creek," it provided the Arapaho and Southern Cheyenne compensation in the amount of fifty thousand dollars per year for fifty years for the encroachment of several buffalo ranges.[20]

With this treaty, the Cheyenne and Arapaho were allowed control of the area from the Rocky Mountains eastward some three hundred miles, including the land between the North Platte and Arkansas Rivers (which included the Oregon and Santa Fe trails). As such, this treaty officially affirmed the separation of both the Arapaho and Cheyenne from their northern counterparts.

Black Kettle must have been pleased with the results of the treaty, as it allowed his people to remain in their traditional territory. However, the peace was short-lived.

In the summer of 1852, over two hundred members of the Cheyenne Dog Soldiers, as well as warriors of the Apache, Arapaho, Kiowa, and Sioux tribes, engaged in fierce battle against their enemy: the Pawnee. For the Cheyenne, it was a battle of revenge, for in 1842, the Pawnee had managed to capture the Cheyenne Sacred Arrows in a battle at the Platte River. The Cheyenne had made numerous attempts to recover the spiritual arrows through peaceful overtures, but to no avail. In this ensuing battle, the Pawnee were defeated and the Cheyenne celebrated the victory.

Bolstered by the victory, the Cheyenne Council Chiefs, including Black Kettle, declared war against their bitter enemy. A messenger was dispatched to bring the news to the many lodges camped at the mouth of Beaver Creek and the South Platte River. Within a few days, the Cheyenne people tore down their lodges and moved in a long single column south toward the Arikara (Arikaree) fork of the Republican River.[21] On the morning of the attack, the chief of the Cheyenne Dog Soldiers, Long Chin, selected to lead the ceremony before the battle, wore the Sacred Buffalo Hat. Black Kettle carried the new prepared Sacred Arrows on the end of his war lance as he rode to the head of the assembled warriors.

The attack was thwarted before it began. One of the warriors, Big Head, led several others away from the main warring party in an attempt to count the first coup against the Pawnee. This action was a violation of Cheyenne law. Not only did it disrespect the power of the Sacred Arrows and the Sacred Buffalo Hat carried by the leaders, the very act was considered to diminish the spiritual power they represented.

Unaware of Big Head's actions, Black Kettle and Long Chin

Black Kettle released these child captives to Wynkoop. Ambrose Asher age 7, Laura Roper age 17, Isabelle Eubanks age 3 and Daniel Marble age 9. *Nebraska State Historical Society.*

led the warriors toward the Pawnee camp. Reaching the camp, Black Kettle was dismayed to find it deserted. Big Head then rode toward Black Kettle with a bloody scalp. He directed the warriors to the site where the Pawnee had retreated. Black Kettle and his warriors followed Big Head to the site. However, due to Big Head's premature action, the Pawnee had assumed an effective defense position. Nevertheless, Black Kettle and his warriors fought furiously throughout the afternoon to penetrate the Pawnee defense. Meanwhile, other warriors were able to enter the Pawnee camp where they burned the lodges and confiscated their property. During this time of destruction, another group of warriors were observed riding toward the camp from the opposite direction. As the riders got closer to the Cheyenne warriors, they were recognized as Potawatomis and opened fire. Several Cheyenne warriors lay dead before the remaining force retreated. The Cheyenne marked this incident as bad medicine due to Big Head breaking tradition regarding the Sacred Arrows.

    A few years later, Black Kettle led a band of warriors into northern Mexico to avenge the death of two hunters from the Scabby Band of the Cheyenne. Included in the group were two women, Red

Eye Woman and Black Kettle's wife, Little Sage Woman. According to his biographer, Thom Hatch, after a successful attack and the stealing of several horses, Black Kettle and the others began the long journey north to their homeland. Somewhere between the Cimarron and South Canadian rivers, the group were overtaken by a band of Utes. George Bent, in his memoirs, recounted the bloody fight that occurred:

> *"This party ran right into the Ute village without seeing it, and in the retreat Black Kettle's wife and another woman were thrown from their horses and captured... Both were young women, and Black Kettle's wife, it is said, was fine looking. Mexican traders were induced to try to find these women, but they could get no trace of them and they were never heard of again."* [22]

During the fierce fighting, Little Sage Woman was thrown from her horse. Black Kettle made several attempts to get to her but as the Utes circled around the area, he was unable to reach her. Shortly after one attempt, in which Black Kettle was wounded, he watched in horror as a Ute warrior grabbed Little Sage Woman and rode away with her.[23] Emboldened by the warrior's action, a few other Ute warriors closed in around Red Eye Woman who lay wounded. Her husband, Frog, who was at her side, fought Utes and died for his efforts, as Red Eye Woman was also taken captive. Then, the Ute warriors abruptly left the scene, taking with them the horses the Cheyenne had stolen in Mexico. Black Kettle constantly searched for his wife and even enlisted Mexican traders to find Little Sage Woman, but to no avail.

Eventually, after a respectful period of mourning, Black Kettle remarried in 1854. He married Medicine Woman Later, a member of the Wu-ta-pi-u or Wotapio band, a small division of the integrated Cheyenne-Sioux band. As was the Cheyenne custom, Black Kettle lived among his wife's people. The Wotapio were known for their fine horses and expert riders. According to George Bent: "Everything they had was clean and of the best quality, and by the other Cheyenne bands they were called 'Stingies,' because they did not like to give away their things as presents like the others."[24] During the winter of 1854, not long after Black Kettle's second marriage, the chief of the Wotapio band, Bear Feather, died. A council was held to elect a new chief. The unanimous choice was Black Kettle to lead the Wotapio people. George Bent recounted the events leading to Black Kettle becoming chief of the Cheyennes:

"The chief of this band at the time was Bear With Feathers, and when he died in 1850, [sic] Black Kettle was elected chief."[25]

This high honor was a testament to Black Kettle's years as a formidable warrior, as well as a loyal and spiritual Cheyenne, despite his personal loss. Among the Indian tribes of the plains, Black Kettle was widely respected as a fierce adversary of the Pawnee and Kiowa, yet he believed in peace with the white man. Black Kettle would draw on that spiritual guidance in the years to come as he dealt with enemies, as well as the white man. His goal never wavered, for Chief Black Kettle spent the rest of his life working for peace.

His chance at peace with the white man came in 1861 with the Treaty of Fort Wise. William Bent, who had served as Indian Agent for the Arapaho and Cheyenne in 1859, wrote:

"The Cheyans and Arrapahos have took my advice to them last Winter and this last Spring. I am proud to say that they have behaved themselves exceedingly well. Thair will be no troble settling them down and start farming. They tell me they have passed theair laws amongst themselves that they will do anything I may advize. It is a pity that the Department can't send Some farming implements and other necessarys this fall Sow as they could commence farming this Coming Spring...After I deliver the Indians theair goods I intend to have a conversations with the Kioways and Commanches. I suppose that will be putary saucy-but as I have bin appointed agent I feel it my dutay to see all of the Indians under my agency-if they sculp me...you Must excuse my bad spelling as I have bin so long in the Wild Waste I have almost forgotten how to spell." [26]

Evidently, Bent's report was either not received favorably, or the federal government saw things quite differently. A. B. Greenwood, Commissioner of Indian Affairs, wrote in his annual report for 1859:

"There is no alternative to providing for them in this manner but to exterminate them, which the dictates of justice and humanity alike forbid." [27]

Therefore, Greenwood's recommendation was to negotiate a new treaty with the Arapaho and Cheyenne. The government agreed. There was also an ulterior reason for a new treaty: land. The previous year, large amounts of gold had been discovered in the Rocky Mountains. Thousands of gold seekers were rushing to the mountains and still others were settling in the area and starting businesses. Denver City had been established near the confluence of the South Platte River and Cherry Creek. The government needed title to the land to further economic development.

Early in 1860, the U. S. Congress appropriated thirty-five thousand dollars for various expenses to hold a council with the tribes along the Upper Arkansas River. Federal government officials drafted a treaty to purchase the Indian title to all lands within the contemplated territory to be negotiated. In August 1860, Greenwood left Washington, D. C., with federal documents in hand, for a long trip to Bent's Fort on the Arkansas River. Included in his party were a group of friends and relatives as well as Colonel Albert Gallitan Boone, the grandson of famed frontiersman, Daniel Boone. Meanwhile, William Bent had sold his fort to the War Department which had originally renamed it Fort Fauntleroy, but then changed it to Fort Wise in honor of Virginia governor, Henry A. Wise, and even later, Fort Lyon, in 1861. Greenwood and his entourage, followed by thirteen wagons loaded with goods and presents, arrived on September 8, 1860. He was surprised to find that the Arapaho were already camped at the fort, awaiting his arrival. A reporter covering the event wrote that the Indians roamed the area, "with blankets, leggings, paint, lice and dirt."[28]

Greenwood was told that the Cheyenne were hunting buffalo some two hundred miles away, but that messengers had been sent out to locate them. Ten days later, Black Kettle of the Cheyenne and White Antelope of the Arapaho rode into the fort. The chiefs explained to Greenwood that members of their tribes would not arrive for several days as they were many miles away. Greenwood elected to begin the council without the other tribal members.

It would be a tactical error that would result in confusion and even denial of agreement among many in both tribes.

As the council began, Greenwood presented the Indians with a portion of the goods and presents, explaining they would receive the remainder when a treaty was signed. Several advocates for peace and friends of the Cheyenne and Arapaho were in attendance, including Charles Autobees and John Hatch. William Bent was there, delighted to be reunited with his old friend, Colonel Albert G. Boone. John Smith served as interpreter.

Following opening remarks, Greenwood displayed a map of the area assigned to each of the tribes. Bent argued, on behalf of the Indians, that they be allowed to remain on their homelands, but to no avail. In the October 4, 1860 of the *Western Mountaineer*, the correspondent for the paper wrote:

"Of course, settlers would object; and if any arrangement is made, the Indians will probably be put over on the Republican, or in some other locality where they will not interfere with 'our manifest destiny.'"

After difficult negotiations, Black Kettle and White Antelope agreed to the new land assignments, but refused to sign the treaty until they held a vote with their respective tribes. As an expressed measure toward the peace proposal, Greenwood presented Black Kettle with an American flag, instructing the peaceful chief to fly it, as a symbol of peace, when and if soldiers should approach his camp.

Disappointed, Greenwood left Fort Wise on September 20, 1860, without the coveted signed treaty. Equally disappointed, William Bent resigned his office as Indian Agent, requesting his old friend, Colonel Boone, replace him. Due to Bent's recommendation, Boone became the new Indian Agent of the Upper Arkansas region.

Boone's first task was to complete the treaty efforts begun by Greenwood. To this end, in February, 1861, he gathered the tribal leaders, once again, at Fort Wise. And once again, only a few of the principal chiefs arrived. Black Kettle, Lean Bear, Little Wolf, Tall Bear, and White Antelope of the Cheyenne participated. The Arapaho representatives included Big Mouth, Left Hand, Little Raven, Shave-Head and Storm. However, the leaders of the Dog Soldiers, defiant in their opposition, refused to attend. Robert Bent, the son of William Bent and Owl Woman, served as the official interpreter for the U. S. government.

The new treaty offered the tribes nearly half a million dollars over a fifteen year period. In return, the treaty required that the Arapaho and Cheyenne relinquish the vast majority of their land appropriated in the Fort Laramie Treaty of 1851. This new proposal reduced their land to one small portion on the Arkansas River, in southern Colorado Territory. However, it also provided each Indian forty acres of land. Perhaps as an enticement to the Indians for their vast loss of land, the treaty included the following clause:

"It is further understood, before signing the above treaty, that it was the particular request and wish of the chiefs and councillors [sic] *in general*

convention, in consideration of Robert Bent being one of their halfbreed tribe, that he should have, as a gift of the nation, six hundred and forty acres of land, covering the valley and what is called the Sulpher Spring, lying on the north side of the Arkansas River and about five miles below the Pawnee Hills, and they wish the general government to recognize and confirm the same; and that Jack Smith, son of John S. Smith, who is also a halfbreed of said nation, shall have six hundred and forty acres of land, lying seven miles above Bent's Old Fort, on the north side of the Arkansas River, including the valley and point of rock, and respectfully recommend the general government to confirm and recognize the same."[29]

The agreement was signed by all in attendance on February 18, 1861. Indian Agent Boone returned to Washington, D. C. with the signed document, which was subsequently ratified in the U. S. Senate and signed by President Abraham Lincoln on December 15, 1861. It was a fabulous treaty for the government. They had acquired the desired land where gold had recently been discovered and confined the Indians to a small piece of land far away from the anticipated economic boom. However, several members of both the Cheyenne and Arapaho bands refused to settle down on the small gameless reserve and continued to hunt buffalo. For the next three years, Black Kettle struggled to maintain the peace between his people and the white man. The Indians began to complain that the dry lands near the Arkansas River held little wildlife and the white settlers encroaching on the land had removed much of the timber in the area.

The young Cheyenne warriors, particularly the Dog Soldiers, over which Black Kettle had little influence, refused to obey the Treaty of Fort Wise. They began to launch raids among the white people. In response, the government formed the Third Voluntary Cavalry regiment to protect the settlers.

Now, in the cool autumn of 1864, as Black Kettle gravely rode toward his camp, following his peace-keeping efforts at Camp Weld, his mind must have been filled with the events of the past summer. He knew from experience that the white man's new militia would eventually set out on a full-scale war and would not relent, even to a peace-seeking Black Kettle and his Cheyenne people. Black Kettle also worried over the coming winter. When the winds brought the snow, would there be enough game to feed his people, and timber to warm the tipi?

Among those in Black Kettle's camp was George Bent, who had written the letter for Black Kettle addressed to Major Colley, requesting peace and offering the release of the seven captives. Bent was the son of William Bent and his Cheyenne wife, Owl Woman. He was born in 1843 at the famous fort his father had built in southern Colorado along the Arkansas River. His grandfather was the great Cheyenne chief, Gray Thunder, the Keeper of the Sacred Arrows. At the age of ten, George, and his siblings, were sent east to St. Louis for their education, where they lived with Albert G. Boone, grandson of the famous frontiersman. In 1861, George enlisted in the Confederate Army, where he saw battle at Wilson's Creek and Pea Ridge. Taken as a prisoner following the siege of Corinth, Bent was released by officers under pressure from his father's influential friends.

Returning to southern Colorado and his home at Bent's Fort, twenty-two-year-old George Bent soon found himself in the middle of the oncoming war between two cultures; cultures of which he was a product.

The Indian deprivations escalated at an alarming rate across the eastern plains, some of which were perpetrated by George's half-brother, Charles, an avid member of the Dog Soldiers. William Bent knew that war was coming. Following the Treaty of Fort Wise, Bent had made the decision to send George and his sister Julia, and their half-brother, Charlie, to their mother's tribe, camped at Sand Creek.

It was a large camp, with more tribes moving in almost daily. Bent later described it as "a good place." High bluffs on the west bank of the creek provided shelter for the growing Indian village. Nearby springs provided clean water, while small pools in the otherwise dry creek bed offered water for the horses. There were nearly a hundred Cheyenne lodges, surrounded by the other tribes. William Bent's old friend, Chief Yellow Wolf, and his band, camped near Black Kettle, and White Antelope camped just north of the peaceful chief's lodge. One-Eye's lodge was upstream from this area, as was War Bonnet's lodge and his Ho-iv-i-ma-nah, or Scabby band.

The Third Colorado regiment, dubbed the "Bloodless Third," by the press, were led by Chivington's and had trained and spent over half of their enlistment time waiting for horses, arms and ammunition. After great publicity in recruiting such a force, Chivington needed to act fast before the troops were uselessly mustered out.

On September 19, 1864, Chivington learned that a supply of firearms and ammunition destined for General Carleton's soldiers in New Mexico had been delayed at Fort Lyon. Chivington immediately sent a wire to Secretary of War, Edwin Stanton, requesting the authority to claim the arms and ammunition for his own military regiments, indicating he wished to use the arms against the "Indian warriors congregated eighty miles from [Fort] Lyon, three thousand strong."

U. S. Army Chief of Staff, Major General Halleck, returned Chivington's wire stating that Chivington follow the military protocol for such requisition requests. Chivington sent an urgent wire to General Halleck:

> "Have regiment of 100 days men ready for field. Train on the way from Fort Leavenworth, but can not get here in time because of the Indian troubles on the Platte Route. Are four hundred miles back, and laid up. The time of this regiment will expire and the Indians will still hold [the] road. This is no ordinary case." [30]

It is clear from this communique that Chivington was desperate to receive the necessary arms for his troops to carry out his mission to annihilate the Indians, thereby gaining an extraordinary political victory: protecting the settlers of Colorado Territory, which, he was sure, would lead to statehood. Several soldiers had been complaining to their superiors that they would not see active service in the Indian war, which they had volunteered for. Irving Howbert, a member of the Colorado Third Regiment under First Lieutenant Joseph Graham, later wrote in his memoirs:

> "A majority of the Third Regiment had been in camp near Denver [Camp Weld] during all this time. This inactivity had caused a great deal of complaint among both officers and enlisted men. The regiment had been recruited principally from the business men, miners and farmers of the Territory, and the understanding was that they were to be given active service against the hostile Indians at the earliest possible moment. However, undoubtedly the delay was unavoidable, due to the fact that the necessary horses had to be driven to Colorado from east of the Missouri River, and this took more than a month." [31]

Time was running out. Their federally authorized "100 days" of service was nearing its end. When the needed firearms were finally issued, through a formal military request, they were outdated Austrian muzzle-loading muskets "of large bore."[32] Chivington immediately sent a request for a shipment of Starr carbines.

In October, one company of the volunteer soldiers finally found action in the field. Captain Nichols of the Third Colorado regiment, stationed at Valley Station on the South Platte River, had been informed of a band of Indians not far from the station. Taking a troop of forty soldiers, on October 10, 1864, Captain Nichols set out to investigate. On the bluffs above the south side of the river, Nichols and his men spotted two lodges camped near a spring on the south side of the river. Nichols and his troops immediately attacked the small Indian camp. When the military fire ceased, six warriors, three women, and one young boy lay dead. The soldiers confiscated their ponies and mules. Searching the lodges, they found the scalp of a white woman, several articles of white women's clothing, as well as bills of lading from St. Joseph to Denver. Captain Nichols later wrote in his report:

"We also found Big Wolf's certificate of good character, friendship for whites, &c., but the lady's scalp and clothing failed to corroborate the statements." [33]

A few weeks after this incident, Chivington received a telegram from Brigadier-General P. E. Connor, commanding the District of Utah. The telegram informed Chivington that Connor had received precise instructions from Secretary of War Stanton, to "do all in his power," to protect the overland stage between Salt Lake City and Fort Kearney. In Connor's communication to Chivington he specifically asked Chivington:

"Can we get a fight out of the Indians this winter? Can you send grain out on road to meet my command? How many troops can you spare for a campaign? Answer." [34]

Chivington, confused by Conner's request, sent a telegram of his own to his superior, General Samuel R. Curtis:

"Have department line changed? If not, will I allow him to give direction to matters within this district? Line perfectly protected to Julesburg. The line this side of Julesburg ought to be in this district, as my troops are taking care of it." [35]

Brigadier-General P. E. Connor, along with Ben Holliday, owner of the Overland Stage Company, arrived in Denver on November 14, to personally speak with Chivington regarding the allocation of military protection for the stage line. Ironically, this was the same day that Chivington had issued orders to his troops to march southeast from Camp Weld. The *Rocky Mountain News* covered the event in the November 16, 1864 issue, under the headline, "Gen. Conner."

> *"This distinguished gentleman was serenaded at the Planter's House last evening by the First Regiment band, attended by the District Commander, Colonel Chivington, and a number of the Colorado officers, as well as by a large delegation of our citizens. The General came out on the portico and made some brief remarks, thanking the people for the kind reception, and telling them that he was not, by profession, a speaker. We knew that, and excuse him. He is, however, a fighter, and a gentleman and a soldier to boot. Gen. Connor is a man that suits the genius of this West, and Colorado will appreciate his mission. He comes here to take a look at the field, and ascertain the feasibility of punishing the hostile Indians on the overland mail route. We congratulate Colorado on the accession of so sagacious an officer to our section of the prairie west."*

The meeting was both cordial and contentious, according to Chivington's account. Years later he told the following to a reporter for the *Denver Republican*:

> *"Several days before the troops left Denver General Conor, [sic] who was in command of the district of Utah, had been in Denver, and my impression from the day of his coming was that he had been ordered here by the secretary or war, to see whether we were efficiently prosecuting this campaign against the Indians. In this conviction I was confirmed when the general came to me, after I had mounted to overtake the troops, and said to me: 'I think from the temper of the men that you have and all I can learn that you will give these Indians a most terrible threshing if you can catch them, and if it was in the mountains, and you had them in a canyon, and your troops at one end of it and the Bear river at the other, as I had the Pi-Utes, you could catch them; but I am afraid on these plains you won't do it.' I said: 'Possibly I may not, but I think I shall.' 'Well,' he said, 'I repeat, if you catch them-but I don't think you will-you will give them a good dressing down.' To which I could only reply: 'I may not general, but I think I will catch them.' And as I was about to ride off he said: 'If you do catch them wire me just as soon as you can get to a telegraph office, for I shall want to know it, and I start by the next coach for Salt Lake.' I promised him I would do so, when he looked back at me and said: 'Colonel, where are these Indians?' I said: 'General, that*

is the trick that wins in this game, if the game is won. There are but two persons who know their exact location, and they are myself and Colonel George L. Shoup." [36]

On that day, November 14, 1864, Chivington was deep in thought as he left that meeting and rode toward his troops. He needed a military victory against the hostile Indians for the citizens of Colorado as well as his own political agenda. In his mind, both goals were the same; the success of victory would lead to Colorado statehood and his own political triumph. Following his contentious meeting with General Conner, Chivington may have even wanted to prove a point. Colonel John M. Chivington guided his horse briskly along the Bijou Creek Trail toward his newly created "100 Day Volunteers," camped along the creek. The one-time Methodist elder and Civil War hero of Glorieta Pass now had the coveted orders from his district commander, General Samuel Curtis:

"The Indians are to be fully subdued or exterminated. There will be no peace until the Indians suffer more." [37]

Colonel George L. Shoup and Major Hal Sayr, along with several companies of both the Colorado First and Third regiments, were awaiting Chivington's arrival at their camp in the Bijou Basin. Finally, after a two-day ride, Chivington arrived in camp. Following a rallying speech to the soldiers, camp was broken and Chivington led the Colorado Third Regiment as well as three companies of the Colorado First Regiment, south toward the Arkansas River. Major Sayr took seven companies of both regiments with him toward Camp Fillmore, near the Arkansas River. Colonel Shoup left Bijou Creek and headed up the Platte River to the Valley Station where the remaining companies of the Colorado Third were stationed.

A severe snowstorm hampered the troop advancement toward the Arkansas River. The troops marched doggedly for over two hundred miles in the cold and wind, often pulling their horses out of snow drifts as much as two feet deep. Finally, on November 18, 1864, Major Sayr and his troops, guided by Jim Beckwourth, arrived at Camp Fillmore and were greeted by members of Company E of the First Regiment. Colonel Shoup arrived with companies C, D, and F of the Third Regiment as well as Company H of the First Regiment, on November 21. Chivington and his troops arrived on Wednesday, November 23, 1864. Chivington wasted no time. The following morning, Chivington led his troops on a long, cold

From this spot Chivington's soldiers first looked down on Black Kettle's camp. Today, the ghost of sorrow haunts Sand Creek. *Sand Creek National Park Service*

march down the Arkansas River. Irving Howbert later recounted the experience:

> "We steadily marched down the valley of the Arkansas River, going into camp between seven and eight o'clock each night; but by the time we had eaten supper and cared for our horses, it was after ten o'clock. Reveille sounded at four o'clock the next morning and before daylight we were on the march again." [38]

By Sunday, November 27, the soldiers had traveled ninety-three miles to a spot along the river where they made camp for the night.

Early the next morning, Monday, November 28, Chivington ordered a group of soldiers from the Colorado Third, under Lieutenant Joseph Graham, to head across the river toward William Bent's ranch at the mouth of the Purgatoire River. Graham's additional order was to "put the place under guard, allowing no one to leave." With the same orders, Captain Cook left the camp with a regiment of the Colorado First, for the John W. Prowers ranch along the Arkansas River, at the mouth of Caddoa Creek. Howbert, who was under Graham's command, recalled:

> *"In order that the news of our approach should not reach the Indians, every man whom we met on the road was taken in charge, and guards were placed at all ranches for the same purpose."* [39]

The siege of the Bent and Prowers ranches was significant to Chivington's secrecy on several levels. William Bent was the father of half-white, half-Indian sons, believed to consort with the enemy. John W. Prowers was married to Amache, the daughter of One-Eye, who had bravely walked into Fort Lyon with the peace letter from Black Kettle, and pledged peace with the white man that led to the council at Camp Weld, something Chivington was strongly opposed to.

At the Bent ranch, the family was ordered inside the home and guards were placed at all doors. The Bent family was told that anyone attempting to escape would be shot. Robert Bent, the eldest son of William, was ordered to aid Jim Beckwourth in guiding the soldiers to the Cheyenne village; ironically, the very village of his mother's people, where his brother George and three younger half-sisters were living.

Forced into such a position, what went through Robert Bent's mind is anyone's guess. Apparently, Chivington didn't trust him as he told Bent:

> *"I haven't had an Indian to eat in a long time. If you fool with me, and don't lead us to that camp, I'll have you for breakfast."* [40]

On that same morning, just two days after Wynkoop had left for his new assignment at Fort Riley, Kansas, Captain Silas Soule was on a reconnaissance mission with twenty troops of the First Colorado regiment. Following the Arkansas River upstream for approximately ten miles from Fort Lyon, Soule and his command came upon a mule team on the north bank of the river. In casual conversation, the driver delivered a stunning piece of news to Soule. He had passed Colonel Chivington and a dozen companies of soldiers further up the river. Curious, as no one at the fort had prior knowledge of such a large military force coming to the fort, Soule traveled further upstream. After a few miles, Soule came upon four columns of advancing cavalry, complete with artillery wagons. Chivington, in the lead, asked Soule if anyone at the fort knew he was coming. Soule replied in the negative. Soule and his men returned to fort, following Chivington's advance.

Once at the fort, Chivington immediately took command and sealed off the fort. No one was allowed in or out. Again, Howbert related the incident:

> "We arrived at Fort Lyons [sic] about four o'clock in the afternoon of November 28, to the great surprise of its garrison, as they were not aware that the regiment had left the vicinity of Denver. A picket was thrown around the Fort at once to prevent the trappers or Indian traders, who generally hung around such places, from notifying the savages of our presence." [41]

Meeting with Major Anthony, Chivington revealed his plan of attack on the Indians. Anthony agreed with Chivington's mission, but requested that three white men camped with the Indians, Watson Clark, Private David Louderback and John Smith, be removed from the camp before the attack. He also asked that the peaceful Indian chiefs, Black Kettle, Left Hand, One-Eye and White Antelope be spared.[42] Enraged at Anthony's request, Chivington replied:

> "Black Kettle is the principal chief of the Cheyenne nation, which has been engaged in bloody war with the whites since April. His claim of friendship seems to have arisen with the ending of the summer season and the approach of cold weather when Indians fight at a disadvantage. However, it is not my intention to attack without warning. Actual operations must, of course, depend on conditions which we find on arrival, but I propose to first immobilize the Indians, if possible, and then to offer them a parley on terms of surrender. Such terms would include the delivering up for punishment of all savages guilty of hostilities, the return of all stolen property, the surrender of all firearms and the giving of hostages to ensure against further hostilities." [43]

With this statement made by Chivington to Major Anthony, a series of deceit and lies were now in the making. For this very statement contradicted a remark Chivington had said to the soldiers when he arrived at Bijou Creek:

> "Scalps are what we're after. I long to be wading in gore." [44]

Tension was mounting that night within the confines of Fort Lyon. Captain Silas Soule later wrote a letter to Major Wynkoop:

"As soon as I knew of their movement I was indignant as you would have been were you here and went to Cannon's room, where a number of officers of the 1st and 3rd were congregated and told them that any man who would take a part in the murders, knowing the circumstances as we did, was a low cowardly son of a bitch. Capt. Y. J. Johnson and Lieut. Hardin went to camp and reported to Chiv, Downing and the whole outfit what I had said, and you can bet hell was to pay in camp." [45]

Twenty-six-year-old Captain Silas Soule immediately went to his commanding officer, Major Anthony, asking the major to dissuade Chivington of such an action.

"I talked to Anthony about it, and he said that some of those Indians ought to be killed; that he had been only waiting for a good chance to pitch it to them. I reminded him of the pledges he had made them, and he said that Colonel Chivington had told him that those Indians in the camp should not be killed; that the object of the expedition was to go out to the Smoky Hill and follow the Indians up. Anthony told me that I would not compromise myself by going out, as I was opposed to going." [46]

Obviously this statement by Anthony would prove not be the case. Either Chivington lied to Anthony, or Anthony lied to Soule. Captain Soule then sent a note to Chivington asking for a meeting. The note was returned unopened.[47]

Lieutenant Joseph A. Cramer also tried to reason with Anthony. He reiterated what Major Wynkoop had previously explained to him: that Black Kettle, Left Hand, and White Antelope, along with their tribes, were peacefully camped at Sand Creek at the very direction of Governor Evans and Chivington himself, following the meeting at Camp Weld the previous month. Anthony told Cramer that the chiefs and their people were in no danger and that Black Kettle will not be killed. Anthony told Cramer that the object of Chivington's mission was to "surround the camp and take any stolen stock."[48]

Again, either Chivington lied to Anthony or Anthony lied to Cramer. That evening, Major Anthony penned a report later delivered to the army headquarters at Fort Riley, Kansas:

> "I have the honor to report that Col. John M. Chivington, First Cavalry of Colorado, arrived at this post this day with 1,000 men of the Third Cavalry and two howitzers, on expedition against Indians. This number of men has been required for some time, and is appreciated by me now, as I believe the Indians will be properly punished-what they have for some time deserved. I go out with 125 men and two howitzers to join his command." [49]

Through this missive, unknown to the soldiers at the time, Anthony's true intentions became clear. He not only agreed with Chivington's proposed action, but lied to his troops.

Major Colley agreed with Wynkoop's policy and said so to Chivington, explaining, action to the contrary was against what was stated at Camp Weld. Chivington, outraged at the mounting opposition, responded to Colley:

> "Damn any man who is in sympathy with an Indian." [50]

Lieutenant Cramer attempted to appeal to Chivington, asking him to reconsider the "mission." He later testified under oath:

> "I had some conversation with Major Downing, Lieutenant Maynard, and Colonel Chivington. I stated to them my feelings in regards to the matter; that I believed it to be 'murder,' and stated the obligations that we of Major Wynkoop's command were under to those Indians. To Colonel Chivington I know I stated that Major Wynkoop had pledged his word as an officer and a man to those Indians, and that all officers under him were indirectly pledged in the same manner that he was, and that I felt it was placing us in very embarrassing circumstances to fight the same Indians that had saved our lives, as we felt they had. Colonel Chivington's reply was, that he believed it to be right or honorable to use any means under God's heaven to kill Indians that would kill women children, and 'damn any man that is in sympathy with Indians,' and such men as Major Wynkoop and myself had better get out of the United States service." [51]

Both Cramer and Soule were put on notice to steer clear of Chivington. The colonel's orders stood. At eight o'clock that night, over seven hundred troops comprised of the First Colorado Cavalry, including Cramer and Soule, as well as the Colorado Third Cavalry under Colonel George L. Shoup, including Howbert, and the additional troops from Fort Lyon, under Major Anthony, marched north from Fort Lyon fourteen miles to the banks of Sand Creek and into infamy.

Howbert later recounted:

"Each man was instructed to get from the commissary a few pounds of bacon and sufficient hard-tack to last three or four days, these articles of food to be carried along in our saddlebags. At eight o'clock that night, the regiment took up its line of march across the prairie in a direction almost due north from Fort Lyon. Each company was formed in ranks of fours, and we traveled rapidly from the start. It was walk, trot, gallop, dismount and lead, all night long. I had slept but little for two or three nights previous to this, and consequently, I found this all night marching terribly exhausting. During the latter part of the night I would willingly have run the risk of being scalped by Indians for a half hour's sleep. Sometime after midnight, the regiment's guide led us through one of the shallow lakes that are so plentiful on the plains of that region. He was suspected of being more friendly to the Indians than to the whites, and it was thought probable that he planned this purposely, hoping that the water would reach and spoil our ammunition, making it ineffective in the anticipated engagement. During the night, in order to keep awake, many of us had been nibbling on the hard-tack that had been issued to us, and were greatly disgusted in the morning when we found it very much alive with worms." [52]

The guide Howbert speaks about was undoubtedly either Jim Beckwourth or Robert Bent, both of whom, obviously friendly to the Indians, would have reason to lead a diversion.

Dawn broke cold and damp on the barren prairie along the banks of Sand Creek as fog danced with the early sunrise on Tuesday, November 29, 1864. Camped in the ravine near the creek were some six hundred Indians, including a great number of women and children, along with chiefs Little Raven, White Antelope, Left Hand and Black Kettle.

Chivington moved his troops into position just south of the Indian camp along the banks of Sand Creek. The creek was but a small trickle of frozen water at this time of year, and years of drought had exposed the sandy creek bottom for several miles.[53] Chivington's troops were soon joined by over a hundred men of the Colorado First Regiment, followed by an additional one hundred troops from Fort Lyon, led by Major Anthony. In addition to the armed troops, nearly seven hundred strong, were four twelve-pound mountain howitzers.

Despite his stated intentions to "surround the camp and take any stolen stock," Chivington deployed his troops for an all-out attack on the village. Chivington rallied his soldiers for battle with a venomous speech, frothed with Indian hatred, ending with, "Remember our wives and children murdered on the Platte and Arkansas."[54] Chivington then divided his forces for a three-pronged attack of the village from the south, the east and the west.

"It was a bright, clear, starlight night, the air crisp and uncomfortably cool, as might have been expected at that time of year. Just as the sun was coming up over the eastern horizon, we reached the top of a ridge, and away off down in the valley to the northwest, we saw a great number of Indian tents, forming a village of unusual size. We knew at once that this village was our objective point. Off to the left, between the place where we were and the village, there was a large number of Indian ponies scattered over the plain grazing. Two or three minute later, orders came directing our battalion to capture this herd. Under command of a major of the regiment we started immediately on the run in order to get between the ponies and the Indian camp before our presence was discovered. We had not proceeded any great distance when we saw half a dozen mounted Indians coming from the direction of the camp, riding rapidly toward the herd. However, upon seeing our large force they hesitated a moment, and then started back to their village as fast as their ponies could take them. We were not long in securing the herd, which consisted of between five and six hundred ponies. The officer in command detailed a small force to take charge of the animals, with instructions to drive them away to a point where they would be in no danger of recapture."[55]

However, a few of the ponies broke from the herd and ran toward the village. Some of the women, building fires and preparing the morning meal in the cold dawn of a new day, heard the thunder of the horses' hooves. As they began shouting the alarm, men, women and even children ran out of their lodges into the confusion.

As the sun rose, Chivington's troops began their charge into the sleepy Indian village, a fight that would last over six hours. Lieutenant Luther Wilson, with over one hundred soldiers from Companies C, E, and F, of the Colorado First Regiment, led the attack. Charging northeast, crossing the creek, the soldiers began firing upon the Indian village. Major Anthony's three companies of the First Colorado Cavalry were used as reinforcements along the battle lines. Chivington then moved his artillery on a ridge over the creek bed.

Cheyenne elder White Antelope, hearing the shots, left his lodge with arms extended, in the traditional sign of peace. George Bent watched in horror as he was shot down in a single round of fire.

John Smith, the trusted Cheyenne interpreter, along with David Louderback, ran toward the soldiers in an effort to make them stop firing. Louderback immediately recognized the soldiers as those of his own company. He quickly grabbed a white handkerchief and attached it to a stick, waving it as a sign of peace. His effort was ignored. The soldiers advanced and shot and wounded John Smith. Horribly frightened and confused, the two men ran for the shelter of their lodge which included Smith's son, Jack, Charley Bent and his brother-in-law, Ed Guerrier, who was half-white, half-Indian.

Black Kettle, too, had emerged from his tipi, telling his people to remain calm. To the soldiers, he made the sign of peace and pointed to the American flag flying above his tipi. It was the very flag that A. B. Greenwood, Commissioner of Indian Affairs, had given to Black Kettle during the initial meeting which later led to the Treaty of Fort Wise. Greenwood had instructed Black Kettle to fly the flag as a symbol of peace should soldiers approach unannounced.

George Bent described the ensuing chaos of the early dawn:

"I looked toward the chief's lodge and saw that Black Kettle had a large American flag tied to the end of a long lodgepole and was standing in front of his lodge, holding the pole, with the flag fluttering in the grey light of the winter dawn. I heard calls to the people not to be afraid, that the soldiers would not hurt them; then the troops opened fire from two sides of the camp." [56]

Bent saw enough. Grabbing his weapons, he ran for the bluffs along the west side of Sand Creek. Unknown to Bent, his brother Robert was nearby watching the horror unfold. He watched as White Antelope was shot by the soldiers.

In governmental sworn testimony during the many investigations following the atrocity at Sand Creek, Robert Bent recounted in vivid detail examples of the many horrors he had witnessed. He said he saw a woman fall to the ground, her leg shattered from a cannonball. He said, as soldiers rode near her, she raised her arm to protect herself as a soldier drew his saber. He watched as the soldier sliced her arm in two. As the woman screamed in agony, the soldier sliced her other arm. He said he saw a group of women, hiding in a sand hole, send out a young female child with a white piece of cloth tied on a tree branch. As soon as soldiers spotted her, Bent said, they shot her. Then, he said, they saw the women and children in the sand hole and shot them all. Bent said he watched the soldiers shoot a pregnant woman and then cut the unborn child from her womb and lay the dead bloody infant next to the dead bloody mother.

Shortly after the shooting started, Ed Guerrier was able to run north to safety. He was picked up by his cousin, one of White Antelope's daughters, who had captured a few head of horses.

By this time, a group of nearly one hundred warriors had assembled a line of defense and were able to defend the village for a time. Then Colonel Shoup and his men advanced into the village at the same time Chivington ordered his men to fire cannonballs from the twelve-pound mountain howitzers positioned on the bluff above the village.

All hell broke loose.

The barrage of fire killed several in camp, including women and children. Hundreds fled north, away from the fire, the wounded crawling in the dry creek bed. George Bent was one of the wounded and later recalled:

> *"The Indians were all running but they did not seem to know what to do. I got my weapons...and joined a group of middle-aged Cheyenne men. We made a stand, but troops came up the west side of the creek and opened hot fire...we ran up the creek with the cavalry following...I was struck in the hip by a bullet but managed to tumble into a hole. Finally they withdrew, killing all the wounded laying in the creek bed."* [57]

As the warriors seemed to initially repulse the first attack, Chivington, Shoup and Anthony then ordered more troops into the Indian village.

On a ridge a short distance from the village, Captain Silas Soule watched in horror as the slaughter of human beings went on and on. When he was ordered to lead Company D into the battle, Soule steadfastly refused. Lieutenant Joseph Cramer also refused to send in his troops.

Remarkably, in the face of death and destruction, Black Kettle and his wife, Medicine Woman Later, remained at their lodge until they were confident that those who were able to escape had done so. Not just Black Kettle's Cheyenne people, but all the people of the peaceful village along Sand Creek. As Black Kettle and Medicine Woman Later made their way out of the village, following those fleeing north through the creek bed, Medicine Woman Later was hit by several bullets. Black Kettle biographer, Thom Hatch, best describes the horrific incident:

> *"Groups of soldiers were rushing to attack that creek bank, and Black Kettle and his wife became prime targets for their rifles. The couple dashed through a gauntlet of bullets and an obstacle course of dead and dying bodies, until finally Medicine Woman Later fell to the ground unmoving."* [58]

Black Kettle knelt down to help his wife. Believing she was dead, he reluctantly left her and ran up the creek bed as the soldiers fired at him. He was able to reach a spot in the sand pits where he took shelter as the warriors continued their attempt at holding back the soldier's onslaught.

Many of the Cheyenne men who bravely fought against the soldiers were themselves wounded. George Bent, who had received a bullet to the hip, was able to look south toward the village. He saw many men, women and children dead in the creek bed. Bent later described the line of defense he and others mounted:

> *"The soldiers concentrated their fire on the people in the pits and we fought back as well as we could with guns and bows, but we had only a few guns. The troops did not rush in and fight hand to hand, but once or twice after they had killed many of the men in a certain pit they rushed in and finished up the work, killing the wounded and the women and the children that had not been hurt."* [59]

Bent witnessed one such incident, when a young warrior next to him bravely defended his wife and daughters against a few soldiers nearing the pits. He later provided a first-hand account:

> *"He jumped out of the hole and ran towards the troops that were coming upon us, and as he came back into the hole he told me and his wife that he was killed. Blood gushed from the man's mouth and he fell face forward into the pit."* [60]

Black Kettle, for his part, although his eyesight was weak,

aided the warriors by reloading their weapons with what precious bullets they had.

As a military operation, the battle was a horrible bungle. Military command was lost early in the day. Soldiers were caught in their own crossfire as Chivington ordered Captain Baxter and his Company G of the Third Regiment to attack the village from the east in direct line of Wilson's troops. Lieutenant Joseph Cramer later testified:

> "There seemed to be no organization among our troops, everyone on his own hook, and shots flying between our own ranks." [61]

As John Smith and David Louderback raised the stick with the white handkerchief attached to it, in an effort of peace, the soldiers fired toward them. A soldier yelled, "Shoot the old son of a bitch."[62] One of Cramer's soldiers, George Pierce, attached to Company F, rode in to rescue the two men from eminent crossfire. He was thrown from his horse in the attempt and when he arose from the ground, he was killed, possibly in the crossfire.[63]

The surprised Indians, the few chiefs and warriors who happened to be in camp during the hunting season, were ill-armed, yet managed to hold their own and kept the soldiers at bay for several hours. Corporal Amos Miksch, with the First Colorado Cavalry, later recalled:

> "There were no rifle pits except what the Indians dug into the sand bank after we commenced firing. I saw them digging out sand with their hands, while the firing was going on; the water came into the trenches as they dug in this manner." [64]

As several troops of Chivington's army pursued the fleeing Indians, others were launching a heinous attack on the Indian village. Those Indians who could not flee the bloody insanity died on the spot, primarily women and children. Several soldiers dismounted and, entering lodges, killed and mutilated anyone they found.

John Smith had managed to move his wife and son, Jack, to what he thought was the safety of Chief War Bonnet's lodge. From the opening of the lodge, Smith saw Chivington. In an attempt to get his attention, Smith hollered at the colonel. Chivington, recognizing Smith, motioned for him to come toward him. Smith was taken to a safe place where he huddled while the battle raged on.

His intent was to return to War Bonnet's lodge to get his wife and son after he reasoned with soldiers. Smith had no idea at the time that Chief War Bonnet had been shot shortly after Chivington had whisked him out of harm's way. Smith described what happened next:

> *"By the time I got up with the battery to the place where these Indians were surrounded there had been some considerable firing. Four or five soldiers had been killed, some with arrows and some with bullets. The soldiers continued firing on these Indians, who numbered about a hundred, until they had almost completely destroyed them. I think I saw altogether some seventy dead bodies lying there; the greater portion women and children. There may have been thirty warriors, old and young; the rest were women and small children of different ages and sizes. The troops at the time were very much scattered. There were not over two hundred troops in the main fight, engaged in killing this body of Indians under the bank. The balance of the troops were scattered in different directions, running after small parties of Indians who were trying to make their escape."* [65]

Smith also recounted the atrocities committed by the soldiers that he had personally witnessed:

> *"All manner of depredations were inflicted...they [the Indians] were scalped, their brains knocked out; the men used their knives, ripped open women, clubbed little children, knocked them in the head with their guns, beat their brains out, mutilated their bodies in every sense of the word... children two and three months old; all ages lying there, from sucking infants up to warriors."* [66]

Meanwhile, as this unspeakable savagery was occurring, the Cheyenne warriors, who had dug a defense position in the sand pits nearly two miles north of the village, had managed to hold off an advance by the soldiers for several hours. This also provided cover for some three to five hundred Indians (accounts vary) to make their escape across the prairie.

However, by the late afternoon of that bloody day, the soldiers were finally able to gain a position where they successfully fired into the pits, killing nearly thirty, including women and children. And then the bullets stopped. "When the sun was high in the sky," as the Indians later recounted, the battle was over.

The soldiers left the sand pit area and returned south to

the village and the rest of Chivington's army. Chivington then assembled his troops in an area of the village and ordered his men to set up camp at the bloody site of the Indian village. Chivington knew that many of the Arapaho and Cheyenne had escaped death and destruction, fleeing in the northeast direction toward refuge with the Cheyenne Dog Soldiers camped at the Smoky Hill River. Therefore, Chivington placed soldiers on alert throughout the night, should warriors move from the Smoky Hill camp to strike in revenge.

A few hours after sundown, the remaining Cheyenne sheltered in the sand pits felt it safe to make their way north to the Smoky Hill camp under the cloak of darkness. George Bent recalled the escape north to safety:

"At last we crawled out of the holes, stiff and sore, with the blood frozen on our wounded and half-naked bodies. Slowly and painfully we retreated up the creek, men, women and children wailing and crying, but not too loudly for they feared the return of the whites." [67]

Among those who left the sand pits was Black Kettle, who did not immediately go north with his people. Instead, he chose to return under the cover of darkness to search for Medicine Woman Later. As he got closer to the village, he could see the camp fires of the soldiers and, according to Bent, could hear their laughter and cheers as they looted the lodges. With Black Kettle's poor eyesight, it must have been difficult to recognize her in the dark, but eventually he did find her. Her bullet-riddled body was covered with blood. As he bent down to pick her up, Medicine Woman Later moaned. Her breathing was sporadic, but she was alive. Black Kettle gently lifted her limp body onto his back and carefully retraced his steps back through the dead. Eventually he caught up with the survivors who were moving quietly through the night toward the Smoky Hill River and refuge with the Dog Soldiers.
On that bitter cold November day on the southeastern plains of Colorado Territory, life as the Cheyenne and Arapaho Indian tribes had once lived, changed forever.

Just after sunrise on that day of November 29, 1864, the sounds of gunfire, followed by cannon fire, billows of hazy smoke, screams, and mass confusion, awakened a sleepy young Cheyenne woman. Realizing her Indian village was under attack by government soldiers, seemingly from all directions, she huddled with fear inside her tipi.

She watched as her people reacted to the surprise attack. Defense and organization was slow to start, as elder chiefs fell to the soldier's bullets, cannon fire blasted tipis apart, children screamed, and people died; all before her very eyes. She noticed some sort of organization was attained eventually, as the few men in camp gathered what weapons they could find, and attempted a defense against the soldiers. Meanwhile, the elderly, the women, and children ran for their lives, as their loved ones lay dead or dying in the village.

As sunlight turned to sunset, the gunfire seemed to ease in and around the village, and moved off toward the north. As the sun set over the death and carnage of the Cheyenne village, the young Cheyenne woman emerged from the smoke and ashes that was her village just hours ago.

Mo-chi, twenty-three years young, carefully walked among the dead bodies of her tribe, shaking with fear and horror. She found the body of her husband, Standing Bull, and pressed on through tears of grief. Finally, she found the body of her father. Her grief turned to anger.

Mo-chi seized her dead father's Hawkens rifle, a previous gift from a grateful white man, and pledged revenge. On that fateful day, as the Cheyenne village smoldered in death and ruin, sadness, anger, and revenge smoldered in Mo-chi.

Mo-chi would become the first female Cheyenne warrior. Cheyenne oral history records Mo-chi's declaration for war:

"This day, I vow revenge for the murder of my family and my people. This day, I declare war on veho - white man. This day I become a warrior and a warrior I will be forever."

"She knew of no other way to handle losing all her family but to fight back, the Old Ones said. On that November morning, the month of the Hard Face Moon, Mo-chi was reborn a Tsistsistas warrior." [69]

However, for the time being, the young female survivor of what would become known as the Sand Creek Massacre, struggled with other survivors to flee the carnage and find a safe lace away from the warring soldiers.

As darkness fell, it was some time before Mo-chi felt safe enough to leave her hiding place near the village, and begin her journey north, along the creek bed. As she did so, she heard the soldier's loud commotions, laughter, and smelled the smoke of what she assumed was the burning of her village. The cold winter night chilled her to the bone, her feet were nearly frozen over the crusted, dried snow, but soon, she met with other survivors, also heading north. Relieved she had found survivors of her village, and no longer alone, Mo-chi pressed on searching for safety. John L. Sipes, Mo-chi's great-great-grandson, and Cheyenne tribal historian, related the Cheyenne oral history:

> *"According to the Old ones, in Cheyenne oral history, the survivors followed the creek north from the slaughter, approximately four miles, then headed northeast, some forty miles, to the head waters of the Smoky Hill River, known by our people as the Bunch of Trees River. They were welcomed into the camp of a group of Dog Soldiers, where they were fed, clothed, and their wounds tended to. The Dog Soldiers sent out Wolves, (scouts) to search for others who may have been lost or wounded along the river trail. Mo-chi remembered it as the worst night of her life."* [70]

After a few days of rest, and fearing the soldiers may be in pursuit, the collective group of survivors, which included Black Kettle and his wounded wife, Medicine Woman Later, and George Bent, were guided by the Dog Soldiers. The group moved to a large Sioux camp on the Solomon River, and then on to Cherry Creek, a tributary that flows into the South Fork of the Republican River in Kansas, near present-day St. Francis. This camp consisted of the Sioux bands of Spotted Tail and Pawnee Killer, as well as several Northern Arapaho. It was here that the survivors of the massacre along Sand Creek were able to receive attention to their injuries, rest and recuperate. They would later move to the Smoky Hill River in Kansas.

Medicine Woman Later had received nine bullets to her body, but amazingly lived. Following the removal of the bullets, she made a slow but steady recovery. She told her husband that after she was hit by the first bullet, she fell to the ground and could not move. Then, she said, soldiers shot her again and again and again.[71]

Meanwhile, anger at the massacre of the Cheyenne people spread like wildfire throughout the Indian societies, and the traditional war pipe was sent out by the runners to all Indian camps. All smoked the war pipe and declared war, including the Dog Soldiers. The Sand Creek massacre proved to be the driving force to unite the Indian camps, including the Arkansas River and Dog Soldier bands, a union that ended decades of warring between the two.[72]

The chiefs held a council, where it was concluded: war against the white man was the only way to avenge the honor of their dead and save their homeland and way of life. The tribes of the Plains Indians were united as never before.

"The tradition of the war pipe, when necessary, was sent out in the spring, but after the slaughter at Sand Creek, the war pipe went out in the winter, December. To my knowledge, from the Old ones, never before had the war pipe been sent in the time of winter until Sand Creek." - John L. Sipes, Cheyenne Tribal Historian

The same day Medicine Woman Later lay in agony as nine bullets were slowly removed from her body, John Smith was leading a few of the soldiers across the battlefield where many lay dead or dying. Smith was able to identify many of the dead Indians, for the soldiers. Those who were still alive were immediately shot dead.

One particular badly-mutilated male body was identified by Smith as that of Black Kettle. Chivington must have felt triumphant over his militant glory at the news that Chief Black Kettle had been killed. He rushed back to his tent and penned the first of several reports regarding the Indian battle. A few days later, reporting to General Samuel Curtis, Chivington wrote:

"After a march of forty miles last night I, at daylight this morning, attacked Cheyenne village of 130 lodges, from 900 to 1,000 warriors strong; killed Chiefs Black Kettle, White Antelope, Knock Knee, and Little Robe. and between 400 hundred and 500 hundred other Indians, and captured as many ponies and mules. Our loss 9 killed, 38 wounded. All did nobly." [73]

Colonel Chivington quickly followed up with a second report to General Curtis:

"In the last ten days my command has marched three hundred miles - one hundred of which the snow was two feet deep. After a march of forty miles last night I, at daylight this morning, attacked the Cheyenne village of one hundred thirty lodges, from nine hundred to one thousand warriors strong. We killed chiefs Black Kettle, White Antelope, and Little Robe, and between four hundred and five hundred other Indians; captured between four and five hundred ponies and mules. Our loss is nine killed and thirty eight wounded. All did nobly. I think I will catch some more of them about eighty miles, on Smoky Hill. We found a white

man's scalp, not more than three days old, in a lodge. J.M. Chivington Col. Com'g District of Colorado, and First Indian Expedition. I am, gentlemen, very respectfully, your obedient servant." [74]

Chivington then followed this report with a letter to the editor, William N. Byers of the *Rocky Mountain News*. The letter was sent with a soldier who immediately left the camp for Denver. Byers, elated over the news of a military victory by his friend, printed the letter, as well as the above report, a copy of which Chivington provided, as well as detailed reports running the length of three columns, under the headline:

"Great Battle with Indians! The Savages Dispersed! 500 INDIANS KILLED Our Loss 9 Killed, 38 Wounded Full Particulars"

Chivington ended his report with the promise of more fighting:

"I shall leave here, as soon as I can see our wounded safely on the way to the hospital at Fort Lyon, for the villages of the Sioux, which are eighty miles from here on the Smoky Hill, and three thousand strong; so look for more fighting."

Byers declared that:

"The Third Regiment boys will probably not be here for a few weeks, as they say they are loaded down with buffalo robes, scalps, strings of silver dollars, etc. - plunder taken from the Indians. Bully for them."

Contrary to Chivington's boisterous account, eyewitness accounts from both soldiers and Indians estimated the number of casualties at approximately one hundred and fifty, with two-thirds of the dead being women and children, laying on the blood-soaked ground. Little Robe was not in the peaceful camp, and while Chief Black Kettle survived Sand Creek, other notable peace chiefs did not. Among those killed were White Antelope, the first to fall by military fire. Others killed were War Bonnet, Yellow Shield, Spotted Crow, Bear Man, Standing Water, Yellow Wolf and One-Eye.

Mystery surrounds the demise of Arapaho Chief Left Hand. He had signed the Treaty of Fort Wise in February 1861, and declared he would no longer fight the white man. On the morning that Chivington's soldiers attacked the peaceful village, Left Hand stood bravely in front of his tipi, instructing his people to remain calm and attempted to reason with the soldiers. It was believed by many at the scene that Left Hand had been killed, but his body was never identified by John Smith or others covering that desecrated ground the following day. He may have managed to escape, an idea his biographer, Margaret Coel, aptly offers. However, it is doubtful that had he escaped, Left Hand would have remained silent regarding the future of his people. In any case, he was never heard of again. Another contradiction in Chivington's report to his superior and the *Rocky Mountain News*, was his promise "look for more fighting," declaring:

> "I think I will catch some more of them about eighty miles, on Smoky Hill."

In fact, Chivington was ordering his troops to prepare to return to Fort Lyon. Later that afternoon, Major Anthony ordered Captain Silas Soule, who refused to participate in the fight, to accompany him back to Fort Lyon. Soule, who was hearing rumors of killing the half-white, half-Indians in camp, requested that Charles Bent be included in the group returning to the fort. His request was granted. Soule led the supply team along the miserable miles to the fort in silence.

As preparations were being made to load the wounded into the wagons, soldiers came into the lodge where John Smith's son Jack was being held prisoner. As they gathered up blankets for the wounded soldiers, Jack protested. This was either the last straw or the soldiers found their excuse to kill the young half-white, half-Indian man. When word of the plot reached Major Anthony, he immediately went to Chivington.

Major Scott J. Anthony later testified:

> "I went to Colonel Chivington and told him that Jack Smith was a young man he might make very useful to him; that he could be made a good guide or scout for us; 'but,' said I to him, 'unless you give your men to understand that you want the man saved, he is going to be killed. He will be killed before tomorrow morning, unless you give your men to understand that you don't want him killed.' Colonel Chivington replied, 'I have given my instructions; have told my men not to take any prisoners.'"[75]

Later that afternoon, nearly a dozen soldiers from both Lieutenant Clark Dunn's and Major Hal Sayr's companies entered the lodge where Jack Smith was being guarded. Private David Lauderback, who was in the lodge with Smith, witnessed the soldiers taunting Smith. Lauderback said they called him a son of bitch, and that he should have been killed long ago. According to Lauderback, Jack Smith replied that he didn't give a damn and that if they were going to kill him, shoot him. Lauderback later testified:

> *"When Jack said this I thought it was time for me to get out of there, as men had threatened to hang and shoot me as well as uncle John Smith, and the teamster Watson Clark that was with us."* [76]

John Smith said that when Jack was taken prisoner following his brief escape during the fighting, he remained in the lodge "sitting quietly." According to his father, Jack remained a hostage in the lodge throughout the night and into the following day. John Smith later testified to the event that led to his son's murder:

> *"About four o'clock in the evening, as I was sitting inside the camp, a soldier came up outside the lodge and called me by name. I got up and went out; he took me by the arm and walked towards Colonel Chivington's camp, which was about sixty yards from my camp. Said he, 'I am sorry to tell you, but they are going to kill your son Jack.' I knew the feeling towards the whole camp and that there was no use to make any resistance. I said, 'I can't help it.' I then walked on towards where Colonel Chivington was standing by his camp-fire; when I got within a few feet of him I heard a gun fired, and saw a crowd run to my lodge, and they told me Jack was dead. Major Anthony, who was present, told Colonel Chivington that he heard some remarks made, indicating that they were desirous of killing Jack; and that he [Chivington] had it in his power to save him, and that by saving him, he might make him a very useful man, as he was well acquainted with all the Cheyenne and Arapaho country. Colonel Chivington replied to Major Anthony, as the Major himself told me, that he had no orders to receive and no advice to give."* [77]

The veteran scout and friend to the Indians, Jim Beckwourth, was also in the lodge when the murder occurred. He later testified:

> *"He [Jack Smith] was sitting in the lodge with me; not more than five or six feet from me, just across the lodge. There were from ten to fifteen soldiers come into the lodge at the time, and there was some person came on the outside and called to his father, John Smith. He, the old man,*

went out and there was a pistol fired when the old man got out of the lodge. There was a pistol shot through the opening and the bullet entered below his [Jack Smith's] right breast. He sprung forward and fell dead, and the lodge scattered, soldiers, squaws, and everything else. I went out myself; as I went out I met a man with a pistol in his hand. He made this remark to me: he said, 'I am afraid the damn son of a bitch is not dead, and I will finish him.' Says I, 'Let him go to rest; he is dead.' We took him out and laid him out of doors. I do not know what they did with him afterwards." [78]

It seems as if the soldiers and their commanders immediately put a plan in place to cover up the murder. Shortly after the soldiers returned to Fort Lyon, Major Anthony penned a letter to his brother describing the Sand Creek affair. Regarding Jack Smith, Anthony wrote:

"We, of course, took no prisoners, except John Smith's son, and he was taken suddenly ill in the night, and died before morning." [79]

Major Hal Sayr originally said that Jack Smith was killed in an accident while handling a gun. As it was known by all that Smith was being held as a prisoner, how he would have even had a gun defies logic. Years later, when the major had curiously changed the spelling of his surname to "Sayre,"[80] he wrote that:

"Some of the boys dragged the body out onto the prairie and hauled it about for a considerable time." [81]

However, Captain Silas Soule and several soldiers spoke quietly of their disdain for what had happened at Sand Creek. Colonel Tappan, who was at Fort Lyon at the time of the attack recuperating from a leg injury, heard the talk of the soldiers and began making inquiries. Meanwhile, Soule and Cramer took on a letter writing campaign to get the truth out. As more and more soldiers began to open up, it became clear the battlefield was not the only site of atrocity.

In a lengthy letter describing the horrible events of the day written to Wynkoop, dated December 14, 1864, Soule said in part:

"Jack Smith was taken prisoner, and murdered the next day in his tent by one of Denn's Co. "E". I understand the man received a horse for doing the job. They were going to murder Charley Bent, but I run him into the Fort. They were going to kill Old Uncle John Smith, but Lt. Cannon

and the boys of Ft. Lyon, interfered, and saved him. They would have murdered Old Bents family, if Col. Tappan had not taken the matter in hand. Cramer went up with twenty men, and they did not like to buck against so many of the 1st." [82]

For his part, Chivington carried on with orders for his men as if nothing had happened. Soldiers were ordered to return to Fort Lyon with the wounded. The remainder of the troops spent another night camped at the former Indian village. That evening, Lieutenant Colonel Leavitt L. Bowen, of the Third Colorado Cavalry Regiment, wrote his formal military report to his superior, Colonel George L. Shoup. Bowen concluded his report with hearty congratulations to Shoup for:

"The signal punishment meted out to the savages on yesterday, 'who so ruthlessly have murdered our women and children,' in the language of the colonel commanding, although I regret the loss of so many brave men. The Third Regiment cannot any longer be called the 'bloodless third.' The war flag of this band of Cheyennes is in my possession, presented by Stephen Decatur, commissary sergeant of company C, [sic] who acted as my battalion adjutant." [83]

However, Decatur would later testify under oath, that he indeed saw a white flag hanging above the village shortly after the battle commenced, but did not say anything about a "war flag," presumably the United States flag given to Black Kettle to fly as a sign of peace should soldiers arrive unannounced. Later that same evening, Chivington sent another dispatch of the events to William Byers of the *Rocky Mountain News*. Chivington then ordered Lieutenant Joseph A. Cramer to burn what remained of the Indian village.

Early on the morning of December 1, Chivington led his men in military march formation, not northeast toward the Smoky Hill River, as he had indicated in his report to both General Samuel Curtis and the *Rocky Mountain News*, but to Fort Lyon. Along the way, Chivington led a few troops east in pursuit of a band of Indians toward the Kansas border. After two days Chivington's soldiers came upon an abandoned Arapaho village and moved south in pursuit. Following the trail for another two days, Chivington again came upon an abandoned Indian camp. On the cold, clear morning of December 7, Chivington gave up his pursuit and led his men back to Fort Lyon, arriving on December 10, 1864. Chivington and a small entourage of soldiers traveled to Denver for a series of meetings with Governor Evans. On December 16, Chivington wrote out his report to General Curtis. In summarizing the failed pursuit of the Indians, Chivington wrote, "It may perhaps be unnecessary for me to state that I captured no prisoners." He also chose to include the following observation and opinion regarding Captain Silas Soule:

> "I cannot conclude this report without saying that the conduct of Capt. Silas S. Soule, Company D, First Cavalry of Colorado, was at least ill-advised, he saying that he thanked God he had killed no Indians, and like expressions, proving him more in sympathy with those Indians than with the whites." [84]

A few days later, several troops of both the First and Third regiments of the Colorado Voluntary Army arrived in Denver for preparations for what promised to be a glorious parade. On December 17, the *Rocky Mountain News* ran a series of articles recounting the military event at Sand Creek.

> "Among the brilliant feats of arms in Indian warfare, the recent campaign of our Colorado Volunteers will stand in history with few rivals, and none to exceed it in final results. Although utterly surprised, the savages were not unprepared, defensive works a half-mile long and a similar line of work on the adjacent bluffs. A thousand incidents of individual daring and the passing events of the day might be told, but space forbids. We leave the task for eye-witnesses to chronicle. All acquitted themselves well, and the Colorado soldiers have again covered themselves in glory."

Because no newspaper reporters were at the scene, it is obvious that the information Byers printed was supplied by Chivington in his dispatch of November 30, 1864. Therefore, the article is instrumental in the beginning stages of what would become the true account of the passing events of the day. For example, the article admits that the Indian village was "utterly surprised." This was an explicit violation of Chivington's very words to the peace chiefs at the Camp Weld council just two months prior to the attack. Chivington told those present at the council:

> "I am not a big war chief, but all the soldiers in this country are at my command. My rule of fighting white men or Indians is to fight them until they lay down their arms and submit to military authority. They are

nearer Major Wynkoop than any one else, and they can go to him when they get ready to do that." [85]

The *Rocky Mountain News* even printed these very words of Chivington's in their paper dated September 29, 1864. The chiefs, led by Black Kettle, believed these words and moved their lodges to Sand Creek as instructed by Major Wynkoop. Another point in the article is that "the savages were not unprepared, defensive works a half-mile long and a similar line of work on the adjacent bluffs." This was not necessarily true, as eyewitness reports and later testimony from several present that day, including the half-white, half-Indian George Bent, and Corporal Amos Miksch with the First Colorado Cavalry, contradicted the statement by the newspaper. This was, however, the first time the claim that the Indians had fortified their position for defense purposes prior to the attack first occurs. It would become one of the many contentious reports that is repeated to this day; one that swirls around the controversy and debate regarding Sand Creek.

Finally, the article's offer of leaving "the task for eye-witnesses to chronicle," would turn out to be quite fortuitous, as future investigations would include much first-hand testimony, testimony that would prove to be the opposite of the account the *Rocky Mountain News*, and Colonel Chivington, attempted to portray for the public.

December 22, 1864, was a triumphant day in Denver. Colonel John M. Chivington led his troops in a parade through the dirt streets of Denver, while crowds cheered the hero's welcome. The *Rocky Mountain News,* in its afternoon issue dated the same day, reported: "Headed by the First Regiment band, and by Colonels Chivington and Shoup, Lieut. Col. Bowen and Major Sayr, the rank and file of the 'bloody Thirdsters,' made a most imposing procession, extending, with the transportation teams, from the upper end of Ferry street, through Larimer, G street and Blake, almost back to Ferry street again. As the 'bold sojer boys' passed along, the sidewalks and corner stands were thronged with citizens saluting their old friends."

The glory of the "bold sojer boys" was somewhat diminished when the *Rocky Mountain News* printed an article which originated in a Washington D. C. paper. It appeared in the *Rocky Mountain News* the following day:

"The affair at Fort Lyon, Colorado in which Colonel Chivington destroyed a large Indian village, and all its inhabitants, is to be made the

subject of congressional investigation. Letters received from high officials in Colorado say that the Indians were killed after surrendering, and that a large proportion of them were women and children."

This caused the Denver rumor mill to spew forth speculation from all corners of the city, including government and military quarters. Citizens were wondering what it might mean for Governor Evans, Colonel Chivington, and the volunteer troops who were at the end of their enlistment period. Major Hal Sayr recorded the following in his report for December 25, 1864:

"In Camp-[Weld] None of our Regiment mustered out yet-Some of the boys trying to have a Merry Christmas by getting drunk." [86]

For the next several issues of the *Rocky Mountain News*, Byers ran editorials defending Chivington's actions:

"It is unquestioned and undenied, that the site of the Sand Creek battle was the rendezvous of the thieving and marauding bands of savages who roamed over this country last summer and fall, and it is shrewdly suspected that somebody was all the time making a very good thing of it." [87]

This defense put forth by the leading paper in the city of Denver would prove to be not only contentious in its inaccuracy, but demonstratively misleading, given the paper's own reporting of the events of the Camp Weld peace council held in the city just two months previously. Nevertheless, Byers held firm, including writings from Chivington who was, by now, feverishly defending himself:

"Several scalps of white men and women in Indian lodges; also various articles of clothing belonging to white persons. On every hand the evidence was clear, that no lick was struck amiss." [88]

This is one of the many contradictions in Byers' editorials. While writing of the Indian atrocities, including the "scalps of white men and women," he also cheered the soldiers who committed the very same act. In the December 29, 1864 issue of the *Rocky Mountain News*, Byers reported the following:

"A very full and fashionable audience was at the Denver Theatre last night to witness that great Indian piece, and well were they repaid for

their investment. The play was put upon the stage in splendid style, with numerous novel trappings, scalps; trophies of the big fight at Sand Creek. The piece will be repeated this evening, when everybody ought to see it for themselves."

Major Edward Wynkoop, stationed at Fort Riley, Kansas, was outraged by Chivington's actions at Sand Creek. He had been kept informed of the atrocities perpetuated by the colonel's orders through letters from both Captain Soule and Lieutenant Joseph Cramer, both of whom had refused to take part in their commander's mission. Wynkoop seethed with anger after receiving more letters from Soule and Cramer.

Shortly after the Indian battle, Captain Soule had written the following letter to his former superior. However, Wynkoop did not receive it until late in December 1864.

"Dear Ned,
The massacre lasted six or eight hours, and a good many Indians escaped. I tell you Ned it was hard to see little children on their knees have their brains beat out by men professing to be civilized. One squaw was wounded and a fellow took a hatchet to finish her, she held her arm up to defend her, and he cut it off, and held the other with one hand and dashed the hatchet through her brain. I saw two Indians hold one anothers hands, chased until they were exhausted, when they kneeled down, and clasped each other around the neck and were both shot. They were all scalped. White Antelope, War Bonnet and others had ears and privates cut off. You would think it impossible for white men to butcher and mutilate human beings as they did there, but every word I have told you is the truth." [89]

This was followed by a letter Wynkoop received from Lieutenant Cramer, dated December 19, 1864:

"Bucks, women and children, were scalped, fingers cut off to get the rings on them, and this as much with Officers as men, and one of those officers a Major: and a Lt. Col. cut off Ears of all he came across, a squaw ripped open and a child taken from her, little children shot, while begging for their lives and all the indignities shown their bodies that ever was heard of, things that Indians would be ashamed to do. Most of the Indians yielded 4 or 5 scalps. But enough! For I know you are disgusted already." [90]

An indignant Major Wynkoop demanded a meeting with General Samuel Curtis. The general agreed to the meeting and Wynkoop traveled to Fort Leavenworth to meet with the general. He methodically and patiently laid out his case for Chivington's removal. Wynkoop then presented Curtis with the letters from Cramer and Soule; the first-hand accounts of the debauchery inflicted on the Cheyenne and Arapaho by soldiers under Chivington's command. The major concluded by again stressing to the general the peace agreement "presumably" reached by all at Camp Weld on September 28, 1864. General Curtis told Wynkoop he would take the matter under advisement and ordered him to return to his post at Fort Riley.

Evidently General Curtis had indeed considered Wynkoop's evidence, as he issued orders to return Wynkoop as commander of Fort Lyon. On December 31, 1864, under General Curtis' order, Colonel James Ford released Wynkoop from his duties at Fort Riley and gave him written instructions to assume command of Fort Lyon. [91]

When word of Wynkoop's return to Fort Lyon, and the circumstances therein, became public, Byers rushed again to defend Chivington and the Colorado Volunteers. In the January 4, 1865 issue of the *Rocky Mountain News*, Byers printed the following:

"Reports of 'high officials' say that a large proportion of the Indians killed were women and children. To those who were present, this would seem too base a fabrication to need contradiction, but fearing that many, hearing only the lie might be deceived by its apparent truth; two hundred and one dead bodies of Indians, among whom we do not think there were over a dozen women and children."

Byers was obviously attempting to spin the story. Where he got his facts is unknown, as even Chivington's reports to his superiors as well as to Byers did not list the Indian casualties at that high number. Moreover, there were several reports available to Byers of the numerous atrocities inflicted, particularly relating to the women and children who died that day.

It was also during this time that Colonel John M. Chivington, quietly and unceremoniously, resigned his army commission on January 4, 1865. He was replaced by Colonel Thomas Moonlight. The following day, Byers again defended Chivington's actions and took exception to a report made public by Major Scott Anthony, which condemned the Sand Creek affair. Byers' editorial appeared in the January 5, 1865, issue of the *Rocky Mountain News*:

> *"Yesterday we published official reports of Col. Chivington, Col. Shoup, Major Anthony and their battalion commanders, of the battle of Sand Creek. We observe no quibble, even in Major Anthony's report, respecting the propriety of attacking that particular camp of Indians. Major Anthony was not stationed in the District of Colorado; he was not subject to the order of Col. Chivington; therefore he joined the expedition of his own free will, and if it was, as he has reported to have said 'an unmitigated massacre of the only band of friendly Indians of the plains,' why did he, knowing the facts, having been in command at Fort Lyon, join in the commission of such a dark deed?"*

While Byers professed "no quibble, even in Major Anthony's report," he went on to do just that. Whether Byers was ill-informed regarding the Districts of the Military, or he was deliberately swaying public opinion, can not be known. The fact is that at the time of the Sand Creek Massacre, Fort Lyon was in the District of Colorado, and Anthony was indeed under the order of Colonel Chivington. Moreover, Colonel Chivington signed his military correspondence as: J.M. Chivington Col. Com'g District of Colorado, and First Indian Expedition. [92] This very signature and title were printed in Byers' *Rocky Mountain News* just a month previous, on December 14, 1864.

It is also interesting to note the apparent change in Major Anthony's position regarding the Sand Creek affair, given his statement, "an unmitigated massacre of the only band of friendly Indians of the plains." It seems as if, given Chivington's recent resignation, and a growing turn in public opinion, Anthony was either giving himself cover for his own part in the atrocity, or once again deceiving those around him as well as the public. The evidence is a letter Anthony wrote to his brother dated December 1, 1864. The *Rocky Mountain News* printed the letter a week later, in the December 8, 1864, issue.

> *"The following from the Major to his brother, in this city, we are permitted to publish:*
>
> SAND CREEK, 25 *miles above Fort Lyon, Dec. 1, 1864.*
> *Dear Web - I am here with the command. We have just had, day before yesterday, an Indian fight. We have nearly annihilated Black Kettle's band of Cheyennes and Left Hand's Arapahoes. I did my share, and I think*

my command did as well as any in the whole brigade, notwithstanding. I lost one man killed and two slightly wounded; I was one of the first in the fight and among the last to leave, and my loss is less than any other battalion. We have forty-seven persons killed and wounded. I will give particulars when I see you. We start for another band of red-skins and shall fight differently next time. I never saw more bravery displayed by any set of people on the face of the earth than by those Indians."

Indeed, Major Anthony may have been reading the winds of change correctly. News of the Sand Creek incident had reached the east coast within days. On December 29, 1864, the *Rocky Mountain News* printed a dispatch from Washington D.C. mentioning the Congressional investigation into Sand Creek.

However, in Colorado, many of its citizenry still approved of the military action against the Indians. Editorials ran in most of the papers supporting the Colorado soldiers, including this example printed in the Black Hawk *Daily Mining Journal*, December 30, 1864:

"A good many of the Third Regiment boys are returning to their old haunts. Some of them do not scruple to say that the big battle of Sand Creek was a cold-blooded massacre. If so, it must be remembered that the individual who gave the order for its commission is alone to blame for it. 'Tis the soldier's part to obey without question, and right nobly was it done on this occasion. We are glad to see the men of the "Third" returning home. They are entitled to credit for their public spirit, and the sacrifices they have made."

Word soon reached Denver that the rumored Congressional investigation was in fact a reality and would begin after the first of the new year. Byers ran the following editorial in the December 31, 1864, issue of the *Rocky Mountain News:*

"We fear that the representations that have been made to the authorities at Washington, respecting the 'Fort Lyon affair,' about which we had something to say yesterday will tell sadly against the prosperity of Colorado, and enhance the difficulties of procuring adequate protection to travel on the plains. It will be hard to prevail upon Congress, or the Departments, to give our Territory and its roads the security they actually need. The representations that have been made by the 'high officials' referred to, place our people, and our military authorities and forces, in the light of aggressors upon the rights of the Indians. The spirit that prompted such representations, is as contemptibly mean as the representations

themselves are outrageously false, as everyone in this country well knows. Unfortunately, Colorado is saddled with a lot of uneasy spirits, among whom are these 'high officials,' who could drag her down to hell, if by so doing they could further their own political ambitions, or put money in their pockets. These are the men who call for 'Congressional investigation' of the 'affair at Fort Lyon.' They care not what difficulties they may throw around the vital question of securing peace and safety along the Platte and Arkansas roads. They care not for the security of Colorado's frontier settlements, nor for the lives of her defenseless women and children. They would blast the prospect of the Territory for years to come, and for what? Solely and simply to vent their spite upon two or three men against whom they have personal animosities, or whose power and popularity they envy and fear."

Edward Wynkoop tried to keep the peace. *DPL*

Major Edward Wynkoop returned to Fort Lyon and resumed command on January 14, 1865. His first act was to dismiss Major Scott Anthony, who had relieved Wynkoop of command the previous fall. Meanwhile, through detailed reports received by Secretary of War Stanton, an investigation by the Joint Committee on the Conduct of War began on January 10, 1865. Ultimately there would be several investigations.

Upon his arrival at Fort Lyon, Wynkoop received further orders, including instructions "to make thorough investigations of recent operations against the Indians and make a detailed report."[93] Wynkoop immediately began a series of interviews, taking testimony and signed affidavits from several who were at Sand Creek on November 29, 1864. He received damning testimony from several, including Wilson Clark, David Louderback, John Smith, Lieutenant James D. Cannon, and Indian Agent Samuel G. Colley. Wynkoop also spoke with the military district inspector, Captain Booth, who had made a detailed examination of the battlefield on January 1, 1865. Incredibly, just over thirty days after the attack, the dead bodies remained on the blood-encrusted ground. Booth told Wynkoop he counted sixty-nine bodies, which was far from the inflated number Chivington boasted to his superiors and the press. Booth also said that the majority of the bodies were women and children. This was also more in line with eyewitness reports from both soldiers and Indians present that day.

On January 15, Wynkoop submitted his report to General Curtis, in which he referred to Colonel Chivington as an "inhuman monster." He also wrote:

"The country presents a scene of desolation; all communication is cut off with the States except by sending large bodies of troops, and already over one hundred whites have fallen as victims to the fearful vengeance of these betrayed Indians." [94]

Samuel G. Colley, as Indian Agent, used his influence as well. He sent a detailed letter to Senator James Rood Doolittle, who served as chairman of the Senate Committee on Indian Affairs. Colley informed the senator that:

"All the chiefs and their families were in camp and doing all they could to protect the whites and keep the peace, when Colonel Chivington attacked them."

Colley's letter covered the horrific slaughter and molestation perpetrated on the victims. Doolittle later said after reading the many accounts that they:

"Made one's blood chill and freeze with horror." [95]

Doolittle demanded a government inquiry. Curtis then forwarded Wynkoop's report, including the testimony denouncing the unwarranted attack, to military personnel in Washington, D. C. Meanwhile, Wynkoop, fearing Indian retaliation, began a stronger defense around Fort Lyon. He fortified the hill above the fort, and constructed a series of breastworks on both the north and east sides. He built a stone wall at the road that led from the river, and ordered cannons placed on both the northeast and northwest corners of the fort. Mrs. Julia S. Lambert, the wife of the Fort Lyon's station master, later recounted:

> *"Every man in the Fort worked on the breast works except the officer of the day and the guard. Major Wynkoop, in a blue flannel shirt, used pick or shovel as it was needed and everybody worked hard to complete the fortifications. We felt greatly relieved when the fortifications were completed. Reports of depredations were coming in from all sides and without these fortifications we had felt that we were not prepared for any trouble which might come. No one who had not had a similar experience can realize what this anxiety and sense of insecurity meant to us."* [96]

With mounting pressure from senators and other government officials, Colonel Thomas Moonlight, Chivington's successor, ordered a military investigation of his predecessor's actions at Sand Creek. The proceedings began in Denver on February 1, 1865, with Colonel Samuel Tappan chairing the committee, charged with: "Investigating the conduct of the late Colonel J. M. Chivington, First Regiment Colorado Cavalry, in his recent campaign against the Indians." [97]

That same day, the *Rocky Mountain News* ran an editorial regarding a report submitted by Major Anthony to the military officers, including Colonel Thomas Moonlight. In it, Anthony admitted that his original report, filed after the Sand Creek affair, "was wrong in many particulars." Editor William N. Byers wrote:

> *"We publish elsewhere in this paper, by request of Col. Moonlight, a letter received by him from Major Anthony, late of the First Colorado Cavalry. It is remarkable in some respects, and mainly in the change of sentiment it reveals since the Major's report of the Sand Creek battle. We know not what to attribute such a change, unless it be to the influence of public sentiment in and about Fort Lyon since Col. Chivington's command returned from that post. The confession that his report 'was wrong in many particulars,' is also strange. It is passing strange that his 'official report' should have been made up from hearsay, and, in that respect, looks a little unmilitary. It is equally strange that Major Anthony, as*

well as many other citizens, have, since the battle of Sand Creek, entirely forgotten the sad and bloody events of the four or five months preceding that battle. They excuse the Indians for their present hostility, by saying, 'it is the result of the Sand Creek fight,' or 'they are provoked to it by the massacre near Fort Lyon.' This is the kind of talk that has been heard from the Judge's bench, in the Auburn Advertiser, and other papers. Its humane authors have forgotten the murders, the heart-rendings, the house burnings, and train and mail robbings of last summer and fall. The blood of the butchered Hungate family, and scores of others, men, women, and children, no longer cries out from the ground in tones that will reach their ears. The ruthless deeds are hidden from their eyes by the smoke of the 'Fort Lyon affair.' They see only the present, and they justify the savages for their acts, because it is in revenge for the 'massacre' by Col. Chivington. How long, O God! should we have endured and suffered in silence? Day by day the murderous tomahawk and rifle were thinning our sparse settlements; night after night the flames of burning homes and moving trains of goods, lighted up the eastern horizon, or gleamed along the Platte and Arkansas. But they tell us it was wrong to strike a blow in return. The first punishment given to the enemy - not half nor quarter equaling their own barbarity - is called a 'massacre.' The officers and men who did it were maligned. High officials misrepresent the facts to blot and disgrace the fair name of our territory, and yet we are commanded to 'suffer and be still.'"

Despite Editor Byer's views, the military investigation, held in Denver in February 1865, would prove to be the most comprehensive and dramatic investigation of the horror of Sand Creek and the darkest day in Colorado history.

Nevertheless, Byers continued to defend Chivington and his actions. Byers ran the following article, under the headline, "Slaughter of Indians," in the February 4, 1865 issue of his *Rocky Mountain News*:

"Some weeks ago, says the Boston Journal, we published a telegraphic dispatch stating that there had been a great Indian fight near Fort Lyon, Colorado Territory, in which about five hundred Indians were killed by Col. Chivington and his command. A Washington Correspondent of the New York Herald publishes part of a letter from a party who is said to hold a highly respectable position in the Territory, which says: 'This attack on the defenseless savages was one of the most cruel in history. The Indians claimed to be quiet and at peace, yet the command pitched into a village of lodges, and the most of these victims were women and

papooses. None were spared. All were killed who could not escape. These Indians, I am assured, molested no travelers who passed among them. The most of them had given up their firearms before the attack was made. If such is a military glory, God deliver me from all such!' And God deliver us from such fools as you down-easters!"

As the proceedings were about to began, Moonlight attempted to keep the investigation to the facts of the incident. However, Chivington hotly contested the entire proceedings and expressed his opposition to Tappan's presence on the committee. He claimed that Tappan was "an open and avowed enemy."[98] Byers backed Chivington's claim. In an article in the February 8, 1865 issue of the *Rocky Mountain News,* Byers wrote:

"By order of Col. Moonlight, commanding this district, the board of military officers appointed to investigate the acts of Col. Chivington and the 'Fort Lyon affair' will meet in this city tomorrow to enter upon the discharge of that duty. They are Lieut. Col. S. F. Tappan, Capt. E. H. Jacobs and Capt. G. H. Stillwell. The first named gentleman has been here for some time past; Capt. Stillwell arrived yesterday by the southern coach and Capt. Jacobs is expected to-day. [sic] We, in common with the public, are glad that the settlement of this issue is at last under way. There has been quite talk about it. None will rejoice more, perhaps, than Col. C. His motives have been impugned and his character maligned; all to answer personal ends, but he will, we are confident, come out of the ordeal unscathed. We are surprised at one thing in the organization of the Commission; that is the appointment of Lieut. Col. Tappan President of the Board. His well-known personal enmity to the Colonel should have excused him from the position he is to occupy in the pending trial. However, we have no fear of the results. The evidence of almost every one who participated in the battle will sustain the Colonel's action, and the opinion of the great public approves it."

Byers could not have been more wrong in his prediction. Several of those who "participated in the battle," did not "sustain the Colonel's action," but testified against it. Witnesses were called to testify on February 11, 1865. The first witness was Captain Silas Soule. He described in graphic detail the brutal killings of the innocent Indians camped at Sand Creek. He told of accompanying Wynkoop to meet with Black Kettle and the return of the four white hostages to Denver. In damning testimony, Soule also related the subsequent peaceful negotiations by Wynkoop and continued under

Anthony, which allowed the tribes to camp at Sand Creek. Soule's testimony lasted for two days, and cross-examination by Chivington lasted another two days. Soule's account was supported by other soldiers of the First Colorado Regiment, as well as officers including Cramer and Wynkoop. Private Naman D. Snyder, with the First Colorado Cavalry, said he had witnessed soldiers scalping Indians. He also testified to seeing the American flag flying "in the lower end of the village. The west end."[99]

W. N. Byers offered his hypocritical reasoning for the investigation against Chivington's actions in his editorial in the *Rocky Mountain News*, dated February 28, 1865:

Colonel John Chivington was only too willing to wage war against the Indians. DPL

> "It is because Chivington did not kill Indians who had been murdering travelers and immigrants, but on the contrary did kill those with whom he had authorized Maj. Wynkoop to enter into a treaty, that his conduct has been made the subject of investigation."

This observation by Byers is a key point to the controversy surrounding the events leading to the Sand Creek massacre. Often overlooked by historians is the fact that Chivington did indeed agree to Wynkoops's actions at the Camp Weld peace council. Chivington had told the Indians, "My rule of fighting white men or Indians is to fight them until they lay down their arms and submit to military authority. They are nearer Major Wynkoop than any one else, and they can go to him when they get ready to do that." This is exactly what Black Kettle and his Cheyenne people did.

The military commission then traveled to Fort Lyon on March 9, to hear additional testimony. It is interesting to note that

Chivington did not testify in his own defense. However, yet again, Byers and the *Rocky Mountain News* stepped up in Chivington's defense. Under the headline, "The Responsibility of the Indian War," dated March 2, 1865, Byers wrote:

> *"Our sympathies are upon the side of the white man, and between the two stories we are inclined to believe his [Chivington.] The [Black Hawk] Journal favors the Indians, excuses the Indians, justifies the Indians, believes the Indians, and its editor probably expects to go to Black Kettle when he dies."*

Ironically, the following day, Senator James R. Doolittle established the Senate Joint Special Committee in Washington D. C., and the U. S. Congress opened a full investigation.

Later that month, Major Wynkoop received word that the United States House of Representatives passed a motion on the House floor:

> *"That the Committee on the Conduct of War be required to inquire into and report all the facts connected with the late attack of the third regiment of Colorado volunteers, under Colonel Chivington. on a village of the Cheyenne tribe of Indians, near Fort Lyon."* [100]

As chairman of the Senate Committee on Indian Affairs, Doolittle's purpose was to investigate the treatment of the Indian tribes and in particular, the Sand Creek incident. Various members of the congressional committee convened to hear testimony from March 13 through March 15, 1865. Governor Evans, Major Anthony, interpreter John Smith, and Samuel Colley all testified before the committee. Major Scott Anthony, under oath, reluctantly testified to incidents of unthinkable atrocities.

> *"There was one little child, probably three years old, just big enough to walk through the sand. The Indians had gone ahead, and this little child was behind following after them. I saw one man get off his horse, at a distance of about 75 yards, and draw up his rifle and fired - he missed the child, Another man came up and said, 'Let me try the son of a bitch; I can hit him' He got down from his horse, kneeled down and fired at the child, but missed. A third man came up and made a similar remark, and the little fellow dropped."* [101]

In the end, Chivington was condemned by the Congressional committee, but because he had resigned his military commission, no further action could be taken against him.

Meanwhile, back at Fort Lyon, Colonel Moonlight resumed the investigation with testimony on March 20, first calling Major Edward Wynkoop. He began by relating the details of his meeting with Black Kettle and the Cheyenne at their village along the Smoky Hill River. He recounted the peace talks which resulted in the relinquishment of the four white prisoners and the chiefs' consent to meet at Camp Weld for a peace conference. At this point, Chivington objected, declaring Wynkoops's account of the peace talks was hearsay. Chivington's objection was overruled. For the next two days, Wynkoop was grilled with questions regarding his attempt at a peaceful solution by bringing the Indian chiefs to Denver, his belief in the desire for peace by the Indians, his conversations with both Chivington and Governor Evans at the time of the Camp Weld peace talks, and his subsequent removal as commander of Fort Lyon.

On March 23, Chivington began his cross-examination of Wynkoop. His first question to Wynkoop was:

"What instructions had you received from the commanding officer of the district, [Chivington] in which Fort Lyon was located, in regard to your intercourse with the Indians?

Wynkoop - *"I had never received any instructions in regard to what the question has reference to. I had received a letter from General Blunt, the effect that on the account of the peculiar position of Fort Lyon, a great deal was left to my discretion, being so far removed from headquarters, and the opportunities for communicating being seldom."*

Chivington - *"Prior to your expedition to the Smoky Hill, had not Field Order No. 2, headquarters department of Kansas, Major General Curtis commanding been received at Fort Lyon?"*

Wynkoop - *"It had not, to my knowledge."*

Chivington - *"Have you [since] seen Field Order No. 2?"*

Wynkoop - *"I have."*

Chivington - *"When did you see it?"*

Wynkoop - *"I can't remember the date or time, but it was since my expedition to the Smoky Hill."*

Chivington - *"When did the order reach Fort Lyon?"*

Wynkoop - *"The first I heard of it being at Fort Lyon was when Major Anthony relieved me from the command on the 5th day of November, 1864. He brought some copies with him."*

Testimony ended for the day with Chivington unable to prove that Wynkoop had disobeyed orders. The following day, Chivington resumed his cross-examination of Wynkoop. After a few general questions regarding the meeting with the Indians at Smoky Hill, Chivington's final question was if Wynkoop allowed "large numbers" of Indians into Fort Lyon. Wynkoop replied:

> *"Large numbers of Indians were not allowed to enter Fort Lyon as they pleased."* [102]

The commission heard more testimony from soldiers of the First and Third regiments, including David Louderback, George Roan, Amos James, and officers, including Sergeant Lucian Palmer and Lieutenant James Cannon, Major Anthony's adjutant during the Sand Creek affair. Lieutenant William Minton testified that Black Kettle and Left Hand were indeed offered military protection if they moved to Sand Creek.[103]

First Lieutenant James Olney, of the First Colorado Cavalry, gave his testimony, which stunned the members of the commission. He stated:

> *"During the massacre, [I] saw three squaws and five children, prisoners in charge of some soldiers; that while they were being conducted along, they were approached by Lieutenant Harry Richmond, of the third Colorado cavalry; that Lieutenant Richmond thereupon immediately killed and scalped the three women and the five children while they were screaming for mercy, while the soldiers in whose charge these prisoners were shrank back, apparently aghast."* [104]

As testimony of this sort by several witnesses continued throughout the day, it became clear that members of the "Bloodless Third," as the press called them before Sand Creek, were anything but. The testimony of the next witness called before the commission proved to be another dramatic moment in the investigation. James Combs, the teamster who had reported the murders of the Snyder wagon group on August 17, 1864, offered his testimony to related events. He stated that he was present at the Spring Bottom stage station near the Arkansas River, on the evening of November 25, when Chivington and his men arrived. Combs said he shared the evening meal with Chivington when the conversation turned to Fort Lyon and Major Wynkoop's transfer to Fort Riley. Combs testified that Chivington replied that it was Chief Left Hand who was really in charge of Fort Lyon. Combs further stated that when the meal was completed, as Chivington rose from the table, he repeated the same rallying phrase he had used at Bijou Creek:

"Scalps are what we're after. I long to be wading in gore." [105]

In cross-examination, Chivington had a few more questions for Combs, and then the transcript says Chivington ended the cross by stating that:

"Remarks [Chivington's] of hatred were in reply to Combs' [supposed] remarks in regard to the Indians."

This insertion of a personal observation by an interrogator was not only unusual in a military proceeding, it also had no merit, as Combs was never asked if such a statement was made.[106]

The military commission adjourned at Fort Lyon on April 8, and preparations were made to travel back to Denver, where the committee was scheduled to reconvene on April 17, 1865.

Meanwhile, Captain Silas Soule had been transferred to the Denver Provost Guard. By testifying against Chivington, which destroyed Chivington's reputation, Soule became the target of Chivington supporters, a strong group in Denver. During a trip to Central City with Captain George F. Price, district inspector and Assistant Adjutant General in Denver, Soule told Price that he knew his "character had been blackened" after his testimony against Chivington and that he "fully expected to be killed."[107]

Although aware of the threats this group posed, by all accounts Soule performed his duties as Provost Marshal without incident, and remained a favorite topic in the March 18, 1864, issue of the *Rocky Mountain News*: "The Regimental Band and Capt. Soule, too, were musically on it yesterday - thanks to their good taste and generosity for a glorious serenade, now mellow as St. Patricks [sic] day."

On April 1, 1865, Silas Soule and Hersa Coberly were married in a private ceremony by Reverend Kehler, the Chaplain of the First Cavalry. And again, the *Rocky Mountain News* covered the event in the April 5th issue:

> *"Married. In this city, at the residence of H.J. Rogers, on the 1st inst., at 8 o'clock A.M. by Rev. Mr. Kehler, Capt. Silas Soule and Miss Hersey [sic] A. Coberly."*

On Sunday evening, April 23, 1865, at approximately 9:30 p.m., Silas Soule and his bride of three weeks had just returned to their home on Curtis Street, when shots rang out. As Provost Marshal, Soule left to investigate. He walked along Lawrence Street, crossed at F Street, and proceeded to Arapahoe Street, where he fired his derringer and was than shot by a man who instantly shot him in the head. Captain Silas Soule fell to the street, dying instantly.[108] He was twenty-six years old.

Silas Soule refused to fire on the peaceful Indian camp at Sand Creek. *DPL*

Although the assassin fled the murder scene on foot, eyewitnesses stated the murderer was Private Charles W. Squiers, of the Second Colorado Cavalry, formerly under Chivington's command. Squiers had previously been accused of attempted murder; however, he was released from the charges based on the recurring obstacle of proper territorial jurisdiction.

Authorities learned from tips and informants that Squiers had fled to New Mexico, after claiming to his friends he had killed Soule. It was suspected at the time that Squiers was either an agent or an assassin paid by Chivington himself. Shortly before Soule was killed, Chivington had given a speech where he offered to his supporters five hundred dollars to any person who would kill an

Indian or one who sympathized with them.[109]

Flame-throwing rhetoric to be sure, however, soldiers and officers of the First Colorado Regiment had previously testified to overhearing Chivington's threats against Soule and Cramer at Fort Lyon. Therefore, a posse was sent to New Mexico to track Squiers and return him to Denver. Meanwhile, the *Rocky Mountain News* covered the horrific assassination in the April 24 issue under the headline: "The Homicide Last Night"

> *"Our city was thrown into a feverish excitement last evening by the assassination of Captain S. S. Soule, of the Colorado First. The sad affair took place about half past ten o'clock, and was evidently coolly and deliberately planned, and as systematically carried out. For some time past the Captain had been in charge of the provost guard of the city and neighborhood, and his duties in that capacity had, as a natural consequence, created many enemies. Threats against his life have been freely and frequently made – so we are informed – and no longer ago than yesterday he said that he was expecting to be attacked. In the evening he and his wife were visiting at the house of a friend and returned home between nine and ten o'clock. Shortly after, a number of pistol shots were fired in the upper part of the city, evidently to decoy him out, and the Captain started to ascertain the cause. Whilst passing along Lawrence Street, Near F, and directly in front of the residence of Dr. Cunningham, he seems to have been met by the assassin, and the indications are that both fired at the same instant, or so near together that the reports seemed simultaneous. Probably the Captain, expecting to be attacked, was in readiness, and when the other man presented his pistol, he did the same, but the intended assassin fired an instant soonest, with but too fatal effect. The ball entered the Captain's face at the point of the right cheek bone, pressing backward and upward, and lodging in the back part of the head. He fell back dead, appearing not to have moved a muscle after falling. The other man, from the indications, was wounded in the right hand or arm; how severely is not known. His pistol was dropped at his feet and he immediately started and ran towards the military camp in the upper part of the city, leaving a distinct trail of blood where he passed along. When the shots were fired they were standing about four feet apart, face to face. Within less than a minute after the fatal shot, one of the provost guard and Mr. Ruter reached the spot. The Captain was already dead, and his murderer had disappeared. They alarmed Dr. Cunningham, and a guard was sent for. A number of persons, soldiers and civilians, soon gathered around, and after a few minutes the body was removed to the building occupied by the officers of the Headquarters of the District. The*

excitement this morning, when the facts became generally known, was intense. Hundreds of citizens visited the scene of the tragedy, and it has formed the burthen of conversation throughout the city all day. Patrols were dispatched in every direction, and it is hardly possible that he will escape more than for a day or two. Probably he will be overtaken today. Of his identity we shall at present refrain from speaking, though there is scarce a doubt but it is clearly known. The cause is said to have grown out of an arrest made by the Captain in the discharge of his duty as Provost Marshal. Captain Soule was highly respected by his brother officers, and beloved by the men in his company. He was married in this city on the 1st inst., and consequently leaves a young wife to mourn this terrible and untimely fate. It is the hope of all that his murderer and his accomplices will be speedily brought to judgment, and a punishment meted out to them such as the base crime deserves."

If it was indeed an assassination, there are a few interesting points in this news article worth mentioning. First, it was no secret that editor Byers backed Chivington and defended his actions in the paper. The fact that Byers chose not to release the name of the suspected murderer to the public is highly suspect of proper journalism of the era. Second, it was a well-known fact that threats had been made against Soule specifically because of his testimony against Chivington. The insertion into the article that the cause of the shooting was "said to have grown out of an arrest made by the Captain in the discharge of his duty as Provost Marshal," is an inaccurate statement and must have been inserted as a distraction to the possibility of an assassination.

As the military investigation into the Sand Creek matter, and Chivington in particular, was still ongoing in Denver, the following statement was entered into the official record: "The members of the Commissions having been requested to assist in making arrangements for the funeral of the late lamented Silas S. Soule, commission adjourned until Thursday morning April 27th, 1865 at 9 o'clock."

The funeral for Captain Silas Soule took place in Denver on Wednesday, April 26, at St. John's church. One of the largest funerals to date in the city, the church was crowded with many citizens who knew of the jovial Provost Marshal by his fine reputation in the city. Also in attendance, surprisingly enough given the political dynamic, was Governor John Evans.[110]

The *Rocky Mountain News* covered the funeral in the April 27 issue in the obituary section, saying in part:

"As a military funeral, this was the finest we have ever seen in the country. The officers and soldiers and Lt. Wilson's Company, made an appearance of style and discipline most "military" indeed. A long line of carriages - almost all the public and private ones in town - were in the citizen cortege. Deceased was about 27 years of age, descended from Irish parentage. His sister and mother reside in Lawrence, Kansas. His young widowed bride - has been draped in weeds before the orange blossoms scarce had time to wither."[111]

Captain Silas Soule was buried with full military honors at Mount Prospect Cemetery, or the City Cemetery as it became commonly known as. A group of generous citizens began a collection drive for a proper memorial for his grave site.[112] There is some evidence that in early July, Wynkoop learned of Squiers' exact location in Las Vegas, New Mexico, and alerted the military forces in that region.[113] In any case, Squiers was arrested in Las Vegas, New Mexico, where Lieutenant James Cannon, who, coincidentally, had served as Major Anthony's adjutant during the Sand Creek affair, traveled to bring the prisoner back to Denver to stand trial for the murder of Captain Soule.

Cannon and his prisoner arrived in Denver on July 11, where Squiers was taken in cuffs and chains to the provost jail on Larimer Street, to face a military trial for murder. The recently completed jail was, ironically, constructed during the tenure of the late Provost Marshal, Silas Soule.[114] Meanwhile, Lieutenant Cannon took a room at the nearby Tremont House, where three days later he was found dead in his room. An incomplete autopsy ruled the death a natural cause. However, several members of the military pushed for an investigation. The *Daily News*, a small Denver paper, reported in their July 14, 1865 issue, "Mysterious Death of Lt. Cannon - Evidence before the Coroner's Inquest."

Sheriff O. O. Kent served as the coroner. As mysterious as the death may have seemed, so was the subsequent coroner's inquest. No reports ever appeared in any of the newspapers. However, the *Rocky Mountain News* did report Cannon's burial, in the City Cemetery, the very next day after the inquest was held.[115] Major Wynkoop would later write what he had always believed, that Lieutenant Cannon was poisoned.[116]

Squiers spent his time in the provost jail in chains as he awaited his trial. However, just days before the trial was set to begin, Squiers escaped. The *Rocky Mountain News* reported the incident in the October 10, 1865 issue:

"It is supposed he [Squiers] was aided from the outside, as the large padlock at the back door was picked. Two men are under arrest for aiding in the escape, one of them, a blacksmith, charged with furnishing the chisels for removing the shackles from the limbs of the prisoner."

Accounts vary as to where Squiers went. The fact is, he was never seen in Denver again and, thus, never held accountable for the murder of Captain Silas S. Soule.

No direct evidence was ever presented implicating Chivington in either Silas Soule's murder or Squiers' escape from the provost jail. However, following the very convenient escape, even the most ardent Chivington supporters came to believe he was behind both crimes. Perhaps Major Wynkoop said it best: "... Col. Chivington never dared to place Capt. Soule in arrest but some months subsequently had him murdered at night in the streets of Denver by an assassin whom he hired for that purpose."[117]

The day after Captain Silas S. Soule was laid to rest, the military commission resumed their investigation promptly at 9 a.m., Thursday, April 27, 1865. This was the day everyone was waiting for, as Chivington now began his own defense.

Chivington presented the commission with a sworn deposition, signed and dated April 7, 1865. It was the testimony of Lipman Meyer, a freighter who had been with Captain Soule on a scouting expedition shortly after the Sand Creek episode. Meyer alleged that on this scouting trip, Soule was drinking heavily and did not know which direction they were going. He further asserted that Soule was afraid of the Indians and accused the captain of theft. This testimony was clearly character assassination and had no relevancy to the investigation regarding Sand Creek.

Chivington attempted to bolster his defense to prove that the Indians were indeed hostile and that interpreter John Smith, Captain Silas Soule and Samuel Colley were acting together against the army to profit from the Indians. Incredibly, given much previous testimony of the horrific atrocities both during the fight and after, by members of the Third Regiment, Chivington called several officers of the Third Regiment to testify in his defense, among them, Captain T. G. Cree, Lieutenant Clark Dunn, Captain Jay J. Johnson, and Captain Presley Talbot. Incredibly, another witness Chivington called was none other than Lieutenant Harry Richmond, the very soldier who First Lieutenant James Olney, of the First Colorado Cavalry, previously testified:

"Lieutenant Harry Richmond, of the third Colorado cavalry; that Lieutenant Richmond thereupon immediately killed and scalped the three women and the five children while they were screaming for mercy."[118]

The testimony of these soldiers did nothing to help Chivington's defense. In fact, a case could be made that their very presence hurt Chivington's efforts. The following day, reports and signed affidavits relating to Major Wynkoop's meeting with the Cheyenne on the Smoky Hill River were presented to the commission. Chivington immediately objected, and just as immediately, he was overruled. The military continued their investigation, finally adjourning on May 30, 1865. Although stunning revelations emerged throughout the process and Chivington was condemned by his former superiors, there was no military prosecution, as Chivington had resigned on January 5 of that year. It would be a different outcome for Governor John Evans.

However, investigations continued. The same day that the military proceedings ended, Senator Doolittle and members of the governmental Joint Special Commission arrived at Fort Lyon to continue their investigation. Major Wynkoop personally welcomed the senator and offered his private living quarters for Doolittle to stay while he was at the fort.

Wynkoop took the group to the death scene at Sand Creek. In his memoirs, he recorded observing: "expressions of horror [over] the bleaching bones of the slain, skulls of infants, several of which Senator Doolittle collected that had bullet holes through the top of the head, showing conclusively the manner of their death."[119]

Major Edward Wynkoop then sent the following testimony to the Congressional committee conducting the "Condition of the Indian Tribes." At Fort Lyon, June 9, 1865:

"Since the massacre I have not been able to hold any communication with the Indians. I have in my possession a statement made by a half-breed, who had been in their camp since the massacre. He was in during the attack, and was among those who escaped; he was also in their camp when the remnant of the tribe got together on the Smoky Hill. Black Kettle, head chief of the Cheyennes, was there, but in disgrace with his tribe; was recognized no longer, and was taunted for having, by putting too much faith in the white man, their women and children murdered. They insult him and threatened his life, asking him why he did not stay

and die with his brothers. The Indians told him that altogether there were one hundred and forty missing, but some wounded afterwards came in. Black Kettle is the only chief left who was in favor of peace. White Antelope folded his arms stoically and was shot down." [120]

Meanwhile, concluding their investigation at Fort Lyon, Doolittle and his group traveled to Denver, where Doolittle sent reports of their findings back to Washington, D. C. Secretary of State William H. Seward sent the following letter to Colorado Territorial Governor John Evans:

"I am directed by the President [Andrew Johnson] to inform you that your resignation of the office of Governor of Colorado Territory would be acceptable, the resignation [should] reach Washington without delay." [121]

The *Rocky Mountain News* carried the story in the June 15, 1865:

"The announcement last evening, that Governor Evans was removed, created something of a sensation. It was received almost universally with expressions of regret. Even those who have differed with him upon political questions, are frank to admit that he has been a faithful, impartial and judicious officer; whilst his urbanity, undoubted ability, exemplary conduct, and high moral standing, have secured him the confidence and respect of the people generally during an administration of great embarrassment and difficulties. In striking contrast with the general demeanor of our citizens over the news, was the conduct of the U.S. District Attorney - Gen. Browne. He embraced the occasion to get 'glorious light,' and until a late hour, made the night hideous on some of the principal streets of the city with his rejoicings over the event, shouting, 'Who is Governor now?'"

With this forced resignation, Governor Evans was the only man who suffered for the atrocities at Sand Creek on November 29, 1864. While Evans was held accountable for his complicity in the actions leading to the massacre, Soule, who refused to take part, paid the price with his own life.

The former army colonel, John Milton Chivington, found work as a Denver undersheriff and, later, as coroner of Arapahoe County. He eventually left Colorado, roaming the country in search of acceptance, yet remained defiant. Throughout his life, Chivington suffered personal tragedies. His son drowned tragically in Nebraska, and his wife died soon after. When Chivington married his widowed daughter-in-law, even W. N. Byers, Chivington's long-time friend and fervent supporter, had had enough of Chivington and his actions. Byers ran the following editorial in the June 9, 1868 issue of his *Rocky Mountain News*:

"It seems to be true that John M. Chivington has married his son's widow. What will he do next to outrage the moral sense and feeling of his day and generation, remains to be seen; but be sure it will be something, if there is anything left for him to do."

Governor John Evans was reluctant to work at peace with the Arapaho and Cheyenne which led to war. *DPL*

In 1883, Chivington gave a speech at an event hosted by the Denver Pikes Peak Pioneers Association. Chivington again attempted to redeem his actions at Sand Creek when he said:

"What of that Indian blanket that was captured, fringed with white woman's scalps? What says the sleeping dust of the two hundred and eight men, women, and children, emigrants, herders, and soldiers who lost their lives at the hands of these Indians? Peaceable? Now we are peaceably disposed, but decline giving such testimonials of our peaceful proclivities, and I say here as I said in my own town in the Quaker county of Clinton, State of Ohio, one night last week - I stand by Sand Creek." [122]

Controversy will forever hang over the Sand Creek Massacre. More important are the reasons for such a tragic affair, thereby gaining an understanding of the truth. That obscure truth most likely lies in deep layers somewhere in the middle of the controversy.

In man ways the tragedy at Sand Creek represented both the cause and effect of the white man's Manifest Destiny and clash with Indian tradition. The massacre at Sand Creek, more than any other Indian conflict at that time, set the stage for the bloody battles yet to come on the American Plains.

In American history, it would remain with the Cheyenne Indians as the most decisive symbol of white-man betrayal, and among the citizens of Colorado, as the worst tragedy in the state's history. John Sipes, Cheyenne Tribal historian said:

> *"Many that survived Sand Creek later died at the Lodge Pole River on an early snowy morning. It was foretold that after Sand Creek there would be no rest and peace for the Cheyenne for they knew to survive it meant to fight and fight and be killed or kill to live."* [123]

The Indians would exact their revenge.

— Chapter Notes —

1. The *Rocky Mountain News*, September 28, 1864.
2. Smith, *The Birth of Colorado*, pg. 213.
3. Berthrong, *The Southern Cheyenne*, pg. 140.
4. United States Congress, Report on the Conduct of War, including testimony,1865, pg. 47.
5. The *Rocky Mountain News*, October 20, 1864.
6. Wynkoop, Edward Estill. Also see Kraft, *Ned Wynkoop and the Lonely Road from Sand Creek*, pg. 126.
7. Official Military Record, Series I, Vol. XLI, pg. 433.
8. ibid.
9. Official Military Record, Series I, Vol. XLI, pg. 912.
10. Official Military Record, Series I, Vol. XLI, pgs. 913-914.
11. Major Scott Anthony testimony, March 14, 1865, "Sand Creek Massacre."
12. ibid.
13. John L. Sipes, great grandson of Mo-chi and Medicine Water, and Cheyenne tribal historian. Documents, records, and correspondence now in possession of the author.
14. Hyde, *Life of George Bent*, pg. 322. Custer's attack of the Cheyenne Indians on the Washita River in the Indian territory of today's state of Oklahoma occurred on November 28, 1868, four years nearly to the day after the massacre at Sand Creek.
15. ibid.
16. Hatch, *Black Kettle*, pg. 22.
17. Hatch, *Black Kettle*, pg. 28.
18. Powell, *People of the Sacred Mountain*, pg. 71.
19. Hyde, *Life of George Bent*, pgs. 96-97.
20. The U.S. Congress later reduced the time from fifty to ten years.
21. Hatch, *Black Kettle*, pg. 35.
22. George Bent Letters. Denver Public Library, Western History Department.
23. Hatch, *Black Kettle*, pg. 41.
24. George Bent Letters. Denver Public Library, Western History Department.
25. ibid.
26. Halaas & Masich, *Halfbreed*, pg. 100.

27. Annual Report of the Commissioner of Indian Affairs, 1859, pg. 507.
28. The September 20, 1860 issue of the *Western Mountaineer*.
29. Fort Wise Treaty, February 18, 1861.
30. Hoig, *The Sand Creek Massacre*.
31. Howbert, *Memories of a Lifetime in the Pike's Peak Region*, pg. 120.
32. ibid.
33. Official Military Record, Series I, Vol. XLI, Part III, pg. 789.
34. Official Military Record, Series I, Vol. XLI, Part IV, pgs 23-24.
35. ibid.
36. The *Denver Republican*, May 18, 1890.
37. Official Military Record, Part 1, pg. 964.
38. Howbert, *Memories of a Lifetime in the Pike's Peak Region*, pg. 121.
39. ibid.
40. Grinnell, *Fighting Cheyennes*, pg. 163.
41. ibid.
42. Hoig, *The Sand Creek Massacre*.
43. ibid.
44. Hoig, *The Sand Creek Massacre*, pgs. 27-28.
45. Roberts, Gary L., and Halass, David F., *Written in Blood: The Soule-Cramer Sand Creek Massacre Letters*, reprinted by Fulcrum Press, 2004. Pages 328-331.
46. Congressional Testimony, March 20, 1865.
47. Hoig, *The Sand Creek Massacre*, pg. 13.
48. Hoig, *The Sand Creek Massacre*, pg. 21.
49. Hoig, *The Sand Creek Massacre*, pgs. 46-47.
50. ibid.
51. Hoig, *The Sand Creek Massacre*, pg. 47.
52. Howbert, *Memories of a Lifetime in the Pike's Peak Region*, pg. 122.
53. This is important to note as several writers of the Sand Massacre have characterized the creek as "full" and "rushing waters." Following a severe snowstorm with freezing temperatures in late November, Sand Creek could not possibly have "full" or "rushing waters."
54. Hoig, *The Sand Creek Massacre*, sworn testimony of Robert Bent.
55. ibid.
56. E.S. Ricker Papers, F.W. Cragin Papers, Denver Public Library, Western History Department. Also see Grinnell, *Fighting Cheyennes*, pg. 177, and Hyde, Life of George Bent, pgs. 151-154.
57. Grinnell, *Fighting Cheyennes*.
58. Hatch, *Black Kettle*, pg. 158.
59. Hyde, *Life of George Bent*, pg. 155. Also see "Sand Creek Massacre," pgs. 50-51.
60. Hyde, *Life of George Bent*, pgs. 177-178.

61. Hoig, *The Sand Creek Massacre,* Cramer sworn testimony, pg. 73.
62. Hoig, *The Sand Creek Massacre,* pg. 138.
63. George Pierce had served honorably beside Colonel Chivington during the Battle of Glorieta Pass.
64. U.S. Senate Executive Documents for the Second Session of the Thirty-Ninth Congress of the United States of America, 1866-67, pgs. 219-222.
65. ibid.
66. ibid.
67. Hyde, *Life of George Bent,* pgs. 156-157.
68. Several writers have confused Mo-chi with with Buffalo Calf Woman. There have been several English spellings of her name. Tribal historian and Mo-chi's great-great grandson, John L. Sipes, said the English translation is Mo-chi, pronounced Mo-Ki. Sipes family records in possession of the author.
69. Sipes, the late Cheyenne Tribal historian.
70. ibid.
71. Hyde, *Life of George Bent,* pgs. 156-157.
72. Wommack, Linda and John L. Sipes, *Mo-chi: The First Female Cheyenne Warrior,* Wild West Magazine, April, 2008.
73. Hatch, *Black Kettle,* pg. 167.
74. Official Military Record, Volume 1, pg. 948, the same report was printed in the *Rocky Mountain News* on December 14, 1864.
75. Hoig, *The Sand Creek Massacre,* pgs. 176-177.
76. Hoig, *The Sand Creek Massacre,* pg. 136.
77. ibid.
78. ibid.
79. United States Congress, Reports of the Committees, 39th Congress session, 1867, pg. 92, 80. Company Muster Roll of July 29 through August 31, 1861. Transcripts of the Colorado Volunteers records, State of Colorado, Division of the Archives and Public Records.
80. Company Muster Roll of July 29 through August 31, 1861. Transcripts of the Colorado Volunteers records, State of Colorado, Division of the Archives and Public Records.
81. Company Muster Roll of July 29 through August 31, 1861. Transcripts of the Colorado Volunteers records, State of Colorado, Division of the Archives and Public Records.
82. ibid.
83. United States Congress, Reports of the Committee, 39th Congress session, 1867, pg. 52.
84. Official Military Record, pgs. 948-950.
85. "Sand Creek Massacre," pgs. 213-15. The *Rocky Mountain News* issue of September 29, 1864, also carried the transcript on its front page.

86. Official Military Record, pgs. 948-950.
87. The *Rocky Mountain News,* December 30, 1864.
88. The *Rocky Mountain News,* December 27, 1864.
89. Wynkoop, "Unfinished Colorado History, 1886."
90. ibid.
91. Kraft, *Ned Wynkoop and the Lonely Road from Sand Creek,* pg. 139.
92. This signature is on several documents submitted during the investigations and are in the Official Military Record. Signature printed in the *Rocky Mountain News* on December 14, 1864.
93. Official Military Record, Series I, Vol. XLI, pg. 971.
94. Wynkoop, "Unfinished Colorado History, 1886," pg.115.
95. Official Military Record, Series I, Vol. XLVIII, pg. 1,511. Also see Kraft, *Ned Wynkoop and the Lonely Road from Sand Creek,* pg. 140.
96. The Trail, "Plain Tales of the Plains," Volume V111, 1916.
97. Hoig, *The Sand Creek Massacre.*
98. ibid.
99. Hoig, *The Sand Creek Massacre,* Snyder testimony, pgs. 77-81.
100. United States Congress, House of Representatives. "Massacre of the Cheyenne Indians." Report on the Conduct of War, 1865.
101. "The Chivington Massacre," Report of the Joint Special Committee. Appointed Under Resolution of March 3, 1865. Hereafter referred to as the "Chivington Massacre."
102. Hoig, *The Sand Creek Massacre,* Wynkoop testimony, pgs. 83-103.
103. Hoig, *The Sand Creek Massacre,* Minton testimony, pgs. 146-159.
104. United States Congress, Reports of the Committees, 39th Congress session, 1867, pg. 61.
105. Hoig, *The Sand Creek Massacre,* pgs, 27-28.
106. Hoig, *The Sand Creek Massacre,* James Combs testimony, pgs. 115-118.
107. Hoig, *The Sand Creek Massacre,* George F. Price testimony, pgs. 188-189.
108. In November of 2010, the Colorado Historical Society placed a memorial plaque in honor of Captain Silas Soule on the building at the northwest corner of Fifteenth and Arapahoe streets in downtown Denver. It was at this exact location where Soule was assassinated on April 23, 1865. The plaque reads: "Silas S. Soule. At this location on April 23, 1865, assassins shot and killed First Colorado Cavalry officer Capt. Silas S. Soule. During the infamous Sand Creek Massacre of November 29, 1864, Soule had disobeyed orders by refusing to fire on Chief Black Kettle's peaceful Cheyenne and Arapaho village. Later, at army hearings, Soule testified against his commander, Col. John M. Chivington, detailing the atrocities committed by the troops at Sand Creek. His murderers were never brought to justice."

109.   Kansas State Historical Quarterly, November, 1939 Vol. 8, No. 4.
110.   Perkins, LaVonne, "Silas Soule and His Widow Heresa [sic], and the Rest of the Story." *Denver Westerners Roundup,* Vol LV, no.2, Mar-Apr, 1999.
111.   Mrs. Hersa Coberly Soule was twenty years old at the untimely death of her husband.
112.   A six-foot-tall obelisk was placed at Soule's grave on June 19, 1866.   When Soule and many other bodies were removed to Riverside Cemetery beginning in 1893, the obelisk was not and thus is lost to history. Perkins, pg. 13.
113.   Wynkoop unfinished manuscript, Colorado Historical Society, Kraft, *Wynkoop,* pg. 151. Although Wynkoop by this time was on his way back to Fort Riley, the message could have been sent.
114.   The *Rocky Mountain News,* February 9, 1865.
115.   The *Rocky Mountain News,* July 15, 1865.
116.   Wynkoop's unfinished manuscript, Colorado Historical Society.
117.   The Denver Police Department Pictorial Review and History, 1859-1985. Also of note is Tom Bensing's biography of Silas Soule in which he maintains Soule was not murdered, rather it was a horrible accident.
118.   United States Congress, Reports of the Committees, 39th Congress session, 1867, pg. 61.
119.   Wynkoop, "Unfinished Colorado History, 1886."
120.   Condition of the Indian Tribes, 39th Congress, 1866-67, Report No. 156.
121.   John Evans Personal Correspondence, Colorado History Center.
122.   Dunn, *I Stand By Sand Creek,* pg.72; also see Thayer, *Marvels of the New West.*
123.   John L. Sipes, the late Cheyenne tribal historian.

— REVENGE, RAIDS AND THE RIVER —

As the survivors of the Sand Creek massacre recuperated along the Smoky Hill River in Kansas Territory, the traditional war pipe had been sent out by the runners to all Indian camps. It was a departure from Indian custom. According to John L. Sipes, Jr., Southern Cheyenne Tribal Historian:

> *"The tradition of the war pipe, when necessary, was sent out in the spring, but after the slaughter at Sand Creek, the war pipe went out in the winter, December. To my knowledge, from the Old ones, never before had the war pipe been sent in the time of winter until Sand Creek."*

George Bent, who had been hit with a bullet in his hip, remembered this time in the Smoky Hill camp with silent resolve bent on revenge.

> *"As we rode into that camp everyone was crying, even the warriors and the women and children screaming and wailing. Nearly everyone present had lost some relations or friends, many of them in their grief were gashing themselves with their knives until the blood flowed in streams."*[1]

Bent watched for nearly a week, as struggling survivors entered the camp known as the "Bunch of Timbers." Through his talks with many of them, he witnessed the severe causalities of his people. Black Bear's wife had been struck with a bullet in her eye. After a long recovery which left her so disfigured, she was forever known as One Eye Comes Together. During her recovery, she told of the horror she had seen: the soldiers killing the innocent children and raping women.

At one point Bent had estimated the dead at fifty-three men and one hundred and ten women and children. However, Bent was unable to learn anything of his stepmother, Island, or his half-brother, Charlie.

> "The Wutapiu clan headed by Black Kettle was the sufferer of most lives lost. The Heviqsnipahis clan headed by Sand Hill had the least loss of lives, mainly because they were camped farther down on Sand Creek. Yellow Wolf's Hevhaitaniu clan lost about half of their people. Yellow Wolf was killed with his people in this camp. He was 85 years old and he also lost his brother, Big Man.
>
> The Oivimana clan also lost half its people. White Antelope with his clan of Hisometainio lost many people. Chief One-Eye (Lone Bear) was killed with many of his band. The Suthai clan lost a few people." [2]

Meanwhile, as the anger over the slaughter of the Arapaho and Cheyenne people spread, several chiefs and warriors of the surrounding Indian societies gathered together for a war council. Black Kettle, as a respected member of the Cheyenne Council of Forty-Four, sat in during the war council.

Black Kettle, who advocated for peace, nevertheless understood the overwhelming vote by the council for war; the attack at Sand Creek must be avenged. All in attendance smoked the war pipe and declared war, including the Dog Soldiers. Black Kettle did not smoke the war pipe, for he believed that a war against the whites could not be won.

Several chiefs and pipe bearers left the camp to carry the war pipe to the Northern Arapaho on the Republican River and the Lakota on the Solomon River. George Bent and his brother-in-law, Edmund Guerrier, eagerly joined the pipe bearers on their journey to the other Indian camps. All agreed with the Cheyenne and smoked the war pipe. War had been declared. An agreement was made that all the tribes would gather at Cherry Creek, a tributary that flows into the south fork of the Republican River, near present-day St. Francis, Kansas. Here, they would plan a war strategy.

As the various tribes packed for the move, George Bent secured a horse and, along with Ed Guerrier and another Sand Creek survivor, fifteen-year-old Howling Wolf, the three rode for the Purgatoire River in Colorado Territory: the home of George's father, William Bent. George wanted to inform his father of the impending war and learn news of any survivors, including his sisters, half-brothers and stepmother.

With Bent's hip wound still healing, the trio rode slowly. Eventually they reached the Arkansas River, just a few miles up-river from Fort Lyon. On a bluff above the river, Bent saw a large military camp. He could hear the soldiers singing and straining to hear the melodies, he recognized Christmas carols. It was Christmas Eve. Bent decided to resume travel after dark, so as not to alert the soldiers. However, Guerrier, fearful of being caught by the soldiers, refused to go on. The only hope as he saw it was to surrender. Bent included this incident in a letter to friend and historian, George Hyde.

> *"He [Guerrier] said he was going right down there and give himself up; that he was tired of the whole business and did not care much what the soldiers did to him. We talked this over a while, and then Guerrier rode down and gave himself up. He was not treated badly, Major Anthony tried to get information from him about the position of our camps but did not give him any information that was of value, and he did not say anything about my being near the fort."* [3]

In the cover of darkness, Bent and Howling Wolf made their way to the Bent ranch along the Purgatoire River. The two arrived just in time for Christmas dinner. The Bent family reunion was an especially joyous one on this holy day of celebration. William Bent thought his son was dead. George was relieved to be greeted by Island, his stepmother, who he feared was dead. His brother Robert was also there, having been released into their father's custody. His sister Mary and her husband, Robison Moore, were also safe at the ranch. George learned that Charlie had been escorted to Fort Lyon by Captain Silas Soule. He was also told that after being held prisoner for nearly a week, Charlie was released and believed to be in one of the Dog Soldier camps at the "Big Timbers" area of the Smoky Hill River. George had news for the family as well. He reported that his sister Julia, married to Edmond Guerrier, was safe and in camp with the Dog Soldiers. He told his father of Guerrier's surrender, but assured him he thought he was being treated fairly.

After nearly a week with his family, Bent's hip wound was nearly healed. He knew it was time to return to Black Kettle's camp. Sometime in the last days of December, 1864, George Bent left his father's ranch. He later recounted:

> *"It was sometime in December when we set out for the camp, and we took with us my step-mother and two women who had been captured at Sand Creek and turned over by the soldiers to my father. We travelled [sic] four days and then found the camp on Cherry Creek, a small stream that flows into the South Fork of the Republican in the present*

Cheyenne County, Kansas. This place is in the extreme northwestern corner of Kansas, right on the Colorado line and not ten miles south of the Nebraska line. Here the Cheyennes were all encamped, and with them were Spotted Tail's and Pawnee Killer's Sioux bands and a camp of eighty lodges of Northern Arapaho." [4]

It was the largest Indian village Bent had ever seen, nearly a thousand lodges strong. Settling into camp, Bent was present as the preparations for raids along the Platte River were made, including a massive raid at the town of Julesburg, Colorado. The immediate concern was fortification of supplies. With Fort Rankin nearby, there would be an ample supply of goods such as food, blankets, fire arms and various necessities.

The fort, originally called Camp Rankin, was established on May 17, 1864, specifically to provide protection for westward travelers. It was strategically located approximately one mile east of the settlement of Julesburg, near several fords of the South Platte River, where a branch of the Overland Trail, as well as the South Platte River Road, continued west. Brigadier General Robert B. Mitchell placed Colonel Christopher H. McNally, of the Third U.S. Volunteer Regiment, in command of the military post. George Bent later described the fort and Julesburg:

"In 1865 Julesburg was an important place on the stage line; here the company had a large station house...with an eating house, a big stable, blacksmith and repair shop, granary, and storehouses, and a big corral enclosed by a high wall built of sod. Besides the stage company's property, there was a large store selling all kinds of goods to travelers and emigrant trains, and the Overland Telegraph Company also had an office at this point. Altogether, Julesburg Station was quite a large place for the Plains in those days. The buildings here were partly built of cottonwood logs and partly of sod." [5]

With the conclusion of a final war council by the chiefs, runners were sent throughout the camp announcing the chiefs' intentions. Warriors from all the tribes readied for war, including the Cheyenne Dog Soldiers. The warriors prepared their lances, shields, bows and arrows: only a few had firearms. George Bent, who rode with the Cheyenne Dog Soldiers, later wrote:

"We set out about one thousand strong, and a number of women came with us with extra ponies to bring back the plunder we would take from

the Julesburg store. We marched in regular order, the soldier societies seeing to it that no one slipped off to go on ahead and do something that might warn the [white] soldiers and put them on guard. The chiefs led the column and the Sioux chiefs were ahead of all the others because the Sioux had smoked the war pipe first and must be given first place. This was the custom, that when a war pipe was sent around, to ask aid in making war, the tribe that smoked first, thus promising their aid, was the tribe that was given the lead in all moves. The chiefs who smoked the pipe first had to be treated with respect, and so they were given the lead in all movements." [6]

The chiefs Bent spoke of were Spotted Tail and his Brule Sioux warriors, and Pawnee Killer and his Oglala Sioux warriors. Chief Black Kettle was there, as well as chiefs of both the Northern and Southern Arapaho. Among the women who traveled with the group, herding the extra horses needed to carry the supplies obtained, mentioned by Bent, was Mo-chi. She insisted on helping her people in whatever way she could. She would prove herself worthy.

It was an incredible attack, thoughtfully planned and executed brilliantly. The collective warriors, led by the Sioux warriors, approached the bluff above Julesburg, hiding in the sand hills. It was a crisp cold night, yet it mattered not. Most of the warriors were deep in thought and preparation. A few hours before sunrise on January 7, 1865, the warriors prepared for the attack. Bent recalled, "My brother Charlie and I both dressed ourselves as warriors, as we intended to take part in the fight."[7]

As the sun rose in the eastern sky, Big Crow, chief of the Cheyenne Crooked Lance Society, led his warriors toward the fort. It was a cognizant ploy to bring the soldiers out of the fort. The ruse worked. The guards saw the Indians approaching and sounded the bugle alarm. The gates of the fort were thrown open and over forty armed, mounted soldiers galloped out of the fort to confront the Indians. They were led in their charge by Captain Nicholas J. O'Brien, with the Seventh Iowa Cavalry, Company F., who was temporarily stationed at Camp Rankin.

Big Crow and his warriors then turned their horses and headed away from the fort, with the soldiers following in pursuit. The decoy effort had worked perfectly. George Bent recounted what happened next:

"As soon as this was seen, the criers rode about camp calling to the warriors to mount and get ready. Big Crow and his men retreated back toward the hills, drawing the soldiers after them. They came nearer and nearer and it began to look like they would ride right into the trap; but as usual, the Indians would not wait for the right moment, and some young men suddenly broke away from the main force and charged out of the hills toward the soldiers. The rest of the thousand followed them, as there was no longer any use in hiding. The soldiers saw us swarming out of the hills and halted at once, than began to retreat. Big Crow and his party at once turned and charged the soldiers, being joined by a large body of Indians coming up from the rear. They struck the soldiers about three hundred yards from the stockade. In this first charge Starving Elk killed the bugler, and several other soldiers fell. Some of the cavalrymen jumped off their horses to fight on foot, but were at once surrounded; the rest of the troops, with their officer, galloped away toward the stockade, the Indians attacking them on all sides but not in strong enough force to cut them off and surround them. Some of these soldiers were killed, and all those who had dismounted also fell. Lieutenant [Eugene F.] Ware, who belonged to the Camp Rankin garrison but was not present during the fight, says that fourteen men were killed, one sergeant, three corporals, and ten privates. He gave all the names. I thought that more than this number fell, and a few weeks later, when the Indians attacked Julesburg again, I counted eighteen fresh graves near the stockade, but all these men may not have been killed in that fight." [8]

Bent also related to historian George Hyde that there were no Indian casualties, although the U. S. Army records reported some fifty Indian deaths. Given the incorrect Indian casualty reports after Sand Creek, this seems to have been a developing pattern by the U. S. Army, most likely an attempt to impress superiors and the public as well. It would later become apparent that it was also a pattern the Indians had adopted.

The Indians who "would not wait for the right moment," as Bent stated, were headed by none other than his brother Charlie. They rushed forward with blood-curdling yells of vengeance. Several years later, Captain Nicholas J. O'Brien recalled the incident and described the Indian yells for a *Rocky Mountain News* reporter:

"The first warning was the weird yelling...As we advanced forward, the Indians retreated toward an arroya known as Devil's Dive, a well known point of ambush." [9]

The warriors must have been amazed when the soldiers (perhaps in confusion), dismounted and staged an ill-conceived counter fight. The Indians pounced on the soldiers, killing many, including a bugler, who many warriors first counted coup on. Old Crow, mounted on a big bay, made the final attack of death. Charging forward with tomahawk at the ready, he instead, fired a bullet into the right cheek of the bugler. The bugler fell off his horse, with blood oozing from his mouth.[10] A noted Cheyenne warrior, Medicine Water, took the reins of the bugler's horse as his prize.

Meanwhile, Indian scouts stationed on the hill sent a signal by sunlight reflected from a mirror to warriors below. This was a sign for the warriors to advance toward the settlement of Julesburg. With the soldiers away in pursuit of the decoys, the remaining warriors were at their leave to plunder the area. George Bent later wrote:

> "The Indians circled around the stockade, yelling and shooting; but they soon turned off and charged down on the stage station, which they began to plunder. At the station breakfast had just been put on the table and was still hot. I sat down with several Indians and ate a good meal. It was the first meal I had eaten at a table in a long time. One old warrior took a great fancy to the big sugar bowl and tied it to his belt. I saw him afterward riding off with the big bowl dangling from his belt behind him. The shelves in the store were packed with all sorts of goods, groceries and canned goods. The Indians took whatever they wanted, but they did not touch the canned goods, as they did not know what they were. The big warehouse belonging to the stage company was also plundered. From it the Indians secured all the flour, bacon, corn, and sugar their ponies could carry.
>
> Some of the warriors found a big tin box and knocked the lock off. It was full of pieces of green paper. The Indians handled the paper but did not know what it was. One man took a big bundle of paper, chopped it into three or four pieces with his tomahawk, and then threw it up in the air, laughing as the wind blew the fragments across the valley. I came up and secured a great deal of the money, but the Indians had already nearly emptied the paymaster's box. The soldiers later had a fine paper hunt and picked up money all over the prairie.
>
> At the station I found an express package addressed to some officer in Colorado, and in the package was a new major's uniform. I took this and

later wore it during the fight on Powder River when we fought General Connor's troops." [11]

According to Bent, the raid continued for the better portion of the day:

"The soldiers did not interfere and could not even come out to pick up the dead bodies of their comrades...We withdrew late that day, January 7." [12]

Charles Griffin Countant was an eyewitness to the Julesburg raid. He later described a somewhat different version of the event:

"Indians under Man-Afraid-of-His Horses and other chiefs made an attack on an incoming stage and came very near capturing it, but fortunately it escaped to the station, having one man and one horse killed. Captain O'Brien discovered the Indians and hastily mounted thirty-seven men and leaving twelve at the fort in charge of two pieces of artillery, he dashed down the savages. Riding to a bluff about a half mile from the fort, they discovered that the Indians were in strong force. The charge was sounded and the gallant heroes, with the clatter of hoofs and shouts, were soon in the midst of the savages. The Indians in their turn, with overwhelming numbers, charged back upon the white men and for a time the carnage went on. At last Captain O'Brien, finding nearly half of his men killed, ordered the remainder to fall back. Fourteen of the thirty-seven enlisted men lay dead on the field. The Indians, with savage shout and maddened fury, now attempted to storm the fort...two pieces of artillery served with telling effect on the advancing savages. The following morning a party was sent out to the battlefield of the day before to gather up the dead. They found them lying where they fell, but their bodies had been stripped and horribly mutilated. The dead soldiers were carried to the fort and buried with honors of war. It was never fully determined how many Indians were killed in this battle, but after peace had been declared they admitted their loss to have been sixty-three." [13]

The *Rocky Mountain News* reported the attack at Julesburg in the January 9, 1865 issue:

"Since our Saturday evening's issue there have been various reports afloat here about Indian matters down the road. A dispatch was received on Saturday evening from Clarks' and Keith & Crook's trains, bound eastward, stating that four of the teamsters had been killed

by Indians. Also, a dispatch was received from the Julesburg office on Saturday evening, saying that the Indians had cleaned out the town, smashed all the windows, doors and furniture in the houses, and robbed everything from the Express coach coming this way, except the package of greenbacks, which the messenger chanced to save, and escaped with to the fort adjoining the town, which the few citizens and soldiers occupied. Also that five dead bodies were lying on the townsite.

The operator further said that the commander of the post desired no dispatches until he would first dispatch his own report of the days fight and consequences. The telegraph machine was taken to the fort before the office was 'cleaned out.' A rumor prevailed here last night, that a train encamped near Bijou station was attacked Saturday night, the train burned and most of the men killed, but today it has not been substantiated or even corroborated."

In the same issue of the *Rocky Mountain News*, a dispatch from Valley Station was printed:

*"Valley Station, Sunday Evening, Jan. 8 -
Men went down the road today to look after the men that were killed by the Indians yesterday. We found men killed and scalped, and horses and wagons burned, all along the road. Post's train from Denver had one man killed, named Andrews, five men severely wounded, two horses killed, and the wagons burned. Marsh's train had one man killed, two wounded slightly, one mule killed, one wagon burned, and the stock and men all missing.*

*One party of Indians are three miles in the bluffs, and we could not catch them. Seven men are missing and cannot be found. The coach today was escorted by soldiers, who saw Indians in the Bluffs [sic] all along the road.
Haines, Operator."*

The paper continued with an added report sent by Captain O'Brien:

"This p.m. we received the following, which is a copy of a dispatch sent by Major [Captain] O'Brien of Julesburg to Gen. Mitchell of Omaha. My scout just in reports an Indian village 10 or 15 miles south of White Man's Fork.

The Indians I fought yesterday were seen by my scout on White Man's Fork, about 60 miles south of here. Indians attacked Dennison's ranch at the same time I was fighting them. They killed 4, and wounded 7 white men. The force on the Republican is not less then 4,000 warriors; this is the report of my scouts and Jewitt, also has 50 of my best men.

A telegram from the Express Messenger at Julesburg, to Mr. Dahler, agent, at this place received at 2 this afternoon, said that he, the messenger, had just found the treasure trunk about two miles from Julesburg, and a small amount of money on the field close by. A diligent search is being made for the articles taken from the Express coach. He also states, 'We buried twenty white men here today.'

As we go to press we learn there is a long and elaborate report of the Indian troubles coming from the Julesburg office. We shall issue it, in an extra, if it contains intelligence, interesting and additional to what we have already received."

Meanwhile, as the victorious warriors made their way back toward the hills, the women, including Mo-chi, came out of the hills with the extra ponies and loaded the goods onto the horses. Then several of the women, led by Mo-chi, gathered the captured horses. Mo-chi led the horses back to the hills and the Cheyenne camp.

Arriving at the camp, Medicine Water turned his prize horse loose with Mo-chi's horse herd. It was their first meeting. From this time forward, the two forged an inseparable bond, bound by sorrow and revenge, eventually entwined by love, family and the Cheyenne spirit of loyalty and endurance.

"During the Moon of the Strong Wind, the attack of Julesburg took place, according to Cheyenne Oral history. The Old ones taught young Medicine Water to respect his elders, to be peaceful with others and to learn to make arrows for possible war. Within the village were a few women warriors, like Mo-chi. They had their own way to prepare for battle. All the while keeping the lodge, having babies, paying attention to passing on the traditions. Mo-chi sang her own songs, painted her own war shield, made her own medicine, all taught to her by the Old ones." [14]

Medicine Water, Mi-Huh-Heu-I-Nup, was a well-respected Cheyenne warrior. The fifth son of six born to Medicine Water and

Old Yellow Hair, he was born in 1835 in the Yellowstone Country. Mo-chi was also born in the Yellowstone Country, in 1841. The two would soon join to fight for their Cheyenne hunting grounds of Colorado and Kansas.

Medicine Water and his brothers became members of the Bowstring Cheyenne Warrior Society and noted chiefs. Two of his brothers, Earrings and Alights-On-Cloud, were killed by the Ho-Nehe-Taneo-O (Wolf People or Pawnee) in 1852 on the South Loupe River in south-central Nebraska.[15]

> *"Following their deaths, Medicine Water proved his right to be chief to this courageous and loyal society of warriors; the Cheyenne Bowstring Warrior Society."* [16]

As the leader of the respected Cheyenne Bowstring Warrior Society, and with fierce devotion to the Cheyenne way of life, Medicine Water was determined to exact revenge for his people killed at Sand Creek. Mo-chi would be at his side as revenge reigned up and down the river.

The attacks along the South Platte River began by several bands of Indians the very day George Bent and the Dog Soldiers were raiding Julesburg. Valley Stage Station, located just south of the South Platte River some sixty miles west of Julesburg and four miles east of today's town of Sterling, was under threat of attack. John Hines sent two wires from the station to Denver that day:

> *"January 7 - From Valley Station - 9:00 A.M.*
> *Indians attacked train in sight of station here. Two men and two Indians killed. Troops chasing Indians. Operator accompanied them. Couch from east fired on four miles below Valley. No one hurt.*
>
> *January 7 - From Valley Station - 9:30 A.M.*
> *Large train which has been encamped for the winter about five miles below attacked by about seventy-five Indians who came from the south. Burned all wagons, killed twelve men, and report says killed some emigrants. I am going to take all my things and go down road until things get more quiet.*
> *Hines, Operator."* [17]

Indeed Hines did move his equipment and took the few lay-over passengers at Valley Station with him to Jim and Charlie Moore's Washington Ranch station, a few miles downstream. The

Medicine Water and Mo-chi rode together as they raided, torched and pillaged along the South Platte River Trail. *John Sipes collection*.

abandoned Valley Station was then raided and plundered by the Indians.

That same morning, a teamster, W. G. Cross, left the American Ranch station, upstream from Valley Station, near today's town of Merino. His wagon included eight passengers who were traveling east from Denver. As the group came upon a spot about half-way between the American Ranch and the Valley Station, they were attacked by Indians. A man by the name of Andrews was killed. The others fell to the floor for protection as Cross urged his four-mule team to full speed. The Indians advanced and were able to ride their ponies alongside the speeding wagon. Cross was hit by a bullet to the elbow which caused him to lose control of the reins. As the mules ran in a haphazard manner, the Indians then shot the animals. As the mules fell, the wagon was now out of control and tumbled over a small hill. The survivors of the attack managed to escape to the river and eventually make their way to Valley Station. Doctor Hamilton attended the survivors at Valley Station and wired a report to the *Rocky Mountain News* which printed it in the January 9, 1865 issue:

> *"All except Andrews were able to make their way to the station...all wounded, some in many places. A young man from Chicago-Bill-will probably die. His skull was fractured by a rifle ball. I amputated Cross' arm."*

Colonel Thomas Moonlight, who had replaced Chivington, sent a message to General Samuel R. Curtis, commander of military operations in the West.

> *"Operators have left stations. Unless troops are hurried out from Kearny, Lyon, or some point, people must starve. Immense excitement. I have no body to re-enforce with."* [18]

Curtis issued orders for Lieutenants J. J. Kennedy and James Olney to reinforce Moonlight's troops. When the order reached the lieutenants, they left for the area with companies C and H of the First Colorado Cavalry. They arrived too late.

The next day, January 8, Hines, the operator at Valley Station, discovered the scalped men of a wagon train. As he hurriedly made his way back to the station, he noticed a group of Indians high on a hill.

Two days later, on January 10, Reuben Thomas, division

agent for the Overland Stage Line between Denver and Julesburg, reported the Indian attack of four men near Valley Station. They had been scalped and horribly mutilated. Thomas was among several men who would later bury the bodies.

The Indian attacks over the past few days caused great fear among the stage drivers and freighters. Travel virtually came to a stand-still along the Platte River Trail as drivers up and down the river route pulled their wagons into the various stations. It is interesting to note that on the very day of January 10, when Thomas reported the scalped bodies of four travelers, the independent passenger transportation firm of Keith & Cook ran an ad in the *Rocky Mountain News:*

"Passengers to the States
We will start five six-mule wagons for the States next Saturday, and will warrant comfortable accommodations, Fare $90. Train supplied with arms and amunition. [sic] *Apply to Keith & Cook."* [19]

The *Miner's Register*, a Central City newspaper, must have elected to down-play the devastation on the plains. The following article ran in the January 14, 1865 issue of the paper, under the headline:

"Troubles Greatly Exaggerated"

"We have been favored by Captain Jones with the perusal of a letter from his sister, Mrs. Clayton of Denver, who started a few days since to go to the river [South Platte] by coach, but after laying at Valley station [sic] for several days was compelled to return to Denver. She says: 'Parties who have just returned from the scene of the recent fight, say there were only seventy-five to one hundred Indians engaged in the fight, and that instead of twelve or twenty being killed as reported, only four were actually killed, the rest having since come in to the various ranches along the route.' She thinks the coaches might pass through without difficulty, and says the whole account of the troubles has been greatly exaggerated. She is not very complimentary to the military there."

Then the Indians attacked again. It was January 15, 1865, the very day after the Central City newspaper printed their article of Indian "exaggerations." William Morris, operator of the American Ranch, along with Gus Hall, and another man, known as "Big Steve," were off gathering wood near Cedar Canyon. As they crossed the frozen river, a large group of Indians converged on the American Ranch. The Indians split their forces. One group attacked the ranch, while another group cut off Hall and his men.

Watson S. Coburn, who owned a ranch along the South Platte River, recalled the Indian attack of the American Ranch:

> *"All the men and family were in the room back of the one where all the goods were kept. Mr. Morris was playing the fiddle when suddenly Mrs. Morris heard a noise in the front part and at once called Mr. Morris' attention to it. On opening the door he saw the room was full of Indians, who immediately gave the war whoop and tried to kill him. He then opened fire with his revolver and killed three of them before they could get out of the door.*
>
> *After barricading the door the men were able to hold their own until the latter part of the day when the Indians set fire to the stables and a large quantity of hay adjoining the house."* [20]

The second group of Indians killed "Big Steve" and shot Hall in the leg.[21] Hall, helpless, watched as the Indians circled around the American Ranch property and set fire to the barn and other outbuildings, as well as the stable and hay stacks. While they did not burn the house, the Indians fired several shots through the windows. Those inside the ranch house, including members of the William Morris family, and others, managed to find cover from the onslaught. As the smoke from the burning structures filtered into the house, those inside began to panic. When the house caught on fire, those sheltered in the house were forced to flee.

Coburn continued his chilling narrative:

> *"The smoke poured into the house in such volumes that the inmates were about to suffocate. Seeing that it would be impossible to stand it much longer, Mr. Morris took half a bottle of strychnine that he kept to poison wolves with, and divided it into two decanters of whiskey behind the counter, after shaking it up; he told his wife to take the children and go out to the front door and give herself up, while he and the men would try to escape out the back way. It was a well known fact that the Indians seldom killed a white woman, hence the plan taken. The men, however, were all killed and scalped a short distance from the house."* [22]

Gus Hall watched as the inhabitants fled from the burning house. As they made their escape, the Indians surrounded them.

Hall managed to raise himself on his good leg, and began to make his way toward the Morris family in an effort to help them. Just as he managed to raise up, he found himself face to face with an Indian pointing a bow and arrow directly at him. The Indian fired the arrow which lodged into the side of Hall, rendering him helpless. He watched as the buildings burned and the Indians finally rode away.

What Hall could not have known was that his friend William Morris would be killed and scalped, or that Sarah Morris and her children would be taken captive.

Meanwhile, with unbelievable self-determination, Gus Hall spent the next seventeen hours painfully crawling down the frozen South Platte river. It was nearly noon on the following day when Hall finally reached Wisconsin Ranch, just two miles upriver from the American Ranch. As he managed to drag himself over the river bank, he wasn't surprised to see the barn and stables burned to the ground. Hall eventually made his way to one of the outbuildings where he could gain shelter from the freezing temperatures and finally rest. What Hall didn't know was that Godfrey and his family had survived.

Holan Godfrey's ranch on the south side of the river was nearly a fortress, specifically designed against Indian attacks. A six-foot-tall adobe wall surrounded the property. Godfrey fortified his defense with an ample supply of food and ammunition. It was very early on the morning of January 15, 1864, when Godfrey noticed the Indians approaching at a fast pace from the southeast. Godfrey immediately sounded the alarm. Ranch hands, with guns and ammunition, ran to the portholes in the adobe walls. Godfrey's wife, Matilda, and their daughters, Celia and Martha, were ushered to safe quarters.

The Indians, both Cheyenne and Sioux, made several attempts to attack the ranch, but were stopped by rapid gunfire. Then the Indians switched tactics. They ran the livestock away from the ranch and set fire to the haystacks. The high winds that day eventually caused a massive blaze of fire that reached the stables and barn. Matilda and the girls worked a bucket brigade of sorts. With Matilda drawing bucket after bucket of water from the well, the girls would then drench roofs of the buildings inside the fortress. This routine went on the entire day. Occasionally, Godfrey managed to sneak out of the fortress when the smoke could conceal him and throw a bucket of water on the ground in an effort to create a fire break. A few Indian braves rode close enough to fire flaming arrows into the roofs of the buildings. When Godfrey killed two of them, the braves retreated. Godfrey then held watch from the rooftop, while Matilda and the girls ran the water buckets up a ladder, where Godfrey then dumped the water all over the rooftop. When night fell, the attack stopped.[23]

Later that night, when all felt it was safe, Eli Perkins left the fort for help. He followed the South Platte River Road west, passing the burned-out Beaver Creek Station, finally reaching the Junction Stage Station, an approximate thirty mile ride. The station master sent an alert by wire to Denver at 11 p.m. that night. The *Rocky Mountain News* printed it the following day:

> "Received from the Junction January 15, 11:00 P.M.
> The American Ranch is burnt to the ground by Indians. About 100 made attack there yesterday morning. Inmates all destroyed. Valley Station burnt and Wisconsin [Station] probably destroyed. A messenger just got here after help. The Indians attacked Godfrey's ranch, two miles this side of the American, and are fighting there now. Messenger got away and is here after help now. Probably where line is down.
>
> I have my horse at door and will start down immediately and get line o.k. as soon as possible. All people in ranches attacked were killed." [24]

This report was not entirely true. As the same morning that the American Ranch was being attacked, another band of Cheyenne raided the Wisconsin Ranch, approximately fifteen miles downstream, on the south side of the South Platte River. The owners of the ranch, brothers, twenty-two-year-old John F., and thirty-three-year-old, Mark M. Coad survived. In fact, John was away in Nebraska Territory at the time of the attack. Mark Coad later recounted the event:

> "Between ten and eleven o'clock in the morning the Indians made an attack on the ranch...About twenty-five or thirty Indians made a dash on the ranch. They were mounted and had guns, bows and arrows, tomahawks and spears with them. Mr. Danielson [Coad's brother-in-law] saw the Indians and ran into the dwelling house from the store to get his wife and children. I was standing at the door and trying to get the horse into the store but the Indians commenced hallowing at me. I could not get the horse in so I let him go and went to the counter to get a gun. The horse ran down to the stable and one or two of the Indians ran after him. They kept shooting at us all the time and we returned the fire until

they fell back. By this time Danielson got into the store with his wife and children. The Indians were all the time firing at him but shot over his head...There were seven Indians coming from the west and seven from the east, all on foot. They were still firing at us and we at them until they came too thick. We kept them away from the corrals and stables all this time...We were skirmishing back and forth for about an hour and a half, when we fell back to the store house and they jumped into the hay corrals and set fire to them...The smoke blew across to the store house and all the time they kept shooting at us but on account of the smoke they could not distinguish where we were...The Indians kept reinforcing all the time. Another crowd had captured the American Ranch about this time and destroyed it.

Toward evening, I think it was about four or five o'clock, they got armfulls [sic] of wood and hay and came around to the back door of the store to set it on fire...We had a string of wagons around the yard forty or fifty steps from the store in a half circle. We had the doors and windows piled up with flour and corn to keep the bullets from getting through. The Indians would shoot at the doors and windows but with the sacks of grain and flour and other stuff which were piled up in front of them the bullets could not come through to us.

There was an old stove by the side of the store and an Indian there was trying to light a fire with some hay which he had in his hand. I saw the Indian and shot him with my gun. I then threw the gun back into the house and took two pistols and rushed among the Indians. The Indian who I first shot, who was lighting the match on the stove, fell. The Indians were all naked except their breech clouts. One Indian had a tomahawk with him. I shot him through the breast and I wounded the other one. They shot at me but shot over my head. I jumped in through the back door but kept on my hands and knees. When I went through the door they fired a volley of bullets into the door. Danielson stood inside the door with an ax ready to assist me if I needed him. That was our plan. That was pretty near the winding up of the fight." [25]

    As the Indian raids continued along the South Platte River corridor, Valley Station operator sent an urgent telegraph dated January 17, 1865:

"The telegraph operator from Junction Station arrived here this morning. He had an escort part of the way. He came the last twenty-two miles alone, and in the night. He found two wounded men at a ranch five miles *west of this place.* [Wisconsin Ranch] *An escort was sent from here, which brought the wounded men in. He found the American Ranch, 17 miles west of here, again on fire, and seven bodies burned to the cinders, among them two children and one woman. A large number of Indians were along the road. Signal fires are burning at night in every direction. It is expected the Indians will butcher every person on the road unless speedy assistance is sent us."* [26]

Eli Perkins accompanied by a troop of soldiers soon came down the South Platte River Road. All along the way, they witnessed death and destruction. The travel stations were burned, the hay stacks still smoldering. Reaching Godfrey's fortress, the men counted seventeen dead Indians outside the adobe walls. Otherwise, Godfrey's place stood, virtually intact. It was the only ranch along the river that had withstood the raids on the South Platte River.

A relieved Holon Godfrey greeted the soldiers.

The Indians, frustrated they were unable to penetrate the fortress, called it "Old Fort Wicked." When Godfrey heard of this, he erected a large wooden board over the entrance with the words, "Old Fort Wicked," the name it was forever known as.

That same day, a wagon train from Denver, bound for Omaha, stopped periodically as they passed the ruins of the ranches, searching for survivors. Miraculously, one member of the party found Gus Hall, barely alive. Watson S. Coburn later recounted:

"While one of the party was looking around he discovered Hall curled up in a corner and holloed to the rest, 'Here is a dead man.' This aroused Hall and he said, 'I am not dead yet, but I think I will be before long.'" [27]

The teamsters continued on to Omaha, taking the near-death Gus Hall with them. Doctors in Omaha amputated Hall's leg, but saved his life.

A few days later, as the soldiers continued down river, they discovered more dead bodies, including both white men and Indians. At the ruins of American Ranch, the bodies of three white men and two Indians were discovered. William's Morris' body would later be found on April 14, 1865. His body, with seventeen arrow wounds, was found on an island in the river. The *Rocky Mountain News* reported the finding in the April 14, 1865 issue under the headline, "Body Found."

Despite the increase of soldiers along the South Platte

Road, the Indian attacks continued. The operator at Valley Station sent a wire to Denver dated January 20, 1865:

"Big train from Denver arrived. 105 wagons. 300 men. Our scouts have run out Indians three times between Junction and here. They fired on our pickets last night, no one hurt. Two dead Indians and three white men found at American."

While the Indian rage and revenge continued with murderous raids along the South Platte River, there was good news to be had further north on the Platte River in Dakota Territory. Joseph Bissonette operated the Deer Creek Station, approximately twenty miles east of Platte Bridge, at the site of present-day Casper, Wyoming. In December 1865, a group of Indians came into his station with news that a band of Cheyenne had a female captive, held by Medicine Arrow, and that they were willing to trade for a variety of goods and provisions. Bissonette learned that the female captive was Nancy Jane Morton, captured on Plum Creek in Nebraska Territory the previous August. He immediately sent a telegraph communique to Major John Woods at Fort Laramie, alerting him of the news. Major Woods replied, giving his consent to Bissonette to pursue the trading negotiations.

Bissonette collected a wagon load of supplies. He then sent his half-white, half-Indian son, Joseph Bissonette Jr., and a local trader, Jules Coffey, with the wagon to trade with the Cheyenne, camped along the Powder River. Apparently the Indians had a change of heart as a few of the warriors chased them away from their village. Shorty after this incident, Medicine Arrow indicated he would trade Mrs. Morton, but his demands for provisions had doubled. Once again Bissonette loaded his wagon with blankets, guns, gun powder and knives. A supply of food included sacks of coffee, corn, flour, rice, and sugar. Bissonette and three hired men took the wagon load as well as four horses for trade, to the Cheyenne camp, now in the Big Horn Mountains of Wyoming Territory. Medicine Arrow and the Cheyenne Indians accepted the goods as well as the added horses and released Nancy Jane Morton from captivity.

After four days of travel in the freezing temperatures and frozen ground, the rescue party arrived at Bissonette's Deer Creek Station. There, Nancy Jane Morton spent the night in a warm bed with a solid roof over her head, the first time since that fateful day of August 8, 1865, in Nebraska Territory.

The following morning, Bissonette and his men loaded Mrs. Morton into the wagon, covered with warm blankets, and continued on toward Fort Laramie. That evening they stopped at Horseshoe Station where they spent the night. Nancy Morton fearfully noticed the few Indian tipis near the station. As the wagon passed, she recognized Big Crow, who had captured her at Plum Creek and abused her brutally during the first days of captivity. Although safe with her benefactors nearby, Nancy didn't sleep as well that night. She was much relieved the following morning when a group of soldiers arrived to escort the rescue party to Fort Laramie. The group finally delivered Nancy Jane Morton to the military safety of Fort Laramie on January 30, 1865.[28]

At Fort Laramie, Lieutenant Jeremiah Triggs, commander of Company D, 7th Iowa Cavalry, conducted a lengthy interview with Mrs. Morton, who described much of what she had been through during her nearly six months of captivity. She also told of seeing her captor, Big Crow, along her journey to the fort. Major Thomas Mackey investigated Mrs. Morton's assertion and ordered the arrest of Big Crow. Soldiers brought the Cheyenne into the fort shackled in chains, where he remained behind bars for several months.

As Nancy Morton rested and gained her strength, she was befriended by another female captive, Sarah L. Larimer. She had also been abducted, by the Sioux, in 1864, but managed to escape after two days of captivity. For whatever reason, she was still at Fort Laramie when Nancy arrived. The two women, sharing a common bond, often confided with one another. Nancy told Sarah of her many ordeals, including the caring for and then losing the young girl the Indians gave her. Sarah Larimer later wrote of Nancy's experience:

> *"She was an intelligent little creature, but alas! Could not understand that her only safety lay in obedience. The child cried continuously for her mother, frequently declaring she knew the Indians were going to kill her. The savages admired the little girl, and evidently intended to take her to their village, but at length, weary of her continual fretting, a council was held to decide her fate. It was decided that she was unprofitable, and, at the close of the council, the child was placed a little apart from the others. 'I believe you are going to kill me,' she cried, as she held her little trembling hands imploring toward her companion in bondage. At this instant a deadly arrow pierced her heart, and she lay dead.*
> *The savages evidently were sorry for what they had done, though conceiving it their duty, and laid her to rest with all honors due to a beloved one of their own tribe."* [28]

When the time came for Nancy Morton to return to her family in Sidney, Iowa, friends and soldiers at Fort Laramie gave her a "going away" party of sorts. As folks gathered around the parade ground, the fort's regimental band played "Home Sweet Home." Then a group of well wishers presented her with a purse of nearly fifteen hundred dollars, collected from many folks at the military post. The wagon train, with a military escort, left the fort on Monday morning, February 26, 1865.

As the wagon train crossed Plum Creek in Nebraska Territory, the driver halted near the site where Morton's husband, brother and cousin were killed on that horrific day of slaughter and where Nancy Morton was captured. She got out of the wagon and walked the area alone, in quiet reflection. When she found the mound of dirt that covered the single grave of her loved ones, she was overcome with grief. She later wrote:

> *"Terrible were the scenes that passed through my mind, as the sight of the savages as they came upon us that morning, came fresh to my memory and were truly appalling. No one only those who have had a personal experience can realize the thoughts that fired my brain, and oppressed my heart, as my memory led back to the sight of the ghastly corpses about me, and the savages with blackened faces, and fierce and uncouth gestures, which seemed to me is to be a never-to-be-forgotten scene. As I know [sic] look back upon that horrifying morn, I wonder that I ever survived, and as I turned to leave the graves of those so dear to me the picture of that fatal morning came repeatedly before me not as a picture in memory but as a present reality."* [29]

Nancy Morton arrived safely at her father's home in Sidney, Iowa on March 19, 1865. She would eventually remarry and live a long life. Years later, Nancy Jane Morton Stevens wrote her memoir of the atrocities she suffered during her captivity.

It is quite interesting to note that on two occasions Morton recounted that she and Lucinda Eubanks were also in the same Cheyenne camp when the warriors came for Laura Roper, Daniel Marble, Ambrose Asher and little Isabelle Eubanks. They were the four hostages that Black Kettle relinquished to Wynkoop the previous September. Of the incident, Morton said the Indians "ordered Mrs. Eubanks and I to the ground with buffalo robes thrown over us so we would not be noticed. And warriors stood near us with bows and arrows drawn ready to murder us if we should make one faint murmur [sic]." [30] As there were no white men in the village, who were the warriors hiding the women from? Could it have been Black Kettle? Black Kettle told Wynkoop he would need time to find out which camp held the remaining hostages he had promised. If this was true, and indeed Black Kettle did not know they were in his village, it clearly showed how much power he had lost with the Dog Soldiers.

The South Platte River, one of Colorado's most important waterways, was used by both settlers and Indians. *DPL*

Meanwhile in Colorado Territory, during this same time period the Cheyenne village moved to a popular camping site at White Butte Creek, near Summit Springs. It would be the campsite from which several of the Cheyenne Dog Soldiers would launch further raids in northeast Colorado. Four years later it would also be the site of a major confrontation known as the Battle of Summit Springs.

On January 26, a missive was sent from Fort Leavenworth to Colonel Moonlight with orders to burn the entire prairie south of the South Platte River from Fort Kearney, Nebraska Territory, west to Denver. This was in an effort to deter the Indians and their ruthless attacks on innocent settlers. In any case, that evening, officers stationed at the different stations along the South Platte River sent out detachments who set fire to the grasslands south of the river, from Fort Kearney to Denver, some three hundred miles along the river. However, there seems to be much evidence that the burning did not have much effect, despite the winds, nor did it dissuade the Indians. George Bent relayed the following observation:

> "Although I was south of the Platte at the time and right in the way of such a fire, I did not see a sign of it, and never saw an Indian who knew anything about such a fire. Meantime, while the General was amusing

his troops with the ten thousand-square miles of prairie fire, we were on our way to clean out the stage line, and this time we did the work thoroughly." [31]

True to his word, George Bent and the Cheyenne Dog Soldiers did just that. Bent continued:

"I think it was January 26 or 27 when we broke camp on the White Butte Creek and started north. The main village with the women and children struck about due north so as to reach the South Platte some miles west of Julesburg, but a large part of the warriors formed themselves into war parties with the purpose of striking the Platte Road simultaneously both east and west of Julesburg. I went with the Cheyennes who intended to strike high up the South Platte, about midway between Julesburg and Denver; the Sioux struck east of Julesburg, and the Northern Arapaho in between the Sioux and Cheyenne." [32]

Evidently the United States Army was watching the movements of the Indians. And according to the following report sent by Brigadier General R. H. Mitchell to Major General Samuel Curtis, the Indians were watching the soldiers. The report was reprinted in the *Leavenworth Times* issue dated January 27, 1865:

"Fort Kearney, Jan. 20, 1865
To Major General Curtis:
Arrived here last night. Have been up nearly to the Arickard [sic] fork of the Republican, east to your trail, and thence where the Indians were frightened away by Col. Chivington's affair. Their main trail is westward along the Republican, and over one hundred smaller ones fall into it from the south. I don't know, as yet, where they crossed the Platte, but one [Indian] told me they passed to the northeast, about twenty miles west of Julesburg.

There is still a rear guard of Indians watching us, about Julesburg. The weather was very severe, but we met with no accidents. The men and horses are in fine condition. There is no game in the country traversed. The overland stages shall run through, and we will protect them.
R. H. Mitchell
Brigadier General"

Both George and Charlie Bent rode with the Cheyenne Dog Soldiers as they continued their raids along the South Platte River Road. George Bent later wrote:

"I did not see a tenth of the things that happened along the South Platte during those stirring days, but I saw many strange things. At night the whole valley was lighted up with flames of burning ranches and stage stations, but these places were soon all destroyed and darkness fell on the valley. Our big village strung along the north bank of the river for some distance, the Cheyennes, Sioux, and Northern Arapahos camped separately, but all the camps near together. In every camp the fires were burned all night, and until daylight feasting and dancing and drumming went on. I remember that when I was out with raiding parties at night, we used to halt and look for the campfires to tell which way the village lay, and when we could not see the fires we would listen for the drums. On a still night you could hear them for miles and miles along the valley." [33]

The Cheyenne Dog Soldiers then crossed the river and headed north where they attacked Harlow's Ranch, just south of the river and east of the present town of Crook. William H. Harlow and his wife, having learned of the Indian raids in the area, left with a neighbor, Hiram Davis, for safety at Mrs. Harlow's father's ranch. Following the river upstream, the group saw a few Indians along the way and decided to return to Harlow's Ranch. The following day the Harlows left with Davis and his partner, John Hiteman, for Julesburg, where they arrived safely at Julesburg Station. The next day William Harlow returned to his ranch to collect a wagon load of valuable possessions.

As dawn broke on the morning of January 29, 1865, Harlow prepared to return to Julesburg. Suddenly, Indians appeared and circled the ranch, running off his stock. Harlow, along with three others, defended the ranch from the house. They were soon joined by fourteen freighters who helped defend the property. By placing their wagons around the ranch house, the freighters were able to keep the Indians away from the house. Nevertheless, the Indians managed to set fire to the stables, the wood yard and the hay stacks. With the fire and heavy smoke, they attempted to reach the house, but were unsuccessful. The fighting lasted until nearly nightfall. The Indians retreated as the sun set on that frightful day. Harlow later ventured out of his home, finding four dead Indians.

It was one of those late nights Bent spoke about when he listened for the drums of the village. He finally arrived at the village and camped on the north side of the river from Harlow's ranch. Bent found that the women had killed and butchered several head of Harlow's cattle and everyone in the village was enjoying the fine meal.

When a group of Cheyenne Dog Soldiers came into the village with the scalps of Cheyenne Indians, the village instantly fell into stunned silence. The warriors told the people of their attack of a small group of soldiers on the South Platte River Road. The warriors easily overtook the group, killing them without hesitation. As they plundered through the dead soldiers saddle bags they found the grisly scalps, two of which were identified as their Cheyenne brothers. A tiny seashell attached to the braided hair of one scalp was identified as that of Little Coyote. The scalp of White Leaf was identified by the unique light shade of hair. [34] Little Coyote and White Leaf had been in camp at Sand Creek; neither men had been seen or heard from since. Enraged, the Cheyenne Dog Soldiers then scalped the dead soldiers, split open their chests, ripped out their hearts and mutilated the bodies. A new sense of revenge gripped the village.

They would ride both sides of the river with rage and raid everything in sight.

As Harlow defended his ranch against the raiding Indians, another group of Indians were making their way toward Julesburg Station and Camp Rankin, their intent being a second attack on the settlement. This time, they would succeed in burning the station to the ground.

On the morning of January 28, 1865, Captain Nicholas J. O'Brien, who had returned to Fort McPherson, Nebraska Territory, received a telegraph from Camp Rankin, detailing the Indian raids along the South Platte River from Julesburg west to Valley Station. As the depredations were continuing, causing the closing of the South Platte River Road, O'Brien was ordered to return to Camp Rankin. He left Fort McPherson with Lieutenant Eugene Ware, who served under O'Brien with Company F of the Seventh Iowa Cavalry. Incredibly, the two officers took with them only five soldiers, but did include a mountain howitzer. On January 31, the soldiers arrived at Alkali Stage Station, where they were met by Captain John Murphy and Captain H. W. Cremer, also of the Seventh Iowa Cavalry, and nearly three hundred soldiers under his command. The following morning the two groups of soldiers set out west toward Camp Rankin, leaving six soldiers behind at Alkali Station.

The same day the soldiers were making their west from Alkali Station toward Camp Rankin, George Bent's group of Cheyenne Dog Soldiers were moving east toward the same destination. Along the way, they attacked the ranch of Lewis B.

Gillette, nearly ten miles west of Julesburg and Camp Rankin. They set fire to all the buildings, including the ranch house, barn, stables and outbuildings. Fortunately, Gillette was uninjured. Captain O'Brien later recounted:

> *"The Indians had approached Julesburg from the south and west, attacking Gillette's ranch ten miles west of the fort, the evening before. A group of plainsmen and others had gathered there for protection and put up a stubborn fight. During the night they had escaped and made a dash for the river in an attempt to reach the fort. The river was ice-covered, with many small islands on which bunches of willows grew. These afforded slight shelter to cover their retreat but they reached the post about daybreak."* [35]

On the morning of January 30, Jim and Charlie Moore's Washington Ranch station was again attacked by Indians. The telegraph operator at Valley Station wired the news to Denver:

> *"Jim Moore badly wounded in neck. Ten soldiers saved ranch. One hundred head of cattle run off."* [36]

Famed Pony Express rider, Jim Moore, would carry a bullet near his jugular vein for the rest of his life.

Meanwhile, the group of soldiers moving west reached Richard Cleave's Big Springs Station in Nebraska Territory, approximately seventeen miles east of Camp Rankin, on February 2, 1865. Cleave, also a former rider for the Pony Express, had opened his own stage station along the old trail shortly after the demise of the famed express enterprise in October 1861.

Incredibly, on that early morning, a large plume of dark smoke rose from the west. Although some distance away, the soldiers and Cleave surmised it was at the vicinity of Camp Rankin and the Julesburg settlement. They would be proven correct.

The Indians had cautiously approached the vicinity of the Julesburg Station and Camp Rankin. As the warriors descended on the unsuspecting settlement, they split their nearly one thousand warriors into three groups, nearly surrounding the area. Lieutenant John Brewer, in temporary command of the military post, had less then fifty soldiers to defend the fort. As such, they realized the futility of an attempt to defend the Julesburg settlement. As the Indian raid continued, Brewer managed to fire cannons from the howitzer at the fort in the direction of the approaching Indians.

While it may have deterred an Indian attack at times, it did not stop the burning of Julesburg.

The Indians took their time burning the town. They set the buildings on fire, one at a time, waiting for one building to be fully engulfed in flame, before torching the next one. This routine was repeated until every building in the small settlement was blazing with plumes of smoke rising in the windblown prairie.

George Bent was with the Cheyenne Dog Soldiers as they burned the town and taunted the soldiers at Camp Rankin:

> *"When the village left the South Platte and started north a big war party, Sioux, Cheyennes, and Arapahos, left the village and started down the river to finish up Julesburg. I went with the party and again the Indians tried the old trick of luring the soldiers out of their stockade by hiding the warriors among the hills and sending out a small party to tempt the soldiers out; but the troops this time were on their guard and would not stir outside their defenses, so after waiting among the sand hills for some time, our whole body charged out and raced across the flats to the stockade. Here we saw the fresh graves of the soldiers who had been killed in our first attack on Julesburg, and I counted eighteen graves in all.*
>
> *The Indians circled around the stockade, yelling and shooting and taunting the soldiers, to get them to come out and fight; but it was no use, so after a while we withdrew east to the stage station. Here, the warriors, about six hundred strong, broke into the store and stage company warehouse, and completely plundered both. In the hope of drawing the soldiers out, as soon as they had plundered the buildings, the Indians set fire to them, one by one, burning the stage station, telegraph office, store, warehouse, stables, etc., each separately. But no one came out. The great column of smoke floated up in the air, and it could be seen for twenty miles along the valley."* [37]

Meanwhile, as O'Brien and the soldiers prepared to move west, Cleave and his wife, fearing for their safety, elected to accompany the soldiers to Camp Rankin. A stage coach with five passengers followed closely behind. Leaving the station, Richard Cleave's decision proved to be a correct one, as he watched a band of Indians surround his cattle and begin to herd them north.

It was nearly noon when the soldiers reached an area known as Devil's Dive, a deep, rugged wash of rock, sand and sagebrush, that was a perilous stretch of road for the stage lines. The area was approximately three miles east of Camp Rankin and the Julesburg settlement. Captain O'Brien later described his first sight of the burning of Julesburg:

"From the summit of the hill above Devil's Dive, where the main part of the first battle was fought, I could see smoke rising above the intervening rise of land and I moved cautiously across to where I could see through my field glasses that the stage station was burning, causing the column of smoke we had observed. Indians covered the area in all directions, circling their horses around the station and other burning buildings at close range. They were circling the fort also, but at a much wider range, remembering their first experience with howitzers in the stockade. Apparently, the main body of Indians was not aware of our coming [as] the wind was blowing from the northwest and driving a pall of smoke from the burning buildings in our direction. The weather was also hazy, which was favorable to our chances." [38]

Captain O'Brien then placed the soldiers in a column advance formation, with the stagecoach, driven by Andrew Hughes, following behind and other soldiers protecting it. Captain O'Brien continued his description of the events that day:

"'Andy,' I told young Hughes, 'we probably won't live through this, but I want to sell our lives as dearly as possible.' 'Go ahead, Captain, I'm ready to sell,' was his short but emphatic reply.

We also determined on a strategy to try and bluff the Indians, and lead them to believe that we were the advance guard of a heavy body of cavalry. The smoke, the haze, and the lay of the land favored this pretense.
The first mile was made at an easy gait until we came into full view of the warriors around the blazing structures in the village. Many must have noticed our party about the same time, but they were busily engaged in carrying off sacks of corn and flour, loading their ponies with foodstuffs to send across the river on a sanded strip of ice.

Drawing closer, the howitzer was fired at the Indians gathering ahead of us, and they drew back from the gun, opening the way temporarily - and through the cleared channel sped our brave band, shooting, and beckoning on the phantom army - which we hoped to make the raiders believe was in close pursuit." [39]

However, Captain O'Brien and his soldiers were still a good mile away from the settlement and the fort. O'Brien ordered his men to continue the advance with sabers drawn in the ready. As a group of Indians attempted to halt the advance, Lieutenant Brewer, still entrenched inside the military post, saw the soldiers approaching and the Indian confrontation. Brewer prudently brought out a howitzer from the fort and fired shells at the Indians. Alerted to the firing, O'Brien ordered shells fired from his howitzer, thus the Indians were caught in a crossfire.

O'Brien related the result of the strategy:

"The post continued firing to keep the path clear. The Indians did not understand the situation. Our appearance had been too sudden and unexpected - they could not know it was a bluff. They could not tell what was coming behind or what the smoke concealed. They did not dare to charge, so hovered on our flanks, disconcerted by the wildly dashing horses and coach as we moved at full speed toward the post and safety. Andrew Hughes and his companion, Supt. Clift - Division Manager of the stage line, kept up in fine style with the prossession. They kept the horses on the run, yelled as much and fired as often as they could. They kept the stage right side up over the rough ground and seemed filled with hilarity. It was a royal bluff with our lives at stake and we were at all relieved and grateful to be spared.

Not one in the party was injured! The marauders, like a hive of disturbed bees, showed great alarm and were galloping around the fort." [40]

The soldiers at the fort were also relieved that help had arrived. There were less than fifty, many of whom had been wounded during the Indian raid on January 7. They had been holding the Indians at bay since nearly noon, but as the Indians grew in numbers, the soldiers feared they would not be able to fend off an all-out attack. Now with reinforcements, Captain O'Brien issued a series of orders to fortify the military post against an attack during the night. Soldiers were placed atop the wall of the garrison for greater observation. O'Brien, along with Lieutenant Ware, then climbed the walls, placing barrels of water on the edges of the walls in an effort to extinguish any fire arrows the Indians might send toward the fort.

Meanwhile, the Indians had left the area, camping on the north of the river bank. George Bent recounted the aftermath:

"After plundering and burning Julesburg, the Indians broke up into three parties; the largest part camped on the north bank of the river with all the plunder that night, holding scalp dances around the fires, in plain sight of the soldiers at Camp Rankin." [41]

Lieutenant Eugene Ware offered his vivid account of the Indian campfire scene just across the river from the fort:

"As the huge campfire blazed up higher and brighter in the the Indian camp we could see cattle being driven in from the east and the west - also bands of American horses prancing about. More and more Indians joined in the war dances and the tum-tum of the native drums sounded across the river in a rhythmic beat. We would hear the yells, then a chorus of shouting, as though the squaws had joined in the excitement. Braves were circling the fires, stamping the ground - then raising their hands in gestures toward the sky." [42]

The news of the Indians burning Julesburg swiftly reached the media at Fort Leavenworth. The *Leavenworth Times* printed Brigadier General Robert Mitchell's report to General Samuel Curtis in the February 5, 1865 issue:

"Omaha, Feb. 3, 1865
To Major General Curtis:
Col. Livingston reports the burning of the stage station at Julesburg. Captain O'Brien and his company with two mountain howitzers, were driven into their works. He says that no one company can do more than hold the garrison against such numbers of Indians. Our forces cannot give protection to coaches or travelers on the route unless we abandon the garrisons and unite the forces, and establish a regular system of escorting trains through the mountains. Our supply posts must be kept up. If we adopt this course the country will be kept a barren waste. On the other hand, if I can be supplied with 2,000 additional men and supplies, in thirty days I will be able to put an end to all these Indian outrages in this district.

At the lowest estimate, there was at Julesburg fifteen hundred Indians; there was at the same time a large force threatening Alkali, fifty miles this side of Julesburg. Colonel Livingston is between the two places with all the spare men he has in his Sub-District, and will do the very best that can be done.
R. H. Mitchell,
Brigadier General"

The *Leavenworth Times* ran the following editorial in the same issue:

"What we said yesterday, we need not repeat today. Gen. Mitchell's report of today confirms, not only our views, but our worst anticipations. Now what can be done?

The trade of the Plains is the life of our cities. That sustains, in part, Atchison and Leavenworth. The present population of the State would neither give them the business they have, nor sustain the people who inhabit them. Let them lose this trade for a year and they would suffer, suffer severely, as would the whole State.

We ask, again, what is to be done?

The answer is more troops. They must be had. We should have them. Let us all unite, press upon Gen. Pope, press upon the War Department and demand more troops, - troops enough to protect our trade and defend the frontier."

It was late in the night of that fateful day of February 2, 1865, that a group of soldiers and citizens felt safe enough to venture out of the fort. Their actions were later described in an account printed in the February 27, 1865 issue of the *Telegrapher*:

"At midnight a pole was erected, topped by a tattered American flag, with an Indian arrow pointed west and a paper buried at the foot of it. The paper was signed by all within the walls of the post. It bore the following words:

'This pole is erected by Philo Holcomb and S. R. Smith, operators for the Pacific Telegraph Line, and Joel F. Wisely, Surgeon, U.S. Army -twenty-six days after the bloody conflict of January 7, 1865, between 1200 Cheyenne warriors and forty brave boys of the 7th Iowa Cavalry under command of Capt. N. J. O'Brien. On this afternoon, the lives of fifteen soldiers and five citizens were lost during this terrible raid, and their remains interred nearby.

With a fervent prayer for the success of the Union cause, and shouts for victory to our arms - we raise this humble memorial, high in the free air. 'Fearing that they would not live to see another day,' these courageous men were determined that the heroic actions of their fallen comrades should not go unrecorded."

The military officers, safely ensconced behind the walls of Fort Leavenworth, were quick to respond in the aftermath of the burning of Julesburg, perhaps due to the media outcry. Less than a week after the destruction in Colorado Territory, the *Leavenworth Times* ran the following notice, dated February 7, 1865:

"RESOLUTIONS"

"The resolutions passed by the Legislature of Kansas, in favor of more vigorous measures by the War Department, for the protection of emigrants and settlers on the routes from the State to Idaho, Colorado and New Mexico, against Indian incursions and depredations, last week, was laid before the Senate by Mr. Pomeroy, and referred to the Committee on Indian Affairs."

The Cheyenne Dog Soldiers, including the Bent brothers, followed the Sioux up Lodge Pole Creek for more raiding, bent on revenge. However, a few bands of warriors remained to wreak further havoc along the South Platte River Road.

On the morning of February 4, 1865, a large wagon train, eighteen wagons and two coaches, escorted by Colonel George L. Shoup and fifty soldiers, arrived at the burned-out American Ranch. One of the passengers, Halie Riley Hodder, wrote in her diary of seeing her first Indian. "He was burned to a cinder," she wrote. Later that afternoon, the wagon train arrived at Valley Station. There, they were warned of the Indians raiding downstream along the river. The soldiers and teamsters elected to push on, arriving at Moore's Washington Ranch station, a few miles downstream. There they found the badly injured Jim Moore. Halie Riley Hodder wrote of seeing Moore in her diary as:

"the most terrible sight I have ever seen with his head swelled almost to the width of his shoulders. Why he didn't die, I can't say." [43]

By February, the telegraph lines were still down in many areas along the South Platte River Road. William N. Byers, owner of the *Rocky Mountain News*, outraged at the lack of protection and deaths of citizens, wrote a scathing editorial, under the headline, "How It Looks To Us," demanding military protection:

"For weeks and months our mails have been interrupted and our commerce destroyed or cut off. The road is marked with the new-made

graves of our citizens. Provisions are at starvation prices. Millions of dollars have been lost, directly and indirectly, to our Territory and the future is still uncertain. Yet not a hand has been raised to give us relief, beyond a few scattered detachments of soldiers usually stationed along the lower road. The Arkansas route is solely and directly beneficial to Kansas; hence it receives protection. The Platte route divides its benefits, hence it is left to fate. More commerce, more money, more mails, more property and more people pass over the Platte route in a week - ordinarily - except New Mexico and Arizona - are dependent upon it for their mails. Three Territories, and a portion of two others, receive all their merchandise and machinery, and a great share of their provisions over it. All the Great West is dependent upon its telegraph line. We want troops...from wherever they can be spared. We want them on the Platte route to protect it." [44]

George Bent headed west with a group of the Cheyenne Dog Soldiers. After a few miles upriver of the South Platte, Bent observed a company of soldiers riding east along the opposite side of the river. As the soldiers came into better view, Bent noticed they were members of the 7th Iowa Cavalry. Evidently they had noticed Bent as well, when suddenly, one of the officers rode toward the bank of the river, pulled his rifle, and fired at Bent. Although the officer missed, Bent was enraged. He boldly rode alone to the river bank and pulled his two pistols. Knowing he was out of range, he wildly fired the guns in the officer's direction, the bullets primarily landing on the ice of the frozen river. So angry was Bent that as he fired his pistols, he let loose a flurry of foul language directed toward the officer. With that, he calmly turned his horse around, and rode back to his people.

It was later revealed that the officer was Captain Eugene Ware, who wrote of the experience:

"He [Bent] began to fire a lot of good American words at me, and they were shot in such good English that I became satisfied that the Indian was not a Cheyenne or a Sioux." [45]

The military resolutions passed by the Legislature of Kansas were quickly put in place. The new commanding officer of the South Platte River area was Brigadier General Patrick E. Connor. Under his command, two companies of one hundred men each were sent to reinforce the military forts along the South Platte River Road. The site of Camp Tyler, located midway between

Denver and Julesburg, on the south side of the river, was fortified with new buildings and strategic overlooks. The new military post was renamed Camp Wardwell, with Captain Thomas Kenny as commander. R. O. Woodward, who was stationed at the newly fortified military post, later described the facility:

> *"We found a lot of adobe buildings nicely plastered inside with mud mixed near the river. They just used alkali water in preparing the mortar and when dry the plastering was nice and white. The quarters were certainly good."* [46]

General Connor also sent several troops, comprised of twelve men each, to guard stations at ten mile intervals along the South Platte River Road. As the soldiers traveled to their various military stations, the dead, both Indians and white men, naked and mutilated, lay rotting on the lonely prairie for miles. As if this evidence of death and destruction were not enough, at Godfrey's ranch, the soldiers learned that Sarah Morris and her two young sons, Charles and Joseph, were missing and presumed abducted by Indians.

With visual evidence of the horrible devastation along the river, and news of an abduction, the soldiers stationed along the South Platte River Road took their duties very seriously. However, in mid-April of 1865, the horribly mutilated bodies of two soldiers were found approximately two miles south of Moore's ranch. They were buried where they fell.

The morale of the soldiers was lifted by the news of the release of another female captive. However, confusion and controversy surround the circumstances of the hostage release. Through the winter of 1864-1865, under the auspice of a peaceful surrender, several bands of the Sioux camped on the north bank of the Platte River, approximately ten miles south of Fort Laramie in Wyoming Territory. Many of these Sioux Indians were responsible for the murderous raids along the Little Blue River in Nebraska Territory the previous summer.

In May of 1865, according to historian George E. Hyde, Black Foot and Two Face, leaders of the Oglala Sioux, came in to Fort Laramie to surrender. To show their sincerity, the two leaders offered to release two of their hostages, Mrs. Lucinda Eubanks and her young son, William Jr., both of whom had been captured during the burning of the Eubanks family home and subsequent brutal murders of most of the Eubanks family members.

Following the release of Lucinda Eubanks and her son, Colonel Thomas Moonlight, commander of the garrison, interviewed Mrs. Eubanks, who recounted her terrible ordeal and the unspeakable brutality she suffered. Enraged, Moonlight ordered the immediate arrest of both Black Foot and Two Face. The two men were accused of brutal mistreatment of Lucinda Eubanks and found guilty. On May 26, 1865, they were escorted outside of the fort where they were hanged. In Lucinda Eubanks' statement, later given at Camp Rankin, it is possible that the two men hung were not the men who had abducted Eubanks and her children.

In an ironic twist of fate, the double hanging occurred on the gallows constructed for the hanging of Big Crow who had horribly mistreated Nancy Jane Morton. General Patrick Connor had sent a telegram to Fort Laramie on April 22, 1865, with orders that Big Crow be hanged and his body to be left hanging from the gallows.[47] The order was carried out on April 24, 1865. Big Crow was led to the gallows with his legs shackled and promptly hanged. In compliance with the General's order, the body of Big Crow was left hanging for nearly a month when Black Foot and Two Face met the same fate.

There were several spectators at the double hanging next to the rotting hanging corpse that day. Harvey Johnson, with an Ohio Cavalry unit, was one of the witnesses. In a letter written a week later, he mentioned the hanging:

> "They [the Indians] *wanted half a bushel of silver and were equally as extravagant in their demands for provisions. The ire of the 'powers that be' at the fort were aroused, (Col. Collins aint in command now) and 'Mr. injen' was swung up, and it didn't cost a cent to get the woman and child. It is 'bad medicine' for an Indian to be hung. They think he never goes to the 'happy hunting ground.*" [48]

Lucinda Eubanks and her son were escorted to Camp Rankin in Colorado Territory, by a company of soldiers, over one hundred (accounts vary), led by 7th Iowa Cavalry Captains William D. Fouts and John Wilcox. The soldiers had a dual mission. While entrusted to deliver the released captives safely to Camp Rankin, they were also escorting a group of some fifteen hundred Sioux Indians to Fort Kearny, Nebraska Territory. The Indians were allowed to keep their guns for shooting wild game along the way, for their meals. After a few days into the journey, on the morning of June 14, a group of Indians lingered behind the soldiers. After a few miles, the soldiers realized that several Indians were missing. Captain Fouts led a group of soldiers back to order the Indians to rejoin the military escort.

Once again, it was a perfectly planned ruse by the Indians. As the returning soldiers came within range, the Indians raised weapons and opened fire on the soldiers. Four of the soldiers were wounded and three were killed, including Captain William D. Fouts. The Indians then made their escape on foot, swimming to safety across the North Platte River.

The now commanding officer, Captain John Wilcox, after sending a dispatch to Fort Laramie regarding the death of the soldiers and the escape of the Indians, pressed his troops on to Camp Rankin without incident. Shortly after her arrival at Camp Rankin, Lucinda Eubanks gave a detailed statement of her horrendous ordeal in captivity. The *Rocky Mountain News* printed the account submitted by Captain E. B. Zabriskie in the September 13, 1865, issue:

> *"Statement of Mrs. Ewbanks, Giving an Account of Her Captivity Among the Indians"* [49]
>
> *"Of Mrs. Ewbanks, giving an account of her captivity among the Indians. She was taken by the Cheyennes, and was one of the prisoners proposed to be given up by Black Kettle, White Antelope and others, in the Council at Denver.*
>
> *Mrs. Lucinda Ewbanks [sic] states that she was born in Pennsylvania; is 24 years of age; she resided on the Little Blue, at or near the Narrows. She says that on the 8th day of August, 1864, the house was attacked, robbed, burned, and herself and two children, with her nephew and Miss Roper, were captured by the Cheyenne Indians. Her eldest child, at the time, was three years old; her youngest was one year old; her nephew was six years old. When taken from her home, was, by the Indians, taken south across the Republican, and west to a creek the name of which she does not remember. Here, for a short time, was their village or camping place. They were traveling all winter. When first taken by the Cheyennes, she was taken to the lodge of an old chief whose name she does [not] recollect.*
>
> *'He forced me, by the most terrible threats and menaces, to yield my person to him. He treated me as his wife. He then traded me to Two Face, a Sioux, who did not treat me as a wife, but forced me to do all menial*

labor done by squaws, and he beat me terribly. Two Face traded me to Black Foot who treated me as his wife, and because I resisted him his squaws abused and ill-used me. Black Foot also beat me unmercifully, and the Indians generally treated me as though I was a dog, on account of my showing so much detestation towards Black Foot. Two Face traded for me again. I then received a little better treatment. I was better treated among the Sioux than the Cheyennes, that is, the Sioux gave me more to eat. When with the Cheyennes, I was often hungry.'

Her purchase from the Cheyennes was made early last Fall, and she remained with them until May, 1865.

Witness: J. H. Triggs, 1st Lt. Comd'g Co. D. 7th Iowa Cavalry
E. B. Zabriskie, Capt. 1st Cav. Nev. Volunteers, Judge Advocate, Dist. of the Plains.
Julesburg, C. T., June 22, 1865."

After a good deal of rest, Lucinda Eubanks was ready to return with her son to her Eubanks relatives on the Little Blue River in Nebraska Territory. However, she was unaware they had all been killed. The soldiers at Camp Rankin were able to pool their money and get passage for her and the boy on a wagon train headed east from the garrison. A few of these dedicated soldiers accompanied the train for added protection.

Lucinda eventually remarried. Following the death of her second husband, she and her son William, who was twenty-five years old, moved to McCune, Kansas. There in 1893, she married for a third time, to Doctor D. F. Atkinson. When the doctor died, after only a few years of marriage, Lucinda was once again a widow. She moved in with her son and his wife, Jennie and their family of eight children, where she remained until her death on April 4, 1913. Later, William Eubank (for some reason he dropped the 's' from the surname) moved his family to Colorado, living for a time in Greeley and Kearsey, before moving to Pierce, Colorado.

During the time of Lucinda Eubanks' release and subsequent statement of events to military officials, dated June 22, there was also news of another release of a female captive.

Sarah Morris, abducted by the Cheyenne at American Ranch, during the Indian raids along the South Platte River, had been released at Fort Rice, Dakota Territory, on June 21, 1865. Colonel Charles Augustus Dimon, commander of the fort, learned from Grass, a Cheyenne, that White White, a Minnecongu traveling with the Cheyenne, was interested in a trade with the soldiers. Dimon learned that White White had traded two horses for a white woman and was now willing to trade her to the soldiers for two horses.

On the morning of June 21, 1865, White White and several Cheyenne Indians appeared at the fort where they were met by Colonel Dimon. As negotiations for the trade commenced, a disturbance from a separate group of Cheyenne occurred. Alarmed, the soldiers stood at the ready. It must have been a dramatic scene as Sarah Morris, filthy dirty, her long black hair in a tangled mess, and dressed in only a buffalo robe, ran with all her might toward toward the soldiers.[50] Sarah Morris was finally safe.

Sarah was taken to the fort hospital where she languished in pain and emotional distress for several weeks. During the raid at her ranch and subsequent capture, she had been shot by five arrows and later stabbed five times. Several whip marks were also evident on her body. A concerned group of soldier's wives stayed with her, giving her clothes and listening as she began to talk of her experiences.

While Sarah lived through the horrendous ordeal, one of her children was taken from her and the other child was murdered. Sarah wept as she told of her young son, Charley, who had barely survived after White White had thrown him him to the ground and stomped on his head. A few weeks later, White White threw the ailing infant into a burlow sack and began to bury him in a shallow grave. Fearing the animals would get him, a hysterical Sarah frantically dug at the soil with her bare hands to cover her lost babe.

She told of the other horrors she went through during the capture:

> "I was living at American Ranch on the Platte River in Colorado at the time of my capture by the Cheyennes. My family consisted of my husband, William Morris, one child, my own, and an adopted one. My child's name was Charley. The adopted on we called Joseph. It was the 10th [15th] of January 1865, the Indians attacked the house where we lived. The party consisted of about one hundred. It was near 10 A.M. We kept a hotel. They set the house and stables afire, and drove us into the pilgrim room. At last the doors of the pilgrim room got in flames, and we had to leave. We ran out towards the river, through the corral, hoping to make our escape. My husband said perhaps we could escape that way. When we got to the corral we found we could not.

He [William Morris] told me to stop, that they would probably take me prisoner, and he possibly might get away. They surrounded him, and killed him and another man as they were running to the river. The Indians stood so thickly about me; I could not see him when he was killed. He had no arms of any kind with him.

My baby, fifteen months old, died about a month ago. The Sioux took Joseph and have him yet. They put me on a pony, and went south about fifty miles. They have been traveling, and I with them most of the time since. At their first camping ground they stayed three or four days, holding their scalp dances. Since they have been moving north. About four days ago they told me they were going to bring me in to the whites, pointing this way, saying 'Sioux, sugar, coffee, heap.' My joy knew no bounds. I certainly know they killed my husband, for they told me there were four men killed at the Ranch and they were all there. At the time of my capture I received five wounds from arrows and six stabs from knives. They also struck me across the head with their whips. My wounds are not entirely healed. The old chief he took me doctored me up and with his medicine, and my wounds partially healed up...He however did not like my little boy. My baby was afraid of him, and would cry. One day he took him by the neck and threw him down, and stamped on him. The child took sick, and died in about three weeks. They wanted to bury him before he was dead. I had hard work to keep them doing it. He sunk away, and I knew he was not entirely dead. After his death they put him in a coffee sack, and laid him in a hole in the ravine, hardly covering him over. I wanted them to dig the grave deeper, but they would not. The chief's name is White White. He is the one that brought me in." [51]

Colonel Dimon later wrote of his experience in the rescue of Sarah Morris, although a somewhat revised version:

"I shall never forget the heart-rending story of a white lady who was captured by them, and passing a living death with them, given to me when she had just been rescued from a fate indescribable and worse than death. On the 21st of June, 1865, White White, leader of a band of Minnecongus, had sent me word that his band wanted to make peace with the whites. Learning that they had a white woman prisoner in their camp, I stipulated that they should give up this woman; they agreed, and the next day the band appeared near the post with a flag indicating peace; we went out to meet them. It seems the woman, not understanding their language, had no knowledge of their intentions. When about two hundred yards from them, a commotion among the Indians was noticed,

and soon a form darted from their midst and flew toward us, with nothing but a buffalo robe girt about her loins, with hair flowing and unkept, with hands extended - this poor woman, flying from the gates of a living hell, with hope long ago left far behind, but now returning so suddenly as to nearly take from her reason, this saved soul threw herself at the feet of my horse, and clinging to the stirrups of the saddle, with streaming eyes, could only say, 'Merciful God! Have you at last heard me? Am I dreaming? God Bless you! God Bless you!'

For many weeks, she lay in our Fort hospital between life and death; her cries during the delirium of her fever were fearful as she seemed to be again going through her terrible sufferings. When reason was restored, she gave me an account of atrocities, that if it were permissible to repeat, you might think possible and probable in some far away wild land of India or Africa, but could NEVER imagine took place in one of our border states or territories. It was learned that this woman's name was Mrs. Wm. Morris, a daughter of Reason Imes, Esq., of Granville, Delaware County, Indiana, a refined educated lady, who had been brought up as an only daughter, amid luxuries and comforts.

She had started with her husband, Mr. William Morris, his brother, a son aged six years, and an infant about one year old, to go to Colorado, there to settle in a new home, with prospects in life before her, and these bright. They were captured by a band of hostile Indians on the 10th [15th] of January, 1865, about one hundred and thirty miles north-east of Denver, Colorado. She was wounded in several places. Her husband was wounded and after tortured, scalped, and murdered, before her eyes; the brother-in-law was killed at the first attack; her son was sold to another band in the second day, and she never saw him again. The fourth day, the Indian possessing her, becoming enraged at the constant crying of her sickly babe, in a passionate moment, took it by its limbs and dashed its brains out on the frozen ground. When opportunity offered, she was sent down to her father in Indiana, who welcomed her as one from the dead." [52]

    While there are a few discrepancies between Dimon's version of events and Sarah's, it is difficult to discern if it was Dimon's dramatic prose, or Sarah's confusion regarding the time frame of events.
    In any case, the soldiers at the various forts along the South Platte River Road were elated that another female victim at the hands of the Indians was freed from their clutches and sent home to the loving protection of her family.

The Cheyenne Dog Soldiers, led by Medicine Water, head chief of the Cheyenne Bowstring Warrior Society, continued to wreak further havoc by raiding the overland stages and destroying some seventy miles of telegraph wire. The route to Denver was crippled. With no travel, communications, or goods coming into Denver, the frontier town became a victim to isolation. As Medicine Water led these raids, his wife, Mo-chi, was by his side. [53]

General Grenville M. Dodge was now charged with keeping the South Platte River Road open for travelers. He was known as "Long Eye" to the Indians because of his ability to see afar through his long "looking glass." During the summer he had received fresh troops from the Sixth United States Infantry Regiment. He stationed Company B at Camp Wardwell, soon to be renamed Fort Morgan, and another group at Camp Rankin, later renamed Fort Sedgwick.

Despite the military reinforcements, there were more Indian raids along the river. On July 6, Colonel Smith reported from Camp Wardwell that a small freighting team had been attacked near Wisconsin Ranch. Later that same month, the Coad brothers lost an entire herd of cattle, stolen by Indians. In August, Elbridge Gerry's place was raided. There, the Indians made off with twenty-one horses. On September 30, a government supply train, led by James H. Temple, was attacked seven miles west of O'Fallon's Bluff, a small settlement, just south of the river, east of the present-day Colorado state line.

During the surprise attack, which occurred in the mid-morning of that day, Temple was instantly killed, and two of his ten men were wounded. One of the men managed to escape and miraculously made his way, on foot, the seven miles to O'Fallon's Bluff, without being discovered by the Indians. There, Captain John Wilcox, in command of a squad of the 7th Iowa Cavalry, immediately dispatched Lieutenants Akin and Parker, with a group of soldiers, to the area described by the teamster. The captain's orders were to fight and defeat the Indians responsible. If the Indians were not found, they were not to pursue, but return to O'Fallon's Bluff. Reaching the site of the attack, the soldiers found no Indians in the area, but did find the two wounded men, still alive, and the body of James Temple. Under the cover of darkness, the soldiers began their return trip east, with the wounded and the dead body, to O'Fallon's Bluff. After traveling some three miles, the men arrived at the station ranch of Lewis Baker, where they were invited to stay the night. The next morning, the soldiers discovered the trail of the Indians, but with such a small force of men, the lieutenants elected to move on to their destination, arriving the following day.

As the summer of 1865 cooled with the autumn winds, so did the Indian raids. The warriors had nearly destroyed every station, ranch and homestead along the river from Julesburg west to Holan Godfrey's Fort Wicked, a distance of some ninety miles. Satisfied with such destruction, most of the Indians moved north into Wyoming Territory and northeast into Nebraska Territory.[54]

The U. S. military reinforced their strong-holds along the river. Camp Rankin, near Julesburg, had been rebuilt. On September 27, 1865, the military post was renamed Fort Sedgwick in honor of Major General John Sedgwick, who commanded Fort Wise prior to the Civil War. He was killed at Virginia at the Spotsylvania fight on May 9, 1864. The new fort was described by General William H. Bisbee as being located "one mile south of the right bank of the South Platte River, opposite a ranch called Julesburg, which was equidistant on the north bank." He described the new military post as "of the customary story-and-a-half and single-story frame and log construction, arranged on four sides of a center parade ground, some acre or two in area." Dallas Williams, a local historian, wrote, "The quarters, if any, were considered unlivable, the food was terrible, pleasures were few and the nearest bath house was the South Platte River."[55]

In October, after months of political intrigue by both the United States government and heads of the various Indian tribes, yet another peace treaty was signed. Colonel Jesse H. Leavenworth, a graduate of West Point, who had served with honor during the Civil War, now served as Indian agent for the Apaches, Comanches and Kiowas. Since February, Leavenworth had been working toward a peace council with the Indians. He had asked the chiefs of the three tribes to remain peaceful and meet for a peace council along the Arkansas River. Meanwhile, Colonel James H. Ford, commanding the troops along the Arkansas River, was preparing his troops to attack the Indians camped along the Cimarron River. Leavenworth appealed to Colonel Ford, who agreed to halt his military strike.

President Andrew Johnson agreed with Leavenworth's efforts. He appointed Major Generals William S. Harney and John Pope along with John B. Sanborn, as well as Secretary of Interior, James Harlan, to assist Leavenworth. William Bent and Christopher "Kit" Carson were personally asked to participate by the Secretary of the Interior. It was through the efforts of Bent and Carson, that

The Cheyenne Dog Soldiers burned Julesburg to the ground. *DPL*

Black Kettle, representing the Cheyenne, although weary of the white man's promises, agreed to the council, with the following statement:

> *"We, the undersigned, chiefs and headmen of the bands of Arapaho and Cheyenne Indians, now south of the Arkansas River, having been forced, in self-protection, to fight the United States troops under the command of Colonel J. M. Chivington, at Sand Creek, Colorado Territory, and having, through the interpretation of a kind providence, escaped our intended massacre, and having heard from our friend Colonel J. H. Leavenworth, through his runners and agents, that we could in safety visit him at the mouth of the Little Arkansas river, [sic] have come to him to ask that he will use his influence to restore kindness between our bands, and if possible between our whole tribes and the government of the United States."* [56]

It is interesting to note the style of the language used. While it is not known who wrote this for Black Kettle, it is highly doubtful it was written by George Bent, who had previously written many of Black Kettle's communiques to the government. The peace council was held on October 12, 1865, at the mouth of the Little Arkansas River, near present-day Wichita, Kansas. Representing the Indian delegation along with Black Kettle, was Arapaho chief, Little Raven.

The council commenced with an opening statement by Sanborn, who issued apologies to the Indians for their sufferings since Sand Creek:

> "We all feel disgraced and ashamed when we see officers or soldiers oppressing the weak, or making war on those that are at peace with us." [57]

Black Kettle extended his hand to each of the commissioners and then said:

> "My shame is as big as the earth. It is hard for me to believe white men anymore." [58]

William Bent also spoke at the peace council. He first acknowledged Black Kettle's remark by stating that Governor Evans and Colonel Chivington had lied to him as well, regarding the horrible atrocity at Sand Creek. He then addressed the Indians directly, speaking in Cheyenne:

> "Friends, I would like for you once more to take my advice. I am satisfied that there is no deception. I am well aware that we have both been deceived at prior times in the execution of our treaty by white men in authority, but we must not judge all white men alike." [59]

Commissioner James Steele addressed the Indians, revealing the true intentions of the U. S. government, and what they would be giving up by agreeing to this treaty:

> "We fully realize that it is hard for any people to leave their homes and graves of their ancestors; but unfortunately, for you, gold has been discovered in your country, and a crowd of white people have gone there to live, and a great many of these people are the worst enemies of the Indians - men who do not care for their interests, and who would not stop at any crime to enrich themselves." [60]

Steele then "promised" the Indians that the U. S. government would "give" the Indians:

> "...a country that is full of game and good for agricultural purposes, and where the hills and mountains are not full of gold or silver." [61]

The land Steele spoke of, in reality a reservation, was a small portion of land. George Bent later described the negotiations:

"All the rest of the lands which had been recognized by the treaty of 1861 as Cheyenne territory was to be ceded to the government by the Indians. This country embraced the eastern half of Colorado, a large portion of western Kansas, and parts of Nebraska and Wyoming." [62]

Black Kettle speaking for the Cheyennes, refused this offer and objected to making any land cessions because there were only eighty lodges of Southern Cheyenne present at the council, the rest of the tribe being north of the Platte. For this reason, Black Kettle said, he did not wish to make any agreement as to land, knowing that it would cause trouble when the rest of his people and the Southern Arapahos returned from the north.

Then he had his wife [Medicine Woman Later] were brought in and showed Generals Harney and Sanborn the wounds she had received at Sand Creek, when after she was wounded and lay on the ground the soldiers shot again and again into her body. The commissioners found nine wounds on the woman's body. General Harney was so impressed with Black Kettle that he presented him with a fine bay horse. "Black Kettle gave me this horse the next year when I married his niece Magpie," wrote George Bent. He went on to recount the events of the meeting:

"Little Raven spoke for the Arapahos and was shrewd enough to remark that the lands offered by the commissioners to his tribe were north of the Platte and had already been given in treaty to the Sioux, while the lands offered south of the Arkansas belonged to the Kiowas and Comanches; he said that if his people accepted these lands and moved upon them they would at once become embroiled with the tribes to whom the lands rightfully belonged.

It was always easy to induce Indians to sign a treaty, even if they did not like its provisions, and on this occasion the chiefs were finally won over and the treaty was signed on October 14.

This treaty of October 14, 1865, was called the Treaty of the Little Arkansas. Though only one-sixth of the tribe was present, the Southern Cheyennes gave up all the lands between the Arkansas and Platte rivers, and while still permitted to hunt in that region, agreed to settle on a reserve to be established for them south of the Arkansas. The Indians *were not to go ten miles of any main traveled road, post, or station without permission. These were the main provisions of the treaty, and it was easy to see that trouble would result from any attempt to carry them out."* [63]

As word reached the Cheyenne Dog Soldiers of the signing of the Treaty of the Little Arkansas and the relinquishing of much of their home lands, a new sense of rage rose among the warriors.

Outraged at the news, Medicine Water, head chief of the Cheyenne Bowstring Warrior Society, declared war:

"Medicine Water and the society were seeking to preserve the traditions and life-styles of The People. With fierce devotion to the Cheyenne way, he was determined to pursue any intrusion into his homeland." [64]

And so, the Indian wars would continue.

— Chapter Notes —

1. Hyde, *Life of George Bent*, pg. 158.
2. John Sipes, Cheyenne Tribal Historian.
3. Hyde, *Life of George Bent*, pg. 165.
4. ibid.
5. ibid.
6. ibid.
7. ibid.
8. ibid.
9. Dunn, *Indian Vengeance at Julesburg*. pg.7.
10. Hyde, *Life of George Bent*, pg. 171.
11. ibid.
12. ibid.
13. Countant, *The History of Wyoming from the Earliest Known Discoveries*, pg.454.
14. John L. Sipes, Cheyenne tribal historian.
15. ibid.
16. ibid.
17. Propst, *Forgotten People*, pg. 75.
18. Official Military Record, Series I, Vol. XLIII, pg. 124.
19. The *Rocky Mountain News*, January 10, 1865.
20. Coburn, W. S., *Raid Up the Platte*, Luella Shaw, pgs. 23-32.
21. Propst, *Forgotten People*, pg. 76.
22. Coburn, W. S., *Raid Up the Platte*, Luella Shaw, pgs. 23-32.
23. ibid.
24. The *Rocky Mountain News*, January 16, 1865.
25. John F. and Mark M. Coad Indian Depredation Claim #7665, courtesy, Dr. Jeff Broome. See also *Cheyenne War*, pg. 149.
26. Reprinted in the *New York Daily Courier* on January 19, 186. Also see Broome, *Cheyenne War*, pg. 143.
27. Coburn, W. S., *Raid Up the Platte*, pgs. 23-32.
28. Broome, *Cheyenne War*, pg. 96.
29. Larimer, *The Capture and Escape*, pgs. 130-131. See also Czaplewski, *Captive of the Cheyenne*, pg. 22.
30. Unpublished manuscript, Nancy Jane Fletcher Morton Stevens, Iowa State Historical Society.
31. Hyde, *Life of George Bent*, pg. 177.

32. ibid.
33. ibid.
34. Halaas & Masich, *Halfbreed*, pg. 172-173.
35. ibid.
36. Broome, *Cheyenne War*, pg.163. Also see Broome, "James Moore. Pony Express Rider, Ranch Owner, Indian Fighter, Livery Operator in the Early Colorado and Wyoming Territory." *Wild West History Association Journal* Vol. XII #4, December 2019.
37. Hyde, *Life of George Bent*, pg. 182-183.
38. Woodward, *With the Troops in Colorado*, 1865, *The Colorado Magazine*, May, 1926. Propst, *Forgotten People*, pg. 82.
39. ibid.
40. ibid.
41. Hyde, *Life of George Bent*, pg. 183
42. Ware, *The Indian Wars of 1864*.
43. Broome, *Cheyenne War*.
44. A copy of this undated article is located in the archives of the Julesburg Museum.
45. Ware, *The Indian War of 1864*.
46. ibid.
47. Hyde, *Life of George Bent*, pg. 183.
48. Propst, *Forgotten People*, pg. 85.
49. The *Rocky Mountain News*, February 13, 1865. Note the misspelling of Eubanks as "Ewbanks."
50. Hodder, "Crossing the Plains in War Time," *The Colorado Magazine*, April, 1933.
51. ibid. Also see Broome, *Cheyenne War*, pg. 174.
52. Charles Augustus Ropes Dimon Papers, Yale Collection of Western Americana. See also Broome, *Cheyenne War*, pg. 145.
53. Wommack, Linda and John L. Sipes, Jr. "Mo-chi: The First Female Cheyenne Warrior," *Wild West Magazine*, April, 2008.
54. Bisbee, "General Sedgwick and Recollections of Fort Sedgwick," *The Colorado Magazine*, May 1933. Propst, *Forgotten People*, pg. 90.
55. The *Frontier Scout* newspaper, June 22, 1865. Information is also had at the Fort Sedgwick Historical Society.
56. Report of the Commissioner of Indian Affairs, 1865. pg. 395.
57. Report of the Commissioner of Indian Affairs, 1865. pgs. 516-517.
58. ibid. page 520.
59. ibid. page 522.
60. ibid. page 523.
61. ibid.
62. ibid.

63. Hyde, Life of George Bent, pgs. 248-249.
64. Wommack, Linda and John L. Sipes, Jr. Mo-chi: The First Female Cheyenne Warrior, *Wild West Magazine,* April, 2008. John Sipes, Cheyenne Tribal Historian and great-great grandson of Medicine Water and Mo-chi.

— FOR PEACE OR WAR —

Revenge for the Sand Creek Massacre continued with attacks along the South Platte River throughout 1866 and into 1867. By the spring of 1867, the Indians were raiding in the southern portion of Colorado Territory, primarily along the Arkansas River.

Once again, the United States government sought peace with the Indians through faulty negotiations and treaties that would not be honored. Colonel Jesse H. Leavenworth, Indian agent for the Comanche and Kiowa tribes, was ordered by the Commissioner of Indian Affairs, Nathaniel G. Taylor, to try to gather all the hostile tribes together for peace negotiations.

However, while Leavenworth was working toward gathering the various Indian tribes together, Major General Winfield Scott Hancock, the former Union commander hailed as a hero during the Battle of Gettysburg, had been assigned to command the Military Department of the Missouri, including Colorado Territory and Kansas. At the same time, the military organized a new cavalry unit for the expressed mission to deal with the Indian uprisings. This unit, known as the 7th Cavalry, was organized and first based at Fort Riley, Kansas, under the field command of Civil War Brevet Major General George Armstrong Custer.

Major Edward W. Wynkoop, former commander of Fort Lyon in Colorado Territory, was now the acting Indian agent, based at Fort Larned. Hancock sent a communique to Wynkoop, dated March 11, 1867, informing the Indian agent of his plans to send a large military force out to meet with the various Indian tribes in the Central Plains region. Hancock was acting under direct orders from his superior, General William Tecumseh Sherman, who sent his letter of authorization, dated March 14, 1867. Sherman wrote in part:

> *"I therefore authorize you to organize, out of your present command, a sufficient force to go among the Cheyenne, Arapahoes, [sic] Kiowas, or smaller bands of Indians, and notify them if they want war they can have*

it now; but if they decline the offer, then impose upon them that they must stop their insolence and threats, and make their conduct conform more nearly to what we [believe] *right."* [1]

Hancock asked Wynkoop to accompany him, saying in part, "We are able to chastise any tribes who may molest people who are traveling across the plains." Hancock went on to say, regarding the Indians, that he would "treat them with justice and accordingly to our treaty stipulations. I desire especially in my dealings with them to act through their Agents as far as possible. And tell them also, if you please, that I go fully prepared for peace or war."[2]

Wynkoop, bewildered by the mixed message from Hancock, was apprehensive about joining Hancock. Did the general mean war or peace? Wynkoop knew that with the Indians, actions spoke louder than words and this action Hancock was about to undertake, in Wynkoop's view, would mean war. Therefore, Wynkoop requested that Hancock use extreme caution in any action he chose regarding the Indians of the Central Plains. Nevertheless, Major General Hancock wasted no time in putting his troops, the 7th cavalry, under the command of Major General Custer, in the field in pursuit of hostile Indians.

In an interesting turn of events, George Bent's closest friend and future brother-in-law, Edmund Guerrier, rode with Custer on this mission. Guerrier was with Bent at Sand Creek and also managed to survive the massacre. Guerrier was also the cousin of Roman Nose's wife, the famed Cheyenne Dog Soldier. Within a year following the horrible event at Sand Creek, Guerrier had expressed his intention to marry Bent's sister, Julia. It was also during this time that Guerrier, perhaps due to a generous salary offered by the military, chose to offer his services as guide and interpreter for the United States Army. Guerrier was assigned to assist Hancock in his dealings with the Cheyenne Dog Soldiers.

Meanwhile, Leavenworth had sent a message to George Bent, who was then living with the Cheyenne camped along a stream in Texas, known as "Bitter Water." The whites called it Sweetwater Creek.

Leavenworth requested Bent's assistance in persuading as many of the head chiefs as he could to attend the peace negotiations. Meanwhile, Leavenworth set about asking head chiefs within his Indian agency to also attend.

At this time, George Bent was living in a lodge with his good friends, Charlie Rath, a former employee of his father's at

Bent's Fort, and Chief Santanta, when he received the request for his help from Leavenworth. Bent immediately set out to visit the various Indian camps and gain support from the chiefs. Bent later recalled:

> *"The first village we visited was Little Raven's Arapaho camp on the Cimarron. I had him send out a crier to call all the chiefs and headmen of the soldier bands together in the center of the camp. Then I read and interpreted the Commissioner's letter to them. The letter said that all the chiefs of the five tribes were to meet Superintendent of Indian Affairs, Thomas Murphy, at Fort Larned to select a place for the great council. The next camp we came to was Black Kettle's, on Wolf Creek. I told Black Kettle to call the chiefs and headmen to the big lodge in the center of the camp circle, and there I read the letter to them. My brother Charlie was in the camp and also read the letter to the chiefs. After visiting Black Kettle's camp I went to the camps of the Kiowas and Comanches and brought back to Fort Larned Black Kettle and a few other Cheyenne headmen, a good many Arapahos, a small party of Kiowas and Comanches, and several Prairie Apaches.*
>
> *At Fort Larned we held a talk with Leavenworth and it was decided to hold the big council on Medicine Lodge Creek, south of the Arkansas, where for many years the Kiowas had held their annual Medicine Lodge."* [3]

Black Kettle, who always advocated for peace, was apprehensive about this meeting. Several members of the Cheyenne Dog Soldiers no longer trusted their chief in the way of peace negotiations and many blamed Black Kettle, indirectly, for the atrocity of the Sand Creek massacre. Black Kettle had another concern, this one regarding many enemy tribes that would also be at the meeting. Earlier in the year, several warriors from Black Kettle's village were involved in a dispute with a band of the Wichita tribe over stolen horses, which had resulted in the death of a Wichita warrior. Tensions were high between the two tribes and Black Kettle worried his Cheyenne delegation would be attacked. George Bent had reassured him that after his talks with Buffalo Goad, the Wichita head chief, there would be no action taken by his tribe, if Black Kettle truly sought peace. Nevertheless, when Black Kettle and his people arrived for the peace conference, he chose to camp far away from the other tribes, at a place called Lake Creek.[4]

The following morning, as Black Kettle prepared for the

George Bent, shown with his wife Magpie, raided alongside Medicine Water and Mo-chi. *DPL*

journey toward Fort Larned, many of the sub chiefs felt the trip through the enemy camps was too dangerous and chose to stay behind in the Cheyenne camp. Determined to attend the council, Black Kettle left the camp with his wife, Medicine Woman Later, his cousin, Lone Bear, and George Bent. The group was delayed by a heavy spring snow storm, and forced to make camp until the storm passed. Black Kettle sent a messenger to his friend, Major Wynkoop, that his group had been delayed.

As the weather cleared, the Cheyenne group resumed their travel toward Fort Larned. During the journey, Black Kettle became aware of an extraordinary happenstance, precipitated by a general hope for peace.

When Black Kettle and his group neared a party of Osage hunters, a long-standing enemy of the Cheyenne, they were surprised when members of the hunting party invited them to their camp. The two tribes shared a fine meal and the chief invited the Cheyenne group to stay the night in his camp. As his journey continued, Black Kettle was greeted warmly and with great respect in every camp, including the camp of the Wichita tribe. It was a testament to the true intentions for peace by these warring tribes. Perhaps, under Black Kettle's leadership and influence, a lasting peace could be gained.

Finally, Black Kettle and his group crossed the river and approached Fort Larned. Henry M. Stanley, a reporter for the *New York Tribune*, who would later gain international fame in 1871 as the man who found the missing internationally celebrated Scottish missionary, David Livingston in Africa, described the event:

"The Indians were dressed in various styles, many of them with the orthodox army coats, some with gorgeous red blankets, while their faces were painted and their bodies bedizened in all the glory of the Indian toilette. To the hideous slits in their ears were hanging rings of brass; they wore armlets of silver, wrist rings of copper, necklaces of beads of variegated colours, breast ornaments of silver shields, and silver medals, and their scalplocks were adorned with a long string of thin silver discs." [5]

Arriving at Fort Larned, they were met by Colonel Leavenworth, and Buffalo Goad, chief of the Wichita tribe, who shook his hand in a show of welcome and peace. From then on, the meeting, held in April, was fraught with several blunders. Despite Leavenworth's efforts, Major General Winfield Scott Hancock, taking charge of the meeting, apparently was unaware of various

Indian customs as well as U.S. policy toward Indian outrages.

Hancock opened the meeting that evening around a huge glowing bonfire. The Cheyenne, particularly the Dog Soldiers who had been reluctant to attend the peace negotiations, as well as Black Kettle, were offended that the meeting took place under the cloak of darkness. It was their belief that such important meetings were to be held in the light of day. Hancock further insulted the Indians by expressing his disappointment that Roman Nose, a member of the Cheyenne Crooked Lance society, was not in attendance, despite the fact that Edmund Guerrier had explained to Hancock that Roman Nose, while a respected Cheyenne warrior, was not a chief and therefore, according to Cheyenne protocol, did not have a say in such matters.[6] Nevertheless, Hancock continued to voice his displeasure, much to the annoyance of Tall Bull, who reportedly glared at Hancock.

Hancock then stood as he addressed the Indians with a very blunt statement:

> *"I have a great many soldiers - more than all the tribes put together. The Great Father has heard that some Indians have white captives, and that many are trying to get up a war to hurt the white man.*
>
> *I am going to visit you in your camp. The innocent and those who are truly our friends, we shall treat as brothers. If we find hereafter that any of you have lied to us, we will strike.*
>
> *I have heard that a great many Indians want to fight. Very well; we are here and we come prepared for war. If you are for peace, you know the conditions. If you are for war, look out for its consequences. If you go to war with the white man, you would lose.*
>
> *For any depredation committed by any one of his tribe, I shall hold the chief and his tribe responsible.*
>
> *I have no more to say. I will await the end of this council to see whether you want war or peace."* [7]

The next day, Hancock again addressed the Indians. In keeping with his previous statements, he announced that he and a large military force would begin immediately visiting the various Indian villages. Hancock then offered the Indian chiefs wagon loads of presents and promises of favorable negotiations for a lasting peace.

In a show of good faith toward the Cheyenne delegation, Hancock returned a young Indian boy who had been captured at Sand Creek, over two years ago. Taking the young lad, the Cheyenne chiefs were bewildered as no one recognized the boy. However, members of the Arapaho delegation did recognize the child as a member of their tribe. He was known as White Shirt, the son of Red Bull. As Hancock had previously insulted the Cheyenne, he had now insulted the Arapaho. Then, curiously enough, the meeting ended with Hancock and Leavenworth requesting the Indians to select a mutual site, near Fort Larned, for further negotiations, where upon the promise of more goods and presents would be delivered.

As the meeting broke up, Tall Bull approached Major Wynkoop for a private meeting. Throughout the peace council, Wynkoop had sat in stunned silence. He was appalled at the arrogance and lack of respect Hancock had displayed. As Indian agent, he readily agreed to meet with Tall Bull. During their short conversation, Tall Bull asked Wynkoop to stop Hancock and his army of soldiers, impressing upon the Indian agent the fear of his people, following the massacre at Sand Creek. After this meeting, Wynkoop requested to meet with Hancock. It was well after midnight when Hancock finally received the Indian agent. Wynkoop relayed his meeting with Tall Bull and his concern for the people of his village. Hancock was not interested in what Wynkoop had to say. He told Wynkoop that his plans were unchanged; he would lead his forces toward the Indian villages in the morning, and expected Wynkoop to join him. [8] Wynkoop later wrote:

> *"I accompanied the column for the purpose of subserving the interests of my department by looking after the interests of the Indians of my agency as far as lay in my power."* [9]

On the morning of April 14, 1867, Hancock and his soldiers began their march toward the Indian village located on Pawnee Fork, approximately thirty miles from Fort Larned. Two columns of troops, one headed by Hancock, the other headed by Custer, rode to the crest of a hill. Below were nearly five hundred Cheyenne and Sioux warriors. Custer later wrote:

> *"We witnessed one of the finest and most imposing military displays, prepared according to the Indian art of war, which it has ever been my lot to behold. It was nothing more nor less than an Indian line of battle drawn directly across our line of march; as if to say; thus far and no further."* [10]

The warriors formed a battle line, led by Bull Bear, Pawnee Killer, Roman Nose and Tall Bull. Tension mounted as the warriors taunted the soldiers to attack. According to Wynkoop biographer Louis Kraft, the Indian agent had been pleading with Hancock for restraint for weeks. Once again he spoke to the general. This time Hancock acquiesced. Wynkoop was granted permission to speak with the Indian leaders.

Wynkoop, along with Edmund Guerrier, rode across the open valley to the line held by the warriors. As the two neared the warrior line, several Indians broke the line to surround them. They were heavily guarded with guns, pistols, bows and arrows. Soon, several of the leaders rode into the circle, including Cheyenne Dog Soldiers Gray Head, Medicine Wolf and White Horse, as well as Oglala Sioux warriors Bad Wound, Little Bear, Pawnee Killer and Tall Bear. Wynkoop, conversing with them through Guerrier, asked them to retreat and the soldiers would do the same. As this dialogue was happening, Roman Nose, painted for war, was riding along the front line, urging the warriors on to a great battle. Following his discussion with the leaders, an annoyed Wynkoop rode his horse directly toward Roman Nose. Wynkoop than confronted Roman Nose and told him, through Guerrier, that no villages would be attacked by the soldiers if Roman Nose backed down.

Evidently the Cheyenne Dog Soldier listened to Wynkoop, for Roman Nose led both Wynkoop and Guerrier to the group of warriors who were discussing what Wynkoop had said them. Wynkoop reiterated to the leaders that the soldiers would not attack if the warriors retreated. Roman Nose agreed to talk with the soldiers and raised a white flag as Wynkoop led the group of soldiers.[11]

When the two warring factions met face to face, it was a classic tête-à-tête. Hancock said he was more than ready to fight. Roman Nose said he would not be speaking to him if he was ready to fight; he was there to talk peace. When Roman Nose reached over and touched Hancock's face, thereby counting coup, he told Bull Bear to return to the warriors. Hancock, bewildered by the action, had no idea what had just transpired. However, Bull Bear was fully aware of the action. His instincts told him that Roman Nose fully intended to kill Hancock. Bull Bear took a bold action when he grabbed the reigns of Roman Nose's horse and led him away from the soldiers. Hancock told the remaining group of warriors that he would not attack but expected a second meeting the following day.

As the two sides retreated, Bull Bear rode forward for another meeting with Wynkoop. He again told the Indian agent that the soldiers should not camp near his village, as his people were fearful of another massacre. When Wynkoop relayed Bull Bear's request to Hancock, the general refused to listen. Hancock ordered his men into formation and led the march toward Pawnee Fork. Late in the afternoon, after traveling over seven miles, the soldiers set up camp. As it turned out, they were less than a mile from the village.

As the sun began to set that evening, warriors rode frantically into the village with news of a large military camp nearby. It was a large village, with over one hundred thirty Cheyenne lodges and one hundred forty Sioux lodges, and several hundred people living there. The village criers quickly made their way to each lodge with the news that soldiers were near. Fearing another massacre, panic swept throughout the village. The women gathered their children, food and clothing and fled the village, either on ponies or on foot. Several warriors led them to safety.

A group of soldiers had been keeping watch on the activity at the Indian village. When they returned to the military camp with the news that the occupants were fleeing, Hancock was furious. He immediately sent Guerrier to the village with a message that Hancock demanded they meet with him immediately. Guerrier conveyed Hancock's instructions to Bull Bear. Once again, in the dark of night, the Indians were expected to attend a meeting, an action that went against their traditional protocol. After some discussion with Roman Nose and Tall Bull, Bull Bear made the decision that the three leaders would ride to the general's camp, despite the cloak of darkness.

Hancock was impatiently waiting when the three Cheyenne Dog Soldiers arrived. Guerrier translated Hancock's first question as to why the women and children had fled the village. Roman Nose countered with asking if white women would not take their children away from danger. When Hancock had no answer, Roman Nose followed with a second question. He asked Hancock of the justification for the massacre of the innocent occupants of the village at Sand Creek in 1864. Hancock did not answer the question but offered a demand. Incredibly, the arrogant general told Roman Nose that the women and children must be returned to the village as he considered their fleeing a treacherous act.[12] Furious at such an outlandish accusation, the leaders of the Cheyenne Dog Soldiers broke off the talk and returned to their village. Guerrier returned with them.

It was nearing midnight when Guerrier again returned to the military camp. He reported to Hancock, telling him that the Indians were abandoning the village. Outraged by this further treachery, Hancock ordered Custer to invade the village. As Custer and his men approached the village, the following morning, it appeared to be deserted. Henry Stanley, the reporter for the *New York Tribune*, was allowed to enter the village with Custer and his men. He reported what he and the soldiers found:

"Dogs half eaten up, untanned buffalo robes, axes, pots, kettles, and pans, beads and gaudy finery, lately killed buffalo, and stews cooked in kettles, things scattered about promiscuously, strewing the ground." [13]

When Hancock entered the abandoned village the following morning, he was furious. As the soldiers further inspected the village, they soon discovered that animal remains and dirty pots and pans were not all that was left behind. In one lodge was found an elderly Sioux warrior with a broken leg and his disabled wife. In another lodge, the feeble-minded mother of White Horse was also discovered. In still another lodge, a young girl estimated to be between the ages of eight or ten, was found in a deplorable condition. The discovery of this helpless little girl stirred a bit of controversy.

Hancock's initial report claimed the child was white and that the girl had told him personally that she had been violated repeatedly by a Cheyenne warrior. This caused renewed outrage among the public, perhaps Hancock's intent. However, when Indian agent Wynkoop read Hancock's report, he wrote his own report to Thomas Murphy, Superintendent of Indian Affairs. Specific to the little girl found in the abandoned Indian village, Wynkoop wrote:

"That she is white is false, that she was ravished is correct. She was found after the camp was occupied by the troops, and the question in my mind is still, by whom was this outrage committed? If by her own race, it is the first instance I have any knowledge of."[14]

Cheyenne historian George E. Hyde wrote, "She [the young girl] may have been outraged, but not by the Indians, for she was a half-witted Cheyenne girl, forgotten by her people in the hurry." [15]

Wynkoop persisted in his efforts to stop Hancock from further antagonizing the Indians. After a few more heated exchanges between the two during a very long night, Hancock told Wynkoop in yet another meeting, this one held at 2:00 a.m., "that he intended to burn the village [the] next morning, as he considered the Indians had acted treacherously towards him, and they deserved punishment."[16]

Wynkoop had enough. He fired off a message to Hancock, in writing, regarding his intention to burn the village:

> *"I am fully convinced that the result would be an Indian outbreak of the most serious nature, while at the same time there is no evidence in my judgment that this band of Cheyennes are deserving this punishment."* [17]

Wynkoop wasn't finished. He changed tactics. After a few hours of sleep, he asked for a meeting with Colonel A. J. Smith. He explained to Smith the dire consequences if Hancock burned the village and retaliated against the Indians. While Colonel Smith agreed with Wynkoop, he was unable to convince Hancock.

Nevertheless, Wynkoop continued his letter-writing campaign. He wrote to his superior, Nathaniel Taylor, Commissioner of Indian Affairs, detailing the events and Hancock's intentions, predicting an Indian war if Hancock proceeded as planned. Wynkoop wrote that the Indians fled out of "fear alone...movement toward their village terrified them."

It seemed as if no one could reason with Hancock. While he did not burn the Indian village, Hancock set into motion a series of events that many historians believe made him responsible for the Indian War of 1867-1868. However, there are plenty of examples in the historic record that reveal Hancock was carrying out orders from his superiors, including this from General Sherman:

> *"You may therefore take these Indians in hand in your own way and let them feel our power and anger."* [18]

Meanwhile, several of the Indians who had abandoned their village, including Charlie Bent, Medicine Water and Mo-chi, retaliated by conducting more raids along the Smoky Hill Trail.

Hancock ordered Custer and his newly formed 7th Cavalry "to pursue and decimate the Cheyenne Dog Soldiers."[19] In early April, Hancock again sent Custer and the 7th Cavalry in search of the hostile Indians along the Smoky Hill Trail. Custer led four companies of troops out of the fort. The major general then split the troop force, with two columns ordered to patrol the area of the Smoky Hill River. The second force went in pursuit of the fleeing

Indians from Pawnee Fork. After a few days of heavy marching, with no luck, the soldiers were caught by a severe snowstorm. When the storm passed, the soldiers, no longer able to track the Indians, and low on provisions, made their way to Fort Hays.

At an Overland stage stop known as Lookout Station, approximately twenty miles west of Fort Hays, Kansas, Custer and his men came upon the aftermath of a horrific Indian attack at Monument Station. John Ferris, a stage driver, had arrived there on April 15, 1867. Ferris found three dead men who had been scalped, stabbed, burned and horribly mutilated. The three men, later identified as employees of the station, had been hastily buried in a haphazard attempt, when Custer later arrived. It was Custer's first exposure to Indian atrocities and he immediately reported the news to Hancock:

"The hair was singed from their heads; the skin and flesh burned from their breasts and arms, and their intestines torn out." [20]

Later, Hancock and a troop of soldiers arrived near the area, west of Lookout Station on April 20, 1867. There, Hancock learned that Indians had attacked Joseph Brown's military wagon near that station on April 16, 1867. It was here that Hancock also learned that the Indians who had killed and mutilated the three men at Monument Station, had returned and burned the station, and stolen all the stock. That very night, following Hancock's departure from Downer Station, the station was again attacked by Indians.

With the added information Hancock learned at Downer Station, and Custer's detailed report, Hancock firmly believed that the Indians responsible were the very band of Indians who had fled the village on Pawnee Fork. Hancock had backed down from his original decision to burn the abandoned village primarily due to Wynkoop's persistence. Now, with full confidence in his decision, Hancock issued a field order to burn the Indian village:

"As a punishment for the bad faith practiced by the Cheyennes and Sioux who occupied the village at this place and as a chastisement for murders and depredations committed since the arrival of the command at this point by the people of these tribes, the village recently occupied by them, which is now in our hands, will be entirely destroyed." [21]

After the village was burned, a satisfied General Hancock and his command set off for Fort Dodge. Meanwhile, when Wynkoop learned of the burning, he wrote to his superior, Nathaniel Taylor, "This whole matter is horrible in the extreme."[22]

As soon as General Hancock arrived at Fort Dodge, he arranged to meet with Kiowa leaders, Kicking Bird, Stumbling Bear and The Man that Moves, who were all camped nearby. The meeting was held in a Sibley tent on April 23, 1867. Hancock was joined by a few officers including Colonel Jesse H. Leavenworth, Indian agent for the Comanche and Kiowa tribes, Colonel A. J. Smith and Major Edward Wynkoop. Richard "Dick" Curtis had been assigned to interpret for Hancock. Hancock opened the meeting with a general statement:

> "We do not come here to make war upon the Indians, but to confirm the good feelings of those who are friendly toward us. We come here however, to fight those who wish to have war with us."[23]

Unfortunately, Hancock then slipped into his usual pattern of bad form and disrespect regarding the Indians. While Hancock professed peace, he also expressed upon them the actions of the military to those who did not conform to the military peace policy. Hancock went into great detail regarding his view of treachery by the Arapaho and Cheyenne tribes and his subsequent burning of their village:

> "We then burned their village and destroyed everything in it except some lodges. We have Bull Bear's tent and that of Roman Nose."[24]

When he was finished, Hancock offered the Kiowa leaders and their warriors "the same pay as our soldiers, horses, guns, blankets, &c.," if they desired to scout for the army.[25] However, there was a caveat; the Kiowa were to have no dealings with the Cheyenne or Sioux.

Kicking Bird spoke for the Kiowa, explaining to Hancock that while they wanted peace, they would first have to hold a council with Santanta and the other Kiowa chiefs. As the Kiowa leaders prepared to leave Fort Dodge, they asked for clothing for their people. Hancock refused, saying he would supply such needs when his warriors "enlist as guides and scouts."[26]

Pleased with his meeting with the Kiowa leaders, the next day Hancock asked Wynkoop to send runners to bring Arapaho chief Little Raven and his leaders to Fort Dodge for a similar meeting.

Wynkoop did as asked and then sent a request to Commissioner of Indian Affairs, Nathaniel G. Taylor, for a transfer back to Fort Larned. The request was granted and Wynkoop left the following day. Thomas Murphy, Superintendent of Indian Affairs, agreed with Wynkoop's position, writing to Taylor:

> *"Hancock's expedition has resulted in no good...*[and] *has been productive of much evil."* [27]

Meanwhile, Little Raven had agreed to the meeting with Hancock at Fort Dodge. The Arapaho chief arrived on April 28, bringing with him several chiefs. Hancock held the meeting the following day. In the meeting, Little Raven spoke of peace and his willingness to work with the white men. Hancock, pleased with Little Raven's words, made Little Raven the same offer as he had to the Kiowa leaders; military benefits if the chief and his warriors enlisted as scouts for the U. S. Army. Little Raven declined.

As Hancock and his men were busy holding meetings and offering bribes to the various Indian leaders, the warriors were continuing with their raids along the South Platte River. Thefts of livestock from Julesburg west to Godfrey's Ranch (Fort Wicked) were reported regularly during the summer of 1867. In Kansas Territory, several murders occurred along the Smoky Hill Trail.

In May Wynkoop traveled to several of the Southern Arapaho and Cheyenne camps within his district as acting Indian agent. He was startled to learn from them, rather than his own government officials, that several troops of soldiers had been riding between the Arkansas and Platte Rivers. This was land that, by treaty, had been given to the Arapaho and Cheyenne.

When Wynkoop returned to Fort Larned, he sent his report to Thomas Murphy, relating what he had heard from the Indians and asked Murphy to respond. Wynkoop wrote:

> *"General Hancock has declared war upon the Cheyennes, and ordered all to be shot who make their appearance north of the Arkansas or south of the Platte Rivers. The question is, what have these Indians done to cause such action? It is well known by every man who has the least knowledge of Indian affairs in this country, that the Pawnees are the hereditary enemies of the Cheyennes and Sioux, and war has always existed between them."* [28]

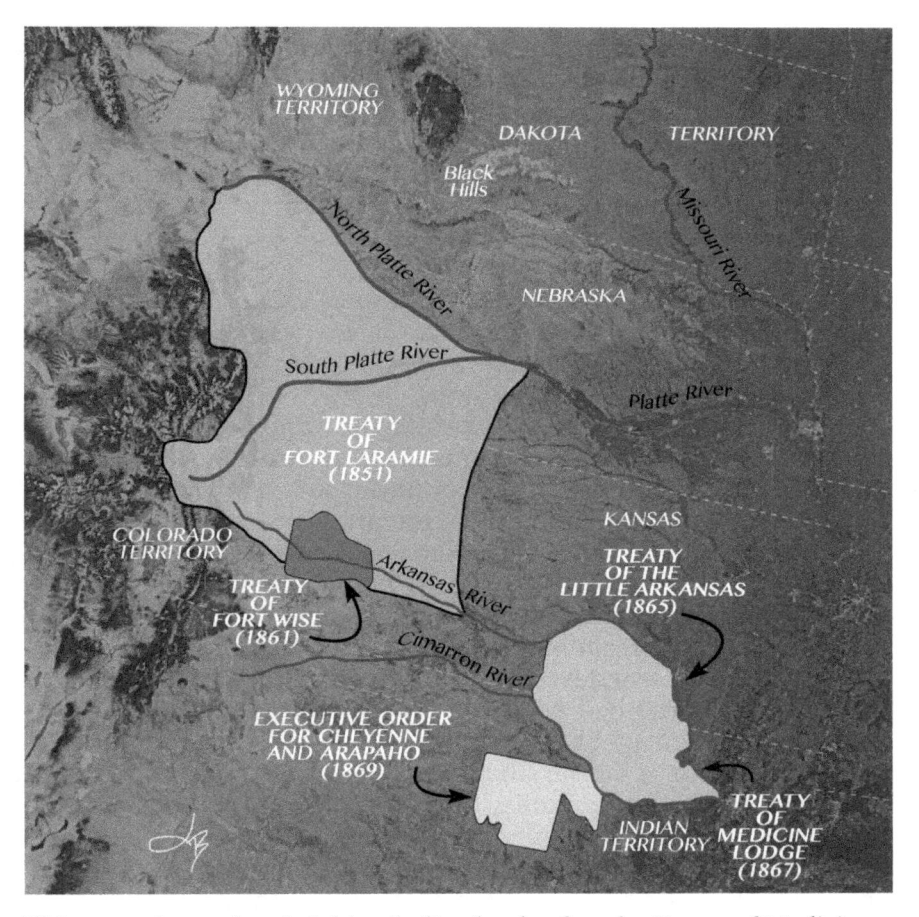

This map shows the shrinking Indian lands after the Treaty of Medicine Lodge in 1867. *Jeff Broome*

This last statement by Wynkoop might well have been in reference to Custer's April 17, 1867 report to Hancock, in which he erroneously claimed that "eight hundred Pawnee, Cheyenne, and Sioux crossed the Smoky Hill road."[29]

Murphy responded to Wynkoop's inquiry in his report that indeed, there were soldiers patrolling the area belonging to the Arapaho and Cheyenne designated lands. Murphy further requested of Wynkoop that he travel to the Washita River area, where the Southern Arapaho and Cheyenne had been told was a safe area to camp. Murphy's orders to Wynkoop were to reassure the Indians that they would be protected at this place, as long as they honored the peace treaty.[30]

As Wynkoop made the long trip from Fort Larned to the Washita River, he became keenly aware that the events unraveling were quite similar to the events prior to the Sand Creek massacre in 1864. His intuition may have eventually proven to be correct.

On July 20, 1867, the United States Congress passed a bill approving the funds to establish a new treaty with the Arapaho and Cheyenne tribes. The bill read in part:

"...to call together the chiefs and headmen of such bands of Indians as were then waging war, for the purpose of ascertaining their reasons for hostility, and to make treaties with them."

Meanwhile, the head chiefs of the various tribes that had attended the April meeting with General Hancock at Fort Larned, had returned to their camps earlier in the summer. Here they held their own councils regarding the white man's peace proposal.

Interestingly enough, Colonel Leavenworth personally requested that George Bent remain behind at Fort Larned as a personal aid to help Leavenworth notify the tribes of the time and place for the peace council once that determination was made. Coming to Fort Larned was a risky decision on Bent's part. He and his brother Charlie had been with the Cheyenne Dog Soldiers as they conducted many of their murderous raids in the territories of Colorado Territory, Kansas and Nebraska. These raids, reported in newspapers across the region, often mentioned the names of the notorious Bent brothers. Despite the actions of George Bent and his half-brother Charlie, Leavenworth, with or without military approval, for history does not record, chose to disregard Bent's past actions.

Black Kettle, returning to his people's village, was unable to immediately gather his chiefs for a council. While many of the braves were away for the summer buffalo hunt, others were with the Dog Soldiers conducting raids along the South Platte River and the Smoky Hill Trail. When George Bent visited Black Kettle's village, at the behest of Colonel Leavenworth, in August, Bent learned from Black Kettle that Stone Forehead, the keeper of the Sacred Arrows, had planned the annual renewal ceremony for later that summer. As Black Kettle was preparing to move the village for the ceremony, he was not able to commit to Bent's request regarding a date for the impending peace council.

Black Kettle's Southern Cheyenne were the first to arrive at Beaver Creek, south of the Arkansas River, where the ceremony would be held. When the other Cheyenne bands had arrived, Black Kettle assembled the chiefs, including Black White Man, Seven Bulls, Little Wolf, and Little Robe, into the Sacred Arrow Lodge, to discuss the peace council with the white man, which would result in a new treaty. There, George Bent read the military letter, relaying the information regarding the upcoming peace council. Bent's brother Charlie then translated the information. All in attendance agreed to attend the peace negotiations. Curiously, those who were not at this meeting, the Dog Soldier chiefs, were outraged that Black Kettle would even consider yet another treaty that in their opinion would only result in further loss of their sacred homeland. Dog Soldier chiefs and headmen, including Stone Forehead, keeper of the Sacred Arrows, Black Shin, Bull Bear, Gray Beard, Tall Bull, and White Horse, declared they would rather fight then surrender their homeland:

> *"The Old ones say Medicine Water and the society vowed to fight the white man, at ultimate sacrifice, and refused their intrusion into the Cheyenne homeland. They were seeking to preserve the traditions and life-styles of The People. With fierce devotion to the Cheyenne way, he was determined to pursue any intrusion into his homeland."* [31]

    The Cheyenne Dog Soldiers as well as the Sioux warriors were spreading their violent attacks across the of Colorado Territory, Kansas and Nebraska. On July 22, 1867, a group of Cheyenne and Oglala Sioux warriors murdered members of a family and captured others.

    Albert Kalus and his hired hand, Joseph Pixta, had left the Kalus homestead, east of Hebron, Nebraska, that morning in a wagon. Mrs. Margaretha Kalus became concerned after nightfall when the two men did not return as expected. She later recounted the experience:

> *"Of course I became then fearful of the safety of my husband and I and my four little children were sitting day in and day out, from week to week, from morning till night and weeping; crying and weeping, when we got the news that the bodies of my husband and Joseph Piexa* [sic] *had been seen by the drivers and passengers of the Overland stagecoaches, frightfully mutilated and buried by the roadside where found by a scouting party of white settlers from Swan Creek, who placed a headboard on the grave and marked it 'Two men killed by Indians.'"* [32]

The day following the disappearance of Albert Kalus and Joseph Pixta, Peter Ulbrich's two oldest children were abducted by Indians from his home. Ulbrich was Mrs. Kalus' brother-in-law, and the Ulbrich homestead was not far from the Kalus' land. Peter Ulbrich recalled the horrific incident years later:

"About 9 o'clock on the morning of that terrible day a roving band of Cheyenne Sioux, [sic] about thirty in number, came galloping down from the direction of Pawnee Ranch on the Fort Kearney road; a squad of them immediately entered my pasture and seized two horses and a mule of mine, grazing therein.

At the same time others in the party jumped over the fence into the field, where my 13 year old daughter Veeney (Veronica) and my 12 year old son Peter were pulling weeds for the hogs in the potato field, pounced upon the terrified children, began whipping them with their rawhides and driving them in the direction of the house, which we had hastily barricaded. Finding the doors and windows barred, the Indians called out the words in plain English: 'Father, father! Come out, we give you papooses.' From upstairs I had observed the Indians on every corner of the house with guns at aim; I could see from their countenances and general conduct and appearances that they were bloodthirsty devils and judged that they would massacre all of us, if I opened the door. Having no other means of defense but an old rusty musket, I preferred to await events. My wife implored them: 'Give the papooses free, you got horses and mule, take it, that is enough.'

Waiting and parlaying quite a while the Indians finally went to my stable and compelled my boy in sight of the house to cut up the double harness hanging there, with a sharp knife they handed him; the bridles, lines and other straps were carried off by them.

About 10 o'clock A.M. the Indians lifted my son and daughter on the horses stolen from me, riding off with them in a due westerly course. Arrived at the eastern shore of the Little Blue River they shot and killed my boy while riding in their midst; they left him, where we found his body 4 or five months later, at the exact spot which his then liberated sister had pointed out." [33]

The next day, another group of Indians, later identified as Northern Cheyenne, under the leadership of Turkey Leg, raided two other farms including the Peter Campbell homestead, some ninety miles from the attack and abduction at the Ulbrich home. The attack occurred early in the day when Peter Campbell and his oldest son were away helping a nearby farmer. Late in the afternoon, neighbors rushed to alert Campbell of the Indian raid at his home.

Campbell immediately raced on horseback to his home. As he passed the home of his nearest neighbor, he was shocked when he "found the mother of the family lying dead on the doorway threshold of the door, clasping her infant in her arms; and nearby a son, fourteen years of age, lay shot through the thigh."[34] When Campbell reached his own home, he discovered his four other children had been abducted by the Indians.

Thirteen-year-old Veronica Ulbrich, who was held captive by Turkey Leg and the Northern Cheyenne for six weeks, experienced horrendous torture and was continually violated by warriors of the band. She later recalled when the Campbell children were brought into the camp:

"I first saw the Campbell children, Jessie about twenty years of age, Catherine about 18 years, Daniel and Peter, both small boys about 5 or 6 years old; I think they were twins. Of course I was glad to have white company in my misery. I was afraid I never could get away and had to stay with these brutes and devils all my lifetime." [35]

Two weeks after the capture of the Campbell children and Veronica Ulbrich, Turkey Leg and his band of Northern Cheyenne warriors were again raiding along the Platte River Road near Plum Creek in Nebraska. During a few of these raids, he likely joined forces with Pawnee Killer and his band of warring Oglala Sioux.

On August 6, 1867, a railroad crew for the Union Pacific Railroad was repairing the telegraph line approximately three miles west of Plum Creek Station in Nebraska when they were attacked by Indians. This was the same area where the Cheyenne Dog Soldiers had raided and where freighters were murdered at the Plum Creek massacre and others were captured, three years previously, and on the same day.

Cheyenne Dog Soldier Porcupine, who continued his father, Porcupine Bear's warrior ways, later spoke of the events of August 6 and 7, 1867:

"We had a fight with the soldiers on Ash Creek [Plum Creek] which flows into the river. There were Sioux and Cheyennes in the fight, and the troops had defeated us and taken everything that we had, and had made us poor. We were feeling angry.

Not long after that we saw the first train of cars that any of us had seen. We looked at it from a high a ridge. Far off it was very small, but it kept coming and growing larger all the time, puffing out smoke and steam; and so it came on, we said to each other that it looked like a white man's pipe when he was smoking.

After we had seen this train and watched it come near us and grow large and pass by and then disappear in the distance, we went down from the ridge where we had been, to look at the ground where the train had passed, to see what sort of trail it made.

We crossed the track, looking carefully at it as we passed, and then went on and crossed the river.

Not long after this, as we talked of our troubles, we said among ourselves: Now the white people have taken all we had and have made us poor and we ought to do something. In these big wagons that go on this metal road, there must be things that are valuable. If we could throw these wagons off the iron they run on and break them open, we should find out what is in them and could take whatever might be useful to us.

Red Wolf and I tried to do this. We got a big stick, and just before sundown one day tied it to the rails and sat down to watch what would happen. Close by the track we built a big fire. Quite a long time after it got dark we heard a rumbling sound, at first very faint, but constantly growing louder. Presently the sound grew loud, and through the darkness we could see a small thing [a handcar] with something on it moving up and down." [36]

As day turned to night, a group of warriors sprang from the tall grass and attacked the engineer. Three of the men were murdered and another was severely wounded. When the next west-bound train failed to arrive at the station at the designated time of 1:50 a.m., Mr. Snyder, the station operator, sent a telegram to Colonel Potter at Fort McPherson. Snyder was concerned that the train may have derailed, and given the Indian uprisings, feared for the crew and passengers.

A group of soldiers were immediately sent to investigate. The sun had not yet risen on the morning of August 7, when the soldiers arrived upon a disastrous scene. Indeed the train had derailed. Brookes Bowers, the engineer, and the fireman, Gregory Henshaw, were found in the remains of the burned train. They had both been shot and scalped.

Porcupine, Red Wolf and the warriors used the same trick with the stick as well as pulling up several of the railroad ties before the next train approached. When the east-bound train approached the damaged track, it jumped the track. The Indians swarmed the wrecked train, killed the crew and plundered the contents of the cars. Then they set fire to the train. As the Indians rode away with their stolen goods, a group of Pawnee warriors gave chase, eventually overpowering a small group of the fleeing Cheyenne. The Pawnee killed one of the men and captured a young girl, Island Woman, and a boy, Pawnee, the nephew of Cheyenne leader Turkey Leg.

Veronica Ulbrich was 13 when she was abducted by the Cheyenne. *Jeff Broome*

    The remainder of the Cheyenne warriors made it safely to their camp at Plum Creek, where they alerted Turkey Leg of the abduction of the girl and his nephew. Two months later, Turkey Leg sent a runner to Fort McPherson to inform the soldiers that Turkey Leg was willing to exchange his white prisoners for the release of his nephew and the young girl, held by the Pawnee.
    Major Frank North received the message through a group of Cheyenne who were enroute to the peace council that was finally set to be held at Medicine Lodge Creek. Major North brokered the exchange of prisoners between the Pawnee and the Cheyenne. When the exchange was made, Major North took charge of the released captives, returning the Indian children to Turkey Leg. The white prisoners, including the children of Peter Campbell and Peter Ulbrich's daughter, Veronica, were cared for until family members could be notified. The children were then sent by train back to their families.

Peter Ulbrich later recalled being reunited with his daughter:

"When I recovered her at the farm of Mr. Campbell, south of Grand Island, she was nothing but skin and bones. Campbell's three or four children and my daughter had been surrendered to the military authorities at North Platte, Nebraska, and forwarded by the Union Pacific Railroad to Grand Island, where Mr. Campbell received them." [37]

Veronica Ulbrich later wrote of her captivity under Turkey Leg:

"Although it is a long time ago I remember yet vividly the hot summer day of 1867 when a band of Cheyenne Indians swept down upon our farm, captured me and my brother Peter. They whipped us with their rawhides and we cried bitterly for help. More dead than alive they took us away from home and three miles later they shot my brother off the horse and left him, where I pointed out the location four months later to my father. They compelled me to travel with them, we were traveling from one place to another, some of the band were on the go all the time. I did not get enough to eat, suffered from thirst, had to wash and do other work; sometimes they whipped me, sometimes they wanted or threatened to kill me. Soon one Indian, soon another belonging to the band forcibly violated my body, causing me immense pain and anguish thereby. This was almost a daily and nightly occurrence which would have killed me, if I had not been liberated almost exhausted." [38]

The various bands of the Cheyenne and Sioux as well as other bands of the central plains had finally agreed to meet in mid-October at Medicine Lodge Creek, some seventy miles southwest of Fort Larned.

Black Kettle, who had received several threats from the Dog Soldiers, was nevertheless determined to attend the peace council. He asked George Bent to escort him and his family to Medicine Lodge Creek. The group stopped at Fort Larned for a meeting with Superintendent Thomas Murphy and Indian agent Edward Wynkoop. [39] The meeting, held on September 8, 1867, was the first meeting for old friends Black Kettle and Wynkoop, who had not seen each other since their meeting at the Smoky Hill Council in September of 1864. During the meeting, which also included Arapaho chief Little Raven and Prairie Apache chief Poor Bear, Black Kettle expressed his wishes for peace and explained that a few bands of the Cheyenne were against the idea. Following the meeting, Murphy included the results of the meeting in a report, writing in part, "If the Cheyennes will agree to be friendly, I would trust them much more than any of the other tribes."[40]

On September 17, 1867, the three chiefs, with nearly forty warriors, escorted Murphy and Wynkoop and their wagon train during the sixty-mile trip south to the Indian camp at Medicine Lodge Creek. It would take three days. George Bent later described the Indian camp:

> *"The great camp was in a beautiful hollow through which flowed Medicine Lodge Creek, with its lovely wooded banks. This was a favorite place for the summer medicine-making of the Indians and also for their winter camps. At the head of the camp were the Arapaho, under Little Raven, with about one hundred and seventy lodges; next, in a fine grove, were the Comanche, with one hundred lodges, under Ten Bears and Silver Brooch; below them were the Kiowa, under White Bear, Black Eagle, Sitting Bear, and Kicking Eagle, with one hundred and fifty lodges; and next were the Apache, eighty-five lodges, under Poor Bear. The council grounds were in the center, in a grove of tall elms. Across the creek from the council grounds was Black Kettle's camp of sixty lodges. The remainder of the Cheyennes were camped several miles away on the Cimarron river, [sic] and when they moved in later on they brought the number of Cheyenne lodges up to two hundred and fifty. Fully five thousand Indians were encamped here, each Indian village being pitched in a circle. Thousands of ponies covered the adjacent hills and valleys near the camp and great was the excitement."* [41]

Soon, newspaper correspondents from across the country began to arrive at the Indian camp site. One of those reporters was Henry M. Stanley of the *New York Tribune*, who had been covering the events from the onset. However, on this occasion, Stanley and other reporters managed to raise the ire of the Indians. George Bent recalled the incident:

> *"The crowd of white camp followers quickly brought down the wrath of Santanta on their heads by the wanton killing of buffalo near the camp. He protested so vigorously against this unnecessary slaughter that the commission ordered the arrest and confinement of several of the wrongdoers."* [42]

The "remainder of the Cheyennes camped several miles away" that Bent spoke of was the village of the Cheyenne Dog Soldiers, located on the Cimmaron River. When Black Kettle arrived

Cheyenne warrior, Roman Nose, was a member of the Crooked Lance Society.

at his village on the evening of September 20, he was greeted by six members of the Dog Soldiers. The warriors requested a meeting with Black Kettle and Superintendent Thomas Murphy, where they voiced their concerns regarding another peace treaty. Following the meeting, interpreter Edmund Guerrier was asked to return with the Dog Soldiers to their camp along the Cimarron River, with a personal letter of invitation from Murphy. Superintendent Murphy wrote in a report to the commissioners:

> *"These Cheyennes, being fooled by whites so often and many of them but recently from war are very timid, and are determined to understand well who they will be expected to meet before they come."* [43]

Superintendent Murphy was either himself a fool, or naive in the very nature of the Cheyenne culture. The Cheyenne Dog Soldiers were anything but "timid." They had been waging war against the white man for the salvation of their land and people for years. Furthermore, they understood very well what was about to occur with this new peace council.

Nevertheless, the chiefs of the Dog Soldiers gathered in the Sacred Arrow Lodge to hear Guerrier read and interpret the words of Superintendent Murphy. After some discussion, Gray Beard and Roman Nose agreed to attend the peace council. Others in attendance, along with Black Kettle, were Brule leader Spotted Tail, Man Afraid of His Horses, Man that Walks Under the Cloud, Pawnee Killer, Standing Elk, Spotted Bear, Big Mouth, Black Deer, Cold Face, Cut Nose, Crazy Lodge, Santanta, and Turkey Leg. John Smith and George and Charlie Bent would interpret for the Arapaho and Cheyenne, while Jesse Chisholm, the half-white, half-Cherokee, would interpret for the Comanche and Kiowa.

During the trip to Medicine Lodge, several members of the Kiowa observed dead buffalo laying across the prairie. When the Kiowa arrived for the peace council, Chief Santanta said:

> *"Have the white men become children, that they should kill meat and not eat? When the red men kill, they do so that they may live."* [44]

The peace commissioners for the government were Brigadier Generals Christopher C. Augar, and William S. Harney, Major General John B. Sanborn, Lieutenant Colonel Samuel F. Tappan, General Alfred H. Terry, Kansas Governor Samuel J. Crawford, Missouri Senator John B. Henderson, and Commissioner of Indian Affairs Nathaniel G. Taylor. Edmund Guerrier would interpret for the government officials. It is interesting to note that Brigadier General Augar, Commander of the Department of the Platte, had replaced General William Tecumseh Sherman. General Ulysses S. Grant, a proponent of Indian peace negotiations, had removed Sherman from the post following statements Sherman had made regarding his position against peace proposals with the Indians.

Taylor opened the peace talks, after the traditional peace pipe had been passed and smoked, by presenting the promised gifts. Many items of clothing and army issue blankets, left over from the Civil War, were distributed among the head chiefs of the tribes, with a promise of more provisions to come following the successful terms of a peace policy. Taylor then expressed his concern for a unified consensus for peaceful negotiations with all the tribes present. With this invitation, the chiefs were encouraged to voice their concerns. There was much dissension among the tribal leaders. Kiowa chief Black Eagle and Comanche chief Ten Bears bickered back and forth while others chiefs would not commit to a peace proposal. Angered and embarrassed by this display of tribal friction, Black Kettle spoke:

"We were once friends with the whites but you [Comanche and Kiowa] *nudged us out of the way by your intrigues, and now when we are in council you keep nudging each other. Why do you not talk, and go straight, and let all be well? I am pleased with all that has been said."* [45]

With that bold comment, the meeting ended for the day, as Black Kettle and the other Cheyenne leaders left to attend the ceremony of renewing of the Sacred Arrows. And then, no sooner had the chiefs left the area for the Cimarron River, nearly fifty Cheyenne Dog Soldiers rode into the camp of the commissioners. Brigadier General William S. Harney stepped from his tent to meet the leaders, Tall Bull and Gray Beard. Harney recognized the chiefs immediately. Both Tall Bull and Gray Beard were helpful to Harney during the 1858 Sioux uprising along the North Platte River. Harney invited the Cheyenne leaders into his tent for a private talk. The Dog Soldiers remained on their ponies, with their guns ready, should the soldiers make a move.

Edmund Guerrier was called to the brigadier general's tent to interpret. Tall Bull and Gray Beard expressed their anger over the deliberate and unnecessary burning of the abandoned villages in April, by Major General Hancock. Brigadier general William S. Harney assured his Cheyenne friends that he would personally request a military investigation regarding Hancock's actions. Satisfied with Harney's gesture, these two leaders of the Cheyenne Dog Soldiers agreed to attend the peace council.

Surprisingly to all in attendance, Harney had appealed to the Commissioner of Indian Affairs, Nathaniel Taylor, and the two opened an investigation then and there, at the camp along Medicine Lodge Creek. Taylor presided over the military investigation. Tall Bull and Gray Beard sat at a table with Brigadier General William

S. Harney as the proceedings progressed. Indian agent Edward Wynkoop was one of the first to give testimony, stating that it was his belief that the present Indian warfare was in retaliation for the horrible atrocity that had occurred at Sand Creek in 1864. Senator Henderson asked Wynkoop a few questions regarding Colonel John M. Chivington, who led the military troops at Sand Creek. Wynkoop replied to the senator's inquiry by saying:

> *"His business was to kill Indians, and not make peace with them. After Sand Creek the Indians were at war everywhere, mostly on the Platte* [River Road.] *Property was destroyed, horses were stolen, and emigrants were killed.*
> *Some annuity goods which Commissioner Goodall bought in New York, three-point blankets which are used as wrappers, and which were charged in the bill, at $13 per pair, were the most worthless things that i ever saw. It was a most shameless affair. They* [the Indians] *were not only killed, but the friendliest were cheated."* [46]

Regarding Hancock's burning of the Cheyenne village, Wynkoop said it was an impulsive act by Hancock; his own retaliation born from frustration at not capturing his enemy. He further stated:

> *"Concerning the disposition of the Sioux, I will state that they were under the impression, previous to the destruction of that Cheyenne village by Hancock, that as the Cheyennes had made peace, they also wanted peace. Hancock stated in my presence that he intended to burn the village next morning, as he considered that they had acted treacherously towards him, and they deserved punishment."* [47]

Next, Wynkoop spoke of the elderly warrior, his disabled wife, and the young girl that were found in the deserted village. Sadly, both the warrior and girl had died a few weeks after they were taken to Fort Dodge. When General John B. Sanborn asked about the brutal raping of the girl, Wynkoop immediately responded:

> *"I firmly believe that the soldiers ravished the child. It was the conclusion I arrived at when I heard that she was ravished. It is my belief now. The Cheyennes I have seen lately gave me to understand that the war this summer was in retaliation for the destruction of their village by General Hancock."* [48]

The *Kansas Tribune*, the *Daily Colorado Tribune* and the *Rocky Mountain News* all covered the investigation proceedings in their October 29, 1867 issues. William N. Byers, editor and owner of the *Rocky Mountain News*, a fierce supporter of former Territorial Governor John Evans and Colonel John M. Chivington and their actions regarding Sand Creek, wrote a scathing editorial regarding Wynkoop's testimony. Byers defended Major general Winfield Scott Hancock's actions and criticized Wynkoop and his damning testimony of the General, by writing in part that Hancock had been:

"...attacked by so consummate a thief and a scoundrel is astonishing. We are able to expect almost anything from Wynkoop. The words and oath of some men are always worthless, and partially aware of the fact, they tell as large a falsehood as possible. Wynkoop is such a man, and whether he swears much or little, it is all the same. No one who knows him will believe his word or his oath." [49]

Editor Byers, who had a long-standing disdain for Major Edward W. Wynkoop, continued his attack in the editorial pages of his *Rocky Mountain News*. In the November 12, 1867 issue of the paper, Byers again attacked his nemesis, Wynkoop.

"Wynkoop, if he wishes to give any more evidence must take care and not have it published, and then no one will know how great a liar he is. Stanley, of the Democrat, [sic] contradicts him. General Smith contradicts him, and all Colorado contradicts him. Under such circumstances, Wynkoop will have to go to places where he is not known to be believed. Let the whole west spot him."

Meanwhile, after Wynkoop's testimony, both Tall Bull and Gray Beard, grateful for his honestly, shook Wynkoop's hand. It was a bold move by Wynkoop, for just a few days before the council began, Roman Nose, on the other hand, still angered by Wynkoop's failed promise that no villages would be attacked by the soldiers, threatened to kill the Indian agent. Undaunted, Wynkoop stuck to his convictions of securing peace.

However, the other leaders of the Cheyenne Dog Soldiers remained leery of the peace council as they learned a treaty would mean more loss of their sacred land. Therefore, with no clear indication as to the results of the investigation, Tall Bull and Gray Beard left the proceedings and rode directly to Black Kettle's camp. Meeting with Black Kettle, they requested he accompany them to the Dog Soldier camp on the Cimarron River, to explain to all the chiefs what the Cheyennes would gain should they sign the treaty. Tall Bull then warned Black Kettle that if he did not go with him, he would shoot all of Black Kettle's ponies. [50]

The peace council reconvened the morning of October 19, following the renewal ceremony of the Cheyenne Sacred Arrows. Black Kettle attended the proceedings but sat in silence. For the next two days, the commission leaders heard from the various tribal leaders. When the leaders of the Indian tribes were finished, Missouri Senator John B. Henderson presented the proposed terms of the peace treaty. In his opening statement, Henderson said:

> *"One day the buffalo* [will] *be all be gone. The Indian must change the road his father trod."* [51]

The Indian delegation were stunned. Finally, Ten Bears, chief of the Comanches, rose in defiance. He said:

> *"I love the open prairie, and I wish you would not insist on putting us on a reservation."* [52]

Then Santanta addressed the commission panel:

> *"When I go up the river, I see a camp of soldiers, and they are cutting my wood down or killing my buffalo. I don't like that, and when I see it, my heart feels like bursting with sorrow."* [53]

Henderson went on to describe the outlines of the peace proposal. Henderson told the Indians they would be allowed to hunt south of the Arkansas River "so long as the buffalo ran." He further promised them annuities, including food and supplies, for thirty years. Henderson explained that the agreed-upon treaty included moving the Cheyenne once again, this time onto two smaller reservations in Indian Territory (present-day Oklahoma). The Comanche and Kiowa would be moved to a new location on the Red River near the Wichita Mountains.

When Henderson noticed members of both tribes angrily conversing among themselves, the arrogant Missouri senator boldly told them that he was prepared for war, should they refuse to move to the new designation area. The peace treaty required that the Comanche and Kiowa relinquish over sixty thousand square miles of their traditional homeland for just under forty-eight thousand square miles of land in a place that was strange to them.

Nevertheless, whether a matter of intimidation on the part of Missouri Senator John B. Henderson, resulting in submission on the part of the Indian tribes, or an extreme act of faith in the peace process, the chiefs of the Comanche and Kiowa tribes agreed to the treaty, signing on October 21, 1867. However, other leaders, Gray Head, Little Robe and White Head, left the council proceedings that evening.

In a driving rainstorm, these head warriors made their way toward Black Kettle's camp. Arriving well before dawn, they went to Black Kettle's lodge, where they aroused him from his nightly sleep. Concerned with the removal to reservations, and the loss of their sacred homeland, the Kiowa leaders asked Black Kettle to return with them for a meeting with Brigadier William S. Harney. When Harney was awakened in his tent in the early morning, he was pleased. Meeting with the small Indian delegation, he had harsh words for them. Ever the peace maker, Black Kettle offered apologies and told Harney he would need a few more days to speak with the Cheyenne Dog Soldiers before he could agree to the proposed peace treaty. Wynkoop was also present during this meeting. He knew the Dog Soldiers were angry, and primarily at his friend, Black Kettle.

On the morning of October 27, 1867, the Cheyenne returned to Medicine Lodge Creek. Henry M. Stanley, the reporter for the *New York Tribune*, wrote:

"Out of the earth issued a vapor, in which distant objects seemed to float and assume monstrous proportions. It was a day which invited unrest." [54]

Runners raced through the Indian camps, alerting the chiefs and warriors that the Cheyenne were approaching. Unsure of the intent of the Cheyenne, particularly the Dog Soldiers, warriors in the various Indian camps prepared for war. Meanwhile, the commissioners and various dignitaries were equally concerned. Soldiers were ordered to prepare for an attack, and civilians in the commissioner's camp were ordered to arm themselves. Stanley's article continued:

"We got ready; loaded our rifles, our revolvers, and our derringers, and then we awaited their coming with what patience we could command."[55]

The Cheyenne Dog Soldiers formed a battle line. Again, Stanley described the scene:

"Five columns of a hundred men each, forty paces apart, dressed in all their gorgeous finery. Crimson blankets about their loins, tall, comb-like headdresses [sic] of eagle feathers, variegated shirts, brass chains, sleigh bells, white, red and blue bead-worked moccasins, gleaming tomahawks, made up the personnel of the scene never to be forgotten." [56]

Major Joe Elliott ordered a squad of the 7th Cavalry to move the Gatling guns into position, while Captain Albert Barnitz ordered his soldiers into battle formation. Barnitz later wrote:

"One portion of the tribe - about a squadron formed in line in front of my camp on a little rise of ground about 150 yards distant, and behind them and on their left flank about 200 Arapahos sat on their ponies, with bows strung, and on the other side of the camp the Comanches, and Kioways, [sic] and Apaches were out in force." [57]

After a long stand-off, the Cheyenne did not attack, as Black Kettle had arrived. Stanley observed the scene:

"Their chief, Mo-ko-va-ot-o, or Black Kettle, mounted upon a wiry horse, sprang forward, dressed in a dingy shirt and dingier blanket, his long hair floating behind him like a bashaw's tail, and waved his hands. In most admirable order they moved by the left flank by divisions; another wave and they marched obliquely across the Neo-contogwa - up to within 50 yards of Commission Camp, where they halted, but still continued their lively exhilarating chant until the commission appeared in full dress and halted within a few paces of the line." [58]

As tensions eased throughout both the Indian camps and the "Commission Camp," General John B. Sanborn requested a meeting with the Cheyenne and Kiowa chiefs. Through John Smith, who acted as the interpreter, Sanborn asked Gray Head to relate the events at Pawnee Fork. Gray Head told of Hancock and his soldiers approaching the Indian camp and the fear and panic that gripped the Indian village. When Sanborn specifically asked about the rape of the young Cheyenne girl, and who was responsible, Gray Head responded, "I was the last one that left the village, and she was not hurt then. She would not go with us, and we had to leave her there."[59]

The peace council resumed mid-morning, the following day. Major Wynkoop joined the commission in an effort to provide reason to the council, concerning the Indian point of view. The

Medicine Water's brothers, Iron Shirt (kneeling) and ManOnCloud, pose for the camera. Both fought alongside their brother. *John Sipes collection*

Indians were represented by Little Raven, of the Arapaho, and Cheyenne chiefs, Black Kettle and Little Robe. Also in attendance were members of the Cheyenne Dog Soldiers, including Buffalo Chief, Bull Bear, Old Little Wolf, Tall Bull, Tangle Hair, and White Horse.

     Missouri Senator John B. Henderson opened the peace talks professing peace. Henderson then apologized for Hancock's burning of the Indian village on Pawnee Fork. Henderson reiterated the new land arrangements as specified in the treaty; that the Indians were to relinquish their sacred land between the Arkansas and South Platte rivers, and move to the new reservation land in the Indian Territory (Oklahoma). Henderson further explained that annuities in the form of food, clothing, and firearms, would be supplied for a period of thirty years.

     Each tribal leader was allowed to speak. Arapaho chief Little Raven was agreeable to the treaty, but requested that his people be allowed to live near Fort Lyon. Buffalo Chief spoke, telling the commission that his people would never relent to the requirements of the proposed treaty, and refused to surrender their land between the Arkansas and South Platte rivers. Remarkably, Black Kettle did not speak. As the Cheyenne tribal leader, he was walking a fine line within his own tribe. As much as he wanted peace, Black Kettle knew the Dog Soldiers were against this treaty.

Following Buffalo Chief's defiant remarks, Henderson suspended the peace talks for a private meeting with the Cheyenne chiefs. George Bent and John Smith were called upon to interpret. Henderson reassured the chiefs that there was plenty of time before they would have to move to the reservation. Henderson further attempted to entice the Indian delegation into signing the treaty by assuring them that there were plenty of buffalo north of the Arkansas River, near their new hunting grounds. This was an important issue to the Cheyenne Dog Soldiers, and Henderson knew it.

On October 28, 1867, the peace papers known as the Medicine Lodge Treaty of 1867 were presented to the Arapaho and Cheyenne tribes in a signing ceremony. Aware of the Cheyenne Dog Soldier's opposition, Henderson felt he had won them over and asked Bull Bear to be the first to touch the paper. Bull Bear, at first reluctant, eventually signed, to the astonishment of many of the Dog Soldiers. However, Bull Bear had this to say following making his mark on the treaty:

"We will hold that country between the Arkansas and the Platte together. We will not give it up yet, as long as the buffalo and elk are roaming through the country." [60]

Cheyenne chiefs who followed Bull Bear in making their mark on the treaty paper were Black Kettle, Black White Man, Buffalo Chief, Crow Chief, Curly Hair, Heap of Birds, Little Bear, Little Robe, Old Little Wolf, Tall Bull and White Horse.

Stone Forehead, the Keeper of the Cheyenne Sacred Arrows, and a leader of the Dog Soldiers, was conspicuously absent from the peace proceedings. It was the first time in sixteen years of peace negotiations that the Sacred Arrows were not present to bless the peace. Many of the Dog Soldiers considered the absence of the Sacred Arrows as a sign that the treaty was not sincere.

Several members of the Dog Soldier society were furious that Black Kettle had agreed to the treaty, thereby giving away their homeland. The late John L. Sipes, Cheyenne tribal historian wrote:

"The Old ones say a member of the Dog Soldiers stepped up to the table at the Medicine Lodge Treaty Council, where he took his knife and stuck

it through the treaty papers and into the table and left the knife there. The Old ones said that was his signature and he walked off." [61]

Captain Albert Barnitz, who witnessed the entire negotiation process, later wrote:

"They have no idea they are giving up, or that they have given up the country which they claim as their own, the country north of the Arkansas." [62]

Conversely, Major Edward Wynkoop felt that Senator Henderson's promises of annuities and hunting were sincere. Wynkoop was shocked when he later learned the details of the ratified treaty. The treaty specified that the Indians would no longer contest the building of railroads, mail stations, and new roads. It also made clear that not only were they to leave their homeland, they would be required to live as white men in the Indian Territory. The treaty further required that the Indians cease their attacks against the white population, and finally, that the Indians would be allowed to hunt south of the Arkansas River, not north, as was promised by Senator Henderson.

When Captain Barnitz learned the details of the ratified treaty, he rightly predicted:

"The treaty amounts to nothing, and we will certainly have another war sooner or later with the Cheyennes." [63]

As Black Kettle and his people settled on their new reservation, near the banks of the Washita River in Indian Territory, several warriors refused to recognize the treaty and did not follow Black Kettle to the Washita River, but continued to hunt on their ancestral lands.

Medicine Water, along with his wife, Mo-chi, led a group of the Cheyenne Dog Soldiers who were conducting raids along the Smoky Hill Trail in eastern Colorado and western Kansas. This latter group, consisting mainly of young warriors, allied with Cheyenne warrior Roman Nose, angered the government by their refusal to obey the Medicine Lodge Treaty.

General William Tecumseh Sherman launched a military campaign to force them onto their assigned lands. Roman Nose and his followers fought back.

Captain Albert Barnitz's fateful prediction of war would indeed come "sooner rather than later."

— Chapter Notes —

1. Department of the Missouri, Letters Received Group 393. Also in Broome, *Cheyenne War*, pg. 251.
2. Hancock to Wynkoop, March 11, 1867, United States House of Representatives, 40th Congress Executive Document #240.
3. Hyde, *Life of George Bent*, pg. 282.
4. Hatch, *Black Kettle*, pg. 217.
5. The *New York Tribune*, October 23, 1867.
6. Roman Nose, the leader of the Cheyenne Crooked Lance society, should not be confused with the Arapaho warrior, Roman Nose, implicated in the Hungate murders in the spring of 1864.
7. Major General Winfield Scott Hancock's April 1867 report, United States House of Representatives, 40th Congress, Executive Document #28.
8. Kraft, *Ned Wynkoop and the Lonely Road From Sand Creek*, pg. 184.
9. Wynkoop to Murphy, June 11, 1867, in Kraft, *Ned Wynkoop and the Lonely Road From Sand Creek*, pg. 184.
10. Custer, *My Life on the Plains*, pg. 27.
11. Kraft, *Ned Wynkoop and the Lonely Road From Sand Creek*, pg. 188.
12. Hyde, *Life of George Bent*, pg. 260.
13. *Rocky Mountain News*, October 29, 1867, also in Kraft, *Ned Wynkoop and the Lonely Road From Sand Creek*, pg. 192.
14. Wynkoop to Murphy, June 11, 1867, included in the House of Representatives investigation, 40th Congress. Document 240, pg. 66.
15. Hyde, *Life of George Bent*, pg. 261.
16. *Rocky Mountain News*, October 29, 1867.
17. ibid.
18. Department of the Missouri, Letters Received, Group 393. Telegram from Sherman to Hancock dated February 19, 1867. Also in Broome, *Cheyenne War*, pg. 251.
19. Halaas & Masich, *Halfbreed*, pg. 218.
20. Department of the Missouri, Letters Received. G. A. Custer, "Camp of the 7th Cavalry, April 17, 1867. Also in Broome, *Cheyenne War*, pg. 251.
21. Department of the Missouri, Letters Received. Hancock Special Field Order #12.
22. Wynkoop to Taylor, April 21, 1867, United States House of Representatives, 40th Congress Executive Document #240.

23.   Hancock meeting with the Kiowa leaders, April 23, 1867, Report on Indian Affairs by the Acting Commissioner for the Year 1867.
24.   ibid.
25.   ibid.
26.   Murphy to Taylor, May 13, 1867. Also in Kraft, *Ned Wynkoop and the Lonely Road From Sand Creek*, pg. 196.
27.   Wynkoop to Murphy, June 11, 1867, United States House of Representatives, 40th Congress Executive Document #240.
28.   Department of the Missouri, Letters Received, Group 393. G. A. Custer, "Camp of the 7th Cavalry, April 17, 1867. Also in Kraft, *Ned Wynkoop and the Lonely Road From Sand Creek*, pg. 197.
29.   ibid.
30.   Report of the Indian Peace Commissioners, United States House of Representatives, 40th Congress Executive Session. Also in Broome, *Cheyenne War*, pg. 305.
31.   John L. Sipes, the late Cheyenne tribal historian.
32.   Margaretha Kalus Indian Depredation Claim #4545, courtesy, Dr. Jeff Broome. Also in Broome, *Cheyenne War*, pg. 306.
33.   Peter Ulbrich Indian Depredation Claim #6220, courtesy, Dr. Jeff Broome. Also in Broome, *Cheyenne War*, pg. 306.
34.   Campbell, *An Indian Raid of 1867*, Nebraska State Historical Society archives.
35.   Peter Ulbrich Indian Depredation Claim #6220, courtesy, Dr. Jeff Broome. Also in Broome, *Cheyenne War*, pg. 308.
36.   Grinnell, *Fighting Cheyenne*, pg. 266-267.
37.   Peter Ulbrich Indian Depredation Claim #6220, courtesy, Dr. Jeff Broome.
38.   Peter Ulbrich Indian Depredation Claim #6220, courtesy, Dr. Jeff Broome.
39.   Berthrong, *The Southern Cheyennes*, pg. 292.
40.   Hyde, *Life of George Bent*, pg. 284.
41.   ibid.
42.   Berthrong, *The Southern Cheyennes*, pg. 294.
43.   Jones, *The Treaty of Medicine Lodge Creek*, pg. 229.
44.   Hatch, *Black Kettle*, pg. 225.
45.   The *Daily Colorado Herald*, October 29, 1867, the *Herald Missouri Democrat*, October 23, 1867, and the *Rocky Mountain News*, October 29, 1867.
46.   ibid.
47.   Kraft, *Ned Wynkoop and the Lonely Road From Sand Creek*, pg. 209.
48.   ibid.
49.   ibid, pg. 227.
50.   Jones, *The Treaty of Medicine Lodge Creek*, pg. 287.

51. ibid.
52. ibid.
53. The *New York Tribune*, October 27, 1867.
54. ibid.
55. The *New York Tribune*, November 8, 1867.
56. Utley, *Life in Custer's Cavalry: Diaries and Letters of Albert and Jennie Barnitz*, pg. 114.
57. The *New York Tribune*, November 8, 1867.
58. The *New York Tribune*, October 27, 1867, also See Kraft, N*ed Wynkoop and the Lonely Road From Sand Creek*, pg. 215.
59. Hoig, *Battle of the Washit*a, pg. 37.
60. ibid.
61. John L. Sipes, the late Cheyenne tribal historian. Documents and research in possession of the author.
62. Utley, *Life in Custer's Cavalry: Diaries and Letters of Albert and Jennie Barnitz*, pg. 115.
63. ibid.

— THE BATTLE OF BEECHER ISLAND —

Cheyenne Dog Soldiers had warned Black Kettle that signing yet another treaty with the white men, as he did with the Medicine Lodge Treaty, would result in losing what was left of their traditional homeland. They were correct.

The Cheyenne had once enjoyed roaming their hunting grounds on the Great Plains from the Canadian border south into Mexico, and from the Missouri River west to the Utah Territory. The 1851 Treaty of Fort Laramie reduced their homeland to an area bordered by the North Platte River and the Arkansas River. In Colorado Territory, the 1861 Fort Wise Treaty reduced the land even further. Then, the 1865 Treaty of the Little Arkansas moved the Indians onto reservation land between the Arkansas and Cimarron rivers in Kansas and Oklahoma Territory. The Medicine Lodge Treaty of 1867 effectively reduced that land to a mere 320 acres, bounded by the 37th parallel and the Arkansas and Cimarron Rivers. The Cheyenne chiefs who signed this latest treaty, particularly Black Kettle, aroused the lingering indignation felt by many of the Cheyenne Dog Soldiers. They openly disavowed their leaders and refused to abide by the treaty. The Cheyenne Dog Soldiers mounted a defense to protect their homeland; a defense that would bring more war and bloodshed on the Colorado prairie. In the spring of 1868, a group of the Dog Soldiers camped near the area known as the Bunch of Trees, along the Smoky Hill River. The warriors, led by Mi-Huh-You-I-Nup, known to the whites as Medicine Water, began scouting for soldiers and other intruders, including overland travelers. According to Cheyenne tribal historian, John L. Sipes:

> *"Medicine Water and the Dog Soldier Society were seeking to preserve the traditions and life-styles of The People. With fierce devotion to the Cheyenne way, he was determined to pursue any intrusion into his homeland."* [1]

Medicine Water was born in 1835 in the Yellowstone Country. He was the fifth son of Medicine Water, one of the original members of the Dog Soldier Society, and his wife, Old Yellow Hair. His parents had a total of six sons. All sons of Medicine Water followed their father's example, becoming members of the Bowstring Cheyenne Warrior Society and noted chiefs. Little information exists about the eldest son, who was killed by the Crow Indians about 1830.

Medicine Water's older brother, Alights-On-Cloud, was part of the Indian delegation sent to Washington, D.C. in 1851 for a peace council which included the Pawnee, the enemy of the Cheyenne. Several politicians and their wives also attended the proceedings. However, according to Cheyenne tribal historian Sipes, the Indians were forbidden to smoke the traditional peace pipe.

> "The Old ones say Alights-On-Cloud would have refused to smoke the pipe with the Pawnee for it would 'make a lie.' But the Great White Father refused to allow the Indians to smoke the peace pipe as it was improper to smoke in front of ladies." [2]

That same year, members of the Pawnee tribe professed peace with the Cheyenne. Alights-On-Cloud and White Antelope, (later killed at Sand Creek), represented the Cheyenne delegation. As the peace pipe was passed, Alights-On-Cloud declined to smoke.

Medicine Water, along with his brothers Alights-On-Cloud, Earrings and Iron Shirt, rode together for several years, protecting their homeland primarily from their archenemy, the Pawnee. They also engaged in hunting buffalo and capturing wild horses. One of their favorite places to capture wild mustangs was north of the Arkansas River, along Black Squirrel Creek, east near present-day Pueblo, Colorado. The brothers worked in pairs, one chasing the sought-after pony, on his own fast horse, the other handling the roped animal. Alights-On-Cloud, mounted on his horse White Antelope, was considered the finest horseman among the Cheyenne. In 1852, Medicine Water and his brothers were involved in a fight with the "Wolf People," the name the Cheyenne called the Pawnee. During the engagement, which occurred on the South Loupe River in south-central Nebraska Territory, two of his brothers, Earrings and Alights-On-Cloud, were killed. After Earrings fell by an arrow through his chest, Alights-On-Cloud bravely moved closer to the

Mo-chi and Medicine Water knew that with the Medicine Lodge Treaty, their land and way of life were threatened. *John Sipes collection*

Wolf People, as a decoy, intentionally drawing fire from the enemy. Alights-On-Cloud was struck by an arrow shot from his people's worst enemy. The arrow went through his eye and lodged in his head. As he fell from his trusted horse, White Antelope, several of the Pawnee warriors attacked the lifeless body. Enraged, Medicine Water killed as many of the enemy as he could before the Cheyenne band realized they must retreat.

The scene was so devastating to the Cheyenne that they retreated, demoralized by the defeat. Later, members of the Cheyenne Dog Soldiers, led by Medicine Water, returned to retrieve what was left of their comrade's bodies. There were only parts of human remains of both Alights-On-Cloud and Earrings. The scalped heads, feet, hands and genitals of both men had been severed from their bodies. Their stomachs had been ripped open, leaving maggot-infested holes in both men. The grisly remains were gathered together in a woven wool blanket and moved from the area of death. Medicine Water found a peaceful place on the prairie where he placed the remains of his brothers on a scaffold erected high in an oak tree, as was the Cheyenne custom for brave warriors.

Following the Pawnee fight, the Cheyenne Council of 44, the governing body of the Cheyenne Nation, felt that Medicine Water had performed admirably, particularly under devastating personal loss. Thus, Medicine Water was elevated to chief of the Cheyenne Bowstring Warrior Society, a position his father once held.

> *"The Old ones said that my great-great grandfather, Medicine Water, proved his right to be chief to this courageous and loyal society of warriors."* [3]

A young, fearless Cheyenne warrior, Roman Nose, had proven himself in several battles. Therefore, Roman Nose, being related by marriage to Medicine Water, was brought into the Cheyenne Dog Soldiers. He would soon prove himself to be worthy of the honor.

Both men were determined to fight for their cultural ways, despite the signing of the Medicine Lodge Treaty. Roman Nose and his warriors carried out raids throughout the Colorado and Kansas territories. After the Sand Creek massacre, as head chief of the Cheyenne Bowstring Warrior Society, Medicine Water waged war against the white men. At his side rode his wife, Mo-chi, the first female Cheyenne warrior.

> *"Medicine Water and Mo-chi fought for their traditional way of life. They fought for their people, the 'Tsistsistas'."* [4]

In early March 1868, members of the Cheyenne and Sioux set up a camp of approximately fifty lodges, along the South Platte River. The camp, located approximately forty miles south of Julesburg and Fort Sedgewick, was the base of operations for a massive raid of homesteads and stage stations along the South

Platte River Road. However, in September 1867, the Union Pacific Railroad had built its rails west. The railroad line, for the most part, followed the old Pony Express route, crossing the northwest corner of the Colorado Territory near Julesburg. From there, the railroad went northwest to Cheyenne in Wyoming Territory. This spelled the beginning of the end for stage line service, and stage stations, along the South Platte River Road. Within two months nearly all the stage companies, including Wells Fargo, had terminated their business in this area. Stage stops along the river were soon abandoned. New routes were built from Cheyenne to Denver.

Nevertheless, the Cheyenne and Sioux warriors commenced their attacks along the river. On March 20, 1868, they raided the Washington Ranch, owned by brothers Charles and James Moore. This was the third time that the Moore's ranch had been attacked by Indians, severely wounding James during one attack. This time the Indian raid destroyed the Washington Ranch. Fortunately, the Moore brothers were not present, as the ranch had been left in the hands of a property manager, who had left the ranch prior to the Indian raid. The Indians burned all the buildings to the ground and even succeeded in destroying the adobe buildings. Charles Moore later described the devastation which finally ended his family's business:

> *"They destroyed for us at that time a two-story, shingle roof, adobe walled house worth $3500, all out buildings including the house, and corral enclosed by an adobe wall 252 by 600 feet. The hay corral was also within the wall, but the Pilgrim house was outside across the road from this enclosure. The Pilgrim house was built of adobe and was 24 by 40 feet and worth $600. There was a frame residence adjoined onto the adobe house inside the corral worth $2100, also an adobe stable 36 feet wide by 250 feet long, with double rows of stalls, and an alley between so that you could drive right through those stalls. Those stalls were made out of pine stuff hauled from Denver and the roof was also covered with pine poles and covered with hay like the thatched roof on top of it...They burned the frame storage room which was about 12 ft. by 20 feet worth $600. On the other side of the river we had a sheep ranch, which they burned, that was worth, what was left of it, $500."* [5]

In June, Cheyenne warrior Tall Bull, along with over two hundred men, joined with Little Robe and his band of one hundred warriors. The two Cheyenne warriors led their men to the Kaw Indian Agency near Council Grove, Kansas Territory. The Cheyenne were now prepared to fight the Kaw in retaliation for an encounter between the two tribes five months previously, near Fort Zarah. Tension mounted among the settlers of the area as the large war party passed their homesteads. Indian agent Albert Gallitan Boone, the grandson of famed frontiersman, Daniel Boone, hastened to the agency as soon as he received word of the impending arrival of the Cheyenne warriors. However, Boone was too late to stop the fight between the two tribal warrior factions. When Boone arrived at the agency, he discovered the Kaw warriors were ready for battle.

On the morning of June 3, 1868, the dry Kansas dirt swirled into the air as a mighty force of Cheyenne warriors, supported by a strong group of Arapaho and Kiowa, descended upon the Indian agency. Reaching the agency, the Indians stopped. What appeared to be a stand-off was actually a taunting action by Cheyenne and their fellow warriors. It worked. After a few tense moments, the Kaws opened fire. Their bullets were wasted, as the enemy was just out of range.

Then, in a diplomatic maneuver, a runner for the Cheyenne was sent to deliver a message to Boone. The Cheyenne trusted Boone and wished to meet with him. Boone, along with Major Stover, rode over meet with the Cheyenne leaders. Following friendly greetings, Boone expressed his desire to prevent a fight. The Cheyenne leaders agreed. As the conversation continued, gun shots rang in the air. Agent Boone later wrote in his report of the incident:

> "Just then the Kaws fired on us and some of the balls passed to Major Stover and myself; some passed over our heads and some fell short; he [Stover] wheeled and went to the Kaws, while the Cheyennes and myself changed position." [6]

The fight between the two enemies had commenced. The Cheyenne surrounded the charging Kaw warriors. After a four-hour battle, the Kaw retreated. The Cheyenne and their supporters remained for two days in a menacing stance, and then left the area. As they made their way back to their main camp, they raided and plundered several ranches and homesteads along the way.
Following the Indian fight at the Kaw Indian Agency, Nathaniel G. Taylor, Commissioner of Indian Affairs, issued an order to Superintendent Thomas Murphy, to suspend the scheduled distribution of arms and ammunition, as designated by the Medicine Lodge Treaty. This did not sit well with the Cheyenne, as they felt

the ensuing fight at the Kaw Indian Agency was started when the Kaws opened fire. After several threats of warfare by the Cheyenne, the government backed down. General Alfred Sully requested that the Indians receive the arms and ammunition. On July 23, Commissioner Taylor sent an order to Superintendent Thomas Murphy, rescinding the order regarding the distribution of arms and ammunition. Many military officers were outraged at Taylor's reversal. However, Captain Myles Keogh, of the 7th Cavalry, was so angered by the initial decision of the Department of the Interior to give out guns and ammunition to the Indians, he went to the *New York Times* with his concerns the previous year. The article, printed in the January 13, 1867, issue, contained the following regarding the arms issue:

> "*He* [Keogh] *asks why is it that the Interior Department, through its agents, should furnish them with the very means of committing massacres, while the War Department is furnishing troops to prevent them. There must be a screw loose somewhere.*" [7]

When Major Edward Wynkoop began distributing the arms and ammunition to the Indians on July 31, 1868, Captain Albert Barnitz witnessed the scene. He wrote to his wife:

> "*I believe - maybe they will feel very brave when they get those arms, and will begin to turn their thoughts to war again! Who knows. It is certainly very foolish to fight Indians with one hand, and to make presents, and give them arms with the other!*" [8]

No sooner had the Cheyenne received the coveted arms and ammunition, than war once again broke out on the Great Plains. The Cheyenne and Arapaho had successfully deceived the Indian agents, including Wynkoop, by expressing to them that guns were needed to hunt wild game, including the sacred buffalo, to feed their people. George Bent later told historian George E. Hyde the traditional Cheyenne ways of hunting wild game:

> "*Arrows were always used by the hunters, to avoid quarrels, for each man had his marks on the arrows and he could tell by the arrows which animals belonged to him. If guns had been used, there would have been constant squabbling.*" [9]

For the next few months, Arapaho and Cheyenne warriors, including the Cheyenne Dog Soldiers, conducted raids along the

Saline and Solomon rivers in Kansas Territory, murdering several homesteaders. In Colorado Territory, Indian raids along the South Platte and Arkansas rivers achieved the same results. Major Wynkoop, clearly duped by the Cheyenne, wrote to his superior, Superintendent Thomas Murphy, in a letter dated August 19, 1868:

"I am sorry to admit, that the Cheyenne are guilty." [10]

On August 10, 1868, the largest raid by the Indians began along the Saline River. Led by Red Nose, a Cheyenne warrior, women were raped and two young girls were captured. One particularly vicious attack occurred near what was known as Bacon Creek named for settler David Bacon. Twenty-two-year-old Mrs. Mary Jane Bacon received a severe blow to the head, resulting in a deep gash in her skull. She was then repeatedly raped and left for dead on the prairie. However, the warriors returned later in the day, taking the near-senseless woman hostage. The warriors then arrived at the homestead of Simon Shaw, along Spillman Creek. They remained there throughout the day, menacing the Shaw family and violating the women. Shaw later reported that he thought there were at least four hundred Indians surrounding his home. In the darkness of night, Shaw took his wife and her sister, Miss Foster, and attempted to escape on horseback. The Indians quickly overtook the fleeing party. One of the warriors rode up to Shaw, striking him with a war club, which knocked him off his horse. Then the warriors easily recaptured the two women. Triumphant in their efforts, the warriors again took their turn at repeatedly violating the women. The warriors continued to have their way with the women, including Mary Bacon, until well after midnight, when they left the area, leaving the ravaged women laying on the cold prairie. Kansas historian, Adolph Roenigk, in his *Pioneer History of Kansas*, wrote:

"Mrs. Bacon was so terribly unnerved by the frightful circumstances attending her capture, that she was unable to sit on the horse, which the savages gave her to ride, and either fell off, or was voluntarily liberated by her captures. The exact details of her horrible experience she could never fully recollect. Her home was on the banks of a small stream, which to this day, is called Bacon Creek. When the Indians made the attack upon her cabin, she and her husband ran to some timber nearby. She was overtaken and carried away with her baby." [11]

Other members of the warring party were incensed by the actions of Red Nose and his men. Wynkoop was later told by this group that while they did not condone such actions, "but finding it useless to contend against these outrages being committed without bringing a strife among themselves, they gave way, and all went in together. They then went to another house in the same settlements, and there killed two men and took two little girls prisoners."

General William Tecumseh Sherman had lost his position as Commander of the Department of the Platte prior to the Medicine Lodge Treaty of 1867. Following the treaty negotiations, General Sherman had been assigned to lead a military campaign to force the out-lying bands of Indians onto their assigned reservation lands. Hearing of this latest vicious act by the Indians, General Sherman launched a military investigation. The general reported his findings in a later report dated November 1, 1868:

"On the 10th they appeared on the Saline, north of Fort Harker, where the settlers received them kindly; they were given food and coffee, but pretended to be offended because it was in 'tin cups,' they threw it back in the faces of the women and began at once to break up furniture and set fire to the houses. They seized the women and ravished them, perpetrating atrocities which could only have been the result of premeditated crime. Here they killed two men. Thence they crossed over to the settlements on the Solomon, where they continued to destroy houses and property, to ravish all females, and kill thirteen men. Going on to the Republican, they killed two more men and committed other acts of brutal atrocity."[12]

Meanwhile, Kansas Governor Samuel J. Crawford traveled by train to Salina and toured the devastation from there to the settlement known today as Beloit, Kansas. In a special dispatch to President Andrew Johnson, dated August 17, 1868, Crawford wrote:

"I have just returned from Northwestern Kansas, the scene of a terrible Indian massacre. On the thirteenth and Fourteenth instant, forty of our citizens were killed and wounded by hostile Indians. Men, women and children were murdered indiscriminately. Many of them were scalped, and their bodies mutilated. Women, after receiving mortal wounds, were outraged and otherwise inhumanely treated in the presence of their dying husbands and children. Two young ladies and two children were carried away by the red-handed assassins, to suffer a fate worse than death."

As a result of the increase in Indian raids, in both Colorado and Kansas Territories, General Philip Sheridan enlisted the help of Brevet Brigadier Major General George Alexander Forsyth. Forsyth led a troop of soldiers, along with scouts and a surgeon, to track down the marauding Indians. Their quest would end in a bloody battle. In mid-August, a large group of Arapaho and Cheyenne boldly rode into Colorado City. While in the city, they proudly showed their papers which represented their peaceful intentions, received at the Medicine Lodge Treaty the previous year. However, the city fathers of Colorado City were apprehensive and wired the Colorado Territorial Governor Alexander Cameron Hunt, asking for verification. Irving Howbert, with the First Colorado Cavalry, later recounted the incident:

> *"He,* [Hunt] *replied that they* [the Indians] *were not hostile and must not be interfered with. Our people were not yet satisfied as to that point, owing to the fact that at the time of their visit to Colorado City, the Indians were noticeably sullen and appeared to be observing everything in a manner that aroused suspicion."* [13]

However, once the Indians left Colorado City, they traveled through Ute Pass, northwest to a place near present-day Hartsell, in Park County. Here they engaged a group of Utes. During the fight, they killed six warriors and two woman, and captured a young boy.

Following the fight with the Utes, the victorious Arapaho and Cheyenne warriors left the area, passing back through the Fountain Valley and Colorado City. Near this area, the warriors divided their forces into three parties. One group conducted raids along Fountain Creek, while another raided and murdered settlers near Colorado City. The third group of warriors conducted raids along Monument Creek. Meanwhile, Cheyenne Dog Soldiers continued raiding north along the South Platte River, and south along the Arkansas River. These warriors also moved northwest of the Arkansas River, conducting a series of raids near the town of Kiowa. On the morning of August 25, 1868, a group of nearly one hundred Arapaho and Cheyenne warriors arrived in the region and set up their lodges in the Bijou Basin. The day would end with murder.

A few miles east of Bijou Basin, along Comanche Creek, was the homestead of German immigrant, Apollinaris Dietemann. He and his young family had just moved to the area from Plum Creek, where Dietemann owned a small cattle ranch and operated a hotel north of the present-day town of Castle Rock. Dietemann sold both operations, moving to the region to join forces with his partner, Anton Schindelholz, in an effort to expand their cattle enterprise. Schindelholz was engaged to marry Dietemann's sister, Maria, who had just recently arrived in America. Joining Dietemann in this move were his thirty-one-year-old wife, Henrietta, pregnant with their third child, five-year-old John and three-year-old Henrietta, called "Hattie." The Dietemann family had lived on their new homestead two short months when their lives were torn apart by murder at the hands of marauding Indians.

On August 23, 1868, Dietemann and his future brother-in-law, Schindelholz, set out for Denver to purchase furniture for the new home, built next to the Dietemann house, for Schindelholz and his soon-to-be bride. The women and children remained behind with two hired hands, Benedict Marki and a man known only as Mr. Lawrence. What happened to the Dietemann family on August 25, 1868, is best described by one of the survivors. Maria Dietemann Schindelholz Wortman wrote the following in 1892:

"On Tuesday morning about eight o'clock, the 25th of August, 1868, about twenty-five or thirty Indians came right near our houses, with a herd of horses that they had stole [sic] all over the country; and one of the Indians came up to the house and took two horses that were picketed in front of the house, one of which was my brother's [Apollinaris] and the other A. Schindelholz's and they took all the horses, about seven or eight in number, that were grazing near the house; and two mares and a colt, belonging to my brother, were taken at that time. I saw the Indians drive them off. I know that they were Indians and the people told me they were Cheyenne and Arapaho Indians. After they had the horses away we got frightened and thought it wasn't safe there, and my brother's wife wanted to go away to some neighbors, and those neighbors were ten miles away; so we took all the valuables along that we had in the house that we could carry, and my brother's wife and children and the two hired men, Benedict Marki and Mr. Lawrence, and myself, started up the creek to the nearest neighbor, which was about ten miles. Before leaving the house we took all valuables along, which was of course the money, and I seen my brother's wife take the money along, and she counted it before going, and she put the paper money in her bosom, and she put the gold in a buckskin belt. She counted it before putting it on her person, and she said it was between seven and eight thousand dollars. She kept the money in the house, as they expected to go down to Arkansas to buy some

cattle after our marriage, so I was positive that she had the money with her. She took the money along. I saw her put the money on her person before we left the house. She took her gold watch and chain, worth about $100.00. It must have been about nine o'clock when we started; as we was about half the way we seen five or six horses grazing in a gulch, and one of the hired men wanted to go and take one of those horses and ride over to Kiowa to tell the people we were in trouble, but as we neared the horses some Indians came out of a ravine and shot at us, about five or six in number, and they commenced to shoot at us and we commenced to run, and my brother's wife wasn't able to run, and the Indians overtook her and shot her, killed her and scalped her, and the little boy I had hold of with my hand, but he run toward his mother, as he thought he was safer with her, and they took a hold of him and killed him. The balance of us turned our course and went to Middle Kiowa [Creek.] All of the white people in that neighborhood was together there at Middle Kiowa, as it was safer, and we stayed there until all the trouble was over and we knew that the Indians were gone. I saw them shoot my sister-in-law with a revolver, in the breast, and they shoot the boy with arrows, and one of them took a hold of him and twist his neck. This occurred about ten o'clock, After we was at Middle Kiowa about two or three hours my brother came from Denver and A. Schindelholz, also, and about half a dozen of the men went with him to hunt the remains, which they found at the place we left them, and the next day they fetched them in to Denver to be buried. I saw the remains when they were brought in to Middle Kiowa."[14]

Dietemann and Schindelholz were returning from their Denver trip when they were stopped by a stage driver near the Running Creek Stage Station near where the town of Bennett is today. The driver told the two men of the recent Indian attack in the Comanche Creek area and that a woman and boy had been killed. Crazed with fright and worry, Dietemann and Schindelholz hastened their pace to Comanche Creek. One of the hired hands for the Dietemann's, Benedict Marki, later recounted his experience:

"On the morning of the 25th I went about two miles north of where Dietemann lived after three head of horses belonging to Dietemann. I brought them home and picketed one of them. The Indians were chasing me and [I] did not have time to picket the other two horses. They cut the horse loose that I had picketed and drove the others off. After the horses were taken Mrs. Dietemann, two children, his sister and the hired man and me, walked up the creek about four miles when we were attacked by

another body of Indians. I was carrying the little girl on my back and Mrs. Dietemann was a little behind. I also had the little boy by the hand. I walked up the hill and looked back and saw the Indians as they grabbed Mrs. Dietemann and shot her in the breast with a pistol. The little boy was with me and ran back [to] his mother and the Indians killed him. We then went where people had gathered and after Mr. Dietemann came we organized a party and went back and found the bodies of Mrs. Dietemann and the boy. Mrs. Dietemann was nearly naked. Her dress was over her face and she was scalped and the little boy had been shot by arrows, lanced and stabbed all over. The bodies were found right close together." [15]

Joining the search party was John Benkelman. He later gave the following information to the *Rocky Mountain News:*

"So we joined in with two men who were present when the deceased were captured. They guided us to the place where it occurred, and we found the little boy about thirty yards from the place where first captured, dead. After making further search, we found the mother about fifteen yards from where the boy lay. We then sent four men after a wagon, to convey the bodies to Denver, where they now lay. These Indians are supposed to be Arapahoes. The deceased were both about four miles from their home, in company with some others, trying to make their escape to a neighbor's house, but from fatigue from traveling, were a little behind their comrades, when they were cut off by some Indians concealed under a bank. When we found the said bodies, they were horribly mutilated; the mother was shot in the front of the right shoulder, her face badly bruised as though she had been beaten with a revolver or club, bruises were also found nearly all over her body; she was also scalped. I think she must have been dead about five hours; she had, also, from evident signs, been ravished, which was the conclusion of myself, and those that were with me, signs of great struggle were also visible where she lay." [16]

Mrs. L. J. Fahrion was one of the local women who attended the deceased bodies. In 1916, Mrs. Fahrion wrote of the experience:

"Bands of Indians raided the country in this locality, then called Douglas County, now Elbert County. Comanche Creek, about six miles from Kiowa, was one of the streams raided. On that day [August 25, 1868] the bodies of a woman named Mrs. Dietemann and a boy, who had been killed by the Indians were brought to Kiowa. I saw the bodies. They were said at the time to be the bodies of the wife of Apollinaris Dietemann and

their boy. This family had just located on Comanche Creek. They were the only persons killed in the raid of that day. I helped lay out the bodies and assisted the two women, both of whom are now dead, who prepared the bodies. I held the washbowl at the time. Her scalp was entirely taken off and her clothes were partially torn off. There was no belt or money on her body at the time."[17]

The bodies of thirty-one-year-old Henrietta Dietemann and her five-year-old son John, were then placed in the bed of wagon and brought to Denver. They were displayed in a window of an empty building across from the Tremont House on Front Street, just as the murdered bodies of the Hungate family had been four years earlier. Years later, when Apollinaris Dietemann filed an Indian Depredation Claim with the United States government, he testified:

"I heard on Running Creek, about fourteen miles from where I lived, that a family had been killed on Comanche Creek. I immediately feared it was my family, as my family was the only ones then living on Comanche Creek. I went on about five miles in the direction of my ranch to Middle Kiowa. At Middle Kiowa I found all the members of my family, except my wife and boy, and was informed by them that my wife and boy had been killed by the Indians. About a half a dozen of the men, and myself amongst the number, went to hunt for the remains of my wife and son. We went five or six miles in the direction of my ranch, and found the bodies about three or four miles south of my ranch.... I found my wife scalped and shot through the breast, and the boy with his neck broken, and with four or five arrow shots in his body." [18]

In the *Rocky Mountain News* issue of August 27, the following article offered a few more details to the horrible murders:

"Last evening about seven o'clock a team came into town bringing the remains of Henrietta Dietermann [sic] and her boy, the persons spoken of yesterday as having been captured, the latter about five years old, killed by the Indians on Comanche Creek, Tuesday. The boy had been shot several times and his neck broken, the woman had been shot through the body, outraged, stabbed, and scalped. Decomposition had set in and the sight was horrible. They were killed near their house, Mr. Dietermann [sic] being absent. A man who was about to marry Mr. Dietermann's sister, and a daughter of the Dietermanns considerably older than the murdered boy, were at the house at the time, but escaped. About thirty

Indians came after the man who brought away the bodies Tuesday night, but he succeeded in getting into the station safely. The remains were taken to an empty house in front of the Tremont House, where for an hour or two people came and viewed them."

Later that day, Doctor W. F. McClelland presided over the coroner's inquest of the Dietemann bodies. Following the inquest, Dr. McClelland concluded that the cause of death of Henrietta Dietemann was a gunshot to the breast. He also disclosed that five-year-old John Dietemann died from the five arrows shot into his body. Doctor McClelland also included in his report the following statement, "I give as my opinion professionally that the mother is pregnant about seven months gone." [19]

Irving Howbert, who was well aware of the Indian presence earlier that month in Colorado City, remarked on the horrendous murders at the hands of the Indians who had professed peace while in Colorado City:

"Mrs. Dietemann formerly had lived near the northern line of El Paso County, and well known to many of the old settlers. The story of her tragic death created a great sensation, not only in this county but in Denver and throughout the Territory. News of this tragedy and of the many outrages perpetrated in the region east of the Pinery, reached Colorado City late in the evening, a day or two afterward. As there was a possibility that the savages might appear here abouts at any moment, messengers were at once sent throughout the county notifying the people of the great danger that confronted them." [20]

Once again the citizens of Colorado Territory were afraid for their safety and demanded the governor do something. At the time of the Dietemann murders, territorial Governor Alexander Cameron Hunt was on the western slope, dealing with the recent Ute uprisings, led by Colorow and Captain Jack. It seemed as if the entire territory of Colorado was under siege by hostile Indians. Territorial Secretary General Frank Hall, as acting governor, sent a request to the United States War Department on August 27, 1868:

"The Arapahoes are killing settlers, destroying ranches in all directions. For God's sake, give me the authority to take soldiers from Fort Reynolds. The people are arming, and will not be restrained." [21]

General Philip Sheridan responded to General Hall's request by stating that no military forces could be spared. Therefore, Sheridan authorized Hall to form his own enforcements, which Hall immediately began to organize. However, Hall was limited in his efforts as there was very little money in the Territorial treasury. Hall called for volunteers. Citizens from all over the territory volunteered, bringing their own horses, guns and ammunition.

On August 29, 1868, Major Jacob Downing led a volunteer company of cavalry to the eastern plains, in pursuit of the hostile Indians. Another troop of soldiers, under the leadership of D. R. Bailey, left Denver the same day for the South Platte River area. This group of volunteers, known as the "Platte Rangers," included men who lived in the area such as Elbridge Gerry, Holon Godfrey, and the former Lieutenant Territorial Governor Jared L. Brush. [22]

Meanwhile, in early September 1868, a group of Cheyenne and Arapaho warriors conducted a raid at Bijou Basin. They attacked the Gomer's Mill, owned by Philip Gomer, near present-day Elbert. This was not the site that the murdered Hungate family were brought to four years earlier. During the raid, as the Indians were stealing horses, a few of their band spotted two little boys playing nearby. One of the boys was shot and killed with no provocation. The boy, Leona Johnson, was the grandson of Gomer's cook and housekeeper, Mrs. Louisa A. Johnson. Mrs. Johnson later described the scene:

"Three Indians dashed in from the timber near the Mill and seeing two little boys out at play a short distance from the house they shot and killed one of them and then rode rapidly away."

Philip Gomer, along with several neighbors, set out in pursuit of the murdering Indians. On September 4, the group finally caught up with two of the warriors. As they chased these Indians, a another large force emerged from a dense thicket of trees. Gomer and his group were chased for nearly five miles before making it to the safety of Gomer's Mill.

At Colorado City, some fifty Indian warriors rode through stealing as many horses as they could. Eighteen-year-old Charley Everhart had left his family home, west of Monument Creek, to check on his father's cattle, grazing a short distance east of the ranch house. As he made his way to the cattle herd, Everhart noticed a party of Indians approaching from the north. Young Everhart jerked his horse around and galloped back toward the family home as fast as the small horse could run. The Indians, on much faster horses, easily overtook the teenager and brutally murdered him. Irving Howbert later recounted the incident:

> "Everhart had reached a point near what is now the intersection of Platte and Cascade Avenues, [in Colorado Springs] when a shot from one of the savages caused him to fall from the pony. One of the Indians then came up, ran a spear through his body and scalped him, taking all the hair from his head except a small fringe along the back part. This tragic occurrence was witnessed from a distance by several persons. An hour later, when the Indians had gone and it was safe to do so, a party went out to where the boy's ghastly, mutilated body lay and brought it in to Colorado City." [23]

After the Indians left the body of Charley Everhart, they happened upon a lone sheepherder, known in the region as "Judge" Baldwin. Noticing the quick advance of the Indians, Baldwin did his best to urge his horse into a run. Again, Irving Howbert related the episode:

> "Having neither spur nor whip, he [Baldwin] took off one of his long-legged boots and used it to urge on the animal. This, however, was ineffectual as his mount was not the equal of those of the Indians, and they overtook and shot him before he had gone very far. The bullet struck him in the shoulder and, as he was leaning forward at the time, angled up through his neck and came out through the jaw. Baldwin fell from his horse. Although badly wounded, he now used the boot to fight off the Indians. The latter evidently thought his wound mortal, so without wasting any more ammunition upon him, one of their number proceeded to take his scalp. The savage ran a knife around the back part of Baldwin's head, partly severing the scalp from the skull, and then discovered that the herder had been scalped at some previous time. For some reason, probably of a superstitious nature, the Indians then abandoned their purpose of again scalping the man, and the entire band rode off, leaving their victim on the prairie to die, as they doubtless thought. It is true that Baldwin had been scalped by Indians in South America some years before, a piece about the size of a silver dollar having been taken from the crown of his head." [24]

Amazingly enough, Baldwin lived. The Indians were not finished with their rampage in the Colorado City vicinity. Not far from where young Charley Everhart was murdered, they attacked and killed two young boys. The Thomas H. Robbins family lived on the south side of Fountain Creek. On this fateful day, Robbins two sons, aged eight and eleven, were tending their father's sheep when they were killed by marauding Indians. Irving Howbert recounted the horrendous murder of two boys:

> "Evidently they saw the Indians coming when still some distance away and were using every possible endeavor to escape, but they had not gone far when overtaken. It was said that one of the boys fell upon his knees and lifted his hands, seeming to be begging the Indians to spare his life, but the savages never heeded any such appeals. Two Indians reached down from their horses, each grabbing a boy by the hair and held him up with one hand, and with a revolver in the other, shot him through the head, and then flung the quivering lifeless body to the ground."

Later, the mutilated bodies of both boys were brought to Colorado City. Hattie L. Hedges Trout was a young girl when she saw the bodies as they were laid out for public view. She later told of the experience:

> "Those were very exiting days as the Indians were on the war path here. People for miles around came and brought their families for protection from them [the Indians] and were forted up in the old Anway house which was located at 2618 West Pikes Peak. As I remember it was a log house with a stairway going up on the south side. It still stands but has been remodeled and sided up and painted so no one could recognize it now. We were with others in the fort while my Father and other men stood guard on the hill north of town. We were all living here when the three boys were killed by the Indians near where the Antler's hotel now stands. They were herding cattle when they were watched by the Indians from the hills. The oldest of the boys was young Everhart. I believe he was twenty years old. The Robbins boys were younger. They were brought here and laid out in the old log building which was the first state house. It was located on the north side on Colorado Avenue between 26th and 27th streets. I can just remember of going with my sister to see the bodies as everyone was flocking there so horrified and grieved over it. Oh they were a terrible sight scalped and speared and they had placed their guns to their eyes and blew them out and faces and necks all powder burnt. Even after all these years I dread to recall the awful sight for at that time I hid behind my sister after a horrified glance at them. Oh those were terrible times for everyone so filled with fear and dread." [26]

Meanwhile, along the South Platte River Road, things were relatively quiet with regard to Indian raids. So much so that Fort Morgan, located on a bluff above the river, had been abandoned on May 18, 1868. Nevertheless, this is where Major Downing set up his military headquarters. The *Frontier Index* newspaper reported a very different situation in the September 5, 1868 issue:

"Reports from all parts of the Territory show that Indian atrocities continue. Ten persons murdered in the last 48 hours. Governor Hunt has been assured by General Sherman that every available man will be used to suppress the outrages. Arms and ammunition have been furnished to the volunteers. He believes this war is unprovoked, and is in favor of continuing it till either the Indians or the whites come out victorious."

Three days later, the *Frontier Index* reported of the growing situation:

"Two scouts sent here by the Gov. of Colorado, arrived yesterday and report the Indians about nearly all the settlements south-east [sic] and north-east [sic] of Denver. The settlers have suffered much; over five hundred head of stock have been carried off in the past week, and twenty or more settlers killed and scalped. The Indians are reported from two to three hundred strong at Sand Creek, three miles east of Big Timbers. Advises from Fort Lyon state that Gen. Penrose and company of cavalry fought two hours on the 8th, killing four Indians, and losing two soldiers killed and two wounded. About 1 o'clock this afternoon the pickets reported two small bands of Indians about six miles north-east of this post, moving westward."

The United States Army had implemented a new strategy in fighting the Indians. They began to recruit experienced civilian scouts and organized them within the various units, as fighting units unto their own. One of these scouts, attached to Major Downing, was Charles Stewart Stobie, a colorful scout who, by 1865, had become known as "Mountain Charlie." However, the majority of the scouts were Civil War veterans or seasoned scouts who had been in the Western Plains region for years. The majority of these scouts, similar to Forsyth scouts, were placed under the command of First Lieutenant Frederick H. Beecher.

Forsyth's scouts were at Fort Wallace in early September 1868, when Indians attacked a group of traders at Sheridan, Kansas, near the end of the Kansas Pacific Railroad, approximately thirteen miles east of Fort Wallace, near the Kansas/Colorado border. The *Leavenworth Times* reported the incident in the September 17, 1868, issue:

> "Fort Wallace, Kans., Sept. 16. *A report brought to this post at noon to-day,* [sic] *says a party of twenty-five Indians ran off twenty mules from Clark & Co., hay contractors within half a mile of Pond City, four miles west of here. They were pursued by the owner and citizens, but could not be retaken, though overhauled and fired on several times. Soon after 12 o'clock Captain Ezekiel saw a dozen Indians making for the Quartermaster's herd, half a mile from the Post. They turned back, going Southwest, the herd having been in the corral as soon as the Indians came in sight. At 2 p.m. a citizen came in and reported that a band of 100 Indians were in sight of Pond City and had just stampeded 1,200 head from a herd of 2,500 cattle, mules and horses, which passed here yesterday en route to California. Capt. Carpenter's Company, the 10th United States Colored Cavalry, arrived here from Fort Hays at 2 p.m. to-day, and were immediately sent after the Indians: no report from him since. Gen. Sheridan visited Sheridan City to-day and returned to Fort Hays this afternoon.*"

This latest series of Indian raids, despite the signing of the 1867 Medicine Lodge Treaty, renewed the Indian wars on the Great Plains. The Cheyenne Dog Soldiers, who had never agreed to the treaty, were joined by the Arapaho, Northern Cheyenne and Sioux tribes to wage war on the whites. Following reports of more depredations by raiding Indians, Brevet Brigidier General George Alexander Forsyth, along with First Lieutenant Frederick H. Beecher, and a unit of fifty soldiers, scouts, and a physician, left Fort Wallace, Kansas Territory, in pursuit of the marauding Indians.

Forsyth, a native of Pennsylvania, had enlisted with the Union Army on April 19, 1861. He was twenty-four years old. He soon rose to the rank of first lieutenant with the 8th Illinois Cavalry. By 1863, Forsyth received a promotion to major. Colonel Forsyth saw action at the battles of Chancellorsville, Fredericksburg and Beverly Ford, where he was wounded. Following his recovery, Forsyth was given an assignment with the military staff at Washington, D. C. Unhappy with a desk assignment, Forsyth requested and received a field assignment. Colonel Forsyth commanded a force of four hundred soldiers, who fought at Spottsylvania and the Battle of the Wilderness with General U. S. Grant. Following these battles, and

Forsyth's distinguished leadership, Forsyth became a staff officer for General Philip Sheridan. Among his many duties, Forsyth was charged with discretely moving dispatches through Confederate lines to the headquarters of the Union Army. Forsyth was present with General Grant during the surrender of General Robert E. Lee and the Confederate Army, at Appomattox, Virginia. Forsyth, now with the brevet rank of brigadier general, was praised by his ranking officer, General Philip Sheridan, as he was mustered out of service, on February 1, 1866:

General George A. Forsyth was in command at Beecher Island. *DPL*

> "I had so much confidence in his soldierly ability that I on several occasions gave him control of divisions and corps under my command."[27]

Forsyth again served under General Sheridan at Fort Hays, Kansas Territory, in the summer of 1868. Once on the western frontier and dealing with the Indian depredations, Forsyth soon formed an opinion regarding the Indians:

> "The Western Man who has lost his horses, had his house burned, or his wife violated or murdered, finds a whole lifetime of hatred and revenge too little to devote to his side of the question. The conception of Indian character is almost impossible to a man who has passed the greater portion of his life surrounded by the influence of a cultivated, refined, and moral society." [28]

Forsyth was given the command of fifty soldiers and scouts, as well as First Lieutenant Frederick H. Beecher, of the Third Infantry, as his second in command.

> "Headquarters Department of the Missouri, Fort Harker August 24, 1868 Brevet Colonel George A. Forsyth, A. A. Inspector-General, Department of the Missouri. Colonel, The general commanding directs that you, without delay, employ fifty first-class hardy frontiersmen, to be commanded by yourself, with Lieutenant Beecher, Third Infantry, as your subordinate. You can enter into such articles of agreement with these men as will compel obedience. I am sir, very respectfully Your obedient servant, J. Schuyler Crosby A.D.C. & A.A. Adjutant General." [29]

Forsyth lost no time recruiting his men. He later recalled:

> "In two days I had enrolled men at Fort Harker, and marching from there to Fort Hayes, sixty miles westward, I completed my complement in two days more. It was no ordinary command, this company of fifty scouts, and I have little doubt but that each and every trooper, both young and old, had a history worth hearing, if he had cared to tell it. All but four of these men were native Americans, and a number of them college graduates, and I never saw but one company of enlisted men who I thought exceeded them in general intelligence: First Lieutenant Fred H. Beecher, Third Infantry, U. S. Army; Acting Assistant Surgeon, J. H. Mooers, Medical Department, U. S. A.; Abner T. Grover, chief scout; Wm. H. H. McCall, first sergeant; W. Armstrong, Thos. Alderdice, Martin Burke, Wallace Bennett, G. W. Chalmers, G. B. Clark, John Donovan, Bernard Day, Alfred Dupont, A. J. Entler, Louis Farley, Hudson Farley, Richard Gantt, George Green, John Haley, John Hurst, Frank Harrington, J. H. Ketterer, John Lyden, M. R. Lane, Joseph Lane, C. B. Nichols, George Oaks, M. R. Mapes, Thomas Murphy, Howard Morton, H. T. McGrath, Thomas O'Donnell, C. C. Piatt, A. J. Pliley, William Reilly, Thomas Ranahan, Chalmers Smith, S. E. Stillwell, S. Schlesinger, Edward Simpson, William Steward, H. H. Tucker, Isaac Thayer, Pierre Truedeau, Fletcher Violett, William Wilson, C. B. Whitney, John Wilson, Eli Ziegler, Louis McLaughlin, Harry Davenport, T. K. Davis." [30]

Five days later, on August 29, General Sheridan ordered Forsyth and his men into the field. The mission was to scout the area between Beaver Creek and Fort Wallace, report any sightings of Indians, and await further instructions. Forsyth later recounted:

"Early on the morning of the 29th of August, 1868, I received the following at the hands of Acting Adjutant-General, Colonel J. Schuyler Crosby: Fort Hays, Kansas, August 29, 1868. Brevet Colonel George A. Forsyth, Commanding Detachment of Scouts: I would suggest that you move across the headwaters of Solomon to Beaver Creek, thence down that creek to Fort Wallace. On arrival at Fort Wallace report to me at that place. Yours truly, P. H. Sheridan, Major General, United States Army." [31]

Forsyth, pleased with the assignment, later wrote:

"The fresh air of the plains, the clearness of the atmosphere, the herds of buffalo, which scarcely raised their heads as we passed, the half haze, half vapory mist that marked the line of the Smoky Hill River, and above all, the feeling that civilization was behind us, and the fascination that the danger of campaigning in the enemy's country ever holds for a soldier was before us." [32]

One of Forsyth's new recruits, nineteen-year-old Sigmund "Sig" Schlesinger, had an entirely different opinion of his first field assignment:

"I will never forget the first day's ride. I was not familiar to the saddle, and my equipment was all the time where it should not have been. My bridle arm became stiff; my equipment would not remain in any one place, and I was sore and galled. I was too exhausted to eat supper, while to cap the climax, I was detailed for guard duty [and] *no sooner was I directed to my post than I dropped on the ground and fell fast asleep."*[33]

Forsyth and his men marched through freezing rain, finally arriving at Fort Wallace on September 5, just after the Indian attack at Sheridan, Kansas. They soon were ordered to again leave the fort, this time in pursuit of the Indians. Forsyth described the equipment and supplies for the regiment:

"Our equipment was simple: A blanket apiece, saddle and bridle, a lariat and picket-pin, a canteen, a haversack, butcher knife, tin plate and tin cup. A Spencer repeating rifle (carrying six shots in the magazine, besides the one in the barrel,) a Colt revolver, army size, and ten 140 rounds of rifle and 30 rounds of revolver ammunition per man - this carried on the person. In addition, we had a pack-train of four mules, carrying camp kettles and picks and shovels, in case it became necessary

to dig for water, together with 4,000 extra rounds of ammunition, some medical supplies, and extra rations of salt and coffee. Each man, officers included, carried seven days' cooked rations in his haversack." [34]

The supplies would prove to be invaluable in the days to come. One of Forsyth's scouts, Thomas B. Murphy, later wrote of his experience on the first day in the field: "We arrived at Sheridan and found the ox freight train had been attacked in the western superb. The train was scattered and the dead oxen and wagons were all around the scene of action." [35] Forsyth also recounted the incident:

"On my arrival there, I carefully examined the ground in the vicinity, and soon reached the conclusion that the attack had been made by a war party of not more than twenty or twenty-five Indians - this from the fact that there were not more than thirty or thirty-five different-sized pony tracks to be seen. I therefore made up my mind that while this party was probably not less than twenty, it did not exceed twenty-five men. This being the case, I assumed that the attack had been made by a scouting party and not by a war party who had cut my trail and followed it towards Fort Wallace, stumbling upon the freight train. We followed their trail until dark, and camped upon it." [36]

As the military troops moved northwest along the Smoky Hill River, Forsyth's scouts again picked up the trail of the Indians. Forsyth's scouts rode some fifty yards ahead of their party. Thomas B. Murphy later recalled:

"After several miles travel this trail became a beaten path, proving that a large part of the Indians dragging their lodge poles had passed this way." [37]

Forsyth wrote:

"I realized that the Indians were dropping out here and there, wherever the ground hardened and their individual trail could not be easily followed. Beecher and Grover kept their eyes fixed on the fast diminishing trail; and knowing that either man was my superior in this especial line of plainscraft, I quietly followed on at the head of the command content to await developments. Within an hour they halted and as the command overtook them Beecher sententiously remarked: 'Disappeared!' Halting and dismounting the command, we held a consultation, in which Grover,

Beecher, McCall and I took part. On one point we were all agreed, and that was that the Indians had seen us, and had scattered on the trail, and it was reasonable to suppose that they would rejoin their main body sooner or later. One thing was certain, they were not strong enough to fight us. Beecher said little, and refused to express an opinion. Grover and McCall were inclined to think that before we could overtake the Indian party it was more than probable that they would be able to mass several of the tribes against us, as the general trend of their trail was toward the north, towards the Republican River. Now, I had already determined in my own mind that it was in that section of the country we would eventually find the Sioux and Cheyenne, who had recently done so much damage to the settlers near Bison Basin, and I therefore cut short the discussion by saying that I had determined to find and attack the Indians no matter what the odds might be against us. If we could not defeat them, we would show them that the government did not propose that they should escape unpunished for want of energy in their pursuit. That I thought, with fifty-one men, even if we could not defeat them, they could not annihilate us. Furthermore, it was expected that the command would fight the Indians, and I meant to do so." [38]

With this determined leadership, Forsyth led his men west, following the trail along the Republican River, where it than followed the Arickaree River into the eastern portion of Colorado Territory.[39] Many of the scouts were concerned that they were following a much bigger band of warriors then their small fifty-three man troop could handle. Determined to advance, Forsyth later recalled:

"Some of my men grew apprehensive and entered a protest upon our further advance into the Indian country. The company was out to fight Indians and that [I] was taking all the risks that they were. It was expected that we would hunt these people down at any rate." [40]

On September 10, Forsyth's scouts located an abandoned Indian camp and knew they were on their trail. Forsyth wrote:

"On the fifth day out of Wallace, on the north bank of the Republican River, we stumbled upon an abandoned 'wickie-up' a shelter formed by pressing over young willows, or alders, interlacing the tops of the branches, and covering the top with hides or long swamp grass. We took up the trail here, and followed it a couple of miles, and we were rewarded by finding a place where three mounted Indians had encamped within

twenty-four hours; and following their trail, we ran into that of a small war party, possibly some of the Indians who had given us the slip a few days since. From this on the trail was easily followed. It led up to the forks of the Republican River, where it crossed to the north side of the stream, and grew steadily larger as various small trails from the north and south entered it, until finally it was a broad beaten road along which had been driven horses, cattle and travois carrying heavy loads of Indian tent poles that had worn great ruts into the earth, showing that all the paraphernalia of one or more large Indian villages had passed that way. Coming to what we then believed to be Delaware Creek, but which we knew later to be the Arickaree fork of the Republican River, we found the trail leading up it along the south bank of the stream." [41]

It was near dusk on Wednesday, September 16, 1868, when Forsyth led his men into a narrow valley near the junction of the Arickaree and Republican Rivers, south of present-day Wray, Colorado. [42] There, the military force set up camp for the night, on the north side of the Arickaree River, across from a small sand bar, or island, in the mostly dry riverbed.

Eli Ziegler was the youngest of Forsyth's scouts. His military records show he was sixteen, although census records show he was born in 1850, when he signed up with Forsyth. Ziegler was also the brother-in-law of another volunteer scout, Thomas Alderdice. The young scout later recalled his first night in the field:

"We unsaddled our horses and picketed them out to graze and built our fires, we saw a signal [arrow] go up south of us and a little east and then we saw more go up in different directions. Forsyth put on more guards that night and ordered us to be ready at any moment."[43]

Forsyth spent a long night filled with apprehension, as he later recalled:

"In my wakeful hours of this September night as I paced the ground to and fro along the river bank in front of the line of my sleeping men, I felt that the coming winter's campaign in the Indian country would result in much hardship outside of actual fighting. I had seen personally to the posting of our sentries, and had given especial instructions not only to hobble the horses, but directed that every scout should be especially careful to see that his horses lariat was perfectly knotted for I was somewhat apprehensive of an attack at daylight. Several times during

the night I rose and visited the sentries, for I was restless, anxious, and wakeful."

The soldiers had no idea what lay in store for them when dawn would bring another day. Roman Nose, a Northern Cheyenne, was a celebrated warrior, greatly admired by the Cheyenne, Arapaho and Sioux tribes, and feared by the Pawnee. Among the military officers who knew him, Roman Nose garnered the same sentiment from them as from the Indians. General Rodenbough described Roman Nose after the two met:

"Roman Nose moved in a solemn and majestic manner to the centre [sic] of the chamber. He was one of the finest specimens of the untamed savage. It would be difficult to exaggerate in describing his superb physique. A veritable man of war, the shock of battle and scenes of carnage and cruelty were as the breath of his nostrils; about thirty years of age, standing six feet three inches high, he towered, giant-like, above his companions. A great head, with strongly marked features, lighted by a pair of fierce black eyes; a large mouth with thin lips, through which gleamed rows of strong white teeth; a Roman nose, with delicate nostrils like those of a thoroughbred horse, first attracted attention, while a broad chest, with symmetrical limbs, on which the muscles under the bronze of his skin stood out like twisted wire, were some of the points of this splendid animal. Clad in buckskin leggings, and moccasins, elaborately embroidered with beads and feathers, with a single eagle feather in his scalp-lock, and that rarest of robes, a white buffalo, beautifully tanned and as soft as cashmere, thrown over his naked shoulders, he stood forth, the war-chief of the Cheyennes." [44]

Theodore Davis, a correspondent for *Harper's Weekly*, had witnessed the hostile encounter between Roman Nose and Major General Winfield Scott Hancock, in the fall of 1867. Davis wrote of this experience:

"I have never seen so fine a specimen of the Indian race as he - quite six feet in height and finely-formed...dressed in the uniform of a United States officer, and provided with a numerous quantity of arms, he rode his well-formed pony up to Hancock and proposed to talk. From this manner it was quite evident that he was indifferent whether he talked or fought. His carbine, a Spencer, hung at the side of his pony, four heavy revolvers were stuck in his belt, while his left hand grasped a bow and a number of arrows - the bow being strung and ready for instant use." [45]

George Bent and Roman Nose were both members of the Crooked Lance Society of the Cheyenne Dog Soldiers. Bent later recounted his knowledge of the early years of Roman Nose:

> "Roman Nose was the most famous Cheyenne warrior of his day. Although Little Wolf, (Okohm-ha-ket,) or Little Coyote, had counted more coups, he was not as widely known as Roman Nose. As a boy Roman Nose was called Sautie (the Bat) but when he became a warrior he was given the name Woqini, meaning Hook Nose, which the whites always interpreted Roman Nose. He had two brothers and one sister; only one of these is still living, a brother, Cut Hair, now at the Tongue River Agency. Contrary to the general opinion, Roman Nose was never a chief, nor was he even the head man of any of any of the soldier societies. He was a member of the Hi-moi-yo-qis, or Crooked Lance Society, so called from the peculiar lance carried by the leader. I also belonged to the Crooked Lances and it was at ceremonies of this society in the North in 1865 that I first made the acquaintance of Roman Nose. At the time of the great wars in the 1860's he was known as a great warrior to all the Indians of the Plains, and his fame so spread to the whites that they credited him with being the leader in all the fights where the Cheyennes were engaged." [46]

Roman Nose was in the large Indian camp that had launched the fire-arrow signals witnessed by Forsyth's men. The Indian village, a few miles from Forsyth's military camp, consisted of several bands of Brule Sioux, Northern Arapaho and Northern Cheyenne. However, the majority of the Southern Cheyenne tribe were with Black Kettle, south of the Arkansas River, in keeping with the Medicine Lodge Treaty. Nevertheless, many of the Cheyenne Dog Soldiers were Roman Nose, including Bull Bear, Tall Bear, White Horse, Medicine Water, his wife, Mo-chi, and his brothers, Iron Shirt and Man on Cloud. Cheyenne tribal historian, and great grandson of Medicine Water and Mo-chi, John L. Sipes, later wrote:

> "Medicine Water and the society were seeking to preserve the traditions and life-styles of The People. With fierce devotion to the Cheyenne way, he was determined to pursue any intrusion into his homeland." [47]

Cheyenne warriors Good Bears and Two Crows estimated nearly three hundred and fifty warriors in Roman Nose's camp. [48] This Indian camp was obviously quite aware of the military camp threatening their traditional homeland. They had been previously warned by a Sioux war party returning from a raid on the South Platte River. On the night of September 16, two Cheyenne warriors came in to the camp reporting that they had spotted a military camp along the Republican and Arickaree rivers.

As Forsyth paced the ground at his camp, the Indian warriors prepared for war, intending to attack at dawn. Sacred rituals such as applying war paint and preparing war bonnets were done carefully and methodically. The warriors formed into two groups to attack the soldiers. The first group left well before daylight. Once they were within range of the soldier camp, they were instructed to wait for the second group of warriors. Despite the instructions, two young and eager Cheyenne warriors, Little Hawk and Starving Elk, along with a small number of Sioux, disobeyed the leaders. George Bent recalled the incident for historian George Hyde:

> *"Cheyennes, with six Sioux, all young men, mischievously agreed to slip out and find the whites. Starving Elk was a great friend of mine and he told me that his party scouted for a long time in the dark, trying to find the light from the camp fires of the whites. It was not until just before daybreak that they located the scouts. Even at this early hour Forsyth's men were moving about camp getting ready to start, and Starving Elk's little party startled them by making a rush toward the horses and mules. The white men opened fire on the raiders, but some of the stock stampeded and was swept off by Starving Elk and his friends. But these wild young men spoiled everything. The white men had their mules all packed, horses were saddled, and they were ready to move away."* [49]

Eli Ziegler was one of the scouts in camp that witnessed the surprise Indian attack.

> *"I believe I heard the first whoop they gave, but I was so sleepy I thought it was a flock of geese; just then the guards fired. I gave a jump and said to Culver, 'They are here.' As we were all dressed and our revolvers and cartridge boxes all buckled on and our carbines lying by our sides we were ready for action as soon as we raised up. We were so close we could see [Indians] by the flash of their guns. The next thing I saw was a few of our horses going over [the hill] with quite a little band of Indians closed in behind them."* [50]

The soldiers and scouts found cover amid the tall buffalo grass along the riverbank. Then, as the sky cast the first light of the morning dawn, the remainder of Starving Elk's group of warriors stormed the area. Forsyth ordered his men to mount their horses. Abner T. Grover was at the side of his commander when Forsyth exclaimed, "Oh heavens look at the Indians." Even Forsyth seemed to be stunned by the enormity of the Indian force. Forsyth later wrote, "The ground seemed to grow them. They appeared to start out of the very earth."[51]

Almost immediately the command was given for the soldiers to move to the sand bar island in the riverbed. George Bent described the riverbed:

"The Arickaree Fork of the Republican River at this season was practically dry; but here and there in the broad bed of dry sand were little pools of water. The sandy island on which Forsyth and his men had taken refuge rose several feet above the dry bed of the stream and was covered with a growth of tall grass, bushy willows and alders, and one cottonwood tree. The banks of the stream bed were well covered with high grass and willows in spots, the land on one side of the stream rising in a gentle slope to a line of low-lying hills about three miles away, while on the other side the land rolled off into the prairie." [52]

Eli Ziegler described the move to the riverbed island:

"Pell-mell, helter-skelter, every man for himself, with a grand rush over the embankment, across the dry creek bottom, up the bank and the island was gained in less time than it takes to tell it." [53]

Once on the island, Forsyth had ordered his men to tie the horses together as a defense perimeter. However, the encroaching Indians crept through the tall grass along the riverbank and shot the horses. John Hurst, disappointed in his commanding officer's decision, later wrote:

"It was unfortunate that some of our horses were located within the zone of fire near where many of the men were fighting. This brought the men in range of bullets that were intended for the horses." [54]

Indeed, a few of the soldiers had taken cover behind the horses and some of them were hit by the Indians bullets. Meanwhile, Martin Burke, Louis Farley, Richard Gantt, Frank Harrington, and Thomas Murphy had made a dash for the north bank of the riverbed, in an effort to escape. Seeing this daring attempt, the Indians opened fire on the men. Gantt, Harrington, and Farley were all wounded in the attempt. Murphy, the only man not hit by the enemy, managed to make his way back to the island. Thomas Murphy wrote of his ordeal:

> "In crossing back to the island I sought the shelter of a wounded horse when [Sergeant] McCall called out, 'Look out Tom, that horse will kick; he isn't dead.' Feeling that a kick from a horse was less to be dreaded than a savage's arrow and bullets, I maintained my position until ammunition at hand was nearly exhausted." [55]

Once on the island, the soldiers began digging pits in the sand for protection. Sigmund "Sig" Schlesinger later recalled:

> "There was nothing but our hands and the knifes at out belts with which to work, but the soil was soft, loose sand, and the light sod was easy to cut. Kicking with toes and heels, and working with knifes and hands, we soon had shallow holes that afforded a slight shelter." [56]

Eli Ziegler added:

> "We all went to digging when we could and shooting when we had to. I moved a little south and got down and tried to dig some, they [bullets] kept coming so fast and so close that it did not seem that there was much chance to dig." [57]

In this manner, Forsyth and his men managed to hold their defense line on the island throughout the early morning hours. However, as the sun rose higher during that day, the command began to suffer casualties. H. H. Tucker was one of the first wounded. A bullet from the enemy broke the bone in Tucker's left forearm. As John Haley was tending to Tucker's wound, Haley received a bullet to his hip. Then, Eli Ziegler, who was attending to the wounded Haley, was grazed by an arrow to his leg. Amazingly, the arrow then became lodged in Tucker's leg, just above the knee. Ziegler managed to push the arrow through Tucker's leg, and bind the wound. Next, Howard Morton was wounded, with a bullet in the back of his head. The bullet passed through one of his eyes and became lodged in his nostril. Bravely, Morton wrapped his head and continued to fight. As the Indians sent another volley of bullets toward the island, a bullet grazed the neck of Sergeant William H. H. McCall. The bullet then struck G. W. Culver in the head. Culver was dead before he hit the ground.

As the casualties mounted on the island, Forsyth, along with First Lieutenant Frederick H. Beecher, sought to restore the morale of their troops. Forsyth was moving among the men, offering encouragement, when he was hit in his right leg by an enemy bullet. Forsyth fell into one of the hastily dug sand pits. Although wounded, Forsyth was able to see some of the fighting action from the sand pit. Doctor John H. Mooers was tending to Forsyth's wound when Forsyth raised up and turned to shout an order to his men. When he did, a bullet hit his other leg, shattering the lower bone. It was nearly noon when the second group of over two hundred Cheyenne and Sioux warriors arrived and immediately charged forth toward the island. John Hurst recalled the horror:

"I thought we were all going to be killed and scalped, and I think this belief was quite general with all the men. I heard Forsyth call out and ask if anyone could pray." [58]

Sigmund "Sig" Schlesinger later recounted the experience:

"No living thing could withstand such a seething hell of flame and lead. With wild cries of rage, the onrushing savages passed [over us] like a tornado." [59]

The soldiers rallied as they knew they were in the fight of their lives. Eli Ziegler wrote:

"Every trooper realized that his time had come and a heroic determination was pictured on the countenance of every man to sell his life as dearly as possible. Volley after volley was poured into the charging foe in rapid succession. Soon horses and warriors were mingled in disorganized confusions." [60]

John Hurst recalled:

"A warrior coming from the north almost ran over me on horseback, and would have done so had not his pony shied to one side and the Indian had hard work to keep his seat, insomuch that he had no chance to fire at me. However, I was glad his pony took him away, for had he fallen off it would have meant death to one of us. I shot at him as his pony rushed along, but [I] did not see the Indian fall. Scout Chalmers Smith noted that Lieutenant Beecher seemed to be exhilarated by the action, as if he were on a holiday. Smith heard Beecher declare it to be 'like shooting sparrows." [61]

Indeed it did appear as if the Indians were disorganized. During the heavy fire from the soldiers, the Indians were surprised and then became disheartened as they were losing many warriors to the soldier's bullets. The Indian accounts have all disputed this claim and many of the soldier claims have been found to have been embellished. However, the fact remains that by late afternoon the Indians had retreated. This was undoubtedly due to the effective weaponry used by the soldiers.

Although the Indians clearly outnumbered the soldiers, under siege on the island, it became apparent that they were at a disadvantage. Each of the soldiers, including the scouts and additional personnel, possessed the latest model of Spencer carbine seven-shot repeater rifles and plenty of ammunition, 56/50 rimfire cartridges. They also had a sidearm, the 1860 Colt revolver. Conversely, the Indians were armed with their traditional bows and arrows, as well as outdated Sharps rifles and older, heavy carbines. George Bent explained the Indian's retreat after that first charge:

LIEUT. FRED H. BEECHER

Lieutenant Fredrick H. Beecher was killed during the battle that bares his name. *DPL*

> *"In a tumult of shouting and shooting, singing war and death songs, the Indians charged up the streambed; many of the Sioux with streaming war bonnets of eagle feathers, the Dog Soldiers wearing their peculiar bonnets of crow feathers without a tail. Many of the warriors wore a war whistle, made from the wing bone of an eagle, hanging by a beaded cord of buckskin strung around the neck; these whistles warded off bullets when blown by the wearer in a fight. But the white men, with*

their new repeating rifles, poured such a hot fire into the Indians that the charge broke down before it reached the island. The rifle fire of those new repeaters was continuous and unlike anything the Indians had ever before experienced, yet, strange to say, was not especially damaging, though a number of ponies were killed. Instead of riding over the sandy island and stabbing and lancing the white men as planned, the Indians swept down the river bed on either side of the island. Wolf Belly, or Bad Heart, half-Cheyenne and half-Sioux, whose medicine was so strong that bullets could not harm him, headed this charge, armed with only lance and shield. He wore a breechcloth and a panther skin thrown over his shoulder. Unlike the others, he never faltered under the terrific rifle fire from the island and rode through the scouts and up the river bank, then turned and, to show his strong heart, charged back again through the entrenched whites. He was never stuck by a bullet." [62]

The Indians had retreated from the island, they maintained a steady watch, occasionally firing on the soldiers from a distance. One of their shots hit Doctor John H. Mooers as he rose from the sand pit to return fire. Forsyth recalled:

"I heard the peculiar thud that tells the breaking of bone by a bullet. Turning to the doctor, I saw him put his hand to his head, saying, 'I'm hit,' his head at the same time falling forward on the sand. Crawling to him. I pulled his body down into the pit and turned him upon his back, but saw at once that there was no hope. A bullet had entered his forehead just over the eye, and the wound was mortal. He never spoke another rational word, but lingered nearly three days before dying." [63]

Not long after Dr. Mooers was mortally wounded, Lieutenant Beecher made his way from his rifle pit, to where Forsyth was giving comfort to Mooers. As he slumped to the ground, Forsyth realized his second in command was also mortally wounded. Forsyth later wrote:

"I could hear him talking in a semi-unconscious manner about the fight; but he was never again fully conscious, and at sunset his life went out." [64]

Due to Beecher's valiant service in the heat of the battle, the island, located south of Wray in Yuma county, was named "Beecher Island." Years later, in commemoration of the battle at Beecher Island, Forsyth wrote of his admiration for Lieutenant Frederick H. Beecher:

"My lieutenant, Fred H. Beecher, of the Third U, S. Infantry, was a most lovable character. He was the son of the Rev. Charles Beecher, brother of Henry Ward Beecher, the distinguished divine. He served through the Civil War with great gallantry, and was lamed for life with a bullet through the knee at the battle of Gettysburg. Energetic, active, reliable, brave, and modest, with a love of hunting and a natural taste for plainscraft, he was a splendid specimen of a thorough-bred American, and a most valuable man in any position requiring coolness, courage, and tact, and especially so far for the campaign we were about to enter upon." [65]

As night fell, the soldiers hunkered into the sand pits. The Indians circled the island, firing their rifles toward the stranded soldiers. Of the Indians, "Sig" Schlesinger wrote:

"Such magnificent horsemanship as I have never seen before or since. Rifle smoke and clouds of dust, shot through with flashes of powder, are ever in my memory when I think of that awful fight." [66]

Colonel Forsyth recalled: *"All night long we could hear the Indians stealthily removing the dead bodies of their slain, and their camp resounded with the beat of drums and the death wails of the mourners."* [67]

Shortly after sunrise on the following day, Forsyth ordered Simpson Everett "Jack" Stillwell and Pierre Trudeau to secure the west side of the island. However, Stillwell led the men to cross the river channel. There, they dug a pit in the sand, shielded by the tall buffalo grass. The men hid in this pit as the Indians again fired on the island. From this strategic location, they were able to defend themselves and provide cover for the soldiers as the Indians charged toward them. During one of the charges, a warrior, White Weasel Bear, rushed forth to the island. His horse jumped over Stillwell's concealed sand pit. As the warrior passed above the sand pit, one of the soldiers shot at him. White Weasel Bear fell from his horse, mortally wounded. The bullet had hit the thigh of the warrior, and then passed up to his back, where it lodged in his spine, near his neck. White Thunder, the nineteen-year-old son of White Horse and nephew of White Weasel Bear, watched in horror as his uncle was shot. White Thunder immediately went toward the dry riverbed in search of his uncle. As he approached the tall buffalo grass concealing the soldiers, one of the soldiers shot and killed White Thunder. Enraged, White Horse went to his other brother, Two Crows, for help in mounting a strong attack. Two Crows, whose horse had been shot by the soldiers, found another horse and joined his brother. Together the brothers led another charge toward the island. Again, the warriors split forces in an attempt to surround the soldiers. A small contingent of these warriors moved toward the island on foot. Shielded by clusters of tall willow branches, the warriors then crawled close to the sand bank, where they dug a rifle pit for themselves. From this spot, the Indians rose up and fired on the soldiers. The soldiers instantly returned the fire, killing a Northern Arapaho, Little Bear, and Prairie Bear, a Cheyenne. Each were killed by a single shot to the head. Another warrior in the group, Good Bear, managed to escape.

Later that afternoon, brothers Two Crows and White Horse, along with a few others, crept toward the river bank in an attempt to retrieve the bodies of White Thunder and White Weasel Bear. As they neared the area, the soldiers opened fire. One of the Indians, Bear Feathers, was hit in the shoulder. Another bullet hit Black Moon, also in the shoulder. A third bullet hit the shield of Two Crows.[68] Still, the Indians crept forward. The soldiers again shot, finding their mark. Cloud Chief was hit by a bullet to the arm. The warriors moved slowly until they found the bodies of their comrades. George Bent later recounted:

> *"Presently they came on White Thunder and White Weasel Bear lying close together. The bullets were still spitting around them whenever they moved. Here Cloud Chief was wounded in the shoulder. The lariat was passed around White Thunder's foot and he was dragged away by those in the rear, Weasel Bear was still alive, and Two Crows, his brother-in-law, spoke to him. Weasel Bear told them that he had been shot in the hips and could not move his legs. They passed the lariat around his body dragged him away. He was a heavy man and over six feet tall. Two Crows says that on account of his wounds they had to rest him frequently as they dragged him out. The scouts were shooting into the grass at them all this time."* [69]

Stunned and demoralized by the number of casualties, runners were sent back to the Indian camp to bring Roman Nose into the fight with the soldiers. Roman Nose had been reluctant to join the battle as he felt he had come upon bed medicine. Roman Nose was held in high esteem by the Cheyenne, and particularly by the Dog Soldiers. He took this recognition very seriously. When he received a particularly sacred gift of a war bonnet, Roman Nose, honored by the gesture, strictly adhered to the sacred rituals that went with such an honor. Perhaps George Bent described the sacred Cheyenne ritual best:

> "Roman Nose always wore in battle the famous war bonnet which was made for him up North in 1860 by White Buffalo Bull, who is still living at Tongue River Agency and is one of the most famous of the old-time Northern Cheyenne medicine men. This war bonnet was the only one of its kind ever made. When a boy, Roman Nose fasted for four days on an island in a lake in Montana, and in his dreams saw a serpent with a single horn in its head. This was the reason White Buffalo Bull came to make this peculiar war bonnet. Instead of having two buffalo horns attached to the head-band, one on each side, it had but one, rising over the center of the forehead; it had a very long tail that nearly touched the ground even when Roman Nose was mounted. This tall was made of a strip of young buffalo bull's hide, and had eagle feathers set all along its length, first four red feathers then four black ones, then four red feathers again, and so on, forty feathers in all. In making this famous war bonnet, White Buffalo Bull did not use anything that had come from the whites; no cloth, thread, or metal. Usually war bonnets required little medicine-making when going into battle, but Roman Nose's bonnet was very sacred and required much ceremony...A strict set of rules of conduct went with the war bonnet; certain things Roman Nose was forbidden to eat, and there were other rules. White Buffalo Bull particularly cautioned Roman Nose never to eat anything that had been touched by metal, and was told that if he neglected this rule he would be killed in the next battle." [70]

A few days before the battle, Roman Nose's medicine was indeed broken when he ate food that had been prepared with metal utensils. Again, George Bent recounted the incident:

> "A feast was given by the Sioux to some of the prominent Cheyennes, and Roman Nose was one of the invited guests. While talking to the chiefs he forgot to warn the Sioux women not to touch his food with a metal fork or spoon. After the feast he remembered that he had neglected to make this request, as was always his custom. So he asked one of the Sioux chiefs to inquire of the women who had cooked the meal. One woman remembered having taken his bread from a skillet with an iron fork. This oversight destroyed the protecting power of Roman Nose's medicine. Certain purification ceremonies must be performed to restore this

power, but these took some time, and before Roman Nose could start his ceremony word was brought that Forsyth's scouts had been discovered. And this was the reason why Roman Nose, always eager for battle, took no part in the fighting during the early part of the day. He firmly believed that his medicine was so weakened that he would be killed if he went into the battle."

When the runners told Roman Nose of the Indian casualties, the great warrior, despite his bad medicine, mounted his fine, spirited horse, and rode toward the fight at the river. At a small hill above the Arickaree River, Roman Nose dismounted from his prized horse. Then, he began the sacred ritual of applying the war paint; yellow for the forehead, red over the nose, and black across the chin and mouth, just as White Buffalo Bull had instructed him many years ago. Next, Roman Nose took his sacred war bonnet from its buffalo-hide case and performed the sacred ritual taught to him by the war bonnet's maker, White Buffalo Bull. Roman Nose asked for blessings, raising the war bonnet to the Cheyenne deities and Mother Earth, four times, to the north, west, south, and east. Then Roman Nose mounted his horse and rode into battle. It would be his last.

The sun was high in the western sky when Roman Nose rode to the front of the Indian defense line. Roman Nose gave the order to charge, leading the Arapaho and Sioux warriors, as well as Tall Bull's Cheyenne Dog Soldiers, into battle.

Forsyth's men were ready. As the warriors approached the island, the entrenched soldiers opened fire. Roman Nose's horse jumped over the riverbank, narrowly missing the camouflaged spot of Stillwell and the other soldiers. However, as Roman Nose passed the concealed rifle pit, rifle shots rang out from the pit. One of those bullets struck Roman Nose in his back.

As the warriors charged on, Roman Nose reared his horse around and managed to ride away from the scene of the battle. George Bent related the following:

"Roman Nose rode near the scouts lying in the hole on the river bank and was shot in the small of the back as he passed. The others weakened under the hot rifle fire and again failed to ride over the whites. Roman Nose did not fall from his horse when shot, but turned and rode back to the Indian line. Here he got down from his horse and lay on the ground. No one knew he had been shot. Bull Bear and White Horse rode up and spoke to him. Then he told them. He said he did not see these men hiding

in the grass, and up to this, the Indians did not know there were any scouts fighting except on the island. Some women had now come up to look after the wounded, and Roman Nose was taken back to camp. He lingered the night and died at daybreak next day." [71]

John Sipes recounted his Cheyenne family oral history of the effect of the death of Roman Nose:

"Co-hoe or Limpy was a warrior, and when he saw the failed medicine he took after the medicine man, Wolf Belly, with a horse quirt and commenced to whipping the medicine man and calling him 'no good' and a fake, and Medicine Water himself pulled the horse and Co-hoe back from the medicine man. They were later able to get the dead warriors off the battlefield and away from the fight area." [72]

The Indians were devastated by the loss of their revered leader. As dusk descended over that fateful day, the Indians again retreated. The stars shown bright in the night sky as the Indians held vigil over Roman Nose and the soldiers mourned the loss of their comrades, including First Lieutenant Frederick H. Beecher.

Colonel George Alexander Forsyth later wrote of his thoughts during this time:

"Considering the fact that my command, including myself, only numbered fifty [some] men, the outlook was somewhat dismal. Lieutenant Beecher, Surgeon Mooers, and scouts Chalmers Smith and Wilson were dead or dying; scouts Louis Farley and Bernard Day were mortally wounded; scouts O'Donnell, Davis, Tucker, Gantt, Clarke, Armstrong, Morton, and Violett, severely wounded, and scouts Harrington, Davenport, Haley, McLaughlin, Hudson Farley, McCall, and two others slightly wounded." [73]

It is interesting to note that in this recount by Forsyth he was more concerned for his men, as he doesn't mention his own injuries. During the night, the soldiers reinforced their position on the island. They stacked saddles against the dead horses and mules. They worked at deepening the rifle pits and connecting them with a series of trenches. Martin Burke led a group of the men in digging deeper into the ground and creating a makeshift well, supplying an abundance of available water.

Sometime during that night, it was determined that someone needed to go to Fort Wallace, nearly one hundred miles away, for reinforcements. Two of the scouts, S. E. "Jack" Stillwell and Pierre Trudeau volunteered for the risky venture. Eli Ziegler later recalled:

> "Jack was the best imitator of an Indian that I ever saw. They fixed themselves up as Indians the best they could and took off their boots and tied on some rags and blankets on their feet so that if the Indians saw their tracks next day they would think it some of their own party and not follow them before they got to the fort. At a late hour they gave us their hand and crawled out." [74]

Sig Schlesinger added:

> "We listened for some time fully expecting every moment to hear the warwhoop which would announce their discovery and capture, but not a sound followed their departure." [75]

As the night wore on, many of the men, unable to sleep, grew restless. Schlesinger remembered a chilling moment when he crawled to his dead horse to retrieve some wild plums he had in his saddlebag:

> "I got out of my hole and creeping on hands and knees to the spot where my dead horse lay, [I] began feeling around in the darkness. I came in contact with something cold, and upon examination found it was Scout Wilson's dead pallid hand. The shivers chased up and down my back, but I got to my horse and tugged until I secured the saddlebags containing the plums. On my way back to my hole I passed where Doctor Mooers lay wounded, moaning piteously. I put a plum in his mouth, and I saw it between his teeth next morning." [76]

By sunrise of the following day, September 18, 1868, Stillwell and Trudeau had made their way to the south fork of the Republican River, dangerously close to the main Indian camp. The two scouts spent that entire day hidden in a ravine along the river, covered by clusters of tall prairie grass. Meanwhile, the Indians made another attack on the island in the dry riverbed. Again, the fighting lasted all day. Colonel Forsyth recalled:

> "At daylight [the Indians] again took up the fight from their former position in ambush, but as we were now fully protected, they did us no particular harm. It was now apparent that they meant to starve us out, for they made no further attempts to attack us openly." [77]

Eli Ziegler also wrote of that day's attack:

"They did come early, just before the sun rose. It seemed to me there were just as many and as bad as the first day and the squaws took their places on the hills just the same as the day before. Our orders were about the same, 'Hold your fire till they get close, but don't let them ride over us.' We were in a good deal better position and could all be together which gave us a better show than we had the day before. [The Indians] *stopped fighting and put up a white flag, but most of us were to old to be scalped alive that way and we showed no signs of a white flag so that did not last long with them.* [The fighting] *soon commenced again and poured in on us as hard as ever the rest of the day."* [78]

As darkness fell on that long day, Allison J. Pliley and Chauncey B. Whitney attempted to escape the island, but were unable, as the Indians had managed to block any path away from the island. However, under the cover of darkness that night, Stillwell and Trudeau were able to cross the river from their hiding place, and make their way slowly, southeast toward Fort Wallace. The following day they again sought a place to hide during the daylight hours, and found safety in the dried and decaying carcass of a buffalo.

John Hurst recounted the experiences of the third day of siege at the island:

"The third day was a repetition of the second, very little firing, but close watching on the part of the Indians. After dark Forsyth again called for volunteers, and Jack Donovan and A. J. Pliley started out, with directions to come back straight across the country with soldiers and an ambulance and medical supplies, together with plenty of food." [79]

Before Donovan and Pliley were sent on their dangerous assignment, Colonel Forsyth wrote out the following dispatch to carried by the scouts:

"On Delaware Creek, Republican River, September 19, 1868. To Colonel Blankhead, or Commanding Officer, Fort Wallace: I sent you two messengers on the night of the 17th instant, informing you of my critical condition. If the others have not arrived then hasten at once to my assistance. I have eight badly wounded and ten slightly wounded men to take in, and every animal I had was killed, save seven, which the Indians stampeded. Lieutenant Beecher is dead, Acting Surgeon Mooers

probably cannot live the night out. He was hit in the head Thursday, and has spoken but one rational word since. The Cheyennes alone number 450, or more. We have killed at least thirty-five of them, and wounded many more, besides killing and wounding a quantity of their stock. I am on a little island, and still have plenty of ammunition. We are living on mule and horse meat, and are entirely out of rations. You had better start with not less than seventy-five men, and bring all the wagons and ambulances you can spare. Bring a six-pound howitzer with you. I can hold out here for six days longer if absolutely necessary, but please lose no time. Very Respectfully, your obedient servant, George A. Forsyth U. S. Army, Commanding Co. Scouts. P. S. - My surgeon having been mortally wounded, none of my wounded men have had their wounds dressed yet, so please bring out a surgeon with you." [80]

Forsyth recounted:

"Shortly after midnight they [Donovan and Pliley] *left our entrenchments, and as they did not return, I felt satisfied that they had eluded the Indians and were on their way to Fort Wallace."*

On the third day of the siege, there was very little fighting. Major Forsyth recounted an interesting incident which occurred that day:

"There were, as a matter of course, queer episodes during the siege. On the third day a large and very fleshy Indian, having, as he thought, placed himself just out of range, taunted and insulted us in every possible way. He was perfectly naked, and his gestures especially were exceedingly exasperating. Not being in a happy frame of mind, the man's actions annoyed me excessively. Now we had in the command three Springfield breech-loading rifles which I knew would carry several hundred yards farther than our Spencer rifles. I accordingly directed that the men using these guns should sight them at their limit - 1,200 yards - and aim well over the sight, and see if by some chance we might stop the antics of this outrageously insulting savage. At the crack of the three rifles he sprang into the air with a yell of seemingly both surprise and anguish, and rolled over stone dead, while the Indians in his vicinity scattered in every direction, and this almost unexpected result of our small volley was a matter of intense satisfaction to all of us." [81]

Meanwhile, Donovan and Pliley had successfully made their way through the Indian's escape blocks. Allison J. Pliley later wrote of his experience:

> "After changing our boots for a pair of moccasins, which we had taken off dead Indians, in order to make as light a trail as possible, and after filling our pockets with tainted horse meat, we bid a silent 'so-long' to our comrades and started to crawl down along the north side of the island, stopping frequently to let a party of Indians surrounded the island pass by. After getting outside of their lines, we straightened up, and taking our course by the north star started on our long, weary walk, and we soon found we had made a mistake by putting on the moccasins." [82]

Jack Donovan picked up his comrade's story of that harrowing experience:

> "The prickly pear [cactus thorns] penetrated the wet leather like needles. Before we had covered ten miles our feet were like pincushions and began to swell. From that time on the trip was like a nightmare. We had to tear up our shirts and tie up our injured feet." [83]

The two scouts found an area of buffalo wallows where they hid for the rest of that day. Pliley remembered:

> "Lying there all day in the hot sun, without water, eating that rotten horse meat in order to keep up strength. About three o'clock in the afternoon our attention was drawn to a party of twenty-five Indians coming around toward us; ten minutes more and they would be upon us. We placed our guns where we could get them easily and prepared for the closing acts of our lives. When they got to within a quarter of a mile of us they halted, and after a short consultation they bore off to the northwest and past [sic] us without seeing us. Jack, who always light hearted in danger, commenced singing 'Oh, for a thousand tongues to sing.' After dark we again took up our weary walk, footsore and almost famished for water. About twelve o'clock that night we struck the south fork of the Republican. After spending an hour drinking and bathing our sore, swollen feet, we hurried on our mission. It appeared that every hour added more thorns in our feet and more pain from those that were already in them, until it seemed impossible to go on, but the thoughts of our comrades who depended upon us spurred us on. When we started from the island we laid our course to hit the Smoky Hill [route] north of Cheyenne Wells and on the fourth night out at three o'clock we struck the road." [84]

The soldiers and scouts stranded on the island were beginning to feel the strain of what looked like a hopeless defense. After the third day, it was apparent to all that the wounded were suffering terribly. The drastic change in temperatures from hot days to chilly nights in the crisp autumn air greatly affected their situation, particularly on the following morning when there was a white carpet of light snow covering the area.

Evidently this change in the weather affected the Indians as well. Shortly after sunrise, the soldiers observed the Indians moving away and hoped they were retreating. Indeed this appeared to be the case as there were no attacks that day. Still, there was a sense of grumbling among the soldiers. John Hurst recalled:

"We who were left on the island were having a serious time. The Indians gave up the siege [and] some of the men were prompted to advise saving the lives of those who were uninjured by striking out for the fort and leaving the wounded to their fate, thinking none of the volunteers would be able to get through. When this talk of abandoning the wounded reached Forsyth's ears he called us together and made a nice talk. It was very touching and soldierlike - so much so that I never heard any more talk about abandoning the wounded. Forsyth told us he expected us to stay with the command until the men he had sent out had time to get to the fort, and that it was our duty to the law of humanity to stick together at least that long. We all then swore we never would desert the wounded, but would die with them if necessary." [85]

On the morning of the fourth day, September 20, 1868, Doctor John H. Mooers died. Sigmund Schlesinger later wrote:

"Our mortally wounded were made as comfortable as possible before they died. As soon as possible we put our dead in the ground. Those that died at one end of the island were cared for by those in that vicinity, and others in their vicinity, so that one part of the island was not aware of the location of the corpses of the other part; at least I did not know where the bodies lay of those killed on the eastern end of the island. So one time, as I walked around among the pits, I noticed something red and round sticking out of the sand, like a half-buried red berry. I kicked it, but by so doing it was not dislodged; I kicked it again, but to no result. I then looked closer and discovered that it was the nose of a dead man." [86]

As for the wounded lingering in agony on the island, the suffering became almost unbearable. Colonel Forsyth recalled his own horrendous ordeal:

"As the days wore on the wounded became feverish, and some of them delirious, gangrene set in, and I was distressed to find the wound in my leg infested with maggots. I appealed to several of the men to cut it [the bullet] out, but as soon as they saw how close it lay to the artery, they declined doing so, alleging that the risk was too great. However, I determined that it should come out, as I feared sloughing, and then the artery would probably break in any event; so taking my razor from my saddle-pocket, and getting two of the men to press the adjacent flesh back and draw it taut, I managed to cut it out myself without disturbing the artery, greatly to my almost immediate relief." [87]

For the soldiers and scouts who were not wounded, the days on the island, waiting for reinforcements, were monotonous and the men began to wander about the area. Forsyth wrote:

"On the fifth or sixth day two of the command quietly stole away down the stream in the hope that they might possibly get a shot at some game, but their quest was in vain. However, they did find a few wild plums. These they brought back, boiled, and gave to the wounded, and I know that the few spoonfuls I received was by far the most delicious food that ever passed my lips." [88]

Sigmund Schlesinger remembered one particular incident:

"On about the fifth day, as the Indians began leaving us, we began to walk about and look around. About fifteen or twenty feet from my pit I noticed a few of our men calling to the rest of us. I ran to the place, and there, against the edge of the island, I saw three dead Indians. Their friends evidently could not reach them to carry them off, which explained to us the persistent fighting in this direction. When I got there, the Indians were being stripped of their equipments, scalps, etc. One of them was shot in the head and his hair was clotted with blood. I took hold of one of his braids and applied my knife to the skin above the ear to secure the scalp, but my hand coming in contact with the blood, I dropped the hair in disgust. Old Jim Lane saw my hesitation, and taking up the braid, said to me: 'My boy, does it make you feel sick?' Then inserting the point of the knife under the skin, he cut around, took up the other braid, and jerked the scalp from the head." [89]

The Indians had removed what dead comrades they could. They moved southwest of the battle site. Approximately twenty miles from the scene of the battle, they found a spot to offer their dead to the Great Spirit. On a high bluff above the Arickaree River the Cheyenne placed their dead warriors on wooden scaffolds, as was the traditional custom. The body of Roman Nose, their revered leader, was placed in a crevice in the hillside, sealed by a circular layer of stones. [90] For Medicine Water and Mo-chi, who by this time were wed in the Cheyenne tradition, the death of Roman Nose was a personal family tragedy, Roman Nose being related by marriage to Medicine Water.

"The Old ones say Medicine Water and Mo-chi greatly mourned the death of Roman Nose. They feared for their traditional way of life. Medicine Water vowed to carry on the fight." [91]

George Bent said of his fellow warrior:

"Roman Nose had never before been wounded except by an arrow in a fight with the Pawnees, yet he was always in front in battle and rarely had a horse shot out from under him. Roman Nose was killed in the prime of life; he was strong as a bull, tall even for a Cheyenne, broad-shouldered and deep-chested." [92]

The stranded soldiers on the island began to suffer from the effects of rancid horse meat, not to mention the smell of dead animals. Forsyth wrote:

"It was very hot, our meat had become putrid, and the stench from the dead horses lying close around us was almost intolerable." [93]

John Hurst related:

"We had no salt and our systems were craving for it. One of the men found a piece of pork rind in his haversack and chewed it until he thought he had all the good out of it and spit it out; and then I took it and chewed it up thought it tasted delicious." [94]

Howard Morton, one of the wounded, wrote the following from his hospital bed at Fort Wallace, shortly after the rescue:

"There was no certainty that our men sent to the fort had reached it. Some of our men found prickly pears on the hills, which we ate with relish. We were a disconsolate looking crowd. It was cold and wet most of the time and one morning it snowed. We hovered over our little fires,

made soup from the strong horse meat, putting in [gun] powder to deaden the taste." [95]

September 22 marked the sixth day for the stranded men. Starvation was becoming a stark reality. John Hurst offered a horrific account:

"We had nothing to eat but the dead horses which were festering and decaying about us, and when cut into this meat the stench was something frightful, and it had green streaks running all through it. The only way it was made at all available for eating was by sprinkling gunpowder over it while it was cooking, which partially took away the bad odor." [96]

Eli Ziegler also recounted the events of that day:

"On the morning of the sixth day everything was quiet, except the howling of wolves and sour horse meat was so rotten and alive with maggots we thought we would try to find some game or something to live on so we rustled out a little and found nothing much but prickly pears. We soon found out they would not do entirely for food so we lingered along on our old butcher shop [the dead horses] *until the eighth night."* [97]

During the eighth day of what must have had seemed as abandonment, John Hurst and a few of the others again wandered about looking for food. Soon, they came upon a few mounds built by prairie dogs. Hurst related the story:

"I went out to the dog town and watched it for awhile, but no dog came out. I kept up pretty well until this time, but now I began to think I would starve to death." [98]

What was not known to the stranded soldiers on the island was that two of their comrades, Jack Donovan and A. J. Pliley, had made the heroic one hundred and fifty mile journey, on foot and unscathed, arriving at Fort Wallace just before sunset on September 22. It was the end of a grueling five-day ordeal for the two men. Years later, A. J. Pliley wrote of the experience:

"On the fourth night out at three o'clock we struck the road at a ranch about three miles east of the wells. Our feet were a sight to look at, swollen to twice their normal size, festered with thorns protruding out of the numerous festering pimples on them, tired out, sick from eating

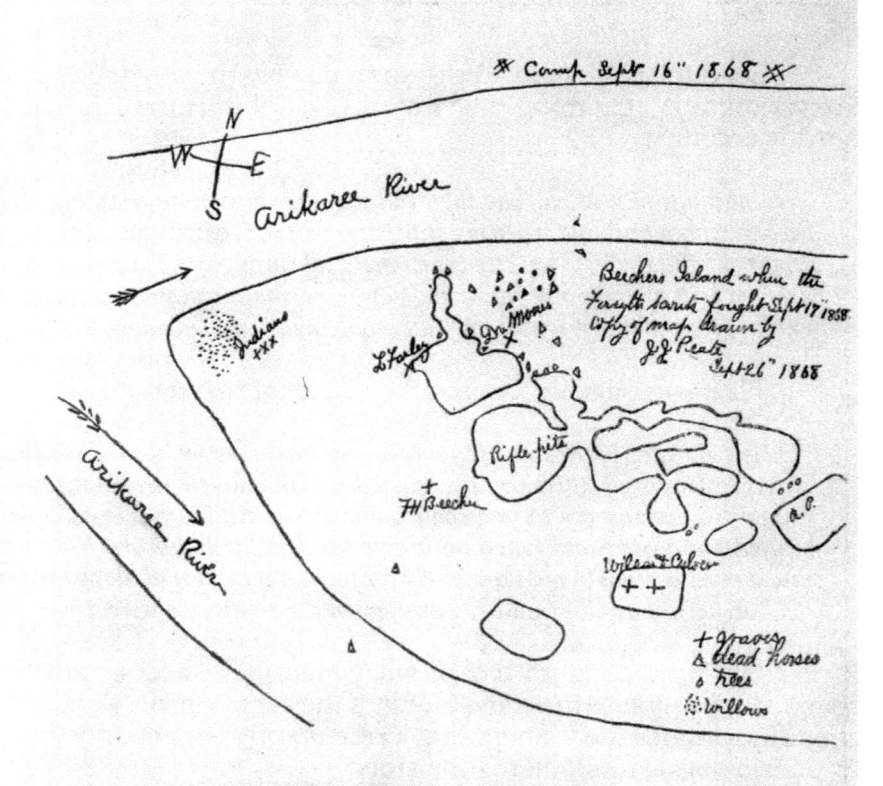

MAP OF BEECHER ISLAND.

The above map is reproduced from a copy drawn by J. J. Peate, of the Relief Expedition, at the time Forsyth and his scouts were rescued by Col. Carpenter's command.

The Island appears today as it did then excepting that the south channel of the river is closed and the trees and improvements, including the monument, appear as the Association has placed them.

This map of the Beecher Island battle was drawn by J.J. Peate. *DPL that putrid horse meat and drinking warm water we were indeed hard looking when we arrived at the ranchmen and explained to them where we were from and what we wanted, which consisted of a little whiskey, something to eat and a chance to lie down and sleep, with their promise to wake us when the stage to Wallace came along, all of which they cheerfully complied with, waking us about six o'clock and we had no trouble arranging terms with the driver for our passage in to Wallace and within an hour after we reported to the commanding officer every available man at the post was galloping to Forsyth's assistance. Donovan went with them as guide. That night with a message to General Bradley at the mouth of the Frenchmans Fork of the Republican river, [sic] I struck his command about eight o'clock the next morning and in a few moments his command was hurrying to the assistance of Forsyth. I then returned to Fort Wallace and I will here say, that Donovan and I beat Stillwell and Trudeau who left the island two nights before we did on the same mission, into Fort Wallace by about an hour."* [99]

After Stillwell and Trudeau had related the plight of Forsyth and his men to Colonel Henry Bankhead at Fort Wallace, the two were given quarters where they could clean up, get their first decent meal in nearly two weeks, and some much needed rest. In the meantime, Colonel Bankhead sent a message to General Philip Sheridan, relaying the news of Major Forsyth. Sheridan ordered Bankhead to exercise the "greatest dispatch to be used, and every means employed to succor Forsyth at once."[100] Officers at Fort Wallace sent news of the Indian fight and Forsyth's men to the United States War Department. The *New York Times* ran the Story in their September 24, 1868, issue. It read in part:

"Fort Wallace, Kansas, Wednesday, Sept. 23, - Two scouts from Col. Forsyth's command, who have been scouring the country towards the headwaters of the Republican River, arrived last night. The scouts could only travel at night, on account of danger from the Indians, they being seen every day. Later - 8 P.M. - Gen. Nichols has just arrived from Fort Reynolds and reports that Lieut. Beecher is dead. Dr. Mooers is mortally wounded, and is dying, and Col. Forsyth is nearly as bad. All are lying there, with Indians all around them, eating their horseflesh and waiting for relief. Cols. Bankhead and Carpenter will reach them tonight."

The *Leavenworth Times*, for obvious logistical reasons, provided the best coverage of the events as they received the information from Fort Wallace. The September 25, 1868, issue did just that under the headline:

> "*Additional Particulars*
> *Col. Forsyth, of Maj. Gen. Sheridan's staff, with forty* [sic] *men, was attacked by seven or eight hundred Sioux, on the 17th of September, while scouting on the Dry Fork of the Republican River. The Indians were well armed, and pressed our troops during the entire day and the following night, when Col. Forsyth effected a retreat to an island in the river, where he was entirely surrounded by Indians. During the night two men were dispatched as messengers to Fort Wallace, a distance of over a hundred miles, to carry the intelligence to Gen. Sheridan. The men made their escape from the beleaguered party by crawling on their hands and knees for more than a mile. Gen. Sheridan, with his usual promptness, sent forward from Fort Wallace reinforcements and provisions.*"

J. J. "Jack" Peate, an original member of Forsyth's scouts, had remained stationed at Fort Hays when the rest of his group left the post on September 16, 1868. Peate was with a command of soldiers ordered to search for marauding Indians when he first learned of Forsyth and the scouts' dire predicament. Years later, Peate recounted:

> "*September 21, 1868, we were ordered out on a scout with Lieut. Col. L. H. Carpenter and his troops of the Tenth United States cavalry (colored.) We were to scout along the Smoky Hill road, as the Indians were doing considerable damage there. We were in camp on Goose creek, north of the stage road and about the Kansas line, when four troopers came to us with a dispatch from Fort Wallace. They told us they had met two of Forsyth's men, that Forsyth had had a battle with the Indians, that half of his men were killed or wounded and all his horses were dead. The dispatch directed Carpenter to proceed at once to a point on the Dry Fork of the Republican 'about seventy-five miles or eighty miles north, northwest from Fort Wallace.' Carpenter communicated the dispatch to all, and ordered the wagon boss to leave any mules that could not keep up, and, if necessary, to abandon wagons.*" [101]

Captain Louis Henry Carpenter and his troops of the Tenth United States Cavalry, along with J. J. Peate, left their camp at noon and traveled northwest, toward the Republican River. On the morning of September 24, 1868, Carpenter's scouts found fresh Indian tracks. Peate again picked up his experience:

> *"About noon we came to a large, sandy-bottomed dry creek, and hunted on it for miles for signs of Forsyth. The first sign we found of a battle was a dead horse that had died of gunshot wounds. This was about a mile south of the south fork of the Republican. Half a mile south of the river we found several dead Indians on a scaffold about eight feet above the ground (some tribe's mode of disposing of the dead.) They were wrapped in blankets and buffalo robes and had their hunting and war paraphernalia beside them. Horses had been killed by the side of the scaffold so the departed warriors would have horses to ride in the happy hunting grounds. We examined the dead warriors and found they had died recently of gunshot wounds. This was about 3 o'clock p. m., and we felt sure we were near where the battle had taken place. We found several other scaffolds with dead Indians upon them that afternoon there was a large fresh trail near the river, and the Indians had traveled east."* [102]

The site of the Indian scaffolds, discovered by the scouts of the Tenth United States cavalry, located in what is today Yuma County, was also (unknown to the scouts at that time) the concealed burial site of Roman Nose. J. J. Peate continued with his account:

> *"Just before day the morning of the twenty-fifth we saw five mounted men coming over the hills from the south. We were glad to find it was Jack Donovan, one of the second of two to leave the island for help, and four other fearless men, who were returning with him to the island. Carpenter took one lieutenant, the doctor, Donovan and his scouts, fifteen troopers, the ambulance, a few rations, and away we went. Even our horses entered into the excitement of the hour and needed very little urging. I was looking in a northwest direction and saw two objects that looked like men walking down a hill a mile and a half away. I called Donovan's attention to them and he said, 'Yes, by God" There is a camp!'"* [103]

September 25, 1868, marked the ninth day for the stranded scouts. Morale was low and the men were not having much luck in their hunt for fresh meat. It was mid-morning on that day when several of the men, either wandering around or hunting for game, noticed something moving toward them in the distance. Major Forysth recounted what happened next:

> *"On the morning of the ninth day since the attack by the Indians one of the men near me suddenly sprang to his feet, and shading his eyes, with his hand, shouted, 'There are some moving objects on the far hills!'*

Instantly every man who could stand was on his feet gazing intently in the direction indicated. In a few moments a general murmur ran through the command. 'By God above us, it's an ambulance!' shouts one of the men; and then went up a wild cheer that made the little valley ring, and strong men grasped hands, and then flung their arms around each other, and laughed and cried. It was a troop of the Tenth Cavalry, under Lieutenant-Colonel L. H. Carpenter, the advance of Colonel Bankhead's command from Fort Wallace, which that officer had fairly hurled forward as soon as news of situation reached him through Donovan and Pliley." [104]

John Hurst was one of the men out hunting, south of the island, for fresh food on that day:

"I had not gone far when I saw some of the men running towards me and motioning for me to hurry [back.] The thought that it was Indians returning for another invasion of the island took possession of me and I started on a dead run for my comrades. I was too faint and exhausted, however, to run very far, and soon fell to the ground, all in, and scarcely caring whether it was Indians or not, so discouraged and disheartened was I. Happening to look up, I saw three horsemen riding toward me. I gazed long and earnestly at the advancing riders and soon saw they were white men. It proved to be Jack Donovan, Jack Peate, a Forsyth Scout who had remained behind at Fort Wallace, and a relief party. The sudden transition from despair to safety was too much for my overtaxed nerves, and I broke down and wept like a child." [104]

Eli Ziegler was also out hunting for food when he and Fletcher Vilott noticed movement from "the far hills to the south":

"We jumped to our feet and walked up the hill a little further, where we could plainly see that [something] *was coming over the hill toward us. We could not make out it was so we hurried back to camp in case it was Indians. We reported in camp that their was quite a large force of something coming over the hill from the south. The colonel said, 'Get the men all in and we will be ready for anything. In a short while, I saw a man at full gallop. When he got a little closer to my great surprise,* [I realized] *it was my old friend Jack Peate."* [105]

J. J. Peate added his own recollections of that day of rescue:

"Down that steep hill we rushed as fast as we could urge our horses. Soon we could see several men running towards us. Nearer us was a

man running toward the island. We were fast overtaking him while he stopped and raised his gun to fire at us. We separated, waved our hats and he came running toward us. Soon we met the others. I put spurs to my horse and rode into that blood-stained island alone. Ne'er received so royal and hearty a welcome as I did. Among those staunch-hearted men, who lifted me from my horse, embraced me and, strong men though they were, wept, as cheer upon cheer arose. How they cheered, again and again, while manly tears coursed down their cheeks." [106]

Private Reuben Waller, with Company H of the 10th United States Cavalry Regiment, and himself a former slave, later wrote of his arrival at the battle scene:

"Colonel L. H. Carpenter, with his Company H, 10th U. S. Cavalry, was at Cheyenne Wells, Colo., 100 miles from Beecher Island. Jack Stillwell brought us word of the fix that Beecher was in and we entered the race for the island, and in 26 hours Colonel Carpenter and myself, as his hostler, rode into the rifle pits. And what a sight we saw - 30 wounded and dead men right in the midst of 50 dead horses, that had lain in the hot sun for ten days. The men were in a dying condition when Carpenter and myself dismounted and began to rescue them." [107]

It should be noted that Reuben Waller wrote this in 1929, at the age of eighty-nine. Given his age and the passing of sixty years, Waller's memory was a bit faulty. Frederick Beecher had died in the early morning of the second day of the siege and Beecher Island had not yet been named at the time of the rescue. Also, Waller obviously using Cheyenne Wells as a point of reference, as the town was not established until 1870.

Private Waller continued his account:

"By this time all the soldiers were in the pits and we began to feed the men from our haversacks." [108]

At the island, Captain Louis Henry Carpenter immediately set out to find his old friend, George Alexander Forsyth. The two former Civil War officers had formed a bond during their service under General Philip Sheridan, both seeing action in the Shenandoah Valley as well as the Wilderness Campaign. When Carpenter found his severely wounded old friend, he must have been shocked. However, he didn't let on, but shook the hand of Forsyth and offered his military services. Meanwhile, a rush of activity was occurring on the island. First Lieutenant Charles Banzof brought in the supply train and very quickly, tents were erected a good distance away from the island, in an effort to relieve the wounded from the horrible stench of the decaying animal carcasses. Jenkins A. Fitzgerald, the military surgeon who had accompanied Carpenter's regiment, set up a makeshift field hospital to attend to the wounded. The wounded soldiers and scouts were carried to this area.

Private Waller provided a somewhat humorous account:

"The men were eating all we gave them, and it was plenty. Sure, we never gave a thought that it would hurt them. You can imagine a man in starvation, and plenty suddenly set before him. He can't think of the results until too late. That is the condition that Company H, 10th Cavalry fixed for the Beecher Island men. We were not aiming to hurt the boys. It was all done through eagerness and excitement." [109]

Doctor Fitzgerald immediately saw to the medical needs of the wounded. In examining the wound of Louis Farley, Fitzgerald felt he had no other choice but to amputate his leg. Captain L. H. Carpenter was present during the procedure. He later recalled:

"I assisted all that I could in the operation, but the poor fellow was so far gone that he could not stand the shock and died the following morning." [110]

Upon examining Major Forysth, Doctor Fitzgerald recommended the amputation of one of the major's legs. However, Forysth adamantly refused. Fitzgerald managed to save Forysth's leg and later said that if another twenty-four hours had passed before help arrived, Forsyth likely would have died. The following day, Colonel Henry Bankhead and his troops, accompanied by Major James S. Brisbin and two troops of the Second Cavalry out of Fort Sedgewick, arrived at the island. As the group approached the area, following the Arickaree River, young Sigmund Schlesinger was the first to notice their arrival. Schlesinger later wrote:

"Nearly all of us ran out to meet the party. Soon Jack [Stillwell] jumped from his horse, and in his joy to see so many of us alive again, he permitted his tears [to] free flow down his good honest cheeks." [111]

This drawing depicts the rescue of soldiers stranded at Beecher Island.
DPL

Over the next two days, Thursday, September 25, and Friday, the 26th, while the wounded were cared for, the soldiers reburied the dead deeper in the ground. Major Brisbin wrote of the event:

"Today we are burying the dead and caring for the wounded. Dead Indians lay within fifteen feet of the breastworks, and the stench from their swollen and bloated bodies and the dead horses is terrible." [112]

For all who participated, the saddest reburial of all was that of First Lieutenant Frederick H. Beecher. All who knew him respected him and those in the relief party who hadn't known him, certainly knew him by reputation. Among those attending to the reburial was Sigmund Schlesinger. Years later, Schlesinger wrote:

"We removed his [Beecher] boots, coat, etc., [when wounded] and of course, these things were not replaced on the body after he was dead, but lay around unnoticed. My shoes were quite badly worn, especially after being used for digging in the sand, so when we were preparing to leave the island, I put on his shoes, which were just about my size, and wore them even after I got back to New York City, leaving my old shoes in their stead on the island." [113]

On Sunday morning, September 27, 1868, Captain Carpenter and the soldiers of Tenth United States Cavalry, along with Colonel Bankhead and his troops, accompanied by Major James S. Brisbin and his cavalry, escorted the wounded and surviving members of Forsyth's scouts back to Fort Wallace. It was a long grueling trip over rough terrain. Following a fork of the Republican River, the entourage reached the area where, on the high bluff above, the Cheyenne had placed their dead warriors on wooden scaffolds. Here, a few of the soldiers had no qualm in desecrating the Cheyenne burial site. J. J. Peate was one of these men and later wrote:

"The Indian was placed on a scaffold that was eight feet high. Fastened to the scaffold was his war bonnet and a large drum. He was wrapped in blankets and a buffalo robe and tied on the scaffold. The posts on one side of the scaffold were torn away by the boys so we could have a better look at the good Indian. The body was then rolled to the edge of the canon and it rolled from there to the bottom." [114]

Sigmund Schlesinger, another active participant, remembered:

> *"All the bodies were pulled down from their lofty perches. This may seem as a wanton sacrilege, but not to those who have suffered bodily torture and mental anguish from those very cruel savages. I had no scruples in rolling one out of his blankets, that still were soaking in the blood from the wounds that evidently caused his death, and appropriating the top one that was least wet. This Indian had on a headdress composed of buckskin beautifully beaded and ornamented, with a polished buffalo horn on the frontal part and eagle feathers down the back. When I took this off, maggots were in the headpiece. I also pulled off his earrings and finger rings, which were of tin. He was so far decomposed that when I took hold of the rings the fingers came along, and those I shook out! I also got his beaded knife scabbard and other trinkets. The blanket, one earring and scabbard are still in my possession. I had great trouble in carrying my souvenirs away, owing to the awful stench. No one would tolerate me near him. When I was mounted I tied the bundle to the saddle girth under the mule's body, and when I rode in a wagon I tied it to the axle, but in spite of these expedients, I had to put up with remonstrances until we finally reached Fort Wallace, where I immediately soaked my trophies in a creek, weighing them down with stones. At Wallace we naturally were objects of interest and our souvenirs no less so. My Indian headdress was an especial curiosity. Jack Donovan interceded for one of the officers and offered me $50 for it, but I refused to part with it. Next morning it was missing from my tent!"* [115]

Back at Fort Wallace, it wasn't long before tales told by the scouts of the Indian battle and siege on the island became front page news across the country. The *Leavenworth Times* reprinted an article from the *Rochester Evening Express* in their September 30, 1868, issue:

> *"Relatives Concerned For Colonel Forsyth*
> *The Rochester Evening Express says of Col. George A. Forsyth:*
> *'His friends and relatives in this city are overwhelmed with grief, and it is to be hoped some favorable intelligence will be received today. A letter was received from him by his mother, dated the 17th, in which he wrote that he had become tired of camp life and had applied for a temporary command, to go out and fight the Indians. It had been given to him, and his friends need not expect another letter from him for several weeks. Col. Forsyth has escaped death a thousand times while in service with*

Gen. Sheridan in the Shenandoah Valley, and distinguished himself for gallantry and bravery in many a hard fought battle. It is to be sincerely hoped that, after passing through so many struggles, and coming through so many unscathed by a rebel bullet or bayonet, that he may now escape being the victim of the wily and crafty red-skins. Col. F.'s father, mother and sisters reside in this city, and he is the brother of Mrs. Wm. H. Ross Lewin."

The *Leavenworth Times* printed an obituary for Doctor John H. Mooers in the September 29, 1868, issue:

"Doctor John H. Mooers, whose death is announced by our special dispatch, had lived at Hays City about one year, and he was a physician and druggist. He belonged in Plattsburg, N. Y., where he leaves a widow and one child. Elias Woodruff, Esq., of this city, is a brother-in-law of the deceased. Dr. Mooers acted as surgeon during the war, serving four years. In Northern New York he stood very high in his profession. He was a cultivated and genial gentleman, and had hosts of friends. He received a fatal shot while dressing the wounds of Col. Forsyth." [116]

The *Cheyenne, Wyoming Leader* newspaper issue of October 22, 1868 reported the news of General Philip Sheridan's General Field Order No. 2, issued from Fort Hays, Kansas, on October 1, 1868:

"The Major General commanding calls attention of the following officers and soldiers under his command to the following record of some of the engagements and pursuits under the present Indian campaign, and desires to express his thanks and high appreciation of the gallantry, energy and bravery displayed by those engaged therein. First. The affair on the Arrickaree [sic] fork of the Republican River, Kansas, September 17, 1868, where a party of forty-seven scouts, under command of Brevet Colonel George A. Forsyth, Major Ninth Cavalry, Acting Assistant Inspector General Department of the Missouri and First Lieutenant Frederick H. Beecher, Third Infantry, defended themselves against about 600 Indians for eight days, successfully repulsing several charges and inflicting a loss upon the savages of over seventy-five killed and wounded, in which Lieutenant Beecher, Doctor Mooers and three others were killed and wounded, all their stock killed, and the party obliged to live on horse flesh during that time. Second. The affair at Big Sandy Creek, Colorado Territory in which Company I Tenth Cavalry, under the command of Captain George Graham and Lieutenant Amick, defended themselves

against the attack of about one hundred Indians, losing a number of horses killed and wounded, and afterwards pursuing the Indians, killing eleven and capturing a number of their ponies. Third. The rapid preparation pursuit and attack made by Brevet Brigadier General W.H. Penrose, Captain Third Infantry, commanding Fort Lyon, Colorado Territory, and First Lieutenant Henry H. Abell, Seventh Cavalry, on September 8, 1868, in which they pursued a party of Indians who had driven off stock, killing four of their number and capturing the stock, having traveled on their return to camp, 120 miles in 25 hours."

When General George Armstrong Custer learned of Colonel Forsyth's ordeal, he remarked on the actions of his fellow officer as:

"One of the most remarkable and successful contests in which our forces on the Plains have ever been engaged; and the whole affair was a wonderful exhibition of daring courage, stubborn bravery, and heroic endurance, under circumstances of great peril and exposure. In all probability, there will never occur in our future hostilities with the savage tribes of the West a struggle the equal of that in which were engaged the heroic men who defended so bravely 'Beecher Island.' Forsyth, the gallant leader, after a long period of suffering finally recovered from the effects of his severe wounds, and is now contentedly awaiting the next war to give him renewed excitement." [117]

For the Cheyenne, the battle was forever known as "The Fight when Roman Nose Was Killed." To some of the Cheyenne, it was considered a minor fight, but for the fact that their renowned warrior, Roman Nose, was killed.

For the Cheyenne Dog Soldiers, the battle at the island, resulting in the death of their warring leader, meant nothing less than revenge.

— Chapter Notes —

1. John L. Sipes, Cheyenne tribal historian.
2. Various writers referring to this incident have misnamed Alights-On-Cloud as "He Who Mounts the Clouds," or "Touching Cloud." John L. Sipes, Cheyenne tribal historian. Also see Grinnell, *The Fighting Cheyennes,* pg. 74.
3. John L. Sipes, Cheyenne tribal historian.
4. ibid.
5. Charles Moore - Indian Depredations Claims Division, Record Group 123, Claim #1246.
6. Annual Report, A. G. Boone, Indian agent, June 4, 1868. Also see Monnett, *The Battle of Beecher Island and the Indian War of 1867-1869.*
7. The *New York Times,* January 13, 1867.
8. Utley, *Life in Custer's Cavalry: Diaries and Letters of Albert and Jennie Barnitz,* pg. 174.
9. Hyde, *Life of George Bent,* pg. 200.
10. Annual Report for 1868, Edward Wynkoop to Thomas Murphy, August 19, 1868.
11. Roenigk, *Pioneer History of Kansas,* pgs. 94-95.
12. Annual Report for 1868, Edward Wynkoop to Murphy, August 19, 1868.
13. Crawford, Samuel J., *Kansas in the Sixties.*
14. Apollinaris Dietemann Indian Depredation Claim #4941. Courtesy, Jeff Broome.
15. ibid.
16. The *Rocky Mountain News,* August 27, 1868.
17. Apollinaris Dietemann Indian Depredation Claim #4941, Mrs. L. J. Fahrion Deposition. Courtesy, Jeff Broome.
18. ibid.
19. The *Rocky Mountain News,* August 28, 1868.
20. Howbert, *Memories of a Lifetime in the Pike's Peak Region,* pg. 184.
21. Report of the Secretary of War, 1868, pg. 13.
22. Brush's cattle ranch, along the South Platte River, had suffered attacks by the Indians. The town of Brush, Colorado would be named for him.
23. Howbert, *Memories of a Lifetime in the Pike's Peak Region,* pg. 195-196.
24. ibid.
25. ibid.

26.   ibid. The cabin where the deceased boys were brought still stands in a park in Old Colorado City.
27.   *Denver Westerners' Roundup*, September 1969. Also see Monnett, *The Battle of Beecher Island*, pg.117.
28.   Forsyth, *The Story of the Soldier*, pg. 200.
29.   Annual Report of the Commissioner of Indian Affairs, 1868, pg. 65.
30.   Forsyth, *A Frontier Fight, The Beecher Island Annual,* 1930, pgs. 34-35.
31.   ibid., pg. 38.
32.   Forsyth, *Thrilling Days in Army Life*, pg. 20.
33.   Monnett, *The Battle of Beecher Island*, pg.124. Also see Brininstool, *The Beecher Island Fight*, pg. 60.
34.   Forsyth, *A Frontier Fight, The Beecher Island Annual*, pg. 35.
35.   Murphy, *The First Day of the Battle of the Arickaree, The Beecher Island Annual*. Thomas B. Murphy should not be confused with Superintendent of Indian Affairs, Thomas Murphy.
36.   Forsyth, *A Frontier Fight, The Beecher Island Annual*, pg. 39.
37.   Murphy, *The First Day of the Battle of the Arickaree, The Beecher Island Annual*.
38.   Forsyth, *A Frontier Fight, The Beecher Island Annual*, pg. 39.
39.   It is interesting to note that today's Colorado state map spells the river's name as "Arikaree."
40.   Forsyth, *The Story of the Soldier*, pgs. 214-215.
41.   Forsyth, *A Frontier Fight, The Beecher Island Annual*, pg. 39.
42.   Propst, *Forgotten People*, pg. 109.
43.   Zigler, *Story of the Beecher Island Battle, The Beecher Island Annual*. Military records, courtesy of Jeff Broome. It should also be noted here that in later life, Eli Ziegler changed the spelling of his surname to Zigler.
44.   ibid., pg. 56.
45.   Davis, "A Summer on the Plains," *Harper's New Monthly Magazine*, Vol. 36, No. 18, 1868, pg. 295. Also see Hoig, *The Peace Chiefs of the Cheyennes*, pg.97.
46.   Hyde, *Life of George Bent*, pg. 306.
47.   John L. Sipes, the Cheyenne tribal historian.
48.   Hyde, *Life of George Bent*, pg. 298.
49.   Hyde, *Life of George Bent*, pg. 299.
50.   Zigler, *Story of the Beecher Island Battle, The Beecher Island Annual*.
51.   Forsyth, *A Frontier Fight, The Beecher Island Annual*, pg. 41.
52.   Hyde, *Life of George Bent*, pg. 300.
53.   Zigler, *Story of the Beecher Island Battle, The Beecher Island Annual*.
54.   Monnett, *The Battle of Beecher Island*, pg.134.
55.   Murphy, "The First Day of the Battle of the Arickaree," *The Beecher Island Annual*.
56.   Brininstool, *The Beecher Island Fight*, pg. 95.

57. Zigler, *Story of the Beecher Island Battle, The Beecher Island Annual.*
58. Monnett, *The Battle of Beecher Island,* pg.137.
59. Brininstool, *The Beecher Island Fight,* pg. 95.
60. Zigler, *Story of the Beecher Island Battle, The Beecher Island Annual.*
61. Hutton, *Phil Sheridan & His Army,* pg. 47.
62. Hyde, *Life of George Bent,* pgs. 300-301.
63. Forsyth, *A Frontier Fight, The Beecher Island Annual,* pg. 46.
64. ibid.
65. Forsyth, *A Frontier Fight, The Beecher Island Annual,* pg. 35.
66. Brininstool, *The Beecher Island Fight,* pg. 81.
67. Forsyth, *A Frontier Fight, The Beecher Island Annual,* pg. 50.
68. Monnett, *The Battle of Beecher Island,* pg.145.
69. Hyde, *Life of George Bent,* pg. 304.
70. ibid., pg. 307-308.
71. ibid., pg. 302.
72. John Sipes, Cheyenne tribal historian. Wolf Belly was later killed in the fight.
73. Forsyth, *A Frontier Fight, The Beecher Island Annual,* pg. 50.
74. Zigler, *Story of the Beecher Island Battle, The Beecher Island Annual.*
75. Brininstool, *The Beecher Island Fight,* pg. 95. Also see Monnett, *The Battle of Beecher Island,* pg.152.
76. Monnett, *The Battle of Beecher Island,* pg.153.
77. Forsyth, *Thrilling Days in Army Life,* pgs. 62-63.
78. Zigler, *Story of the Beecher Island Battle, The Beecher Island Annual.*
79. Hurst, *The Beecher Island Fight,* Kansas State Historical Society, Volume 15, 1919.
80. Forsyth, *A Frontier Fight, The Beecher Island Annual,* pg. 51. It should remembered that Forsyth and his men thought the Arickaree Creek was the Delaware Creek.
81. ibid., pg. 52.
82. Pliley, *The Journey of Pliley and Donovan to Fort Wallace for Relief, The Beecher Island Annual,* pg. 74.
83. Monnett, *The Battle of Beecher Island,* pg.156.
84. Pliley, *The Journey of Pliley and Donovan to Fort Wallace for Relief, The Beecher Island Annual,* pgs. 74-75. It should also be noted that Pliley wrote this in 1930; thus the town of Cheyenne Wells was used as a reference point, as it did not exist in 1868.
85. Hurst, *The Beecher Island Fight,* Kansas State Historical Society, Volume 15, 1919.
86. Monnett, *The Battle of Beecher Island,* pg.160.
87. Forsyth, *Thrilling Days in Army Life,* pgs. 70-71.
88. Forsyth, *A Frontier Fight, The Beecher Island Annual,* pg. 53.
89. Brady, *Indian Fights and Fighters,* pg. 118.

90. Wommack, *From the Grave*, pg. 65. The site, discovered years later, is located west of Bonney Reservoir in Yuma County. Also see the WPA Colorado Cemetery Directory, as well as the archives of the Burlington Public Library.
91. John L. Sipes, Cheyenne tribal historian.
92. Hyde, *Life of George Bent*, pg. 308.
93. Forsyth, "A Frontier Fight," *The Beecher Island Annual*, pg. 53.
94. Hurst, "The Beecher Island Fight," Kansas State Historical Society, Volume 15, 1919.
95. Morton, *The Beecher Island Annual*, pg.100.
96. Hurst, "The Beecher Island Fight," Kansas State Historical Society, Volume 15, 1919.
97. Zigler, "Story of the Beecher Island Battle," *The Beecher Island Annual*. pg. 65.
98. Hurst, *The Beecher Island Annual*, pg. 72.
99. Pliley, *The Journey of Pliley and Donovan to Fort Wallace for Relief, The Beecher Island Annual*, pgs. 74-75.
100. Monnett, *The Battle of Beecher Island*, pg.169.
101. Peate, J.J., "Peate Tells of the Relief," *The Beecher Island Annual*, pg. 89. The Tenth United States Cavalry of which Peate referred to was the famous unit known as The Buffalo Soldiers.
102. ibid., pg. 90
103. ibid.
104. Hurst, "Scout John Hurst's Story of the Fight," *The Beecher Island Annual*, pg. 73.
105. Zigler, "Story of the Beecher Island Battle," *The Beecher Island Annual*, pg. 66.
106. Peate, J.J., "Peate Tells of the Relief," *The Beecher Island Annual*, pg. 90.
107. Waller, "History of a Slave Written by Himself at the Age of 89 Years," *The Beecher Island Annual*, pg. 116.
108. ibid.
109. ibid.
110. Monnett, *The Battle of Beecher Island*, pg.172.
111. ibid. Page 175.
112. Anderson, "Stand at the Arickaree," the *Colorado Magazine*, Fall 1964, pg. 42.
113. Brady, *Indian Fights and Fighters*, pg. 120.
114. Peate, J.J., "Peate Tells of the Relief," *The Beecher Island Annual*, pg. 91.
115. Schlesinger, "The Beecher Island Fight," Kansas State Historical Society, 1919.
116. It is interesting to note that the state of New York has two towns bearing the Mooers name: Mooers and Mooers Forks, New York.
117. Custer, *My Life on the Plains*, pg. 143.

— BATTLE OF SUMMIT SPRINGS —

Following the Indian's departure from what they called "The Fight when Roman Nose Was Killed," the Cheyenne Dog Soldiers again split their forces. Many went north toward the Solomon and Saline Rivers under Tall Bull, where they continued raiding in Kansas Territory. Others went south to settle in for the winter with Black Kettle at his camp north of Antelope Hills in the Indian Territory. Medicine Water, along with his daughter, Measure Woman, and Mo-chi were among those who joined Black Kettle's camp. Here their first child, a girl, Tah-nea, was born in their lodge.[1]

A few bands of the Dog Soldiers returned to the South Platte River Road, raiding and terrorizing travelers and homesteaders. Other bands of the Dog Soldiers remained along the Arkansas River, their sacred homeland, which they intended to defend. It would be a defense which included raiding, murder and the taking of hostages.

Richard Foote and Clara Isabel Blinn operated the way station at the junction of Sand Creek and the Arkansas River, just northeast of present-day Lamar, in Colorado Territory. Blinn, a Union veteran of the Civil War, had mustered out of service when the war ended, but suffered from a wound to his arm, which would plague him the rest of his life. Nevertheless, he married sixteen-year-old Clara Isabel Harrington, August 12, 1865. The newlyweds settled into their new life near Clara's parents, in Perrysburg, Ohio. Here, their first (and only) child, William, was born in 1866. Two years later the young family decided to journey west, where Blinn would start his own business, along with his brother, Hubble, and brother-in-law, John Buttles. Leaving Ohio in March 1868, they traveled west by train to Kansas City. From there, they made their way to the Colorado Territory, arriving on April 20, 1868. For the next six months, Richard and Clara Blinn tried to make a go of their operation, but Blinn's arm injury became more painful. In early October, they decided to return to the East. On October 5,

1868, the Blinn family left Fort Lyon with a small wagon train, following the Santa Fe Trail eastward. The journey seemed fairly routine until the fourth day of their travel.

Shortly after noon, on October 9, 1868, their wagon train was attacked by a party of nearly one hundred Cheyenne Dog Soldiers near the border of Colorado and Kansas. As the Indians split their forces, they charged the wagon party, One group circled the back half of the wagon train, firing their rifles and shooting arrows at the men driving the wagons, while other warriors were able to overtake the lead wagon, driven by Clara Blinn, with her two year old son sleeping in back. As the Indians drove the wagon across the Arkansas River, and away from the rest of the group, Richard and his brother, Hubble, gave chase on horseback. In an attempt to stop the wagon, they tried to shoot the oxen, but failed in their efforts. The men watched in horror as the wagon containing their family was driven away.

Richard and Hubble Blinn, along with the other men in the wagon train, were now trapped. They circled their wagons and constructed barriers as best as they could. The Indians remained in a menacing stance, but did not attack. On the fifth day of the siege, one of the men in the wagon party managed to break away and make his way back to Fort Lyon, arriving before daylight on October 14, 1868. That morning, troops led by Captain William H. Penrose left the military post and rescued the remaining members of the stranded wagon train. The soldiers, along with Richard Blinn, set out to search for Blinn's wife and son. They found the wagon, burned and abandoned.

Leaving the area, the warriors had taken nineteen-year-old Clara Blinn and two-year-old Willie, who were now captives of the Cheyenne Dog Soldiers. A troop of soldiers followed the Indian trail which led southeast. Not far on the trail, a soldier found a note in the brush. It was written by Clara Blinn and read:

> "Dear Dick, Willie and I are prisoners. They are going to keep us. If you live, save us if you can. We are with them. Clara Blinn." [2]

The soldiers soon lost the trail, gave the note to an obviously upset Richard Blinn, and eventually returned to Fort Lyon.

Meanwhile, Major General Philip H. Sheridan, commander of the Military Department of the Missouri, realized the futility of special military units in the field, such as the Forsyth scouts, who came under siege at the Battle of Beecher Island. Sheridan became convinced that winter campaigns against the Indians, such as that carried out by Colonel Chivington at Sand Creek, nearly four years previous, was the strategy to implement within his command. While it was a common phrase of the era, "The only good Indian is a dead Indian," most historians believe it originated from a statement made by Sheridan.

In any case, Sheridan theorized that due to the Indian's constant movements in the summer months they were hard to catch, but during the winter months, when the Indians were in camp, they were easily located. Therefore, Sheridan would eventually consolidate eight companies of the Seventh Cavalry as well as a company the Third Cavalry, under the command of Alfred M. Sully, District Commander of the Upper Arkansas District. Sully was not Sheridan's ideal selection for this military endeavor; however, Sully was the only officer available at the time of Sheridan's implementation.

Sully had raised the ire of Sheridan when he had authorized the distribution of arms and ammunition to the Indians in August 1868. From then on, the two were often at odds. One officer who observed the contention between the two, later recalled that Sully was:

"A very pleasant, genial sociable man in manner and appearance, whose only common characteristic with Sheridan was that he always took a little whiskey very regularly." [3]

During a pursuit of Indians along the Cimarron River, Sully's scouts were attacked by a group of Cheyenne warriors. A few members of Sully's troops rescued the scouts and then set out in pursuit of the Indians. Unable to catch them, the soldiers returned. Incredibly, Sully arrested two of the officers who led the pursuit. A few days later, Sully and his troops were again attacked by the same group of warriors. Sully ordered the soldiers to retreat and move back toward Fort Dodge. By this time, General Sheridan was disgusted with Sully and his performance as an officer. [4] Sheridan strongly felt he needed new leadership if his plans for a winter campaign against the hostile Indians was to be successful.
General Sheridan sent a request to his commander, Lieutenant General William Tecumseh Sherman, for additional troops as well as aggressive field commanders. Sherman was only too happy to oblige his old friend, as he, too, wished to wage war against the marauding Cheyenne Dog Soldiers. General Sheridan was given

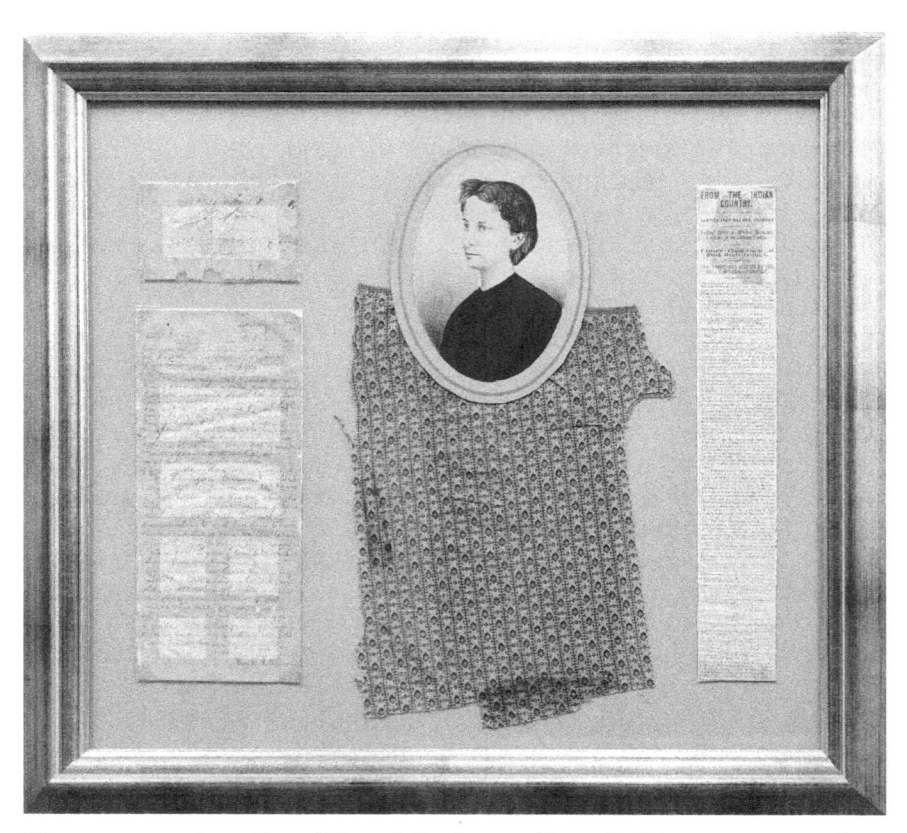

Cheyenne captive, Clara Blinn, left pieces of her clothing on trees and bushes in hopes her path could be tracked by her husband or soldiers. She was found dead at Black Kettle's camp on the Washita River. *Washita National Park Service.*

six companies of the Twenty-Seventh Infantry and two companies of the Second Cavalry from the Department of the Upper Platte. In addition, Samuel J. Crawford, governor of Kansas, pledged his assistance by putting a call out for volunteers to form a militia. The federal government promised to supply the arms, ammunition and horses for this regiment.

Sheridan used Fort Harker as his command headquarters. He appointed Brevet Major Colonel William B. Royall and Brevet Major General Eugene Asa Carr to command the Republican River Expedition. Sheridan had the utmost respect for Carr, an 1850 graduate of West Point. His admiration stemmed from the Civil War Battle of Pea Ridge, where Carr led the Fourth Division of the Army of the Southwest in a critical battle for the Union, later earning him the Congressional Medal of Honor. Carr had later been assigned to serve on the frontier, leading several engagements against the Apache, Comanche, Kiowa, and Sioux. These actions led to Carr's promotion to Brevet Major General. Carr's proven experience against the hostile Indians was exactly what Sheridan was looking for. He would be proven correct in his selection.

Carr received his first order from General Sheridan at Fort Wallace on October 12, 1868. He was instructed to join Major Royall's troops at Beaver Creek and scout the area in search of Indians. Two days later, on October 14, Carr left the fort with nearly one hundred troops of the Tenth Cavalry, the famed Buffalo Soldiers. His scout was Abner T. "Sharp" Grover, one of Forsyth's scouts who had survived the Beecher Island battle. Arriving at Beaver Creek, the troops traveled along the creek for over fifty miles, without locating Royall and his men. Continuing their search, they were attacked on the morning of October 17 by a Cheyenne war party led by Tall Bull. After eight hours of fighting, the troops of the Tenth Cavalry defeated the Indians who retreated from the area.

Meanwhile, Royall and his command had also been attacked by a group of Tall Bull's Cheyenne Dog Soldiers on the very day Carr left Fort Wallace to join him. Two soldiers were killed and twenty-seven horses were taken.

Carr and his troops joined Royall and his soldiers on October 22, and set out in pursuit of Tall Bull and the Cheyenne Dog Soldiers. Three days later the soldiers discovered the Indians camped on Beaver Creek. Carr ordered the attack, but Tall Bull's warriors were ready. For five days the soldiers waged a fierce battle against the Indians. In the end it appeared to be a standoff. On the morning of October 31, the soldiers discovered Tall Bull's warriors had left the area. Carr's troops returned to Fort Wallace. Pleased with Carr's efforts, Sheridan was convinced that Carr would succeed after Sully's repeated failures.

Still, Sheridan wanted another officer with grit, fearless determination and the tenacity to implement a strong war strategy against the hostile Indians. In short, Sheridan wanted twenty-eight-year-old, General George Armstrong Custer. However, Custer had been court-martialed the previous year for absence without leave, and sentenced to suspension from rank and pay for one year. [5] General Sheridan wired General Sherman, requesting the services of Custer and asking that the remaining two months of time of Custer's sentence be lifted. Sheridan then telegraphed Custer, at his home in Monroe, Michigan, informing him of his actions. Custer, wasting no time, for he knew Sheridan's request would be granted, boarded the next train bound for Fort Hays, Kansas. Indeed, Sherman lifted Custer's suspension. At Fort Hays, Sheridan gave Custer field command of the Seventh Cavalry, now comprising eleven companies, and the two began their plans for a winter campaign against the Cheyenne.

Meanwhile, as Tall Bull and many of the Cheyenne Dog Soldiers continued their raids in the Kansas Territory, Black Kettle and the Council of 44 believed it would be prudent to move their village to the Indian Territory, as a sign of peace. Medicine Water and Mo-chi went with Black Kettle's people to spend the winter on the Washita River, or the Lodge Pole River, the Cheyenne name for the river. As the winter season approached, several bands of the Arapaho, Comanche, Kiowa and Prairie Apache gathered together at this site. By early November, there were nearly six thousand camped along the river; forty-seven lodges were in Black Kettle's Cheyenne camp. Here, the Indians found abundant wild game to sustain them through the winter.

Early in November, Black Kettle received word that Cheyenne Jennie, a trusted ally who had often helped the Cheyenne and Black Kettle in particular, had died. Her husband, the equally trusted ally and Indian trader, William "Dutch" Griffenstein, had requested that Black Kettle travel to Fort Cobb to collect Cheyenne Jennie's possessions for distribution among his people.

The runner sent by Griffenstein to deliver the message to Black Kettle had news of his own when he returned to Fort Cobb. The runner told Griffenstein that there was a white woman and child in Black Kettle's village. Griffenstein sent Cheyenne Jack, a young half-white, half-Indian boy, to Black Kettle's camp. Obtaining access to the woman, Cheyenne Jack gave her a piece of paper and a pencil.

The woman was Clara Blinn, captured by the Cheyenne Dog Soldiers the previous month. Clara wrote out a letter, stating who she was and that her young child was with her, but was weak. She also wrote that the Cheyenne had her and she implored the governor of Kansas to make peace, as the Indians told her that "when white men make peace we can go home." Clara ended the letter with, "Do all you can and God will bless you." [6] The letter was dated November 7.   While this was transpiring, Black Kettle and a small group began the journey to Fort Cobb. George Bent was among those traveling with Black Kettle. He later recalled:

"The party was made up of Black Kettle and his wife, Lame Man and his wife, Lone Bear, Sylvester, and myself. No other chiefs or headmen would go. It was considered too dangerous. Griffenstein, the Wichita trader, was married to a Cheyenne woman, called by the whites Cheyenne Jennie. Lame Man was her step-father and his wife was Cheyenne Jennie's mother. So, Lame Man and his wife, went with our party. Lone Bear was not a chief, but was a cousin to Black Kettle and went along with him for company, willing to share the risks." [7]

Black Kettle and his party were met on the journey by Little Robe and Big Mouth, as well as Spotted Wolf, of the Arapaho tribe. Together, the group made the eighty mile journey to the Fort Cobb. Arriving at the fort, on November 20, 1868, they were greeted by Griffenstein, who relinquished his late wife's belongings to Black Kettle.

Black Kettle then had a meeting with Colonel William B. Hazen, commander of Fort Cobb, where the two discussed peace. During this meeting, Black Kettle said:

"I always feel well while I am among these Indians, the Caddoes, Whichitas, kichais, as I know they are all my friends; and I do not feel afraid to go among the white men, because I feel them to be my friends also. The Cheyennes, when north of the Arkansas, did not wish to return to the north side, because they feared trouble there, but were continually told they had better go there, as they would be rewarded for so doing. The Cheyennes do not fight at all this side of the Arkansas; they do not trouble Texas, but north of the Arkansas they are almost always at war. When lately north of the Arkansas, some young Cheyennes were fired upon and then the fight began. I have always done my best to keep my young men quiet, but some will not listen and since the fighting began, I have not been able to keep them all at home. But we all want peace, I would be glad to move all my people down this way. I could then keep them all quietly near camp. My camp is now on the Washita, forty miles east of Antelope Hills, and I have there about 180 lodges. I speak only for my own people. I cannot speak for nor control the Cheyennes north of the Arkansas." [8]

Colonel Hazen believed Black Kettle was sincere in his desire for peace. Yet Hazen was caught in the middle, as he was fully aware that General Sheridan had declared the Arapaho and Cheyenne tribes as hostile enemies. Therefore, Colonel Hazen choose his words very carefully as he replied to Black Kettle:

"I am sent here as a peace chief. All here is to be peace, but north of the Arkansas is General Sheridan, the great war chief, and I do not control him, and he has all the soldiers who are fighting the Arapaho and Cheyenne. Therefore you must go back to your country, and if the soldiers come to fight you must remember they are not from me, but from that great war chief, and with him you must make peace. I am glad to see you, and glad to hear that you want peace and not war. I cannot stop the war, but will send your 'talk' to the 'Great Father,' and if he gives me orders to treat you like the friendly Indians I will send out to you to come in; but you must not come in again unless I send for you, and you must keep well out beyond the friendly Kiowa and Comanche. I am satisfied that you want peace, that it has not been you but your bad men who have made the war, and I will do all I can for you to bring peace: then I will go with you and your Agent on to your reservation, and care for you here. I hope you understand how and why it is that I cannot make peace with you." [9]

With that explanation, Black Kettle and his group left the fort on November 21, 1868. Captain Alvord witnessed the departure of the Indians and later wrote:

"Parties of the Cheyennes and Arapahoes leave here after in vain attempting to arrange with General Hazen for a removal of their people to this vicinity to remain peaceable. They seem quite astounded at the novel fact that the war is not to cease at their pleasure." [10]

Not long after Black Kettle's departure, Cheyenne Jack returned to the fort with Clara Blinn's handwritten letter. Griffenstein read the letter and immediately turned it over to Colonel Hazen, who then sent it to General Sheridan. Hazen's message to his commander also said that he had requested that Griffenstein handle the negotiations for the release of Clara Blinn and her child. Unfortunately, Griffenstein's effort would not prove successful. When William T. Harrington, Clara's father, learned of the Indian capture of his daughter and grandson, he also wrote a letter to General Sheridan, imploring him to do all he could to save his loved ones.[11] The heartrendering plea was not lost on the general. During this time Black Kettle had returned to his people camped along the Washita. It was a grueling six day trip as the small Indian party encountered a severe north wind that first brought with it freezing ice and then swirling snow. As Black Kettle was traveling through blizzard conditions, Major Edward Wynkoop was also traveling. He had been visiting his mother in Philadelphia and had also made time to meet with politicians who shared his vision of Indian rights. While on leave from his duties as Indian agent, Wynkoop was abruptly ordered by the Department of the Interior to report to Fort Cobb, Kansas, immediately and see to those Indians under his authority to "keep them out of the war."[12]

Wynkoop arrived by train at Lawrence, Kansas. Here, he was given additional orders and briefed by Thomas Murphy, Superintendent of Indian Affairs. Wynkoop was outraged by what he was told. He learned that five columns of troops were already marching toward the Indian country. Wynkoop never reached Fort Cobb. Instead, he tendered his resignation, writing in part:

> *"I most certainly refuse to again be the instrument of the murder of innocent women and children...All left me under the circumstances is now to respectfully tender my resignation."* [13]

Wynkoop's words were fortuitous. On November 21, 1868, General Philip H. Sheridan and Lieutenant Colonel George A. Custer met at Camp Supply, on the south banks of the Canadian River, in Indian Territory. During the meeting, the two officers discussed their strategy toward defeating the hostile Indians. Custer also reported to his commander of the lackluster performance of Colonel Alfred Sully, (who out-ranked Custer) during the march to the Indian country. Custer explained that along the way, his Osage scouts had discovered a fresh Indian trail near Beaver Creek. Requesting permission to lead a troop to follow the trail, Sully refused. Coincidentally, Sheridan had also observed the same trail on his journey to Camp Supply, and assumed troops were following it.

Sheridan, fully aware of Sully's inadequacies as a soldier, let alone an officer, had finally had enough. Sheridan promptly dismissed Sully from his command and ordered him back to Fort Harker. He then formally placed Lieutenant Colonel George A. Custer in command of the Seventh Cavalry, reportedly saying, "Custer, I rely on you in everything."[14] Sheridan's final orders to Custer read:

> *"To proceed south in the direction of Antelope Hills, thence towards the Washita River, the supposed winter seat of the hostile tribes; to destroy their villages and ponies; to kill or hang all warriors, and bring back all women and children."*[15]

Meanwhile, Colonel Hazen, in a strange event given his previous words of peace to Black Kettle, approved of Captain Alvord's request to send Padouca Comanche spies to the Cheyenne villages. Within a few days, the captain received his first report:

> *"The camps of all the Cheyennes and Arapahoes south of the Arkansas River have been consolidated, from 16 to 20 miles west-southwest [sic-east-southeast] from Antelope Hills [and] the Washita forks. At the fork, the large main camp of these hostile Indians, with their families and all their stock was situated on the night of the 22 inst - four days ago."* [16]

Captain Alvord also reported that his intelligence reports had confirmed that Clara Blinn and her child were being held captive within this camp. Finalizing the preparations for attack, Custer had readied his regiment for deployment against the "hostile" Indians. Promptly at 6 a.m. on the morning of November 23, 1868, despite a steady snowfall, Custer formed his Seventh Cavalry in front of General Sheridan and gallantly rode off as the military band played "Garry Owen."

As the sun slowly rose over the frozen prairie on November 27, 1868, Lieutenant Colonel George Armstrong Custer attacked Black Kettle's Cheyenne village on the Washita River, camped in Indian Territory.

The village was caught by total surprise, as only the day before Black Kettle and Little Robe had finally returned from Fort Cobb amidst the swirling blizzard conditions. The attack was swift, killing more than a hundred men, women and children, including leaders, Black Kettle and Little Rock. Black Kettle mounted a horse, and with Medicine Woman Later clinging to his back, the two attempted to escape the unspeakable horror they were again going through four years after Sand Creek. Approaching the river, Black Kettle was hit in the back by a soldier's bullet, but managed to stay on his horse. Another bullet hit his stomach. This time the peaceful Cheyenne chief Black Kettle fell from his horse. He was dead before he hit the ground.

> *"The Old ones say Black Kettle was the first to die. The Old ones say it was the end of the Tsistsistas' way of life. The Old ones say 'For a time, this day broke their spirit.'"* [17]

George Bent, who was not at the Washita camps that fateful day, later wrote:

> "Black Kettle was sixty-seven years old when he lost his life. I married his niece [Magpie] in 1866 and lived with him until the early summer of 1868, when I went to Colorado and never saw him again." [18]

Medicine Woman Later managed to remain on the horse, perhaps for only seconds, as soldiers' sent a volley of fire in her direction. Just like four years earlier, Medicine Woman Later's body was riddled with bullets. Although she survived her injuries at Sand Creek, Medicine Woman Later died in the icy waters of the Washita River.

> "Both the chief and his wife fell at the river bank riddled with bullets," one witness reported, "the soldiers rode right over Black Kettle and his wife and their horse as they lay dead on the ground, and their bodies were all splashed with mud by the charging soldiers." [19]

Before the sun had risen high in the sky on that dreadful day, the freezing river banks were littered with dead bodies, the cold creek waters flowed over the bodies of Black Kettle and his wife, Medicine Woman Later, as the soldiers rode their horses over the death and carnage.

Both Medicine Water and Mo-chi, along with their children, were in Black Kettle's camp on that horrible day. Mo-chi must have been horrified as she watched her village attacked, reliving the same unbelievable circumstances as that of Sand Creek. The similarities were striking. Again, it was an attack at dawn on a bitter cold snowy day, and again, the soldiers attacked from all sides of the peaceful village. John Sipes later recounted his family's oral history of this event:

> "Black Kettle had no wolves [scouts] out to guard the sleeping village, although Iron Shirt and Man on Cloud, brothers of Medicine Water, had returned to the village the night before the attack, warning the village of troop movement in the area. Medicine Water and Mo-chi took heed, tying their war horses, as did many other warriors." [20]

Medicine Water and Mo-chi's actions the previous night would prove to be a wise precaution. In the meantime, the couple were trying to escape the soldiers onslaught along with the rest of their people. The young brave held vigil as best he could at the river, protecting and aiding several, including Mo-chi, across the river. Standing between his fleeing family and the troops, Medicine

Water stood with his war horse at his side, the two were a team and never flinched amid the onslaught of gun fire. That is, until their five-year-old daughter, Measure Woman, was struck with a bullet in her hip. [22] Mo-chi managed to escape the destruction with her wounded child, and her infant. As they did so, they were aided by a family member, Red Bird. Again, John Sipes picks up the oral family history:

"As Red Bird stood in the river firing at the soldiers, the return fire from the soldiers eventually brought him down. Medicine Water, seeing Red Bird fall, turned his horse toward the river and shot Red Bird's war horse, a Cheyenne custom so the two would be together in the Spirit World."

Later that day, when the soldiers had successfully annihilated Black Kettle's village, Custer ordered a few of his officers into the camp. There were several women who had remained in their lodges with their children. The soldiers also found a few women who had killed themselves. Custer's men gathered the surviving women and children together, a total of fifty-three, in a central area away from the village. Then in an effort to thwart those who had escaped, including Medicine Water and Mo-chi, Custer ordered the village to be burned. Custer then ordered the captured horses to be shot. Cheyenne oral history, according to John Sipes, is that:

"The Tsistsistas' lodges and winter supplies of food, tipis, [sic] and buffalo robes were burned, while over eight hundred horses were shot through the head. When the carnage ended and the survivors reunited, sorrow swept the Tsistsistas people to the very core."

Custer, triumphant in his recent engagement with the Indians, led his Seventh Cavalry, along with his captured prisoners, back to Camp Supply, where he received a heroe's welcome. General Philip Sheridan sat among the spectators as Custer arrived. A bizarre parade of jubilant soldiers, followed by forlorn Indian scouts leading warriors in chains, entered the wooden gate of the fort. Sheridan biographer Paul A. Hutton best described the scene as the gallant, yet arrogant, "Boy General," Colonel George Armstrong Custer paraded before his commander:

"First came a dozen Osage trailers, wildly painted and chanting their shrill war songs. Their ponies and lances were decorated with the

scalps of the Washita victims. Little Beaver, their chief, rode quietly but haughtily in the front, followed by the young warrior Trotter, who carried on his spear the prize trophy of the battle - the scalp of Black Kettle. Suddenly Little Beaver broke his proud silence and shouted, 'They call us Americans: we are Osages!' - and his warriors whooped in approval."[23]

Following the parade, Custer and Sheridan met to discuss their next campaign against the Indians. It would be a series of engagements covering parts of the western plains that would last for the next decade.

On December 2, 1868, General Sheridan and Colonel Custer and his Seventh Cavalry, with fresh provisions, left the military post to return to the Washita River and recover their dead soldiers. A second mission was to scout for Major Joel Elliott and his troops who were missing. Along with Sheridan and Custer rode Colonel Samuel J. Crawford, leading the Nineteenth Kansas Volunteer Cavalry. Crawford had resigned as governor of Kansas, just the previous month, to lead the newly formed volunteer regiment.[24] The men arrived at the river after a grueling trip in sub-zero temperatures, on December 10. The following morning, a detail of soldiers set out to gather their dead while a separate group scouted the area.

A short distance east of the now burned Indian village, Captain Milton Stewart discovered the bodies of Clara Blinn and her son, William Blinn, near the river at one of the abandoned villages. Clara had been scalped, her skull fractured, and there was a bullet hole above her left eyebrow. Her face, disfigured by the gunpowder, indicated she had been shot at close range. Two year old Willie's head had been horrifically bashed and his body was covered with severe bruising. [25] One of the soldiers identified them and told General Sheridan. Sheridan, recalling the pleading letter he received W. T. Harrington, Clara's father, could do nothing more then personally wrap the bodies of Clara and William Blinn in blankets. A reporter for the *New York Herald*, Randolph DeBenneville Keim, was with the soldiers when the bodies were found. He described Clara Blinn's appearance in an article for the paper, which ran in the issue dated December 24, 1868:

"Mrs. Blinn's body was dressed in the ordinary garments of a white woman; on the feet were a pair of leather gaiters, comparatively new. Upon the breast was found a piece of corn-cake, and the position of the

hands indicated that the woman was eating when she, unexpectedly, received the fatal blow."

On the morning of December 12, 1868, the military expedition departed the Washita River with the bodies of Major Joel Elliott and the bodies of Clara and William Blinn. The remains of the dead soldiers were buried at the battle site. They traveled to Fort Arbuckle, southeast of the river, deep in the Indian Territory. There, a military funeral was held on Christmas day as the bodies were interred. General Philip Sheridan feeling a personal sense of duty to Clara's family, attended the services. Paying his final respects to the deceased, before the internment, General Philip Sheridan, snipped off a lock of hair from both Clara and Willie, which he would later send to Clara's father.

Just as the actions of Colonel John M. Chivington, at Sand Creek, had stirred controversy, particularly in the East, so had the actions of Custer and his Seventh Cavalry, at what became known as the Battle of the Washita. However, the leading newspaper of the country, the *New York Times*, fell on the side of the famed Union Army "Boy General," Colonel George Armstrong Custer. The editorial ran in the December 22, 1868, issue:

"The truth is, that Gen. Custer, in defeating and killing Black Kettle, put an end to one of the most troublesome and dangerous characters on the Plains. Black Kettle was one of the most active chiefs in stirring up the tribes to war. From the beginning of the war in 1864, this Black Kettle, of the Cheyennes, aided by...Little Raven, of the Arapahoes, has been always most active in mischief, and it was a fortunate stroke which ended his career and put the others to flight."

Nevertheless, for those Cheyenne tribal members who had survived the attack on the Washita River, they were now in a precarious situation. The Indians that had been rounded up at the camp site were eventually transported to Fort Hays, where they remained as prisoners for the next few months. Not long after the construction of Fort Sill, in Oklahoma Territory, on January 8, 1869, these prisoners were then moved to the new military fort. During this time, messages were sent out to the various hostile Indian camps to come in to Fort Sill. However, the Indians, particularly the Cheyenne Dog Soldiers, ignored the invitation. George Bent explained the situation:

"The husbands and relatives of these prisoners waited on the chiefs of the tribes and asked that no war parties be sent out, as this would make the case of the prisoners worse; for this reason, no raiding was permitted." [26]

Meanwhile, many of the survivors had moved south to the Red River in Texas. In the spring of 1869, several of these warriors, including Medicine Water and Mo-chi, as well as bands of the Cheyenne Dog Soldiers, began to make their way north. The raids would continue.

The Cheyenne Dog Soldiers, led by Tall Bull, soon made their presence known. They were spotted near Beaver Creek, in northwest Kansas, by scouts serving under Major General Eugene A. Carr. One of these scouts was none other than William Frederick "Buffalo Bill" Cody. He had been assigned to Carr's regiment at the recommendation of General Philip Sheridan. In Sheridan's written recommendation, he cited Cody's service during the previous year, including a particular incident when Cody rode horseback over 350 miles in under sixty hours. Sheridan wrote:

"Such an exhibition of endurance and courage was more than enough to convince me that his services would be extremely valuable in the [upcoming] campaign, so I retained him at Fort Hays till the battalion of the Fifth Cavalry arrived, and then made him chief of scouts for that regiment." [27]

At a spot known as Elephant Rock, Major General Carr ordered his regiments of the Fifth Cavalry into battle on May 13, 1869. Carr and his men were successful, defeating the warriors handily. Twenty-five warriors were dead, while Carr's losses were four soldiers killed. Three days later, Carr's men again attacked the Cheyenne group and were again victorious. Again, Cody proved his skills as a scout, prompting Major General Carr to write:

"Our Scout William Cody, who has been with the Detachment since last September displayed great skill in following it [the trail] and also deserves great credit for his fighting in both engagements, his marksmanship being very conspicuous. He deserves honorable mention for this and other services, and I hope to be able to retain him as long as I am engaged in this duty." [28]

Cody had been injured during this fight, with a bullet that cut an inch gap in his scalp. Obviously painful and bleeding profusely, Cody nevertheless volunteered to ride through the night the fifty miles to Fort Kearny for reinforcements. Cody would remain with Carr's regiment and again prove himself in his scouting and fighting abilities. As for Tall Bull, he would not be defeated so easily. By this time, Sioux warrior Pawnee Killer and Cheyenne warrior Whistler and their bands had joined with Tall Bull's band. Together, they and Tall Bull's Dog Soldiers, along with Good Bear, and brothers Two Crows and White Horse, would retaliate with immeasurable death, destruction, and torture. Within days after the fight near Elephant Rock, the Dog Soldiers formed small groups of warriors and raided, stole, and murdered homesteaders in the Kansas valleys of the Saline and Solomon Rivers. On a tributary of the Saline River, known as Spillman Creek, Thomas and Susanna Alderdice and their young family lived on a homestead claim near a developing Danish colony. [29] Nearby, several of Susanna's family members had also homesteaded, including her brother Eli Ziegler and her sister Mary and her husband, John Alverson.

William Frederick "Buffalo Bill" Cody served as a scout under Major Carr. *DPL*

At the age of fifteen, Susanna had married twenty-year-old James Alfred Daily in 1860. Not long after President Abraham Lincoln signed into law the Homestead Act of 1862, the young couple moved to Salina, Kansas Territory, where they took advantage of the new Homestead Act. Here, Susanna gave birth to their first child, John, on July 1, 1863. Not long after, Susanna's family, the Zieglers, joined them. As the Civil War continued, Daily

314

decided to enlist with the Seventeenth Kansas Infantry in July 1864. Susanna, pregnant with their second child, stayed with her family while her husband was away fighting the war. Her second child, Willis, was born on October 5, 1864. [30] James Daily had only served with the Seventeenth Kansas Infantry for four months when he contracted typhoid fever. Daily died on November 25, 1864, at Fort Leavenworth. He never saw his second son, Willis, born the previous month.

Thomas Alderdice had served his country as a soldier in the Confederate Army during the Civil War. At some point during the war, while stationed in Salina, Kansas, he met the young widow, Susanna Ziegler Daily.

Following the end of the Civil War, Susanna Ziegler Daily and Thomas Alderdice were married on June 28, 1866. A veteran of the Civil War, Alderdice had served with the Forty-Fourth Mississippi regiment. During the 1863 battle at Chickamauga, Alderdice was captured by Union soldiers. He was taken to Rock Island, Illinois, and held as a prisoner of war. Alderdice later swore an oath of allegiance to the Union, effectively becoming a member of the "Galvanized Yankees." These former Confederate soldiers joined the Second U. S. Volunteers, a regiment that was used to fight the Indians on the Great Plains. After some time with this Volunteer regiment, Alderdice and his young brother-in-law, Eli Ziegler, had answered Colonel George A. Forsyth's call for volunteers prior to what became known as the Battle of Beecher Island. Both Alderdice and Ziegler had served admirably as scouts and soldiers under Colonel Forsyth's command. Settling into their new life on the plains, the Alderdice family grew. Along with Susanna's two children from her previous marriage, Thomas and Susanna welcomed children of their own; Frank, in 1867, and Alice in 1868. In May 1869, Susanna was in her fifth month of pregnancy with her fifth child.

Not far from the Alderdice and Ziegler homesteads, on Spillman Creek, a young couple, George and Maria Weichell, in her first trimester of pregnancy, had only been in the area a few short months. The Weichells had only recently arrived in the area, having immigrated from Luneburg, Hanover, Germany.

May 30, 1869, was a typical pleasant Sunday full of bright sunshine in the Saline valley area. It was also the day Americans observed the new national holiday of "Memorial Day," honoring American soldiers who had died in the line of duty, previously known as "Decoration Day."

Then, as now, many Americans across the country were simply going about their daily lives. Such was the case in the Saline valley. Many of the men were doing chores and the women were tending to their children, or visiting with neighbors. Their lives changed forever in mid-afternoon of that fateful day.

Nineteen-year-old Eli Ziegler and his brother-in-law, John Alverson, were following Spillman Creek upstream to check on a possible homestead claim approximately ten miles from the Alderdice homestead. The two were traveling by wagon, full of building supplies should the land claim prove worthwhile for young Ziegler to strike out on his own. Along the way, they stopped at the homestead of Michael Haley, west of their homesteads, also on the Saline River. There, they joined in the noon meal with Susanna Alderdice and her four children, who were staying at the Haley residence. On that pleasant valley Sunday, Susanna's husband Thomas was away on business. As Ziegler and Alverson were leaving, Susanna hugged her brother Eli and her brother-in-law John, and warned them of the rumors of various Indian sightings in the area. [31]

From the Haley place, Ziegler and Alverson headed north, following Lost Creek for a few miles, and then turned west toward Trail Creek. Crossing Trail Creek, Eli Ziegler, who was driving the wagon, noticed a large group of men on horses off in the distance. Ziegler watched as the group split its forces, with one group riding off from the other. Ziegler believed them to be soldiers. Ziegler later recalled:

"The sun glistened on their guns so plain that I still thought they were soldiers, but John would have not have it that way, and I had about made up my mind that they were." [32]

Ziegler was sadly mistaken. It was not long thereafter that the remaining group charged across the creek, headed toward Ziegler and Alverson. Ziegler quickly reacted. He turned the wagon around in an attempt to escape the pursuing Indians. Years later, Ziegler recounted:

"When we got to the creek the Indians were close behind us. I looked across the creek and thought there was a little bank on the other side that would protect us some. So I drove across, but John misunderstood me and jumped out into the creek and I drove up the bank. John ran along under the bank on the side I was on; the Indians were coming across the creek

within a few yards of us, shooting and yelling. John was calling for me to get out of the wagon, when I got to that little bank, I stopped the horses, seeing nothing more could be done to save the team and that we must defend ourselves, I dropped the lines, grabbed my gun and jumped out on the off side of the wagon. Reaching in the box for my cartridges, I could only get the box, about 20 rounds. While I was getting the cartridges the Indians were close all around. One of them rode up and picked up the lines just as I had laid them down and he held the horses. I thought sure I'll put a hole in through you, but before I could get my gun around he jumped off his pony beside the wagon, and still held the horses. The Indians were shooting all this time. John was calling for me to get under the bank. Just then another Indian darted up right close to the wagon and I thought I would let him, but before I could cover him with my gun he jumped his pony on the opposite side of the wagon, so I could not get him. John was still begging me to jump over the bank and I had about made up my mind to. As I stepped out from the wagon I looked toward the rear and behind the wagon and saw three Indians standing about four rods away, having me covered with their guns. I had no time for a shot, so made a spring for the creek bank; my foot slipped and I fell just as they fired. I think they over shot me. I also think that the slip is what saved me. I kept going on my hands and knees over to the bank. As they were pouring their shots right at us at short range we saw a log lying up the bank a little below us, we ran to that, thinking that would protect us on the side." [33]

Sometime in the late afternoon the two men were able to move undetected, along the bank of the river. Eli Ziegler continued with his account:

"We got to the bank of the river, one of the bends which points to the north. When they got opposite and close enough we were going to fire toward them. By this time they were north of us, but quite a ways out of the bottom. All at once they commenced hallooing and fired several shots. As the last shots were fired, we heard a woman scream one loud piercing scream more of horror than of agony, then all was still. There was no one living in the direction from which the scream came...we listened... but no sound reached us...we crossed the river in the direction of Bullfoot [Creek.]" [34]

The warriors had obviously soon tired of firing at the two men and had moved on. Instead they plundered the abandoned wagon, while Ziegler and Alverson scampered for the better hiding spot. Here they stayed until nightfall, then quietly made their way toward the Saline River. Ziegler recalled, "We got on high ground, saw several fire arrows into the sky, from up Bullfoot west and south of us." As the sun began to rise the following morning, the two men left the river and headed on foot for the settlement. Ziegler and Alverson had no idea that as they had been hiding from the Indians the previous day, the other group of Indians that Ziegler had noticed before they were attacked had gone on to the small settlement where his sisters were.

This second group of warriors was none other than Tall Bull and a band of the Dog Soldiers. They followed the bank of the Spillman Creek to Spillman Creek, first attacking Esrkild and Stine Lauritzen. The Danish couple were surprised while taking a Sunday walk on the north side of the creek, as their bodies, found the following day, were some distance from their small cabin, on the side of the creek.

It was approximately 2 p.m. when the Indians attacked George and Maria Weichell, and Fred Meigerhoff, who were also out on that peaceful Sunday. Both men were armed and fired at the warriors as they and Maria fled, running along the south bank of Spillman Creek. It was a harrowing run of nearly three miles, southeast, with the Dog Soldiers in close pursuit, when Meigerhoff and Weichell both ran out of ammunition. There, the Indians quickly overpowered the men and killed them. Maria was grabbed by one of them and swung onto the back of his horse. A small group of the warriors rode away with Maria. After some distance they stopped and threw Maria to the ground. There, as warriors held her arms and legs, the men took their turn in raping the defenseless woman. [35] This was a long held practice of the Cheyenne, known as Noha's-w-stan, translated as "staking a woman on the prairie." The origin of the horrendous practice was used as punishment for adultery among Cheyenne women. The accused woman would be taken outside the Cheyenne village where the warriors of the village would have their turn raping the woman. As the Cheyenne Dog Soldiers became more aggressive with their murderous raiding among white settlements, the taking of white women as captives more often then not included this horrific act upon their person. [36] For the white female captive it was truly a fate worse than death.

Meanwhile, the remaining group of Dog Soldiers continued their reign of terror along Spillman Creek. Approximately a mile south, they came to the Michael Haley home, approximately a quarter of a mile north of the Saline River. This is where Susanna

Alderdice was staying and had bid her brother Eli and brother-in-law John a fond goodbye after sharing the noon meal together.

The Indians first set their sights on the horse corral, capturing the horses. Bridget Kine watched the Indians steal the horses from a window in the Haley home. Ms. Kine was staying at the Haley home with her two-month-old daughter, Katherine, while her husband, Timothy Kine, was away on business.

Realizing the danger, Susanna Alderdice had gathered her four children and ran for the Saline River. Bridget Kine grabbed her infant daughter and quickly followed Susanna. The two women struggled with the children as they tried to make their way through the tall grass along the river. Just as they reached the river bank, the Indians spotted them. What happened next is described in Timothy Kine's Indian Depredation Claim:

Maria Weichell was captured by Tall Bull's band and rescued by soldiers on July 11, 1869 at Summit Springs. *Jeff Broome*

> *"Being already exhausted from her long flight and carrying the children, in her arms she saw that she could not hold out unless she disposed of part of her burden. With great presence of mind she concealed, as she thought, the Alderdice child* [she had been carrying] *in the tall grass, at a time when the Indians were not in sight, and then made another rush to the river. She reached the river bank and upon looking back she saw the Indians driving a spear into the defenseless body of the child. They had carried the child a short distance in the direction in which she had gone. During the time that the killing of the Alderdice child was taking place the Indians were yelling and riding round and round in the tall grass looking for Mrs. Kyne but in a few minutes they made straight for the river at a point near where Mrs. Kyne had disappeared. Into the water Mrs. Kyne plunged to her waist and crawled beneath the bank. It*

is difficult to imagine how she managed to prevent the infant child from making some outcry but as Mrs. Kyne often stated afterward there 'was never a whimper.' A few feet above her stood the Indians, shouting and screaming, one of them in plain view of Mrs. Kyne. In one arm clasped to her breast she held the child and with the other she took up her apron and was prepared in case the child should attempt to cry, to thrust the end of the apron in the mouth of the child. But for this she had no occasion. After some parlaying among themselves the Indians went east along the north bank of the river." [37]

The Alderdice child referred to in this depredation claim was two-year-old Frank.

Bridget Kine sat quietly in the river water, holding her infant child, as best she could, above the water. Bridget heard the Indians walking around her hiding spot, yet she remained undetected. But they did discover the twenty-four-year-old pregnant Susanna Alderdice and her three remaining children. She had struggled with her children to get to the river when she was surrounded by the warriors. Susanna fell to the ground, clutching eight-month-old Alice. She grabbed for her two sons, but the Indians got them first. Within a matter of minutes the boys were killed. Five-year-old John was shot with four bullets, and Frank, just two-years-old, was shot with five arrows, and then his lifeless body was bashed against the ground. Willis had been shot twice, five arrows were in his back and a spear through his left hand. After this, the Indians put Susanna Alderdice, still holding her baby tight against her, on a horse, tied her to it, and departed the area.

While Susanna Alderdice and Bridget Kine were suffering unspeakable horrors at the hands of the marauding Indians, another band of Dog Soldiers were conducting more murderous raids two miles east, along the Saline River.

Not far from the river, two of the warriors, one a young teenager, approached two teenaged boys, Arthur Schmutz and John Strange, who were digging turnips. What happened next was most likely a young Indian warrior's lesson in counting coup on the enemy.

Schmutz and Strange were understandably frightened as the two Indians advanced. However, the older warrior spoke to the young lads in broken English. He told them that they were friendly Pawnee Indians. Then, in what the boys thought was a gesture of good will in the Indian way, the man touched each of them on the shoulder with his spear, and rode his pony to a spot behind the boys. At this point, the younger warrior nudged his pony forward to meet with the boys. Suddenly, the teenaged warrior rose up, and with his war club high in his hand, he slammed it against the head of John Strange. The innocent teenager managed to utter his last words, "Oh Lord," before he died. Seconds later, the teenaged warrior dropped his war club, broken by the force of the blow to Strange's head, and grabbed his bow and arrow, firing an arrow into the left breast of Arthur Schmutz. Gravely injured, and stunned, Schmutz had the presence of mind and stamina to run away as fast as he could. The young warrior chased him and managed to put another arrow into him. Still, Schmutz continued to run. As Schmutz approached the Strange cabin, two of John Strange's younger brothers were watching from the window. They grabbed their guns and ran from the cabin, firing at the pursuing young Indian warrior. Missing their target, the warrior rode away. Strange's cousin, C. C. Hendrickson, who had been watching from his cabin window, later recalled seeing:

> *"The Schmutz boy running around the point of the bluff west of our house, and an Indian after him. From the Strange house they* [the Strange brothers] *could see them* [the Indians] *before we could and two of the Strange boys, Riley and Marion, took their guns and went to meet the Schmutz boy. He had been shot with an arrow in his back. He pulled the arrow out as he ran but the arrowhead was left in his back. When the Indians saw the Strange boys coming, they gave up the chase and started for the house. There were two Indians in sight by this time and in less time than it takes to tell it there was another one or two of them coming toward the house. One was driving off our work horses. They were shot at from the house so they turned back and went to drive the horses off. About that time one of the women looked south and saw a band of men on horses coming and said, 'My God, look at the Indians coming from the south. We are gone.' But it proved to be a company of soldiers that had come from Fort Harker."* [38]

Just before dusk, a group of men met at the ranch of Lon Schermerhorn to form a search party for their missing neighbors and loved ones. During their discussion, they were suddenly interrupted by a harrowing call for help. It was Bridget Kine with her daughter Katherine in her arms. Bridget had managed to leave her hiding place in the Saline River and made her way east, along the south side of the river, five miles to the Schermerhorn ranch on Elkhorn Creek, a mile south of the Saline River.

Later that morning, Eli Ziegler and John Alverson had made their way back to the settlement. The two had noticed the presence of soldiers near Bullfoot Creek, just south of the Saline River, not far from the Hendrickson homestead. Ziegler approached the soldiers. In their discussion, Ziegler spoke of the Indian raids of the previous day. Eli Ziegler later recalled:

> "We reported to the Captain what we had seen - told him what we had heard that night, out on the Saline River bottom, and of the fire arrows we had seen just a little above on the Bullfoot. I begged him to saddle up at once to furnish me a horse and I would lead them right to the Indian's camp, where I thought we could catch them if we moved at once and moved quickly. He replied, 'I cannot move any further until I get orders to do so. The Indians were in the settlements over the river yesterday afternoon, but I do not know how much damage they have done!' He had sent a dispatch to Fort Harker for orders and would wait there until he received an answer. We were disgusted with his reply, drank a cup of coffee, ate a hard tack, and started on home, keeping on the south side of the river." [39]

The military camp Ziegler and Alverson came into was that of Lieutenant Edward Law and his company of the Seventh Cavalry. In fact, the soldiers were in the area not to protect the settlements, as they learned of the Indian raids, murders, and taking of captives after the fact, but to pursue marauding Indians who had committed previous raids. Why Lieutenant Law refused Ziegler's offer to take the soldiers to the Indian camp, and further, why he told Ziegler he had to wait for orders from Fort Harker, is a mystery. For on May 31, 1869, the day after the raids on Spillman Creek, Second Lieutenant T. J. March sent a report to his superior, Lieutenant Law, noting his recent actions in pursuing the Indians. Evidently from his report, March didn't feel it necessary to await orders, so the question remains a mystery as to why Lieutenant Law told Ziegler he must await further orders.

Lieutenant March's report reads as follows:

> "Camp of Troop 'G' 7th Cav. On the North side of Saline River Near mouth of Bullfoot Creek 1st Liet. Edward Law, Comdg. Troop 'G' I have the honor to submit the following report concerning pursuit made by me yesterday with a detachment of 'G' Troop after a party of Indians who attacked the settlers near our encampment. Soon after going into camp it was reported to me that the Indians were attacking the settlers not more

than a mile from us. I immediately ordered the horses to be promptly and quietly brought in and saddled up, I ordered a detail of fifteen men to remain at the encampment. After passing the place of the attack we could see nothing of Indians for more than two and a half miles. Could only follow the general direction of the course they were reported to have taken viz: (southwest.) At this time it was reported that some of the horses were giving out, as they had already made a hard march before coming into camp. I took the advance ordering the remainder to act as a reserve and move up as fast as the horses would allow. After moving about a mile further and while ascending a gentle slope we saw a small party grazing their ponies near some ravines beyond. I dismounted the men with me and fired into the party, but with no effect. Immediately commenced pursuit and continued it at a rapid pace, but our new horses soon commenced fagging out and appeared to be gaining but little upon them, night coming on we finally lost sight of them. After scouting the different ravines and satisfying ourselves that further pursuit would be useless, I ordered a return march after having pursued them for more than fifteen miles after dark. Returning to Camp [sic] after midnight. On my return I ascertained the following facts from the Settlers: 'that this was a war party of about 9 warriors; that we were pursuing but a detached portion of about four or five; that the Settlers report one women and three children missing and one supposed to have been taken away by the remaining portion of this band; one other boy is lying dangerously wounded, having an 'Arapaho' arrow sticking in his back and another lance wound in his left side. The latter case I have seen." [40]

Earlier that morning same morning of the 31st, the local search party left the Schermerhorn ranch, in the direction of Spillman Creek. J. J. Peate, one of Forsyth's scouts who fought at the Battle of Beecher Island, took part in the search. He later wrote:

"In the first bend of the Saline river [sic] about a mile west of the mouth of Lost Creek [were] found two murdered children of Mrs. Alderdice and one that was badly wounded." [41]

The wounded child, shot with multiple arrows, was four-year-old Willis, who with mutiple wounds, was incredibly still alive. Bridget Kine had reluctantly left him behind as she ran with her infant child toward the river. The men carefully gathered the two dead boys and injured child and placed them in a wagon.

One of the men rode over to the soldier's camp at the junction of the Saline River and Bullfoot Creek. There, he asked

Lieutenant Law for the services of his surgeon. Incredibly, the surgeon refused to treat the two wounded boys. J. J. Peate wrote:

"I have met many army officers and found them to be honorable men, and grand comrades. This one was in the shape of a man, but it ended there."[42]

The search party had no other choice but to continue their search and make their way back to the settlement. The men found the body of John Strange, which was also placed in the wagon. Sadly, they were unable to find Susanna Alderdice and her infant child.

Arriving back at the Schermerhorn ranch, a few of the men gathered provisions and prepared for the trip to Fort Harker with the wounded teenage boy, Arthur Schmutz. Four-year-old Willis remained behind.

The deceased children had earlier been taken to the Martin Henderickson home, on the north side of the Saline River. Esrkild and Stine Lauritzen were buried on the prairie where they had been murdered, as were George Weichell and Fred Meigerhoff. When the men found the bodies of Meigerhoff and Weichell, they noted that the left ring finger of Weichell had been cut off and his wedding ring was missing.

Meanwhile, Thomas Alderdice and John Strange were returning from their business trip at Junction City, Kansas, when they were informed by a rider of the Indian raid. The two were then escorted to the Henderickson's home. There, Henderickson met the men and said:

"Strange, your boy is killed. Alderdice, your family is all killed or captured." [43]

Once the shock of this news wore off, many of the men rode in pursuit of the Indians. John S. Strange stayed behind to see his deceased son. Thomas Alderdice also remained at the Henderickson home, where he was soon shown the bodies of his deceased sons, as well as his severely injured stepson, Willis. C. C. Henderickson was there and later recalled:

"I can never forget the sad look of my uncle J. S. Strange, when he looked on the lifeless form of his boy. I also cannot forget the heart rending cry of Alderdice when he came into the house." [44]

The close-knit community grew closer as Thomas Alderdice and John S. Strange prepared to bury their children. Thomas Alderdice later recalled this sad time in an interview for the *Lincoln Republican*, printed January 25, 1923.

> *"I placed the children side by side and covered them and the next morning went back and was preparing to make a coffin for them. Mike Haley came over to where I was and said 'It's hard Tom for a man to be making a box for his own children.' He helped me to make the coffin."*

Thomas Alderdice attended the funeral of his son Frank and stepson, John. Both boys were laid to rest in the family cemetery at the homestead of Michael and Mary Ziegler, the parents of Susanna Alderdice. John Strange was laid to rest on his family's homestead.

Grief among the neighbors turned to anger as word leaked out of the army surgeon's refusal to give medical aid to the injured boys, rescued by the local search party. Soon, Kansas newspapers, including the *Kansas Daily Commonwealth* and the *Junction City Weekly Union*, were reporting the story. However, the *Topeka Commonwealth* took it a bit further, demanding answers in their June 12, 1868, issue:

> *"We would like to know the name of the surgeon who accompanied the company of Seventh Cavalry on the march from Fort Harker to Asher Creek. We would like to see what kind of a name is disgraced by such an ownership. We are informed that this company was within a mile or two of the scene of the massacre on the Saline a week ago Sunday evening. A Mr. Alderdyce, [sic] who happened to be away from home had two boys killed, his wife and babe carried off, and his only remaining child, a little boy four or five years of age, seriously wounded, and two arrows left sticking in his back. Word was sent to the surgeon and he was urged to go to the assistance of the wounded, a boy named Smart, [Schmutz] and the one already referred to. He steadfastly refused, and no entreaties could prevail him to go. The Lieutenant in command wanted him to go, but had no authority to order him. After failing to procure a physician at Salina and at Fort Harker, one was finally obtained at Ellsworth. These boys laid without medical attendance from Sunday evening until last Saturday night. Meantime, the arrows were pulled out of the little Alderdyce by unprofessional hands, and he withstood the agony of the operation with the heroism of a youthful martyr. The boy Smart, [Schmutz] having been in feeble health at the time he was wounded. is*

not likely to recover. Decent humans will want appropriate epithets with which to characterize this surgeon, if his conduct be correctly reported. He is a wretch, who would deserve little sympathy were he disemboweled by the savages and hung up by the sinews of his limbs."

Four-year-old Willis lay in agony that first night at the Henderickson home. Four arrows were pulled from his back, but the fifth arrow had penetrated his entire body, lodged below his breast bone. Another day passed while Thomas Alderdice and the others waited for a doctor that never arrived. On the morning of the third day, with the child crying out in excruciating pain, one of the neighbors, Philip Lantz, offered to do what he could for the boy. Young C. C. Henderickson witnessed the agonizing ordeal Willis went through, later writing:

"...begged so hard to have it [the arrow] *taken out that a man by the name of Phil Lantz said that if someone would hold him down, he could pull it out and a man by the name of Washington Smith said he would hold him. Lantz pulled the arrow out with a pair of bullet molds of my father's and as luck would have it, the spike came out but no one thought he would live."* [45]

Amazingly, young Willis did live. However, his recovery was long and painful. Susanna's parents, Michael and Mary Ziegler, brought Willis to their home as Thomas Alderdice aided the military in the search for his wife and infant daughter.

Amidst the sadness of the grieving Alderdice and Strange families, it was a very different outcome for Timothy Kine. He reunited with his wife Bridget and their two-month-old daughter, Katherine. They had survived their harrowing ordeal hiding in the Saline River from the Indians.

However, the experience traumatized Bridget Kine for the rest of her life. In 1896, after the death of a child, Bridget's mental stability deteriorated. By a court order issued by A. Artman, in Lincoln County, Kansas, Bridget Kine was to be institutionalized at the Kansas Insane Asylum in Topeka. After six months, Bridget was released. Evidently her mental state remained problematic, as she again went to the same institution in 1900, and again in 1906. Bridget seemed to suffer from delusion, lashing out violently and at times was restrained. Eventually she was released, but died from severe burns in her home in 1913.[46]

Following the burial of his boys, Thomas Alderdice left

on June 1, 1869, to track the Indian trail, in a determined search for his wife and child. An experienced scout, having served under Colonel Forsyth, Alderdice was confident in his abilities. Alderdice included his account in a letter written to the U. S. Department of the Missouri, dated June 21, 1869:

> "I started in pursuit on the 1st of June, traveled from Saline River three miles east of Spillman Creek, north by west striking the north branch of Salt Creek. Distance 12 miles. Traveled west by north up north branch of Salt Creek, striking Spillman Creek about 1/2 mile above main fork. Distance 9 miles. Traveled up west fork of Spillman to head of creek traveling west by north, crossed to Wolf Creek striking east fork; went up east fork about 4 miles, crossed to west fork. Found trail. Followed trail to creek, name unknown. Traveled north to Solomon up north fork of Solomon. Saw Indians (3 in number) hunting, still further up creek Indians. I supposed a large camp above, secreted myself in ravine to watch movements. Could see nothing but Indians going out and returning to creek. Returned back to settlement for help." [47]

Alderdice carefully retraced his nearly one hundred mile trip, staying hidden in creek banks as much as possible. It took several days to reach the settlement at Spillman Creek. Learning that Lieutenant Law and his regiment of the Seventh Cavalry had left the area, Alderdice immediately set out for Fort Harker. There, he reported his discovery of the Indian camp. Alderdice was told that there were no troops that could be spared. Undaunted, Alderdice then rode east, to Fort Leavenworth. He intended to meet directly with General John Schofield, commander of the U. S. Department of the Missouri. Alderdice, arriving at the fort on June 19, was not able to meet with General Schofield. However, he did happen to meet General George Armstrong Custer. During their brief meeting, Alderdice told Custer of the Indian raids at Spillman Creek and of the capture of his wife and infant daughter. He also informed the general of his recent scouting expedition and the discovery of the Indian camp. General Custer told Alderdice he would take the information to his superiors, but warned Alderdice he didn't know if anything could be done to help his plight.

News of this meeting and the desperate situation of Thomas Alderdice quickly reached the reporters of the *Leavenworth Daily Commercial*, which printed the story the following day, June 20, 1869:

"There are times when what is known as 'red tape' may be excusable in military as in other matters. There are times, however, when its observance in military matters is likely to prove productive of a great wrong. A case in point was reported to us yesterday. A gentleman living on the frontier, whose wife and youngest child, together with a young Swede girl, had been captured by Indians, and whose other children had been killed by these murdering savages, arrived in the city Friday afternoon, for the purpose of securing military aid in recovering those thus captured. The gentleman meeting General Custer in the city shortly after his arrival, told his story and appealed to him for aid. The General told him he had no power to act in the matter, but advised him to go at once to the Commanding General of the Department, remarking at the same time that as it was nearly five o'clock, he might not be able to see him that evening, as the offices were usually closed at that hour. The gentleman, terribly grieved at his loss and at the threatened and probable fate of the captured, would not rest until he had made an effort to do have done all that was possible for their relief, and hence posted off at once to the Fort. As had been suggested by General Custer, it was after five at the time he arrived there, and he, in accordance with custom, was refused an audience until nine o'clock the following morning. The distress of the gentleman in question at his failure to get an audience and an order for troops to follow hard in pursuit of the flying Indians was very great, eliciting the profound sympathy of all who saw him and heard his story. From five o'clock in the evening till nine in the morning is a long time to wait, with such weighty and soul-harrowing thoughts resting upon one. With two helpless women in the hands of these red devils, the one a wife, with a young child, who will wonder the man was nearly distracted on being refused an audience on Friday afternoon."

The following morning, while Thomas Alderdice waited to meet with General Schofield, a group of reporters gathered to get his story. Alderdice granted an interview with a reporter from the *Leavenworth Times* that day, which was carried by newspapers across Kansas and reprinted in the June 26, 1869, issue of the *New York Times*. Alderdice described, in graphic detail, his personal tragedy:

"We received a call yesterday from Mr. Thomas Alderdice, who resides - or did reside, before his family was murdered and his property destroyed by Indians - on the Saline River, about one and a half miles below the mouth of Spillman Creek. On Sunday, the 30th day of last May, as Mr. Alderdice was returning from Salina, [Junction City] and when about three miles from his home, he heard that a band of Indians had been

into the settlement and murdered a large number of people and destroyed considerable property. On arriving at his home he found it deserted, and was almost paralyzed with grief at finding one of his children dead... with four bullets in his body, and another of his children dead, shot with five arrows. A third child had five arrows in his body, one entering his back to the depth of five inches. Mrs. Alderdice and her babe, aged eight months, were carried away captive by the Indians."

Alderdice finally met with General Schofield on June 21, 1869. Alderdice was not optimistic regarding military aid following the meeting, but did leave the general with a hand-written description of his wife and child:

"Description of Mrs. Susanna Alderdice, captured by Indians on the Saline River, Lincoln County, Kans, May 30th, 1869. Height: Medium Complexion: Light Hair: Light Brown Age: Twenty Two years Eyes: Blue Female child eight months old, with her, when captured." [49]

The "red tape" the *Leavenworth Daily Commercial* referred to in their June 20, 1869, article, proved to be an accurate representation. General Schofield believed the Indians had left the area and were most likely headed northwest to Powder River country in Wyoming. And, as was the case at Fort Harker, Schofield could not spare any troops for a search of Indians he felt were long gone. It should also be noted that the cavalry capable of pursuing the Indians was not in Schofield's jurisdiction, but fell under the Department of the Platte, with General C. C. Augur in command.

However, Schofield was aware that General Eugene Carr and his Fifth Cavalry were in the area of the Republican River valley. He and his men had been scouting for the Indian trails since the engagement with Tall Bull and the Cheyenne Dog Soldiers the previous month. Therefore, Schofield wired Alderdice's description of his wife and daughter to General Augur. Schofield also sent the description to the commander at Fort Supply with the message to alert Little Robe, now considered the chief of the Cheyenne, that if he had not already released his hostages as previously agreed upon, Little Robe would "be retained as a hostage for the captives in question."

There was nothing else to be done at Fort Leavenworth, so Thomas Alderdice began his long return trip to his no longer happy home on Spillman Creek. Along the way, Alderdice detoured a bit, returning home. When he returned to the Indian camp he found it was deserted, just as General Schofield had thought would be the case. Alderdice spent some time rummaging through the discarded things left behind, looking for clues that might somehow lead him to his wife and child. As Alderdice wandered about the abandoned camp, he happened to glance across at the few trees in the area. He noticed something odd hanging in one of the trees. With what must have the deepest sense of dread, Alderdice approached the tree. His worst fear was realized. There, hanging from a tree branch, was the lifeless body of his eight-month-old daughter, Alice. She had been strangled with bowstring and then hung in the tree.

Weary with fatigue and distraught over the murder of his baby daughter, Alderdice removed his child from the tree and dug a grave. Meanwhile, General C. C. Augur, having received Schofield's wire regarding Thomas Alderdice's desperation in finding his captured wife and daughter, sent it via a courier in the field to General Carr. Augur added a message that read in part, "with request that such efforts as may be practable [sic] be made by the troops in his department to rescue these captives." With the information and location of the Indian village provided by Alderdice, Major General Eugene Carr was ordered to pursue the Indians in that vicinity. Carr understood that not only was this a military expedition, it now became a rescue mission. Carr's Fifth Cavalry, with William F. "Buffalo Bill" Cody as chief scout, was reinforced with a company of Pawnee Scouts, under the command of Major Frank Joshua North, as well as a subordinate officer, his brother, Captain Luther H. North. Carr's troops totaled nearly five hundred. On June 28, Carr and his men reached the Republican River, which they followed west. Along the way, with Carr in the lead, he discovered the Indian trail. Carr later described the incident:

> "I dismounted the command so as not to hurt the tracks and sent for 'Buffalo Bill,' who was hunting antelopes off to the right, and told him to look at that! He said, 'By Gee Hosaphat, that is the trail!' And I felt quite cocky at being the first to find it. It had drawn close together, to make as little show as possible, when it had to cross the river, and went into the bluffs on the north side. It then went parallel with the line of the valley to the westward, crossing the ridges and ravines, keeping five or ten miles away from the river bottom, and camping on hidden springs, which the Indians knew." [49]

Carr and Cody both concurred that the lodge pole trails found were not over a week old. The trail also revealed tracks made by shod animals. As the soldiers followed the river southwest in Nebraska Territory, Carr divided his command. On July 2, 1869, Carr and his troops, camped on the south fork of the Republican River, had a skirmish with a group of Dog Soldiers. Major Frank North kept a journal of the expedition. Although he does not mention the Indian skirmish, his account of this day offers an insight to the life of the soldier and officer:

> *"July, Friday 2. this morn moved at 6 a.m. and marched about 15 miles and camped on Republican near thickwood.* [sic] *Jim Murie is quite sick today. I am really sorry I did not send him home with the train. The boys killed an antelope today."* [50]

The following day, Carr and the soldiers moved further west along the river. Soon, Carr and his men came upon Indian tracks that were no more than twenty-four hours old. Believing they were in the vicinity of Tall Bull's Dog Soldier camp, Major North sent a group of the Pawnee scouts to search for their trail. North's journal entry for this day reads:

> *"July, Saturday 3, 1869 moved this morn at 5:30 marched up north fork of Republican River. I sent Sam and ten men out on scout they found trail of thirty Lodges. two white men went with them and one has not returned. George is out on little scout. marched 15 miles, good camp."* [51]

Originally Major General Carr did not care for the Pawnee scouts. Carr, early on in the expedition, had lost confidence the Pawnee's abilities. As the Pawnee scouts led the soldiers in the first days of the expedition, their ponies could not perform. Of this situation, Carr later commented that the ponies "could hardly keep out of the way of the troops on an ordinary march." Carr also felt that the Pawnee scouts were not familiar with the Republican River and that they were "rather lazy and shiftless, but I hope to make their Indian qualities useful."[52]

Nevertheless, the Pawnee scouts returned, reporting to Carr that they had located the Indian camp, but that it had been abandoned within the past twenty-four hours. As the scouts, along with a troop of soldiers were sent to check the area, they found evidence in the ground revealing there had been possibly two hundred tipis staked at the site. The following day, July 4, Carr ordered Brevet Major Colonel William B. Royall and Companies

A, E, and M, as well as a group of the Pawnee scouts, to track the Indian trail. Major North's journal entry for this day reads:

> "Sunday 4 Moved at 5:30 marched 25 miles camp on same stream as last night. sent Gus, Barclay and Wallace with 50 men out on Scout with Col. Royal [sic] to follow Indians trail. Sam came in tonight. nothing of interest from the camp. killed 5 buffalo today." [53]

Royall and his men scouted northwest of the Republican River, while Carr, with the remaining troops, moved up to the north fork of the river, known as Rock Creek. At that point, Carr turned his men southwest to a small tributary he called Black Tail Deer Creek. [54] Here, Carr found a recently deserted Indian camp. Royall and his men bivouacked and rejoined with Carr and his troops at this area. Royall informed Carr that his intelligence, gleaned from his scouts, indicated that there were a large number of Cheyenne and Sioux heading north to the South Platte River region.

Receiving this news Major General Carr made a critical decision. Carr chose to lead his men south, where they set up camp that evening, July 5, just a few miles from the mouth of the Arikaree River. This was near the site of the 1868 Beecher Island fight. Later that night a courier from Royall's camp delivered a massage to Carr. It reported that a troop of soldiers under Royall's command had a fighting encounter with approximately twelve Cheyenne warriors of Tall Bull's band. Royall reported no casualties or wounded, and that the Pawnee Scouts had killed three and wounded three of the warriors. This fight occurred approximately thirty miles north of the Republican River, near today's town of Holyoke, Colorado.

Now that Carr knew Royall's soldiers, not to mention the Pawnee Scouts he did not trust, were on the trail of Tall Bull and the Cheyenne Dog Soldiers, Carr ordered his men to prepare to march north at daybreak. Major North wrote of the events of this day, evidently unaware of the fight with the Indians:

> "today lay in camp all day no excitement drew 15 days rations. one of Lute's [Luther North] parties came in at 1 p.m. with news from Col. Royal. [sic] I think he has found the Indians before this time." [55]

Following the fight that day, and after the soldiers had departed, the warriors retrieved their dead and wounded from the windy prairie. George Bent later recalled the incident and the fight that led up to it, for historian, George Hyde:

"The Dog Soldiers and Sioux were camped at this time at the head of Cherry Creek, a small stream which flows into the Republican River from the north. The soldiers were camped near the mouth of this creek, news of which was brought in by a small scouting party of young Dog Soldiers. A number of young Dog Soldiers went out to make a night attack on the camp, hoping to stampede some horses. This was on July 8, 1869. Yellow Nose, the Ute captive, then a young boy of about twenty, was in this raid and says that they charged the camp at midnight, yelling and shooting. White Horse, one of Cheyennes, shot a Pawnee scout doing guard duty. Yellow Nose said that his war horse ran against a picket rope and threw him in among the frightened cavalry horses. His arm was broken and his horse got away from him, leaving him on foot. He lost his lance and shield when he fell and could not find them in the dark. The cavalry horses were thrashing around wildly, making it very dangerous for Yellow Nose. The soldiers and Pawnee scouts were shooting and shouting, but Yellow Nose had no trouble in slipping through them, though at times they were very close. The rest of the Cheyenne party thought Yellow Nose had been killed in among the cavalry horses. Hawk caught Yellow Nose's war horse and brought it back to camp. Much to the surprise of everyone Yellow Nose turned up two days later, his arm in a sling which he had cut from a shirt, having made the trip on foot. Mr. J. J. White, who was down here some time ago getting stories from the old people, told me that many years ago he bought the shield and lance, which Yellow Nose lost, from one of the officers of Carr's command present at this night fight." [56]

Of this incident, Bent also said that the Cheyenne Dog Soldiers had run-in fights with Carr's soldiers almost daily. In one of the attacks, Bent recounted:

"In one of these fights, Howling Magpie was shot through both thighs. He was too weak to ride, so two of his cousins with this was party pushed on to the Indian village, the cousins following with a mule dragging Howling Magpie's travois. When the war party reached the village they were to send out relatives to care for the wounded man. But the soldiers and Pawnee scouts jumped the village before anyone could go out and Howling Magpie and his cousins, Shave Head and Little Man, were never again seen alive. Another war party found their dead bodies some time later. Years afterward, when the Pawnees and Cheyennes made peace, some Pawnees who were scouting with Major Carr at this time told how they come on these three Cheyennes and killed them. The Pawnees say they were scouting in advance of the troops and jumped the little Cheyenne party. Shave Head and Little Man put up a good fight *and, refusing to leave their wounded cousin, were soon killed. Howling Magpie, crippled by his wounds, was killed lying in the drag. After the little night fight Carr left his wagons under strong guard and pushed on after the Dog Soldiers. William F. Cody (Buffalo Bill) was chief of scouts for Major Carr, and Major Frank North commanded the Pawnee scouts. The reason this command did so much damage, the Indians say, was because of the presence of the Pawnee scouts. They always showed up first and the Cheyennes mistook them for friendly warriors."* [57]

Major Frank North's journal entry for July 7, 1869, seems to corroborate Bent's account:

"Wednesday 7 today has been a great day for the Scouts. Gus returned at 2 p.m. with scalps from three Indians and 8 captured animals. 2 with U.S. brand which I turned in. 6 I gave to the men. I am in hopes we can find the small village in a few days, heap of dance." [58]

On July 8, Carr and his command set up camp a few miles east of the Arikaree River. As Royall led his troops to Carr's camp, a group of nearly fifty Dog Soldiers gave chase. The soldiers and scouts were able to keep them at bay. However, once the soldiers returned to their camp, a few of warriors attempted to attack the camp. The Pawnee scouts easily fought off the Dog Soldiers. One of these Pawnee scouts, Mad Bear, charged out of the military camp to confront the attacking Indians. However, in the fading light of the evening and the confusion of the situation, Mad Bear was shot in the back with a bullet from one of Carr's soldiers. The critically wounded Pawnee scout was taken to the ambulance wagon. Later, Carr would recommend Mad Bear for the Congressional Medal of Honor, the first time in history that such an honor would be bestowed on an American Indian. Major Frank North's journal entry for this day reads:

"this morn moved at 6 a.m. marched 15 miles back to our old camp on north fork no game today. I camped on north side of Creek opposite the General. misquetoes [sic] very bad. went to bed at 9 p.m. and was awoke at 11 by firing in camp. five Cheyennes charged our camp. one of Fred's men was shot by our own men not bad." [59]

Incredibly, another act of exceptional bravery occurred earlier that same day. This, too, would later result in a recommendation for the Congressional Medal of Honor. The day after the Indian attempt to attack the soldier camp, Royall mentioned that in being chased by the Dog Soldiers, he was forced to leave behind a worn down horse, belonging to Company M of the cavalry regiment. When Corporal John Kile heard this, he immediately volunteered to ride to the area, approximately fifteen miles northeast, to retrieve the horse. With three other volunteers the soldiers set out on their mission. The men were successful in finding the horse. However, on the return trip back to camp the three soldiers were charged by a band of the Cheyenne Dog Soldiers. The warriors quickly surrounded the soldiers. Kile did not hesitate, but fired at the Indians as the other two soldiers made a breastwork for cover. They were able to kill three of the warriors and injured others before the Dog Soldiers retreated. Kile and the two volunteers returned safely back to Carr's camp. One of the soldiers in the camp, First Lieutenant George F. Price, witnessed the return of Kile and the two soldiers, and later wrote:

"On the afternoon of the 8th Corporal Kyle [sic] and three men [sic] of Company M had a brilliant affair on Dog Creek, where although surrounded by thirteen Sioux [Cheyenne] warriors, they succeeded in killing three and compelling the others to retreat north of the Republican River, where they leisurely retired and rejoined the command twelve miles below." [60]

When Major Carr learned of Corporal John Kile's heroic actions in defending the Indian attack he immediately extended his thanks and congratulations. Kile's heroics would not go unnoticed. In his field report, Carr related Kile's experience:

"During the day three men of Company M who were several miles in the rear of the column bringing in a given-out horse, were attacked by eight Indians. They got near a large rock for a breastwork on one side, and killed the horse as a defense on the other, and beat off the Indians, wounding two badly. Corporal John Kyle, [sic] Company M 5th Cavalry was in charge of the party; he showed especial bravery on this, as he had done on previous occasions." [61]

Carr would later include this report in his recommendation for the Congressional Medal of Honor for Corporal John Kile, which would be awarded to Kile in August 1869. One year later, Kile was killed in a drunken brawl in Hays, Kansas, with "Wild Bill" Hickok. On July 9, Carr and his troops, as well as the scouts, made their way some thirty miles northwest into Colorado Territory. Following the Indian trail, Major Frank North and a group of his Pawnee scouts had discovered several signs of Indian movement. The soldiers pushed on. It was long journey in the hot prairie winds of summer and no water in sight. The following day, the scouts easily picked up the trail of Tall Bull and his Cheyenne Dog Soldiers. Major North recounted the day in his journal:

> "Saturday 10 this morn moved at 6 a.m. and followed Indian trail 35 miles passed three of the Indian camps. water poor, in the morn we move early and take 3 days rations on pack mules and light out for the Indians. we will have a fight tomorrow sure. I hope we may come out victorious. I shall be careful for the sake of dear ones at home." [62]

That night the soldiers set up camp near Frenchman Creek, with plenty of water, approximately five miles south of present-day Holyoke, Colorado.

Meanwhile, Tall Bull had sent scouts south to track the soldiers' movements, not knowing that Carr had turned his men northwest. George Bent later recounted Tall Bull's tactical error:

> "The Dog Soldiers now decided to go north and join the Northern Cheyennes and Sioux under Red Cloud. They had no trouble in distancing Carr's outfit, but when they reached the South Platte the river was so high that they were compelled to lie in camp waiting for the flood to subside. Tall Bull sent scouts south, in which direction the Indians had their last fight with Carr, but no scouts were sent to the east, as they did not expect any troops from that direction. Pawnee scouts came up on two Cheyenne men and one old woman who were following the village and they killed the two men. The Pawnees told the Cheyennes later that the woman refused to be captured and they were compelled to kill her also. These scouts told Carr which way the trail went. Tall Bull was anxious to cross the Platte river [sic] and get up into the Black Hills country. He sent Two Crows and five others on ahead to try the South Platte and found the river so high in some places that the water ran over their horses backs. It was evening when they returned to the village and reported to Tall Bull. There was a great deal of excitement in the camp at this time, as a war party of Sioux had come in and reported troops following the trail. Nevertheless Tall Bull sent criers through the camp to announce that they would camp where they were for two days; then they would cross over and camp in the high bluffs near the square butte, known to the whites as Court House Rock, where they could watch for soldiers and could not

be surprised. Many of the Sioux, however, insisted on crossing the river that evening. But the Cheyennes went into camp at this place, called by the whites Summit Springs. This is at the base of Freemont Butte [sic] or White Butte, and here heads a little stream called White Butte Creek. The Cheyennes say it was poor judgment for Tall Bull to insist on going into camp instead of crossing the South Platte that evening and that this error was the cause of the village being surprised next day." [63]

The area of Summit Springs was so named because of the its high location between the Republican and South Platte Rivers. However, Bent's location of the site was off by about eight miles. Because Tall Bull had not sent scouts east of his encampment at Summit Springs, he had no idea that Carr and the soldiers were fast on their trail. As the sun set that night on his village, Tall Bull could not have known it would be the last sunset he would ever see.

Before sunrise on Sunday, July 11, 1869, Carr and his men were on the march. Following the Indian trail, they approached a ridge overlooking the South Platte River, approximately six miles east of present-day Sterling. [64] Here, the soldiers dismounted, and leading their horses, crossed the ridge, all the while concealing themselves along the ridges as was possible. After six miles of travel the men reached the river, following it at a distance amidst the sand hills for concealment.

All the while, the Pawnee scouts, with Cody, were ahead of the soldiers and soon spotted mounted warriors not far off to the south and what was believed to be a herd of horses off to the north. At this point, close to the noon hour, Carr divided his troops. Royall and three companies moved north, while Carr led the rest of his command southwest. Not long after Carr's men were again on the move, Cody quickly reported the site of Tall Bull's camp. After a four-mile ride on the hot windy prairie, at approximately 1:30 in the afternoon, the troops were able to see the village in the distance, less than a mile away.

Carr took some time to rest the weary horses and gather the military force into formation for an attack on the Indian village. Carr ordered his troops into two columns, each ready to charge the Indian camp from separate directions.

Lieutenant William Volkmar was one of Carr's soldiers. He kept a daily journal of this military excursion and wrote of the charge on Tall Bull's camp:

"All being ready the trumpets rang out the 'charge' and with hurrahs the columns and reserve dashed over the hill, down the slope towards the village, the columns forming lines as they ran. The surprise was complete - the Indians having made a desperate attempt to run off their stock, offering the most resistance on the left, [north] but half the reserve being thrown in there, the fight was quickly over and ended with a running pursuit of six or eight miles when it had to be abandoned on account of the exhausted horses." [65]

Amidst a howling prairie wind, the soldiers charged from the northeast toward the Indian camp. As they approached, a young teenaged boy, tending to the herded ponies, noticed the soldiers and ran to the village, yelling all the while. His voice was lost in the howling wind. The soldiers charged on and the boy was killed. Captain Luther North later said of the boy, "No braver man ever lived than that fifteen-year-old boy." [66]

George Bent later recounted the surprise attack:

"The Cheyennes agree that the Pawnee and soldiers took them completely by surprise. The day was a misty one, 'smoky' the Indians say. They had been burning the grass to destroy their trail; they say everything looked indistinct. Brave Bear and Two Crows say they were eating the mid-day meal when Carr attacked them. Some of the Indians were lounging on a little hill, but most were eating. The Pawnee scouts were in the lead in the charge on the camp, shooting and yelling. Most of the horses were herded close to the camp, and many were tied near the lodges. At the first sound of firing all ran to catch horses before they stampeded. Those with horses in camp quickly mounted with the women and children, while the men got ready to fight. Brave Bear and Two Crows ran out of their lodge toward the horses just in time to see all of Tall Bull's own herd stampede." [67]

The soldiers were quickly able to overtake the village. Panic and pandemonium caused the people of the Indian village to run out of the lodges, only to be shot down before they knew what was happening. Those that were able to escape went south of the village, as the soldiers continued their onslaught of fire.

Carr later reported one soldier slightly wounded, and estimated the Indian dead as between fifty and seventy-five, and reported over eighty tipis in the camp. However, a group of the Dog Soldiers, including Tall Bull, had gathered at the southeast area of the Indian camp. Here, they wielded their lances, shields and clubs, as well as what few firearms they possessed, in a brave but futile attempt to fight the soldiers. George Bent recounted the fight as related to him by Two Crows:

> "Tall Bull called in a loud voice, 'All of you that are on foot and cannot get away follow me.' A number of people ran with Tall Bull and his two wives to a little ravine with sharp high banks. By this time the troops were all around, except on the south side of the camp, and the excitement was terrifying. Horses were stampeding in all directions, the Pawnees and soldiers yelling and shooting, women and children screaming with fright, Cheyenne and Sioux men shouting orders to the women and fighting off the attackers. Many people, mounted and on foot, streamed out the south and scattered over the prairie in little groups, the men fighting off the pursuing Pawnees. Tall Bull's party in the ravine helped divert the soldiers and scouts from the fleeing Indians. The Pawnees, the Cheyennes say, did most of the killing and also captured the greater part of the pony herd. Two Crows ran across the prairie with a party of Cheyennes and Sioux, who covered the flight of a number of Cheyennes and Sioux, women and children. Some were mounted, many on foot, and they were strung along the open prairie. The Pawnees followed, shooting and killing, but their horses seemed very tired. Fighting in the rear of these women and children were Kills Many Bulls, Two Crows, and Lone Bear, the latter mounted, the other two on foot. Lone Bear was very brave, Two Crows says, charging again and again into the party of Pawnees chasing them, thus covering the flight of Two Crows and Kills Many Bulls as well as the women and children they were protecting. These three kept turning and fighting off the Pawnees; men in other groups did the same. Once Lone Bear charged right in among the Pawnees and went down fighting like a wild animal. Other Cheyennes say Two Crows was very brave, though he speaks sadly of running away and leaving so many Cheyennes and Sioux women and children to be killed by the Pawnees. After killing Lone Bear, Two Crows says, the Pawnees seemed to have stopped chasing the people. Two Crows had been badly kicked in the shins by a Pawnee horse he was trying to catch. In some way this horse got away from its rider and ran past Two Crows." [68]

George Bent continued, relating the death of Tall Bull:

> "Tall Bull, the Dog Soldier chief, had three wives. One of those he put on a horse when the shooting started and she got away with a daughter of the first wife. The other two wives, the youngest and the eldest, went with Tall Bull to the ravine. In the fighting here the youngest was killed

and the other captured. A young Dog Soldier, named Wolf with Plenty of Hair, was very brave and staked himself out with a dog rope at the head of the ravine. It was the custom for the Dog Soldier wearing a dog rope to pin himself down in running fights or when a party was taken by surprise as in this case. The fighting was so hot around the ravine that no one had time to pull the picket pin for Wolf with Plenty of Hair, and after the fight was over he was found where he had staked himself out. The Cheyennes in the ravine put up a desperate fight. Bill Cody and Frank North claim they killed Tall Bull, but the Pawnees say no one knows who killed him, as they were all shooting at him. White Buffalo Woman, [a] wife of Tall Bull and sister of Good Bear, was allowed to come out of the ravine and surrender. The rest of the Cheyennes were killed in the ravine."

Major Frank North's journal entry for this day read:

"Sunday 11 Marched this morn at 6 a.m. with 50 of my men and 200 whites with 3 days rations followed trail till 3 p.m. and came up to the village made a grand charge and it was a complete victory took the whole village about 85 lodges killed about 60 Indians took 17 prisoners, and about 300 ponies and Robes, etc. innumerable. rained pretty hard tonight." [69]

It is interesting to note this journal entry by North. Despite Bent's assertion that Frank North claimed he killed Tall Bull, North makes no mention of it. In fact, in North's later writings and in his very few interviews, he never made such a claim. Years later, when Cody launched his world-wide famous Wild West Show, he included the reenactment of the battle of Summit Springs, with himself as the killer of Tall Bull. This led to decades of controversy as to who actually killed Tall Bull that day of July 11, 1869. However, Bent's statement that "the Pawnees say no one knows who killed him, as they were all shooting at him," is very accurate. Even Carr mentioned three different possibilities over the ensuing years.

One of the soldiers, Captain Sylvanus E. Cushing, a brother-in-law to Frank and Luther North, entered Tall Bull's lodge, where he discovered a severely wounded Maria Weichell. Maria had been shot in the back as she attempted to flee the lodge, and blood was oozing from her breast. Captain Luther North described Cushing's experience in a 1917 interview:

"When we charged into the village, Cushing stopped in a teepee to get a drink of water out of a keg and the wounded white woman ran up and grabbed hold of him almost frighting him to death. She afterwards said Tall Bull in person had shot her."

Captain North later expanded the incident in his memoirs:

"About this time a woman came crawling out of the lodge, and running to Capt. Cushing fell on her knees and threw her hands about his legs. We now saw she was a white woman. She was bleeding from a bullet wound through her breast. She was a Swede [German] and could not speak English, and had been taken prisoner several months before, when this band of Cheyennes had raided a Swedish settlement in Kansas. Tall Bull had taken her for his wife, and when we charged his camp he tried to kill her." [70]

After the fighting had ended, as storm clouds gathered over the eastern plains, a troop of soldiers entered the camp, searching for the reported white female captives, Alderdice and Weichell, and other survivors. It was nearly four o'clock, according to Lieutenant William Volkmar's daily journal. Shortly thereafter, a horrific thunderstorm descended on the dry prairie. The storm, carried by high winds, brought heavy rain as lightning strikes crackled in the sky. Soon, large hail fell so fast that the soldiers ran inside the tipi for shelter.

Maria Weichell had been held captive for a horrific six weeks before she was finally rescued. Maria was transported to an army tent set up for the wounded. There, the military surgeon, Louis Tesson, removed the bullet from Maria's back.

Meanwhile, the soldiers had also made another discovery, this one sadly different than finding Maria Weichell alive. Captain Luther North, during the fight and while scouting the area, came across the body of the pregnant Susanna Alderdice, also taken captive by the Cheyenne that fateful Sunday in Kansas, six weeks previous, on May 30, 1869. North found Alderdice near White Butte Creek at the southern end of the village. General Carr later reported the manner in which Susanna Alderdice died.

"She [Alderdice] was shot over the eye and had her skull broken in. She was of middle age and looked badly, and evidently had been hardly [badly] used and treated as a slave." [71]

One of the captured Indians was Sun Dance Woman, one of Tall Bull's wives. She later said that Tall Bull had killed Susanna Alderdice, striking her on the head with the butt of his rifle. Sun Dance Woman told the soldiers, through an interpreter, that she:

> "...knew that Susanna was dead or would die, from the sound of the rifle blow when it hit her head. It cracked like a split from a ripe pumpkin." [72]

The soldiers took the body of Susanna Alderdice to the army tent, where field surgeon Louis Tesson prepared her body and wrapped it in a buffalo robe for burial at the site of the battle. Through an interpreter, German Henry Voss, Maria Weichell told the soldiers that both she and Susanna had been violated repeatedly. Maria also said that it was after the third day of their capture that the Indians had killed Susanna's baby, Alice Alderdice, by strangling her. Maria, now in the fifth month of her pregnancy, was tenderly cared for in a private tent, where the bullet was removed from her chest and she was given to rest as comfortably as possible.

After the thunderstorm had moved away from the area, small groups of cavalrymen and scouts patrolled for signs of returning warriors. Just as the sun was setting on that fateful day, one of the soldiers spotted some sort of movement near the bluff where the heaviest fighting had taken place earlier in the day, and where Tall Bull had been killed. A group of soldiers mounted their horses and galloped over to investigate. They were startled to discover a small Indian boy, no more than four years of age, wandering about, most likely attempting to make his way back to his village. The soldiers brought him to the military camp, where he was given food and shelter among the other sixteen Indian women and children captured after the battle.

The following morning, before the soldiers burned the Indian village to the ground, they went through the contents in each tipi. Among the expected items found, such as knives, bows and arrows, tomahawks, buffalo robes, clothing and moccasins, a gruesome item was also recovered. It was a necklace strung with human fingers. When George Weichell's body had been found, it was noted that his left ring finger had been cut off and his wedding ring was missing. While it can never be known if one of the fingers on the necklace was Weichell's, his wedding ring was indeed recovered from the same tipi and returned to his widow, Maria Weichell. With the discovery of such items, there was now no doubt that Tall Bull and his band of Dog Soldiers were responsible for the raids, murders and kidnappings along the Saline River and Solomon Creek. It was something the now widower, Thomas Alderdice had known from the day his wife was captured and his children murdered.

Major Carr, under Special Order No. 17, from the headquarters of the Republican River Expedition, ordered his men to complete a written inventory of the contents found. Major Royall provided that inventory, along with the following comments:

> *"Besides the above mentioned articles the Board is of the opinion that there was at least ten (10) tons of various Indian property, such as clothing, flour, coffee, corn meal, saddle equipments, fancy articles, etc., destroyed by the command before leaving the camp by burning. There was also found in the different lodges, articles which had undoubtedly been stolen from white settlements: albums, containing photographs, daguerreotypes, watches, clocks, crockery ware, silver forks and spoons, etc. In making examination preparatory to to burning the camp, quite a number of white scalps were found attached to wearing apparel, lances and children's toys, some of which appeared to be fresh."* [73]

Not listed on the official inventory compiled by Major Royall was the discovery of what looked to be a common accounting or ledgerbook. This was most likely one of the many items taken after the plundering of the Julesburg station following the raid on January 7, 1865. As a soldier thumbed through it, he saw it was full of Indian pencil drawings which depicted various activities, but primarily Indian fights. Somehow the ledgerbook became the possession of Lieutenant Peter V. Haskins, with Carr's Fifth Cavalry. The following day, July 12, 1869, at eight o'clock on a misty morning, Louis Tesson presided over the solemn burial of Susanna Alderdice and her unborn child. Nearly all of the soldiers attended. After her body was lowered into the ground, the soldiers fired three shots in tribute, over her grave. One soldier later recalled:

> *"The cavalry sounded the funeral dirge, and as the soft, mournful notes died away many a cheek was wet that had long been stranger to tears."* [74]

Another soldier, perhaps even Major Carr, renamed the area "Susanna's Springs," in honor of Susanna Alderdice. And for a time the name remained, at least among the soldiers who, sadly, arrived too late to save her.

Following the solemn burial, the soldiers prepared for the

burning of the Indian village. First Major Carr ordered the gathered inventoried items loaded into six wagons. Next, over one hundred and sixty small fires were set in and around the large village, in an effort to ensure the entire camp site would be completely destroyed. As the village burned, Major Carr led his troops out of the area, heading north toward the South Platte River. As the soldiers departed, Carr recalled seeing several dogs "gathered on a hill and set up a Wagnerian accompaniment in a gamut of discontent howls." Major North's journal entry of this day read:

General Eugene Carr led his men on an expedition that resulted in the battle at Summit Springs. *DPL*

"July Monday 12, 1869. Invoiced property today and burned what we did not want and started on the march at 12 m. for the Platte River arrived in camp at 4 p.m. find good grass and plenty of wood such as telegraph poles. we are 65 miles from Julesburgh. [sic] George and ten men went to Julesburgh with dispatches." [75]

The soldiers rode the long sixty-five miles back to Fort Sedgwick, with wagons carrying the Indian prisoners, and ambulance wagons carrying the injured, including Maria Weichell. The first group of troops arrived at the military post on July 14, 1869. Major North and his troops, at the rear of the command, arrived a day later. North wrote of the day's event's in his journal:

"Wednesday 14 Marched at 6:30 a.m. came down to antelope station on the Platte distance 20 miles. nothing of importance transpired today. roads good. Gus with 4 men goes to Sedgwick tonight at midnight I telegraph home as I write. I hope I can go home in a few days." [76]

After meetings with military officers, Major General Eugene Carr included the following in his final report to Brigadier General George D. Ruggles, Assistant Adjutant General:

"It may be imagination, but there is a general feeling that the services and hardships of the regiment have not been appreciated for want of any brilliant list of killed and wounded. We have, however, no pleasure in killing." [77]

The news of the battle at Summit Springs was on the front page of newspapers across the country, including the *New York Times*. Locally, the *Atchison Champion & Press* was one of the first to report the news in their July 15, 1869, issue:

"The Department Headquarters at Omaha received intelligence from the expedition on the Republican, on Thursday night. General Carr, after pursuing the Indians ten days, effected a complete surprise of a large body of Cheyennes, on Sunday morning; killed fifty-two of their warriors and captured seventeen of their women. The Indians abandoned their entire camp, leaving three hundred and fifty-nine animals, eighty lodges, a large quantity of arms, robes and other supplies. They attempted to murder two white women captured in Kansas, and succeeded in killing one and wounding the other. The wounded woman will probably recover. Gen. Carr's loss is not stated."

The *Atchison Champion & Press* continued their coverage in the July 20, 1869, issue:

"Omaha dispatches say that Gen. Auger returned from Fort Sedgwick on Sunday morning. Gen. Carr's victory is more complete than first reported. Over four hundred horses and mules were captured, with a large quantity of powder, and nearly four tons of buffalo meat. Among the killed is the noted chief 'Standing Bull.' [Tall Bull] *About nine hundred dollars in money was found in the camp, which was given to Mrs. Weisel,* [Weichell] *a white woman recaptured. They were the same Indians who last year fought Gen. Forsyth and recently committed depredations in Kansas. Lieutenant Beecher, of the Pawnee scouts, reports meeting small numbers of Sioux Indians on the Republican. Three of them were killed and three wounded."*

Before the soldiers left Fort Sedgwick for the long journey to Fort McPherson, one of their last acts was to bid farewell to

Maria Weichell. Maria was to accompany a troop of soldiers with the Indian prisoners to Omaha, Nebraska. There, she would give birth to a daughter two months later. Still later, Maria would remarry. She married a man named John Mantz.

Major North recorded the last day at Fort Sedgwick in his journal:

"Friday 16. This morn went up to the Fort and had 1 game of Billiards and came to Camp just in time to see Gen. Auger. we had a council today with the prisoners. The Gen. will take them to Omaha. divided the ponies tonight." [78]

Major North had received orders to pursue the fleeing Indians. Along with the regiment rode William F. "Buffalo Bill" Cody as chief scout. General Carr also received the same order. However, just as the expedition was about to depart, on July 23, 1869, Carr received word of the death of his five-month-old son, George. Carr was relieved of his duties and rushed for home in St. Louis, Missouri. Colonel Royall then commanded the regiment, following the Indian trail along the Republican River, and then north, crossing the South Platte River. After crossing the North Platte River, the soldiers lost the trail. The Indians had escaped north to the White River.

For the Cheyenne Dog Soldiers, their defeat in battle at Summit Springs, and the death of Tall Bull, nearly broke the spirit of Cheyenne people. So devastated by the loss and many deaths, the Cheyenne fled the area, and never returned to gather the dead.

In late September, two months after the battle, a small group of Indians, led by Sioux leaders Pawnee Killer and Whistler, returned to the site. There, the bodies of their fallen comrades, including Tall Bull, still lay on the wind-blown Colorado prairie. The small Indian band did their best to tend to the badly decayed bodies, and prepare them for the spiritual afterlife. Cheyenne historian John Sipes remarked of this sad affair in Cheyenne history, by repeating the words of Sweet Medicine, the first leader of the Cheyenne people, "Some day the Earth Men will come. Do not follow anything they do." For the Cheyenne, this marked the end of their traditional way of life on the plains of Colorado. Most of the Dog Soldiers remained in the north country. Those who had managed to escape from the battle at Summit Springs, and had not followed the Dog Soldiers north, slowly began to arrive in small groups at Camp Supply. Here, they surrendered to the soldiers. A

Susanna Alderdice, a captive of the Cheyenne, was killed by Tall Bull during the fight at Summit Springs. General Eugene Carr and his men buried her at the site. *Jeff Broome*

few bands of the Dog Soldiers, including Medicine Water and his wife, Mo-chi, would continue raiding in the Kansas and Nebraska areas. John L. Sipes, great-great grandson of Medicine Water and Mo-chi, once said:

> *"Our Cheyenne family fought to the bitter end for their values of life, their beliefs of the customs and the will to survive."* [79]

However, a historical legacy for the Cheyenne people and the Dog Soldiers in particular, a piece of their history, was preserved from that day of July 11, 1869. It was the ledgerbook, containing the Indian drawings found in Tall Bull's camp at Summit Springs. Lieutenant Peter V. Haskins, with Carr's Fifth Cavalry, had obtained the ledgerbook. He had written the following on page nine, "This book was captured." On the next page, he wrote:

> *"This book was captured by the 5th US Cavalry on their charge through the Indian village July 10 [11] 69. 60 Indians killed and many wounded. 400 head of stock also captured. Immense destruction of Indian property."* [80]

At some point during Lieutenant Haskins' time at Fort McPherson, the ledgerbook came into the possession of Second Lieutenant Hohn Henry Filler, with the 29th U. S. Infantry. Lieutenant Filler's name also appears on page nine of the ledgerbook, but with no date. Later, Ira W. LaMunyon, a railroad supervisor for the Union Pacific Railroad, living in North Platte, Nebraska, acquired the historic ledgerbook.

A decade later, LaMunyon moved his family to Dumont, Colorado, where he eventually served as a justice of the peace in Clear Creek County. Then, on November 3, 1903, LaMunyon donated the Cheyenne ledgerbook of drawings, along with several other items, to the State Historical and Natural History Society of Colorado. Many of LaMunyon's items, including rocks and minerals from Clear Creek County, were placed on display, but the Cheyenne ledgerbook was relegated to storage for the next sixty years.

Through the efforts of Jean Afton, the wife of Ira W. LaMunyon's great-great-grandson, the historic Cheyenne ledgerbook was rediscovered. After a long process of analyzing the 144 drawings, and historic research as to the artists and the events depicted, the history of the Cheyenne Dog Soldiers emerged.

Today, the historic Cheyenne Dog Soldier ledgerbook of drawings is housed at the Colorado History Center and occasionally on display, an account of their side of history.

— Chapter Notes —

1. Measure Woman was the first child of Medicine Water and his first wife. She joined the lodge of her father and Mo-chi. John L. Sipes, the great-grandson of Medicine Water and Mo-chi. Genealogical records in possession of the author.
2. Justice, "The Saga of Clara Blinn at the Battle of the Washita," Research Review, *The Journal of the Little Big Horn Associates,* Winter, 2000, pgs. 11-12.
3. Hutton, *Phil Sheridan & His Army,* pg. 48.
4. ibid.
5. Hutton, *The Custer Reader,* pg.105.
6. "Justice, The Saga of Clara Blinn at the Battle of the Washita," Research Review, The Journal of the Little Big Horn Associates, Winter, 2000, pgs. 12-13.
7. Hyde, *Life of George Bent,* pg. 279.
8. Records of the 40th session of U.S. Congress, Executive Document #18. Also see Hatch, *Black Kettle,* pg. 240.
9. ibid.
10. Alvord to Forsyth, Report of the Officers in the West and Southwest, November 21, 1868. Also see Greene, *Washita,* pg. 108.
11. W.T. Harrington to P.H. Sheridan, November 8, 1868, Division of the Missouri Records, the United States Army. Also see Hutton, *Phil Sheridan's Army,* pg.52.
12. Kraft, *Ned Wynkoop and the Lonely Road from Sand Creek,* pg. 244.
13. Records of the 41st session of U.S. Congress, Executive Document 240.
14. Custer, *Elizabeth Bacon, Following the Guidon.*
15. Hutton, *Phil Sheridan & His Army,* pg. 63.
16. Alvord to Forsyth, Report of the Officers in the West and Southwest, November 26, 1868. Also see Greene, *Washita,* pg. 108.
17. John L. Sipes, the great-grandson of Medicine Water and Mo-chi, and Cheyenne tribal historian. Hereafter cited as John L. Sipes, Cheyenne tribal historian.
18. Hyde, *Life of George Bent,* pg. 322.
19. Wommack, Linda and John L. Sipes, "Tragedy at Sand Creek." *True West Magazine,* August 2003.
20. ibid.

21. John L. Sipes, Cheyenne tribal historian.
22. Measure Woman would later have a daughter, Cleo, who would later have a son, John L. Sipes. Genealogical records of Medicine Water and Mo-chi, in possession of the author.
23. Hutton, *Phil Sheridan & His Army*, pg. 70.
24. Broome, *Dog Soldier Justice*, pg. 54.
25. Justice, "The Saga of Clara Blinn at the Battle of the Washita," Research Review, *The Journal of the Little Big Horn Associates*, Winter, 2000, pgs. 17-18. Also see Hutton, *Phil Sheridan & His Army*, pg. 89.
26. Hyde, *Life of George Bent*, pg. 324.
27. Carr, Report to General G.D. Ruggles, Received 1869. Also see Broome, *Dog Soldier Justice*, pg. 75.
28. ibid.
29. This Danish colony would later be established as the town of Denmark, Kansas.
30. Broome, *Dog Soldier Justice*, pg. xi.
31. ibid., pg.91.
32. ibid.
33. ibid.
34. Sparks, *Reckoning at Summit Springs*, pg. 35.
35. ibid.
36. Llewellyn, *The Cheyenne Way: Conflict and Case Law in Primitive Jurisprudence*, pg. 202. Also see Hoebel, *The Cheyennes: Indians of the Great Plains*, pg. 95.
37. Timothy Kine Indian Depredation Claim, courtesy, Jeff Broome. Broome notes that by the time of the Depredation Claim, Timothy had changed the spelling of his surname from "Kyne" to "Kine."
38. Hendrickson, C.C., "Memories," *The Lincoln-Sentinel Republican*, February 1st and 8th, 1934. Also see Broome, *Dog Soldier Justice*, pg. 102.
39. Sparks, *Reckoning at Summit Springs*, pg. 35. Also see Broome, *Dog Soldier Justice*, pg. 103.
40. T.J.March, Report of May 31, 1869, Division of the Missouri Records, the United States Army.
41. ibid., pg. 188.
42. ibid.
43. Roenigk, *Pioneer History of Kansas*, pg. 94.
44. ibid.
45. Hendrickson, C.C., "Memories," *The Lincoln-Sentinel Republican*, February 1st and 8th, 1934.
46. *The Lincoln Sentinel*, April 24, 1913. Also see Broome, *Dog Soldier Justice*, pg. 100.
47. U. S. Department of the Missouri. Also see Broome, *Dog Soldier Justice*, pg. 118.

48.   U. S. Department of the Missouri. Also see Broome, *Dog Soldier Justice*, pg. 122.
49.   Carr, Reminiscences, pgs. 15-16. Also see Broome, *Dog Soldier Justice*, page 122.
50.   Frank J. North Papers, Series 3, Box 1, *The Journal of an Indian Fighter: The 1869 Diary of Major Frank J. North*. Nebraska State Historical Society. Hereafter listed as *The Journal of an Indian Fighter: The 1869 Diary of Major Frank J. North*. Nebraska State Historical Society.
51.   ibid.
52.   Carr, Official Report of Operations, Republican River Expedition, 1869.
53.   *The Journal of an Indian Fighter: The 1869 Diary of Major Frank J. North*. Nebraska State Historical Society.
54.   Carr, Official Report of Operations, Republican River Expedition, 1869.
55.   *The Journal of an Indian Fighter: The 1869 Diary of Major Frank J. North*. Nebraska State Historical Society.
56.   Hyde, *Life of George Bent*, pg. 330.
57.   ibid., pg. 331
58.   *The Journal of an Indian Fighter: The 1869 Diary of Major Frank J. North*. Nebraska State Historical Society.
59.   Carr, Official Report of Operations, Republican River Expedition, 1869. Also see Broome, *Dog Soldier Justice*, pgs. 157, 158.
60.   Price, *Across the Continent With the Fifth Cavalry*, pg. 136. Also see Broome, *Cheyenne War*, pg. 454.
61.   ibid.
62.   *The Journal of an Indian Fighter: The 1869 Diary of Major Frank J. North*. Nebraska State Historical Society. It is also interesting to note that several writers have perpetuated a myth regarding this incident. It is said by some that North discovered a woman's shoe print along the trail. This is preposterous. There are many accounts, including from George Bent as well as Buffalo Bill Cody, that relate that the first thing the Indians would do with female captives was to remove their shoes. Replaced with moccasins, there would be no shoe prints to follow. See Hyde, *The Life of George Bent* and Broome, *Dog Soldier Justice*, page 152-153.
63.   Hyde, *Life of George Bent*, pgs. 331-332.
64.   Propst, *Forgotten People*, pg. 118. Also see Broome, *Cheyenne War*, page 456.
65.   Volkmar's journal, entry dated July 11, 1869. Also see Broome, *Cheyenne War*, pg. 457.
66.   Broome, *Cheyenne War*, pg. 458.
67.   Hyde, *Life of George Bent*, pg. 332.

68. ibid.
69. *The Journal of an Indian Fighter: The 1869 Diary of Major Frank J. North*. Nebraska State Historical Society.
70. Danker, *Man of the Plains*, pgs. 115-116.
71. Carr, *Reminiscences*, pgs. 15-16.
72. Cox, "Summit Springs," *Denver Westerners Roundup*, March 1970., pg. 21.
73. Royall, Major W. B., Camp, Republican River Expedition, dated July 11, 1869, Department of the Platte, Letters Received, 1869. Also see Broome, *Cheyenne War*, pg. 466, and Berthrong, *The Southern Cheyennes*, pg. 343.
74. U. S. Department of the Missouri. Carr to General G. D. Ruggles, July 20, 1869.
75. *The Journal of an Indian Fighter: The 1869 Diary of Major Frank J. North*. Nebraska State Historical Society.
76. ibid.
77. The United States Department of the Platte, Letters Received, 1869.
78. ibid.
79. John L. Sipes, Cheyenne tribal historian, correspondence with author, April, 2002.
80. Cheyenne Dog Soldier Ledgerbook, Colorado History Center.

— DEFIANCE, DEATH AND DESPAIR —

Following the Indian decimation at Summit Springs, much to the satisfaction of the United States military, the majority of the Cheyenne left the territory of Colorado. While many moved to the reservations in Oklahoma Territory, others defied the government and pledged to fight on for their peoples' rightful heritage of their homeland. Medicine Water, along with his warrior wife Mo-chi, were among the Cheyenne to continue the fight. It was a futile attempt that only resulted in more bloodshed and cold-blooded murder.

As chief of the Cheyenne Bowstring Warrior Society, also known as the Dog Soldiers, Medicine Water had pledged to do whatever was necessary to protect the homeland of his people. Medicine Water strongly believed in the words of Sweet Water, the prophet and first Keeper of the Cheyenne Sacred Arrows:

> "Though your son might be killed in front of your tepee, you should take a peace pipe and smoke. Then you would be called an honest chief. You chiefs own the land and the people." [1]

However, Medicine Water had watched as Black Kettle had used Sweet Water's suggestion of diplomacy with the white man. And he had witnessed the result, not once, but twice. First was the massacre at Sand Creek and then again four years later, at the Washita River, where Black Kettle lost his life. Now, Medicine Water would adhere to only the last portion of the prophet's wise words, "You chiefs own the land and the people."

Therefore, Medicine Water chose to fight for his people, the Tsis-tsis-tas, Cheyenne for "The People." With Mo-chi at his side, Medicine Water led his warriors to the "Bunch of Trees" area near the Smoky Hill River in Kansas. There, he and his warriors roamed the area, scouting for soldiers and other intruders, including westward travelers and, especially, the hated white buffalo hunters who were killing the animals merely for sport. John Sipes, Cheyenne tribal historian and great-great-grandson of Medicine Water and Mo-chi, recounted Cheyenne oral history:

> "The People believed the Heammawhio [Buffalo] were created by the Great Spirit for them. The meat sustained the People. They made their lodges from skins, clothing and blankets from the hides and tools, weapons from the bones. From the horns, dishes and spoons were made. From the long hair of the head, lariats and ropes were made. No part of the sacred animal was wasted by the People." [2]

Mo-chi still carried her father's rifle which she took when she found his body in the smoldering aftermath of Sand Creek. Ironically, it had been given to him in this very area known as the "Bunch of Trees" by a goldseeker he had once rescued. [3] Medicine Water instructed his warriors to attack all buffalo hunters when discovered, for he knew that without the buffalo his people faced starvation in the coming winters. As head chief of the Cheyenne Bowstring Warrior Society, Medicine Water had declared war.

Early in 1874, a large concentration of perhaps the last of the buffalo hunters gathered together in a bold attempt to establish their coalition in the very center of the Comanche hunting grounds. The site chosen was the old Adobe Walls trading post in the Staked Plains area of the Texas Panhandle. Ironically, an early post had been built in 1842, on the south fork of the Canadian River, and operated by William Bent, the man who long advocated for peace between the two cultures, married into the Cheyenne tribe, and fathered children of Cheyenne descent.

Understandably, the Indian tribes were furious, including Medicine Water and the Cheyenne. In the summer of 1874, Medicine Water led the Cheyenne Dog Soldiers band, the Bowstring Warrior Society, during a combined Indian attack against the hated buffalo hunters, at Adobe Walls. [4] The Cheyenne camped at Palo Duro Canyon with the Kiowa and Comanche. There, Medicine Water smoked the war pipe with Quanah Parker and his band of Comanche, along with a band of the Kiowa. With this honored act, Medicine Water, as well as his brothers Iron Shirt and Man-On-A-Cloud, and other members of the Cheyenne Bowstring Society pledged their support. The Cheyenne joined forces with the Kiowa and Quanah Parker's Comanche warriors to wage war against the buffalo hunters, who were killing the animal so sacred to the Indian way of life. Adobe Walls was a small cluster of sod buildings which included a saloon and blacksmith shop. Twenty-

Medicine Water waged war to keep the Cheyenne tribal lands and way of life. The murder and mayhem that ensued cost all their freedom. *John Sipes collection*

seven hunters, including sharpshooter William "Billy" Dixon, one woman, and later famed lawman, William Bartholomew "Bat" Masterson, occupied the post.

The Indian coalition, over six hundred strong, attacked the fortress at dawn on June 27, 1874. Medicine Water, with Mo-chi at his side, led the Cheyenne in the attack, along with Quanah Parker's Comanche and the Kiowa. Three of the hunters were killed outside of the fortress. The attack turned into a standoff lasting three days.

When it was over, the buffalo hunting group lost four men. Indian casualties were estimated at over seventy warriors, including the son of Stone Calf, the respected Cheyenne leader following Black Kettle's murder.[5] The triumphant buffalo hunters beheaded many of the corpses and placed the heads atop the corral gateposts.[6]

The Indian coalition, devastated by the loss of so many, immediately left the vicinity. Medicine Water and the Cheyenne rode back to the Smoky Hill River country in Kansas. Along the way, they attacked a small wagon train near present-day Hennessy, Oklahoma, killing the teamsters. Sipes recounted the traditional oral history of his people:

> *"Medicine Water intended to continue the war. He and the Cheyenne Bowstring Warrior Society, preferred death in battle to death by starvation."*[7]

Back on the Smoky Hill River Trail, the Cheyenne continued to raid travelers and buffalo hunters. On August 24, 1874, at Spring Creek, approximately six miles southwest of Meade, Kansas, and twenty miles west of Dodge City, a railroad crew of twenty men, led by Oliver F. Short, was attacked and brutally murdered by Medicine Water and his Dog Soldiers. The men, working for the Atchison, Topeka & Santa Fe Railroad, were found scalped and the dead animals had been butchered for food. Nearly three weeks later, the warriors struck again near the Colorado-Kansas border. It would become the worst massacre in the region.

John and Lydia Cox German were originally farmers on a small piece of land near Morganton, Fannin County, Georgia. When the Civil War broke out in 1861, German enlisted in the Confederate Army, and was eventually taken prisoner. While he was imprisoned, his wife Lydia did her best to maintain the farm, however, the heavy fighting in the area had taken a heavy toll on the land, the buildings, and their family. Following the war, German was released from prison and returned to his farmland, which was devastated by the ravages of war.

Encouraged by reports of the tremendous opportunities in Colorado, with its strong economy due to the rich mining in the area, John and Lydia German saved enough money to purchase a covered wagon and oxen. On April 10, 1870, the German family left their beloved Blue Ridge Mountains of Fannin County, Georgia, bound for Colorado. The German family made their way to Howell County, Missouri. Financially insecure, they stayed with relatives for a few years. There, the couple worked various jobs until they had saved enough money to resume their westward travel.

On August 15, 1874, the German family finally left Missouri, bound for Colorado. According to the army bulletins and newspaper reports the couple had read prior to their departure from Missouri, they believed their journey to Colorado Territory no longer contained the threat of Indian raids. Therefore, John German felt safe in traveling the Smoky Hill River Trail westward to Colorado. At Ellsworth, Kansas, the German family followed the railroad to Fort Hays. Stopping for supplies, they were assured by the soldiers and others that there would be no danger of Indian attacks. Continuing on their journey, the family followed the trail west.

It was a slow trek across the wind-blown prairie. John German often walked the trail ahead of the wagon, in search of hazardous road conditions ahead. Their wagon, loaded with all their provisions, moved slowly, as Lydia German carefully drove the oxen onward. Nineteen-year-old Stephen, the couple's only son, walked along the oxen, guiding them along the route. The older daughters, Rebecca Jane, age twenty, seventeen-year-old Catherine Elizabeth, fifteen-year-old Joanna, and twelve-year-old Sophia Louisa often walked the trail as well, in an effort reduce the weight of the wagon. The younger daughters, seven-year-old Juliana, and five-year-old Adelaide, generally stayed in the wagon with their mother.

At a point approximately fourteen miles east of Fort Wallace, on September 10, nearly a month into their westward journey, the family made camp for the night. It was a pleasant spot on the Kansas prairie, just northwest of the Smoky Hill River. John German had been told by a group of eastward travelers that he was within a day's travel of the fort. This was good news, as the journey from Fort Wallace into Colorado Territory would be achieved within a day of good travel conditions.

At daybreak the following morning, September 11, 1874, John and Lydia German gathered their children, broke camp, and prepared for the final leg of their journey to Colorado. With Lydia driving the wagon, her five daughters inside, John led the way as Stephen and Catherine herded the cows and their calves behind the wagon. Only moments into the journey, Catherine and Stephen heard the sound of Indian war cries.[8] Sophia German Feldman would later recall, "It appeared as if nineteen Indians came out of the ground from the high bluff." She continued:

"First I watched the hatchet enter father's head, then I watched it enter my mother's head." [9]

John L. Sipes recounted the Cheyenne oral history of the incident:

"During the month of the Cool Moon [September,] Medicine Water and his warriors encountered a white family that had camped on the Bunch of Trees River. This was on the land the Cheyenne considered theirs, and the whites were seen as intruders. Medicine Water reacted in retaliation for members of his family who had been murdered at Sand Creek and the Washita River." [10]

Before the family had a chance to react and set up a defense, Medicine Water and seventeen of his warriors, including his brothers Iron Shirt and Man-On-A-Cloud, had descended upon the westward travelers. John German was the first to die followed by his son, Stephen, who received a lance driven through his chest. Lydia jumped from the wagon. As she ran toward her husband and son, one of the Indians raised his tomahawk and broke open Lydia German's skull. As Catherine fled for cover, another warrior shot an arrow into her thigh. Catherine fell to the ground in agony.[11]

Seven-year-old Julia hid under the feather bed in the wagon. She later recounted the incident:

"When father heard the Indians coming, he turned black in the face and could not get his gun up to shoot. They came and took an axe after taking hold of pa's horse and struck him in the head, cutting it open. They cut into the heads of all, except my biggest sister, and scalped them. Then, they dragged me out from under the feather bed in the wagon where I was with sister. She commenced and set up crying. I crawled in again and went to sleep. I could not cry. There wasn't enough tears in my eyes." [12]

Then Mo-chi joined the murderous warriors and yielded a hatchet to kill and scalp those that the Dog Soldiers had missed. After killing Rebecca Jane, Mo-chi then killed and scalped Joanna, as her long blond hair was considered a prized trophy. With five dead bodies laying on the ground and a few head of livestock roaming aimlessly, Medicine Water's Dog Soldiers set about gathering the animals and ransacking the wagon. Inside the wagon, five-year-old Adelaide began crying uncontrollably. Just as a warrior was about to shoot the child to stop the annoying crying, Mo-chi grabbed the little girl, saving her life.

Sipes, later reflected on Mo-chi's actions of that day:

"Mo-chi I do not think of the rage in her as much as she had sadness and anger from the losses and deaths of her family and when she was attacking the German family I think she saw no difference in what the soldiers did at the [Sand Creek] *massacre to her family and her people."*[13]

While gathering the animals, Medicine Water discovered Catherine hiding in the tall grass along the river. He grabbed the teenager, pulled out the arrow from her leg and threw her on his horse. He took her to the wagon where her sisters were. There, Mo-chi took charge of the four German girls, seventeen-year-old Catherine, twelve-year-old Sophia, seven-year-old Julia, and five-year-old Adelaide, who were now hostages of the murderous Cheyenne band of Dog Soldiers. Sophia recalled the terror years later:

"We girls huddled together while the braves argued about something - probably what to do with the rest of us. Sister Joanna and myself were placed side by side, and they came up to inspect us and see which one they should kill. The choice fell on poor Joanna, and she was shot through the head." [14]

After the warriors had plundered the wagon and set it afire, Medicine Water placed each one of the German girls on horses with his trusted comrades. Then they fled the scene. Medicine Water led his warriors south, crossing the Canadian River in the Texas Panhandle. A heavy rain fell that afternoon and the Indians searched for shelter. Whether it was due to the late hour when camp was finally made, neglect, or mistreatment, the four German girls did not eat that night.

Of her early captivity, Catherine recalled:

"One day as we crossed a river, which now was a small stream, I noticed the sand quiver under the weight of the ponies and horses carrying our captors. I wished that the earth would open and swallow them all. I felt so bitter toward the Indians at that time, that if I had the poison, I believe I would have made an attempt to kill them." [15]

Medicine Water and the warriors resumed their journey on to Grey Beard's village at McClellan Creek, near today's town of

Pampa, Texas. The military soon learned of the Cheyenne presence in the Texas Panhandle. Major William Price led his Eighth Cavalry into the area, while Colonel Nelson A. Miles and his Fifth Cavalry arrived a few days later. Both regiments had supply wagons and howitzers. On September 28th, the soldiers attacked a small village near the creek. Several Indians were killed in the skirmish. According to Sipes, Medicine Water claimed:

> *"The Kiowa and Comanche lie big of the attack and make blame on us. We honored them by picking up their war pipe so we went first. The other two tribes did not follow so we left them there after losing five men."* [16]

Meanwhile, on September 30, nineteen days after the horrific slaughter of the German family, a lone buffalo hunter, scouting along the Smoky Hill River, came upon the dead and rotting corpses. Leaving the gut-wrenching scene, the man rode north to the nearest settlement, known as Sheridan, where he reported his discovery. A telegram was immediately sent to Fort Wallace. The *Topeka Commonwealth* newspaper carried the story as reported to the editor by Kansas State Senator John H. Edwards, in the October 9, 1874, issue. The article read in part:

> *"On Wednesday last a hunter arrived at Sheridan from the north fork of the Smoky Hill River and reported having found the bodies of three men and one woman [sic] who had been killed by the Indians and their wagon burned. The news was telegraphed to Fort Wallace and a squad of soldiers sent down to investigate the matter. They returned on Saturday [October 3] to Monument Station, bringing the bodies. They had apparently been dead ten or twelve days. An axe was sticking in the woman's head, all the bodies were more or less mutilated. They had apparently been surprised and killed without resistance. From the tracks in the vicinity, there must have been at least three or four children in the party. None of their bodies having been found, however, the supposition is that they were carried off. The wagon had been burned and everything carried off. A Bible was found nearby, the family record of which proves the to have come from the town of Blue Ridge, state of Georgia, and the name of German."* [17]

While the article reported incorrect information regarding the number of dead bodies, the dead were two males and three females. Further information gleaned from the retrieved family bible revealed that four daughters of the German family were missing.

By this time, the United States Army had deduced, through military intelligence and briefings with the various Indian agents, as well as the Commissioner of Indian Affairs, that it was Medicine Water, chief of the Cheyenne Dog Soldiers, who was responsible for the murder of the German family. As a result, Medicine Water was now considered by the United States War Department to be the "worst of the Cheyenne Warriors." However, he succeeded in eluding the troops each time they attempted to close in on him. From late fall into early winter, the soldiers patrolled the Indian Territory in search of Medicine Water and his murderous Dog Soldiers. Sipes recounted the oral history as told by Medicine Water:

"The soldiers were in the field seeking out Medicine Water as he was the war chief so it was their objective to capture him first. The war party, including my great-great grandmother, Mo-chi, went to Antelope Hills and camped in a beautiful little area tucked away just west of the Antelope Hills in northwestern Oklahoma." [18]

However, with an early cold winter, Medicine Water and his band, near starvation and desperate, again moved to Grey Beard's village on McClellan Creek in the Texas Panhandle. Sipes recalled the Cheyenne oral history of this time as:

"It was the time of Hik' o min i, [the Freezing Moon] *and the winter and no food and white soldiers were descending on the Cheyenne."* [19]

The time Sipes spoke of was November 1874, six years after the Washita killings and ten years after the horrific massacre at Sand Creek. Medicine Water and Mo-chi were present at both atrocities and witnessed the horror of the slaughter of their people.

Catherine later wrote extensively of her captivity with the Cheyenne. She kept a journal that she hid but it was later lost. Years after her release and subsequent marriage, she again took up writing of that time period. Here is one excerpt:

"Little Squaw [Wasati] *always showed more kindness to us than the larger squaw. Sometimes Little Squaw roasted a piece of meat well and divided it among us, for she saw we could not eat the half-raw meat that her people enjoyed. The large squaw, whom I called Big Squaw,* [Mo-chi] *seemed delighted to see us tortured or frightened. Once when I was roasting a piece of liver over the camp fire, Big Squaw snatched it from the stick which held it and ate it just before I had finished cooking it."* [20]

Five year old Adelaide cried uncontrollably when captured by the Cheyenne. Mo-chi saved her from being killed by a Cheyenne warrior. *Fort Wallace Museum*

United States Army Colonel Nelson A. Miles had been following Medicine Water and his Cheyenne band for months. Learning the Cheyenne warrior leader was in the Texas Panhandle, Miles led his Fifth Infantry along with Lieutenant Colonel Thomas Neill and his Sixth Cavalry, toward the Indian camp near McClellan Creek. During the early morning of November 8, 1874, Miles quietly divided his troops, surrounding the silent Indian village.

Lieutenant Frank D. Baldwin led the attack on the Indian encampment. Fortunately, the Cheyenne, were alerted to the attack and somehow were able to flee undetected by the soldiers. As the soldiers entered and investigated the captured Indian camp, they were astonished at one particular discovery. In one of the lodges, Lieutenant Baldwin discovered the two youngest German daughters, Julia and Adelaide, alive, but near starvation. [21] During the three weeks at McClellan Creek, heavy rains, pounding hail, and even snow had prevented the warriors from hunting for food. Perhaps thinking the younger girls were near death, thereby no longer valuable as hostages, they were abandoned. In any case, Medicine Water, Mo-chi and several of the Dog Soldiers had left the camp with the older German daughters still held hostage.

Catherine, Sophia and many of the squaws in camp thought Julia and Adelaide had been killed. Catherine wrote of that time. She also spoke of her disdain for Mo-chi, although she would not learn until her rescue that it was Mo-chi who wielded the axe that killed her mother.

"The long, hard ride that day made everyone weary, and especially sister and me. The Indians stopped and set up a rude camp at least an hour before sunset. They killed and prepared a horse for the evening meal. Sophia and I remained close to Little Squaw [Wasati] who kindly

prepared meat for us. She took thin strips of meat and browned them well on both sides. We appreciated her friendly, sympathetic spirit. I noticed the tears in her eyes and knew that she also grieved for our little sisters. Because of her grief, Big Squaw [Mo-chi] laughed at her. I felt a great dislike for that large squaw, almost equal to what I felt toward her brutal buck [Medicine Water] who captured and claimed me." [22]

Meanwhile, unbeknownst to Catherine and Sophia, their sisters were alive and well. Colonel Nelson A. Miles personally took charge of little Julia and Adelaide. During his conversations with them he later wrote:

"Their story of woe and suffering is simply too horrible to describe." [23]

Young Julia gave the following statement to the attending officers:

"My name is Juliana Arminda German. I am aged seven years. My sister, here, Nancy Adelaide, is aged five and a half years. My father's name was John German, and my mother's name Catherine Lydia, and two older sisters Catherine Elizabeth, aged fifteen [seventeen] years and Sophie Louisa aged twelve years. My older sisters are yet with the Indians. I have only seen Catherine once since. I could hear her voice sometimes, but could not see her ever. They didn't treat me well. They bridled up the horse and put sister in front of one young buck and me in front of another on horseback. We were jolted so that our necks got stiff. After a while, they took us out one day and left us on the prairie all alone. I don't know what they did it for. After a while, sister and I got up and found a wagon trail, and we followed it six miles to where there had been a camping party and we found some corn and crackers with a little grain of meat. We got an old broken cup and bucket and went down to the creek and got some water. Then some Indians came that day and took us away again and put us down in a camp where there were Indian squaws - where your soldiers came and found us on the day of the firing. We heard the firing but did not hear the yelling. We are getting over our fright." [24]

Evidently Sophia and Catherine were still in the same camp as Sophia later recalled:

"There was a great commotion in camp, the Indians shouting that soldiers were coming. I was visiting with the little [Indian] girls at the time Captain [Frank] Baldwin made his charge on the Indians. They

were very much excited and rushed me away ahead of them for I was old enough to ride horseback." [25]

Of the incident, George Bent recounted:

"Medicine Water arrived at the Grey Beard encampment early on the morning of the 8th. Camp was hurriedly broken and the little girls placed on the ground eating hackberries while a Cheyenne rear guard watched the soldiers pick up the sisters. Evidently, a rear guard shot toward Julia under the robe." [26]

It had been a long, terrifying six weeks of captivity for Julia and little Addie. On November 8, 1874, it was finally over. After the girls had a few days of rest, proper care, and nutrition, Miles placed them in an army wagon, gently covering them with warm blankets. Then he drove them to Camp Supply, the nearest army camp in the area, located approximately forty miles northeast, near the Washita River. There, Miles placed Julia and Adelaide in the care of the army surgeon at the post. After proper medical attention, the youngest pair of the German girls were then cared for by the officers' wives until they were well enough to be taken to Fort Leavenworth, Kansas. On December 15, Agent John D. Miles sent his report to Commissioner Edward Smith in Washington D.C. It contained the following information:

"I have the honor to report that the following information has just been received from Eagle, Hawk Leader and Man Bear, who arrived here on the 11th, and Bears Heart and Little Shield, who arrived on the 12th, from the hostile camps. These Indians report one of the elder girls was in Medicine Water's camp. She is now the property of Long Neck [Long Back] a Cheyenne buck. The other young lady is with Sand Hill, Cheyenne Chief, and at last account was the property of a son of Sand Hill. Latest reports place Medicine Water on Sergeant Majors Creek, a tributary of the Washita where they have been camped for some time and Sand Hill's [group] are camped on a tributary of the Red River on the Staked Plains in north western Texas. The Indians believe that peace will soon be declared and a large ransom approved." [27]

By January 1875, the harsh winter conditions had forced many of the Comanche and Kiowa to surrender at Fort Sill, in Indian Territory. Medicine Water and his band were also nearly destitute, but refused to surrender. Medicine Water sent word to Stone Calf, whom the soldiers had a cordial relationship with, to negotiate a peaceful meeting with the soldiers and as a gesture of good will, Medicine Water would release the two older German sisters, Catherine and Sophia. Sipes recounted Cheyenne oral history:

> "The Cheyenne were facing starvation and experiencing the erosion of their traditional way of life." [28]

Stone Calf sent a runner to deliver the message to Colonel Nelson Miles. Meanwhile, while awaiting word from Colonel Miles, Medicine Water led his people to Stone Calf's village, near a tributary of the Pecos River by the Texas/New Mexico border.

Seven-year-old Julia and her younger sister, Addie, survived being left alone on prairie. *Fort Wallace Museum*

Despite the possibility of the prisoner exchange, life in the Indian village was no better for Catherine and Sophia German. The girls were forced to do nearly all of the Indian women's work and were beaten when they didn't. Several of the young warriors also had their way with the teenaged girls.

Finally, word was received that Colonel Miles agreed to the exchange. However, Miles stipulated to Stone Calf that peace between the government and the Cheyenne people depended on the safe delivery of the German sisters. With this warning, Stone Calf immediately moved the German sisters into the safety of his lodge. The exchange was to take place in early February, at the Darlington Indian Agency, in Indian Territory. Unexpectedly, Stone Calf and his people failed to appear. [29] Catherine described this event:

> "When I entered the lodge Chief Stone Calf gave a grunt of welcome. He was very friendly and spoke a few words in my language and from his gestures and because I knew a good many words of his tongue, I understood that he was very sorry for me and regretted that some of his tribe had committed the crime against my people. He said that he would

try to have sister and myself taken to our own people. This good news greatly cheered me." [30]

Finally, Sophia and Catherine were reunited and spoke of the hardships they had endured as well as happy moments. Sophia informed Catherine that she had seen Julia and Adelaide some time ago. Catherine was relieved as she was sure they had been killed. Neither knew of the hardships the younger girls had endured alone on the prairie or of their subsequent rescue until they received a photograph of the younger sisters from Colonel Miles.

Catherine German was 17 when captured by Medicine Water and Mo-chi. She later wrote about the experience. *Fort Wallace Museum*

Nearly three weeks later, in late February 1875, Stone Calf and his band, with the German sisters in their care, led the Cheyenne group, including Medicine Water and Mo-chi, from the Pecos River east to the Darlington Indian Agency in Indian Territory, a distance of nearly four hundred miles. John Sipes recounted the family oral history of this event:

> "The Old ones say our family fought to the bitter end until they could fight no more and just had to surrender because their horses gave out and five columns of troops were moving in on Medicine Water from all directions and five different forts. So it was best for his people and his family that he and Mo-chi and the warriors follow the Arrow Keeper and surrender." [31]

Years later, Sophia recounted this long trip in her unpublished manuscript:

> "My Indian clothing was not made for the extremely cold weather in New Mexico, where I could find no firewood to build a fire. I was so

cold and hopeless, I looked forward to dying and have never feared death since. I saw old Indians and little children die that terrible winter." [32]

News of the Indian arrival and subsequent release of the German sisters caused an outpouring of local citizens to witness the event. On March 6, 1875, as the Cheyenne group, led by Stone Calf, approached the Darlington Indian Agency, crowds lined the road to get a glimpse of the girls held hostage by the Indians, cheering at their safe return. [33]

Stone Calf, carrying the white flag of surrender, led the Cheyenne people into the yard of the agency. Three rows of Cheyenne followed, all on foot, their children in the rear. Sipes continued:

"This was done in the traditional way of the Cheyennes. The women with the babes hid the little ones by covering their heads with blankets as to not allow them to witness the arrest of their people. The surrender was formed with a center and two wings on each side of the center group. The soon to be prisoners of war stopped and threw their arms on the ground and all sat down on Mother Earth." [34]

John Sipes continued with the oral history as told to him by his elders:

"The surrender was orderly but the officer in charge [Lieutenant Colonel Thomas H. Neill] *told Stone Calf he knew the count was off and that not all the arms were surrendered. He insisted he wanted all the arms and the men, women and children and he intended to have it this way. Stone Calf reminded the Cheyennes that they agreed to this the night before and must hold to the agreement and give all arms up. The officer told them he would return at midnight and expected what he ordered."* [35]

General Miles also reflected on the historic moment:

"The Indians had gone out in the summer splendidly attired and equipped with grand paraphernalia, beautiful lodges, and thousands of ponies. They came back in the winter, many of them on foot and poverty stricken, leaving most of the ponies as well as many of their people dead upon the plains." [36]

Meanwhile, Catherine and Sophia German were taken to the agency's infirmary, where medical staff gave them a complete exam. The girls were in a very weak condition. Having purposely been denied food by the Indian women, including Mo-chi, the girls had very nearly starved to death. The day they were examined was Catherine's eighteenth birthday; she weighed less than eighty pounds. Despite suffering from extreme malnutrition, the girls also suffered physical and mental conditions due to the repeated raping and beatings. The girls remained in the infirmary, where several women looked after them. Later the girls regretted not keeping their Indian clothing although Sophia did keep her moccasins. [37]

Six days later, on March 12, 1875, Lieutenant Colonel Thomas H. Neill brought several of the prisoners forth with the intent that the German sisters would be able to identify those who had harmed them. Colonel Miles later recounted:

"The two elder German girls went along down the line pointing out to the officers the different men who had been engaged in the murder of their family. In total, they identified Medicine Water, and sixteen Indian bucks." [38]

Catherine remembered:

" Sister and I later waited in Captain Bennett's tent when guards brought in the arrested Indian I knew well as my captor [Medicine Water]. *When he saw us he turned an ashy color and seemed much frightened. I recognized him at once as the husband of Big Squaw* [Mo-chi] *and the one who had been active in the raiding and responsible for the death of my folks. Later I found Big Squaw and was not sorry to see them take her as prisoner, for as you know, she was never kind to us girls."* [39]

Sophia Louisa German specifically pointed her finger at Mo-chi stating that she was the person who "chopped my mother's head open with an axe."[40] Subsequently, Mo-chi, Medicine Water and thirty-two of his Cheyenne warriors, including the sixteen the German girls had implicated, along with nine Comanche, and twenty-six Kiowa, were then ordered to be placed in irons before taken back to the guardhouse. On April 6, 1875, Wesley, ironically a former slave and now employed by the army, dutifully began to perform the task.[41]

However, during the long, tedious task, one of the Cheyenne prisoners, Black Horse, a tall, muscular warrior, overpowered Wesley, kicking him in the chest, and made a clean escape from the agency. Seizing the moment, several of the Cheyenne prisoners followed Black Horse.[42] Soldiers immediately gave pursuit.

Despite the soldiers firing, a defiant Black Horse ran for his life, as did his comrades. Although one of the soldier's bullets hit the fleeing warrior, his comrades also fleeing managed to grab Black Horse and carry him to the safety of White Horse's village. Cheyenne historian Sipes recounted the incident:

> "Black Horse who was wounded during the onslaught, escaped with the other Cheyenne and ran into the sand hills across the river and the soldiers pinned them in these hills until late that same night. The Cheyenne recovered the hidden weapons in the plum bushes near the sand hills. These arms were used to fight back when the soldiers brought out the gatling guns. Then the Cheyenne waded across a small lake under the cover of night and a thunderstorm to escape." [43]

Sophia German, age 12, watched in horror as Mo-chi took an axe to her mother. *Fort Wallace Museum*

The escape of Black Horse and the other Cheyenne prisoners was an obvious miscalculation on the part of the military personnel at the agency. The ensuing pursuit, which also proved unsuccessful, was something that evidently the officers in charge chose to cover up. In the reports of the incident, it was stated that Black Horse had been killed by the soldiers.

White Horse, along with Chicken Hawk, Little Bull and Spotted Wolf, eventually made their way back to the Smoky Hill River. There, they vowed in defiance to fight rather than surrender. Eventually, Wesley completed his task of placing the remaining prisoners in irons. Included among the shackled prisoners was Mo-chi, the first woman as well as the first Native American female to be accused of war crimes against the United States of America. Lieutenant Colonel Thomas N. Neill had brought fourth four distinct charges against Medicine Water:

"Being engaged in the murder of four teamsters on the Cimmarron, March 19,1873; in the murder of the Germain [sic] family, October 20, 1874, [sic] and the abduction of the surviving female children." [44]

As the prisoners of war awaited their fate, their children were cared for in barracks separate from the guardhouse, and had no contact with their parents. One of these children was Measure Woman, (Tah-nea in the Cheyenne language.) She was the eldest daughter of Medicine Water who, at the age of five, was wounded but survived the massacre at Sand Creek. Now, at the age of eleven, she witnessed her parents being taken away from her in chains. Through family oral history, Measure Woman related to her great-grandson, John Sipes that:

"She [Measure Woman] could only see Mo-chi from a distance with leg irons and shackles. She could not see Medicine Water because the soldiers were surrounded on all sides of him with rifles pointed toward him." [45]

Later that month, under U. S. Army escort, Catherine and Sophia German were taken to Fort Leavenworth, Kansas, where they were eventually reunited with their younger sisters, Adelaide and Julia. After an emotional reunion, the four sisters underwent a series of interviews by various military officers.

When much of the sisters' horrendous ordeal became public, a *Kansas City Times* reporter interviewed General William T. Sherman. He specifically asked the general of the fate of Medicine Water, and those that had murdered the German family. General Sherman replied:

"I can hardly tell as yet, but they will probably be sent to a reservation in Florida, where they will be held as prisoners of war." [46]

Learning of the horrific tales told by the German sisters and sympathetic to their plight, Colonel Miles and his wife offered to become the guardians of the four German sisters. While in their care, the girls eventually began to speak more openly of their experiences, particularly Catherine. She told Mrs. Miles of being traded three times, the last time to Long Back, who would allow young warriors to have their way with her, after payment of property, including horses. Catherine related how Long Back's wife would order her to do all the work required in their lodge and beat her mercilessly if she showed any resistance. Often, when Catherine was ordered to go to the stream for fresh water she would be attacked and raped by as many as six warriors. [47]

Eventually, after years of lobbying, Congress authorized a ten thousand dollar withdrawal from the annual Cheyenne annuities to set up an endowment fund for the four sisters. When the girls reached the age of twenty-one, they would then receive a lump sum payment of twenty-five hundred dollars. In the meantime, Mr. and Mrs. Patrick Corney raised the girls in their Kansas home. Medicine Water, Mo-chi and the other prisoners remained incarcerated at the Darlington Indian Agency, while the government held meetings with military officers regarding the fate of the Indian prisoners of war. On a routine visit through his jurisdiction, Indian Agent John D. Miles inspected the guardhouses where the prisoners were being detained. John Miles was appalled at what he observed. Due to the cramped quarters, the humid conditions because of the heavy spring rains, the lack of a proper diet and water, many of the detainees were suffering from sickness and malnutrition. In his report to the Commissioner of Indian Affairs, Agent Miles wrote in part:

> *"A more wretched and stricken* [group] *than these people would be difficult to imagine. They seemed to realize the power of the government"* [48]

Subsequently, Lieutenant Richard Henry Pratt ordered the prisoners of war to be moved to Fort Sill. The prisoners, a total of thirty-three Cheyenne, including the only female, Mo-chi, remained shackled as they were all loaded into covered wagons. The children of the prisoners were placed in a separate wagon. The trip to Fort Sill was done under the cloak of darkness. After their arrival, the prisoners were placed in two long guardhouses constructed of hewn logs. Inside, several Kiowa and Arapaho were also in chains. Once the Cheyenne were incarcerated at the new location, the soldiers ordered the hand chains removed from the men and again placed in leg irons.

After weeks of government wrangling, regarding the definition of war and thereby prisoners of said war, lawyers at the United States War Department advised President Ulysses S. Grant: "A state of war could not exist between a nation and its wards." [49]

However, the lawyers also noted that the prisoners being held could be held for their crimes against the innocent victims.

Thus, President Grant ordered those guilty of such crimes be transported to the military prison at Fort Marion, in St. Augustine, Florida.[50] When Lieutenant Pratt learned of the impending move, he wrote to Lieutenant General William T. Sherman, on April 26, 1875, requesting that he be placed in charge of the Indian removal to the Florida prison:

> *"If, in the care of these Indians east, the government requires an officer of my rank, I want to go, because I have been down here eight years and am hungry for a change...some of them* [Indian prisoners] *ought to be tried and executed here in the presence of their people."* [51]

Pratt received the coveted assignment and prepared two companies each from the Fourth Cavalry. On April 26, 1875, Lieutenant Pratt informed the thirty-three Cheyenne prisoners of the charges brought against them by the United States War Department. The charges ranged from criminal activity and theft against civilians and military personnel, to kidnapping and murder. In particular, Medicine Water was charged with:

> *"Willful and deliberate murder and did kill or assist in killing a party of surveyors, i.e. white men consisting of Captain F. Short and his son, F. D. Short, James Shaw and his son, J. Alan Shaw, J. H. Renchier, Patrick Hennessy, also Henry C. Jones; also charged with abduction, illegal detention, and kidnapping and did carry off or assist in carrying off Catherine, Sophia, Julianne* [sic] *and Mary* [sic] *Germain* [sic.]*"* [52]

Thirty-four-year-old Mo-chi was charged with the same crimes, the first female Native American to be charged with war crimes against the United States government. Pratt noted in his subsequent report that his list also included those he considered: "turbulent, disobedient, agitators, stirrers up of bad feelings, and otherwise troublesome." Following the reading of the charges, Lieutenant Pratt then informed the prisoners of their fate: imprisonment at Fort Marion in Florida. Sipes recounted Cheyenne oral history:

> *"The Old ones say our people did not understand this. The Cheyenne way was to kill the captured war enemy. Medicine Water, Mo-chi and the others that surrendered expected this. Instead they were put in irons and forced into cages."* [53]

In the late night hours of April 28, 1875, Lieutenant Pratt and his troops, under orders from the Bureau of Indian Affairs, placed the thirty-three shackled prisoners of war into eight wagons, where they were then chained together. At midnight the wagons, under heavy military guard, rolled out of the confines of Fort Sill and headed to the town of Caddo, a distance of over one hundred fifty miles. After a six-day journey the troops and their prisoners arrived on May 4, 1875. At Caddo, the prisoners were escorted aboard the M. K. & T. railroad. The Cheyenne prisoners were terrified, having never ridden the "Iron Horse." Lieutenant Pratt and his selected officers also boarded the train. As the train whistle blew, announcing the departure from the depot, many of the Cheyenne shrieked in fear. As the train rolled on, several of the prisoners suffered from motion sickness and fainted.

The train rolled on and on as it made its thousand-mile trip to the Florida prison. During one of the many stop-overs, it was discovered that the Cheyenne warrior Grey Beard had managed to free himself from the chains and escaped. Lieutenant Pratt ordered the train to come to a stop. A group of Pratt's troops left the train and pursued the fleeing warrior. It wasn't long before one of the soldiers spotted Grey Beard hiding in a palmetto tree. Just as Grey Beard jumped from the tree in an effort to escape, the soldier shouted at him to halt. When Grey Beard refused, the soldier shot him. The bullet went through his back and lodged in his chest. In his official report, Lieutenant Pratt wrote:

> "He [Grey Beard] *was still living. We fixed a place and lifted him into the rear of the last car and brought Manimic* [sic] *his old friend and war chief and others of his tribe to see him. The interpreter stood by and told me what they said. Among other things Grey Beard said he wanted to die ever since being chained and taken from home."* [54]

On May 8, the train arrived at Fort Leavenworth, Kansas, where Grey Beard, as well as several seriously ill prisoners were taken to the fort's hospital. The other prisoners were then taken to a guardhouse. The citizens of the small community, anxious to see the Indian prisoners, were denied entry into the fort. However, a reporter for the *St. Louis Daily Globe* did get access to the fort. Accompanied by soldiers, the reporter was able to observe the prisoners inside the guardhouse. In his article which appeared in the May 11, 1875, issue, the reporter wrote of seeing Mo-chi during his visit:

> *"She rose up and looked at them eagerly, almost wildly, as though some chord in her heart had been touched, but said nothing, and after a little time sat down in silence. If ever crimes deserved punishment their bloody deeds merit the fullest demands of justice."*

While incarcerated at Fort Leavenworth, emotional despair must have overtaken the wounded Grey Beard. Despite Cheyenne spiritual beliefs against suicide, Grey Beard attempted to take his own life. Sipes recounted:

> *"The Cheyenne believed that suicide would doom the tassoom [spirit] from walking among the Great Mother Earth."* [55]

One evening, as the sun began to set, Grey Beard managed to cut the edge of his blanket. He then tied one end to an iron bar in the cell, stood on a chair, and tied the other end around his neck. When he kicked the support out from under him, the noise alerted the guards. Grey Beard was immediately released from the tied blanket and placed on the cot. He was still alive. Grey Beard was taken to the fort hospital where he lingered between life and death. Eventually he recovered well enough to continue the train journey to his imprisonment.

On May 11, 1875, Lieutenant General Philip Sheridan, bound by the United States War Department Special Order No. 88, instructed Pratt to proceed with his orders to transport the prisoners of war to Fort Marion. Six days later, on May 17, Pratt and soldiers escorted them aboard the train, which departed the station that afternoon. The following day, the *Leavenworth Daily Commercial* editorialized:

> *"No more will these dusky sons of the forests be allowed the sacred privilege of murdering women and children. So many of them have gone and the frontiersmen need stand in fear of these seventy-five no longer. We hope they will become accustomed to the climate and settle down with a fitting resignation to their daily toil. Goodbye. We should have been much more pleased to have filled this space with a fitting obituary for you all, but as it can not be so, we humbly submit and grant you godspeed on your journey South and may you never return."*

On the morning of May 19, as the train had just rolled through Nashville, Tennessee, soldiers became suspicious of Lean Bear. When Lean Bear, with his blanket covering his head, did not respond to verbal commands, one of the soldiers slowly approached Lean Bear. As the blanket was carefully lifted off the face of the prisoner, the soldiers immediately noticed blood. It was everywhere. It looked as if Lean Bear had slit his throat. As the soldiers leaned down to see if he was still alive, Lean Bear raised up from his seat, and, with a pocketknife, managed to stab both soldiers. As he tried to grab one of the soldier's weapon out of his hands, he was finally subdued and wrestled to the ground. Pratt, who was in another railcar, arrived at the scene and quickly sent for the army doctor, also in another railcar. When the physician finally arrived, he stated that Lean Bear was dead. The two soldiers had suffered minor wounds.[56]

Pratt ordered the train to stop at the Nashville depot. There, Pratt and four soldiers, along with the army physician, carried Lean Bear's body, wrapped in a blanket, off the train. Leaving the body on the train's platform, the military men began conversing with the depot manager, when suddenly Lean Bear wrestled free of the blanket and ran, literally for his life. Two of the soldiers immediately gave chase. Because he was still shackled, Lean Bear was quickly apprehended and thrown to the ground. When the soldiers attempted to raise Lean Bear off the ground and take him back to the train depot, his body was limp. Again, the army doctor examined him and pronounced Lean Bear dead. It was not long afterwards that the coroner's wagon arrived, originally requested for the transportation of Lean Bear's body for burial. After the body was loaded onto the wagon, two soldiers accompanied the driver to the military post for burial.

However, along the way, Lean Bear again arose from his covered blanket. He pleaded with the soldiers to kill him. The soldiers refused, subdued the Cheyenne prisoner, and ordered the wagon driver to return to the train station. After the army doctor made his third exam of Lean Bear, it was determined he was fit for continued travel.

The iron horse continued on its journey. After nearly three weeks of travel and turmoil, the train finally crossed into the state of Florida. It would not be the end of the turmoil and death on this long road. At 2:00 a.m., on the morning of May 21, as the train slowed to pass through two towns, Grey Beard seized the opportunity. He opened the window, and although still shackled, managed to make his way out of the window.

One of the soldiers saw the escape at the last minute and immediately alerted Pratt, who ordered the train to stop. Soldiers disembarked the train and searched for the fugitive. They found his discarded blanket, but were unable to find his trail in the darkness. During this delay, the train engineer alerted Pratt that the steam engine was dangerously low in water. The train had to move on to the next water tank station. Reluctantly, Pratt gave the order for the train to resume travel, but left several soldiers behind to pursue the prisoner.

Just as the train began to move, one of the soldiers shouted an alarm. Looking through his window, he noticed movement in the brush and heard the clanging of metal, unlike that of the rail irons. Hollering at the soldiers on the ground, they moved toward the bushes. Incredibly, Grey Beard left his hiding spot in the bushes and ran toward the train tracks. One of the soldiers fired and Grey Beard fell to the ground in a pool of blood. Still alive, he was carried back to the train. Shortly before Grey Beard died, Cheyenne warrior Minimic spoke with the dying warrior. Pratt included this event in his officer's report which included the statement:

> "He [Grey Beard] told Manimic [sic] what to tell his wife and daughter and soon died." [57]

At Jacksonville, Florida, the iron horse made its final stop. From there, the prisoners were taken to a steamer for the final journey by water to imprisonment. Army soldiers guided the terrified prisoners as they walked the plank to board the steamer on the St. Johns River. Finally, at 5:00 on the evening of May 22, 1875, the three-week journey was over.

For added security, the prisoners were shackled together as they were escorted to the yard of Fort Marion. As they looked around their new surroundings, they must have been overcome with despair. As far as the eye could see was the largest body of water they had ever seen. The large stone castle-like structure was also foreign to the Cheyenne prisoners. As they were led through the arches of the fortress, the large, thick, wooden doors slammed shut behind them. The heavy metal chains were then placed through the door handles and securely locked by the guards.

As the prisoners went through the military process of assimilation into the government prison system, they were required to relinquish their clothing, including moccasins, and don army issue prison uniforms and white man's shoes. Pratt then ordered that each of the Cheyenne were to have their hair cut. John Sipes recounted:

> "The Cheyenne custom in grief and mourning is to cut their hair. The Cheyenne prisoners believed this act meant great sorrow would follow." [58]

Indeed this seemed to be true, for the overwhelming sorrow not only lingered among the prisoners at Fort Marion, but with their children as well. When the Cheyenne prisoners left the confines of Fort Leavenworth, Kansas, their children were forced to remain at the fort. In effect, they became prisoners as well. Measure Woman, the sixteen-year-old daughter of Medicine Water and Mo-chi, later related her experiences to her great-grandson, John Sipes:

> "The military and the Indian agent were mean to the children because their parents were prisoners of war and sent to Ft. Marion, Florida. The children were made to make mud brick for the Ft. Reno and Darlington Agency. Their little hands were so blistered and they were so tired that many nights they just went to sleep hungry and exhausted." [59]

Meanwhile, at Fort Marion, Medicine Water, as the known leader of many of the atrocities of which the Cheyenne were accused of (but were never legally tried) was held in solitary confinement for several months. It was a small room where the only way to enter was to crawl through the small opening. This the officers did every day, along with an interpreter by the name of Romero. The officers would interrogate Medicine Water, demanding he reveal the others who were involved with their war against the United States government. Daily the officers threatened Medicine Water with death threats. Sipes recounted the Cheyenne family history:

> "The Old ones say Medicine Water was told daily he would be killed if he did not tell. He never told. He only told them he wished he could die on the Plains like a warrior and let the wolves scatter his remains about the earth and die honorably as a Cheyenne war chief should fighting for his people." [60]

Of Mo-chi's prison ordeal, Sipes learned:

> "Mo-chi told of sitting in her jail cell awaiting death. She felt it was near as she had seen the first of the Four Great Rivers one crosses to reach the route of Seyon, the Place of the Dead. She had heard the ve hoes [white men] call this river 'ocean' and the vastness was overwhelming. Mo-chi smelled death in the salt spray and in the dank solitude of her mildewed cell.. As a warrior she had prepared herself, she was ready to die for land the whites called Colorado and Wyoming." [61]

In late 1875, a popular Florida writer, Sidney Lanier, visited the Fort Marion prison and took pity on the Cheyenne prisoners. He later described his visit and expressed his opinion:

> *"And so here they are - Medicine Water, a ringleader, along with White Man, Rising Bull, Hailstone, Sharp Bully, and others, in the terrible murder of the Germain* [sic] *family, and in the more terrible fate of the two Germain girls who were recently recaptured from the Cheyennes; Come See Him, who was in the murder of the Short surveying party; Soaring Eagle, supposed to have killed the hunter Brown, near Fort Wallace; Big Moccasin and Making Medicine, horse thieves and raiders; Packer, the murderer of Williams; Mochi, the squaw identified by the Germain girls as having chopped the head of their murdered mother with an axe. Besides these, who constitute most of the criminals, are a lot against whom there is not a particular charge, but who are confined on the principle that prevention is better than cure."* [62]

This sentiment began to fuel the flames of injustice of the Cheyenne prisoners. In January 1877, Pratt listened earnestly to the concerns of the prisoners, particularly their desire to return to their homeland, even if it meant life on a reservation. Pratt had succeeded in his attempt to break the will of the prisoners. Perhaps not Pratt's intention, it would also break the spirit of the Cheyenne people.

Eventually in April 1878, forty of the Cheyenne prisoners were released, including Medicine Water and Mo-chi. During the train trip west, a stop was made at Fort Leavenworth, where the captive children of Medicine Water and Mo-chi joined their parents aboard the train. After a short stay at the fort for reassimilation back into society, the Cheyenne were taken back to the Darlington Agency, in Indian Territory, at the request of Lieutenant Pratt.

Although delighted to have returned to their traditional homeland after nearly three years of imprisonment, it was not an easy adjustment period for the couple. No longer were they free to roam the land, hunt the buffalo, or raise their children in the Cheyenne ways. Their traditional way of life had been lost; they were now living on a government-run reservation, which was a hard adjustment for Mo-chi and Medicine Water.

Struggling to conform to this new way of life was evidently harder for Mo-chi. She had suffered incredible hardship while imprisoned. Due to the damp, cold conditions, it is believed she contracted tuberculosis, as she was very ill following her release

It is said Mo-chi died of a broken heart over the loss her way of life. Her children and grandchildren lived on with a broken heart. *John Sipes collection*

from prison. Just three years later, at the age of forty-one, Mo-chi died in 1881. She was buried with all honors of a Cheyenne Indian warrior woman on high ground near the Washita River, where she had lived through and survived the second massacre of her people. John Sipes, Mo-chi's great-great-grandson spoke of Cheyenne oral history involving his great-great-grandmother:

> *"After her death, the Old ones sang songs and told stories of her great bravery in battle. In one battle Mo-chi saved her brother from a Pawnee war party. The Old ones named the battle 'The time the girl saved her brother from the Pawnee.' Her journey across the Four Great Rivers ended at the Place of the Dead, Seyon. The memory of Mo-chi is alive, for it is said, "As long as your name is spoken, you will never die"* [63]

For Medicine Water, life went on without his soul mate for another forty-five years. Ironically, he eventually found work with the very government he once waged war against. Medicine Water hauled supplies between Caldwell, Kansas, and the Darlington Agency. He remained true to his Cheyenne people, serving faithfully with the Native American Church, and working with the community for better education for the tribal youth. Medicine Water received a land allotment in 1891 near Watonga, Oklahoma, where he lived into old age. He remained close with his family until the day he died. In his own way, he would talk of his experiences, hoping the Cheyenne spirit would live on in his family. John Sipes, Medicine Water's great-great-grandson recalled the family oral history:

> "The Old ones, including my great-uncle Pete Bird Chief, Jr., said that Medicine Water had permanent scars on his ankles from the irons. The Old ones would listen to Medicine Water's stories of Ft. Marion, pointing to the scars and say, "This is what the government did to us to get control of our land, buffalo, ways of life as people and took away our freedom as Cheyennes." [64]

When Medicine Water died in 1926, at the age of ninety, he was buried next to Mo-chi, with all honors of a Head War Chief of the Cheyenne Bowstring Warrior Society. It is said he died of a broken heart. Sipes again recounted:

> "It is said the death and will to fight runs strong in lives such as Mo-chi and Medicine Water. The Old ones have taught us that to endure the hardships of surviving, while maintaining the love and courage to stand beside each other in overwhelming odds was tremendous. In the end, it was the love and dedication to their people, their family and their Cheyenne way of life." [65]

Conversely, with Cheyenne people now placed on government reservations, the United State military considered the Indian wars on the western plains to be over. They were sadly mistaken.

— Requital —

In early 1990, Arlene Jauken, a great-granddaughter of one of surviving German sisters, Sophia Louisa, sent several inquiries to historical institutions. She was seeking information regarding the Cheyenne involvement in the murder of her great-great-grandparents and the hostile capture of her great-grandmother, Sophia, and her three sisters. One such inquiry reached John L. Sipes, who was then employed with the Oklahoma Historical Society. Sipes, the great-great-grandson of the Cheyenne couple responsible for the murder of the German family, thought long and hard before he picked up the phone. In the end he made the call. Arlene Jauken later recounted the conversation:

> "I was so shocked. He called me early in the morning and said, I'm a descendant of Medicine Water and Mochi [sic] who killed your great-great grandparents. I didn't need my first cup of coffee to wake me up."[66]

    For the next several months the two corresponded. Soon they were telling each other the various family stories of the horrible episode. Jauken grew up near the Nebraska farm of her great-grandparents, Albert and Sophia German Feldman. She and her siblings learned of the murder of their great-great-grandparents and what happened to the surviving children over time. Evidently, it was not easy for Sophia to talk about. In turn, Sipes related the Cheyenne oral history as told to him by his great-grandmother, Measure Woman. Through their correspondence, Sipes learned that Jauken and her brothers had inherited the 1880 family farm after Sophia's death in 1947. Conversely, Jauken learned that Sipes had remained on or near the Indian reservation at Watonga, Oklahoma, where his great-great-grandparents lived out their lives following imprisonment for the German murders.[67]
    Over time, the two also began sharing additional information each had learned through independent research. While Jauken reached out to historical societies and libraries, Sipes had utilized his resources through the Oklahoma Historical Society, where he worked in the Archives and Manuscript Division. Sipes also had

the copious amount of research and documents he and noted Cheyenne historian, Donald J. Berthrong, had amassed over years of their work together.[68]

As Jauken and Sipes traded oral stories and research, they began to conceive a plan for a reunion of the descendants of the two families. Sipes recalled:

"It was an opportunity to find peace between our two peoples." [69]

Jauken and Sipes began by reaching out to their respective families and various contacts. Many letters were sent and phone calls made. Local newspapers carried the story of the impending reunion. Through their constant efforts, and perhaps with the help of the media attention, Jauken and Sipes were able to attract the attention of officers at Forts Leavenworth, Riley and Wallace. As the attention and interest mounted, descendants of General Nelson A. Miles expressed interest in attending such a reunion.

With this support, Jauken and Sipes went forward with their plans for a reunion. The date was set for September 9, 1990. The location was the approximate spot in Cheyenne County, Kansas, where the murder of the German family, at the hands of Cheyenne warriors Medicine Water and Mo-chi had occurred.

Jauken and Sipes had done well in getting the word out. Jauken was interviewed the day before the event and stated:

"It was a tragedy for both the German family and the Sand Creek victims. My message will be about love and forgiveness." [70]

On the morning of September 9, a caravan of cars and buses began to arrive at the reunion site. After the guests parked their vehicles they walked a distance of an eighth of a mile in the 100 degree heat to the speaking platform. Over eight hundred people were in attendance.

Before the reunion the Cheyenne held their traditional spirit ceremony. While the guests were allowed to observe the Cheyenne ceremony, they were required to stand apart at a distance of seventy-five feet. Following the Cheyenne ritual, everyone gathered and took their seats before the speaker's platform. Master of Ceremonies Captain Michael L. Baughn, president of the Butterfield/Smoky Hill Trail Association, welcomed the descendants of the German family, over one hundred, as well as thirty-five Cheyenne descendants of Medicine Water and Mo-chi present. Then the 7th Cavalry Fort Wallace Drill Team performed the presentation of the colors, after which the audience sang the national anthem. Following the invocation, given by Reverend Paul McNall, Captain Baughn introduced the descendants of the German family and the families of the Cheyenne warriors. He also recognized the descendants of General Nelson A. Miles. Baughn then introduced those who had also been involved in facilitating the reunion, including Commander Mark Magee of Fort Leavenworth, and Colonel LaGrange of Fort Riley, as well as the many historical organizations.

Baughn introduced the first of the two keynote speakers, Arlene Jauken, Sophia German's great-granddaughter. Jauken spoke of the murder of her family and shared a few of the stories Sophia had told her. Arlene Jauken concluded with this statement:

> *"The last time our families met, 116 years ago, John's great-great-grandmother killed my great-grandfather. John and I have promised to do better."* [71]

The second keynote speaker, John L. Sipes, approached the podium. Sipes related to the audience the Cheyenne oral history of how his great-great-grandmother, Mo-chi, watched as Colonel Chivington and his soldiers butchered her family at Sand Creek in 1864. He also recounted the slaughter of the many innocent Cheyenne four years later, at the Washita River, where his great-great-grandparents barely escaped, and their five-year-old daughter, Measure Woman, who was seriously wounded by a soldier's bullet. Sipes went on to recount the Cheyenne oral history of rage and revenge among his people. Sipes told the audience that in time, through his research and work with respected historians such as Donald J. Berthrong, he learned of the true atrocity of the German family at the hands of his great-great-grandparents. Sipes then graciously acknowledged Arlene Jauken, and thanked her for her leadership in spearheading the reunion of the two families. He concluded by saying:

> *"It is the hope of those who planned the reunion that future historians will endeavor to portray our history in an unbiased and fair manner to both the Indian and white man, leading to a better understanding and that barriers can be removed."* [72]

A few years after this historic reunion, John L. Sipes told this author that it was an "incredible experience." He also described his feeling of being in the Smoky Hill River area where his Cheyenne ancestors considered to be their homeland. Sipes said:

> *"I was overcome by a feeling that I was coming home when I saw the Smoky Hill River. The sight of the hackberry trees were just as the Old one described. A sense of peace overcame me and I was deeply moved."* [73]

John L. Sipes then recalled his Cheyenne oral history when he said:

> *"The Old ones say it was Medicine Water who waged war to protect his people. It is now a time for peace."* [74]

— Chapter Notes —

1. Cheyenne Oral History. Also see Grinnell, *The Cheyenne Indians*, and Hoig, *The Peace Chiefs of the Cheyenne*.
2. John Sipes, conversation with author.
3. ibid.
4. Grinnell, *Fighting Cheyenne*, pg. 319. This was the second fight at the historic site, the first being in 1864, involving Christopher "Kit" Carson.
5. Hoig, *The Peace Chiefs of the Cheyennes*, pg. 154. Also see Hyde, *Life of George Bent*, pg. 360.
6. Lookingbill, *War Dance at Fort Marion*, pg. 21.
7. John L. Sipes, Cheyenne tribal historian.
8. Catherine German's interview at Fort Leavenworth, Kansas, 1875. Courtesy, Fort Wallace Museum.
9. Feldman, Sophia German. *My Capture and Captivity by Cheyenne Indians-1874*.
10. John L. Sipes, Cheyenne tribal historian.
11. Wommack, Linda. "Mo-chi: The First Female Cheyenne Warrior," *Wild West Magazine*, 2008.
12. Interview with the *Leavenworth Daily Times*, December 3, 1874.
13. John L. Sipes, Cheyenne tribal historian.
14. Feldman, Sophia German. *My Capture and Captivity by Cheyenne Indians-1874*. Also see Meredith, *Girl Captives of the Cheyennes*. pg. 25, and Jauken, *The Moccasin Speaks*.
15. Meredith, *Girl Captives of the Cheyennes*, pg. 25.
16. John L. Sipes, Cheyenne tribal historian.
17. Despite the German family Bible recordings and the written account of Vince Rogers, the grandson of Catherine German, who survived the ordeal, many writers continue to spell the surname Germain or Germaine. This may also be because many officer's reports and government records spell the name incorrectly.
18. John L. Sipes, Cheyenne tribal historian.
19. ibid.
20. Meredith, *Girl Captives of the Cheyennes*, pg. 25.
21. Rogers, *The German Family Massacre*. Lieutenant Baldwin later received the Congressional Medal of Honor for rescuing the two German sisters.

22. Meredith, *Girl Captives of the Cheyennes*, pg. 27.
23. Indian Affairs Annual Report 1875. Oklahoma Historical Society.
24. *Leavenworth Times*, December 31, 1874.
25. Feldman, Sophia German. *My Capture and Captivity by Cheyenne Indians-1874*.
26. Hyde, pg. 363.
27. Report of the Commissioner of Indian Affairs for the Year 1875, pg. 268. Indian Agent John D. Miles should not be confused with Army Colonel Nelson A. Miles.
28. John L. Sipes, Cheyenne tribal historian.
29. Indian Affairs Annual Report 1875. Oklahoma Historical Society.
30. Meredith, *Girl Captives of the Cheyennes*, pg. 29. Lookingbill, *War Dance at Fort Marion*, pg. 24.
31. John L. Sipes, Cheyenne tribal historian.
32. Feldman, Sophia German. *My Capture and Captivity by Cheyenne Indians-1874*.
33. Lookingbill, *War Dance at Fort Marion*, pg. 24. The agency was developed and run by Brinton Darlington.
34. John L. Sipes, Cheyenne tribal historian.
35. ibid.
36. Indian Affairs Annual Report 1875. Oklahoma Historical Society.
37. Today, Sophia's right moccasin is on display at the Fort Wallace Museum in Kansas.
38. Nelson A. Miles, *A Documentary Biography 1861-1903*.
39. Meredith, *Girl Captives of the Cheyennes*, pg. 55.
40. Feldman, Sophia German. *My Capture and Captivity by Cheyenne Indians-1874*. Meredith, *Girl Captives of the Cheyennes*. pg. 55, and Jauken, *The Moccasin Speaks*.
41. Lookingbill, *War Dance at Fort Marion*, pg. 28.
42. Black Horse is the great-grandfather of former Colorado state Senator Ben Night Horse Campbell.
43. John L. Sipes, Cheyenne tribal historian.
44. Report of the Commissioner of Indian Affairs for the Year 1875, pg. 268.
45. John L. Sipes, Cheyenne tribal historian.
46. The *Kansas City Times*, April 9, 1875.
47. Rogers, *The German Family Massacre*.
48. Indian Affairs Annual Report 1875. Oklahoma Historical Society. Also see Lookingbill, *War Dance at Fort Marion*, pg. 28.
49. Indian Affairs Annual Report 1875. Oklahoma Historical Society.

50. Report of the Commissioner of Indian Affairs for the Year 1875, pg. 268.
51. Report of the Commissioner of Indian Affairs for the Year 1875, pg. 50. Also see Records of the Office of Indian Affairs, National Archives, Washington, D. C.
52. ibid. Also see Lookingbill, *War Dance at Fort Marion*, pg. 32. Also see Pratt, Battlefield and Classroom.
53. John L. Sipes, Cheyenne tribal historian.
54. Indian Affairs Annual Report 1875. Oklahoma Historical Society.
55. John L. Sipes, Cheyenne tribal historian.
56. Lookingbill, *War Dance at Fort Marion*, pg. 41.
57. Report of the Commissioner of Indian Affairs for the Year 1875, pg. 50. Also see Records of the Office of Indian Affairs, National Archives, Washington, D. C.
58. John L. Sipes, Cheyenne tribal historian.
59. ibid.
60. ibid.
61. ibid.
62. Lookingbill, *War Dance at Fort Marion*, pg. 85. During World War II, Fort Marion was renamed Fort Mantanzas and designated as a National Monument.
63. John L. Sipes, Cheyenne tribal historian.
64. ibid.
65. ibid. Also see Mendoza, *Song of Sorrow*, pg. 147.
66. *Gazette Telegraph*, Colorado Springs, Colorado, September 8, 1990. Also Sipes documents, letters and notes in the possession of the author.
67. ibid.
68. Sipes and Berthrong used their research to promote unbiased accounts of historical events involving the Cheyenne people. This research is now housed at the University of Oklahoma. Additional documents are in the possession of the author.
69. John L. Sipes, Cheyenne tribal historian.
70. *Gazette Telegraph*, Colorado Springs, Colorado, September 8, 1990.
71. *Gazette Telegraph*, Colorado Springs, Colorado, September 9, 1990.
72. ibid.
73. John L. Sipes, Cheyenne tribal historian.
74. ibid.

— THE BATTLE OF MILK CREEK AND THE MEEKER MASSACRE —

A few years after the United States War Department declared an end to the Indian wars in Colorado, an Indian uprising on the western slope showed the error of the claim.[1] For the Ute Indian nation, it ended their traditional way of life. What resulted in the Meeker Massacre on October 1, 1879, was a fundamental clash of cultures, ignorance, and defiance. Because of or despite the peaceful actions and negotiations of Ute Chief Ouray, war along the Milk Creek tributary to the White River, on Colorado's western slope, was inevitable.

The Nunt'z or Ute Indians are considered the oldest continuous residents of Colorado. While it is not known exactly when the tribe or their ancestors arrived in the area, ancient fire pits, stone tools, petroglyphs, and even stone foundations for fortification, dating as far back as 6,000 B. C., have been found and documented by archaeologists from Pikes Peak, south to the present state of New Mexico. It is possible, according to archaeologists, that the arrival of the Ute people into the area caused the Anasazi to leave the sandstone caves of the area. The ancestral Utes may also have displaced the earlier Native Americans who inhabited the region during the early Basketmaker stage through the Developmental Pueblo stage, including the classic Mesa Verde period.

The Nunt'z people, roughly translated by white men as the "Utah/Uintah" people, later shortened to "Ute," came to be known as "The Blue Sky People," "The People of the Shining Mountains," or the "Mountain People." Within the culture of the Ute tribe, the horse became the most important possession, not only for hunting and fast mobility, but also as a symbol of wealth and progress. The Utes became skilled horsemen, developing their raiding and fighting abilities against the Arapaho and Cheyenne tribes who were beginning to migrate into Ute country. With their expert horsemanship, the Utes were mighty in defending their homeland against their enemies.

Several bands of Utes constituted the Ute Indian nation.

Since approximately 1830, the Ute territory covered the western portion of today's Colorado.[2] Their native homeland also stretched west, into the eastern portion of today's Utah, named for the Native American tribe. The Uintah band occupied the northeast area of Utah, while the Weeminuche band roamed the southeast area of Utah and east into the San Juan mountain range of Colorado. [3] The Yampa band occupied the northwest corner of Colorado, the Grand band occupied the Continental Divide range of the Colorado Rocky Mountains, along with the Tabeguache band. The Mouache and Capote bands occupied the south center portion of Colorado and into today's New Mexico.

In 1859, with the news of the Pikes Peak gold rush, the gamble for gold brought prospectors, surveyors, and hordes of miners to the Colorado high country. For the Ute Indians, this was the core base of their homeland. The "Shining Mountain," later named Pikes Peak, was considered sacred to Utes, as was the nearby natural springs of the Manitou.

Startled by the invasion of white civilization, the Ute tribes united to defend their land. The *Rocky Mountain News* featured a story of Indian brutality in the July 9, 1859, issue:

> "Trouble with the Indians - Our miners shot and scalped by the Utah savages without provocation."

Christopher Houston "Kit" Carson, who was serving as a government Indian agent at the time, was working with the Utes, whom he had known for nearly twenty years. While his goal was peace, he knew it would not be easy to attain. The *Rocky Mountain News* ran a statement from Carson in the September 10, 1859, issue:

> "The Tabewache [sic] *are now on the waters of the Grand River. They are hostilely disposed and I would advise all to be cautious of their intercourse with them. The Utes are the most dangerous of the mountain Indians, excellent shots with the rifle and if hostile, will be likely to destroy many small prospecting parties and solitary travelers next season."* [4]

In an article published in the *Rocky Mountain News,* of November 2, 1859, the reporter wrote:

> "While in Taos, New Mexico, I was requested by Kit Carson, government agent for the Ute Indians, to say to the miners here, that he hoped to visit

this region early next spring, with several leading 'braves' of the tribe, to conclude a permanent peace between them and the whites. He deems this very desirable, as the Utes are the most dangerous of the mountain Indians..."

On the west side of the Continental Divide, the San Juan mountains were most inviting to gold seekers. The government ordered prospectors to stay away from the San Juan country, but to no avail. Eventually military posts were built in the area to protect the prospectors and westward travelers over the passes. As the violence escalated, it was left to Ouray, a powerful sub-chief of the Tabeguache Ute band, to work for peace between the two cultures.

Ouray, the Ute name, "Ulay," meaning "Yes" or "Arrow," was a very unique individual.[5] Perhaps prophetically, he was born on the night of November 13, 1833, the night "over 200,000 shooting stars appeared, illuminating the earth." This date is known in Ute history as "The Year of the Shooting Stars." Ouray's father, Guera Murah, a Jicarilla Apache, and his mother, a Tabeguache Ute, raised their son in the ways of the Tabeguache Ute, his mother's tribe, as was the Ute custom. It was also Ute custom to name their children after they showed some sort of trait or sign. Thus, they gave their first born son the name of "Ulay" pronounced "Oo-lay" as this was the first word he learned. It would not be until his first meetings with the white man many years later, that the name became "Ouray." Because there is no "r" sound in the Ute language, this new pronunciation must have been a white man's interpretation of name.

A few years after Ouray was born, his mother gave birth to a second son. As the boy learned to pick up objects, he did so with his left hand. His parents named him Queashegut, meaning "little left hand" in the Ute language. The name would later be translated in English to "Quenche." Unfortunately, the boys' mother died in childbirth. Both Ouray and Quenche were raised by other women in the village.

After a few years, Guera Murah took another wife, also of the Tabeguache Ute band, and left to join her tribe in the San Juan mountains of Colorado's western slope. There, in 1845, the couple had a daughter, Susan, Ouray and Quenche's half-sister. Because they did not live together, it would be years before the siblings would meet. Ouray spent his childhood living in his birthplace of the Taos Valley, in northern New Mexico. Ouray and Quenche stayed in the Taos area, living with a wealthy Spanish couple. Through their benefactors, Ouray and Quenche were able to receive an education in the predominately Spanish area. They were sent to Ranchos de Taos, a Spanish missionary colony, approximately four miles south of the Taos square. There, Ouray became fluent in both the Spanish and English languages. He was encouraged to attend Catholic Mass regularly, where the Catholic friars attempted to convert him to their religion, to no avail.

Nevertheless, Ouray's traditional Ute upbringing and his proficiency in the Ute and Apache languages, coupled with his education in English and Spanish, prepared him for later life. His intellect would impress those of the Ute nation, as well as the great white leaders of Washington, D. C. In 1846, Ouray was not yet thirteen years of age when the winds of war were blowing strong between the United States and Mexico. In May of that year, Mexican troops crossed the border and fired on United States soldiers protecting the southern border. On May 13, President James Knox Polk went before the United States Congress, asking for a declaration of war against Mexico.

General Stephen Watts Kearny and soldiers from Fort Leavenworth, Kansas, followed the Santa Fe Trail toward Mexico. On August 18, 1846, Kearny and his troops captured the town of Santa Fe, the center of the northern government, and claimed the northern portion of Mexico for the United States. Governor Manuel Armijo almost immediately relinquished his position and under orders of President Polk, General Kearny appointed Charles Bent, an influential Taos businessman and part owner of the famed Bent's Fort enterprise, to the office of civilian governor for the new territory, known as New Mexico.

As the new government was formed, Ouray witnessed the power of the white man's government, with the large number of soldiers, over sixteen hundred strong. The massive firepower, including cannons, was something Ouray had never seen before. Ouray must have been stunned by not only the quick and decisive takeover of his homeland by the white man, but at the power and might of this foreign government.

To facilitate a peaceful arrangement with the Ute tribe in the Taos Valley area, General Kearny instructed Major William Gilpin to contact the leaders of the Ute tribes in an attempt to appease them. [6] A month later, Gilpin led a delegation of the southern Ute leaders from the San Luis Valley to meet with General Kearny in Santa Fe. This group of Ute leaders agreed to peaceful negotiations. However, on the cold morning of Friday, January 16, 1847, bedlam broke out on the streets of Taos. Several native Mexicans, as well as many of the local Taos Indians, resented the American takeover of their land. Rioting in the streets of Taos rose to revolt, violence, and murder. One group of Taos Indians, led by Tomasito Romero, stormed into the local jail and broke out two of their tribal members, held on petty charges. By the time Sheriff Stephen Louis Lee arrived at the jail, a large group of angry and quite inebriated men had formed a mob. The group grew larger by the hour, Sheriff Lee was powerless to stop them. As the rioting progressed during the morning hours, more joined the cause. Soon there were over fifteen hundred rioters on the streets of Taos.

Cornelio Vigil, Governor Bent's brother-in-law and a member of the government, tried to reason with the unruly men. Suddenly a few of the men grabbed Vigil and began beating him. Then, others brought out weapons, including knives. When the men stabbed Vigil repeatedly, others began cutting off body parts; ears, fingers, legs and arms. Terrified, Sheriff Lee attempted to flee the horrific scene but was caught and killed.

Feeling victorious, Romero led the murderous rioters through Taos to the home of Governor Bent. They stormed the house, terrorized the Bent family and their guests, one of which was Kit Carson's young wife, Josefa Jaramillo Carson. [7] Bent was shot several times. As his wife, Maria, rushed toward him, she too was shot with an arrow through her arm. Rumalda Luna Bent Boggs, who was holding her mortally wounded stepfather, watched in horror as Tomasito Romero jerked Bent from Rumalda's clutches, and threw him to the floor. Romero then scalped Bent who was still alive, and mutilated the then lifeless body of Governor Charles Bent.

While it is doubtful that Ouray was a witness to such brutality on the streets of Taos, it is most certain that he knew about it. It is also likely that Ouray witnessed the overwhelming might of the United States military when Colonel Sterling Price and three hundred troops ended the riots, killing over one hundred Indians in a single day.

With the increasing military presence in the traditional Ute homelands, leaders of the Mouache and Capote Utes met with Indian agent James S. Calhoun, at Abiquiu, New Mexico. After the obligatory promise of gifts and annuities by the government, the Ute leaders signed their first formal peace treaty on December 30, 1849. Capote chief Quiziachigiate was the principal signer for the two Ute tribes.[8] In return for their promise of peace, the Utes were given free reign of their homeland, with the stipulation that the white man would be free to pass through.

Perhaps due to the encroachment of the military presence, in 1850, seventeen-year-old Ouray and his younger brother Quenche left the Taos Valley of his childhood and joined his father's Tabeguache Ute band on the Uncompahgre Plateau of the southwestern Colorado mountain range; the center of the Ute homelands.[9] Now reunited with his father, Ouray also met his half-sister, Susan, for the first time. Not long after Ouray's arrival, his father, Guera Murah, a respected tribal leader, died. As was the Ute custom, the sons inherited their father's property. In this case, Ouray and Quenche each inherited a dozen prized horses.

Ouray, as the oldest son of the deceased tribal leader, was expected by tribal custom to fulfill his father's role. Because he had not been raised in the Ute traditions of his people, Ouray was belatedly initiated into adulthood, traditionally done when the male reaches the age of fourteen.[10] The ceremony began with Ouray's body being smeared with the blood of a mountain lion; the Ute spiritual belief that this produced strong will in the young male. When the ceremony ended and with the tribal leader's approval, Ouray became a sub-chief of the Tabeguache Ute band. He was then taken to his new tipi, where a Ute maiden awaited.

Three years later, Ouray took his first Ute wife, a Tabeguache Ute maiden, Tukukavapiapi, translated in English as "Black Mare." As was the Ute custom, Ouray moved into the lodge of his wife's family. Ute custom dictated that Ouray would bring the hides of the buffalo he had killed to Black Mare, who would then cure them. After Black Mare had cured and tanned ten hides, the other warrior wives gathered to help Black Mare sew the hides together to cover the lodge of the couple's new home. It was a happy time for Ouray and Black Mare, as they soon welcomed their first child. Sadly however, the daughter, not yet named in accordance to Ute custom, died shortly after birth.

Through his many hunting trips with the tribe Ouray quickly gained a reputation as an aggressive young warrior, despite some among his people who considered him no more than "half Ute." Ouray participated in several battles with his fellow warriors, the most notable occurring in the summer of 1854. Ouray and a band of his warriors came to the assistance of fellow Ute Colorow, who recently had nearly forty horses stolen from him by a group of Arapaho and Cheyenne raiders. Following their tracks, Ouray found the enemy camped on the south side of the Arkansas River, near its juncture with Huerfano Creek. [11]Ouray, aware his group were outnumbered, boldly chose a surprise attack on camp. It was a fierce combat. When it ended, the remaining Arapaho and Cheyenne fled the area on foot, leaving Colorow's forty horses, as well as their own, behind. Before Ouray, Colorow and the other Ute warriors left the scene, they scalped the eight dead enemy and took the scalps as trophies for their successful battle.

In the fall of 1854, Kit Carson, as acting agent of Indian Affairs, was instructed by his superior, David Meriwether, Superintendent of Indian Affairs, to gather leaders of the southern Ute tribes for yet another peace council. It was during this time that Ouray and Carson most likely met for the first time. Because the two men of different cultures could converse with one another in Spanish as well as the Ute language, there was an instant connection between them.

While the leaders of the southern tribes refused to attend the peace council, the effort by Carson at seeking peace was not lost on Ouray. He was fully aware of the military power of the government and began to see that the only way for his people to live among the white man was through peace. As autumn turned to winter, several bands of the southern Utes and Jicarilla Apache began raids among the settlers of southern Colorado. Then, the raids turned to murder.

Fort Pueblo was a crude trading post constructed by noted trappers Alexander Barclay and Joseph B. Doyle, in 1841. The post was located at the confluence of Fountain Creek and the Arkansas River. The adobe quadrangle had eight-foot-high walls, topped with picket fencing, and small bastions. The ceiling was supported by rough logs, with protruding edges, used to hang clothing, dry chili peppers and Indian corn. A corral for horses was erected near the fort, while cattle grazed along the river. The men would tend the livestock and work with the traders and the Indians. Inside, the walls were plastered with adobe and whitewashed, then brushed with sheep skin. The floors were of the area's natural soil, sprinkled with water twice daily and swept until an eventual hard dirt crust formed. The rooms were small, ten feet square, with no beds. Three to five people slept on the floor in blanket rolls in each room. The women spent the day cooking and sewing. Meals were served on the floor, where the guests sat on handmade Native American blankets.

Because Fort Pueblo was the only trading post in the upper Arkansas Valley, it became the major stop to and from Bent's new fort, located several miles downstream along the Santa Fe trail. However, it evidently didn't meet the standards of Francis Parkman. Following his brief visit in 1846, he described the fortress as "a wretched species of a fort." Nevertheless, Fort Pueblo was a busy and popular stopover. Many frontiersmen of the era stopped there and traded their goods before resuming their travels. Among these men were Charles Autobees, Jim Bridger, Kit Carson, Richens Lacy "Uncle Dick" Wootton. Famed trapper George Frederick Ruxton spent part of the winter of 1847 at Fort Pueblo, later wrote:

> "We struck the Arkansa [sic] at the little Indian trading-fort of the Pueblo,' which is situated on the left bank, a few hundred yards above the mouth of the Fontaine-qui-buille, or Boiling Spring River, so called from two springs of mineral water near its headwaters under Pike's Peak, about sixty miles from its mouth. Here I was hospitably entertained in the lodge. I turned my animals loose and allowed them to seek for themselves the best pastures. In the immediate vicinity of the fort game is very scarce, and the buffalo have within a few years deserted the neighboring prairies, but they are always found in the mountain-valleys, particularly in one called Bayou Salado, which abounds in every species of game, including elk, bears, deer, bighorn or Rocky-Mountain sheep, buffalo, antelope, etc. Shortly after my arrival on Arkansa, and during a spell of fine sunny weather, I started with a Pueblo hunter for a load or two of buffalo-meat, intending to hunt on the waters of the Platte and the Bayou, where bulls remain in good condition during the winter months, feeding on the rich grass of the mountain-valleys." [12]

Indeed the wild "game" was becoming scarce, particularly the spirited buffalo, essential to the Indian way of life. It was the slaughter of this "wild game" as well as the continued westward migration, that led the Utes and Jicarilla Apache to attack the fort. "Uncle Dick" Wootton and a party of hunters were headed toward the fort on December 23, 1854. At Coal Creek, Wootton noticed a large gathering of Indian warriors. Arriving at the fort, Wootton told the inhabitants of seeing the warriors and advised them to stay inside.

Despite Wootton's warning, the following day the Christmas Eve celebration proceeded without a care, while a few of the men kept a lookout. The party broke up just before daylight on Christmas Day, 1854. Guero Pais left the fort on horseback, traveling just beyond the ford of Fountain Creek, where he saw the band of Indian warriors Wootton had warned of. Reporting the fact to nearby farmer Marcelino Baca, Pais raced back to the fort to give a warning, then ran to the corrals to check the horses. There he hid as the Indians suddenly thundered down from a hill. It was a grueling five hour ordeal as Pais heard the screams of those being murdered as he hid in silence.

As the Indian raid was taking place at Fort Pueblo, Baca attempted to raise a group of men to go to the fort. Along the way, Baca came across the body of Jose Ignacio Valencia on the east side of Fountain Creek. After crossing the creek, he was met by a staggering Juan Rafael Medina, clutching his belly, his blood spilling. Before Baca could get to him, Medina collapsed and died. As the group got closer to the fort, two more men were found dead, with arrows in their bodies. At the gate of the fort, the horror continued. Three men lay dead. The courtyard of Fort Pueblo was deathly still as Baca and his three companions entered. On the bloodied earthen floor lay the bodies of three men. In an another room, a father and son were found dead, along with two Ute Indians. Behind the fort, four men were found, dead from arrows and gun shots. There were no survivors, although it was later learned that two boys and a woman were taken captive.

The remainder of that Christmas Day was spent burying the dead. It seemed to never end, as two more bodies were found near the river. That night a wake was held at the home of Marcelino Baca. The fort was never again occupied.

In March 1855, the full force of the United States military marched into the heart of the Ute homelands. It was what Ouray had feared all along. Colonel T. T. Fauntleroy led four companies of troops into the area, followed by Colonel Ceran St. Vrain with his company of volunteers. Ironically, it was Christopher "Kit" Carson, a friend of Ouray's, who served as a guide on this expedition.

On March 19, 1855, near Saguache, Colorado, the troops killed nearly forty Ute warriors. As the remaining warriors fled the area, the troops gave chase.[13] It was a long protracted military effort, but after seven separate engagements, the Ute warriors were defeated. The result was another peace treaty, signed in September 1855. The Mouacha Ute tribe agreed to a reduction of their land. They were allowed to keep a thousand-square-mile area west of the Rio Grande River and north of La Jara Creek. Ouray could no longer stand by and watch as the traditional homeland of his people was being systematically taken by the white man. A keen, observant man, Ouray understood the extreme differences between the Indian and the white man. As such, Ouray chose the diplomatic approach in dealing with the white man's government. Ouray's first act as a sub-chief of the Tabeguache Utes became quite controversial to a few Ute tribes, while the white man's government praised his actions.

In the summer of 1855, Kaneache, a Mouache Ute warrior, had been leading raids along the Conejos River in the southern portion of Colorado, an area they had relinquished in the previous treaty. When settlers in the area reported the theft of livestock, a company of troops from the U.S. Third Cavalry of the were dispatched to the area. When Kaneache sent a runner to Ouray's camp for additional warriors, not only did Ouray refuse the request, he detained the runner. After previously seeing the government's military might first hand, Ouray instinctively knew that sending his warriors to join Kaneache would be a fool's errand. Ouray then asked his close friend Shavano, a Ute warrior chief, to bring a few of his men and accompany him to Fort Garland. Ouray's intention was to meet with his friend, Kit Carson, who as Indian agent was known to be in the area.

As Ouray, Shavano, and his warriors came upon the Conejos River, they discovered Kaneache and the Mouache Ute warriors engaged in combat with the soldiers nearby. Ouray and his warriors joined the fight, but aiding the soldiers. During the encounter, Ouray managed to shoot an arrow into Kaneache and take him as a prisoner.

With the defeat of the Mouache Ute warriors, Ouray transported his prisoner to Fort Garland. Following this incident, Carson sent a report to his superior, David Meriwether, Commissioner of Indian Affairs, stating in part that the recent Indian encounter had been "disposed as ever," and that "most of the depredations were committed from absolute necessity when in a starving condition. If the government will not do something for them to save them from starving, they will be obliged to steal."[14] In the end, Ouray's calculation, while causing discontent in his own tribe, ultimately proved to help his people.

Carson distributed food and blankets to the wounded Ute warriors Ouray had brought in to the fort. However, Carson seemed to have concerns as he wrote to Meriwether the following:

> "I cannot see how the Superintendent [sic] can expect Indians to depart satisfied. They are given a meal by the Superintendent, then presents are

given. Some get a blanket; those that get none are given a knife or a hatchet or some vermilion, a piece of red or blue cloth, some sugar, and perhaps a few more trinkets. They could more than earn the quantity they receive in one day's hunt, if left in their country. They could procure skins and furs and traders could furnish the same articles to them and they would be saved the necessity of coming such a distance. If presents are given them it should be taken to their country. They should not be allowed to come into the settlements, for every visit an Indian makes to a town it is of more or less injury to him." [15]

In the summer of 1856 a baby boy was born to the lodge of Ouray and Black Mare. Again, according to Ute custom, the child was not yet given a name, however, his parents must have been overjoyed at the baby's good health. It was also during the summer of 1856 that a young Ute girl known as Chipeta, and her family joined Ouray's village. It was an event that would eventually change both Ouray and Chipeta's lives forever.

Most Ute historians agree that Chipeta was born in the summer of 1843, to a Kiowa Apache couple. [16] Chipeta was approximately two years of age when Ute hunters happened upon the small Kiowa Apache village. After observing the village for some time, the Ute hunters determined the village had been abandoned. The men cautiously approached the village. Along the way, they discovered a few dead bodies in the tall grass. Entering the village, to their horror, they found slain bodies throughout. Women, children, and babies were all dead. Most of the men had weapons in their hands. The Utes surmised that the village had been attacked and no one survived. As the warriors left the village of death, one of the Utes heard the cries of an infant. Chipeta was discovered crawling in the tall grass just outside of the village. One of the hunters gathered the little toddler into his arms and took her back to the Ute camp. There, he and his wife raised the little girl as their own.

The couple named their "adopted" daughter "Guadalupita," meaning "White Singing Bird." [17] The name was later translated by the white man to "Chipeta." Chipeta's Ute family followed the traditional nomadic lifestyle, spending the winter season in northern New Mexico and the summer in the Colorado region. Chipeta enjoyed the seasonal movement, gathering berries in the summer and playing in the winter snow. When the Utes signed the peace treaty in 1849, the nomadic lifestyle of Chipeta's family changed.

The wildlife and sacred buffalo were disappearing, causing hardship, starvation and despair among Chipeta's people. It was during this time that her family moved their lodge to Ouray's camp in the Arkansas River Valley. [18] Chipeta was happy in her new homeland and with her outgoing personality she made many new friends, young and old. One of the older Ute women who befriended Chipeta was Ouray's wife, Black Mare. The two often took long walks together, gathering nuts and berries along the way. Chipeta particularly looked forward to her visits at Ouray and Black Mare's lodge, where she could spend time with the couple's little boy. [19]

Ouray and Black Mare doted on their young son who, by this time, had displayed several delightful characteristics. When it became clear that the child was left-handed, as was Ouray's brother, Queashegut, Ouray gave his son the same name of his brother. The English translation of the Ute name became "Quenche." As the boy grew older, his round, pudgy face reminded Ouray of an apple and gave the child the nickname of Pahlone, the Ute word for apple. It would be the name the child would become known by as he grew to adulthood. Later, the white man would translate the name to "Paron." In the spring of 1858, Black Mare became ill. Despite the efforts of the Ute medicine man, her condition gradually worsened. Several of the Ute women, including Chipeta, offered their help with cooking, cleaning, and caring for both Ouray and young Paron. As the woman most familiar to the young child, fifteen-year-old Chipeta spent much of her time with Ouray and Paron, as well as tending to her ailing friend, Black Mare. Over the next few months Black Mare's condition became dire.

Shortly before the first winter snow, Black Mare died. Chipeta assisted in preparing Black Mare's body for burial. Her blanketed body, tied with rawhide rope, was transported to a small rock crevice a few miles from the village, where it was solemnly placed. After a few days Chipeta returned to Ouray's lonely lodge and offered to care for his young son. Over the next few months, Chipeta's presence became a constant comfort to Ouray. Although the two never spoke of Black Mare, as this was believed to bring death to the mourner, they began to form a spiritual bond. Chipeta came to love Paron as her own and came to love Ouray as well. Ouray felt the same and in 1859, the twenty-six-year-old Ute sub-chief married sixteen-year-old Chipeta. Known as "The laughing maiden of the Utes," Chipeta became Ouray's constant companion and confidant in his capacity as sub-chief of the Tabeguache Utes.

With the onslaught of the white man into the Ute territory following the discovery of gold in the Rocky Mountain region, it was only natural that the Ute warriors would want to fight to protect their land. In short amount of time the government sent military troops to protect the miners and the settlers that quickly filled the region. During 1861 and into 1862, when the Civil War was raging in the East, Colorado Territory faced a shortage of military troops. Volunteer centers were established in various towns and communities across the territory. During this same period, the government began implementing the Indian reservation system. The Weeminuche Ute tribe were assigned to the jurisdiction of the Tierra Amarilla Indian Agency in northern New Mexico Territory. [20] The Mouache and a large group of the Jicarilla Apache were taken to a temporary area in southern Colorado Territory on a portion of the historic Maxwell Land Grant. Ouray's Tabeguache Ute band remained, temporarily under the jurisdiction of the Indian agency at Denver. [21]

Meanwhile, Ouray and Chipeta delighted in watching young Paron grow up and develop his natural attributes; Ouray was particularity pleased with Paron's interest in horses. By the age of five, Paron had not only learned to ride well, he displayed a keen sense of stalking wild game and shooting his prey while astride his horse. Paron also displayed another of his attributes; that of youthful courage. In the summer of 1861, the five-year-old fearless Paron mounted his father's prized powerful and feared war horse, Thunder Cloud. [22] Just as Paron managed to sit the horse, Thunder Cloud bolted and took off at a rapid stride. In an instant, young Paron's fearlessness turned to fear. He clutched the mighty horse's mane with all his might in an effort to stay astride the horse. When Thunder Cloud ran under a tree, incredibly, a limb fell from the tree and lodged itself in the boy's right shoulder, the jolt causing Paron to fall from the war horse. In the end, both boy and horse survived the ordeal. While Paron's shoulder healed, although scarred, his proud father bestowed yet another name for his son, "Little Chief."

Not long after this episode in Ouray's family life, in October 1861, the government established a new reservation for the Unitah Ute tribe in Utah, just west of the Colorado Territorial border. This would later figure prominently in the life of Ouray's wife, Chipeta. It was also during this time that Christopher "Kit" Carson resigned as Ute Indian agent to serve in the war effort. Major Lafayette Head was appointed to replace Carson. It would become a controversial appointment as will be shown later. It would affect the reputation of Ouray, still debated among historians today. Ouray worked diligently for peace with the new Indian agent despite rumors of the new agent's corrupt dealings.

In the summer of 1862, Ouray's half-sister Susan was kidnapped during a raid by the Ute's enemy, the Arapaho. Fortunately, a group of white men from the nearby Indian agency interceded and were able to gain Susan's release.

The summer of 1863 held more tragedy for Ouray and Chipeta. Because of Paron's exceptional horsemanship and hunting skills, Ouray felt it was time Paron joined the Ute annual buffalo hunting party. Father and son, along with approximately thirty Ute hunters, traveled to the eastern plains. After a successful two weeks of hunting, the group spent the last day camped near the South Platte River, near present-day Kersey. They packed the dried meat and hides for the return trip to the mountain camp. Late in the night, nearly one hundred Sioux warriors attacked the Ute camp. Why the Utes did not place sentries around the camp in a foreign country is a mystery. Because of the oversight, three Utes were killed before the rest of the camp had a chance to react to the attack. Ouray quickly hid young Paron under a blanket before grabbing his rifle to fight the hated Sioux. It was no use. The Sioux had surrounded the camp. While one group made off with nearly half of the Utes' horses, a smaller group raided tipis and abducted little Paron. Stunned and full of rage, Ouray and several of the hunters went in pursuit of the Sioux and, in particular, Paron. After a few hours of hard riding, the sun began to rise. With the illumination, Ouray realized they had lost their prey. Grieving over this personal disaster, Ouray returned with the rest of the Utes to their mountain camp for the winter. Chipeta was heartbroken, and for years Ouray tried to find his son.

Occasionally Ouray learned small bits of information. An example is revealed in a statement he made in 1872, nearly nine years after the abduction of his son:

> *"The Utes had a fight with the Sioux on the Platt. [sic] We killed one Indian, and knew it was a Sioux by the shirt, which was of a peculiar kind worn only by the Sioux. After the fight, my boy, about five years old, was missing; and a Mexican who traded with the Sioux has since told me that Friday [an Arapaho chief] had my boy, and a Mexican woman who was married to a Sioux also told me a year ago that she had seen my boy, and that Friday still had him."* [23]

Ouray was never able to find his son. He and Chipeta would suffer this loss the rest of their lives. As the years went on, it became evident that Chipeta was unable to conceive a child. As was the Ute custom, Ouray was free to take another wife, yet he did not. It was a testament to the strong bond and love of the Ute couple.

Following the abduction of Paron, Ouray focused on the welfare of his people. He worked in good faith with Indian Agent Head in maintaining peace. In 1862, Head brokered a meeting with the new Colorado territorial governor, John Evans. When the meeting concluded, Evans agreed to allow Ouray's Tabeguache Ute band to remain in their homeland of the San Juan mountains, as well as the Uncompahgre range, and west into Utah. The governor also agreed to rations and annual payments to the Tabeguache Ute band in return for peace, which Ouray also agreed to.

Although it was a peace agreement between the governor of the Colorado Territory and Ouray's Tabeguache Utes, it did not have the approval of the United States government. Therefore, Agent Head persuaded Hiram P. Bennet, the first senator for Colorado Territory, to use his power in Washington, D. C., to garner support for legislation in the matter. However, Governor Evans took matters into his own hands and contacted President Abraham Lincoln, who agreed to receive a delegation of the leaders of the various Ute tribes in the Colorado and Utah regions. When Head received the news of an impending visit to the nation's capital, he sent runners to the Ute camps to inform the leaders. Many agreed to the trip, including Ouray.

In mid-January 1863, when the government bureaucrats finally set a date for the Utes' trip to Washington, D. C., the Ute leaders prepared to meet at Head's Indian agency, recently relocated to the small Hispanic community of Conejos. However, two interesting events occurred at the agency before the trip east began. When the Tabeguache Ute leaders, including Pabusat, Puwich, Showasheit, Tuepuepa, Tupuwaat, Ouray and his brother, Quenche, arrived at the Indian agency, they discovered that they were the only Utes present. Whether this was intentional on the part of Governor Evans or Head in an effort to gain governmental agreement to the local peace agreement of the previous year, is unknown. However, according to Finis Downing, who wrote extensively on the Ute delegation to Washington, the Ute leaders of the other tribes in the region were never informed of the trip to meet the "Great White Father."

On February 3, 1863, Head led the Tabeguache Ute leaders on the long journey from Conejos to Denver. There, Governor Evans provided a military escort as the group traveled along the Platte River Trail toward the railroad stations at St. Joseph, Missouri. At St. Joseph, Head assisted as the Utes boarded the train. It was the first time Ouray and the other Ute leaders had ever seen or ridden the feared iron horse. The long train trip took six weeks, with stops at various towns including Chicago and Detroit, finally arriving in Washington on March 28.

For the next month, the Ute delegation met with various politicians, including President Abraham Lincoln. When Lincoln met Ouray, he presented him with a gift of a silver-tipped cane. It was a gift that the president often bestowed upon chiefs professing peace. During the negotiations, the politicians promised annuities in the form of food supplies, clothing and blankets, in return for the promise of peace. Between the meetings, Ouray and the other Ute sub-chiefs were shown the sites of the government power, including the many military camps in the area, currently engaged in civil war. There is little doubt that the tour was designed to intimidate the tribal leaders by showing them their military might. This fact was not lost on Ouray.

Before the trip was concluded, the Utes sat for several pictures for the press. In the historic photographs, Ouray is seen with the silver-tipped cane, a gift from President Lincoln. Ouray is dressed in his finest clothing, each piece, from the leggings, shirts, and beaded belts, to the moccasins, all were handmade by Chipeta.

During the last meeting, Ouray and the sub-chiefs professed their friendship and desire for peace, but nothing more. Ouray let the politicians know that he would rather keep the Ute homelands than accept the government's empty promises of presents. The Ute delegation, along with Agent Lafayette Head, finally left Washington on April 27, 1863. During the return trip back to Ute territory, the group faced a delay at St. Joseph, Missouri. Tensions were high as William Clark Quantrill and his force of Confederate guerrilla compatriots were terrorizing Union sympathizers across Missouri and Kansas. [24] During their unexpected stay in St. Joseph, Ouray was interviewed by a reporter for the *St. Joseph Herald* newspaper. The reporter wrote an article regarding the plight of the Ute nation:

"These Utes are noble specimens of the Native Americans, with all the pride and obstinacy peculiar to the race. While in Washington they

threw themselves upon their 'reserved rights' refusing to make a treaty, and when an intimidation was given to their spokesman that he had better conduct himself with propriety and not be so haughty he promptly told the Commissioner something like this: 'I and my party came here because we wished to come. You may give presents to other Indians, but we don't want any presents. You want our land because there is plenty of gold there, but all that you are willing to give us is copper. Do you think we are fools? You talk as if you could whip us. You are now fighting with your own brothers and can't whip them. You will find it harder work to whip us. We wish to go home, and when we get there we may be willing to make a treaty."

It is quite obvious that the reporter chose to use his own words, rather than the interpreter's translation of Ouray's words. While Ouray spoke English, it was not his first language. Moreover, particular words such as "whip" and "haughty," to name a few, would not have been words in Ouray's limited English vocabulary. The Ute entourage was finally able to resume their journey westward with a military escort comprised of volunteer troops from the First Colorado Cavalry. Returning to his Colorado homeland, Ouray began working with the various bands, in conjunction with Agent Lafayette Head, in effort to secure a lasting peace with the white man.

Soon, rumors of corruption at the Conejos Indian agency began to circulate. It just so happened that Agent Head had received a government contract to supply the beef for the agency. Head had established a ranch and stage stop enterprise located across the Trinchera River from Conejos. When members of the Ute nation began to complain of receiving spoiled meat, and not receiving their allotted annuities such as blankets, clothing and food, it was rumored that Lafayette Head was stealing Indian rations. It was further alleged that those supplies were actually being sold at Head's own general store at his stage stop. As the Conejos Indian agency was located in the remote area of the Rio Grande Valley in southern Colorado, very near the New Mexico border, there was no government investigation. Because there was no government inquiry initiated into the Ute's allegations the tribal leaders once again distrusted the government.

This distrust extended to Ouray. Many of the sub-chiefs, particularly those of the northern bands, refused to attend the long-planned peace treaty conference held on October 1, 1863. The Utes believed Ouray was complacent in the agency's corruption, when he agreed to Head's offer of a five hundred dollar yearly salary to act as official interpreter for the Utes. While Ouray went on to strive for peace with the white man and was admired by them as a great Ute, many of his fellow tribesmen would forever consider him a traitor.

Incredibly, the scheduled peace treaty conference took place at the ranch of Lafayette Head. Sub-chiefs of the Mouache and Ouray of the Tabeguache Utes were the only Native Americans present. Indian agents, Simeon Whitely of the Grand River and Unitah agencies as well as Michael Steck, superintendent of the Southern Ute agency, and Lafayette Head for the Tabeguache Utes, dominated the meeting. The significance of the peace treaty conference was particularly evident by the presence of President Abraham Lincoln's secretary, John Nicolay, as well as Governor John Evans, along with members of the press.

Chief Ouray worked for peace for his people. *DPL*

As the talks commenced, Ouray translated the words into Spanish and a Spanish translator then translated the dialogue into English. As such, it was a long, tedious conference. A reporter for the *Denver Commonwealth* reported the following in the October 3, 1863, issue:

> *"The Governor, Col. Chivington, Lieut. Col. Tappan, and other prominent officers of the Colorado troops are here. It is the current belief of those who ought to know that the Utes will make no acceptable treaty, unless force be used to compel them to; and it is equally the general opinion that force will be used. We are expecting six companies and a battery of artillery from Fort Union, added to the troops already here, will make a force capable of whipping two Ute nations."*

Despite the reporter's melodramatic reporting, a peace treaty was negotiated without a shot being fired. Because only the Mouache and the Tabeguache Ute bands were represented by sub-chiefs, the government officials either were not aware of Indian politics within individual tribes, or assumed that Ouray spoke for all the tribes. Thus, when Ouray placed his mark on the Treaty of 1863, he was instantly elevated to "Chief of the Utes" in the minds of the government officials.

For his part in the negotiations, Ouray refused to relocate either the Mouache Utes or his own Tabeguache Ute members to unknown lands or reservations, as was happening with the Arapaho and Cheyenne tribes. Ouray was quoted as saying:

"We do not want to sell a foot of our land that is the opinion of our people. The whites can go and take the land and come out again. We do not want them to build houses here." [25]

However, Ouray, according to the government officials, did agree to relinquish a large portion of the Ute homelands. This area included the San Luis Valley, as well as the land from the Utah border east to approximately the site of present-day Gunnison, Colorado. The new Ute boundary had been reduced to include only the mountain range along the Continental Divide. According to the treaty, Ouray also agreed to allow the government to construct roads through their land and build military posts. In return, the government promised ten thousand dollars annually in the form of supplies and food provisions. They also agreed to provide five stallions to improve the Ute's prized horse herd. Then, in a sign of things to come, a clause in the treaty provided for over seven hundred head of cattle and three thousand sheep for the Ute tribes, provided they engage in farming.

Irving Howbert, a member of the Colorado Third Regiment under First Lieutenant Joseph Graham, later wrote in his memoirs:

"To the west the Ute Indians held undisputed sway to the border of the Great Salt Lake Valley. On the south, with the exception of a small part of New Mexico which was sparsely settled by feeble and widely scattered communities of Spanish speaking people, wild tribes roamed over every part of the country for hundreds of miles. From the foregoing it would be seen that the settlements of Colorado at this time were but a small island of civilization in a sea of savagery." [26]

When news of this new treaty with the white man and the agreement of Ouray reached the other Ute tribes, they immediately rejected it. Their trust in Ouray as a leader was also diminished considerably. When Agent Whitely of the Grand River and Unitah agencies, and Michael Steck, superintendent of the Southern Ute agency, learned that the Utes under their jurisdiction had no intention of abiding by the treaty, they immediately alerted the superintendent of Indian Affairs, John Evans, who also served as the governor of Colorado Territory. Therefore, the Treaty of 1863 was never enforced. It would be renegotiated in 1868, setting up a series of events that would lead to disaster.

In the meantime, Ouray struggled to regain the confidence of the Ute people. It was not easy, nor ever completely accomplished. While he professed peace among the Ute tribes, those that listened to his words did not trust him, and those who had refused to abide by the treaty were scattered across Ute lands and refused to hear Ouray's words of peace.

With the first spring thaw, the Ute bands that rejected the white man's treaty moved to their traditional hunting lands along the front range and eastern plains. There, they set up their lodges and remained throughout the summer. When the cool crisp winds of the fall season blew, the displaced Ute people returned to the government's designated areas. Here they received the provisions supplied by the government through the treaty they opposed, and were able to survive the winter. The routine was repeated in the spring of 1865, but was met with much resistance by the white settlers. A large Ute camp near Fountain Creek, just south of Colorado City, brought much consternation among the residents of the town. Believing that the Utes were in clear violation of the treaty and posed a threat to modern civilization, a committee of local citizens took their concerns to Governor John Evans, who by this time was under investigation for his part in the Sand Creek Massacre, which occurred the previous winter.

Perhaps due to Evans' preoccupation, or the fact Ouray and Chipeta were among those camped very near Colorado City, the Indian agent responsible for the Tabeguache Utes, Lafayette Head, responded to the citizen's concerns. The *Rocky Mountain News* published his response in the April 19, 1865, issue of the paper:

"I met the Tabeguache on the 5th [of April] at Colorado City and had no trouble whatever, in prevailing upon them to leave and return to their reservation. I found them in a truly destitute condition and issued to

them a reasonable amount of flour for the support of their families on the journey home. The current report of their aggressions towards whites in the vicinity of Colorado City was without foundation and to a person familiar with these Indians, no trouble need be apprehended from that quarter. Owing to the difficulties on the plains, these Indians did not receive their presents from the Government last season and are therefore poor and needy."

It is quite possible that Lafayette Head may also have known more of the political negotiations of Governor John Evans during the government investigation regarding the Sand Creek Massacre than he ever let on. Perhaps seeing the writing on the wall, as it were, with regard to the investigation of Evans, who was also his superior, Head began making arrangements to vacate his post as Indian agent. Head found his replacement in a young man by the name of Otto Mears, who happened to speak the Ute language fluently. Through the tutelage of Head, Mears was able to secure a government contract with which to trade with the Ute tribes.

Meanwhile, Governor Evans continued to face grueling Sand Creek Massacre investigations. As the evidence mounted against Evans' complicity in the outrageous disaster, Evans put forth a last-ditch effort to save his governorship, not to mention his reputation. Evans informed the members of Congress that in his current negotiations with the Ute bands in the West, he could bring about peace. He further boldly stated that, as territorial governor, through his friendship with the Utes, he was the only man that could do so.[27] With this final statement from Evans, the congressional Sand Creek Massacre investigation ended. Meanwhile, Senator James Rood Doolittle, chairman of the Senate Committee on Indian Affairs, along with members of the governmental Joint Special Commission, were concluding their own investigation at Fort Lyon. Doolittle and his group traveled to Denver, where Doolittle sent a report of their findings back to Washington, D. C. Receiving the report, coupled with the less than convincing testimony of Governor Evans, Secretary of State William H. Seward sent the following letter to Governor Evans:

"I am directed by the President [Andrew Johnson] to inform you that your resignation of the office of Governor of Colorado Territory would be acceptable, the resignation [should] reach Washington without delay." [28]

Following Evans' removal, President Johnson appointed Alexander Cummings as the new territorial governor of Colorado. Meanwhile, the United States government was making an earnest effort toward persuading the Utes to abide to a lasting peace. Several renegade bands had raided settlers on the western slope and in more than one raid the victims were murdered. When the Civil War ended in April 1865, and the soldiers returned to the west, it was only a matter of time before the government would use their greatest asset, the military, to convince the Ute nations to comply with their treaties. To this end, the government recruited Christopher "Kit" Carson, who was known to be a friend to the Utes, Ouray in particular. Not long after Carson returned to his wife, Josefa, and his children, he received the commission as Commander of Fort Garland. The appointment came from a recommendation by Major General John Pope, commander at Fort Union, to his superior officer, Lieutenant General William Tecumseh Sherman. In Pope's opinion, Fort Garland was the most important post "on the Ute frontier." In his recommendation to Sherman, Pope wrote:

"Carson is the best man in the country to control these Indians and to prevent war if it can be done. He is personally known and liked by every Indian of the bands likely to make trouble." [29]

Lieutenant General Sherman was quoted in the *Rocky Mountain News* issue dated October 10, 1865:

"Those redskins think Kit twice as big a man as me. Why his integrity is simply perfect. They know it, and they would believe him and trust him any day before me."

Carson accepted the command of Fort Garland, arriving on May 19, 1866. With the assistance of his adjutant, James W. Tanfield, as Carson could barely read or write, Commander Carson submitted his first official reports to his superiors. Carson agreed with Pope's assessment of the importance of Fort Garland. However, his assessment of the army garrison was that it was severely undermanned. Carson provided the following information to his superiors:

"Within 50 miles of the post range 3 bands of Utes, numbering 800 warriors, and Jicarilla Apaches with another 250 fighting men. To restrain this large body I have but a Command of Some 60 Men. [sic]

Chief Ouray and Chipeta were a strong couple that worked together to save their homeland for the people. *DPL*

This is inadequate for the proper protection of Government property Alone. [sic]" [30]

In the late summer of 1866, General Sherman journeyed west to Fort Garland for a personal conversation with Commander Carson and to see firsthand the situation at the military post.

During the conversation, Carson explained to Sherman the perilous situation regarding the various Ute tribes; those who were fighting against the government takeover of their land, and those that were faithfully abiding by the Treaty of 1863, but were struggling because the government was not adhering to their faithful promise of providing the promised annuities. Carson and Sherman formed the idea of yet another peace council with the Utes.

Colorado Territorial Governor Alexander Cummings, who had the support of D. N. Cooley, Commissioner of Indian Affairs, arranged for a peace council with representatives of the Ute nations. The meeting took place in October 1866, at a site near present-day Alamosa, Colorado. Governor Cummings opened the peace talks with his desire for peace and his recommendation that the Ute tribes move on to the reservation lands designated by the government. Ouray, speaking for the Utes, and translated by Kit Carson, boldly stated:

> "Long time ago, Utes always had plenty. On the prairie, antelope and buffalo so many. In the mountains, deer and bear, everywhere. In the streams, trout, duck, beaver, everything. Good Manitou give all to red man; Utes happy all the year. White man came, and now Utes go hungry. Game much go everywhere - hard to shoot now. Old man often weak for want of food. Squaw and papoose cry. Only strong brave live. White man grow. Red man no grow - soon die all. Utes stop not in one place, and Comanches no find. But Utes settle down; then Comanches come and kill. Tell Great Father, Cheyennes and Comanches go on Reservation first; then Utes will. But Comanches first." [31]

Due to Ouray's bold statement and the fact that the other Ute bands were not present, the peace council was a failure.
During the year of 1867, the government faced economic hardships, primarily due to the debt of the Civil War. This greatly effected the annuities promised to the Indians who abided by the treaties including the Utes.

The northern Ute tribes were having political problems of their own. In the summer of that year, Nevava, the recognized leader, died. Several noted sub-chiefs including Antelope, Jack, Douglas and Colorow, all vied to be Nevava's successor. In a controversial maneuver, Ouray suggested that all the men remain as sub-chiefs. As Ouray had become the official head chief of the seven Ute tribes, despite his lack of popularity among some, this act did not please the northern bands. Colorow took particular offense to Ouray's suggestion.

A most unusual Ute, Colorow, a slurred version of "Colorado," had an immense ego. Colorow was actually a Comanche Indian. During a fight with their bitter enemy, the Utes, Colorow was captured by the Utes as a young child. However, as he grew older, his expertise as a horseman garnered respect among his northern Ute elders. As a strapping adult, he stood over six feet tall and weighed nearly two hundred pounds. Colorow became a leader among the Ute warriors who waged war against their enemies, including the white intruders, with great force.

However, Colorow's renegade methods and indignant attitude caused hesitation with the Ute elders. Members of his tribe referred to him as a meddler, as his ego knew no bounds. This inner fighting with the Ute elders led to consternation and disrespect. Thus, with Ouray's suggestion of sub-chief, rather than chief of the northern Utes, Colorow became very bitter. In the end, he accepted Ouray's suggestion, yet the two Ute men would forever be at bitter odds.

In the meantime, Carson resigned as commander of Fort Garland in November. At the age of fifty-eight, Carson's health was beginning to decline, and after six years of service, he felt he was no longer able to maintain a military garrison. However, with several children and a wife to care for, Carson needed an income. With the assistance of former employer and friend, William Bent, Carson actively pursued the position of superintendent of Indian affairs for Colorado Territory. [32] When Alexander Cameron Hunt succeeded Alexander Cummings as territorial governor, it began to look as though peace might actually be attainable. With Governor Hunt's endorsement, who was also the acting Superintendent of Indian Affairs, Carson received the coveted appointment.

Governor Hunt respected Carson and admired his ability to work with the Ute nations, and particularly with Ouray. Carson made several trips to Denver from his new home at Boggsville, not far from Bent's Fort, to work with the new governor. Because the Treaty of 1863 had never been enforced, with Carson's help, Governor Hunt believed that a new peace treaty could be achieved. To this end, Hunt and Carson worked feverishly. Through Carson's dealings with the Utes, Ouray expressed interest in a renegotiation of the previous treaty. With this news, Governor Hunt proposed the idea of a new treaty to officials in Washington, D. C. When Hunt received word that a Ute delegation would be welcomed in the nation's capital for the purpose of peace talks, Governor Hunt informed Carson, who in turn informed Ouray.

Ouray gathered together the sub-chiefs who would accompany him to Washington. Included in the entourage were Mouache, Kaneache, Jack, Capote, and Sowerwich. Also included was Piah, the nephew of the deceased northern Ute leader, Nevava. Despite the inclusion of Piah, sub-chiefs of the northern tribes, particularly Colorow, objected to the lack of representation. The southern Utes and their sub-chief, Ignacio, also objected to Ouray's selection of Ute representatives. It would be another act by Ouray that would bring distrust among various members of the Ute tribes.

In January 1868, Ouray and his Ute representatives, along with Governor Hunt and Kit Carson, as well as D. C. Oakes, who served as interpreter, traveled by train to the nation's capital city. After nearly a month of meetings, councils and negotiations, the Ute representatives made their mark on the Treaty of 1868. By agreeing to the treaty, dated March 2, 1868, the United States government ceded, in essence, over fifteen million acres of Colorado's western slope region to the Ute nations "forever." However, the treaty also allowed for the building of "roads, highways and railroads as authorized by law."[33]

The western boundary was the Utah border, and the eastern border was the 107th meridian, near present-day Gunnison, Colorado. The southern Ute land was bordered on the north by the eventual Rio Blanco county line, and on the south by the border with New Mexico Territory. The new boundaries in effect eliminated the front range region as well as the Yampa River Valley, as well as the North and Middle Parks along the Continental Divide. The Ute nations lost their traditional homeland in the San Luis Valley, north to their sacred land of the Manitou and Shining Mountain of their people, which the white man called Pikes Peak. Once again, the boundaries of the Ute homelands were reduced. Later, perhaps as Ouray realized what the Utes had lost, he said:

"The agreement an Indian makes to a United States treaty is like the agreement a buffalo makes with his hunter when pierced with arrows. All he can do is lie down and give in." [34]

In fact, by the government establishing two additional Indian agencies within the new boundaries, the Ute land was, in effect, reservation land. The White River region became the location for the agency serving the Grand River and Yampa bands, and an agency near Saguache, Colorado, served the Mouache, Tabeguache, and Weeminuche tribes. Each location would also provide a schoolhouse, as well as farming equipment, in an effort to "civilize" the Ute people.

However, Ute politics required that all male adults were to vote on the treaties. A three-fourths majority was needed to either approve or disapprove of any treaty negotiations made by their leaders. In yet another controversial act by Ouray, an amendment was added to the treaty, agreed to by the government and signed by the officials, as well as Ouray, on August 15, 1868. This amendment not only gave Ouray complete authority to approve the treaty, but also granted the Ute leader an annual pension of one thousand dollars.[35] According to Ouray's biographer, P. David Smith, the Treaty of 1868 was exactly what Ouray had been working toward. In Ouray's estimation, the Utes had succeeded in retaining much of their land, the Indian agents would provide the promised government annuities, and peace would finally prevail between the two cultures. A noble gesture, to be sure, however, Ouray did not take into account the backlash of his own people. When the two-month stay in Washington ended with the formal peace treaty signed, the Ute delegation from Colorado Territory made their journey home. Back in Colorado Territory, friends Ouray and Carson bid goodbye to one another. It would be the last time the two would see each other.

As Ouray returned to his homeland along the Uncompahgre River and Chipeta, Carson, quite ill by this time, managed to make his way home to Boggsville and his family. Just two days after his arrival, Carson's wife, Josefa, went into premature labor. On April 13, 1868, Josefa gave birth to a healthy baby girl. Sadly, a few days after the birth, Josefa died. Carson, who sat by his wife as she died, named his baby girl Josefita, in honor of her mother and his beloved wife. Perhaps due to his grief over the loss of his wife, and the fact that his health was rapidly declining, Carson died a month later, at 4:25 in the afternoon of May 23, 1868, at the army hospital at Fort Lyon.

A group of soldiers rode to the Los Pinos Indian Agency on the south side of Cochetopa Pass, to personally inform Ouray of Carson's death. With the death of Ouray's only ally in the white man's world, Ouray faced a future of turmoil within both cultures.

Those that opposed Ouray's actions defied him. Colorow, now angry and bitter, was one of the many who had no intention of keeping peace with the white man. During the spring and summer months, Colorow and his renegades roamed much of the valley of the Shining Mountain. Many early settlers on both sides of Pikes Peak, including Private Irving Howbert, observed Colorow's tipi along the various rivers throughout the warm seasons. Colorow and his men would terrorize the settlers with threatening gestures as if they were ready to scalp them. As more settlers moved into the area, Colorow and his men changed their threatening tactics. From their camp near the "red rocks" (later named the "Garden of the Gods"), Colorow would make nearly daily horse rides to the homes of the settlers where he would demand food, clothing, and firearms. In time, Colorow and his men amassed several Manard rifles, becoming as effectively armed as the Colorado volunteer army.

As Colorow's antagonizing tactics continued, he became enamored with the white man's use of sugar in their food. Many pioneer housewives came to know Colorow fairly well. He would often poke his head into kitchen windows, demanding biscuits, sugar, and molasses. Dora I. Foster recalled such an encounter with Colorow while she was visiting her aunt in Bradford City. Colorow arrived at the home of Foster's aunt, demanding biscuits and syrup. The frantic women baked biscuits for the Indian, but he demanded more. As Dora and her aunt prepared the biscuits as quickly as was possible, they were careful to conceal the location of their flour. After baking several batches of biscuits, Dora's aunt finally told Colorow that she had no more flour for making the biscuits. Undaunted, Colorow produced a "greasy skin pouch wrapped in bits of dirty rags," and demanded that the women continue with their baking. [36] Colorow enjoyed his reward for harassing the homesteaders, but he would soon move on to more terror tactics against the white settlers, including allegations of murder.

Meanwhile, Governor Edward McCook appointed the first Indian agent who would also live on the Ute reservation. Lieutenant Calvin T. Speer arrived at the Los Pinos Indian Agency on June 26, 1869. Once the Indians realized that Speer intended to live on "their" land, fifty warriors led by Unaneance, a Ute sub-chief, threatened Speer's life. Ouray intervened and he was able to reason with the warriors. Not long after this incident, a four-room adobe home was built for Ouray and his wife, Chipeta. The government then hired Otto Mears to build a road from the small settlement of Saguache to the agency at the base of Cochetopa Pass, a distance of nearly sixty miles. Within a year, the agency was fully operating. In his final report to the U. S. Bureau of Indian Affairs, Governor McCook, still serving as Colorado Superintendent of Indian Affairs, wrote of the inequities still very much present at the agency:

> *"One-third of the territory of Colorado is turned over to the Utes who will not work and will not let others work. This great and rich country is set aside for the exclusive use of savages. A white man secures 160 acres by paying and preempting: but one aboriginal vagrant, by virtue of being head of a family, secures 12,800 acres without preemption of payment."* [37]

Not long after Governor McCook sent his report, dated September 30, 1870, he relinquished his position as Colorado Superintendent of Indian Affairs and appointed his brother-in-law, James B. Thompson, to the position. There would be more turmoil and turnover at the Los Pinos agency, a foreshadow of things to come.

In the spring of 1871, Jabez Nelson Trask, a business graduate of Harvard University and a staunch member of the Unitarian Church, was selected to replace Speer as Indian agent. On May 3, when news reached members of the Ute tribe that Trask was on the road Otto Mears built toward the agency, Ouray organized nearly one hundred Tabeguache Ute warriors to intercept Trask before he arrived at the agency. Included in this group were sub-chiefs Ahanash, Chavis, Sawawatsewich, Shavano, and Sapovanero, Ouray's brother-in-law. Approximately six miles from the agency, Ouray and his men encountered Trask and through intimidation tactics, and strong words from Ouray, it was made clear that Trask was not welcomed at the agency.[39] Despite the Ute intimidation, Trask assumed his duties as Indian agent. However, it seemed as if the Utes had a point. Shortly after his arrival, Trask reviewed the government expenditures and determined that the rations to the Indians should be drastically reduced, which only infuriated the Utes. Ouray and the other sub-chiefs demanded that Colorado Superintendent of Indian Affairs, Thompson, replace

Trask with an honest agent who would uphold the Treaty of 1868. Ouray suggested his friend, Colonel Albert H. Pfeiffer, with whom he worked with in New Mexico. Ouray's suggestion fell on deaf ears in Washington.

After a year of Ute unrest and rumors of financial fraud on the part of Trask, the government finally sent J. F. Jocknick to the agency. Jocknick, a government accountant, found several discrepancies in Trask's bookkeepping, as well as a Denver bank account, previously unknown to the government officials. It seemed as if, in Jocknick's estimation, the inaccuracies in the bookkeeping methods matched the deposits to the Denver bank account. In speaking with Ouray, Jocknick became keenly aware of many of the Utes' concerns. With the constant increase in white settlement, the Ute boundaries were unclear to the Indians. Jocknick wrote, "No man knows within ten miles the location of the 107th meridian." [40]

Jocknick was not only referring to the eastern border of the Ute reservation as stipulated in the Treaty of 1868, but the fact that the Ute Indians had no concept of a "meridian," not to mention that the government officials had no idea where the 107th meridian was. Jocknick wrote of his meetings with Ouray and described the man:

> *"He is of little account as an interpreter for he has but limited use of English and Mexican. He speaks with remarkable facility. I think he has been much overestimated. He is a remarkable Indian, but would not be much above mediocrity had his lot been cast among civilized Americans. Everybody lauds him as a sort of habit, but I do not think him above lending his influence to schemers, to seekers after the office of agent, or after opportunities to make money out of Agency business, and I know that the stuff he was represented as dictating to Governor McCook last summer was a mass of fabrication conceived for no good end. Still he is with all his self-conceit and self-will a man of good sense and of good advice among the Utahs, and is said to make a charitable use of the stipend he receives as interpreter."* [41]

Jocknick seems to imply a level of corruption on the part of Ouray, something several members of the Ute tribes had believed for years. Even so, following Jocknick's official government report which recommended the removal of agent Trask, Ouray, who never trusted Trask and once threatened him, got his wish. Following his removal from the office, Trask, in his defense, weak and inaccurate as it was, wrote:

"I did my work faithfully and efficiently, reduced expenses, had the confidence of the Indians, paid for Speer's cheats in invoice; and I shall see what is the honor of working in peril of health and life, working successfully, too, without a shadow of protection from my Government." [42]

By the summer of 1872, the government finally found a man they could trust, and a man that Ouray would not only trust, but formed a friendship with that would last a lifetime. He was General Charles Adams, another brother-in-law of Governor McCook. Adams and his wife Margaret arrived at the agency in May 1872. Adams, whose given name was Karl Adam Schwanbeck, shortened his surname to "Adams" when he arrived in America from his native Germany. Following his honorable service in the Colorado State Militia, Adams was given the title of "General" as an act of respect. However, when Adams arrived at the Los Pinos Indian Agency, he faced the same problems that his predecessors had, particularly the constant confusion of the eastern border of the Ute reservation. In the spring of 1872, following the rich discoveries of gold and silver in the San Juan mountains, miners swarmed into the region, creating consternation among the Utes. Almost immediately, a government commission was formed to negotiate with the Ute tribes for possession of the San Juan mountains. Ouray flatly refused, stating:

"We do not want to sell a foot of our land that is the opinion of our people. The whites can go and take the land and come out again. We do not want them to build houses here." [43]

It was only a matter of time before Ouray realized that he either had to negotiate with the white man's government to keep as much of his people's sacred land as he could, or the government would wage war. To Ouray's way of thinking, war would only lead to bloodshed and the strong possibility that the government would revoke the treaties and simply take the land. To avert that possibility, Ouray began to seriously consider relinquishing the San Juan mountain range. It was a bold step, one that weighed heavy on Ouray. When Ouray's native enemies learned of this possible negotiation, several plotted his assassination. Within the span of five weeks, Ouray was able to thwart five attempts on his life, killing all of his attackers including Ute renegades Dynamite, Jack of Clubs, Hot Stuff, Old Nick and Suckett. Later that same year, another assassination attempt was also stopped, yet this particular incident had wide ramifications for both Ouray and his wife, Chipeta. Sapovanero, Chipeta's brother, and a Ute sub-chief, whom Ouray considered his second-in-command, led this conspiracy to assassinate Ouray. Sapovanero and four other like-minded sub-chiefs hid inside the agency's blacksmith shop, awaiting Ouray's daily arrival. However, just as Ouray approached the shop, leading his horse, the blacksmith, George Hartman, gave Ouray a subtle warning. As Sapovanero ran out of the blacksmith shop, swinging an axe toward Ouray, Ouray dodged the blow. Sapovanero raised the weapon again and as he swung it toward Ouray, the axe handle broke. Seizing the opportunity, Ouray grabbed his brother-in-law and threw him into a ditch. Then Ouray pulled his knife and, leaning over Sapovanero, was about to slash his throat, when Chipeta rushed upon the scene, pleading with her husband to exercise restraint; Ouray finally relented.

While Chipeta supported her husband's peace policy, she also believed in the traditional Ute beliefs and the value of their sacred land. Through a long council with both her husband and her brother, Chipeta managed to arrange a truce between her two family members. [44] It took time for both men, but eventually Sapovanero proved himself to be very loyal to Ouray, and was able to regain Ouray's trust. So much so, that Ouray ultimately returned his brother-in-law to his position as second-in-command. This act of forgiveness on the part of Ouray was in no small part due to the love and devotion Ouray had for Chipeta.

Meanwhile, just as Ouray had feared, the further encroachment of miners and settlers in the San Juan mountains brought a new outcry among many to remove the Utes from the region. An editorial in the *Boulder News* reflected the thoughts of many Colorado citizens:

> *"The Los Pinos Ute Indian council has failed in its object. The Utes would not resign their reservation, so the fairest portion of Colorado and some of the richest mining country is closed by force of arms. So settled we believed it will be and should be. An Indian has no more right to stand in the way of civilization and progress than a wolf or bear."*

Naturally, Governor McCook agreed with the public sentiment, calling for a new treaty with the Utes in his biennial address to the Colorado State legislature on January 3, 1873. In his speech, the governor expressed the idea that either the current Ute reservation be reduced in land allocation, or the Utes should be removed to another reservation. Following a meeting in Denver with Governor McCook, Ute Indian agent Charles Adams, along with Ouray, agreed to a formal peace council to be held at the Los Pinos Indian Agency later that summer.

During the first several days of August 1873, members of the various Ute tribes began to arrive at the agency, followed a few days later by reporters from various Colorado newspapers. Ouray and Chipeta invited the sub-chiefs into their home for private talks. However, only a few accepted the invitation, as most felt Ouray's white man's home was yet another indicator of Ouray's betrayal to his people. As a sign of their distrust for Ouray's leadership, the Weeminuche band refused to attend the conference.

A reporter from the *Rocky Mountain News*, who in all likelihood witnessed the disconcertion among the Ute leaders, wrote a scathing article regarding his preconceived attitude of the Ute leader and his wife, Chipeta. Under the headline, "Queen of the Utes," the first printed reference to the moniker by which Chipeta would often be referred, the article, printed in the September 11, 1873, issue, dripped with sarcasm:

> *"This afternoon the commissioners were waited upon by the queen of the Utes - Madame Ure I suppose she is called - who swept down in all her royal stations, attired in a skirt of buckskin, a pair of moccasins, an old shawl, and a lot of uncombed hair. She was very coquettish in her ways and manifested many of the freaks of the worldly-minded in her fashionable call. Royalty among the Utes has its disadvantages as well as advantages. It gives the chief's family position among the others but it doesn't bring sufficient revenue to keep them in affluent circumstances. Mrs. Ure's household is probably just the same as that of her meanest subject; royalty doesn't change the Ute nature any."*

Despite the reporter's obvious disdain, his words also reflected the sentiment of many of the Ute sub-chiefs who disagreed with Ouray's peace policy.

After the Ute delegations had arrived, there was a seven-day delay, as the United States Commissioners, requested by President Ulysses S. Grant, had not yet arrived. Finally, on August 26, the government representatives, led by General A. J. Alexander, commander of Fort Garland, arrived at the agency. When news spread throughout the Indian camps that the annual annuities had not arrived with the government officials, a sense of ambivalence swept among the Ute delegation, including Ouray.

The meeting began the following morning, with Ouray speaking to the government representatives. He expressed to them the Ute desire to retain what land they had left, and reminded them of the Treaty of 1868, in which the Utes had faithfully abided by. Ouray asked the representatives of the government, "Is not the United States government strong enough to keep its treaties with us?"[45]

Then, in a show of good faith, Ouray allowed the Ute sub-chiefs to speak at length, each one professing their objection to yet another treaty. Ouray stood firm in his objective, and in a display of force, refused the government officials the chance to speak. Thus the formal peace council came to an abrupt end.

William Byers, owner of the *Rocky Mountain News*, in an editorial, placed the failure of the peace council on the previous governor, Alexander C. Hunt. Byers editorialized that Hunt's involvement with the Treaty of 1868 codified any possibility of future "reduction of the Ute land," and that it resulted in "an obstacle to territorial progress." Byers negatively concluded, "The riches of Colorado were wasted on a few thousand Utes whose presence in the territory is an annoyance." [46] Following the failed peace council, Governor McCook sent a proposal to President Grant, requesting a formal meeting with the Ute leaders in Washington. President Grant agreed to the meeting, as did Ouray. By November, Ouray had assembled a delegation of sub-chiefs to accompany him to the nation's capital. Included in the group were Coho, Guero, and Tomserick, representing the Tabeguache, as well as Ignacio, for the Weeminuche. Sabeta, sub-chief of the Mouache, finally agreed to be a part of the peace process. The Indian group, led by Charles Adams with Otto Mears as interpreter, and Thomas Dolan, Indian agent for the Southern Utes, arrived in Denver on November 10, 1872. Ironically, just two days before the Colorado Utes arrived in Denver, the Uintah Utes had passed through Denver on their return trip from Washington. The Utah band of Utes, including Antero, Tabbecuna, and Wanderodes, at the invitation of President Grant, attended a series of talks during their visit. The meetings, ostensibly to extend peace, were in reality the government's subtle way of securing more land. It would be the same with the Colorado Ute delegation.

Despite the fancy meals, entertainment and tours of the city, and sight-seeing trips to New York, Ouray and the Ute delegation remained firm in their resolve to keep their land. After ten days of talks, both sides agreed to meet again in the new year. After the rigorous two-month stay in the East, the Ute delegation finally returned to their homeland on January 10, 1873. Forced to abide by the Treaty of 1868, the United States government issued general orders through military channels to prohibit the ore prospectors from entering the Ute Indian territories, which included the San Juan mountains. General A. J. Alexander, commander of Fort Garland, instructed his soldiers to obey the orders and also sent notices to various newspapers across the territory. Outcry among the protesters as well as the citizens of Colorado Territory was loud and strong. The *Denver Tribune* printed the following editorial in the March 26, 1873, issue:

> *"Now, however, that the valuable mines have been discovered and opened up in San Juan with the prospect that a certain portion of the disputed district can be made available for agricultural as well as mining purposes, and hardy bands of pioneers have gone there with the avowed intention of staying and developing its resources - barbarism steps in, supported by the U.S. bayonets and says to civilization - 'Stand back.' Did there ever before exist such an anomalous condition of affairs; government interposing in behalf of a few straight-haired vagabonds against the property rights of a brave, energetic, intelligent class of white men? That seven hundred Americans pioneers should be prodded out of the country by American bayonets, in order that a small band of dirty nomads can idly roam over 20,000,000 acres of hunting ground is an atrocity no other Government on the face of the earth but for our own would be guilty of committing."*

The *Denver Tribune* followed this editorial with an article in the April 23, 1873, issue, reporting on the various meetings held in the region of contention by the Southwestern Cooperative Association, the San Juan Miners' Cooperative, and the newly formed Protective Association. Included in the article was the following letter, signed by various officials, to the United States Secretary of the Interior:

> *"For three years, we have occupied this country, unmolested; we have developed a greater wealth of minerals than has ever been seen upon this continent in so small a compass. Most of us have all our worldly possessions now invested in this country and to force us from it would be doing us an injustice and a wrong. We firmly believe that a treaty could be made with these Indians, by which they will be willing to relinquish their claim upon the southern portion of this reservation, to the southern boundary of Colorado."*

Possibly due to citizen outcry, the government sanctioned a team of leading surveyors with the Army Corps of Engineers to conduct a comprehensive survey of the Ute territory as established by the Treaty of 1868. Why this was not done at the time of the treaty is unknown. However, the fact that the survey was being conducted at this time, after the Utes had repeatedly refused to relinquish the white man's coveted land, was a clear sign that the government was not finished dealing with the Ute tribes. In his report of the survey to the Corps of Engineers, E. H. Ruffner described the Utes he had encountered as:

"Mostly well-armed, well-mounted, well-dressed; uncommonly clean, smiling and civil. They were short men with broad muscular shoulders; good working for Indians; bland, courteous, and great beggars." [47]

By the summer of 1873, Felix Brunot, Commissioner of Indian Affairs, was sent to Colorado Territory to discuss the possibility of a new round of negotiations with agent Charles Adams. Brunot's instructions were:

"The reservation is unnecessarily large, comprising upwards of fourteen million acres of the best agricultural and mineral lands in Colorado. The number of Indians occupying it is comparatively small, not exceeding four or five thousand. The people of Colorado desire to have that portion of the Reserve not needed for Indian purposes thrown open to entry and settlement as public land in order that the agricultural and mineral resources may be developed - especially the portion lying between the southern boundary and the 38th degree of north latitude." [48]

This clearly explains the motivation behind the land survey conducted by the Army Corps of Engineers earlier in the spring. During the meetings between Adams and Brunot, along with input from Governor McCook, it was suggested to President Grant that the government offer to purchase the San Juan mountain region from the Ute tribes. To this end, Adams provided information that could possibly persuade Ouray to agree to the purchase proposal.

Adams had information, gleaned from his fellow Indian agents, that Ouray's son, Paron, originally taken by the Sioux, had been traded to the Northern Arapaho, and then to the Southern Arapaho. Through his contacts, Adams felt that there was a possibility of finding Ouray's son. Adams had a long discussion with Ouray, detailing his information. Following the meeting,

Ouray agreed to meet with Indian Commissioner Brunot.

In June 1873, Adams and Ouray traveled to Cheyenne, Wyoming, where they met with Brunot. During this meeting, Brunot informed the men that he was working on leads he had regarding the location of Ouray's son. Then, in a clever tactical use of persuasion, he indicated to Ouray that further investigation by the U. S. Indian Bureau may lead to finding his son, but that he needed Ouray's cooperation in the current land negotiations. Ouray replied to Brunot's request saying:

> *"The government is strong and can do what it wants; if the government will do what it can for me and get my boy, I will do what I can for the government in regard to our lands."* [49]

Whether Brunot's intelligence regarding the whereabouts of Paron was actionable or not, the emotional tactic used on Ouray worked. Adams later wrote that the meeting was "very satisfactory," but added an interesting suggestion; that the meeting remain private. [50] Why Adams chose to keep the meeting private can only be surmised by the events which followed.

In short order, Brunot had not only arranged for the council to be conducted in August, he had also been actively pursuing the location of Ouray's son. Finally, Brunot received word from his Wyoming contacts that Paron had been found. A meeting was scheduled in Denver, where the now grown man would be taken by Brunot to the Los Pinos agency and reunited with his father. Brunot related the news and the planned Denver meeting with Ouray.

Before Brunot left for Denver, Ouray requested that Brunot bring as few government officials back with him to the agency as was necessary for the council that was to take place. Ouray explained that due to the personal circumstances involved, he wanted as peaceful a process as was possible. Not long after Brunot left the agency, representatives of the various Ute tribes began to arrive at the agency for the council talks. The Utes, camped nearby, stayed for nearly a month before Brunot finally returned.

When Brunot arrived at the Los Pinos agency on September 5, 1873, he was alone. Brunot explained to Ouray and Chipeta that he had waited in Denver for his Wyoming contact, who was bringing Paron to him, for over two weeks. Finally, by September 1, Brunot had decided to return to the agency. He further related to Ouray that he thought the Arapaho might be hiding Paron in the Indian Territory in Oklahoma. Whether any of this was true or just a ruse to gain Ouray's support for the impending peace talks, Brunot told Ouray the council would begin the following morning and that he would serve as interpreter.

Following cursory opening remarks, Brunot explained the government's position regarding the "land in question," and the offer to purchase the San Juan mountains from the Utes, leaving them the rest of the land as stipulated in the Treaty of 1868. Immediately, the Ute sub-chiefs, including Ankatosh, Guerno, Shavano and Warency, Ouray's most trusted allies, voiced their objections. In particular, Shavano objected to the white man's recent survey, saying that the San Juan mountains were the Ute boundary. After much discussion, Ouray finally spoke:

> "They are measuring, and whenever they find a mine, they take a little piece more of our country. I interpreted to the Utes when the treaty was made that the line would be from the Rio Grande to the head of the mountains. We understood it so until the present time. The rivers that run to the east from the mountain range are off the reservation; those that run west are on it. The miners have come to San Juan and Washington Gulch, and the miners will gradually settle down on the lands in the valleys." [51]

Ouray's words suggest that he was still willing to keep his end of the bargain in supporting Brunot and the government purchase. Evidently, after a conversation with the Ute sub-chiefs, Ouray had a different position. When the second day of talks began, Ouray opened with the following statement:

> "We want you should tell Governor Elbert and the people in the territory, that we are well pleased and perfectly satisfied with everything that has been done. Perhaps some of the people will not like it because we do not wish to sell our valley lands, but we think we have good reason for not doing so. We expect to occupy them ourselves. We feel that it would be better for all parties for a mountain range to be between us." [52]

Brunot and Ouray then engaged in a back-and-forth argument regarding the San Juan mountains, as well as the valleys below. When Ouray, frustrated by Brunot's non-answers, ended the discussion, Brunot then stated:

"I have done the best I can for you. It is all over and we part good friends and we may as well adjourn the council." [53]

It was a stalemate, and both sides knew it. Brunot enlisted the advice of Otto Mears, a known friend to the Utes. Understanding Brunot's dilemma, Mears suggested that the government hire Ouray as an interpreter and "peacekeeper." Mears felt that in return, Ouray would be in a more favorable mood to part with the contested mountain range. Brunot presented the idea to his superiors, who in due course approved of the strategy. Brunot and Mears personally met with Ouray, who after much discussion, finally agreed to the proposal.

A week later, Ouray brought representatives of the seven Ute bands together for a council with Charles Adams, Thomas Dolan, Otto Mears and Felix Brunot. Ouray explained that the government agreed to purchase the San Juan mountain "mining" area for an annual stipend of twenty-five thousand dollars for ten years, and twenty thousand dollars annually for the next twenty years. Perhaps under the misguided impression that the Ute sub-chiefs were only relinquishing the portion of the sacred mountain range where white men had built ore mines, Ouray and seven sub-chiefs signed the agreement.

In fact, the "Agreement With Tabeguache, Mauache, Capote, Weeminuche, Yampa, Grand River, and Uintah Bands of Ute," also known as the "Brunot Treaty of 1873," specified distinct boundaries in the form of latitude and longitude, something the Utes had no concept of. [54] In short, the Ute bands had indeed ceded their sacred mountains. By signing the agreement, dated September 13, 1873, the Ute land, now designated as a reservation, had been reduced to a third of what it once was. With the new boundaries, the Indians had relinquished from the Utah lands on the west, to the entire western slope of Colorado which included today's counties of Ouray, San Juan, Hinsdale, Archuleta, Delores, La Plata, Montezuma and San Miguel. Three new Indian agencys were established. One, the northern agency, would be built near the Ute's Smoking Earth River, referred to as the White River by white man, located in Rio Blanco County. The second, a middle agency, would be located along the Gunnison River, but was later moved to the Uncompahgre River in Montrose County. The third, the southern agency, would be built a few miles north of the New Mexico border, in Archuleta County. Several writers have stated that the government agreed to Mears and Brunot's original suggestion of an annual salary for Ouray as a "salary for the rest of his life." This is incorrect. In Article VI of the agreement, Ouray's promised annual salary is clearly specified:

> *"In consideration of the services of Ouray, head chief of the Ute Nation, he shall receive a salary of one thousand dollars per annum for the term of ten years, or so long as he shall remain head chief of the Utes and at peace with the people of the United States."* [55]

Following the signing of the Brunot Treaty, Indian Agent Charles Adams provided a glowing and somewhat embellished report to the *Rocky Mountain News* of the Utes' relinquishment of the San Juan mountain region. The newspaper ran the report in the October 1, 1873, issue:

> *"The Utes ceded the San Juan mining country and received $25,000 annually forever. It was hard work to overcome the stubbornness of the Indians and I am heartily glad that it has ended so well for all."*

Shortly after the signing of the treaty, in addition to Ouray's generous salary, the government also gave Ouray one hundred and sixty acres of land, complete with a new six-room house and furnishings shipped from Washington, D.C.[56] Ironically, the land Ouray received was located in the very San Juan region Ouray had ceded to the government. According to J. F. Jocknick, Ouray later admitted that he realized what he had done had wronged his people, and that Ouray took the money and the property as:

> *"An offset to the loss of dignity which was the penalty he paid for exercising 'a straw-boss's' authority over his subjects."* [57]

Ouray and Chipeta's new home, the last that the couple would share, was located a few miles from present-day Montrose.[58] It was very near one of the largest springs in the area, sacred to the Utes. The flowing water was not only therapeutic to the Ute spirit, but also provided irrigation to the five acres of planted fields including hay, grain and vegetables on Ouray's land.

In late September, just a few weeks following the treaty signing, Colorado's new territorial governor, Samuel H. Elbert, sent word to Charles Adams that government officials wished to meet with Ouray and the sub-chiefs in Washington. The purpose was yet another peace council; this one with the Arapaho. The

Ute delegation, along with Ute Indian agent Adams and Otto Mears, arrived in the nation's capital in early October, ahead of their enemy, the Arapaho. President Grant personally met with Ouray and the others on October 24, 1873. During this meeting it was suggested that rather than the government send their annual delivery of annuities to the reservations, Ouray place an order of the goods needed. Almost without hesitation, the Ute delegation unanimously agreed.

In November, 1873, the Ute delegation had their first meeting with the Arapaho. Commissioner for the Department of the Interior, E. P. Smith, opened the meeting with a bloviated speech regarding peace between the two enemy tribes. Then, in what Smith must have considered a noble gesture toward that peace, he allowed the Arapaho representative, Powder Face, to address Ouray. In what can only be described as dramatic and quite emotional for Ouray, Powder Face brought forth a seventeen-year-old Arapaho brave by the name of Friday, telling Ouray that the boy was his son.

Ouray, who must have been shocked, asked the young man what his Ute name was. Friday said he did not know, only that he was Arapaho and hated the Utes, to which Ouray then asked Powder Face of the circumstances that the boy came into the Arapaho tribe. Powder Face described a fight between the two tribes at a location several miles north from where Ouray's son was actually abducted. When Ouray pointed out this fact to Powder Face, the Araphaho leader had to acknowledge that fact. However, Powder Face countered by stating that there was another Ute boy in his camp that was captured during the fight at the location Ouray spoke of. With this stunning admission, Commissioner E. P. Smith's gesture for peace back-fired. An outraged Ouray stood before the members of the council and boldly stated:

> "The whites have tried to have me get this boy. But he is not my boy. If he was he would not talk that way. Would speak differently. They [the Arapaho] acknowledge hunting Utes. The Utes never hunt the Arapaho. We let them alone, but we must defend ourselves." [59]

In an effort to salvage any possibility of continuing the peace process, Commissioner Smith asked Powder Face if Ouray's allegations were true. Powder Face replied, "That is true." With that admission, Ouray and the Ute delegation ended the "peace" council.

What began as a true and faithful agreement by the Utes with the signing of the Brunot Treaty of 1873, now became a source of contention among the Ute tribes. Their rage would simmer, and eventually boil over to violence, leading to another massacre.

"The Utes Must Go"

This was the glaring headline in *Harpers Weekly,* dated October 30, 1878. In the five years since the Ute bands had signed the Brunot Treaty, in good faith, the rush of miners into the area was unstoppable. Although Ouray tried to keep the peace between his people and the white man, several renegade warriors began raiding and terrorizing the miners and settlers in the San Juan region. Chief among this group was Colorow.

Not long after the failed peace council between the Arapaho and Ute tribes, facilitated by the government, Ouray strengthened his leadership with sub-chiefs he could trust. Colorow had regained Ouray's respect over the years and had proven himself loyal to the Ute leader. After much consideration, Ouray appointed Colorow as his second-in-command. In the ensuing years of Colorow's new-found authority, he showed respect for the elders and their efforts at peace with the white man. It was a sentiment that would not last long with the unpredictable Colorow. During the summer seasons of 1877 and 1878, Colorow led his renegade warriors on raids against the white settlers all along the San Juan mountain range and northeast, to both sides of Pikes Peak, the Ute's beloved Shining Mountain. There, Colorow, often with fellow Ute warrior Buckskin Charlie, set up camps in the vicinity near and around the Florissant area. [60] At first, Colorow and his followers would simply terrorize and antagonize white settlers. Colorow would often ride his horse up to a settler's cabin and shout, "This is Ute land! One, two sleep - you go!" Some historians believe Colorow's actions were secretly sanctioned by Ouray. If true, Ouray eventually realized the error of his ways.

Emboldened by the fear he elicited from the settlers, Colorow led his warriors, which by this time included Piah, Chipeta'a brother, and the nephew of the late Nevava, to further raids including burning and looting of many settlers' property. While Colorow tended to stay in the mountainous areas of Colorado, causing fear, he moved on to the North Park area, where he was suspected in a murder in the Granby area, and implicated of another murder in the Pikes Peak region. However, Colorow was never apprehended, and no formal charges were ever brought. Perhaps Ouray intervened on Colorow's behalf. Nevertheless, Colorow soon gave up his raiding in favor of the threats and intimidation toward the white settlers he so despised.

The constant threats, intimidation, raids and looting by the Ute Indians led to the national outcry referred to in the *Harpers Weekly* article of October 30, 1878. The government understood the national unrest and appointed a new Indian agent for the Colorado Ute White River reservation. At the recommendation of Colorado Senator Henry M. Teller, Nathaniel Cook Meeker became the new Indian agent of the troubled White River Indian agency.

Colorow disliked Meeker and his control over the Utes. *DPL*

Nathaniel C. Meeker was born in Ohio in 1817. At the age of seventeen, Meeker obtained employment as a copyboy for several newspapers in New Orleans, Louisiana, most notably, the Picayune newspaper. For the next eight years, Meeker supported himself in the lower Mississippi Delta area until the climate began to effect his heath.

In 1843, Meeker returned to his home state of Ohio, where he acquired similar work. It was during this time that he met and eventually married Arvilla Delight Smith, the daughter of a retired sea captain. [61] The couple had five children, Ralph, George, Rozene, Mary and Josephine. When the Civil War broke out, Meeker left his family in Ohio, taking a position with the Union Army as a war correspondent.

Following the war, Meeker, looking for employment, sent several of his articles to newspaper publishers, including Horace Greeley, owner and publisher of the *New York Tribune*, the largest newspaper in the country. After reading Meeker's articles, Greeley remarked to his editor, "This is the man we want." Meeker moved his family to New York, where he began his employment as an agricultural reporter for Greeley's *New York Tribune.*

In time, Meeker's articles in the *New York Tribune* were so creditable that he became a leading authority on agricultural issues throughout the country. Meeker wrote a series of pamphlets focusing on the experimental agricultural communities in New York, as well as a book on the subject. Horace Greeley, who had traveled west on several occasions, was a political reformer who used his paper to promote support for labor, homesteads and the western frontier. Meeker, who also adhered to the same philosophy, eagerly accepted his employer's assignment to venture west and write of the possibilities of economic prosperity and the idea of a utopian colony in the West. In 1869, Meeker left New York, traveling by train to his ultimate destination of Utah, where he intended to observe and write about the farming experiences and community life of the Mormons. Along the way, he visited several areas, but wrote extensively of the Colorado Rocky Mountain area. While his glowing articles were printed in the pages of the *New York Tribune,* it was Greeley's words in an editorial that would spark a new movement toward westward expansion: "Go West Young Man."

During one of his visits to the Colorado Territory in 1869, Meeker happened upon a site for the conceived utopia he and Greeley envisioned. It was fertile land, near the confluence of the South Platte and Cache la Poudre rivers, in Weld County, in the north central area of Colorado Territory. With an abundance of water, good soil, and close proximity to trade and commerce, Meeker pitched the idea of a cooperative farming community in this area to Greeley, who immediately signed onto the idea. They called it "Union Colony."

The idea of the Union Colony was first written in a favorable article, "A Western Colony" for the *New York Tribune's* December 14, 1869, edition, in which Meeker encouraged "educated, wealthy, and temperance individuals with high moral standards" to join him in a colony venture in Colorado Territory. The response was enormous, with over seven hundred of the best applicants selected as members, at a membership fee of one hundred fifty dollars each. The Union Colony, with Meeker as president, was founded in 1870. The membership fees were used to purchase land west of the rivers' confluence, encompassing some twelve thousand acres at a cost of sixty thousand dollars, with much of the land being purchased from the Denver Pacific Railroad. By April of that year, the first group of fifty families arrived in the Union Colony. Each member received one town lot, which included farm land, and the colony was incorporated under territorial laws. A town of sorts was established, appropriately named Greeley. The first year of colonization was spent in unity; planting trees, laying out streets, and establishing oversight.

In the spring of 1870, Meeker's wife, Arvilla, and their three daughters Rozene, Mary and Josephine, joined Meeker and his son, George. Their oldest son, Ralph, remained in New York, where he was also employed as a newspaper reporter, like his father, but for the competition, the *New York Times*. The Meeker family had high hopes that the high altitude and drier climate would improve their son George's health, who suffered from tuberculosis. Unfortunately this was not the case, as George died soon after reaching his father's dream land. Ironically, the death of Meeker's son was the first in the new utopian colony.

Not long after settling his family into temporary quarters, Meeker paid fifty dollars for a corner lot at the edge of the new town. He then founded the town's first newspaper in the area, the *Greeley Tribune*. To facilitate the success of the new enterprise, Meeker borrowed fifteen hundred dollars from his Union Colony partner, Horace Greeley, for a printing press and supplies. He also constructed a small adobe building in the downtown area of Greeley, where he operated his newspaper business.

As Meeker began to prosper in the Union Colony, he liquidated his entire savings of six thousand dollars to build his family a fine home. The two-story Meeker family home was the first mansion in the growing town. The Meeker daughters enjoyed growing up in the West, particularly thirteen-year-old Josephine. The adventurous young teen enjoyed wearing trousers and riding astride her horse. One of the city elders wrote a stinging letter to Meeker's *Greeley Tribune*, complaining of the unladylike behavior. To his credit, Meeker published the letter. Not long after this incident, Josephine left the family home for a short time to attend business college in Denver and then Oberlin College.

During the next few growing seasons, agricultural production was so great that Meeker and the colonists were successful in negotiating with the railroad for reasonable rates to ship their produce to market. Because of the successful farming, the colony expanded the network of irrigation ditches and constructed reservoirs for greater crop production. Union Colony and the

Indian Agent Nathaniel Meeker tried to bring his Union Colony beliefs to the Ute Indians. *DPL*

community of Greeley survived the locust plagues and blizzards of the 1870s, as well as the subsequent crop reduction. However, it could not survive the coming of social change. As the crop fields grew, the cattle from surrounding ranches seemed to create problems. Under Meeker's direction, wire fencing went up, enclosing the fields. Natural animosity grew within the community at such an act of separation. The colonists were ridiculed for their "saintly" behavior. Soon social division began to affect the families and businesses; the very fabric of what Meeker and Greeley had tried to create.

In time, the original Union Colony charter expired and was not renewed. While the town of Greeley maintained its firm business foundation, even expanding Meeker's vision of family community, Meeker himself soon fell out of public favor. When a second newspaper enterprise began to rival Meeker's *Greeley Tribune*, Horace Greeley loaned Meeker a thousand dollars to keep his paper viable. However, Greeley died before Meeker was able to repay the loan. Greeley's widow filed suit for payment of the loan, and Meeker's other debts were quickly mounting.

Seeking a way out of his financial predicament, Meeker contacted several influential leaders he had come to know and was able to secure steady employment. On the recommendation of President Rutherford B. Hayes, Meeker was appointed as the new Indian agent at the White River Indian Agency in the northernmost region of the Ute Reservation. Meeker's appointment, replacing H. B. Danforth, broke away from the long-standing policy of the Bureau of Indian Affairs to elicit recommendations for such a post from religious entities. This change in policy may also have had to do with a new treaty the government was negotiating with the Ute tribes. Meeker may or may not have been aware of the Ute Commission in Washington, D. C., to deal with the Utes in Colorado. The commission, formed on May 24, 1878, consisted of Acting Commissioner William Leeds, Colonel Edward Hatch, N. C. McFarland of Kansas, and William Stickley of Washington, D. C. Nevertheless, Meeker was pleased with his new appointment and left Greeley in May 1878.

The sixty-one-year-old Meeker traveled alone, following the Cache la Poudre River from the eastern plains, upstream toward the highest mountain range on the North American continent. As much of the higher range was impassable, despite Otto Mears' sparse road building, Meeker boarded a train at Cheyenne, Wyoming. From there, the train traveled west through the arid lands of southern Wyoming, to Rawlins. At Rawlins, Meeker drove south in a spring wagon, following the rugged road some one hundred seventy miles to the isolated White River Indian Agency. It was a long, slow trip. Snow still fell in this high country and Meeker spent many sleepless nights trying to stay warm in the only shelter he had: the bed of the spring wagon. Finally, Meeker arrived at the agency and was appalled by what he saw. The buildings were falling down and broken fencing was everywhere. Perhaps most astonishing to Meeker, given his agricultural background, was the sight of approximately twenty acres of a once-plowed field, filled with weeds. [62]

Meeker, who had big plans for the Indian agency, must have been incensed by the lack of care given to the agency property, and his attitude would soon reflect his disdain. Meeker had developed his own theory regarding Indian diplomacy through his work with Secretary of the Interior Carl Schurz. Meeker and Schurz had long conversations regarding the act of "land allotment," or "severalty," which was a radical plan for absorbing the Indians individually, rather than collectively, into American customs, such as farming. It was thought that this "individual" method would break the Indian tribal system. They believed that the Indian tribal system, which held authority over the land, was the enemy of their very individual freedom. Meeker further believed that adult Indians possessed the mental development of a young child.

With this working theory, he was prepared to push forth the radical idea. Not long after he arrived, Meeker penned an article for the *New York Tribune*, titled "Lonely."

> "Altogether there are six of us, one a lady, four employes, [sic] often during the day all are gone. So the sun goes down over the mountains, covered with grass to the top, and one looks down the narrow valley which opens up a little mile or so to the north, looks along the wagon road where only one track has been made this year, as if some one were coming, tired and ready for a warm supper, looks out through the gap in the range as if a four-horse might be discovered in a hurry to make the five or six miles before dark, but not a soul is seen, nothing moves. If there were neighbors five miles away, or ten, or twenty, it would be quite cheerful, and one could ride over for a visit once a month, but it is sixty-five miles to the nearest house, where, by the way, no family is now living, the woman having gone east because it was lonely." [63]

Meeker's objective, as the U. S. Indian Bureau made clear, was to establish a school for the Indian children, teach the adults farming skills, and assimilate them into the white man's civilization. Operating from an agricultural mind set, it was Meeker's thought that the Utes should also be transformed into his idea of an agricultural society. However, Meeker knew nothing of the Indian way of life and was less than understanding. Just six months into his new position as Indian Agent, he wrote to Senator Henry Teller on December 23, 1878:

> "When I get around to it, in a year or so, if I stay as long, I shall propose to cut every Indian down to a bare starvation point if he will not work. The 'getting around to it' means to have plenty of tilled ground, plenty of work to do, and to have labor organized so that whoever will shall be able to earn his bread." [64]

In an effort to bring his ideas to the settlers in the area, Meeker, relying on his journalist background, established the *Meeker Herald* newspaper. He printed the weekly publication on the printing press he brought with him to the agency. [65]

Meanwhile, in November 1878, the government was again successful in securing an agreement with the Ute bands for further consolidation of their lands. The Agreement With the Capote, Mauache, and Weeminuche Bands of Ute, consented to by the Yampa, Grand River, Uintah, and Tabeguache Bands, was signed on November 9, 1878. In effect, this new agreement not only reduced the land once occupied by the Ute nation, it also separated the Utes to two reservations, the southern Utes with the agency at Ignacio, and the northern Utes with their Indian agency along the White

River. Article I of the agreement appropriated twenty thousand dollars for upgrades to the White River agency. [66] Among the Utes who signed their name or made their mark on the agreement papers with the government was Ignacio and Douglas for the northern Utes. Uriah H. Curtis, in his last act as the Ute interpreter, and Albert W. Pfeiffer, as Special Commission Interpreter, served as witnesses to the signatures of the Ute Indians.

Among the many Ute signees, conspicuously absent was that of Ouray. In 1876, after a protracted illness, Ouray traveled to Canon City, where he consulted a white man's doctor. After a complete exam, Dr. John H. Lacey diagnosed Ouray as suffering from chronic nephritis. In essence, Ouray's kidneys were failing. Therefore, he was unable to attend the negotiations for the new agreement.

Meanwhile, during that first winter, Meeker and the agency's interpreter, a fellow known only as Henry Jim, repaired the outbuildings. [67] Meeker transformed the agency house into something a bit more suitable for his family and also made improvement on another building to be used for the children's school. In the spring of 1879, Meeker's wife, Arvilla, and twenty-year-old daughter Josephine, arrived at the agency along with several wagonloads of food and supplies, both for the agency and the Indian's annuity goods. After getting his family settled, Meeker requested that Henry Jim summon the Indians from the camps to the agency to receive their annuity goods. It would be his first formal meeting as their new agent.

As the Indians arrived, Henry Jim pointed out the various influential leaders among the two Ute bands, including the sub-chiefs; Jack, a man approximately forty years of age, and Douglas, an older man near the age of sixty.[68] After Meeker introduced himself and handed out the annuities, he looked forward to speaking with the two sub-chiefs. However, only a few of the Indians remained at the agency, including Douglas. Jack and his people immediately left the area. Through Henry Jim's translation, Meeker learned from Douglas that Jack and his people preferred their traditional way of life and only came to the agency when the annuities were distributed. Meeker further learned that Jack was adamantly opposed to any white man's further interference in the Ute way of life. Douglas then began to relate Jack's background for Meeker. Douglas said that Jack had been raised in Utah, by a Mormon family, and received a fine education.[69] Meeker could not understand how an educated man such as Jack was said to be, could be so against the progress for his own people that Meeker and the government proposed.

In the meantime, Meeker stocked the agency store, which was run by his wife, Arvilla. The sixty-four-year-old matriarch of the Meeker family also took on the duties of providing what medical assistance she could to the sick and elderly. Meeker also formally opened the school, and installed his daughter Josephine as the teacher. Unfortunately, very few children attended. Josephine took it upon herself to get acquainted with the Ute families camped nearby. She would ride a horse out to their camps and engage various Ute women into conversation, through Henry Jim's interpreter skills. The women were kind to her and Josephine enjoyed playing with the children. She spent as much time as she could with them and became absorbed in learning the culture. After one particular visit when Josephine was given a handsome pair of beaded moccasins, Meeker reminded his daughter that she was at the agency not to be friends with the Indians, but to teach them.[70]

As Meeker went about organizing the agency that spring, the government had been quietly in negotiations with the southern Ute bands. The long, yet narrow, strip of land which straddled the southern Colorado border with New Mexico, was so remote that it was hard for the government to manage. Therefore, a new agreement was needed to consolidate unto one manageable Indian agency. However, the southern Ute bands, under the leadership of Ignacio and Buckskin Charlie, refused to attend the talks.

Frustrated, the government simply entered legislation which was passed into law on May 3, 1879. This new law allowed the President of the United States, in this case, President Hayes, to personally intercede in the negotiations. Newly elected Governor Frederick W. Gilpin was in full support of this new law. In his first speech before the Colorado legislature, Governor Pitkin laid out his ideas regarding the Utes and more importantly, in his mind, the land:

> *"Along the western border of the state lies a vast tract [of land] occupied by the tribe of the Ute Indians, as their reservation. It contains about twelve million acres and is nearly three times as large as the state of Massachusetts. It is watered by large streams and rivers, and contains many rich valleys and a large number of fertile plains. The climate is milder than in most locales. Grasses grow there in great luxuriance, and nearly every kind of grain and vegetable can be raised without difficulty.*

> *No portion of the state is better adapted for agricultural and grazing purposes than many portions of this reservation. Within its limits are large mountains, from most of which explorers have been excluded by the Indians. Prospectors, however, have explored some portions of the country, and found valuable lode and placer claims, and there is reason to believe that it contains great mineral wealth. The number of Indians who occupy this reservation is about three thousand. If the land was divided up between individual members of the tribe, it would give every man, woman, and child a homestead of between three and four thousand acres. It has been claimed that the entire tribe have had in cultivation about fifty acres of land, and from some personal knowledge of the subject I believe that one able-bodied white settler would cultivate more land than the whole tribe of Ute Indians. These Indians are fed by the government, are allowed ponies without number, and except when engaged in an occasional hunt, their most serious employment is horse racing. If this reservation could be extinguished, and the land thrown open to settlers, it will furnish homes to thousands of people of the state who desire homes."* [71]

Although a bit exaggerated, the governor's ideas were reflective of the general population of the state. Ute agent Nathaniel C. Meeker certainly held the same views as the governor and set forth to comply with Pitkin's policy. Early in the summer of 1878, the Ute Commission had completed their tedious negotiations with the Southern Ute tribes, including Ouray's Tabeguache band, the Mouache and Capote bands, and Buckskin Charlie's Weeminuche Utes. The leaders of the Southern Utes had unanimously agreed to move to the headwaters of the Blanco, Chama, Navajo, Piedra, and San Juan Rivers. By agreeing to this move, the Southern Utes relinquished yet another portion of their sacred homeland. The Ute Commission then began informal negotiations with the Northern Utes.[72] With the government's constant attempt to take more of the Ute's land, tensions were running particularly high among the northern Utes at the White River agency. Nevertheless, Meeker went forth with his plan for assimilating the Indians into the white man's world.

The summer of 1878 was incredibly hot all across the state. On the western slope fires raged in June and well into July. In due course, many newspaper editorials accused the Ute Indians of causing the fires in an effort to drive the settlers and miners out of the area. The citizens demanded action. On July 5, Governor Pitkin sent a telegram to Indian Commissioner H. A. Hayt in Washington:

> "Reports reach me daily that a band of White River Utes are off their reservation, destroying forests and game near North and Middle Parks. They have already burned millions of dollars of timber, and are intimidating settlers and miners. Have written agent Agent Meeker, but fear letters have not reached him. I respectfully request you to have a telegraphic order sent to troops at nearest post to remove Indians to their reservation. If general government does not act promptly the state must. Immense forests are burning throughout western Colorado, supposed to have been fired by Indians. I am satisfied there is an organized effort on the part of Indians in Colorado to destroy the timber. The loss will be irreplaceable. These savages should be removed to Indian Territory where they can no longer destroy the finest forest in this state. Frederick Pitkin, Governor of Colorado" [73]

The following day, July 5, 1878, Meeker received a telegram from the office of Commissioner of Indian Affairs in Washington, D. C. Signed by E. J. Brooks, the message read:

> "Governor of Colorado reports your Indians depredating near North and Middle parks. [sic] If correct take active steps to secure their return to reservation. The secretary directs that if necessary you will call upon nearest military post for assistance." [74]

Meeker took this message as an opportunity to gain the assistance he had so desperately sought from the government. Now he had the attention of both the Indian Bureau and the military. Meeker immediately responded to the missive from Washington, sending a letter to H. A. Hayt, Commissioner of Indian Affairs:

> "You are witness that I have repeatedly reported to you of the absence of the Indians from the reservation, being generally on the Snake and Bear rivers; and I have, agreeably to your directions, often requested the military at Fort Steele, through the commandment, to clear those valleys, but no attention was paid, and no answers given. North Park is the best hunting ground in America, but it is too elevated for general farming. Recently gold discoveries have been made; a great many miners have gone in, and the Indians wish to occupy the ground. A collision is by no means improbable." [75]

Meeker continued to send his monthly reports to Commissioner Hayt. Yet, as summer faded into fall and with cooler temperatures allowing for the fires to die out, Meeker received no further communication regarding the matter from Washington.

Perhaps taking his cue from Governor Pitkin's speech regarding the horse racing reference, in the fall of 1879, Meeker set about plowing up the pastures for the Utes' ponies as well as the race track. Enraged, Douglas rode toward the pasture, aimed his rifle and fired several shots at Meeker, all of which missed. Undaunted, the next day Meeker was back at the pasture with his plow. When he completed the task of destroying the pasture, Meeker also began plowing the race track. This time, Johnson, the husband of Ouray's sister, Susan, shot the horses pulling the plow. The following day, September 10, Meeker confronted Johnson for shooting his horses. Johnson shoved Meeker against a hitching post. Meeker fought back and eventually, Johnson left. Then, Parviet and Antelope came upon Meeker.

Meeker resisted them as best he could, but the two men severely beat Meeker to near unconsciousness. Unnerved by the incident, that very day, Meeker wrote to Hayt:

> *"Hon. E. A. Hayt Commissioner, Washington, D. C. I have been assaulted by a leading Chief, Johnson, forced out of my house, and injured badly, but was rescued by employees. It is now revealed that Johnson originated all the trouble stated in letter September 8th. His son shot at the plowman, and the opposition to plowing is wide. Plowing stopped. Life of self, family, and employees not safe; want protection immediately; have asked Governor Pitkin to confer with General Pope. N. C. Meeker Indian Agent"*

Meeker believed his actions were justified, given his orders from the Indian Bureau to teach the Ute Indians the ways of agricultural farming. Indeed he was within his official authority as Indian agent. However, his governmental authority left no room for tolerance or understanding Ute culture. Thus, this misguided authority became intolerable to the Utes, and further uprisings began to occur. The tyrannical behavior and disregard for the Ute Indian way of life so incensed the Utes, that a conflict that Meeker himself ignited would end with his death. It would be the most violent retaliation by Native Americans in resentment of the government reservation system.

As Meeker faced daily threats from the Utes camped near the agency, Meeker's old friend and mentor, Secretary of the Interior Carl Schurz, received Meeker's telegram and sent it to the of the office of the Secretary of War with a personal note, "I respectfully recommend that the matter be referred to the honorable Secretary of War."

Schurz's recommendation was received and acted upon. On September 16, Lieutenant General Philip H. Sheridan, commander of the Army Division of the Missouri, received his orders from the Headquarters of the Army at Washington, D.C.

> *"Secretary of War approves request of Interior Department, just received, and General of the Army directs that necessary orders be given the nearest military commander to the agency to detail a sufficient number of troops to arrest such Indian chiefs as are insubordinate, and enforce obedience to the requirements of the agent, and afford him such protection as the exigency of the case requires; also that the ringleaders be held as prisoners until an investigation can be had."* [76]

That same day, Meeker received the following telegram from the Washington office of the Indian Bureau:

> *"War Department requested commanding officer nearest post to send troops for your protection immediately. On their arrival cause arrest of leaders in late disturbance and have them held until further orders from this office. Report full particulars as soon as possible. E. J. Brooks, Acting Com'r"* [77]

Sheridan forwarded the order to General John Pope at Fort Leavenworth, Kansas, who ordered Major Thomas Tipton Thornburgh, a West Point graduate, to command a squad of cavalry in the aid and protection of Meeker and his family.

On September 22, 1879, Major Thornburgh, with the Fourth Infantry, and Lieutenant S. A. Cherry, adjutant of the command, departed Fort Fred Steele, near Rawlins, Wyoming. Under their command were Captain J. S. Payne and two companies of cavalry, as well as one company of infantry, commanded by Captain B. D. Price. Along with Thornburgh's nearly two hundred soldiers were nearly thirty supply wagons carrying weapons, ammunition, as well as food and forage for thirty days. It was a journey of approximately one hundred and twenty miles to the White River Indian agency.

As Thornburgh had never been in the Ute country before, he relied on his chief scout, Joseph Rankin. Rankin had previously spent time running the mail route from Rawlins south to the White River Indian agency and knew the area well. Rankin also had personal knowledge of many of the Ute leaders camped at the reservation. After four days of travel southward, the soldiers entered the valley of the White River. On that day, September 26, Thornburgh and his men were confronted by Jack, Colorow, and several other Ute warriors. A conversation ensued in which Jack informed Thornburgh that he had restored the peace with his people and the soldiers were not needed or welcomed on the Ute reservation land, in accordance with the peace agreement signed the previous year. Thornburgh replied that he and his men would continue on toward the Indian agency to assure that Meeker and his family were safe. Reluctantly, Jack let the soldiers pass.

After a few more miles into their journey, the army troops were again stopped by Jack and Colorow. Jack explained that a third man in his group, E. W. "Wilmer" Eskridge, had a message from Meeker, requesting a meeting with Thornburgh. Jack suggested that the soldiers camp in a nearby area and he and Colorow would escort Thornburgh to the Indian agency. Thornburgh took Jack's invitation to camp nearby, but declined to go to the agency alone with the Ute warriors.

Major Thornburgh and his troops would remain camped at the little grassy area along Deer Creek for the next three days. On the early morning of the third day, Thornburgh wrote out a message to N. C. Meeker:

> *"I have carefully considered whether or not it would be advisable to have my command at a point as distant as that desired by the Indians, and have reached the conclusion that under my orders, which require me to march my command to the agency, I am not at liberty to leave it at a point where it would not be available in case of trouble."* [78]

Wilmer Eskridge took the message to the agency that morning and personally delivered it to Meeker. That evening, Sunday, September 28, Thornburgh ordered his men to prepare to march the following day toward the White River agency. Unknown to Thornburgh, Jack, Colorow and their group of warriors were watching the soldier's camp. The next morning, as the soldiers broke camp and began their march, they were immediately confronted by Jack and his warriors.

Jack considered Thornburgh's advance as an act of war and warned Thornburgh not to cross Milk Creek, or his warriors would attack. A defiant Thornburgh disregarded the Ute leader's words and ordered his men to cross the creek. Again, unknown to Thornburgh, Jack and Colorow had several warriors strategically hidden in the crest of a hill, behind rocks and in the tall grass along the river. More warriors were ready to attack near Milk Creek, the border of the Ute Indian reservation.

Just as Thornburgh's command entered an area known as Red Canyon, Jack and Colorow's warriors opened fire on the soldiers. Then another group of warriors emerged, launching an attack on the soldiers from both sides. In the fight that followed, nine of Thornburgh's troopers were killed. As Major Thornburgh attempted to get to the supply wagon, he was caught in a deadly crossfire. Thornburgh's bullet-riddled body would lay near the supply wagon during the remainder of the fight.

Unbeknownst to Meeker, the battle at Milk Creek was raging, while he was busy answering Thornburgh's message. Meeker wrote the following:

"U. S. Indian Service White River Agency, Col. Sept. 29, 1879 - 1 p.m. Major T. T. Thornburgh White River Expedition, in the field, Colorado: Dear Sir: I expect to leave in the morning with Douglas and Serrick to meet you. Things are peaceful, and Douglas flies the United States flag. If you have trouble getting through the canon let me know. We have been on guard three nights, and shall be tonight, not because we know there is danger, but because there might be. I like your last programme. It is based on true military principles. Most truly yours, N. C. Meeker, Indian Agent" [79]

This message would be the last words Nathaniel Cook Meeker would ever write. It was also a message that Thornburgh would never read. The death of Major T. T. Thornburgh rendered his troops and the defense lines disorderly at best. Captains Cherry and Price ordered the soldiers to move the wagons into a circular formation. However, some of the soldiers were unable to make their way to the wagons, and as the Utes had shot several horses and mules, the men had no choice but to move the animal carcasses to form a breastwork in order to have protection.

Then the Ute warriors, led by Colorow, set fire to the grass and sagebrush to an effort to force the troops out of their holding position. While the soldiers fought the flames that caught wagons on fire, the Utes continued to their assault on the soldiers. The grass fires and gunfire raged until well after dark. A few hours later, when the Indian's firing ceased, the soldiers dug trenches around the wagons as well as a pit in the center of the corralled wagons for a makeshift hospital.[80] At some point during that night, the chief army scout, Joseph Rankin managed to escape on horseback in an effort to get help. He rode due north, over one hundred fifty miles, back to Fort Fred Steele in Wyoming. It would be two days before he would make it to safety and get reinforcements for his fellow soldiers. Meanwhile, the fighting would continue at this area for the next four days.

As the battle at Milk Creek continued, Ute sub-chief Douglas had plans of his own. Indian Agent Meeker was keeping himself busy in the agency storeroom as he awaited the arrival of Douglas who would escort him to Thornburgh's camp for the scheduled meeting. When Douglas finally arrived, he told Meeker he would take him to the soldier's camp, but that he must come alone. Meeker refused, as he wanted Wilber Eskridge to come along as well. At this point, a frustrated Douglas left the agency house. Douglas soon returned with a group of warriors, including Ebenezer, Powvitz, and Antelope. What happened next is best described by Josephine Meeker in her later testimony before the United States Congress:

"It was about fifteen or twenty minutes after Douglas had gone out when we heard very suddenly several guns fired off. I ran and looked out the window in the direction from which the sound of the firing came, and I saw the Indians firing at the employees, who were running in every direction and trying to escape." [81]

In the well-planned attack, a group of nearly twenty Utes, led by Douglas, gained entry to the agency storeroom. Without attracting attention, the Indians managed to take all the firearms and ammunition. They then took their positions and began firing, killing two agency employees, Price and Thompson. Pandemonium erupted within the agency household. An agent employee, Frank Dresser, eventually was able to get most of the women and children to the milk house undetected by the Indians. As the sun began to set, the Indians set fire to the agency house. Josephine Meeker later described the horrific incident:

"Around sundown - about five o'clock - we discovered that the house had been fired. Then our room [the milk house] commenced to fill with smoke and we ran out. The Indians were so busy carrying off blankets and goods that they did not see us at first. We ran into father's room. Everything was just as he left it: a book lay open on the desk where he had been reading; nothing was disturbed." [82]

However, N. C. Meeker was not in the room. His wife, Arvilla Meeker later described the sight of her murdered husband:

"I saw Mr. Meeker stretched out on the ground. He had been shot in the forehead. Blood was running from his mouth. His head was leaning back, and he was lying very straight, as if laid out; with his hands right down beside him, just as if laid out. I went right up to his head...stooped to kiss his face." [83]

The women, including Arvilla Meeker and her daughter Josephine, quickly grabbed what they could from the burning house and with their children, followed Frank Dresser as they attempted to make their escape from the madness. Mrs. Flora Ellen Price, along with her two small children, Johnnie and May, was one of the women who survived the ordeal. Mrs. Price later recounted the failed escape:

"I ran outside the fence; Josie, Mrs. Meeker and Frank opened the gate and went into the field, and I crossed over through the wire-fence. Then they saw us; we had not got ten steps from the corner of the fence before they saw us and fired, and hit Mrs. Meeker. The bullets whizzed by my head and hit beside me. They shot at Frank, and as he would take a step, the dust would fly." [84]

Arvilla Meeker later added her recollections:

"We were running away and had got into the sagebrush; when the ball struck me. I dropped on the ground so that I would not be so much of a mark, and as I lay there I saw them capture Josie and Mrs. Price. I thought they would not see me, but as soon as they had captured the others they came to me. The one who came after me [saw] that I was wounded as I lay on the ground. He said, 'I am heap sorry, I am heap much sorry.' He was a young, smart, good-looking Indian, who spoke English pretty well. He said, 'Can you get up?' I said 'Yes, sir.' He gave me his arm just as nice as anybody, and took me to Douglas." [85]

Josephine Meeker recalled the immediate aftermath of their capture:

"The Indians told us to stop. Pah-sone called to me and said, 'Come to me; no shoot you.' I said, 'Going to shoot?' He said, 'No.' He said, 'Come to me.' I looked back; one had hold of Mrs. Price and one had hold

of mother. They took us down toward the river where each one of them had his pile of goods. Pah-sone placed me on the blankets he had stolen. Douglas came and tried to take me away from Pah-sone. He tried to push Pah-sone away and take me away by the arm, but Pah-sone pushed him away, and they had a pretty hot [sic] in Ute. I thought they were going to quarrel, but Douglas turned away and went off. Pah-sone packed his things on a government mule, and I was put on a horse with the little Price girl tied on behind me in a blanket. An Uncompahgre Ute whom we did not know took Mrs. Price. She was taken to another camp. I did not see her at all. Just at dark, we started across the river directly south." [86]

On October 1, Joseph Rankin arrived at Fort Fred Steele. After reporting the siege at Milk Creek, orders were immediately given for troops to depart to the area. A formal military order was also sent by the War Department to Fort D. A. Russell, located three miles west of Cheyenne. Colonel Wesley Merritt, along with a cavalry of two hundred, and over one hundred infantry soldiers, boarded the Union Pacific railroad at Cheyenne, bound for Rawlins. A dispatch was also sent to Captain Francis S. Dodge who, along with Company D of the Ninth Cavalry, also known as the Buffalo Soldiers, were camped along the Grand River in the Middle Park area. Captain Dodge and Lieutenant M. B. Hughes immediately ordered the soldiers to break camp and prepare to march south. Dodge, Hughes, and their thirty-five Buffalo Soldiers rode through the night, arriving at the Milk Creek battle site just after dawn on October 2, much to the relief of the besieged soldiers.

The Ute warriors, unaware of a military advance under the cloak of darkness, watched in amazement that morning as the Buffalo Soldiers rode boldly into the fight. Claims of "woolly head," and "all same as buffalo," floated among the Utes. Captain Dodge's Buffalo Soldiers fought off the onslaught of the Indian's fire with valor throughout that day.

Late in the afternoon of the fifth day of the battle, under heavy fire, Sergeant Henry Johnson emerged from his trench and was able to make his way to the river, gather water in his containers, and returned unscathed to the soldiers' entrenchment. Sergeant Henry Johnson, a twelve-year veteran whose service included the original formation of the Tenth Cavalry's F Company of the Buffalo Soldiers, would be awarded the Medal of Honor for his bravery. [87]

On the morning of October 5, 1879, Colonel Wesley Merritt and his command of five companies of the Fifth Cavalry arrived at the Milk Creek battle site. The Ute warriors, observing so many

The aftermath of the Meeker Massacre. *DPL*

military troops approaching, made a hasty retreat. The battle at Milk Creek was finally over.

After securing the area, the army doctor began treating the forty-three wounded soldiers. Several of Merritt's men worked to gather the dead. Including Major T. T. Thornburgh, a total of fourteen soldiers had lost their lives. Later in the day, Merritt split his company of troops. While half remained at the battle site, Merritt and the remainder of his command proceeded on to the White River Indian Agency. When he arrived, Merritt only found death and destruction.

The soldiers found Meeker's body near the agency house. Evidently the Indians had mutilated the body sometime after Arvilla found her dead husband. A chain was wrapped around Meeker's neck and his face had been smashed with some sort of heavy object. A barrel stave had been driven into his stomach and a large piece of it, broken off, was shoved into his mouth.

Nine other bodies, all men, were also discovered, strewn about the agency grounds. The body of Frank S. Price was found with two bullets lodged in his left breast, and he had been stripped naked. Price was the husband of Flora Ellen Price, who had been abducted along with their two small children, Johnnie and May. The burned bodies of Frank Dresser, an agency employee, as well as his son, Eaton, were found near one of the torched buildings.

Dresser's other son, Harry, was found near a local coal mine with a bullet in his chest. W. H. Post's body, Meeker's personal secretary, was discovered near the river with two bullet holes near his left ear. The naked body of E. W. Eskridge, the trusted messenger of both the Utes and Meeker, was found with a bullet hole through his skull. Two more bodies were discovered, but were so badly burned as to be unrecognizable. The body of a man identified as "Mr. Sheppard" was also found, "his face eaten more or less by wolves, body partially burned and a bullet hole in his left breast."[88]

There were no signs of the women and children. A further search of the burned buildings yielded no results. Merritt concluded, correctly, that the women and children had been taken hostage by the Ute warriors. The soldiers tidied the bodies as best they could and buried them on the agency property.

News of the Ute attack at Milk Creek and the brutal death of Nathaniel Cook Meeker reached Denver and the front range that day. On October 2, 1879, the *Rocky Mountain News* ran a two-page series of dispatches from the area, as well as eyewitness accounts of the carnage. One of Thornburgh's scouts, unnamed by the newspaper, provided such an account under the headline:

> *"The Milk Creek Massacre The White River Utes On the War Path Agent Meeker and Family Murdered and the Agency Buildings Burned The wagons were some distance in the rear and the*
> *Indians were now discovered to be between the command and the wagons. Rankin approached the major and begged him to open on them, saying, 'If you don't we will all be murdered. We must fight now or never.' Thornburgh turned in his saddle and said, 'Joe, under my instructions I dare not fire a shot. Should I open this ball I would not only be court-martialed and cashiered, but would be disgraced'. Just at this time two Indians came out of the brush, and rode up to within a hundred yards of the command. One of them dismounted, took deliberate aim and fired. Thornburgh immediately ordered the troops to fire, and in a few moments he ordered the 'charge' which he himself gallantly led. When the command had reached a point within about five hundred yards of the wagons Major Thornburgh received two shots through the head, which killed him instantly."*

Another dispatch from Georgetown, sent by General William A. Hamill, reported the probable death of N. C. Meeker. The *Rocky Mountain News* printed the dispatch in the same two-page series:

> *"Meeker Reported Killed Georgetown, October 1. - Considerable excitement prevails here over the telegram of Governor Pitkin to General Hamill on the Indian question. It is rumored here to-night that Agent Meeker was killed at the agency Sunday night. No particulars."*

Governor Pitkin summoned all officers of the state militia to his office. After a short meeting, the officers quickly left the governor to assemble their respective units. Next, the governor summoned all local newspaper editors to his office. Notifying the editors that he was invoking martial law, Pitkin instructed the editors to print the instructions, rules and regulations of such law in their newspapers. Governor Pitkin also issued a statement which was printed in all the Denver newspapers the following day:

> *"It will be impossible for the Indians and whites to live in peace hereafter. This attack had no provocation and the whites now understand that they are liable to be attacked in any part of the state. My idea is that, unless removed by the government they must be necessarily be exterminated."*

It seemed as if Governor Pitkin, who long supported the removal of the Indians from Colorado, now saw his opportunity. The governor then sent couriers, by train, to the various areas of the state that did not have telegraph service. Finally, Governor Pitkin sent the following telegram to Washington to the attention of the Secretary of War:

> *"Dispatches just received from Laramie City and Rawlins inform me that the White River Utes attacked* [Brevet] *Col. Thornburgh's command twenty-five miles from agency. Col. Thornburgh was killed, and all his officers but one killed or wounded, besides many of his men and most of his horses. Dispatches state that the whole command is imperiled. The state of Colorado will furnish you, immediately, all the men you require to settle permanently this Indian trouble."* [90]

In effect, Governor Pitkin was asking the United States government to declare war against the White River Utes. Regardless of what the government's ultimate response would be, the citizens of Colorado were armed and ready to fight.

Meanwhile, as the White River Utes were fighting the soldiers at Milk Creek, news of the Ute uprising reached Ouray at his home along the Uncompahgre River, well over a hundred miles south of the White River Indian Agency. Runners from the area, including Joseph W. Brady, an employee at the Los Pinos Indian Agency, had arrived late on the afternoon of October 1. It was three days after the Ute warriors, under Jack, had opened fire on Major Thornburgh and his soldiers.

Ouray was conflicted on how to respond or if he should respond. For the past several months there had been a few incidents of Utes committing crimes against the white man, including those by his own brother-in-law, Piah. While Ouray felt these aggressions were wrong, he also believed that the soldiers' march across Milk Creek had violated the treaty. He first consulted with William M. Stanley, Indian agent at the Los Pinos agency. [91] After much discussion with his most trusted sub-chiefs, Ouray chose to send his brother-in-law, Sapovanero, with a group of Ute braves, as well as Joseph Brady, with a message to the White River Utes to cease the fighting. Ouray then sent telegrams to various town officials in the San Juan area, including mining towns of Lake City and Ouray, ironically, given the present circumstances, named for the leader of the Ute Indians.

On October 4, the day after Pitkin enacted martial law, a united group of citizens at Lake City sent Governor Pitkin the following telegram: "The Indian Chief Ouray has notified the whites to protect themselves, that he is powerless and can afford no protection. The town of Ouray is under arms, and the country is all on fire. We will do all we can, but want arms, can you send them? We must have protection of some kind."[92]

Sapovanero and his men arrived at the battle site on Milk Creek the morning of October 5. Their arrival was just a few hours before Colonel Wesley Merritt and his command of nearly five hundred soldiers with the Fifth Cavalry arrived at the battle site. Sapovanero immediately sought out Jack. During a short discussion between the two, along with Colorow, Sapovanero conveyed Ouray's desire for a cease-fire. Brady then handed the written message from Ouray to Jack. The message read:

"Los Pinos Indian Agency October 2, 1879 To the chief captains, headmen, and Utes at the White River Agency: You are hereby requested and commanded to cease hostilities against the whites, injuring no innocent persons or any others farther than to protect your own lives and property from unlawful and unauthorized combinations of horse-thieves and desperadoes, as anything farther will ultimately end in disaster to all parties." [93]

This message was followed by a second one which read:

"Los Pinos Indian Agency October 2, 1879 To the officers in command and the soldiers at the White River Agency: Gentlemen: At the request of the chief of Utes at this agency, I send by Jos. W. Brady, an employe, [sic] the inclosed [sic] order from Chief Ouray to the Utes at the White River Agency. The head chiefs deplore the trouble existing at White River, and are anxious that no further fighting or bloodshed should take place, and have commanded the Utes there to stop. I hope that you will second their efforts so far as you can, consistent with your duties, under existing commands. This much for humanity. Very respectfully, your obedient servant, W. M. Stanley United States Indian Agent." [93]

It was shortly after receiving these messages that Jack and the warriors retreated under a white flag. Colorow and a band of renegades remained on the hill above the battle site. Several of Jack's warriors spotted Colorow and Jack on the hill. Colorow and this group would eventually continue their war against the white man.

Meanwhile, an active search for the hostages taken from the White River agency was underway in earnest. On October 14, Secretary of the Interior Carl Schurz, Meeker's former mentor, enlisted General Charles Adams to assist in the effort. Schurz knew of Adams' work as former Indian agent for the Utes at the Los Pinos agency, and of his friendship with Ouray. Adams later recounted his involvement:

"On the 14th of October I received a telegram from the Secretary, and also a telegram from my department, the latter detailing me temporarily to the Interior Department and the former giving me instructions how to proceed. I was to go to the Southern Ute Agency, see Ouray, the chief of the Utes, put myself in communication with the hostile Utes, and try to obtain the release of the women and children who were then supposed to be in their camp. If that was agreed to without any conditions, I was to ascertain whether the Indians wanted to prolong the fight, or whether they would be willing to give up the principal instigators of the massacre and resume their relations with the government." [94]

General Charles Adams, along with his wife Margaret, and a group of men including Captain M. W. Cline, George Sherman, clerk of the Indian agency, and William Saunders, a local newspaper reporter, made their way west. The group arrived at Ouray and

Chipeta's home along the Uncompahgre River on October 18. Despite Ouray's advanced kidney disease, the two couples spent the evening together renewing their friendship. The following morning Ouray summoned his trusted sub-chiefs, Colorow, Shavano, and his brother-in-law, Sapovanero, to meet with General Adams.

Adams explained the government's desire to end the current conflict peacefully by securing the release of the hostages. After much discussion, the Ute leaders agreed to assist Adams in the effort. Early on the morning of October 20, Adams and his men were escorted by Colorow, Sapovanero, Shavano, and a group of Ute braves, to Douglas' camp along Plateau Creek. It was believed that this was where the captives were being held. As the entourage approached the White River valley, a Ute brave rode ahead to alert Douglas that the Ute leaders were arriving, along with General Adams. Adams later recounted his arrival at Douglas' camp:

> "I arrived there on the 21st of October, about ten o'clock in the morning, at the small camp; there were only about ten or fifteen lodges of Indians there. A boy that met me about a quarter of a mile away told me that the prisoners were scattered - that is, one woman was in one house at the lower end of the camp; another one in the center, and another above."[95]

When the group arrived at the Indian camp, Douglas received Adams and the Ute leaders in his tipi. During the long council, Adams again explained the government's position regarding ending the conflict with the release of the captives. Douglas made further demands which Adams said he was not authorized to agree to. An obstinate Douglas pressed on with more demands. Finally after several hours of discussion, Sapovanero exploded in anger. He told Douglas that if he did not release the hostage that Ouray was prepared to allow the soldiers to attack Douglas' camp.

Just as Sapovanero finished his vocal tirade, Ouray's half-sister, Susan, in a bold move, interrupted the all-male formal council. Undaunted, Susan pleaded for the release of the hostages.[96]

Following the broken council, General Adams was allowed to retrieve the captives. Adams later recounted the event:

> "I went to the lower end of the camp first, and by inquiring I saw Miss Meeker peeping out of a tent. I dismounted and asked her who she was, not knowing her personally at the time, and told her I had come to release her, and asked her where her mother and the other woman

were. I then mounted again and told Miss Meeker to get ready to leave, if possible, that afternoon. I went up to the upper camp and found all the Indian men, probably about thirty or forty, in a tent together talking very boisterously. I went inside. I inquired for the other captives and was told that they were hidden in the brush about 200 yards distant down a steep bank toward the river. I waited for about an hour, when Chief Douglas, with probably five or six other chiefs, rode up. He informed me that soldiers were advancing from White River, and that the whites were hostile, and he did not see why he should give me the women. He again asked whether I had any conditions to offer for the release of them. I told him I had not; but after he had given them to me I might have something further to say. He then invited me inside the lodge where all others were talking, and I believe we talked there until about four or five o'clock in the afternoon. Finally they agreed to give them to me. They said: 'We don't want to have anything more to do with the government. All that we want is that the soldiers shall not pursue us in our own country. We can live on game, as we have lived before, and not desire to have anything to do with the government, but we give these women to you, and if you can do anything for us afterwards, all right.' So I immediately had the old lady, Mrs. Meeker, and Mrs. Price brought up out of the brush. I then said that I wished the three women to come together that night, Miss Josephine and the other children having been kept in another part of the camp, and that they should start the first thing in the morning." [97]

For the women and children, their horrific ordeal as Indian captives was finally over. It had been twenty-three agonizing days. Adams personally saw to their safety, helping them into the tent he erected, which had been given to Adams by Chipeta just for this purpose. After the women had settled in, Adams began asking them questions regarding their treatment during captivity. Unfortunately, Douglas and two of his men were also present. Adams later detailed the conversations in his narrative:

"I asked Miss Meeker the question, 'Do you know who of these Indians killed your father and the other employes?' [sic] She answered No, she could not tell. I then asked her how the Indians had treated her. She said, 'Well better than I had expected.' I asked her whether they had offered any indignities to her person. She made the off-hand remark, 'Oh, no, Mr. Adams, nothing of that kind.' Then later on Mrs. Meeker asked me whether their release would make peace with the government for the Indians. I said, 'No.' Mrs. Meeker was very willing to talk of who had abused her, but Chief Douglas and other chiefs stood around *her so close, that with her I could not possibly speak about the murders, because if they had thought that I was making an investigation there I considered my life and the others in danger too. But I got Mrs. Price, the other captive, accidentally alone, and I asked her the question whether any indignities had been offered to her. She said, 'No.' I thereupon wrote the dispatch to the Secretary that the women had been given up, and no indignities had been offered them."* [98]

Many writers have stated that Arvilla Meeker was "weak-minded," or "unstable," and that her recollections of her horrific ordeal could not be relied upon as "accurate." Due to the circumstances of this conversation with General Adams, and the fact that Douglas and his men were within earshot of the conversation, it is perfectly understandable why Mrs. Meeker had little to say at the time. Further, given what the sixty-year-old injured woman had endured over the past twenty-three days, not to mention dealing with the anguish of her murdered husband, it is a testament to her strength that she even survived the ordeal.

True to his word, the following morning, General Adams gathered the women and children and helped them prepare to leave the Indian camp. Josephine Meeker later recounted the exit:

"Next morning we left for Uncompahgre to Chief Ouray's house on the Uncompahgre River near Los Pinos. We rode on ponies forty miles the first three days and reached Captain Cline's wagons on a small tributary of the Grand. [River] Here we took the buck-board wagon and traveled next day to the Gunnison River and the next and last day of fear we traveled forty-five miles and reached the house of good Chief Ouray about sundown. Here Inspector Pollock and my brother Ralph met me, and I was happy enough. Chief Ouray and his noble wife did everything possible to make us comfortable. We found carpets on the floor and curtains on the windows, lamps on the tables and stoves in the rooms, with fires burning. We were given a whole house, and after supper we went to bed without much fear, though mother was haunted by the terrors she had passed through. Next morning we breakfasted with Mrs. Ouray who shed tears over us as she bade goodbye." [99]

Regarding the kind treatment provided by Ouray and Chipeta, Mrs. Flora Price later said:

"We were well treated at Ouray's house. It had Brussels carpets, window curtains, good beds. We were received as old and long lost friends.

Mrs. Ouray wept for our hardships and her motherly face, dusky but beautiful with sweetness and compassion, was wet with tears. We left her crying."[100]

Ralph Meeker, the oldest child of the Meeker family, arrived from Greeley to escort his mother and younger sister back to the Meeker family home on the plains. Before they left the area, Meeker made arrangements with the employees at his father's former agency to have the body of Nathaniel C. Meeker disinterred and shipped to Greeley for final burial.[101] General Adams also made the trip east with the Meeker family.

Meanwhile, the government worked quickly to form a commission to investigate what was now being called the "Meeker Massacre." The purpose was to determine who among the Ute leaders at the White River agency were responsible for the death and destruction and bring them to justice. The Committee on Indian Affairs, headed by General Edward Hatch, also hoped to interview the former hostages as to what they might know of the perpetrators.

As it would not be possible for the commission to interview Arvilla Meeker or her daughter Josephine, General Adams conducted the interview from the comfort of the parlor in the Meeker home in Greeley. On November 4, 1879, Adams began his interview process with Josephine. After dutifully swearing to tell the truth, the interrogation began:

Adams: "How long did Pah-sone keep you?"

Josephine: "All the time."

Adams: "Did he at any time feel willing to let you go back?"

Josephine: "Well, they often told me they maybe we would go to Uncompahgre and see a white man. 'Maybe so go; maybe so no go,' he did not know."

Adams: "Did Pah-sone treat you well while you were with him?"

Josephine: "Well, I do not know. No better than what I expected when I was first captured, because I knew the Utes and know their natures pretty well."

Adams: "This of course is an official investigation and I must get all the facts. It is not to be published in the newspapers or anything of that kind. I wish to hear the full truth in regard to the matter. Just consider yourself on the witness stand. It is a matter of life and death with some of those Utes. The government will punish them if guilty and we must know the truth."

Josephine: "Of course we were insulted a good many times; we expected to be."

Adams: "What do you mean by insult, and what did it consist of?"

Josephine: "Of outrageous treatment at night."

Adams: "Am I to understand that they outraged you several times at night?"

Josephine: "Yes, sir."

Adams: "Forced you against your will?"

Josephine: "Yes, sir."

Adams: "Did they threaten to kill you if you did not comply?"

Josephine: "He did not threaten to kill - Pah-sone did not - only on one occasion. I asked him if he wanted to kill me. He said, 'Yes.' I said, 'Get up and shoot me, and let me alone.' He turned over and did not say anything more that night."

Adams: "He was the one who did it first?"

Josephine: "Yes, sir."

Adams: "How long after the capture?"

Josephine: "The same night - Monday. Of course they were drunk, and we dared not refuse them to any great extent. A good many times I pushed him off, and made a fuss, and raised a difficulty."

Adams: "Did any others do the same thing?"

Josephine: "No sir, not to me. He took me as his squaw, and of course the rest dared not come around."

Adams: "Did he say anything when he finally released you?"

Josephine: "The day you came?"

Adams: "Yes. Did he say that you must not tell?"

Josephine: "He asked me the day before what I was going to tell about the Utes. He said, 'You go back and tell them that they are no good.' I said no."

Adams: "Have you told this to anybody besides your mother?"

Josephine: "Yes sir; Mr. Pollock interviewed us. And I believe, also Dr. Avery of Denver. She is a lady physician in Denver; of course we don't want the newspapers to get ahold of it."

Adams: "Did you tell Mrs. Avery that she must not make it known?"

Josephine: "She will not. But the Indians delight in telling such things. It is generally talked around at the camp. You know how low they are."

Adams: "They kept it from me very strictly."

Josephine: "Of course they would not tell you."

Adams: "Did they not seem to think it was very wrong?"

Josephine: "No, they thought it was a pretty good thing to have a white squaw. Pah-sone's squaw told me I must not make a fuss about it; it was pretty good. I do not think she dared to do anything. I think she felt sorry for me, but she did not dare do anything for me."

Adams: "Did Douglas ever offer you any insult?"

Josephine: "No, he did not to me, but he did on one occasion to my mother. I think that is what made a good deal of the trouble - his squaws were jealous; they did not want her there."

Adams: "Where did they take you to camp that first night?"

Josephine: "About twelve miles. It took us until one or two o'clock to get in, but we stopped on the way."

Adams: "You remarked once or twice about the Indians having whiskey?"

Josephine: "Yes, sir."

Adams: "Where did they get it?"

Josephine: "They must have bought it at the stores, some of them. There are a good many stores at the agency - all of them outside - trading stores on the Bear and Snake Rivers. I think that it did not come from the medicine supplies, because that comes in these round bottles and is labeled."

Adams: "Did you see it?"

Josephine: "It was in flat whiskey flats."

Adams: "Did they have several bottles?"

Josephine: "What I saw - the bottle was about half full. They took two or three drinks and passed it around while taking me to the river. Douglas had whiskey. Mother said a good many of them had. I smelt their breath."

Adams: "Did you ever see your father's clothes in anybody's possession?"

MISS JOSEPHINE MEEKER, PHOTOGRAPHED BY BATES & NYE.

Josephine Meeker was held hostage by the Utes. Following her release, she worked tirelessly for the Indian plight. *DPL*

Josephine: "One Indian had father's shoes on; I forget what his name was; I know him well enough."

Adams: "Did you see his coat?"

Josephine: "No, but I saw his pants; I do not know who had them."

Adams: " Did you hear them say who killed your father?"

Josephine: "No, sir."

Adams: "Did you hear any one say who killed any of the other men?"

Josephine: "No, I do not think any one knew who killed them,"[102]

General Adams then interviewed the widowed Mrs. Arvilla Meeker, still recuperating from her ordeal and bullet wound she received to her leg. Her daughters, Rozene and Mary, stayed close to their mother. Adams began his questioning of Mrs. Meeker by asking her what happened after the attempted escape when she was shot. Mrs. Meeker provided the following account:

"In the first place I asked Douglas if I could go and get [the] Spirit Book. They would not let either of the others go back. The house was burning and this Indian with me did not want to go in. All the time I was in the building, he kept saying, "Hurry, hurry; got to go a great ways tonight.' I got my shawl, blankets, and hat that I have worn since. I thought of getting some other things, but knew it would not do. There was thirty dollars there; I counted it; some of it was silver. I handed it to this Indian and he took it to Douglas. Douglas asked me many times where the agent was, and kinda laughed. His breath smelt strongly of whiskey. Douglas as he rode along sang what seemed to be an obscene song in slow measure. When he finished he asked how I liked it. My limb ached so terribly that I could scarcely sit on the horse. Douglas held it awhile; then he strapped it in a kind of sling to his saddle. As we rode, a villainous looking Indian trotted alongside and slapped me on the shoulder, and asked if I would like to be his squaw, and he made indecent proposals. Douglas listened and laughed. We rode four or five mile miles and then stopped. It was in a little canyon, with rocks high all around except where we went in. They had us dismount and lay down, and they put a gun to Josie's head. As I lay on the ground not knowing when I should be butchered, I thought

of my daughter who was not far away, and wondered if she had already been slaughtered. Suddenly I heard Douglas' voice standing close by me, with the muzzle of his gun pointed directly at my face. I involuntarily cried out and said, 'Oh!' Josie heard me, and her voice came out of the night, saying, 'Don't be afraid, Mama, I'm all right.' Douglas lowered his gun, raised it again, and took aim. I said nothing and he walked away. An Indian standing nearby said, 'Douglas no hurt you. He only playing soldier.' They asked Josephine if she was afraid, and she said, 'No.' She thought the Indians were not pleased because Douglas failed to frighten her. They all laughed at him. Then they saddled their horses, and Pah-sone led Josie's horse to her and knelt down on his hands and knees for her to mount from his back. We then moved out to Douglas' camp, I think about ten or twenty miles. We got in a little after midnight." [103]

Reporters from across the country were covering the investigative proceedings and filing daily reports. An example of the reporting on the east coast is the October 25, 1879, issue of *Harpers Weekly* which printed the following article regarding the White River events: "Captain Jack had made a trip to the agency in Denver to complain that Meeker was causing trouble and was unfit as agent. He and Johnson had served as scouts for the army. They had seen troops sent against Indians before and realized the Indians would come out the losers. Major Thomas T. Thornburgh was in command of the troops sent to aid Agent Meeker at the White River Agency. He agreed to halt his troops outside the reservation, but for some unknown reason pushed on and was ambushed at Milk Creek, where he was killed in the first outburst of firing. The troops were held trapped for two days. Old Chief Douglas was held responsible for the attack on the soldiers and the killing of Meeker and his employees at the agency. Antelope, Chief Ouray's runner, was sent to the White River Utes with a message from Ouray advising them to release the captives. Former agent friend of the Utes Charles Adams traveled to the White River Camp, where he succeeded in bargaining for the captive's release."

The government investigative committee convened at the Los Pinos Indian Agency on November 12. General Hatch was able to review the sworn affidavits Adams collected from both Mrs. Arvilla Meeker and her daughter, Josephine. General Hatch was also privy to the sworn testimony of Mrs. Flora Ellen Price:

"Mr. Price, Thompson, and Frank Dresser were working on the new building. After talking with us, Douglas went out and laughed and

talked with the men. Then he left the boys, and started down to his camp. I went out after May, and saw twenty or twenty-five Indians coming up with their guns to meet Douglas, then all came together; Pow-vitz, Douglas, Ebenezer and Antelope. Ebenezer said something to me in Ute as I went into the house with my girl, and I did not understand. He went to hitch up his horse, and then they fired at the men in the building. An Indian was about ten feet from me when he fired at Price, Frank, and Thompson. He crippled Frank in the leg. I ran in the house, picked up the baby, went to my bedroom, and Frank Dresser came in. I gave him a gun. Just as we got to my bedroom door both windows were smashed in. Dresser shot through the window and hit Johnson's brother. We ran to Josie's bedroom and hid under the beds, but Josie said, 'It is not safe here; let's go to the milk house,' and so we did. The shooting kept up for awhile. We did not want to look out. We looked out to the north. The Indians were busy taking the blankets, shirts, and everything else they could. I said, 'Let's try to escape to the north, in the sage-brush.' [sic] Frank said, 'Let's go now, while they are so busy,' and so we went. After I left the river with the Uncompahgre Ute, he riding on the horse behind me, he pulled out a gold watch which I recognized as belonging to Mr. Post. He put the guard over my head and strung it around my neck, saying it was my watch. When we arrived at camp that night, a squaw came and took my little boy from the horse, and cried over him like a child. I sat down in Pah-sone's camp. I wasn't at all hungry, and when they offered me coffee, cold meat and bread, I could not eat. After awhile the squaw got over her weeping, when they talked and laughed. All I could understand was when they related the soldier's names and counted what number of men they had killed at the agency. They said they had killed nine. They spread some blankets for me to lie on, but I could not sleep. The moon shone very brightly, and everything looked ghastly." [104]

As General Hatch's investigation continued, several Ute leaders in attendance felt that the government interpreter was not being fair in the translation of the Ute rebuttals to the claims offered through the testimonials of the three female former captives. Chief among those Utes upset with the proceedings was Ouray. Although quite ill, Ouray felt the need to attend the government hearing and traveled to the Los Pinos Indian Agency. He voiced his objection to the testimony of the three women against his men, as this was contrary to Ute beliefs.

Ouray had also been grieving over the loss of his nephew and an uncle during the time of the battle at Milk River. Ouray had been told that family members were killed before the fighting started.

However, military reports suggested that the two men died during the fighting. Ouray chose to rely on his own intelligence reports and felt that his relatives were killed without provocation. Ouray believed that the Utes could not be tried fairly in this manner.[105]

Perhaps due to his ailing health, his grief over the death of his relatives, or the frustration of the government proceedings, Ouray had had enough. On November 16, four day into the government investigation, Ouray took the floor. In a speech fraught with frustration and despair, Ouray said:

Major Thomas T. Thornburgh led his command during the Milk Creek battle. *DPL*

"I do not want to be chief. I grow old am tottering. Let some young man with the fire of youth in his veins take my place. I have my farm which I would rather cultivate and watch the seed planted by me grow up to maturity than to be head chief. They all come to me with their troubles. I know everything and have all the burdens to bear. Washington no want me to give up my position, wants me to stay and govern Utes. I want only to be known as Ouray, the friend of the white man." [106]

Following Ouray's passionate speech, General Hatch adjourned the proceedings for the day. Reconvening the following morning, Hatch asked Ouray if he stood by his statement made the previous days. Ouray responded, and the following exchange between the two men occurred:

Ouray: "I cannot do more than I have at present. The Indians will not testify any more. If you give me time, say two or three months, I can find out the guilty ones and punish them."

Hatch: "If we grant you this time, will you accompany us, in the meantime, to Rawlins to hear the evidence of the officers and soldiers?"

Ouray: "No, I will go to Washington, but no where else."

Hatch: "Do you mean you wish to go to Washington to settle these difficulties?"

Ouray: "Yes. I want to take other chiefs and go to Washington to talk over this matter. I know the Indians will not say anything here, but believe they will speak the truth in Washington."

Hatch: "How many chiefs do you want to go to Washington?"

Ouray: "I think eight of the principal chiefs will be enough." [107]

At the conclusion of this exchange between Ouray and Hatch, the commission proceedings ended for the day. Later that evening, General Hatch sent a telegram to Secretary of the Interior Carl Schurz, explaining Ouray's position and requested to reconvene the commission's work in Washington. While awaiting a response from Schurz, Hatch continued taking testimony from other witnesses including soldiers involved in the battle at Milk Creek. Whether it was due to his illness, or more likely his refusal to participate in the government proceedings unless they were held in Washington, Ouray was not present for any further testimony.[108]

Hatch finally received a telegram from Schurz on November 20. The Interior Department had agreed to General Hatch's request to reconvene in the nation's capital, with the Ute leaders present. In the meantime, General Hatch proceeded with the commission's work at the Los Pinos Indian Agency. On December 7, with a list of twelve Ute suspects gleaned from the testimony of the three former captives, General Hatch, with the assistance of General Charles Adams, ordered Ouray to bring the twelve accused Utes to the agency at Los Pinos for trial. Hatch further told Ouray that if he refused, Hatch would order his soldiers onto the Ute land and arrest the accused men.

David Day's *Solid Muldoon*, the leading newspaper of Ouray, Colorado, the San Juan mining town named for the Ute chief, had a reporter at the Los Pinos proceedings. The following day, the paper reported the events after General Hatch delivered his ultimatum:

> "A death sentence fell upon everything. Nothing was said and no one moved for a few minutes. Then Colorow lighted a long pipe and each Indian present drew his knife and laid it on his knee. Each Indian present dropped his hand down to his waist and laid it upon his knife or revolver. Each white man did the same, and the two parties remained in this position, each urging the glittering gage of battle and each waiting an aggressive movement on the part of the other. Twenty-five Indians to six whites were terrible odds and the fifteen soldiers in the next room could not have gotten into the room in time to rescue the endangered commission. Finally Ouray spoke: 'We can not deliver up to you these Indians unless they are tried in Washington. They must not be tried in Colorado. The Colorado people are all our enemies, and to give our men up to be tried in this state would be as if we gave them up, knowing that they would be hung instantly. We will bring these men here for you to see, and those whom you decide to be guilty shall be taken to Washington, and the President shall determine their guilt or innocence. Douglas will have go. None of us deny that he was engaged in the White River troubles, and you shall decide who else is to go. Upon this condition and no others will we deliver these Indians. You three (pointing to Hatch, Adams and [Gustavus] Valois, the legal advisor,) all are my enemies. I am one against three. You hate me. You are residents of Colorado and New Mexico and a French devil (alluding to Valois,) I have not one friend among you. You will not give me justice, and that is why I want to go to Washington where I will, at least have one friend.'"

Ouray also spoke that day to the reporter for the *Ouray Times*, which printed his statement the same day as the remarks were printed in the rival newspaper:

> "The Utes are not to blame for this. I told you when we were hunting that I was having trouble in restraining my young men. White prospectors and hunters came on the reservation and shot the Utes when they saw them. You know yourselves that this happened. My uncle and my nephew were killed by the soldiers while they were hunting. Meeker made the Utes work for his own glory and refused to feed them when they did not work as he wanted them to work. He had no right to do that. The Government in our treaty said nothing about work, but agreed to give us these lands and to give us supplies, blankets and food. They have violated that treaty and my men were angry. They heard that Meeker had sent for soldiers to punish them for not working and coming to church, they always remember what Chivington did to the Cheyennes, and they tried to prevent the soldiers from getting to the agency and killing them. Then

they went crazy and killed Meeker and the other white men, and took the women and the children. They should not have done that."

Ouray and his ten chosen Utes left for Washington, on January 16, 1880. Among those Ouray chose to include were Buckskin Charlie, Ignacio, Severo, Sowerwich, and his trusted advisor Shavano to accompany him on the trip to Washington. In an unusual move, given Ute tradition, Ouray allowed his wife, Chipeta, to accompany him to the nation's capital city. Curiously, the two principal Utes believed responsible for both the Milk Creek battle and the Meeker massacre, Jack and Douglas, both agreed to the trip. Also included in the Ute entourage was Otto Mears, who served as Ouray's trusted interpreter. General Charles Adams went along, providing military protection.

As the train carrying the Ute entourage made various stops along the eastward journey, the Utes were greeted with verbal insults and threatened. Shortly after their arrival in Washington. Ouray and the Ute delegation met with Secretary of the Interior Carl Schurz. When Schurz realized that the Utes accused of the crimes in question were not present, he sent a directive, dated January 23, 1880, to General Charles Adams:

"Sir, You are to proceed Saturday Jan. 24 from Washington to Los Pinos, taking with you Jack, Sowawick of the White River Utes, and Wash of the Uncompahgre Utes and two Indian boys who accompanied Ouray to Washington and are not to return. You will then return to Washington together with Jack, Sowawick and Wash, who have promised to return with you, and other chiefs whose presence here may be desirable for the purpose of further conference and negotiation. You are authorized to employ an interpreter to be compensated at the rate of $5 per diem and necessary traveling expenses." [109]

Following this meeting with Secretary Schurz, Ouray, along with the other Utes present in Washington, were summoned to appear before a Congressional committee. The hearings started with the testimonies of soldiers from the Milk Creek battle, and the testimonies of the three former captive women, Mrs. Arvilla Meeker, her daughter Josephine, and Mrs. Flora Ellen Price. Ouray and the other Utes present never spoke. Secretary Schurz had a private conversation with Ouray shortly before he left Washington. Schurz later reflected on that visit, giving insight to Ouray's lack of participation during the Congressional hearings.

> "In conversation of Ouray's talk was quite different from that of the ordinary Indian chief. He spoke like a man of a high order of intelligence and of larger views who had risen above the prejudices and aversions of his race. He had evidently pondered much over the condition and future of the Indians of North America and expressed his mature conclusions with the simple eloquence of a statesman. He comprehended perfectly the utter hopelessness of the struggle of the Indians against the progress of civilization. He saw clearly that nothing was left to them but to accommodate themselves to civilized ways or perish. He admitted that it was very hard to make his people understand this; that so long as they did not fully appreciate it, they should, as much as possible, be kept out of harm's way; that it was the duty of influential chiefs to cooperate with the government to make the transition as little dangerous and painful as possible; that he, therefore, recognized the necessity of removing the Utes from Colorado, hard as the parting from their old haunts might be, and that he depended on me to bring about that removal under conditions favorable to his people. Ouray was by far the brightest Indian I have ever met." [110]

In effect, the great Ute leader Ouray had surrendered his people to the will of the United States government. Perhaps he knew there was nothing that could be done. It was a forgone conclusion in the eyes of many Washington officials, including those with the Indian Commission under General Hatch, as well as several members of the congressional committees.

Secretary of the Interior Schurz refused to talk to members of the press regarding the governmental proceedings concerning the Colorado Utes. In the January 30, 1880, issue of the *Washington Post*, an editorial suggesting that Schurz' actions were representative of "gagging and obstructing the press." The editor also wrote:

> "There is a strong disposition, in some quarters, to hold a whole tribe responsible for the crimes of a few of its members. It would be as reasonable and humane to call for the hanging of all citizens of Washington because murders and brutal outrages on women have been perpetuated here and the authors of these crimes have not been given up to justice."

Back in Colorado, the sentiment of many in the press was quite the opposite of the eastern journalists. David Day, editor of the *Solid Muldoon*, wrote his own editorial, published the same day as the *Washington Post's* editorial; January 30, 1880:

"The Utes are highly pleased with Washington. Well, we are perfectly willing they should stay there."

A few weeks later, it was announced in the Washington press that General Adams was successful in finding the accused Utes. The *Washington Post* broke the news under the headline, "Jack Keeps His Word," in the February 18, 1880, issue. The article read:

"Promptly at the expiration of ten days as promised, Jack rode up to the agency with three of the twelve prisoners demanded by the Government, viz: Chief Douglas, Jim Johnson, and Thomas. Jack is very reticent and declines to say how or in what manner the capture was effected. Sowawick returned several hours later but brought no prisoners, and Jack assured Gen. Adams that owing to the depth of the snow on the mountains and the scattered location of the camps, he would take at least three weeks to capture the remaining nine. Johnson sent his regrets giving as a reason that he was a medicine man and had a very sick patient whom he could not leave. Jack insists that the women were mistaken in the names of certain Indians, who, they testified, were present at the time of the outbreak. Douglas is ill at ease and extremely nervous, and says but little. Military preparations for the protection of the prisoners are complete. Gen. Adams will leave tomorrow with his prisoners for Washington." [111]

General Adams and his armed men guarded the Ute prisoners as best they could. However, during a stop at Fort Leavenworth, Kansas, Douglas fought back against agitators who were throwing rocks and sticks at the Utes. Military personnel arrested Douglas and took him to Fort Leavenworth. Incredibly, the military held Douglas at the fort for nearly a year, rather than have the accused Ute face the government interrogators in Washington. With the arrival of two of the accused Utes, the government's work continued. The accused were allowed to testify, although the testimony largely fell on deaf ears. Despite the reasons the accused offered for their actions on that fateful day of September 29, 1879, an attack occurred under their direction against the United States military. Other members of the Utes, including Douglas, then murdered several men, including Indian agent Nathaniel Cook Meeker and kidnapped three women and two children. In the eyes of the government officials, these facts were indisputable.

With this final testimony, the members of Congress concluded their interviews. Nearly two weeks later, news of the Congressional outcome was leaked to the press. On March 4, 1880, the *Washington Post* broke the story under the headline, "The Ute Matter Settled."

On March 6, the leaders of the Colorado Utes signed the Agreement with the Confederated Bands of Utes. By signing the agreement, the Utes agreed to the following:

> "The said chiefs and headmen of the confederate bands of Utes agree and promise to use their best endeavors with their people to procure their consent to cede to the United States all the territory of the present Ute Reservation in Colorado, except as hereinafter provided for their settlement. The Uncompahgre [Tabeguache] Utes agree to remove to and settle upon agricultural lands on Grand River, near the mouth of the Gunnison River, in Colorado, if a sufficient quantity of agricultural land should be found there, if not then upon such other unoccupied agricultural lands as may be found in that vicinity and in the territory of Utah. The White River Utes agree to remove to and settle upon agricultural lands on the Uintah Reservation in Utah. In consideration of the cession of territory to be made by the said confederate bands of the Ute Nation, the United States, in addition to the annuities and sums for provisions and clothing stipulated and provided for in existing treaties and laws, agrees to set apart and hold, as a perpetual trust for the said Ute Indians, a sum of money, or its equivalent in bonds of the United States, which shall be deemed sufficient to produce the sum of fifty thousand dollars per annum, which sum of fifty thousand dollars distributed per capita to them annually forever." [112]

Again, it was an agreement of empty promises by the government, which opened the door for eventual permanent removal of all Northern Utes from the state of Colorado, as the next provision of the agreement clearly pointed out:

> "Fourth. That as soon as the President of the United States may deem it necessary or expedient, the agencies for the Uncompahgres and Southern Utes be removed to and established at suitable points, to be hereafter selected upon the lands to be set apart, and to aid in the support of the said Utes until such time as they shall be able to support themselves, and that in the mean time the United States Government will establish and maintain schools, in the settlements of the Utes, and make all necessary provisions for the education of their children." [113]

The Ute leaders who signed the epochal agreement were Alhandra, Chavanaux, Galota, Sawawick, Wass, Ignatio of the

Southern Utes, and Ouray of the Tabeguache Utes. [114] It was also stipulated in the agreement that until the perpetrators responsible for both the Meeker massacre and the Milk Creek battle were brought to justice, no annuities or provisions would be available to the White River Utes. It was further stipulated that the land the Utes were leaving would be sold to the settlers and miners; the money going to pay for the provisions allocated in the agreement.

Before the Agreement with the Confederated Bands of Utes could be ratified by Congress, three-fourths of the Ute Nation had to agree and sign the document. On March 22, 1880, the Ute delegation, led by Ouray, left Washington, returning to their people in Colorado to gain their support.

David Day of the *Solid Muldoon*, was not happy with this news. In an editorial dated May 7, 1880, Day wrote:

> *"For seven months have we been hemmed in by a few hundred murderous and treacherous Utes. For seven long months has Secretary Schurz been dilly-dallying with a tribe of villainous and superstitious Utes, whose only object in life is murder and plunder."*

Nevertheless, the members of Congress continued to hold meetings and hearings, while the United States Senate attempted to do their due diligence by introducing new legislation. Colorado's United States Senator Henry M. Teller, felt the agreement was too liberal toward the Utes. He believed these Indians had violated the previous treaty by the actions at the White River Indian Agency. [115] Teller, therefore, was entirely in favor of the complete removal of the Utes from the state of Colorado. On the other hand, Colorado Senator Nathaniel Hill was more sympathetic to the plight of the Utes. During a verbal exchange between the two on floor of the senate, Senator Hill asked Senator Teller what he thought Ouray's impression of the Uintah land in Utah was. Teller responded, "I doubt whether Ouray can comprehend and understand what is intended." Infuriated by Teller's attitude, Senator Hill stated:

> *"Ouray lived in a house on a farm with eighty acres under cultivation. He has as good an eye for farming land as any man I know and I would trust his judgment as soon as any man I know on good location for farming land. Did Ouray choose this* [Uintah] *land?"* [116]

Senator Teller countered by offering the following argument:

> "I understand that Ouray dictates this legislation to us, that the interests of three hundred thousand people in Colorado are left to this renegade chief. Gentlemen may talk as they choose of his ability and his devotion to the whites; he is an Indian, with an Indian heart and with Indian blood; and he is working for what he thinks is in the interest of his tribe. He knows his people do not want to be civilized; he is looking to keep his government stipend." [117]

While the Colorado senators were vigorously debating the removal of the Utes, General Charles Adams, working on behalf of the United States Department of the Interior, was experiencing a wide range of Ute opposition to their removal from Colorado. Concerned and frustrated over the possibility of rising hostility, General Adams wrote an open letter to Interior Secretary Schurz, which appeared in the May 26, 1880, issue of the *Washington Post*. The letter read in part:

> "The Utes believe the government does not intend to act in good faith toward them, and that they expect to be dispossessed of their reservation without remuneration. They do not understand why a solemn agreement urged upon them, which seemed so urgent and was considered as preventing a war two months ago has not been acted upon."

Indeed this was the view of many of the Utes in Colorado. Even so, Ouray felt obligated to meet with them and do what he could for his people. In the summer of 1880, Ouray, along his wife, Chipeta, made the journey to the Los Pinos Indian Agency. Ouray now found himself explaining to his people why they must leave their land. On July 28, Ouray held a council meeting at the Los Pinos Indian Agency. Otto Mears served as the negotiator for the government, as agreed to by Congress. After much discussion and persuasion, Ouray was able to get thirty-six of the Tabeguache leaders and ten of the White River Utes to sign the ratified agreement.

Mears and a group of government officials, as well as Ouray, Chipeta and her younger brother, John McCook, then left for the Southern Ute Reservation, at Ignacio. The entourage arrived at Ignacio on August 17. [118]

Ouray completed the journey, but not the mission. William Burns, an interpreter at the Southern Ute Indian Agency, visited Ouray in his tipi. It was a short conversation, Ouray laying on blankets spread on the floor, informed Burns he was ill. Burns immediately left in search of a doctor. The agency's physician, Dr. E. F. Smith, accompanied Burns back to Ouray's tipi. Smith found Ouray in great discomfort and after examining the respected Ute leader, he discovered his abdomen was swollen. Dr. Smith diagnosed Ouray's illness as Bright's Disease, an advanced condition of his previously diagnosed kidney ailment, chronic nephritis.

A messenger was immediately dispatched to Animas City, the nearest town, to get another physician for consultation, while another messenger was sent to summon the services of Ouray's personal physician, Dr. John Lacey, who by this time was working for the Indian agency. In the meantime, as Ouray's condition grew worse, newspaper reporters sent to cover the events of the potential Ute agreement, quickly learned of Ouray's ill health. A reporter for the *Denver Times* sent the following report, which appeared in the August 20, 1880, issue:

"Indian runners from the Southern Ute agency arrived this morning, and report Chief Ouray dangerously ill and not expected to live. They came with a message from Ouray to Dr. Lacey, in whom he has the utmost confidence, requesting him to come immediate. The Indians will furnish relays of horses, and the doctor intends to make a distance of one hundred and twenty miles in fifteen hours. Ouray went to that point to assist the commission in prevailing upon the Utes to sign the treaty: if Ouray dies, the treaty will never be signed by the White River Utes."

The following day the *Denver Times* printed a dispatch sent by S. B. Beaumont:

"When I left the Southern Ute agency on the 20th there was grave apprehension on the part of the Commissioners that success in concluding the treaty depended largely on Ouray's recovery, and his illness was regarded with serious alarm. My knowledge of the Southern Utes induces me to believe that they will not be influenced to decline the treaty by the death of the Uncompahgre Chief, and that if any serious difficulty arises it will come from the White River bands."

As the agency awaited the arrival of the doctors, Ute subchiefs, including Ignacio and Buckskin Charlie, brought in the Ute medicine men. Unfortunately, not even the Utes medicine was able to relieve Ouray's condition. Chipeta did what she could for her husband and sang traditional Ute songs to sooth him.

During one of his many visits to Ouray's tipi, Buckskin Charlie had a long conversation with the dying Ute chief. Ouray, knowing he was about to enter the spirit world, asked Buckskin Charlie to succeed him as the leader of the Ute nation. A humbled Buckskin Charlie agreed and after a council with other sub-chiefs, the transfer of leadership was approved, should Ouray indeed die.

When Dr. Lacey entered Ouray's tent, he found the ill Ute leader in the care of the tribe's medicine men. Ouray had slipped into an unconscious state. As the medicine men held vigil, Dr. Lacey checked on his patient routinely for the next four days. There was little hope for Ouray. On Monday, August 23, Dr. Hopson, finding no reason to remain, left the agency and returned to Animas City. That same day, the reporter for the *Denver Times* sent a dispatch which was printed in the August 24, 1880 issue:

> *"Ouray is at the Southern Ute agency sick with Bright's Disease and will probably die before morning. It is likely his death will affect the treaty with the Southern Utes. No treaty has been signed yet."*

At mid-morning on Tuesday, August 24, a runner from Ouray's camp arrived at the agency house. Dr. Lacey was summoned to Ouray's tipi. As the doctor approached, a Ute sub-chief stopped Lacey from entering. Ouray, the respected Ute leader, was dead.[119] Chipeta, wrought with grief, let out an ear-piercing mourning cry that alerted the camp that their leader was dead.

The reporters at the Southern Ute Indian Agency all sent dispatches to their editors. The news of Ouray's death was on the front page of newspapers across the state. The *Denver Tribune* ran the following in the August 25, 1880, issue:

> *"In the death of Ouray, one of the historical characters passes away. He has figured for many years as the greatest Indian of his time, and during his life has figured quite prominently. Ouray is in many respects a remarkable Indian - pure instincts and keen perception. A friend to the white man and protector to the Indians."*

Within twenty-four hours, the entire country learned of Ouray's passing. A correspondent with *Frank Leslie's Illustrated Newspaper*, sent a report to his editor. It was printed in the August 25, issue:

> *"Special from Los Pinos Agency, Colorado August 25, 1880 The death of Ouray 24th was a blow from which the Ute Nation will never recover.*

The greatest Indian that ever lived is dead. And there is no one to fill his place. The Utes seem to realize they have suffered an irreparable loss."

In the same issue of *Frank Leslie's Illustrated Newspaper* appeared another dispatch:

"Special from Southern Ute Agency August 25, 1880 As I telegraphed yesterday, Ouray, the great chief of the Utes died. In one hour they had wrapped him in blankets, tied him on one of his ponies, which was led by an Indian on horseback and followed by Chipeta and four other Indians. The procession moved quietly down the Pine River, to some secret spot, unknown, where he was buried with all his belongings and five horses were sacrificed near his grave. It is well that Ouray died away from his comfortable home in the Uncompahgre valley, which was well furnished, as all his articles would have been burned and sacrificed to this strange superstition of the race. The friend of the white man and the protector of the Indian, ever boldly asserting the rights of his tribe and as continually doing all his power to create favor for the whites with the Indians. He dies as he as lived, in the mutual service of the Government and the Indians."

The unnamed Indians referred to in participating in the burial of Ouray included Chipeta's brother John McCook, Buckskin Charlie, Colorow, and Naneese. Chipeta was also among the burial group. [120] Despite her enormous grief, Chipeta began preparing Ouray's body for the journey to the Spirit World. With the assistance of Haseekep, Chipeta's sister-in-law, the women were able to quickly complete the task. In Ute tradition, Chipeta painted her husband's body with red stripes, for protection against possible enemies. White stripes represented the soaring spirit. [121] With this act completed, Ouray's body was then wrapped in new blankets, rolled tight and placed in a buffalo robe, which was tied with rope made of horse hair. Then, Buckskin Charlie, the new leader of the Ute Nation, along with John McCook, placed Ouray's wrapped body on a horse.

As Buckskin Charlie led the horse, followed by McCook, Colorow, and Naneese, Chipeta chanted ancient Ute prayers. The group slowly walked along Pine River to a spot approximately two miles south of Ignacio. On a high ridge, the men placed Ouray's body in a deep rock crevice, and placed rocks atop the crevice to seal the opening.

Meanwhile, as this group tended to Ouray's burial, the

other Utes camped near the Indian agency had moved down river from Ouray's tipi "of death" as was Ute custom. Not long after Chipeta, McCook, Colorow, and Naneese arrived back at the Ute camp, they burned Ouray's tipi, another Ute custom. As the tipi burned, along with all of Ouray's possessions, Chipeta took a knife to her hair, cutting it off; an act of Ute mourning. Then she applied "widow's paint" to her face, a mixture of charcoal and pitch. The widow would not wash her face until the mixture wore off. [122]

The news of Ouray's death quickly became front-page news for newspapers cross the state, and carried throughout the nation. One the many examples is the coverage in the August 25, 1880, issue of the *Denver Times*:

> *"In the death of Ouray, one of the historical characters of Colorado passes away. He has figured for many years as the greatest Indian of his time, and during his life has figured quite as prominently before the country as has any white man in the Rocky Mountains. It is therefore neat and proper that on the occasion of his death, his life should be remembered. The record of his deed is one of simple parts, yet he has proven himself elevated so far above other men of his race and time that his acts stand out in bold relief. Ouray is in many respects - indeed, we may say in all respects - a remarkable Indian; a man of pure instincts, of keen perception, and apparently possessed very proper of ideas of justice and right, the friend of the white man and the protector of the Indian, ever standing up and boldly asserting the rights of his tribe, and as continually doing all in his power to create favor for the white man with the Indians."* [123]

The following morning, McCook, along with his wife Haseekep, escorted Chipeta back to the Los Pinos Indian Agency. From there, they would make the journey to the Uncompahgre River and the adobe home Chipeta had shared with her now deceased husband. As the trio made their way along Otto Mears' road to the agency, they were met by Indian Agent William Berry. Berry offered his condolences to Chipeta, and in a private conversation, aware of the Ute custom of burning the deceased person's home and possessions, made a plea with Chipeta not to do this with her home along the river. Berry very gently explained to Chipeta that the home she had shared with Ouray was a symbol of his hard work in bringing two cultures together. By the end of the conversation, Chipeta graciously agreed with the Indian agent. In traditional Ute custom, Chipeta gave away her husband's possessions. During this daunting task, Chipeta placed the fringed shirt she had made for Ouray, worn on his last trip to Washington, along with his powder horn and his beaded tobacco pouch, which she had also made, in a package and took it to Berry. She asked the Indian agent to send it to the Secretary of the Interior Carl Schurz. Berry included a letter dictated by Chipeta with the package. Years later, Schurz recalled the gift and Chipeta's letter:

> *"I received from a government agent on the Ute Indian reservation a letter from Ouray's widow Chipeta. In it, she told me that I had done much to save Ouray's people from disaster and was, therefore, their best friend. She wished to give me a memory of her husband as a present - the things he most valued. A few weeks later I received a box accompanied by a letter from Chipeta giving me the message: If I accepted the present, to keep it while I lived and for my children, it would be regarded by Chipeta and her people as proof of true friendship on my part, and they would esteem that friendship very highly. But if I made a present in return it would be understood by them as signifying that I did not value their friendship much and simply wished to get rid of an obligation and be quit with them."* [124]

After a respectable amount of time had passed following Ouray's death, the Commission reconvened at Ignacio. When the leaders of the Southern Utes still refused to sign the agreement, Otto Mears, on behalf of the government, held several private meetings with William H. Berry, the Southern Ute Indian agent. In turn, Berry met with the Ute leaders, including Buckskin Charlie, Ignacio, White Eye and Tapuch. The leaders stood firm in their resolve not to give up their land. They also wanted the release of Douglas, still held at Fort Leavenworth. Mears sent a telegram to Washington, explaining the stalemate. Congress had stipulated that the ratified agreement had to be signed by the Ute leaders by October 15, 1880, or the document would become null and void. In an effort to avert this from happening, not to mention losing the opportunity to gain the coveted Ute land, members of Congress quickly reconvened the commission. In an unusually short amount of time, given government proceedings, Congress provided a solution. Because the Southern Utes, originally led by Ouray, refused to sign the agreement, Congress simply removed that article from the original document. Whether it was actually due to the lack of support from the Southern Ute leaders, or the fact that the Southern Ute reservation land was so remote as to be deemed useless to the government, is up for speculation. Nevertheless, the end result was that the 1880 Agreement with the Confederated Bands of Utes was signed by three-fourths of the Northern Ute Nation, before the Congressional deadline. The ratification of the agreement, signed on September 25, read as follows:

> *"We the undersigned, members of the commission appointed in pursuance of an act of Congress, entitled 'An act to accept and ratify the agreement submitted by the confederated bands of Ute Indians in Colorado for the sale of their reservation in said State, and for other purposes, and to make the necessary appropriations for carrying out the same,' do hereby certify that said act of Congress and the agreement therein referred to, and the foregoing instrument of ratification were read, submitted, and fully explained to the Uncompahgre Ute Indians and the White River Ute Indians, of the state of Colorado, at Los Pinos Indian Agency, in said State, by all members of said commission. That several persons whose names are attached to the foregoing instrument of ratification are adult males of the confederated bands of the Ute tribe of Indians in the State of Colorado, and that they respectively signed the same, as shown by the several certificates thereto attached, after said acts of Congress, agreement, and instrument of ratification had been fully read and explained to them as aforesaid, and after having been fully interpreted to them by the persons whose names are attached to and who signed the foregoing certificates as interpreters. And that the said instrument of ratification is signed and executed by three-fourths, and more, of the adult males of the confederated bands of the Ute tribe of Indians, in the State of Colorado. In witness whereof we have hereunto set our hands this 25th day of September, A. D. 1880, at Alamosa, State of Colorado. Geo. W. Manypenny John J. Russell Otto Mears, commissioners."* [125]

The end: result was, in essence, what the government wanted all along the removal of the Utes from the state of Colorado. Curiously, the stipulation in the original agreement regarding no annuities or provisions for those responsible for both the Meeker massacre and the Milk Creek battle was not included in the ratification of the final version of the 1880 Agreement with the Confederated Bands of Utes. Therefore, Jack, implicated before Congress in eyewitness testimony, as the leader of the attack on the soldiers at Milk Creek, was never brought forth by the leaders of the Ute Nation. Nor was Douglas, identified through the testimony of the three captive woman that he was the leader in the Meeker Massacre, and responsible for the abduction of the women and children. The reports from those sitting on the government's investigative committee, submitted to General Edward Hatch and included in the official Congressional record, bore out the aforesaid line of reasoning:

> *"The reports of the agents among the Ute Indians, made from year to year since our first treaty relations with them, bear evidence of their orderly disposition and desire to avoid complications and conflicts with the white people. Some of them, it is true, committed deeds of violence deeply to be deplored. In such cases, and they are but few, a careful investigation of surrounding circumstances will show that the Indians were inspired by events that aroused their savage passions and them to commit the crimes referred to. In our intercourse with them for several months during the past summer and fall we can without hesitation confirm all that their agents have said in relation to their disposition and general good conduct."* [126]

George Washington Manypenny, one of the signers of the agreement, was of the firm belief that there should be allotments of the Indian lands and advocated for the creation of the Department of Indian Affairs, which later became a reality. In the meantime, the government officials with the Department of the Interior had already begun their work for the eventual removal of the Ute bands from the state of Colorado before the agreement was even signed. Captain James Parker, with Colorado's Fourth Cavalry, later wrote of his personal experience:

> *"In March, 1880, I was ordered to join Mackenzie's command at Fort Garland. We learned about this time that the State of Colorado, desiring to develop its western territory and impatient at the outrages continually being committed on miners, teamsters, and demanded of the general Government that all the Utes should be removed into Utah, to the Uintah Reservation of 270 square miles. The Indians fiercely resented the demands of the Commission, and the whole summer of 1880 was absorbed in protracted negotiations; the troops, cavalry and infantry, under Mackenzie, standing idly by. These parlayings were conducted by the Interior Department; Mackenzie under the War Department, having no part in them. They were finally apparently crowned with success. The Indians, in exchange for a certain sum of money, agreed to move to Utah the following summer. As the spring of 1881 advanced we heard rumors of threatened hostilities on the part of the Utes. Having signed the treaty to evacuate, they now claimed that they were deceived and did*

not understand the treaty. Accordingly, on May 9th, the [government] *Commission appeared, and began to parley. The negotiations dragged on all summer without success. Finally in September the commission found that their efforts were useless, and notified the Government to that effect. The matter was turned over to the War Department to settle, and Mackenzie was ordered to take such steps as were in his opinion necessary and proper. Upon receipt of the telegram from Washington, the force of troops present, about ten companies of infantry and cavalry was ordered to stand equipped with two hundred rounds of ammunition per man and three day's cooking rations. This done, Mackenzie sent word to the chiefs to come in for a conference. It took place the following morning. Mackenzie informed the chiefs that the matter had been turned over to him for settlement; they had promised to move to Utah, and he wished to know whether or not they were going. The lead chief commenced an oration in which he denounced the whites for wanting to deprive the Indians of their land, and was proceeding to more violent expressions when Mackenzie, with his hat in his hand, stood up. 'It is not necessary for me to stay here any longer,' he said. 'You can settle this matter by discussion among yourselves. All I want to know is whether you will go or not. If you will not go of your own accord, I will make you go. After a debate lasting several hours they sent for Mackenzie. They proposed a compromise. They said they had concluded they must go, but first they wished to go back to their camp and talk with their old men. "No," said Mackenzie. 'If you have not moved by nine o'clock tomorrow morning, I will be at your camp and make you move.' The next morning, shortly after sunrise, we saw a thrilling and pitiful sight. The whole Ute nation on horseback and on foot was streaming by. As they passed our camps their gait broke into a run. Sheep were abandoned, blankets and personal possessions strewn along the road, women and children were loudly wailing. It was inevitable that they should move, and better then, than after a fruitless and bloody struggle. They should think, too, that the land was lost beyond recovery. And so as we march behind the Indians, pushing them out, Mackenzie sent word to all the surrounding whites, who hurried after us, taking up the land. Our task at the mouth of the Uncompahgre River was to hold back the civilians. They followed us closely, taking up 'locating' the Indian land thrown open for settlement. For obvious reasons it was not desirable to let these civilians come in contact with the Indians; thus we were holding a crowd of these people on the south side of the Gunnison until the Indians had passed Kahnah Creek, thirteen miles distant. As we pushed the Indians onward, we permitted the whites to follow, and in three days the rich lands of the Uncompahgre were all occupied, towns were being laid out and lots being sold at high prices. With its rich soil and wonderful opportunities for irrigation, the Uncompahgre Valley - before a desert - soon became the garden spot of Colorado, covered with fruitful fields and orchards."* [127]

David Day, who had been advocating the removal of the Utes through his editorials in the *Solid Muldoon*, could not have been more pleased. In an editorial in the September 12, 1881, issue, Day wrote:

"Chief Colorow, famous for profound stubbornness and resistance to this removal, was the last to leave the valley - a dull, prosaic dash of copper at the end of a long Indian sentence. Sunday morning the Utes bid adieu to their old hunting grounds - this is an event that has long devotedly been prayed for by our people. How joyful it sounds and with what satisfaction one can say, 'The Utes have gone.'"

Arriving in eastern Utah, the White River Utes were sent to the Uintah Reservation. In a split, designed by the government, the Uncompahgre band was sent to an adjoining reservation, created and symbolically named "Ouray," near the banks of the Green River. William H. Berry, the Ute's most trusted Indian agent, became the agent of the new reservation. The Ute landscape was a stark contrast to their once traditional homelands of Colorado. One of the first visitors to the reservation, John B. Lloyd, described the area:

"The bottom land lying along the Green River and White River contains all the farming land within the lines of the reservation. There is not a stream outside of the two mentioned that has running water in it two months during the year; the fact is, it is nothing but a desert, and it is an utter impossibility to keep the Indians within the bounds of this reservation, as on three sides it is bounded by mountains where there is plenty of game, grass, and water." [128]

Later, Sidney Jocknick wrote in is autobiography of his observations of the Uintah Reservation:

"Today it is easy to see how harsh has been the [Ute] tribe's punishment. Their superb lands have been taken from them and they are herded on a barren reservation where there is a scarcity of water and where successful farming is impossible. When they try to escape from their miserable

surroundings they are called 'marauders' and are herded back under military guard after suffering all the tortures that can come through insufficient protection against the weather and insufficient food. As for Chipeta, the brave and womanly, she has not been given the page in history of which Field wrote, but is suffering, old and feeble with her broken and despairing tribe. If there are any Utes left who took part in the Meeker massacre, it would appear that they have been made to pay the penalty many times over." [129]

As far as the government was concerned, the Ute matter in Colorado was settled. During his last speech before the United States House and Senate, in December 1881, President Rutherford B. Hayes said:

"An agreement has been made with the Utes by which they surrender their large reservation in Colorado in consideration of an annuity to be paid to them, and agree to settle in severalty on certain lands designated for that purpose, as farmers, holding individual title to their land in fee simple, inalienable for a certain period. In this way a costly Indian war has been avoided which at one time seemed imminent, and for the first time in the history of the country an Indian nation has given up its tribal existence to be settled in severalty and to live as individuals under the common protection of the laws of the country. I hope that Congress will at this session take favorable action on the bill providing for allotment of lands on the different reservations in severalty to the Indians. This measure, together with a vigorous prosecution of our educational efforts, will work the most important and effective advance toward the solution of the Indian problem, in preparing for the gradual merging of our Indian population in the great body of American citizenship." [131]

Senator Henry M. Teller strongly disagreed with President Hayes. On January 20, 1881, Teller stood on the senate floor and, in opposition of the bill the president referred to, gave the following speech:

"I know the enormity of the crime of differing with such high and intelligent authority on this matter. I am running amuck against all the intelligence and all the virtue of the country, and therefore, I must be wrong. If I stand alone in the Senate, I want to put upon the record my prophecy in this matter that when thirty or forty years shall have passed and these Indians shall have parted with title, they will curse the hand that was raised professed in their defense to secure this kind

of legislation. Indians differ as much one from another as civilized and enlightened nations of the earth differ from the uncivilized and unenlightened nations of the earth. If those clamoring for severalty understood the Indian character, and Indian laws, and Indian morals and Indian religion, they would not be here clamoring for this at all... [this bill] is in the interest of the speculators; it is in the interest of the men who are clutching up this land, but not in the interest of the Indian at all." [131]

Following Teller's speech, a vigorous debate between the senators took place. Before the session ended for the day, Teller said:

"I say it in no unkind spirit, the bill ought to be entitled a bill to despoil the Indians of their lands and make them vagabonds on the earth, and a few years will demonstrate that what has been true heretofore with the Indians will be true hereafter." [132]

Despite Senator Teller's noble opposition, the bill later passed both houses and was signed by President James A. Garfield. Although Senator Teller lost the debate, he felt strongly about the issues. Remaining involved in the aftermath of the White River atrocities, Teller reached out to the Meeker family in Greeley. After a few conversations, he offered Josephine Meeker employment as a secretary for legislators in Washington. Josephine accepted the position and moved to the nation's capital city. She excelled at her position and in the summer of 1882, Teller gave her a promotion, making her his assistant private secretary. After serving just six months as Teller's secretary, Josephine contracted pneumonia. Twenty-five-year-old Josephine Meeker died on December 29, 1882. Teller arranged for her body to be shipped by train back to her family in Greeley, Colorado, and accompanied the body as well.

The funeral for Josephine Meeker was small, primarily family and close friends, including Senator Teller. It was held in the parlor of the Meeker family home. Burial followed in the Meeker family plot, near her father, N. C. Meeker, in the Linn Grove Cemetery in Greeley. [133] During his time in Greeley, Teller was regaled with several stories of the plight of the Indians from Josephine's older sister, Rozene. Despite the atrocious indignities both her mother and sister suffered at the hands of the Indians, Rozene Meeker had taken up their cause. She wrote several articles and even went on somewhat of a lecture circuit for a time. Back in Washington, many who had previously opposed Senator Teller's staunch position against the Agreement with the Confederated Bands of Utes now seemed to have changed their positions. Within a year, Teller was appointed as Secretary of the Interior, replacing Carl Schurz. Just a few short months after his appointment, Secretary Teller began receiving letters from another Colorado woman who had taken up the cause of "reforming the Indian," Helen Hunt Jackson.

Helen Hunt Jackson, who resided in Colorado Springs, was well known as a champion for the plight of the American Indian. This was primarily with her most popular book, "A Century of Dishonor," published the year before Teller's appointment. Jackson, a fierce critic of former Secretary Schurz, had sent a copy of her book to every member of Congress. Through her letters to Teller, she emphatically urged that the government take a stronger stance in the ongoing struggles of the Indian people. [134] Although Teller and Jackson disagreed on many points, they managed to develop a working relationship on the areas where they found agreement. Teller granted her an appointment as a special agent to visit and report on the conditions she found with the Mission Indians in California, of which she had come in contact during her research for her novel, "Ramona."

Jackson sent regular reports to Hiram Price, the Commissioner of Indian Affairs. In her final report, dated July 13, 1883, Jackson listed several areas for improvement, including establishing more schools, and offering instruction and training for agricultural farming. After reading and analyzing Jackson's fifty-six pages of recommendations, Teller took the most feasible of the recommendations and submitted a bill to Congress on January 14, 1884. However, the bill was defeated. Both Jackson and Teller were disappointed. Nevertheless, Jackson's novel, "Ramona," was published later that year. Three years later, on August 12, 1885, Helen Hunt Jackson died of cancer. Sadly, she had not lived to see the bill she had inspired finally become law. Later that year, Teller open a school for Indian children in Grand Junction, the Teller Institute.

It was also in 1885 that a few local settlers in the White River valley came together to establish a new town. With the leadership of William H. Clark, John C. Davis, J. W. Hugus, Newton Major and Susan C. Wright, the town of Meeker was incorporated. Named in honor of Nathaniel Cook Meeker, the murdered Indian agent, the town of Meeker became the county seat of Rio Blanco County and for the next twenty years remained the only incorporated town in northwestern Colorado. Many of the buildings that were not destroyed by fire during the Indian raid at the White River Indian Agency were sold by the government to the town founders for fifty dollars each, and one hundred dollars for the officer's quarters. These structures were moved to the fledging town. [135]

In 1891, Henry M. Teller, again elected as Colorado's United States senator, reintroduced the bill inspired by Helen Hunt Jackson, which provided for the "relief of the Mission Indians in the State of California." The bill finally passed both houses of Congress and was signed into law by President Benjamin Harrison in January 1891. [136]

Unfortunately, while the Indian Reform movement did much to bring the plight of the American Indians to the public's attention, it was too little, too late for those who had been forced from Colorado to live on the Uintah Reservation in eastern Utah.

While Chipeta, the esteemed and respected wife of the late great chief of the Utes, Ouray, was forced to move to the new reservation, she was promised a house as fine as she had in Colorado. It was another empty promise by the government. Chipeta's new life on Uintah Reservation soon became a new clash of cultures for her. Over the years she had grown accustomed to the ways of living in the white man's world. Now, the "Queen of the Utes," so dubbed by the Washington reporters, was forced to live again among her own people as she had in her youth.

However, given her former status, the government did allow Chipeta to leave the reservation. She was known to make several trips to Ignacio to visit with her brother, Sapovanero, a sub-chief of the Southern Utes. Most likely, during these visits Chipeta made the two mile trek to her husband's burial spot.

Not long after Chipeta and her people were forced onto the Uintah Reservation, Denver's most popular literary figure, Eugene Field, brought a new awareness to Chipeta's plight. During the 1882 Colorado Press Convention, Field read aloud a poem he had penned, entitled, "Chipeta":

> "She is bravest and best of a cursed race, Give her a lodge on the mountainside
> And when she is gone on the hill provide, The Queen of the Utes' last resting place.
> She rode where old Ouray dare not ride, A path through the wilderness rough and wild, She rode to plead for woman and child, She rode in the valleys, dark and chill, O!

*Such a ride as a woman can
By the God-like power which in her lies
Or inspiration from the skies, Achieve for woman and son of man.
They live, and through the country wide,
Where'ere they come, where'ere they go
Though their heads grow white as wintery snow
They will tell of brave Chipeta's ride.
She is bravest and best of a cursed race - Give her a lodge on the mountainside
And when she is gone on the hill provide
The Queen of the Utes' last resting place."*[137]

While several Denver citizens were sympathetic to Chipeta, many journalists of the city were not. In the April 1, 1883, issue of the *Denver Republican*, a two-column story of Chipeta's remarriage appeared. Rife with hilarious prose, it was an obvious April Fool's joke, as Chipeta's new husband was named "Too-much-a-gut." In fact, Chipeta lived alone and lonely on the reservation in Utah.

In time, due to the lack of a sufficient food source for the reservation, another failure of the government, the Ute braves were allowed to leave the reservation to hunt for wild game. Unfortunately, a few renegade warriors traveled far from the reservation and back into Colorado.

In the fall of 1887, following the unprovoked attack on a small party of Ute hunters near the town of Meeker, Colorado, where a young Ute brave, Augustine, was killed, the Utes were outraged. The Ute leaders, including Colorow, were allowed to travel to Meeker to take part in the investigation of the shooting. As Colorow and his group made their way east to Meeker, the sheriff, James Kendall received reported incidents of horse thefts along the very trail Colorow's group were traveling. Sheriff Kendall along with a posse, rode out to intercept the Ute party. Achieving his objective, Kendall confronted the Ute leader. During the conversation, one of Kendall's men opened fire on the Utes. Colorow and his men immediately retreated, leaving the area.

Colorow, with good reason, was incensed by the hostile confrontation. In what would become known among the Utes as the Last War Trail, Colorow launched an attack against whites and the Indian agents. Soldiers at nearby Fort Crawford were alerted to what they believed could be an attempted repeat of the White River attack of 1879. In an effort to stop another Ute uprising, Governor Alva Adams ordered seven brigades of the Colorado

National Guard to the area. Many settlers were ordered to leave their homes for their own safety.

Actually, in this new rebellious effort, later dubbed the "Colorow War," the renegade Utes committed very few crimes against the settlers as Colorow quickly realized that any fight with the whites would be a losing one. Colorow counseled moderation and caution.

Despite Colorow's peace efforts, hostilities broke out in August 1887, near a fork of the White River. As Colorow predicted, the event did not go well. Most of the women and children at the nearby Indian camp, including Chipeta, were moved to safety, although there were a few casualties. During the fight twelve of Colorow's men were killed. Several soldiers were also killed, and many were wounded. A company of soldiers, led by Major Leslie of the First Colorado Cavalry, moved into the area and surrounded the Ute encampment. Eventually, Major Leslie and a few of his officers approached the Indian camp on foot. Colorow and John McCook, Chipeta's brother, went out to meet the soldiers, and a peace of sorts was formed. With this mutual agreement between Colorow and his people and the United States soldiers, with no government bureaucracy involved, the Colorado Indian wars came to an inglorious end.

For the Ute nation, life on the reservations, both in Utah and southern Colorado, was a bitter experience. Living conditions and the lack of fresh water made several ill, including Chipeta. In the cold winter of 1890, the Uintah Reservation was struck with diphtheria. Within a month so many had died of the illness that the agent's physician, Doctor Howard C. Reaves, informed the Secretary of the Interior, Hoke Smith, that the health conditions at the reservation had reached epidemic levels. Dr. Reaves received additional help to care for the sick and dying. However, it was the fresh spring weather that eventually drove the disease from the reservation.

In 1895, Ignacio, leader of the Weeminuche band of Southern Utes, moved his people to the western edge of the Southern Ute Reservation. It was a protest move due to the health concerns, as well as what he believed to be the government's encroachment of reservation lands through a policy of land allotments. Through Ignacio's advocacy for his people, the Bureau of Indian Affairs later created the Ute Mountain Reservation. Encompassing over a half million acres of land, the agency headquarters was established at Towac, Colorado. [138]

Chipeta was forced to leave her homeland and lived the rest of her life on the Ute Reservation in Utah. *DPL*

By the turn of the century, ironically enough, the public became enamored with the American Indian. Much of this new adoration was due in no small part to the enormous popularity of William F. Cody, better known as "Buffalo Bill," and his "Wild West Show." Soon, Native Americans were featured attractions at county fairs, town parades and local rodeos.

The demand for appearances by Native Americans was not lost on the various town leaders across the state of Colorado. Because Chipeta was allowed to leave the reservation, her presence at many events in Colorado was in high demand. For the next several years, Chipeta made appearances in Colorado from Grand Junction to Manitou Springs. In 1907, the elderly "Queen of the Utes" appeared at a county fair in Montrose, close to the home she and Ouray once had. She was photographed among several Indian blankets.

In August 1911, Buckskin Charlie, along with several distinguished Southern Utes including Chipeta, were honorary guests of the mayor and city councilmen of Colorado Springs. The occasion was a Native American festival, they called "Shan Kive," created to boost the depressed economy of the area. Newspaper

Chipeta and Margaret Adams remained friends for the rest of their lives. *Pioneer Museum*

and professional photographers took several pictures of the aging Chipeta in various locales including the Manitou springs and the Garden of the Gods. During her stay, Chipeta visited with her longtime friend from the days at the Los Pinos Indian Agency, Margaret Adams. The two women, both widows now, were featured in the Shan Kive parade which ran for two miles through the town of Colorado Springs. It was also during this time that Buckskin Charlie and Chipeta worked with the El Paso County Pioneer Society to mark the ancient Ute Pass Trail which originated in the area and continued north into the mountains.

During a survey of the area in 1820, Major Stephen H. Long wrote of the historic trail in his famous journal:

"A large and much frequented road passes the [Manitou] *springs and enters the mountains, running to the north of the high [Pikes] Peak. It is traveled principally by bison, sometimes also by the Indians who penetrate here to the Columbia."*

After a few days in the hills above the spring waters, Buckskin Charlie and Chipeta were able to identify much of the trail although it no longer resembled what it once was. Joel Palmer, a trapper and trader who frequented the area, described the trail as he first saw it in 1847. The entry appears in his later published "Journal of Travels over the Rocky Mountains:" "These paths are remarkable in their appearance, being about fifteen inches wide, and four inches deep, and worn into the soil as smoothly as they could be cut with a spade."

In 1912, during the second Shan Kive festival, the El Paso County Pioneers Society dedicated the historic Ute Pass Trail with fifteen white marble markers, etched with the letters U.P.T. placed at various locations along the trail above the springs of Manitou. Buckskin Charlie and several Ute leaders, including Eagle Eye, Moon Face, and Naneece, rode on horseback along the trail. It had been thirty years since Buckskin Charlie had ridden this trail of his homeland. Just before making their entry into the town of Manitou Springs, Buckskin Charlie and Naneece stopped at a chokecherry tree. Breaking off branches from the tree, they continued their ride into the town. The Ute leaders then offered the chokecherry branches to the town officials as a symbol of peace. Then they rode to the sacred springs in the center of the little town where they gave offerings and asked for blessings from the Great Spirit. Following an elaborate ceremony, Buckskin Charlie told a reporter, "I am now seventy years old. I never so happy in all my life." Indeed, for Buckskin Charlie, now the leader of the Southern Utes, was born near the Garden of the Gods and had ridden the trail many times in his childhood. [139] Unfortunately, due to deteriorating eyesight, Chipeta was unable to attend this grand occasion with her people. Troubled by her failing vision, during one of her many visits to Grand Junction, Chipeta consulted Doctor Guy Gary, an optometrist. The doctor recommended immediate surgery. Although terrified, Chipeta consented. Following the surgery, Chipeta returned to her meager home on the Uintah Reservation. Chipeta's eyesight had not improved, but grew worse. When she was able, she made the trip to Dragon, Utah, to consult with another optometrist, Doctor Daniel W. White, who worked in conjunction with the United States Bureau of Indian Affairs. One of Dr. White's nurses, Mrs. W. G. King, took a keen interest in the new patient. Nurse King later wrote of her time with Chipeta:

> "Chipeta, Ouray's widow, was among the first Indians to come to our home. Her eyes were getting bad, and she was worried about them. A doctor in Grand Junction had removed a cataract from one eye. One day Chipeta came in to see me about her eyes. I telephoned to her doctor, and he gave me instructions for treatments. Hot packs were to be placed on her eyes, and he sent medicine to be dropped into them. It was explained she must have treatment for a long period of time in order to get relief and to have improved eyesight. The Indians were very cooperative. They moved down from their camp on Bitter Creek, and made camp up on Vack Creek, a short way. At last the eye treatments for Chipeta were

over and her eyes were improved. The Indians moved back to Bitter Creek where the summer Indian camps were." [140]

Even with her poor vision, Chipeta still enjoyed visiting Colorado towns on the western slope and those near the Ute spiritual area of the springs of the Manitou. During an appearance in 1913, in the town of Ouray, named for her husband, Chipeta rode in an open Ford automobile during a parade. The August 1, 1913, issue of the *Ouray Plainsdealer* reported Chipeta's presence:

"Accompanied by four bucks, five squaws and a single papoose the famous Chipeta visited her husband's old haunting place here last Sunday. The band was entertained by the Commercial Club and gave a full dress parade on Main Street in the afternoon."

In 1916, Superintendent of Indian Affairs Cato Sells took an interest in Chipeta. That summer Sells traveled to the Uintah Reservation where the seventy-three-year-old woman was living an exiled life along Bitter Creek. During their meeting, Sells inquired if Chipeta needed anything. Chipeta replied:

"I desire nothing; what is good enough for my people is good enough for me. And I expect to die very soon." [141]

Chipeta also made such a strong statement that Sells felt compelled to include it in his annual report:

"Never have I had an unkind feeling or an unkind thought toward the Government in Washington, and if I were to express what I have in my mind, someone would misunderstand and I think that Chipeta's heart has changed and that she is no longer friendly toward the Government." [142]

A few years later, Mrs. Margaret Adams, the widow of former Ute Indian agent Charles Adams, paid her old friend a visit; it would be their last visit together. By this time, Chipeta's eyesight was so bad that she followed a rope from her tipi out to the bushes where she could relieve herself. Margaret Adams later wrote that Chipeta was:

"...living on a barren bit of Utah land where even the experienced farmer could not make a living much less an old woman. She [Chipeta] was clever at making certain things, but it is late in the day for her to

learn to till the ground where Uncle Sam has placed her and said make a living or starve. Winter is coming on. Her little log house would be more comfortable." [143]

Chipeta continued to live in her tipi on the "barren bit of Utah land" where "Uncle Sam had placed her," for the next eight years. In 1924, at the age of eighty-one, Chipeta, now totally blind, also suffered from arthritis and severe stomach ailments. On August 16, Chipeta died from chronic gastritis. She had lived a poor, lonely and unhappy life for nearly forty years after the death of Ouray. Chipeta died eight days before the fortieth anniversary of Ouray's death; August 24, 1880. Chipeta, once crowned as the "Queen of the Utes" by the national press, was unceremoniously buried in a shallow grave in the sand wash of Bitter Creek, on the Uintah Indian Reservation.

After receiving news of Chipeta's death, the following year Buckskin Charlie, chief of the Southern Utes following Ouray's death, determined it was time to reveal Ouray's burial spot. In conversations with L. M. Wyat, a Ute trader, and E. E. McKean, Superintendent of the Consolidated Ute Indian Agency at Ignacio, the idea of erecting a monument was originally discussed. However, with the death of Chipeta the previous year, the idea of reburying the two together was also discussed. John McCook, Chipeta's brother, was brought into the conversation, and readily agreed. McCook had visited his sister's grave and knew that shallow burial would either attract predatory animals, or the site would eventually be washed away.

Superintendent McKean sent a request to the Secretary of the Interior for the appropriation of funds for a proper memorial. Meanwhile, several citizens of Montrose, Colorado, learned of the impending possibility of Chipeta's remains being removed and reinterred at Ignacio. The group formed a committee to have Chipeta's body brought to Montrose and buried on the land once owned by her and Ouray. Why the group of concerned citizens did not act when Chipeta was buried in the shallow grave a year earlier is up for speculation.

Nevertheless, the movement went forward while the government bureaucracy, ever slow in its actions, was still dealing with McKean's request for funds for the erection of a memorial to Ouray. Frustrated at the bureaucratic process, McCook consented to the removal of his sister's remains, to be reinterred on the land once owned by Chipeta and Ouray. Although Superintendent

McKean was obviously disappointed, he approved the transfer of Chipeta's body across the state line into Colorado. The exhuming of transfer of the body was assigned to Superintendent F. A. Gross of Fort Duchesne, in Utah. Fort Duchesne, established as a trading post in 1905, also served as an Indian agency.

C. E. Adams, editor of the local Montrose newspaper, was one of the town's citizens working with those supporting Chipeta's reburial in their community. On March 3, 1925, Adams received word from Gross that Chipeta's body had been exhumed and was ready for transporting to Montrose and that McCook was eager to begin the trip east. However, the work on the Chipeta's memorial was not complete. Adams, not wanting to offend the Utes, replied to Gross that same day:

> "F. A. Gross, Supt. Fort Duechesne, [sic] Utah Dear Sir; Men at work on tomb. Weather fierce, but we will have it ready. Wire when you start or when ready. We want to make the Indians feel we are in earnest and thereby inspire them to make a diligent search for enough of Ouray's remains to make a tomb for him. Better wire." [144]

Apparently, from this missive, Adams, and perhaps others on the Montrose committee, thought that with Chipeta's reinterment at the old Ouray farm the Southern Utes would acquiesce to the reburial of Ouray at the same memorial spot.

On March 15, Chipeta's body arrived in Montrose. The body was accompanied by her brother, John McCook, a few Ute leaders, as well as representatives of the Fort Duchesne Indian agency.

At 2:30 p.m., that very afternoon, nearly five thousand citizens of Montrose lined up along the town's Main Street, to observe the nearly mile long ceremonial procession. Led by a military honor guard, Chipeta's casket passed through the town. On foot and in the lead was John McCook, as the procession passed slowly south along the icy and snow-packed road for two and a half miles. Finally, they arrived at the new Ouray Memorial Park, established on the very land of Ouray and Chipeta's farm. [145] There, the group were met by members of the local chapter of the Daughters of the American Revolution. The chairwoman then led McCook and Reverend Milton Hersey to the fresh water spring. The woman filled a cup with water and presented it to the reverend, who then offered a blessing:

"In the name of God, Ouray and Chipeta, I sup from this cup, this water emblematic of the purity of your lives. May the memory of your heroic and humanitarian deeds be kept fragrant in the hearts and thoughts of the white people, whom you so faithfully served. Amen." [146]

The cup of fresh spring water was then passed to Chipeta's brother, John McCook. McCook lifted the cup high above his head and declared:

"Chipeta, I have brought you home." [147]

Reverend Milton J. Hersey, who had baptized Chipeta in the Episcopal Church nearly twenty-seven years earlier, conducted the burial ceremony. Following the ceremony, McCook spoke his final words to his sister in Ute. Chipeta's body was then placed in the tomb erected by the citizens of Montrose. The eleven foot oblong tomb, constructed of Salida granite, was engraved with one word: "Chipeta."[148] Following the ceremony, the Montrose committee, led by editor C. E. Adams, approached John McCook on the possibility of securing Ouray's remains so that they could also be reinterred next to his wife and at the site of his former home. McCook indicated to the group that he would take their request to Buckskin Charlie at Ignacio.

However, when McCook arrived at the Indian agency in Ignacio, he learned that Buckskin Charlie had recovered the remains of the great Ute chief and had no intention of a reburial in Montrose. The bones of Ouray, now removed from the heretofore secret burial site by Buckskin Charlie, were authenticated by sworn affidavits provided by Buckskin Charlie, Naneese, Joseph Price, and John McCook, the group that had participated in the burial in 1880. All four men were present at the site when Ouray's remains were exhumed.[149] Ouray's remains, including the skull and some two dozen bones, were placed in a wooden casket and kept at the Consolidated Ute Indian Agency at Ignacio while his reburial was being planned.

On May 20, 1925, a four-day Indian burial ceremony began. It was the largest Indian gathering ever to assemble at the agency. Following the event, on May 24, Buckskin Charlie, Naneese, Joseph Price, and John McCook, all dressed in their finest ceremonial clothing and wearing full headdresses made of eagle feathers, led the procession to the Ute cemetery located at the edge of the reservation. A pickup truck followed, carrying Ouray's remains.

At the cemetery the largest gathering of both Indians and whites to assemble, then or since, attended the historic event. A Christian burial service was then conducted with both a Catholic priest and a Protestant minister officiating. This decision came about following a dispute over Ouray's religion. While it is known that Ouray attended the Catholic mission as a child in Taos, New Mexico, he never joined the church. There seemed to be some speculation that Ouray had joined the Episcopal Church, largely based on the fact that his wife Chipeta had done so. There is no evidence that Ouray joined this church either. Nevertheless, the controversy was alleviated at the cemetery when the fence dividing the Protestant and Catholic sections was removed and Ouray was reburied lengthwise so that he lay on both sides of the Christian portions. The four men present at Ouray's original burial, Buckskin Charlie, Naneese, Joseph Price, and John McCook, participated in the final burial of Ouray. A small cement headstone, made by the Utes, was placed to mark his grave site.

Buckskin Charlie remained the chief of the Utes, and like his predecessor, Ouray, Buckskin Charlie worked for the continued peace between the two cultures. He kept his people together, continuing Ouray's work and never fought against the white man. In 1905, he led the Utes in the inauguration parade for President Theodore Roosevelt in Washington, D.C.

Following the death of Buckskin Charlie at his ranch near Ignacio in May 1936, he was given a full Ute burial ceremony at the Ute cemetery. Following the ceremony, the body of Buckskin Charlie was laid to rest next to the grave of his predecessor, Ouray. Later, two tall natural white stone monuments were erected to mark the burial sites of the two great Ute leaders, Ouray and Buckskin Charlie.

Three years later, in 1939, again at the behest of L. M. Wayt, and with assistance of the government's Works Project Administration, a memorial park was built in Ignacio to honor the great Ute leaders. Designated the "Ute Memorial Park," located on the original grounds of the Southern Ute Indian Agency, the park was dominated by an eighteen-feet-tall monument. The native stone structure was marked on four sides with bronze busts memorializing four Ute leaders, including:

"Severno, Chief of the Capote Utes, Ignacio, the great Ute chief, Buckskin "Charley", chief of the Moache Band of Utes, and Chief Ouray, the man with a vision." [150]

Many writers have referred to the "Ute Memorial Park" as the burial site of Ouray. In fact, the land where the memorial park is located was where historians and archeologists believe Ouray died. To the east of the monument is a small whitewashed stone marking the approximate site of Chief Ouray's death.

It was also in 1939 that the "Ouray Memorial Park" was established at the burial location of Chipeta, south of Montrose. Two years earlier, in 1937, Chipeta's brother John McCook died. Following an elaborate funeral in Montrose, the funeral procession made the two-mile journey to the site of Chipeta's grave site on the old Ouray farm, where McCook was buried next to his beloved sister. His grave was marked with a simple white wooden cross, etched with the words, "Chief John McCook."[151]

Again, with the assistance of the government's WPA program, a tall natural stone obelisk was placed at the site, a few feet to the left of Chipeta's grave, in honor of Ouray. A cement tipi was built over the spring which provided Ouray and Chipeta with fresh water. The new Ouray Memorial Park, under the direction of the Colorado Historical Society, operated and maintained the nearly nine-acre site for several years. It is indeed a very appropriate spot for a memorial park to a great Ute leader, who spent a lifetime working for peace between two cultures, and his wife, Chipeta. This site, given to them, then taken away, finally memorialized the great Ute couple.

Following the death of Ouray's chosen successor, Buckskin Charlie, his son, Antonio Buck, became the first elected Ute tribal chairman (a term coined by the white man, following the institution of the reservation). Buck served as the leader of the Southern Ute nation for the next quarter-century. When Buck died in 1961, he was given the traditional Ute burial ceremony. Interment followed the traditional ritual at the Ute Cemetery, by this time known as the Ouray Memorial Cemetery.[152] Chief Antonio Buck was buried with honor, just behind the two white stone monuments marking the burials of his father Buckskin Charlie, and Ouray. His brown granite headstone, one of the few granite stones in the cemetery, reads: "Antonio Buck Sr. 1870 - 1961 Last Chief of the Southern Utes." At the time of his death, the remaining Southern Ute leaders bestowed Antonio Buck with the honor of Head Chief, a highly regarded position among the Indians, despite the effort of the white man.

It is was an act steeped in Ute tradition; something not even the white man could take away from these proud people known as the "The People of the Shining Mountains."

The Southern Ute and Mountain Ute reservations are all that remain of the sacred ancestral Ute lands.

— Chapter Notes —

1. Report of the Commissioner of Indian Affairs for the Year 1875, pg. 50. Also see Records of the Office of Indian Affairs, National Archives, Washington, D. C.
2. Smith, Ouray, *Chief of the Utes*, pg. 32.
3. "Utah" is Ute for "the people." Uintah means "edge of the pine." "Yampa" means "the water."
4. The Grand River was later renamed the Colorado River.
5. In 1863 when Ouray made his mark on the Treaty of 1863, a handwritten notation next to it was the word "Arrow." United States Government Documents, Bureau of Indian Affairs, Document #0246.
6. Major William Gilpin would later be appointed by President Abraham Lincoln as the first Territorial Governor of the Colorado Territory in 1861.
7. Simmons, *Kit Carson and His Three Wives*, pg. 72.
8. Documents of American Indian Diplomacy . Also see Smith, Ouray, *Chief of the Utes*, pg. 39.
9. Uncompahgre is Ute for "red lake."
10. Smith, Ouray, *Chief of the Utes*, pg. 43.
11. This location was very near Bent's Fort.
12. Ruxton, *Life in the Far West*.
13. The Ute word, Saguache, means "Blue Earth."
14. Bureau of Indian Affairs, Letters Received, National Archives. Also see Dunlay, *Kit Carson and the Indians*, and Sides, *Blood and Thunder*.
15. Bureau of Indian Affairs, Letters Received, National Archives. Also see Dunlay, *Kit Carson and the Indians*, and Sides, *Blood and Thunder*.
16. The archives of both the Southern Ute Cultural Center and Museum, Ignacio, and the Ute Museum archives in Montrose. Of particular note, the Ute Museum fixes Chipeta's exact date of birth as June 10, 1843.
17. Becker and Smith, *Chipeta*, pg. 3.
18. The archives of both the Southern Ute Cultural Center and Museum, Ignacio, and the Ute Museum archives in Montrose.
19. Archives of the Ute Museum, Montrose, Colorado.
20. In an effort to gain loyalty among its northern citizens, the Mexican government allowed for land grants in northern Mexico. Four of these were in today's Colorado state borders, including the Beaubien-Miranda-Maxwell land grant.

21. Tabeguache is Ute for the "warm side of the mountain."
22. Smith, Ouray, *Chief of the Utes*, pg. 56.
23. ibid.
24. Quantrill and his confederate guerrilla forces were responsible for one of the most heinous acts during the Civil War with the raid on Lawrence, Kansas, in August 1863. The town was nearly burned to the ground and one hundred fifty innocent people were murdered. It occurred just four months after Ouray and the Ute sub-chiefs passed through the area.
25. Smith, Ouray, *Chief of the Utes*, pg. 56.
26. Howbert, *Memories of a Lifetime in the Pike's Peak Region*, pg. 109.
27. Condition of the Indian Tribes, 39th Congress, 1866-67, Report No. 156.
28. ibid.
29. Colorado History Center, Fort Garland Museum, pg. 45.
30. ibid.
31. Smith, Ouray, *Chief of the Utes*, pg. 68.
32. Dunlay, Kit Carson & The Indians, pg. 406.
33. Documents of American Indian Diplomacy , Treaty of 1868.
34. Smith, Ouray, *Chief of the Utes*, pg. 72.
35. ibid.
36. Dora I. Foster personal papers located in the archives of the Colorado History Center.
37. Documents of American Indian Diplomacy , Treaty of 1868.
38. Smith, Ouray, *Chief of the Utes*, pg. 87.
39. Jocknick, *Early Days on the Western Slope of Colorado*.
40. ibid.
41. ibid.
42. Smith, Ouray, *Chief of the Utes*, pg. 88.
43. ibid.
44. Becker and Smith, *Chipeta*, pg. 114.
45. Smith, Ouray, *Chief of the Utes*, pg. 103.
46. The *Rocky Mountain News*, September 11, 1873.
47. Smith, Ouray, *Chief of the Utes*, pg. 107.
48. Pritzker, *A Native American Encyclopedia*.
49. Smith, Ouray, *Chief of the Utes*, pg. 109.
50. Hafen, "Efforts to Recover the Stolen Son of Chief Ouray," *Colorado Magazine*, March 1939.
51. Smith, Ouray, *Chief of the Utes*, pg. 110.
52. ibid.
53. ibid.
54. The United States government official changed the term of "treaty" to "agreement" in 1871. See Documents of American Indian Diplomacy, pg. 233.

55. Documents of American Indian Diplomacy, Agreement With Tabeguache, Mauache, Capote, Weeminuche, Yampa, Grand River, and Uintah Bands of Ute, pgs. 258-260.
56. Smith, Ouray, *Chief of the Utes*, pg. 115.
57. Jocknick, *Early Days on the Western Slope of Colorado*.
58. This house burned in 1944.
59. Smith, Ouray, *Chief of the Utes*, pg. 116.
60. Several tools used by the Utes, such as spoons, carving instruments and grinding stones have been found over the years in the area of Cripple Creek, Divide and Florissant. Celinda Reynolds Kaelin, Pikes Peak Historical Society.
61. Some writers spell Mrs. Meeker's first name as "Arvella." I have chosen to refer to her as "Arvilla," as this is the spelling on the majority of documents, including death certificate, burial record, and her tombstone in Greeley's Linn Grove Cemetery.
62. Emmitt, *The Last War Trail*, pg.51.
63. ibid.
64. ibid.
65. *The Meeker Herald*, established by N. C. Meeker, continues to be a weekly publication, today known as the *Herald Times*.
66. Documents of American Indian Diplomacy, Agreement With Tabeguache, Mauache, Capote, Weeminuche, Yampa, Grand River, and Uintah Bands of Ute, pgs. 258-260.
67. Henry Jim replaced the first interpreter for the agency, Uriah Curtis.
68. Smith, Ouray, *Chief of the Utes*, pg. 143.
69. Emmitt, *The Last War Trail*, pg.55.
70. The moccasins Josephine Meeker received as a gift just prior to the Meeker Massacre, as well as her Indian dress, are on display at the Meeker House Museum in Greeley, Colorado.
71. Smith, Ouray, *Chief of the Utes*, pg. 143.
72. Annual Report of the Commissioner of Indian Affairs for the Year 1878, pg. 70.
73. Bureau of Indian Affairs, Letters Received, National Archives.
74. ibid.
75. ibid.
76. ibid.
77. ibid.
78. Smith, Ouray, *Chief of the Utes*, pg. 143.
79. Emmitt, *The Last War Trail*, pg.191.
80. Burke, "The Thornburgh Battle With the Utes on Milk Creek," *True West Magazine*, March 2019.

81. United States Congress, Committee of Indian Affairs. Testimony in Relation to the Ute Commission, 1880.
82. ibid.
83. ibid.
84. ibid.
85. ibid.
86. ibid.
87. Leckie, *The Buffalo Soldiers*, pg. 210.
88. *The Denver Daily News*, October 13, 1879.
89. Bureau of Indian Affairs, Letters Received, National Archives. Note the governor's incorrect reference to Thornburgh's military rank.
90. Annual Report of the Commissioner of Indian Affairs for the Year 1878, pg. 187.
91. Emmitt, *The Last War Trail*, pg.236.
92. Emmitt, *The Last War Trail*, pg. 240.
93. ibid.
94. White River Ute Commission Investigation, 46th U. S. Congress, Washington, D. C., 1880.
95. ibid.
96. Smith, Ouray, *Chief of the Utes*, pg. 164.
97. White River Ute Commission Investigation, 46th U. S. Congress, Washington, D. C., 1880.
98. ibid.
99. Smith, Ouray, *Chief of the Utes*, pg. 165.
100. ibid.
101. Meeker's body was eventually reinterred in the family plot at Greeley's Linn Grove Cemetery. See Wommack, *From the Grave*.
102. White River Ute Commission Investigation, 46th U. S. Congress, Washington, D. C., 1880, pgs. 43-50.
103. ibid.
104. ibid.
105. Smith, Ouray, *Chief of the Utes*, pg. 168.
106. Annual Report of the Commissioner of Indian Affairs for the Year 1879.
107. ibid.
108. Smith, Ouray, *Chief of the Utes*, pg. 170.
109. United States Congress, Committee of Indian Affairs. Testimony in Relation to the Ute Commission, 1880.
110. ibid.
111. Jim Johnson, mentioned in the article, should not be confused with Johnson, the husband of Susan, Ouray's half-sister.
112. Documents of American Indian Diplomacy, pg 278.
113. ibid.

114. ibid.
115. Smith, Henry M. Teller, *Colorado's Grand Old Man*, pg. 103.
116. United States Senate Executive Documents for the Second Session of the 46th Congress of the United States of America, 1880-81, Washington, D. C.
117. ibid.
118. Smith, Ouray, *Chief of the Utes*, pg. 179.
119. ibid, pg. 182.
120. Wommack, *From the Grave*.
121. Becker and Smith, *Chipeta*, pg. 149.
122. ibid. pg. 150.
123. Ouray's image is one of the original sixteen stained-glass portraits to grace the newly completed state capitol building in Denver.
124. Jocknick, *Early Days on the Western Slope of Colorado*.
125. Documents of American Indian Diplomacy , pg 283.
126. Report of the Commission of Indian Affairs, December 1880, United States Congress.
127. Parker, *The Old Army*.
128. Becker and Smith, *Chipeta*, pg. 164.
129. Jocknick, *Early Days on the Western Slope of Colorado*.
130. 46th Congress of the United States of America, 1880-81, Washington, D. C.
131. United States Senate Executive Documents for the Second Session of the 46th Congress of the United States of America, 1880-81, Washington, D. C.
132. ibid.
133. Josephine Meeker's dress, made from an Indian blanket during her captivity by the Ute Indians, as well as her typewriter, a rare piece, with a glass encasement and glass keys, are on display at the Meeker Memorial Museum in Greeley.
134. Smith, Henry M. Teller, *Colorado's Grand Old Man*, pg. 133.
135. Three of the officer's buildings moved to the new town now serve as the White River Museum. Among the many artifacts on display are the wooden plow Meeker used that ignited the fury of the Utes, as well as his printing press used to print the *Meeker Herald*. Colorow's peace pipe is also among the Ute collection.
136. ibid, pg. 134.
137. Becker and Smith, *Chipeta*, pg. 168.
138. The Ute word, "Towaoc," means "all right."
139. Pettit, *Utes: The Mountain People*, pg. 24.
140. Smith, Ouray, *Chief of the Utes*, pg. 199.
141. ibid, pg. 201.
142. United States Department of the Interior, Bureau of Indian

Affairs. Annual Report, 1916.
143. Smith, Ouray, *Chief of the Utes*, pg. 203.
144. Smith, Ouray, *Chief of the Utes*, pg. 204.
145. The Ute Museum, located on the property, offers great insight to the Ute Indians and the life of Chipeta.
146. Becker and Smith, *Chipeta*, pg. 244.
147. ibid.
148. Wommack, *From the Grave*.
149. Smith, Ouray, *Chief of the Utes*, pg. 204.
150. There are many misspelled words on the bronze plaques, including Buckskin "Charley."
151. Roland McCook, Sr., the great-great-grandson of John McCook, served as vice chairman of the Native American Graves Protection and Repatriation Act.
152. Wommack, *From the Grave*.

— EPILOGUE —

The battle of Sand Creek triggered a culture war that lasted for years. For the white man, it was domination with military, political and social control. For the Cheyenne and Arapaho, it was a fight to hold on to their land and traditional way of life. What became the massacre at Sand Creek, more than any other Indian conflict, set the stage for the ensuing bloody conflict on the Plains. In history, it would remain with the Indians as the most decisive symbol of white-man betrayal.

In the end, both sides lost their objective and much, much more. The repercussions are still being felt today.

Today, the Sand Creek Massacre National Park site attempts to interpret that conflict with signage, tours and quiet reflection. Located in Kiowa County, the site is sacred to the Native Americans. For decades descendants of the Sand Creek victims have made pilgrimages to the area to honor their loved ones.

In 1950, the Lamar and Eads Chamber of Commerce, in conjunction with the Colorado Historical Society (now History Colorado), erected a monument on the bluff overlooking the traditional massacre site. It reads in part, "Sand Creek Battle ground." The memorial at Sand Creek briefly tells the story of this American tragedy. Yet the silence of the area speaks volumes to the sacrifices and courage of that awful day over a century and a half ago.

This site is on land once owned by William Dawson. In 2000, backed by Senator Ben Nighthorse Campbell, Congress authorized the establishment of the Sand Creek Massacre National Historic Site. Three years later Dawson finalized the sale of his land to the National Park Service. In 2007, the Sand Creek Massacre National Park Historic site opened to the public. Brochures, walking trails and guided tours are available. Visitors can also walk independently along the trails where interpretive signs are posted to offer historic information.

The park is located twenty-three miles east of Eads and

forty miles north of Lamar at the junction of county roads 54 and W.

The memorial site of the Beecher Island Battle is located sixteen miles south of Wray at 20697 County Road KK. A monument was erected in 1905 but was washed away in the flood of 1935 that altered the flow of the Arikaree River.

Dr. Jeff Broome and other noted archeologists and historians have long disputed this site. Broome cites an 1873 government survey map placing the actual site five miles northeast, following the Arikaree River. This spot was noted in the USGS report during a homestead survey in 1873, some five years after the battle. According to the report, filed on January 24, 1874, the area was identified by remaining human and animal bones, as well as battle relics.

It was thirty years later, in 1898, that three scouts of Forsyth's command, including J.J. Peate who had come to the soldiers' rescue, returned to the area and apparently misidentified the actual battle site. Confused by the lay of the land and thirty-year-old memories, the men relied on the local homesteaders' accounts.

Nevertheless, that meeting in 1898 marked the first reunion of Beecher Island soldiers. The following year the Grand Army of the Republic organized the Beecher Island Memorial Association for annual reunions, a tradition that reoccurs every September at the marked site. A two-day event, it is sponsored by the Beecher Island Battleground Society in conjunction with the Fort Wallace Memorial Association.

A second monument still stands, replacing the original which washed away in the 1935 flood. A marker for J.J. Pete Hill stands where it was thought that the relief column arrived on September 25, 1868 to rescue the soldiers. An auditorium was erected for such events in 1940 as well as a one-room schoolhouse. Today, a marker lists the names of the wounded soldiers.

The site was listed on the National Register of Historic Places on October 29, 1976. A new monument was erected in 2018 honoring the Buffalo Soldiers who were involved in the rescue of the soldiers.

The site of the Summit Springs battle is located near the Logan/Washington County line. Follow Highway 63 south from Atwood for five miles. Take County Road 43 left at the sign to Summit Springs. The site is on private property.

A 1933 memorial marker is visable, erected by the Sterling

Lions Club. A Cheyenne stone marker erected in 1970 reflects peace and harmony. Two markers are visable amid the prairie grass and are in memory of Susanna Alderdice, a captive murdered by her captor at the onslaught of the battle. She was buried by the soldiers at the site although the exact location is unknown. A monument erected by Dr. Jeff Broome in honor of Susanna was dedicated in 2004.

Three miles west of the town of Meeker, on Highway 65, is the site of the Meeker Massacre. A large wooden site, erected in 1927, gives a brief description and marks the site. A plaque set in a natural granite boulder memorializes the area and lists the names of the dead including Nathan C. Meeker and ten employees of the White River Indian Agency. Although the site is on private land, there is a pull-off from the highway for observation.

— BIBLIOGRAPHY —

Abbreviations Used in Sources

CHC - Colorado History Center
DPL - Denver Public Library
GPO - Government Printing Office
OMR - Official Military Record

Government Publications and Sources

The War of the Rebellion Official Records Sand Creek Massacre - Report of the Secretary of War, 39th Congress session, Washington D. C.,1867.
Bureau of Indian Affairs, Letters Received, National Archives. Indian Affairs Annual Report 1875. Report of the Commissioner for 1875.
Records of the Office of Indian Affairs, National Archives, Washington, D. C.
Report of the Commissioners of Indian Affairs for the Year 1865, Washington D. C.
Report of the Commissioners of Indian Affairs for the Year 1866, Washington D. C.
Report on Indian Affairs by the Acting Commissioner for the Year 1868, Washington D. C.
The War of the Rebellion, A Compilation of the Official Records of the Union and Confederate Armies. 128 volumes, Washington D. C., 1880-1901.
United States Congress, House of Representatives, "The Chivington Massacre," Report of the Joint Special Committee. Appointed Under Resolution of March 3, 1865.
United States Congress, House of Representatives. Joint Committee on the Conduct of War. 38th Congress, 1865, Washington, D.C.
United States Congress, House of Representatives. "Massacre of the Cheyenne Indians." Report of the Committee on the Conduct of War, 38th Congress, 2nd Session, Washington, 1865.
United States Congress, Reports of the Committees, 39th Congress session, Washington D. C.,1867. United States Department of the Interior, Bureau of Indian Affairs. Annual Report, 1865.
United States Department of the Interior, Bureau of Indian Affairs. Annual Report, 1916.

United States Senate Executive Documents for the Second Session of the 39th Congress of the United States of America, 1866-67, Washington D. C.
United States Senate, "Sand Creek Massacre," Report of the Secretary of War, 39th Congress session, Washington D. C.,1867.
White River Ute Commission Investigation, 46th U. S. Congress, Washington D. C., 1880.
Report of the Commission of Indian Affairs, December 1880, United States Congress.
United States Senate Executive Documents for the Second Session of the 46th Congress of the United States of America, 1880-81, Washington D. C.

States and Federal Documentary Archives and Sources

Arapahoe County District Court Records. Colorado State Archives Correction Records.
Colorado State Division of Vital Statistics Company Muster Roll of July 29 through August 31, 1861. Transcripts of the Colorado Volunteers records, State of Colorado, Division of the Archives and Public Records.
Darlington Indian Agency Department of Anthropology, 1900 U.S. Census of Southern Cheyennes, J.J. Chou, University of Oklahoma.
Department of the Interior, Indian Field Office, Concho, Oklahoma 1928.
Department of the Interior, Seger Indian Agency, Colony, Oklahoma. Census Records Documents of American Indian Diplomacy, University of Oklahoma Press, 1999.
The National Archives and Records Administration. Denver Federal Center.

Unpublished Works and Manuscripts

Berthrong, Donald J./Sipes, John L. Cheyenne and Arapaho Collections/ Land Allotment Files, Cheyenne Prisoner Files.
Bushyhead, Ruby, Cheyenne Indian Family Genealogies.
Bushyhead, Ruby/Sipes, John L., Cheyenne and Arapaho Family Heirship and Estate Testimonies, dating from 1902.
Czaplewski, Russ. *Captive of the Cheyenne: The Story of Nancy Jane Morton and the Plum Creek Massacre*. Dawson County Historical Society, Kearney, Nebraska, 1993.
Fletcher, Nancy Jane Fletcher Morton Stevens, Upublished manuscript. Iowa State Historical Society. Hemphill, Anne E. Collection, Silas Soule and Hersa Coberly Soule Letters, Byron Strom, custodian. Sipes, John L., Cheyenne Files, Cheyenne Tribal Historian, now in the possession of Linda Wommack.
Wynkoop, Edward W. "Unfinished Colorado History, 1886." Colorado History Center, MSS II-20.

Newspapers

The various local newspaper archives accessed for this work are noted in the exact quotes used throughout the text.

Historical Archives and Resources

Chavez History Library, Palace of the Governors, Santa Fe, New Mexico.
Angelico Fray Collection Colorado College Tutt Library collections.
Colorado History Center, George Bent letters to George E. Hyde.
William N. Byers Papers.
First Regiment of Colorado Volunteer Records and Company Muster Roll.
John Evans Personal Correspondence.
"Indian Affairs Ledger Book" - John Evans Collection.
Edward W. Wynkoop. Unfinished Manuscript, MSS II.
United States Military Commission reports at Camp Weld.
Wynkoop Unfinished Colorado History 1876 Manuscript Collection No. 695.
Scott J. Anthony Manuscript Collection No. 14.
George Bent Manuscript Collection No. 54.
Samuel F. Tappen Manuscript Collection No. 617.
Denver Public Library Western History Collection E. S. Ricker Papers F. W. Cragin Papers George Bent Letters.
Rocky Mountain News Archives.
Silas Soule Papers, MSS 982.
Thayer, William M. *Marvels of the New West*. The Henry Bill Publishing Company, 1886. Courtesy, Denver Public Library, Western History Research Room.
Photos, courtesy, Coi Gerhig, DPL Photo Editor.
Fort Collins Museum of Local History.
Fort Garland Museum Archives.
Kansas State Historical Society.
Nebraska State Historical Society.
Oklahoma Historical Society.
Sterling, Colorado Museum of Local History.

Primary Sources

Feldman, Sophia German. "My Capture and Captivity by Cheyenne Indians-1874." *The Westerners Brand Book*, April 30, 1930.
Miles, Nelson A. *A Documentary Biography 1861-1903*. Aurthur A. Clark, CO. 1905.
Meredeth, Grace E. *Girl Captives of the Cheyennes*. Gem Publishing Company, 1927.
Jauken, Arlene Feldman. *The Moccasin Speaks, Living as Captives of the Dog Soldier Warriors*. Dageforde Publishing, Inc. 1998.

Periodicals and Historical Journals

Ashley, Susan Riley. "Reminiscences of Colorado in the Early 'Sixties" *The Colorado Magazine*, Volume X111, 1936, pg. 219-30.

Burkey, Elmer R. "The Thornburgh Battle With the Utes on Milk Creek," *The Colorado Magazine*, 1936.

Cobb, Frank. M. "The Lawrence Part of Pike's Peakers and the Founding of St. Charles," *Colorado Magazine*, September, 1933, pg. 194-97.

Cobern, W. S. "Raid Up the Platte," included in *True History of Some of the Pioneers of Colorado*. Cobern, Patterson and Shaw. 1909.

Cox, C. Jefferson. "Summit Springs," *Denver Westerners Roundup*, March 1970.

Downing, Finis E. "With The Ute Delegation of 1863 - Across the Plains and at Conejos" *Colorado Magazine* September 1945.

Hafen, Ann. "Efforts to Recover the Stolen Son of Chief Ouray," *Colorado Magazine*, March 1939.

Justice, Judith P. "The Saga of Clara Blinn at the Battle of the Washita," Research Review, *The Journal of the Little Big Horn Associates*, Winter, 2000, pgs. 11-12.

Carr, Official Report of Operations, Republican River Expedition, 1869.

Kraft, Louis. "When Wynkoop Was Sheriff," *Wild West Magazine*, April 2011.

Milavec, Pam. "Alias Emma S. Soule: Corrected Historical Fictions Surrounding Silas Soule and the Sand Creek Massacre." *Denver Westerners Roundup*, July-August, 2005.

Perkins, LaVonne. "Silas Soule, His Widow Heresa (sic), and the Rest of the Story." *Denver Westerners Roundup*, Mar-Apr, 1999.

Prentice, C. A., "Captain Silas S. Soule, a Pioneer Martyr." *Colorado Magazine*, Nov-Dec, 1935.

Sayre, Hal. "Early Central City Theatrical and Other Reminiscences." *The Colorado Magazine*, Volume VI, 1929, pgs. 47-53.

Wommack, Linda. "Tragedy at Sand Creek," *True West Magazine*, September, 2003.

Wommack, Linda. "In The Eye of the Storm: The Sand Creek Massacre," *True West Magazine*, November, 2003.

Wommack, Linda and Sipes, John. "Mo-chi: The First Female Cheyenne Warrior," *Wild West Magazine*, 2008.

Books

Abbott, Carl, Leonard, Stephen and Noel, Thomas J. *Colorado: A History of the Centennial State*. Fifth Edition, University Press of Colorado, 2013.

Becher, Ronald. *Massacre along the Medicine Road*. Caxton Press, 1999.

Bensing, Tom. *Silas Soule, A Short, Eventful Life of Moral Courage*. Dogear Publishing, 2012.

Berthrong, Donald J. *The Cheyenne and Arapaho Ordeal; Reservation and Agency Life in the Indian Territory, 1875-1907*. University of Oklahoma Press 1976.

Berthrong, Donald J. *The Southern Cheyennes*. University of Oklahoma Press 1963.
Broome, Jeff. *Cheyenne War, Indian Raids on the Roads to Denver 1864-1869*. Aberdeen Books and Logan County Historical Socity, 2013.
Broome, Jeff. *Dog Soldier Justice*. Lincoln County Historical Society, 2003.
Byers, William N. *Hand Book to the Gold Fields of Nebraska and Kansas*. D. B. Cooke of Chicago, 1859.
Campbell, John R. *An Indian Raid of 1867*. Nebraska State Historical Society.
Countant, Charles Griffin. *The History of Wyoming from the Earliest Known Discoveries*. Chaplin, Spafford and Mathison, 1899.
Craig, Reginald S. *The Fighting Parson*. Westernlore Press, 1959.
Custer, George Armstrong. *My Life on the Plains*. Promontory Press, 1874. Reprinted 1995.
Dunn, Ruth. *Indian Vengence at Julesburg*. Self-published, 1972.
Dunn, William R., Lt. Colonel. *I Stand By Sand Creek: A Defense of Colonel John M. Chivington and the Third Colorado Cavalry*. The Old Army Press, 1985.
Ellenbecker, John C. *Tragedy at the Little Blue: The Oak Grove Massacre and the Captivity of Lucinda Eubank and Laura Roper*. Morris Press, Revised Second Edition, 1993.
Emmitt, Robert. *The Last War Trail*. University of Oklahoma Press, 1954.
Fort Garland. Colorado Historical Society, *Fort Garland Museum*. 2005.
Forsyth, George A. *Thrilling Days in Army Life*. Harper & Brothers, 1901.
Frazer, Robert W. *Forts of the West*. University of Oklahoma Press, 1972.
Greene, Jerome A. and Scott, Douglas D. *Finding Sand Creek: History, Archeology, and the 1864 Massacre Site*. University of Oklahoma Press, 2004.
Greene, Jerome A. *Washita: The U.S. Army and the Southern Cheyennes*. 1867-1869. University of Oklahoma Press, 2004.
Grinnell, George Bird. *The Fighting Cheyennes*. University of Oklahoma Press, 1956, (New York 1915).
Grinnell, George Bird. *The Cheyenne Indians Volumes 1 and 2*. University of Nebraska Press, 1923
Hafen, Leroy. *Pikes Peak Gold Rush Guidebooks of 1859*. Arthur Clark Publishers, 1941.
Halaas, David F. and Masich, Andrew E. *Halfbreed: The Remarkable True Story of George Bent*. Da Capo Press, 2004.
Hall, Frank. *History of the State of Colorado. Volumes I through IV.* Blakely Printing Company of Chicago, 1889.
Hatch, Thom. *Black Kettle: The Cheyenne Chief Who Sought Peace but Found War*. John Wiley & Sons, Inc., 2004.
Hoig, Stan. *The Sand Creek Massacre*. University of Oklahoma Press, 1980.
Hoig, Stan. *People of the Sacred Arrows: The Southern Cheyenne Today*. Cobbellhill Books, 1992.
Hoig, Stan. *The Peace Chiefs of the Cheyenne*. University of Oklahoma Press, 1980.

Hollister, Ovando J. *Boldly They Rode: A History of the First Colorado Regiment of Volunteers*. Golden Press, 1949.
Hollister, Ovando J. *History of the First Regiment of Colorado Volunteers in New Mexico, 1862*. R.R. Donnelley & Sons, 1962.
Howbert, Irving. *Memories of a Lifetime in the Pike's Peak Region*. G. P. Putnam's & Sons, 1925.
Hutton, Paul Andrew. *The Custer Reader*. University Press of Nebraska, 1992.
Hutton, Paul Andrew. *Phil Sheridan & His Army*. University Press of Nebraska, 1985, reprinted by University of Oklahoma Press, 1998.
Hyde, George E. *Life of George Bent: Written From His Letters*. University of Oklahoma Press, 1968.
Kraft, Louis. *Ned Wynkoop and the Lonely Road From Sand Creek*. University of Oklahoma Press, 2011.
Krudwig, Vickie Leigh. *Searching for Chipeta*. Fulcrum Publishing, 2004.
Lamm, Richard D. and Smith, Duane A. *Pioneers & Politicians, 10 Colorado Governors in Profile*. Pruett Publishing, 1984.
Lavender, Davis. *Bent's Fort*. University of Nebraska Press, 1954.
Lookingbill, Brad D. *War Dance at Fort Marion*. University of Oklahoma Press, 2006.
Leckie, William H. *The Military Conquest of the Southern Plains*. University of Oklahoma Press, 1963.
Leckie, William H. and Leckie, Shirley A. *The Buffalo Soldiers: A Narrative of the Black Cavalry in the West*. University of Oklahoma Press, 2003.
Madigan, Michael. *Heroes, Villains, Dames & Disasters:150 Years of Front-Page Stories From the Rocky Mountain News*. Madideas, LLC., 2009.
Mendoza, Patrick M., Strange Owl-Raben, Ann, and Strange Owl, Nico. *Four Great Rivers to Cross*. Libraries Unlimited, Inc. 1998.
Monnett, John. *The Battle of Beecher Island and the Indian War of 1867-1869*. University Press of Colorado, 1992.
Perkins, Robert L. *The First Hundred Years*. Doubleday & Company Publishers, 1959.
Pettit, Jan. *The Mountain People*. Johnson Books, 1990.
Powell, Father Peter J. *People of the Sacred Mountain: A History of the Northern Cheyenne Chiefs and Warrior Societies,1830-1879*. 2 volumes, Harper & Row, 1981.
Pratt, Richard Henry. *Battlefield and Classroom: Four Decades With the American Indian, 1867-1904*. Yale University Press, 1964.
Pritzker, Barry M. *A Native American Encyclopedia: History, Culture, and Peoples*. Oxford University Press, 2000.
Propst, Nell Brown. *Forgotton People*. Pruett Publishers, 1979.
Prucha, Francis Paul. *The Great White Father: The United States Government and the American Indians*. University of Nebraska Press, 1984.
Roberts, Gary L. *Sand Creek, Tragedy and Symbol*. University of Oklahoma Press, 1984.
Roberts, Gary L. and Halass, David F. *Written in Blood: The Soule-Cramer Sand Creek Massacre Letters*. Reprinted by Fulcum Press, 2004.

Roenigk, Adolph. *Pioneer History of Kansas*. Self-published, 1933.
Rogers, Vince. *The German Family Massacre*. Self-published, 1974.
Ruxton, George F. *Life in the Far West*. 1927, George F. Ruxton.
Seger, John H. *Early Days Among the Cheyenne and Arapaho Indians*. University of Oklahoma Bulletin, 1924 (edited by Stanley Vistal).
Smiley, Jerome C. *History of Denver*. Times-Sun Publishing Company, 1901.
Smith, Duane A. *The Birth of Colorado; A Civil War Perspective*. University of Oklahoma Press, 1989.
Smith, Duane A. *Rocky Mountain Mining Camps*. University Press of Colorado, 1992.
Smith, Duane A. *Henry M. Teller, Colorado's Grand Old Man*. University Press of Colorado, 2002.
Sprague, Marshall. *Massacre: The Tragedy at White River*. Little Brown & CO. 1957.
Whiteley, Lee. *The Cherokee Trail, Bent's Old Fort to Fort Bridger*. Johnson Books, 1999.
Ubbelohde, Carl, Benson, Maxine, and Smith, Duane. *A Colorado History*. Pruett Publishing, 1976.
Utley, Robert M. *The Indian Frontier of the American West 1846-1890*. University of Nebraska Press, 1984.
Utley, Robert M. *Life in Custer's Cavalry: Diaries and Letters of Albert and Jennie Barnitz, 1867-1868*. Yale University Pres, New Haven, Connecticut, 1977.
Utley, Robert M. *Frontier Regulars: The United States Army and the Indian, 1866-1890*. McMillan Publishing Company, New York, 1973.
Ware, Eugene F. *The Indian Wars of 1864*. Crane & Company, 1911. Reprinted by St. Martin's Press, 1960.
Wommack, Linda. *From the Grave: A Roadside Guide to Colorado's Pioneer Cemeteries*. Caxton Press, 1998.
Zamonski, Stanley W. and Keller, Teddy. *The '59er's*. Platte 'N Press Books, 1961.

— INDEX —

A

Abell, Henry H., 293
Abiquiu, New Mexico, 393
A Company, 16
Adams, Alva, 485
Adams, C. E., 492, 493
Adams, Charles, 419, 421, 422, 424, 425, 427, 428, 429, 452, 453–455, 456–460, 461, 464, 466, 468, 471, 490
Adams, Margaret, 419, 452, 488, 490–491
Adobe Walls trading post, 354–355
Afton, Jean, 348
Ahanash, 417
Akin, Lieutenant, 186
Alamosa, Colorado, 412, 477
Alderdice, Alice, 315, 330, 342
Alderdice, Frank, 315, 320
Alderdice, Susanna, 314, 315, 316, 318–319, 320, 324, 325, 329, 341, 343, 347, 505
Alderdice, Thomas, 256, 260, 314, 315, 316, 324, 325, 326–330, 343
Alexander, A. J., 421, 423
Alhandra, 469
Alights-On-Cloud, 155, 236–237, 238
Alkali Stage Station, 170
Alverson, John, 314, 316, 317–318, 319, 322
Alverson, Mary, 314
Alvord, Captain, 306, 308
Amache, 43, 93
American Ranch station, 157, 158, 159, 160, 161, 163, 177, 182, 183
Amick, Lieutenant, 292

Anasazi, 389
Andrews, Mr., 157
Animas City, 472, 473
Ankatosh, 426
Antelope, sub-chief, 413, 445, 461, 462
Antelope Hill, 299, 307, 308, 361
Antero band (Ute Indians), 422
Anthony, Scott J., 75, 76–77, 94, 95, 97, 98–99, 109, 110, 111, 117, 118, 119, 120, 122–123, 125, 126, 128, 133, 147
Antler's hotel, 252
Anway house, 252
Apache Indians, 19, 35, 39, 78, 80, 187, 219, 303, 392, 399
Appomattox, Virginia, 255
Arapaho/Douglas County line, 69n14
Arapahoe County, 136
Arapahoe Street, Denver City, 142n108
Arapaho Indians, 19, 22, 28, 29, 30–31, 33, 34, 35, 39, 44, 46, 47, 48–49, 50, 52, 54, 57, 58, 60, 61, 62, 63, 67, 68, 74, 75, 76, 77, 78, 79, 80, 83, 84, 85, 86, 104, 106, 112, 117, 118, 137, 142n108, 146, 172, 190, 199, 203, 209, 210, 211, 212, 218, 219, 221, 227, 228, 229, 2 31n6, 241–242, 244, 245, 247, 249, 250, 254, 272, 304, 305, 306, 308, 312, 371, 389, 394, 402, 407, 424, 425, 428, 503
Archuleta County, 427

Arickaree/Arikaree River, 259, 260, 263, 264, 272, 280, 288, 332, 334, 504
Arikara (Arikaree) fork, 80
Arizona, 178
Arkansas River, 28, 33–34, 35, 36, 37, 38, 47, 56, 64, 78, 79, 80, 85, 86, 87, 91, 92, 93, 106, 123, 129, 146, 187, 188, 190, 197, 210, 212, 225, 228, 229, 230, 235, 236, 242, 244, 262, 299, 300, 305, 306, 308, 395
Arkansas River Valley, 74, 400
Arkansas Road, 120
Arkansas Valley, 396
Armijo, Manuel, 392
Armstrong, W., 256, 273
Army Corps of Engineers, 424
Army Division of the Missouri, 442
Army of the Confederacy, 17
Arrow Keeper, 366
Artman, A., 326
Ash Creek, 215
Asher, Ambrose, 41–42, 46, 49, 67, 81, 166
Asher Creek, 325
Ashley, Susan Riley, 26–27
Atchison, Kansas, 67
Atchison, Topeka & Santa Fe Railroad, 356
Atchison Champion & Press, 345
Atkinson, D. F., 182
Auburn Advertiser, 123
Augar, Christopher C., 221, 345, 346
Augur, C. C., 329, 330
Augustine, 485
Autobees, Charles, 38, 58, 84, 396
Avery, Dr., 458

B

Baca, Marcelino, 397
Bacon, David, 242
Bacon, Mary Jane, 242
Bacon Creek, 242
Bad Heart, 268
Bad Wound, 204
Bailey, D. R., 250
Baker, Lewis, 186
Baldwin, Frank, 363
Baldwin, "Judge," 251
Baldwin, Lieutenant, 362
Bankhead, Henry, 283, 286, 288, 290
Banzof, Charles, 288
Barclay, Alexander, 395
Barnitz, Albert, 227, 230, 241
Basketmaker stage, 389
Battle of Beecher Island, 300, 315
Battle of Gettysburg, 197, 269
Battle of Pea Ridge, 302
Battle of Summit Springs, 167
Battle of the Washita, 312
Battle of the Wilderness, 254
Baughn, Michael L., 382
Baxter, Captain, 102
Bayou Salado, 396
Bear Feathers, 82, 270
Bear Man, 21, 108
Bear River, 90, 440, 459
Bears Heart, 364
Bear With Feathers, 83
Beaubien-Miranda-Maxwell land grant, 497n20
Beaumont, S. B., 472
Beaver Creek, 34, 80, 212, 256, 257, 303, 307, 313
Beaver Creek Station, 161
Becher, Ronald, 67
Beckwourth, Jim, 91, 93, 97, 110
Beecher, Charles, 269, 273, 283, 345
Beecher, Frederick H., 253, 254, 256, 258, 259, 266, 267, 268–269, 275, 287, 290, 292
Beecher, Henry Ward, 269
Beecher Island, 268, 282, 287, 288, 289, 293, 332
Beecher Island Battle, 504
Beecher Island Battleground Society, 504
Beecher Island Memorial Association, 504

516

Beloit, Kansas, 243
Benkelman, John, 247
Bennett, Colorado, 246
Bennett, Wallace, 256
Bent, Charles, 32, 33, 87, 99, 109, 111, 145, 147, 149, 150, 168, 177, 207, 212, 213, 221, 392, 393
Bent, George, 29, 33, 39, 41–42, 52, 77, 78, 79, 82–83, 84–85, 86–87, 93, 99, 101, 104, 106, 114, 145, 146–150, 151–152, 155, 167–169, 170, 172, 174–175, 177, 178, 188, 198–199, 200, 201, 212, 213, 218, 219, 221, 229, 241, 262, 263, 264, 267–268, 270–271, 272–273, 280, 304–305, 308–309, 312–313, 332–334, 336–337, 338, 339–340, 351n62, 364
Bent, Island, 145, 147
Bent, Julia, 87, 147, 198
Bent, Maria, 393
Bent, Robert, 85, 86, 93, 97, 99–100, 147
Bent, William, 83, 84, 85, 87, 92, 93, 146, 147, 187–188, 189, 354, 413
Bent's Old Fort, 37, 78, 84, 86, 87, 198–199, 392
Berry, William, 475, 476, 480
Berthrong, Donald J., 382, 383, 387n68
Beverly Ford, battle of, 254
Big Crow, 149, 150, 165, 180
Big Head, 80, 81
Big Horn Mountains, 164
Big Man, 146
Big Moccasin, 378
Big Mouth, 44, 62, 85, 221, 305
Big Sandy Creek, 292
Big Springs Station, 171
Big Steve, 158
Big Timbers, 147, 253
Big Wolf, 44, 89
Bijou Basin, 244
Bijou Creek, 19–20, 21, 59, 91, 94, 129

Bijou Creek Trail, 91
Bijou Station, 153
Bisbee, William H., 187
Bison Basin, 259
Bissonette, Joseph, 164, 165
Bissonette, Joseph, Jr., 164
Bitter Creek, 489–490
Bitter Water Creek, 198
Black Bear, 145
Black Deer, 221
Black Eagle, 219, 222
Black Foot, 41, 179, 180, 182
Black Hawk, Colorado Territory, 119
Black Hawk Journal, 126
Black Hills, 336
Black Horse, 368, 369
Black Kettle, 22, 36, 39, 44, 45–47, 48, 52, 53, 55, 57, 61–62, 63, 64, 67, 77–78, 79, 80–81, 82–83, 85, 86–87, 92, 93, 94, 95, 97, 99, 100–102, 104, 106, 107, 108, 112, 114, 118, 124, 125, 126, 127, 128, 135–136, 142n108, 146, 149, 166, 167, 181, 188, 189, 190, 199, 201, 202, 212, 213, 218, 219–220, 221, 222, 224–225, 226, 227, 228–229, 230, 235, 262, 299, 302, 304–307, 308, 309, 310, 311, 312, 353, 356
Black Mare/Tukukavapiapi, 394, 399, 400
Black Moon, 270
Black Shin, 213
Black Squirrel Creek, 236
Black Street, Denver City, 114
Black Tail Deer Creek, 332
Black White Man, 213, 229
Blanco River, 439
Blankhead, Colonel, 275
Blinn, Clara Isabel Harrington, 299–300, 302, 304, 306, 308, 311–312
Blinn, Hubble, 299, 300
Blinn, Richard Foote, 299–300
Blinn, William, 299, 300, 311, 312

Blue Ridge, Georgia, 360
Blue Ridge Mountains, 356
Blue River, 49
Blue River valley, 30
Bluffs Canyon, 33
Boggs, Rumalda Luna Bent, 393
Boiling Spring River, 396
Bonney Reservoir, 298n90
Boone, Albert Gallatin, 71n35, 84, 85, 86, 87, 240
Boone, Colonel, 37
Boone, Daniel, 71n35, 240
Booneville, Colorado, 37, 50, 71n35
Booth, Captain, 121
Bosse, 47, 52
Boston Journal, 123
Boulder News, 420
Bowen, Leavitt L., 112, 114
Bowers, Brookes, 216
Bowstring Cheyenne Warrior Society, 21, 32, 34, 51, 52, 55, 63, 68, 78, 79, 80, 85, 86, 87, 104, 106, 146, 147, 148, 155, 167, 168, 169, 170, 172, 177, 178, 186, 188, 191, 198, 199, 202, 204, 205, 207, 212, 213, 215, 218, 219, 220, 221, 222, 224–225, 226, 228, 229, 230, 235, 236, 237, 238, 241–242, 244, 254, 262, 267, 271, 272, 293, 299, 300, 303, 304, 313, 314, 318, 329, 331, 332, 333, 334, 335, 336, 338, 340, 342–343, 346, 347, 348, 353, 354, 356, 358, 361
Box Elder Creek, 22, 23, 24, 25, 61, 70n17
Bradford City, 416
Bradley, General, 283
Brady, Joseph W., 451, 452
Brave Bear, 338
Brewer, John, 171, 174
Bridger, Jim, 79–80, 396
Bright's Disease, 472
Brisbin, James S., 288, 290
Brondsall, Dr., 64

Brooks, E. J., 440
Broome, Jeff, 25, 69n14, 70n16, 504, 505
Brown, John S., 24, 25
Brown, Joseph, 208
Browne, General, 136
Brule Sioux Indians, 149, 221, 262
Brunot, Felix, 424, 425, 426–428
Brunot Treaty of 1873, 427, 428, 430
Brush, Jared L., 250
Buck, Antonio, 495
Buckskin Charlie, 430, 438, 466, 472–473, 474, 476, 487, 488, 489, 491, 493, 494, 495
Buffalo Calf Woman, 141n68
Buffalo Chief, 228, 229
Buffalo Goad, 199, 201
Buffalo Soldiers, 303, 447, 504
Bull Bear, 29, 44, 45, 47, 52, 53, 60, 63, 64, 204, 205, 209, 213, 228, 229, 262, 272–273
Bullfoot Creek, 322, 323
Bunch of Timbers, 44, 48, 145
Bunch of Trees, 235, 354
Bunch of Trees River, 106, 358
Bureau of Indian Affairs, 373, 417, 486, 489
Burke, Martin, 256, 264, 273
Burns, William, 471–472
Burton, Augustus W., 22
Butterfield/Smoky Hill Trail Association, 382
Buttles, John, 299
Byers, William Newton, 17, 27, 51, 62, 69n15, 73, 75, 108, 112, 113, 115–116, 117–118, 119–120, 122–124, 125, 126, 132, 137, 177, 224, 422

C

Cache la Poudre River, 28, 432, 435
Caddoa Creek, 93
Caddoe Indians, 305
Caldwell, Kansas, 380
Calhoun, James S., 393
California, 79
Cameron, Simon, 16

Campbell, Ben Nighthorse, 503
Campbell, Catherine, 215
Campbell, Daniel, 215
Campbell, Jessie, 215
Campbell, Peter, 214, 215, 217
Campbell, Peter, Jr., 215
Camp Collins, 28
Camp Fillmore, 37, 91
Camp Rankin, 148, 150, 170, 171, 172, 173, 175, 180, 181, 186, 187
Camp Sanborn, 21
Camp Supply, 307, 310, 346, 364
Camp Tyler, 178–179
Camp Wardwell, 179, 186
Camp Weld, 16, 19, 51, 57, 62, 63, 64, 73, 74, 76, 86, 88, 90, 93, 95, 96, 113, 115, 117, 125, 127
Canadian River, 307, 354, 359
Canby, Edward R. S., 19
Cannon, James D., 111–112, 121, 128, 133
Canon City, 437
Capote band (Ute Indians), 390, 393, 414, 427, 436, 439
Captain Jack, 249
Carleton, General, 48, 87–88
Carpenter, Captain, 254, 283, 290
Carpenter, Colonel, 282
Carpenter, Louis Henry, 284, 285, 286, 287, 288
Carr, Eugene Asa, 302–303, 313, 329, 330–331, 332, 334, 335–336, 337, 343, 344, 345, 346, 347
Carr, George, 346
Carson, Christopher "Kit," 187–188, 390, 395, 396, 397, 398–399, 401, 410–411, 412, 413, 414, 415
Carson, Josefa Jaramillo, 393, 410, 415
Cascade Avenue, Colorado Springs, 251
Casper, Wyoming, 164
Castle Rock, Colorado, 245
Cedar Canyon, 158

Central City, Colorado Territory, 15, 16, 158
Chalmers, G. W., 256
Chama River, 439
Chancellorsville, battle of, 254
Chavanaux, 469
Chavis, 417
Cherry, S. A., 442, 444
Cherry Creek, 24, 25, 29, 69n15, 84, 106, 146, 147, 333
Cheyenne, Wyoming, 425, 447
Cheyenne, Wyoming Leader, 292
Cheyenne Council of Forty-Four, 146, 238
Cheyenne County, Kansas, 148
Cheyenne Crooked Lance Society, 78, 149, 202, 220, 231n6, 262
Cheyenne Dog Soldiers, 21, 32, 34, 51, 52, 55, 63, 68, 78, 79, 80, 85, 86, 87, 104, 106, 146, 147, 148, 155, 167, 168, 169, 170, 172, 177, 178, 186, 188, 191, 198, 199, 202, 204, 205, 207, 212, 213, 215, 218, 219, 220, 221, 222, 224–225, 226, 228, 229, 230, 235, 237, 238, 241–242, 244, 254, 262, 267, 271, 272, 293, 299, 300, 303, 304, 313, 314, 318, 329, 331, 332, 333, 334, 335, 336, 338, 340, 342–343, 346, 347, 348, 353, 354, 356, 358, 361
Cheyenne Indians, 17, 19, 20, 21, 22, 28–29, 30–31, 33, 34, 35, 36, 38, 39, 40, 41, 42, 44, 47, 48–49, 50, 52, 54, 55, 57, 58, 59, 60, 61, 62, 63, 68, 74, 75, 76, 77, 78–79, 80, 81, 83, 84, 85, 86, 99, 103, 104, 105, 106, 117, 118, 125, 126, 127, 135, 137, 138, 139n14, 142n108, 146, 151, 154, 155, 160, 161, 164, 166, 168, 169, 170, 172, 176, 181, 182, 183, 188, 190, 201, 202, 203, 205, 208, 209, 210, 211, 212, 213, 214, 215, 217, 218, 219, 221, 222, 223,

519

226, 227, 228, 229, 235, 236, 237, 238, 239–242, 244, 245, 250, 259, 262, 263, 266, 268, 270, 271, 273, 276, 280, 290, 293, 301, 303, 305, 306, 308, 312, 313, 314, 318, 333, 337, 338, 339, 340, 341, 345, 346, 353, 354, 355, 356, 358, 364, 367, 368, 372, 373, 376, 377, 378, 380, 381, 382, 384, 387n68, 389, 394, 407, 412, 465, 503, 505
Cheyenne Jack, 306
Cheyenne Jennie, 304, 305
Cheyenne Sacred Arrows, 80, 81, 212, 213, 222, 225, 229, 353
Cheyenne-Sioux band, 82
Cheyenne Wells, Colorado, 277, 287, 297n84
Chickamauga, battle at, 315
Chicken Hawk, 369
Chipeta, 399, 400, 401, 402, 403, 404, 408, 411, 415, 417, 420, 421, 428, 430, 453, 454, 455–456, 466, 471, 474, 475–476, 481, 484–485, 486, 487, 488, 489–491, 492, 493, 495
Chivington, John Milton, 16, 18–19, 20, 21, 24, 26, 27, 33–34, 36, 38, 43, 50, 51, 52, 57, 61, 62, 63, 68, 74, 75, 87–88, 89–92, 93–94, 95, 96, 97, 98, 100, 102, 104, 107–109, 110, 112–114, 115, 116, 117, 118, 121, 122, 123–124, 125–128, 129, 130–131, 132, 134, 135, 136–137, 142n108, 157, 188, 189, 223, 224, 301, 312, 383, 406, 465
Cimmaron River, 82, 187, 219, 222, 225, 235, 301
City Cemetery, 65, 67, 133
Civil War, 19, 27, 187, 222, 253, 269, 314–315, 356, 401, 410, 412, 431, 498n24
Clark, G. B., 256
Clark, Watson, 94, 110

Clark, William H., 483
Clark, Wilson, 121
Clark & Co., 254
Clarke, Mr., 273
Clayton, Mrs., 158
Clear Creek County, 348
Cleave, Richard, 171, 172
Cleo, 350n22
Clift, Supt., 174
Cline, M. W., 452, 455
Clinton County, Ohio, 137
Cloud Chief, 270
Coad, Mark M., 161–162
Coal Creek, 25, 396
Coberly, Hersa, 130
Coburn, Watson S., 159, 163
Cochetopa Pass, 416, 417
Cody, William Frederick "Buffalo Bill," 313–314, 330, 334, 337, 340, 346, 351n62, 487
Coel, Margaret, 109
Coffey, Jules, 164
Coho, 422
Co-hoe (Limpy), 273
Cold Face, 221
Colley, Samuel G., 28, 39, 61, 62–63, 86–87, 96, 121, 126, 134
Collins, Catherine Weaver, 33
Collins, Col., 180
Collins, William O., 33
Colorado City, 244, 249, 250, 251, 252, 408–409
Colorado Historical Society, 142n108, 495, 503
Colorado History Center, 29, 348
Colorado National Guard, 485–486
Colorado Springs, Colorado, 487, 488
Colorado Territory, 15–16, 19, 20, 21, 26, 28, 34, 36, 49, 62, 68, 73, 74, 77, 85, 87, 88, 104, 108, 120, 146, 148, 155, 167, 177, 190, 197, 212, 213, 230, 235, 238, 239, 242, 244, 249, 254, 259, 292, 299, 336, 353, 357, 389, 390, 401, 413, 415,

423, 424, 432, 438, 465, 470–471, 477, 497n20
Colorado Third Regiment, 88
Colorado Volunteer Artillery, 20, 117
Colorado War, 486
Colorow, 249, 394, 413, 414, 416, 430–431, 443–444, 451, 452, 453, 465, 474, 475, 480, 485, 486
Comanche Creek, 244, 246, 247, 248
Comanche Indians, 19, 28, 35, 39, 56, 59, 67, 78, 83, 187, 190, 197, 199, 209, 219, 221, 225, 226, 227, 303, 304, 306, 354, 355, 360, 364, 368, 412, 413
Combs, James, 128, 129
Come See Him, 378
Commercial Club, 490
Commissary building, 26–27
Commission Camp, 227
Committee on Indian Affairs, 456
Company A, 331–332
Company B, 186
Company C (First Colorado Cavalry), 157
Company C (First Regiment), 98
Company D (First Regiment), 100, 113
Company D (Ninth Cavalry), 447
Company D (Seventh Iowa Cavalry), 165
Company E (First Regiment), 91, 98, 102, 111, 331–332
Company E (Seventh Iowa Cavalry), 149
Company F (First Regiment), 98
Company F (Seventh Iowa Cavalry), 170
Company F (Tenth Cavalry), 447
Company G (Third Regiment), 102
Company H (10th United States Cavalry Regiment), 287, 288
Company H (First Colorado Cavalry), 157

Company H (First Regiment), 91
Company M, 331–332, 335
Conejos community, 403, 404, 405
Conejos River, 398
Confederate Army, 87, 255, 315, 356, 404
Confederated Bands of Utes, 469, 470, 477, 483
Connor, Patrick E., 89–90, 91, 152, 178, 180
Consolidated Ute Indian Agency, 493
Continental Divide, 390, 391, 407, 414
Cook, Captain, 92
Cooley, D. N., 412
Coon village, 20
Corbin, D. C., 24
Corinth, 87
Corney, Patrick, 371
Cottonwood, 60
Council Bluffs, Iowa, 65, 70n29
Council Grove, Kansas Territory, 239
Council of 44, 304
Countant, Charles Griffin, 152
Court House Rock, 336
Cramer, Joseph A., 37, 44, 50, 52, 95, 96, 100, 102, 111, 112, 116, 125, 131
Crawford, Mr., 38
Crawford, Samuel J., 221, 243, 302, 311
Crazy Lodge, 221
Cree, T. G., 134
Cremer, H. W., 170
Cripple Creek, 499n60
Crooked Lance Society, 78, 149, 202, 220, 231n6, 262
Crosby, J. Schuyler, 256, 257
Cross, W. G., 157
Crow Chief, 22, 229
Crow Chief village, 20
Crow Creek, 21, 28
Crow Indians, 236
Culver, G. W., 264, 265
Cummings, Alexander, 410, 412, 413

521

Cunningham, Dr., 131
Curly Hair, 229
Curtis, Richard "Dick," 209
Curtis, Samuel R., 19, 48–49, 50, 62, 68, 75, 89, 91, 107–108, 112, 113, 117, 121–122, 127, 157, 168, 175
Curtis, Uriah H., 437, 499n67
Curtis Street, Denver City, 130
Cushing, Sylvanus E., 340, 341
Custer, George Armstrong, 77–78, 139n14, 197, 198, 203, 206, 207, 208, 211, 293, 303–304, 307, 308, 310–311, 312, 327, 328
Cut Hair, 262
Cut Nose, 221

D

Dahler, Mr., 154
Daily, James Alfred, 314–315
Daily, John, 314
Daily, Willis, 315, 320, 323, 324, 326
Daily Colorado Tribune, 224
Daily Mining Journal, 74
Daily News, 133
Dakota Territory, 164
Danforth, H. B., 434
Daniels & Brown, 23
Danielson, Mr., 161–162
Darlington Indian Agency, 365, 366, 367, 371, 377, 378, 380
Darrah, Thomas J., 24, 25–26
Daughters of the American Revolution, 492
Davenport, Harry, 256, 273
Davidson, Joseph C., 24, 70n16
Davis, Hiram, 169
Davis, John C., 483
Davis, Theodore, 261–262, 273
Davis, T. K., 256
Dawson, William, 503
Day, Bernard, 256, 273
Day, David, 464, 467–468, 470, 480
Decatur, Stephen, 112

Decoration Day, 315
Deer Creek, 443
Deer Creek Station, 164
Delaware Creek, 275
Delores County, 427
Delware Creek, 260
Denison, Lieutenant, 68
Dennison's ranch, 154
Denver City, Colorado Territory, 15, 18, 19–20, 22, 24, 26, 27, 29, 30, 34–35, 37, 47, 48, 49, 50, 51, 53, 66, 70n19, 74, 84, 89, 94, 108, 113, 114, 124, 129, 131, 132, 158, 161, 164, 171, 179, 181, 186, 246, 253, 404, 422, 425, 433, 458
Denver Commonwealth, 23, 69n15, 406
Denver Pacific Railroad, 433
Denver Pikes Peak Pioneers Association, 137
Denver Provost Guard, 129
Denver Theatre, 115–116
Denver Times, 472, 473, 475
Denver Town Company, 29
Denver Tribune, 423
Department of Indian Affairs, 478
Department of the Interior, 241, 307, 442, 464, 471, 478
Department of the Platte, 243
Department of the Upper Platte, 302
De Smet, Pierre Jean, 79–80
Developmental Pueblo stage, 389
Devil's Dive, 150, 172, 173
Dietemann, Apollinaris, 244–245, 246, 247, 248
Dietemann, Henrietta, 245, 247, 248
Dietemann, John, 245, 248, 249
Dietemann, Maria, 245
Dimon, Augustus, 182, 183, 184–185
District of Utah, 89
Divide, 499n60
Dixon, William "Billy," 355
Dodge, Francis S., 447

Dodge, Grenville M., 186
Dodge City, Kansas, 356
Dog Man, 44
Dog Soldiers, 21, 32, 34, 51, 52, 55, 63, 68, 78, 79, 80, 85, 86, 87, 104, 106, 146, 147, 148, 155, 167, 168, 169, 170, 172, 177, 178, 186, 188, 191, 198, 199, 202, 204, 205, 207, 212, 213, 215, 218, 219, 220, 221, 222, 224–225, 226, 228, 229, 230, 235, 237, 238, 241–242, 244, 254, 262, 267, 271, 272, 293, 299, 300, 303, 304, 313, 314, 318, 329, 331, 332, 333, 334, 335, 336, 338, 340, 342–343, 346, 347, 348, 353, 354, 356, 358, 361
Dog Soldier Society, 236
Dolan, Thomas, 422, 427
Donovan, Jack, 275, 276, 277, 281, 283, 285, 286, 291
Donovan, John, 256
Doolittle, James Rood, 121–122, 126, 135, 136, 409
Douglas, sub-chief, 413, 437–438, 441, 444, 445, 447, 453, 454–455, 458, 459, 460–462, 465, 466, 468, 476, 477–478
Douglas County, 247
Downer Station, 208
Downing, Finis, 403
Downing, Jacob, 95, 96, 250, 253
Doyle, Joseph B., 395
Dragon, Utah, 489
Dresser, Eaton, 448
Dresser, Frank, 445, 446, 448, 461–462
Dresser, Harry, 449
Dry Fork, 284
Dumont, Colorado, 348
Dunn, Clark, 21, 109, 134
Dupont, Alfred, 256
Dynamite, 419

E

Eads, Colorado, 503–504
Eads Chamber of Commerce, 503
Eagle, 364
Eagle Eye, 489
Eagle Feather, 78
Earrings, 155, 236, 238
East Fourteenth Street, Denver City, 26
Eayre, George S., 20, 21, 22
Ebenezer, 445, 462
Edwards, John H., 360
8th Illinois Cavalry, 254
Eighth Cavalry, 360
Elbert, Samuel H., 426, 428
Elbert County, 247, 250
Elephant Rock, 313, 314
Eliza, Aunt, 37
Elkhorn Creek, 321
Elliott, Joe, 227
Elliott, Joel, 311, 312
Ellsworth, Kansas, 357
El Paso County, 249
El Paso County Pioneer Society, 488, 489
Entler, A. J., 256
Eskridge, E. W. "Wilmer," 443, 445, 449
Eubanks, Andrew, 31
Eubanks, Fred, 31
Eubanks, Harriet, 30
Eubanks, Henry, 31
Eubanks, Isabelle, 40–42, 46, 49, 63, 64–65, 67, 81, 166
Eubanks, James, 31
Eubanks, Jennie, 182
Eubanks, Joseph, 30–31, 42, 67
Eubanks, Joseph, Jr., 30–31
Eubanks, Lucinda, 40–42, 47, 64, 65, 67, 166, 179, 180, 181–182
Eubanks, Meldora (Dora), 32
Eubanks, Sarah, 32
Eubanks, William, 30–31, 41, 65–66, 182
Eubanks, William, Jr., 40–41, 47, 65, 179
Eubanks family, 39, 65

Eureka, Colorado Territory, 16
Evans, John, 18, 19, 22, 24, 26, 27–28, 29, 34, 35, 36, 44, 45, 47, 49, 50, 51–69, 73, 74, 75–76, 95, 113, 115, 126, 127, 132, 135, 136, 137, 189, 224, 403, 406, 408, 409, 410
Everhart, Charley, 250–252
Express Messenger, 154
Ezekiel, Captain, 254

F

Fahrion, L. J., 247–248
Fairmount Cemetery, 70n19
Farley, Hudson, 256, 273
Farley, Louis, 256, 264, 265, 273, 288
Fauntleroy, T. T., 397
Feldman, Albert, 381
Ferguson, Mr., 25
Ferris, John, 208
Ferry Street, Denver City, 26, 63, 114
Field, Eugene, 484–485
Fifteenth Street, Denver City, 142n108
Fifth Cavalry, 313, 329, 330, 335, 343, 347, 360, 362, 451
Filler, Hohn Henry, 348
First Colorado Cavalry, 19, 21, 22, 33–34, 36, 65, 77, 96, 97, 98–99, 102, 113, 114, 122, 128, 142n108, 244, 405, 486
First Colorado Regiment, 125, 131
First Indian Expedition, 108, 118
First Regiment of Colorado Volunteers, 15–16, 17–18, 19, 90, 91, 92–93
Fitzgerald, Jenkins A., 288
Fitzpatrick, Thomas (Broken Hand), 79
Fletcher, John, 32
Fletcher, Susan, 40
Fletcher, William, 32, 40
Fletcher/Morgan group, 32, 33, 39
Florida, 11
Florissant area, 430, 499n60

Follett, Mr., 24
Fool Badger, 59
Ford, James, 117
Ford, James H., 187
Forsyth, George Alexander, 244, 253, 254, 255–261, 263, 264, 265, 266, 268–269, 272, 273, 274, 275–276, 278–279, 280, 282, 283, 284, 285–286, 287, 288, 291–292, 293, 303, 315, 323, 327, 345
Fort Arbuckle, 312
Fort Cobb, 304, 307, 308
Fort Crawford, 485
Fort D. A. Russell, 447
Fort Dodge, 209
Fort Dog, 223
Fort Duchesne, 492
Fort Fauntleroy, 84
Fort Fred Steele, 442, 445, 447
Fort Garland, 398, 410, 412, 413, 421, 423, 478
Fort Harker, 243, 256, 302, 307, 321, 322, 324, 325, 329
Fort Hays, Kansas, 208, 254, 255, 256, 257, 284, 292, 304, 312, 313, 357
Fort Kearney, 32, 89, 167, 180, 214, 314
Fort Laramie, 28, 33, 79, 164, 165, 166, 179, 181
Fort Laramie Treaty, 85–86
Fort Larned, 28, 61, 197, 199, 201, 203, 210, 212, 218
Fort Leavenworth, 68, 75, 88, 117, 167, 175, 177, 315, 327, 329, 364, 370, 373, 374, 377, 378, 382, 383, 392, 442, 468, 476
Fort Lyon, 28, 35, 36–37, 38–39, 42, 43, 44, 45, 47, 50, 52, 55, 61–62, 63, 66, 68, 74, 75, 76, 77, 88, 93, 94, 95, 97, 108, 109, 111, 112, 114–115, 117, 118, 119, 120, 122, 123, 125, 126, 127, 128, 129, 131, 135, 136, 146, 147, 197, 228, 253, 293, 300, 409, 415

Fort Marion, 372, 374, 376, 377, 378
Fort McPherson, Nebraska Territory, 170, 216, 217, 345, 348
Fort Morgan, 186, 253
Fort Pueblo, 395, 396, 397
Fort Rankin, 148
Fort Reno, 377
Fort Reynolds, 249, 283
Fort Rice, 182
Fort Riley, Kansas, 75, 93, 95, 116, 117, 129, 197, 383
Fort Sedge, 238
Fort Sedgwick, 186, 187, 288, 344, 345
Fort Sill, 312, 364, 371, 373
Fort Steele, 440
Fort Supply, 329
Fort Union, 18, 406, 410
Fort Wallace, 253, 254, 256, 257, 273, 275, 280, 283, 284, 286, 290, 291, 303, 357, 360, 378
Fort Wallace Memorial Association, 504
Fort Wicked, 187, 210
Fort Wise, 22, 84, 85, 187
Fort Wise Treaty, 235
Forty-Fourth Mississippi Regiment, 315
Fort Zarah, 240
Foster, Dora I., 416
Foster, Miss, 242
Fountain Creek, 252, 395, 397, 408
Fountain Valley, 244
Fourth Cavalry, 372, 478
Fourth Division of the Army of the Southwest, 302
Fourth Infantry, 442
Fouts, William D., 180, 181
Frank, Thomas, 32
Frank Leslie's Illustrated Newspaper, 473–474
Franktown, Colorado, 70n16
Fredericksburg, battle of, 254
Freeman, Daniel, 32

Freemont Butte, 337
Fremont, John C., 69n9
Fremont's Orchard, 21, 58, 69n9
Frenchman Creek, 336
Frenchmans Fork, 283
Friday, Chief, 402, 429
Frog, 82
Frontier Index, 253
Front Street, Denver City, 248
F Street, Denver City, 130, 131

G

Galota, 469
Galvanized Yankees, 315
Gantt, Richard, 256, 264, 273
Garden of the Gods, 416, 488, 489
Garfield, James A., 482
Gary, Guy, 489
Gentle Horse, 78
German, Adelaide, 357, 358, 359, 362, 363, 364, 365, 370
German, Catherine Elizabeth, 357, 358, 359, 361, 363, 365–366, 367–368, 370–371, 372, 385n17
German, Joanna, 357, 358
German, John, 356–357, 358
German, Juliana, 357, 358, 359, 362, 363, 364, 365, 370, 372
German, Lydia Cox, 356–357, 358
German, Rebecca Jane, 357, 358
German, Stephen, 357, 358
German Feldman, Sophia Louisa, 357–358, 359, 362, 363, 365, 366–368, 369, 370, 372, 381
Gerry, Elbridge, 22, 28–29, 33–36, 38, 59, 70n32, 186, 250
"Gettysburg of the West," 18
Gillette, Lewis B., 170–171
Gilpin, Frederick W., 438
Gilpin, William, 15, 16, 17, 18, 392
Glorieta Pass, 16, 18, 69n6, 91
Godfrey, Celia, 160
Godfrey, Holan, 160, 161, 163, 179, 187, 250
Godfrey, Martha, 160

Godfrey, Matilda, 160
Godfrey's Ranch (Fort Wicked), 210
Gomer, Philip, 25, 250
Gomer's Mill, 25, 26, 250
Goodall, Commissioner, 223
Good Bears, 262, 270, 314, 340
Good Manitou, 412
Goose Creek, 284
Graham, George, 292
Graham, Joseph, 88, 92, 93, 407
Granby area, 430
Grand Army of the Republic, 504
Grand Island, Nebraska, 218
Grand Junction, Colorado, 483, 487, 489
Grand River, 447, 469
Grand River Ute Indians, 51, 390, 406, 415, 427, 436
Grant, Ulysses S., 221, 254, 255, 371, 372, 421, 422, 424, 429
Gray, Captain, 37
Gray Beard, 213, 221, 222, 224
Gray Head, 204, 226, 227
Gray Thunder, 87
Great Father, 53, 54, 63
Great Salt Lake Valley, 407
Great Spirit, 280
Great White Father, 236
Greeley, Colorado, 182, 433, 434, 482
Greeley, Horace, 431–432, 433, 434
Greeley Tribune, 433, 434
Green, George, 256
Green River, 480
Greenwood, A. B., 83, 84, 85, 99
Grey Beard, 359, 361, 364, 373, 374, 375, 376
Griffenstein, William "Dutch," 304, 305, 306
Gross, F. A., 492
Grover, Aber, 303
Grover, Abner T., 256, 258, 264
G Street, Denver City, 114
'G' Troop, 322–323
Guadalupita, 399
Guerno, 426

Guero, 422
Guerrier, Edmund, 99, 100, 146, 147, 198, 202, 204, 205, 206, 220, 221, 222
Gunnison, Colorado, 407, 414
Gunnison River, 427, 455, 469, 479

H

Hail, Gus, 158
Hailstone, 378
Haley, John, 256, 265, 273
Haley, Michael, 316, 318
Hall, Frank, 249, 250
Hall, Gus, 159–160, 163
Halleck, General, 88
Hamill, William A., 449, 450
Hamilton, Dr., 157
Hancock, Winfield Scott, 38, 197, 198, 201–203, 204, 205, 206–207, 208–209, 210, 212, 222, 223, 224, 227, 261
Hardin, George, 45, 95
Harlan, James, 187
Harlow, William H., 169, 170
Harlow's Ranch, 169
Harney, William S., 187, 190, 221, 222–223, 226
Harper's Weekly, 261, 430, 431, 461
Harrington, Frank, 256, 264, 273
Harrington, William T., 306, 311
Harrison, Belle, 67
Harrison, Benjamin, 484
Hartman, George, 420
Hartsell, Colorado Territory, 244
Harvard University, 417
Haseekep, 474
Haskins, Peter V., 343, 347, 348
Hatch, Edward, 435, 456, 461, 462, 463–465, 467, 478
Hatch, John, 84
Hatch, Thom, 78, 82, 101
Hawk, 333
Hawkens, 105
Hawk Leader, 364
Hayes, Rutherford B., 434, 438, 481

526

Hays City, 292
Hayt, H. A., 439–440
Hazen, William B., 305–306, 307, 308
Head, Lafayette, 401, 403, 404, 405, 406, 408, 409
Heap of Birds, 229
Heap of Buffalo, 47, 52
Hebron, Nebraska, 213
Henderickson, C. C., 326
Henderickson, Martin, 324, 326
Henderson, John B., 221, 223, 225, 226, 228, 229, 230
Hendrickson, C. C., 321
Hennessy, Oklahoma, 356
Hennessy, Patrick, 372
Henning, B. S., 75
Henry Jim, 437, 438
Henshaw, Gregory, 216
Hersey, Milton, 492–493
Heviqsnipahis clan, 146
Hickok, "Wild Bill," 335
High Black Wolf, 79
Hill, J. J. Pete, 504
Hill, Nathaniel, 470
Hi-moi-yo-qis, 262
Hines, John, 155
Hinsdale County, 427
Hisometainio clan, 146
Hiteman, John, 169
Hodder, Halie Riley, 177
Ho-iv-i-ma-nah band, 87
Holcomb, Philo, 176
Holliday, Ben, 89–90
Hollister, Ovando J., 18
Holyoke, Colorado, 332
Homestead Act of 1862, 314
Ho-Nehe-Taneo-O (Wolf People or Pawnee), 155
Hook Nose (Roman Nose), 262
Hopson, Dr., 473
Horse Creek, 79
Hoseshoe Station, 165
Hot Stuff, 419
House of Representatives, 126
Howbert, Irving, 88, 92, 93, 94, 96, 97, 244, 249, 251, 252, 407, 416

Howell County, Missouri, 356
Howling Magpie, 333, 334
Howling Wolf, 146, 147
Huerfano Creek, 395
Hughes, Andrew, 173, 174
Hughes, M. B., 447
Hugus, J. W., 483
Hungate, Ellen Eliza, 22–27
Hungate, Florence, 22–27
Hungate, Laura, 22–27
Hungate, Nathan Ward, 22–27
Hungate family, 22–27, 58, 61, 70n19
Hunt, Alexander Cameron, 244, 249, 413, 414, 422
Hunt, Governor, 253
Hurst, John, 256, 264, 266, 275, 278, 280, 281, 286
Hutton, Paul A., 310–311
Hyde, George, 147, 150, 241, 263, 332–333
Hyde, George E., 179, 206

I

Idaho, 177
Ignacio, 422, 438, 466, 471, 472, 474, 476, 484, 486, 491, 494
Ignacio, Colorado, 491, 493, 494
Ignatio, 469
Independent Battery of Colorado Volunteer Artillery, 20
Indian Depredation Claim, 248
Indian Territory (Oklahoma), 225, 228, 230
Indian War, 36
Iron Shirt, 228, 236, 354, 358
Irwin, Jackson, & Company, 19
Island Woman, 217

J

Jack, Captain, 461
Jack, sub-chief, 413, 414, 437–438, 443–444, 451, 452, 466, 468, 477
Jack of Clubs, 419
Jackson, Helen Hunt, 483, 484
Jackson Hole, 28

Jacksonville, Florida, 376
Jacobs, E. H., 124
James, Amos, 128
Jauken, Arlene, 381, 382, 383
Jicarilla Apache Indians, 391, 395, 396, 401, 410
Jim, Henry, 499n67
Jimmy's Camp, 58
Jocknick, J. F., 418, 428
Jocknick, Sidney, 480–481
Johnson, Andrew, 187, 243, 409, 410
Johnson, Harvey, 180
Johnson, Henry, 447
Johnson, Jay J., 134
Johnson, Jim, 25, 441, 461, 468
Johnson, Leona, 250
Johnson, Louisa A., 250
Johnson, Y. J., 95
Joint Committee on the Conduct of War, 120, 126
Jones, Captain, 158
Jones, Henry C., 372
Jones, Jack, 29
Julesburg, Colorado Territory, 29, 32, 33, 89, 148, 150, 152, 154, 155, 158, 168, 170, 171, 173, 175, 177, 179, 187, 188, 210, 238, 239, 344
Julesburg Station, 148, 169, 170, 171, 343
Junction City, Kansas, 324
Junction City Weekly Union, 325
Junction Stage Station, 161, 162
Junction Station, 34

K

Kahnah Creek, 479
Kalus, Albert, 213, 214
Kalus, Margaretha, 213
Kaneache, 398, 414
Kansas City Times, 370
Kansas Daily Commonwealth, 325
Kansas Insane Asylum, 326
Kansas Pacific Railroad, 253
Kansas Territory, 36, 68, 75, 106, 145, 155, 178, 190, 197, 212, 213, 230, 235, 238, 242, 244, 254, 299, 300, 304, 313, 404
Kansas Tribune, 224
Kaw Indian Agency, 239, 240, 241
Kaw Indians, 240
Kearny, Stephen Watts, 392
Kearsey, Colorado, 182
Keeper of the Sacred Arrows, 87
Kehler, Reverend, 130
Keim, Randolph DeBenneville, 311–312
Keith, 61
Keith & Cook, 158
Kelly, Michael, 32
Kendall, James, 485
Kennedy, J. J., 157
Kenny, Thomas, 179
Kent, O. O., 133
Keogh, Myles, 241
Ketterer, J. H., 256
Keynon, Ordnance Sergeant, 37
kichais, 305
Kicking Bird, 209
Kicking Eagle, 219
Kile, John, 335
Kills Many Bulls, 339
Kine, Bridget, 319–320, 321, 323, 326
Kine, Katherine, 319, 321, 326
Kine, Timothy, 319–320, 326, 350n37
King, W. G., 489–490
Kiowa County, 503
Kiowa Indians, 19, 28, 35, 39, 56, 59, 61, 67, 78, 80, 83, 187, 190, 197, 199, 209, 210, 219, 221, 222, 225, 226, 227, 246, 247, 303, 304, 306, 354, 355, 360, 364, 371, 399
Knock Knee, 107
Kraft, Louis, 204
Kuner canning plant, 70n32

L

Lacey, John H., 437, 472, 473
LaGrange, Colonel, 383
La Jara Creek, 397

Lake City, 451
Lake Creek, 199
Lakota Indians, 146
Lamar, Colorado Territory, 299
Lamar Chamber of Commerce, 503
Lambert, Julia S., 37–38, 47, 122
Lame Man, 305
LaMunyon, Ira W., 348
Lane, Joseph, 256
Lane, M. R., 256
Lanier, Sidney, 378
Lantz, Philip, 326
La Plata County, 427
Larimer, Sarah L., 165
Larimer Street, Denver City, 114, 133
Last War Trail, 485
Las Vegas, New Mexico, 133
Latham, Colorado Territory, 35
Lauritzen, Esrkild, 318, 324
Lauritzen, Stine, 318, 324
Law, Edward, 322, 324, 327
Lawrence, Kansas, 133, 307, 498n24
Lawrence, Mr., 245
Lawrence Street, Denver City, 130, 131
Lean Bear, 45, 60, 85, 374–375
Leavenworth, Jesse H., 187, 188, 197, 198, 201, 203, 209, 212
Leavenworth Daily Commercial, 327–328, 329, 374
Leavenworth Times, 168, 175, 176, 177, 283, 291, 292
Lee, Robert E., 255
Lee, Stephen Louis, 393
Leeds, William, 435
Left Hand, 44, 45, 47, 60, 64, 77, 85, 94, 95, 97, 108–109, 118, 128
Legislature of Kansas, 177, 178
Leslie, Major, 486
Lewin, Mrs. William H. Ross, 292
Liberty Farm, 49
Limpy (Co-hoe), 273
Lincoln, Abraham, 15, 16, 17, 18, 86, 314, 404, 406

Lincoln Republican, 325
Linn Grove Cemetery, 482, 499n61
Little Arkansas River, 188
Little Bear, 204, 229, 270
Little Beaver, 311
Little Blue River, 30, 40, 59, 64, 65, 179, 181, 182, 214
Little Blue Valley, 31
Little Bull, 369
Little Chief, 21, 22, 401
Little Coyote, 170, 262
Little Hawk, 263
Little Man, 333–334
Little Mountain, 78
Little Raven, 38, 44, 45, 77, 85, 97, 188, 190, 199, 209, 210, 218, 219, 228, 312
Little Robe, 107, 108, 213, 226, 228, 229, 239, 305, 308, 329
Little Rock, 308
Little Sage Woman, 78, 79, 82
Little Shield, 364
Little Squaw, 361
Little Wolf, 85, 213, 262
Living Creek, 23
Livingston, Col., 175
Livingston, David, 201
Lloyd, John B., 480
Lodge Pole Creek, 177
Lodge Pole River, 138, 304
Logan County, 504
Lone Bear (One-Eye), 146, 201, 305, 339
Long Back, 370–371
Long Chin, 29, 34, 80–81
Long Eye, 186
Long Neck, 364
Lookout Station, 208
Los Pinos Indian Agency, 416, 419, 421, 425, 451, 452, 461, 462, 464, 471, 473–474, 475, 477, 488
Lost Creek, 316
Louderback, David, 94, 99, 110, 121, 128
Lyden, John, 256

M

Mackenzie, Mr., 478, 479
Mackey, Thomas, 165
Mad Bear, 334
Madison, James, 29
Mad Wolf, 21
Magee, Mark, 383
Magpie, 77, 190, 200, 309
Major, Newton, 483
Making Medicine, 378
Man-Afraid-of-His Horses, 152, \ 221
Man Bear, 364
Manifest Destiny, 138
Manitou Mountain, 414
Manitou Springs, Colorado, 390, 487, 488, 489
Man-On-A-Cloud, 228, 262, 354, 358
Man-Shot-By-A-Ree, 34
The Man that Moves, 209
Man that Walks Under the Cloud, 221
Mantz, John, 346
Manypenny, George Washington, 477, 478
Mapes, M. R., 256
Marble, Ann, 65, 70n29
Marble, Charlotte Ann, 32
Marble, Daniel, 32, 40, 46, 49, 65, 81, 166
Marble, Joel, 32, 70n29
Marble, William, 32
March, T. J., 322–323
Marki, Benedict, 245, 246–247
Massachusetts, 28, 29
Masterson, William Bartholomew "Bat," 355
Maxwell Land Grant, 401
Maynard, Captain, 25, 96
McCall, H. H., 256, 259, 265, 273
McClellan Creek, 359, 361, 362
McClelland, W. F., 65, 249
McCook, Edward, 416, 417, 418, 419, 420, 421, 422
McCook, John, 471, 474, 475, 486, 491, 493, 494, 495, 502n151

McCook, Roland, Sr., 502n151
McCune, Kansas, 182
McFarland, N. C., 435
McGaa, William W., 29
McGrath, H. T., 256
McKean, E. E., 491–492
McLaughlin, Louis, 256, 273
McNall, Paul, 383
McNally, Christopher H., 148
Meade, Kansas, 356
Mears, Otto, 409, 417, 422, 427–428, 429, 435, 466, 471, 475, 476, 477
Measure Woman, 299, 310, 349n1, 370, 377, 381, 383
Medicine Arrow, 164
Medicine Lodge Creek, 199, 217, 218, 219, 221, 222, 226
Medicine Lodge Treaty, 229, 230, 235, 237, 238, 240, 243, 244, 254, 262
Medicine Lodge Treaty Council, 229–230
Medicine Man, 58
Medicine Water, 139n13, 151, 154, 156, 186, 191, 200, 207, 213, 228, 230, 235–236, 237, 238, 262, 273, 280, 299, 304, 309–310, 313, 347, 349n1, 353, 354, 355, 356, 358, 359, 360, 361, 362, 363, 364–365, 366, 368, 369–370, 371, 372, 377, 378, 379–380, 381, 382–383, 384
Medicine Wolf, 204
Medicine Woman, 82, 350n22
Medicine Woman Later, 100–101, 104, 106, 107, 190, 201, 308, 309
Medina, Juan Rafael, 397
Meeker, Colorado, 483–484, 485, 505
Meeker, George, 431, 433
Meeker, Josephine, 11, 431, 433, 437, 438, 445, 446–447, 455, 456–461, 466, 482, 499n70, 501n133

530

Meeker, Mary, 431, 433
Meeker, Nathaniel Cook, 431–432, 434, 435–436, 438, 439, 440–441, 441–442, 444, 445, 446, 448, 449–450, 456, 465–466, 468, 482, 483, 501n135, 505
Meeker, Ralph, 431, 433, 455, 456
Meeker, Rozene, 431, 433, 482
Meeker Herald, 436
Meeker House Museum, 499n70
Meeker Massacre, 389, 448, 456, 466, 470, 477, 481, 505
Meeker Memorial Museum, 501n133
Meeker Smith, Arvilla Delight, 431, 433, 437, 438, 446, 448, 453–455, 456, 460–461, 466, 499n61
Meigerhoff, Fred, 318, 324
Memorial Day, 315
Merino, Colorado, 157
Meriwether, David, 395, 398–399
Merritt, Wesley, 447, 449, 451
Mesa Verde period, 389
Mexicans, 35, 82
Mexico, 392, 497n20
Meyer, Lipman, 134
Middle Kiowa Creek, 246, 248
Middle Park, 414, 440, 447
Miksch, Amos, 102, 114
Miles, John D., 364, 368, 370, 371
Miles, Nelson A., 360, 362, 363, 365, 382, 383
Military Department of the Missouri, 197
Military District of Colorado, 19
Military District of Nebraska Territory, 19
Milk Creek, 389, 443, 444, 445, 447–448, 449, 451, 461
Milk Creek Massacre, 449, 466, 470, 477
Miner's Register, 158
Minimic, 32, 39, 42, 44, 376
Minnecongus tribe, 184
Minnesota, 60
Minnesota River, 78
Minton, William, 128
Mission Indians, 483
Mississippi Delta area, 431
Missouri, 404
Missouri River, 88
Missouri River Sioux Indians, 60
Mitchell, Governor, 153
Mitchell, Robert B., 19, 33, 148
Mitchell, Robert H., 168, 175, 176
M. K. & T. Railroad, 373
Mo-chi, 11, 105–106, 139n13, 141n68, 149, 154, 155, 156, 186, 200, 207, 230, 237, 238, 262, 280, 299, 304, 309–310, 313, 347, 349n1, 353, 354, 355, 358–359, 361, 362, 363, 366, 368, 369, 371, 372, 373–374, 377, 378–379, 380, 381, 382–383
Monroe, Michigan, 303
Montana, 271
Montezuma County, 427
Montrose, Colorado, 491, 495
Montrose County, 427, 428, 487
Monument Creek, 244, 250
Monument Station, 208, 360
Mooers, John H., 256, 266, 268, 273, 274, 275, 278, 283, 292
Moon Face, 489
Moonlight, Thomas, 117, 122, 124, 127, 157, 167, 180
Moon of the Strong Wind, 154
Moore, Charles, 155, 171, 177, 239
Moore, James, 239
Moore, Jim, 155, 171, 177
Moore, Mary, 147
Moore, Robison, 147
Morgantown, Fannin County, Georgia, 356
Morris, Charles, 179
Morris, Charley, 183
Morris, Joseph, 179, 183, 184
Morris, Sarah, 160, 179, 182, 183–185
Morris, William, 158, 159, 163, 183, 184

531

Morton, Frank, 39, 273
Morton, Howard, 256, 265, 280–281
Morton, John, 40
Morton, Mrs., 164, 165
Morton, Nancy Jane, 32, 39–40, 42, 164, 165, 166, 180
Morton, Thomas, 42
Morton, William, 40
Mouache band (Ute Indians), 390, 393, 397, 398, 401, 406, 407, 414, 415, 422, 427, 436, 439, 494
Mountain Ute Reservation, 496
Mount Calvary burial site, 70n19
Mount Prospect Cemetery, 26, 133
Murah, Guera, 391, 394
Murah, Susan, 391, 394, 402, 441
Murphy, John, 170
Murphy, Thomas, 199, 206, 210, 211, 218–219, 220–221, 240, 241, 242, 256, 258, 264, 265, 307

N

Naneese, 474, 475, 489, 493, 494
Narrows, 65, 181
Nashville, Tennessee, 374
Na-ta-nee, 52
National Register of Historic Places, 504
Native American Church, 380
Native American Graves Protection and Repatriation Act, 502n151
Navajo River, 439
Nebraska City, 66
Nebraska Nelson Gazette, 65
Nebraska Territory, 19, 30, 32, 34, 36, 42, 63, 136, 148, 161, 164, 166, 167, 171, 179, 180, 182, 187, 190, 212, 213, 215
Neill, Thomas, 362, 367, 368, 369
Neva, 44, 46, 47, 52, 58–61, 64
Nevava, 413, 414, 430
New Mexico Territory, 18, 35, 48, 88, 130, 177, 178, 366–367, 389, 390, 399, 401, 405, 407, 414, 418, 438, 465
New Orleans, Louisiana, 431
New York City, 290
New York Herald, 123, 311
New York Times, 241, 283, 312, 328–329, 345
New York Tribune, 201, 206, 219, 226, 431, 435
Nichols, Captain, 89
Nichols, C. B., 256
Nichols, General, 283
Nicolay, John, 406
Nineteenth Kansas Volunteer Cavalry, 311
Noha's-w-stan, 318
North, Frank, 217, 331, 332, 334, 336, 340, 351n62
North, Frank Joshua, 330
North, Luther, 338, 340–341, 344, 346
North, Robert, 19, 35, 61
Northern Arapaho Indians, 146, 148, 149, 168, 169, 262, 270, 424
Northern Cheyenne Indians, 214, 215, 254, 261, 262, 271, 336
Northern Ute Indians, 439, 469, 477
North Park, 414, 440
North Peak area, 430
North Platte, Nebraska, 218, 348
North Platte River, 28, 80, 181, 222, 235, 346
Notnee, John, 61

O

Oak, Colorado Territory, 30
Oakes, D. C., 414
Oaks, George, 256
Oberlin College, 433
O'Brien, Nicholas J., 149, 150, 152, 153, 170, 171, 172, 173, 174, 176
O'Donnell, Thomas, 256, 273
O'Fallon's Bluff, 186

532

Oglala Sioux Indians, 149, 179, 204, 213, 215
Ohio Cavalry, 180
Oivimana clan, 146
Oklahoma Historical Society, 381
Oklahoma Territory, 225, 228, 230, 235, 312, 353, 426
Old Crow, 151
Old Fort Wicked, 163
Old Little Wolf, 228, 229
Old Nick, 419
Old Yellow Hair, 155, 236
Olney, James, 128, 134–135, 157
Omaha, Nebraska Territory, 163, 346
"100 Day Volunteers," 91
One-Eye (Lone Bear), 39, 42–45, 47, 87, 93, 94, 108, 146
One Eye Comes Together, 145
Oregon Trail, 30, 32, 80
Osage Indians, 201, 307, 310–311
Ouray, Chief, 389, 391–392, 394–395, 397–398, 399, 400, 401, 402, 403, 404–406, 407, 408, 411, 413, 414–415, 416, 417, 418, 419, 420, 421, 422, 424–425, 426, 429, 430, 431, 439, 441, 451, 452–453, 455–456, 461, 462–464, 465–466, 467, 470, 472–476, 484–485, 492, 493, 494, 495, 497n5, 498n24
Ouray, Colorado, 464–465, 490
Ouray County, 427
Ouray Memorial Park, 492, 495
Ouray Plainsdealer, 490
Ouray Times, 465–466
Overland Stage Company, 33, 35, 89, 213
Overland State Line, 158
Overland Telegraph Company, 148
Overland Trail, 14, 79, 148
Owl Woman, 33, 85, 87

P

Pabusar, 403
Pacific Telegraph Line, 176
Packer, 378
Padouca Comanche Indians, 308
Pah-sone, 446–447, 456–457, 458, 462
Pais, Guero, 396–397
Palmer, Joel, 488
Palmer, John, 30–31
Palmer, Lucian, 128
Palo Duro Canyon, 354
Pampa, Texas, 360
Parker, James, 478–479
Parker, Lieutenant, 186
Parker, Quanah, 354, 355
Parkman, Francis, 396
Paron, 400, 401, 402, 424, 425–426
Paul Revere of the Plains. *See* Gerry, Elbridge
Pawnee, 217
Pawnee Fork, 203, 205, 208, 227, 228
Pawnee Hills, 86
Pawnee Indians, 80, 81, 83, 211, 217, 236, 237, 261, 320–321, 331, 333, 334, 336, 337, 338, 339, 340, 379
Pawnee Killer, 33, 106, 148, 149, 204, 215, 221, 314, 346
Pawnee Ranch, 214
Payne, J. S., 442
Peare, J. J., 282
Pea Ridge, 87
Peate, J. J. "Jack," 284–285, 286–287, 290, 323, 324, 504
Pecos River, 365, 366
Pennsylvania, 66
Penrose, William H., 253, 293, 300
Perkins, Eli, 161, 163
Pfeiffer, Albert H., 418, 437
Phillips, Charles, 44
Piah, 414, 430, 451
Piatt, C. C., 256
Picayune newspaper, 431
Piedra River, 439
Pierce, Colorado, 182

Pierce, George, 102
Pikes Peak, 32, 389, 390, 396, 414, 416, 430
Pilgrim house, 239
Pine River, 474
Pioneer History of Kansas (Roenigk), 242
Pitkin, Frederick, 438–440, 441, 450, 451
Pi-Ute Indians, 90
Pixta, Joseph, 213, 214
Plains Indians, 14, 107
Plains Indian War, 22
Planter's House, 90
Plateau Creek, 453
Platte Avenue, Colorado Springs, 251
Platte Bridge, 164
Platte Rangers, 250
Platte River, 30, 32–33, 56, 59, 79, 88, 91, 123, 148, 164, 179, 183, 190, 210, 229, 242, 336, 344, 396
Platte River Road, 40, 215, 223
Platte River Trail, 404
Platte Road, 120, 168
Plattsburg, New York, 292
Pliley, A. J., 256, 275, 276–277, 281–282, 286, 297n84
Pliley, Allison J., 275
Plum Creek, 30, 33, 34, 39, 42, 70n29, 164, 165, 166, 215, 217, 244
Plum Creek Station, 32, 33
Polk, James Knox, 392
Pollock, Inspector, 455, 458
Pomeroy, Mr., 177
Pond City, 254
Pony Express, 171, 239
Poor Bear, 218
Pope, John, 176, 187, 410, 442
Porcupine, 215–216, 217
Porcupine Bear, 215
Post, W. H., 449
Potawatomi Indians, 81
Potter, Colonel, 216
Powder Face, 58, 429

Powder River, 152, 164, 329
Powvitz, 445, 462
Prairie Apache Indians, 199, 218, 304
Prairie Bear, 270
Pratt, Richard Henry, 371, 372, 373, 375–376, 378
Price, B. D., 442, 444, 445
Price, Flora Ellen, 446–447, 455–456, 461–462, 466
Price, Frank S., 448
Price, George F., 129, 335
Price, Hiram, 483
Price, Johnnie, 446, 448
Price, Joseph, 493, 494
Price, May, 446, 448, 462
Price, Sterling, 393
Price, William, 360
Protective Association, 423
Prowers, John, 43, 92–93
Pueblo, Colorado Territory, 37, 236
Purgatoire River, 92, 146, 147
Puwich, 403

Q

Quantrill, William Clark, 404, 498n24
Quenche/Queashegut, 391–392, 394, 400, 403
Quiziachigiate, 393–394

R

Ranahan, Thomas, 256
Ranchos de Taos, 392
Rankin, Joseph, 442–443, 445, 447
Rath, Charlie, 198–199
Raven, 58, 60
Rawlins, Wyoming, 435, 442, 464
Reaves, Howard C., 486
Red Bird, 310
Red Bull, 203
Red Canyon, 444
Red Cloud, 336
Red Eye Woman, 81–82
Red Nose, 242, 243

Red River, 225, 313, 364
Red Wolf, 216, 217
Regimental Band, 129
Reilly, William, 256
Relief Association, Denver City, 63, 67
Relief Expedition, 282
Renchier, J. H., 372
Republican River, 20, 22, 33–34, 39, 40, 60, 80, 85, 106, 146, 147, 154, 168, 181, 243, 259, 260, 264, 274, 275, 277, 283, 284, 285, 290, 292, 329, 330, 331, 332, 333, 335, 337, 345, 346
Republican River Expedition, 302, 343
Richmond, Harry, 128, 134, 135
Rio Blanco county, 414, 483
Rio Grande River, 397, 426
Rio Grande Valley, 405
Ripley, W. D., 21
Rising Bull, 378
Roan, George, 128
Robbins, Mr., 18
Robbins, Thomas H., 252
Rochester Evening Express, 291–292
Rock Creek, 332
Rock Island, Illinois, 315
Rocky Mountain News, 16, 27, 29, 34, 51, 62, 64, 69n15, 73, 75, 90, 108, 109, 112, 113,114-115, 117, 118, 119–120, 122, 123–124, 125, 126, 129, 130, 131–134, 136, 150, 152–153, 157, 158, 161, 163, 177–178, 181, 224, 247, 248–249, 390–391, 408–409, 410, 421, 422, 428, 449–450
Rocky Mountains, 80, 83–84, 390, 401, 432
Rodenbough, General, 261
Roenigk, Adolph, 242
Rogers, H. I., 130
Rogers, Vince, 385n17
Roman Nose, 58, 61, 198, 202, 204, 205, 209, 220, 221, 224, 230, 231n6, 238, 261, 262, 270–271, 272–273, 280, 285, 293, 299
Romero, 377
Romero, Tomasito, 393
Roosevelt, Theodore, 494
Roper, Laura, 41–42, 46, 47, 49, 63, 64, 65–66, 81, 166, 181
Royall, William B., 302, 303, 331, 332, 334, 335, 337, 343, 346
Ruffner, E. H., 424
Ruggles, George D., 345
Running Creek, 22, 24, 25, 58, 70n17, 248
Running Creek Stage Station, 246
Russell, John J., 477
Ruter, Mr., 131
Ruxton, George Frederick, 396

S

Sabeta, 422
Sacred Arrow Lodge, 213, 221
Sacred Arrows, 80, 81, 212, 213, 222, 225, 229, 353
Sacred Buffalo Hat, 80
Saguache, Colorado, 397, 415, 417
Salina, Kansas, 315
Saline River, 242, 243, 299, 314, 315–316, 318, 320, 322, 327, 328, 329, 343
Salt Creek, 327
Salt Lake City, District of Utah, 89
Sanborn, George L., 21, 189, 190
Sanborn, John B., 187, 221, 223, 227
Sand Creek, 20, 37, 43, 77, 87, 92, 95, 97, 99, 106, 107, 108, 111, 113, 114, 115, 116, 118, 121, 122, 124, 133, 136, 140n53, 142n108, 146, 147, 155, 188, 203, 205, 224, 299, 301, 312, 358
Sand Creek Massacre, 69n6, 105, 117, 118, 119, 122–123, 125, 128, 137, 139n14, 142n108, 145, 197, 199, 212, 223, 236, 309, 353, 354, 361, 370, 383, 408, 409, 503

Sand Creek Massacre National Park, 503
Sand Hill, 146, 364
Sanford, Mollie Dorsey, 63, 67
San Juan County, 391, 427
San Juan Miners' Cooperative, 423
San Juan Mountains, 391, 419, 420, 423, 426, 427, 428, 430
San Juan River, 439
San Luis Valley, 392, 407, 414
San Miguel County, 427
Santa Fe Trail, 79, 80, 300, 392, 396
Santanta, Chief, 199, 219, 221, 225
Sapovanero, 417, 420, 451, 484
Sawawatsewich, 417
Sawawick, 469
Sayr, Hal, 91, 109–110, 111, 114, 115
Scabby Band of the Cheyenne, 81, 87
Schermerhorn, Lon, 321, 323, 324
Schindelholz, Anton, 245, 246
Schlesinger, Sigmund "Sig," 256, 257, 265, 266, 269, 274, 278, 279, 288, 290, 291
Schmutz, Arthur, 320, 321, 324
Schmutz, Smart, 325–326
Schofield, John, 327, 328, 329, 330
Schurz, Carl, 435, 441–442, 452, 464, 466–467, 471, 476, 483
Schwanbeck, Karl Adam, 419
Second Cavalry, 302
Second Colorado Volunteer Cavalry Regiment, 36, 130, 288
Second U.S. Volunteers, 315
Sedgwick, John, 187
Sells, Cato, 490
Senate Committee on Indian Affairs, 121, 126
Senate Joint Special Committee, 126
Sergeant Majors Creek, 364
Seven Bulls, 213
Seventeenth Kansas Infantry, 315

Seventh Cavalry Fort Wallacce Drill Team, 383
Seventh Iowa Cavalry, 149, 170, 176, 178, 197, 207, 227, 241, 301, 304, 308, 310, 311, 312, 322, 325, 327
Severo, 466
Seward, William H., 136, 409
Seyon, the Place of the Dead, 377, 379
Shai ena, 78
Shan Kive, 487, 489
Sharp Bully, 378
Shavano, 398, 417, 426, 453, 466
Shave-Head, 85, 333–334
Shaw, James Alan, 372
Shaw, Simon, 242
Shenandoah Valley, 287, 292
Sheppard, Mr., 449
Sheridan, Kansas, 253, 257, 258, 360
Sheridan, Philip, 244, 250, 254, 255, 256, 257, 283, 284, 287, 292, 300–302, 303–304, 306, 307, 308, 310, 311, 312, 313, 374, 442
Sheridan City, 254
Sherman, George, 452
Sherman, William Tecumseh, 197–198, 207, 221, 230, 243, 253, 301, 370, 372, 410, 412
Shining Mountain, 414, 416, 430
Shirt, 262
Short, F. D., 372
Short, Oliver F., 356
Shoup, George L., 52, 58, 91, 96, 100, 112, 114, 118, 177
Showasheit, 403
Sibley, Henry H., 17
Sibley's Brigade, 17, 18
Sidney, Iowa, 166
Silver Brooch, 219
Simpson, Edward, 256
Sioux Indians, 19, 22, 28, 30–31, 32, 33, 34, 35, 39, 41, 48, 53, 56, 59, 60, 67, 78, 79, 80, 106, 108, 148, 149, 160, 165, 168,

169, 172, 177, 179, 181, 182, 184, 190, 203, 205, 206, 208, 209, 210, 211, 213, 214, 215, 218, 222, 238, 239, 254, 259, 261, 263, 266, 267, 268, 271, 272, 284, 303, 314, 333, 335, 336, 337, 339, 345, 346, 402, 424
Sioux War, 33
Sipes, John L., 106, 107, 138, 139n13, 141n68, 156, 229–230, 235, 262, 273, 309, 310, 346, 347, 349n1, 350n22, 353–354, 356, 358, 361, 365, 366, 367, 369, 370, 372, 374, 376–377, 379, 380, 381–382, 383–384, 387n68
Sipes, John L., Jr., 145
Sitting Bear, 219
Sixth Cavalry, 362
Sixth United States Infantry Regiment, 186
Slough, John P., 15, 16, 18–19
Smith, A. A., 65
Smith, A. J., 207, 209
Smith, Chalmers, 256, 266, 273
Smith, Edward, 364
Smith, E. F., 472
Smith, E. P., 429
Smith, Hoke, 486
Smith, Jack, 86, 99, 109, 110–111
Smith, James, 32, 40
Smith, John, 29, 38–39, 43, 44, 45–46, 50, 52, 59, 84, 94, 99, 102–103, 107, 109, 110–111, 121, 126, 134, 221, 227, 229
Smith, John S., 86
Smith, Mrs., 40
Smith, P. David, 415
Smith, S. R., 176
Smith, Washington, 326
Smith, William F., 67
Smoking Earth River, 427
Smoky Hill, 20, 48, 76, 95, 107–108, 127, 277
Smoky Hill Council, 47, 50, 218
Smoky Hill River, 42, 43, 104, 106, 112, 127, 135, 145, 147, 207, 235, 257, 258, 356, 360, 369, 384
Smoky Hill River Trail, 356, 357
Smoky Hill Road, 211, 284
Smoky Hill Trail, 79, 207, 230
Snake River, 28, 440, 459
Snyder, Mr., 37, 38, 216
Snyder, Mrs., 38, 47
Snyder, Naman D., 125
Snyder teamsters, 77
Snyder wagon group, 128
Soaring Eagle, 378
Solid Muldoon, 464–465, 467–468, 470, 480
Solomon Creek, 343
Solomon River, 33, 106, 146, 242, 243, 257, 299, 314, 327
Soule, Silas, 15, 16, 18, 19, 36, 44, 46, 50, 52, 63, 64, 93–94, 95, 96, 100, 109, 111–112, 113, 116, 117, 124–125, 129, 130, 131–132, 133, 134, 142n108, 147
South America, 251
South Canadian River, 82
Southern Arapaho Indians, 149, 210, 211
Southern Cheyenne Indians, 80, 190, 212, 262
Southern Ute Indian Agency, 473, 494
Southern Ute Indians, 422, 439, 469, 470, 476–477, 484, 487, 491
Southern Ute Reservation, 471, 486, 496
South Fork (Republican River), 106
South Loupe River, 155, 236
South Platte River, 17, 20, 21, 28, 49, 80, 84, 89, 148, 155, 158, 159, 160, 161, 162, 164, 167, 168, 169, 170, 172, 178, 182, 187, 197, 210, 212, 228, 238, 244, 250, 263, 332, 336, 337, 344, 346, 402, 432

South Platte River Road, 14, 148, 161, 163–164, 168, 170, 177, 179, 185, 186, 238–239, 253, 299
South Platte River Trail, 156
South Platte Trail, 29, 33, 34
Southwestern Cooperative Association, 423
Sowerwich, 414, 466
Special Order No. 88 (War Department), 374
Speer, Calvin T., 416–417, 419
Spillman Creek, 242, 314, 315, 316, 318, 322, 323, 327, 328, 329
Spotted Bear, 221
Spotted Crow, 108
Spotted Tail, 106, 148, 149, 221
Spotted Trail, 33
Spotted Wolf, 305, 369
Spottsylvania, 254
Spring Bottom stage station, 129
Spring Creek, 356
Squiers, Charles W., 130, 133–134
Staked Plains, 354, 364
Standing Bull, 105
Standing Elk, 221
Standing Water, 108
Stanley, Henry M., 201, 206, 219, 224, 226–227
Stanley, William M., 451, 452
Stanton, Edwin M., 36, 61, 74, 88, 89, 120
Starving Elk, 150, 263–264
State Historical and Natural History Society, 348
St. Augustine, Florida, 372
St. Charles Town Company, 29
St. Clair, Mr., 32, 40
Steck, Michael, 406, 408
Steele, James, 189–190
Sterling, Colorado, 155
Sterling Lions Club, 504–505
Steward, William, 256
Stewart, Milton, 311
St. Francis, Kansas Territory, 106, 146

Stickley, William, 435
Stillwell, G. H., 124, 272
Stillwell, Simpson Everett "Jack," 256, 269, 274, 275, 283, 287, 288
'Stingies,' 82
St. Johns Church, 132
St. Johns River, 376
St. Joseph, Missouri, 89, 404
St. Joseph Herald, 404–405
St. Louis, Missouri, 87
St. Louis Daily Globe, 373
Stobie, Charles Stewart, 253
Stone Calf, 355, 364–366, 367
Stone Forehead, 212, 213, 229
Storm, 85
Stover, Major, 240
Strange, John, 320, 321, 324, 325
Strange, Marion, 321
Strange, Riley, 321
Stumbling Bear, 209
St. Vrain, Ceran, 397
Sublette brothers, 28
Suckett, 419
Sully, Alfred, 241, 301, 307
Sulpher Spring, 86
Summit Springs, 167, 319, 337, 340, 345, 346, 347, 353, 504
Sun Dance, 78
Sun Dance Woman, 342
"Susanna's Springs," 343
Suthai clan, 146
Swan Creek, 213
Sweet Medicine, 346
Sweet Water, 353
Sweetwater Creek, 198
Swift Hawk Lying Down, 78
Sylvester, 305

T

Tabbecuna band (Ute Indians), 422
Tabegauche band (Ute Indians), 390, 391, 394, 398, 400, 403, 404, 406, 407, 408, 415, 422, 427, 436, 439, 469, 471
Tah-nea, 299

Talbot, Presley, 134
Tall Bear, 85, 204, 262
Tall Bull, 29, 202, 203, 204, 205, 213, 222, 224, 228, 229, 239, 272, 299, 303, 304, 313, 314, 318, 319, 329, 331, 336, 337, 338, 339–340, 342–343, 345, 346, 347
Tanfield, James W., 410
Tangle Hair, 228
Taos, New Mexico, 390, 392, 393, 394, 494
Taos Indians, 393
Tappan, Samuel, 15, 16, 18–19, 48–49, 111, 112, 122, 124, 406
Tappan, Samuel F., 221
Tapuch, 476
Taylor, Nathaniel G., 197, 207, 209, 210, 221–222, 240, 241
Teller, Henry, 74, 431, 436, 470–471, 481–482, 483, 484
Teller Institute, 483
Temple, James H., 186
10th United States Colored Cavalry, 254
Ten Bears, 219, 222, 225
Tenth United States Cavalry, 284, 285, 286, 287, 288, 290, 292, 303, 447
Terry, Alfred H., 221
Tesson, Louis, 341, 342, 343
Texas, 17, 56, 313, 354, 359, 361, 364
Thayer, Isaac, 256
Third Cavalry, 398
Third Colorado Volunteer Calvary Regiment, 36, 51, 62, 87, 89, 91, 92, 96, 108, 112, 113, 119, 134, 301
Third Regiment of Colorado Volunteers, 74, 407
Third U.S. Volunteer Regiment, 148
Third Voluntary Calvary, 86
Thomas, Reuben, 157–158
Thompson, James B., 417–418
Thompson, Mr. (agency employee), 445
Thornburgh, Thomas Tipton, 442, 443–444, 445, 448, 450, 451, 461, 463
Thunder Cloud, 401
Tierra Amarilla Indian Agency, 401
Tobin, Thomas Tate, 38
Tomserick, 422
Tongue River Agency, 262, 271
Topeka Commonwealth, 325, 360
Towac, Colorado, 486
Towne, D. T., 73–74
Trail Creek, 316
Trask, Jabez Nelson, 417, 418–419
Treaty of 1863, 414
Treaty of 1868, 424, 426
Treaty of Fort Laramie, 80, 235
Treaty of Fort Wise, 83, 86, 87, 99
Treaty of Horse Creek, 80
Treaty of Medicine Lodge, 211
Treaty of the Little Arkansas, 190, 191, 235
Tremont House, 133, 248, 249
Triggs, Jeremiah, 165
Triggs, J. H., 182
Trinchera River, 405
Trotter, 311
Trout, Hattie L. Hedges, 252
Trudeau, Pierre, 256, 269, 274, 275, 283
Tsistsistas, 78, 105, 310, 353
Tucker, H. H., 256, 265, 273
Tuepuepa, 403
Tupuwaat, 403
Turkey Leg, 214, 215, 217, 218, 221
29th U. S. Infantry, 348
Twenty-Seventh Infantry, 302
Two Butte Creek, 78
Two Crows, 262, 270, 314, 336, 338, 339
Two Face, 41, 179, 180, 181–182

U

Uintah Reservation, 478, 480–481, 484, 486, 489, 490
Uintah Ute Indians, 51, 390, 422, 427, 436, 469
Ulbrich, Peter, 214, 218
Ulbrich, Veronica (Veeney), 214, 215, 217, 218
Unaneance, 417
Uncompahgre Plateau, 394, 403, 474
Uncompahgre River, 415, 427, 450, 453, 455, 479–480
Uncompahgre Ute Indians, 462, 466, 477, 480
"Union Administration Association," 73
Union Army, 254, 255, 315, 404
Union Colony, 432, 433–434
Union Pacific Railroad, 215, 218, 239, 348, 447
Unitah agency, 406
Unitarian Church, 417
United States Congress, 212
United States Senate, 470
University of Nebraska Library Special Collections, 31
University of Oklahoma, 387n68
Upper Arkansas River, 79, 84, 85
Upper Platte River, 28
U.S. Army, 150, 168, 198, 210, 253
U. S. Congress, 84, 126
Ute Commission, 439
Ute Indians, 35, 50, 82, 244, 249, 333, 389–391, 392–393, 394, 396, 397, 399, 402, 404–406, 407, 408, 410, 412, 413, 414, 418, 420–421, 422–423, 424, 426, 427, 429, 430, 431, 435, 436, 438, 441, 442–443, 444–445, 447–448, 449, 451, 453, 462, 464, 465–466, 468, 469, 475–476, 478–479, 485, 486, 495, 499n60, 501n133
Ute Memorial Park, 494–495
Ute Mountain Reservation, 486
Ute Pass, 244
Ute Pass Trail, 488, 489

V

Vack Creek, 489
Valencia, Jose Ignacio, 397
Valentine, William H., 77
Valley Stage Station, 155, 157, 158, 162, 164, 170, 171, 177
Valley Station, 34, 89, 91, 153
Valois, Gustavus, 465
Van Wormer, Isaac, 23, 26, 61
Vigil, Cornelio, 393
Vilott, Fletcher, 286
Violett, Fletcher, 256, 273
Viriginia, 187
Volkmar, William, 337–338, 341
Voss, Henry, 342

W

Wakely, George, 51
Waller, Reuben, 287, 288
Wanderodes band (Ute Indians), 422
War Bonnet, 87, 103, 108, 116
War Department, 69n6, 177, 241, 249, 283, 361, 371, 372, 389, 447, 478, 479
Ware, Eugene F., 150, 170, 174, 175, 178
Warency, 426
Wasati, 361
Washington, D. C., 16, 17, 27, 53, 54, 55, 59, 84, 86, 114, 119, 122, 126, 136, 236, 254, 403, 409, 414, 435, 464, 465, 466, 482–483
Washington County, 504
Washington Gulch, 426
Washington Post, 467, 469
Washington Ranch station, 155, 171, 177, 239
Washita Indians, 311, 361
Washita River, 78, 139n14, 212, 230, 302, 305, 307, 308, 309, 311, 312, 353, 358, 364, 379, 383

Wass, 469
Watonga, Oklahoma, 380
Wayt, L. M., 494
Weeminuche band (Ute Indians), 390, 401, 415, 422, 427, 436, 486
Weichell, George, 315, 318, 324, 342
Weichell, Maria, 315, 318, 319, 340, 341, 342, 344, 345, 346
Weld County, 432
Wells Fargo, 239
Wesley, 368, 369
Western Mountaineer, 85
West Point, 187
Whichita Indians, 305
Whirlwind, 58
Whistler, 314, 346
White, Daniel W., 489
White, J. J., 333
White Antelope, 22, 29, 44, 47, 52, 54, 55–56, 57, 58, 60, 63, 64, 84, 85, 87, 94, 95, 97, 99, 100, 107, 108, 116, 136, 146, 181, 236, 237
White Bear, 219
White Buffalo Bull, 271, 272
White Butte, 337
White Butte Creek, 167, 168, 337, 341
White Eye, 476
White Head, 226
White Horse, 204, 206, 213, 228, 229, 262, 269–270, 272–273, 314, 333, 369
White Leaf, 170
Whiteley, Simeon, 51–52, 61
Whitely, Simeon, 406, 408
White Man, 378
White Man's Fork, 153, 154
White River, 346, 389, 415, 427, 437, 443, 453, 454, 465, 469, 482, 483, 485, 486
White River Expedition, 444
White River Indian agency, 431, 435, 437, 439, 442, 448, 450, 451, 452, 456, 461, 470, 484, 505

White River Indian Agency, 434
White River Museum, 501n135
White River reservation, 431
White River Ute Indians, 450, 461, 470, 472, 477, 480
White Shirt, 203
White Thunder, 269, 270
White Weasel Bear, 269, 270
White White, 182–183, 184
White Wolf, 47
Whitman, Walt, 18
Whitney, Chauncey B., 256, 275
Wichita, Kansas, 188
Wichita Mountains, 225
Wichita tribe, 199, 201
Wilcox, John, 180, 181, 186
Wilderness Campaign, 287
Wild West Show, 340, 487
Williams, Dallas, 187
Wilson, John, 256, 273
Wilson, Lt., 133
Wilson, Luther, 98, 102
Wilson, William, 256
Wilson's Creek, 87
Wind Woman, 78
Wisconsin Ranch, 160, 161, 163, 186
Wise, Henry A., 84
Wisely, Joel F., 176
Wolf, 78
Wolf Belly, 268, 273
Wolf Coming Out, 21
Wolf Creek, 78, 199, 327
Wolf People, 236, 237
Wolf with Plenty of Hair, 340
Wolves, 106
Woodruff, Elias, 292
Woods, John, 164
Woodward, R. O., 179
Wootton, Richens Lacy "Uncle Dick," 396, 397
Woqini (Roman Nose), 262
Works Project Administration, 494
World Herald, 67
Wray, Colorado, 260, 268, 504
Wright, Susan C., 483
Wu-ta-pi-u (Wotapio) band, 82
Wutapiu clan, 146

Wyat, L. M., 491
Wynkoop, Edward, 15, 16, 19, 36–37, 38, 39, 42–52, 50, 61, 62, 63, 64, 67, 68, 74–77, 81, 93, 95, 96, 111–112, 114, 116, 117, 120–122, 124–125, 127–128, 133, 134, 135–136, 166, 197, 198, 201, 203, 204, 205, 206–207, 208, 209, 210, 211–212, 218, 219, 223, 224, 227, 230, 241, 242, 243, 306–307
Wynkoop, Edward Estill, 75
Wynkoop, Frank, 15
Wynkoop, Louise, 50
Wyoming, 28, 329
Wyoming Territory, 164, 179, 187, 190, 239

Y

Yampa band (Ute Indians), 415, 427, 436
Yampa River Valley, 414
Yankton Indians, 60
Yellow Nose, 333
Yellow Shield, 108
Yellowstone, 28
Yellowstone Country, 155, 236
Yellow Wolf, 87, 108, 146
Yuma County, 268, 285, 298n90

Z

Zabriskie, E. B., 181, 182
Ziegler, Eli, 256, 260, 263, 264, 265, 266, 274, 275, 281, 286, 314, 315, 316–317, 317–318, 319, 322
Ziegler, Mary, 325, 326
Ziegler, Michael, 325, 326

— ABOUT THE AUTHOR —

A Colorado native, Linda Wommack is a Colorado historian and historical consultant. An award-winning author, she has written sixteen books on Colorado history, including *Murder in the Mile High City, Colorado's Landmark Hotels, From the Grave: Colorado's Pioneer Cemeteries, Our Ladies of the Tenderloin: Colorado's Legends in Lace, Colorado History for Kids, Colorado's Historic Mansions and Castles, Ann Bassett, Colorado's Cattle Queen, Haunted History of Cripple Creek and Teller County, Cripple Creek, Bob Womack & the Greatest Gold Camp on Earth, Ranching Women of Colorado* and *Growing Up With the Wild Bunch: the Story of Pioneer Legend Josie Bassett*. She has also contributed to two anthologies concerning Western Americana.

Linda has been a contributing editor for *True West Magazine* since 1995. She has also been a staff writer, contributing a monthly article for *Wild West Magazine*, since 2004. She has also written for *The Tombstone Epitaph*, the nation's oldest continuously published newspaper, since 1993. Linda also writes for several publications throughout her state.

Linda's research has been used in several documentary accounts for the national Wild West History Association, historical treatises of the Sand Creek Massacre, as well as critical historic aspects for the Lawman & Outlaw Museum as well as the Heritage Center, both in Cripple Creek, Colorado.

Linda feeds her passion for history with activities in many local, state, and national preservation projects, participating in historical venues, including speaking engagements, hosting tours, and is involved in historical reenactments across the state.

CPSIA information can be obtained
at www.ICGtesting.com
Printed in the USA
JSHW020850250322
24203JS00002B/2